Springer-Verlag Berlin Heidelberg GmbH

Thomas Lehmann   Volker Metzler
Klaus Spitzer   Thomas Tolxdorff (Hrsg.)

Bildverarbeitung für die Medizin 1998

Algorithmen – Systeme – Anwendungen

Proceedings des Workshops
am 26. und 27. März 1998 in Aachen

Springer

Herausgeber

Thomas Lehmann
Volker Metzler
Klaus Spitzer
Institut für Medizinische Informatik
Universitätsklinikum der RWTH Aachen
D-52057 Aachen

Thomas Tolxdorff
Institut für Medizinische Statistik, Epidemiologie und Informatik
Universitätsklinikum Benjamin Franklin der FU Berlin
D-12200 Berlin

Die Deutsche Bibliothek - CIP-Einheitsaufnahme

Bildverarbeitung für die Medizin 1998 : Algorithmen - Systeme -
Anwendungen / Hrsg.: Thomas Lehmann ... - Berlin ; Heidelberg ;
New York ; Barcelona ; Budapest ; Hongkong ; London ; Mailand ;
Paris ; Santa Clara ; Singapur ; Tokio : Springer, 1998
    (Informatik aktuell)
ISBN 978-3-540-63885-8   ISBN 978-3-642-58775-7 (eBook)
DOI 10.1007/978-3-642-58775-7

CR Subject Classification (1998): A.0, I.4, I.5, J.3, I.3.3, I.3.5, I.3.7,
I.6.3

ISBN 978-3-540-63885-8

Satz: Reproduktionsfertige Vorlage vom Autor/Herausgeber

SPIN: 10661418   33/3142-543210 – Gedruckt auf säurefreiem Papier

Veranstalter

DAGM   Deutsche Arbeitsgemeinschaft für Mustererkennung

DGBMT Fachgruppe Medizinische Informatik
der Deutschen Gesellschaft für Biomedizinische Technik

GI   Fachgruppe Imaging und Visualisierungstechniken
der Gesellschaft für Informatik

GMDS   Arbeitsgruppe Medizinische Bildverarbeitung der Dt. Gesellschaft
für Medizinische Informatik, Biometrie und Epidemiologie

IEEE   Joint Chapter Engineering in Medicine and Biology (German Section)
The Institute of Electrical and Electronics Engineers

RWTH   Institut für Medizinische Informatik
der Rheinisch-Westfälischen Technischen Hochschule Aachen

Tagungsleitung

Dipl.-Ing. Thomas Lehmann
Abteilung Medizinische Bildverarbeitung
Institut für Medizinische Informatik der RWTH Aachen

Organisation

Dipl.-Inform. Volker Metzler
Abteilung Medizinische Bildverarbeitung
Institut für Medizinische Informatik der RWTH Aachen

Programmkomitee

Priv.-Doz. Dr. R. Brennecke, Universität Mainz

Dr. H. Handels, Medizinische Universität Lübeck

Dr. A. Horsch, Technische Universität München

Prof. Dr. K.H. Höhne, Universitätskrankenhaus Hamburg/Eppendorf

Priv.-Doz. Dr. H.-P. Meinzer, Deutsches Krebsforschungszentrum Heidelberg

Prof. Dr. D. Meyer-Ebrecht, Technische Hochschule Aachen

Prof. Dr. H. Müller, Universität Dortmund

Prof. Dr. H. Niemann, Universität Erlangen-Nürnberg

Prof. Dr. W. Oberschelp, Technische Hochschule Aachen

Prof.em. Dr. R. Repges, Universitätsklinikum Aachen

Prof. Dr. D. Saupe, Universität Freiburg

Prof. Dr. Dr. K. Spitzer, Universitätsklinikum Aachen

Prof. Dr. T. Tolxdorff, Universitätsklinikum Benjamin-Franklin FU Berlin

Prof. Dr. H. Witte, Universität Jena

Die Arbeitsgruppe Medizinische Bildverarbeitung der GMDS sowie die Fachgruppe Imaging und Visualisierungstechniken der GI haben seit nunmehr 5 Jahren jedes Frühjahr in Freiburg einen Workshop zur medizinischen Bildverarbeitung veranstaltet. Im November 1996 hat am Institut für Medizinische Informatik und Biometrie der RWTH Aachen mit Unterstützung des Joint Chapters Engineering in Medicine and Biology (IEEE German Section) ein Workshop Bildverarbeitung für die Medizin stattgefunden. Der Workshop Bildverarbeitung für die Medizin 1998 führt die Tradition beider Veranstaltungen gemeinsam fort.

Hauptsponsor

Sun Microsystems GmbH
Brandenburger Str. 2
D-40880 Ratingen

Industrieausstellung

Advanced Visual Systems GmbH
Heinrich Hertz Str. 40
D-40699 Erkrath/Düsseldorf

best Systeme GmbH
Münchnerstr. 123a
D-85774 Unterföhring

Carl Zeiss Vision GmbH
Brüggelmann Str. 16–18
D-50679 Köln

CREASO GmbH
Talhofstr. 30
D-82205 Gilching

Dresden Informatik GmbH
Tannestr. 2a
D-01099 Dresden

Dressler Computertechnik GmbH
Adenauerstr. 20
D-52146 Würselen

HIKO GmbH
Teichstr. 15-19
D-66953 Pirmasens

Leica GmbH
Lilienthalstr. 39-45
D-64625 Bensheim

LuRaTech GmbH
Rudower Chaussee 5
D-12489 Berlin-Adlershof

MEDAV GmbH
Gräfenberger Str. 34
D-91080 Uttenreuth

MEVA GmbH
Röllingheider Str. 6
D-58285 Gevelsberg

Parsytec Computer GmbH
Auf der Hüls 183
D-52068 Aachen

SAM GmbH
Wielandstr. 28a
D-32545 Bad Oeynhausen

Soft Imaging Systems GmbH
Hammerstr. 89
D-48153 Münster

Sun Microsystems GmbH
Brandenburg Str. 2
D-40880 Ratingen

Transferzentrum Mikroelektronik e.V.
In den Weiden 7
D-99099 Erfurt

VITRONIC GmbH
Hasengartenstr. 14a
D-65189 Wiesbaden

Volker Tympel Ingenieurbüro
Konrad-Zuse-Str. 3
D-07745 Jena

Vorwort

Durch die zunehmende Digitalisierung bildgebender Systeme in der medizinischen Diagnostik hat die digitale **Bildverarbeitung für die Medizin** in den letzten Jahren eine immer stärkere Bedeutung erlangt. Dabei bestehen besondere Anforderungen an **Algorithmen**, **Systeme** und **Anwendungen** der medizinischen Bildverarbeitung, die sich aus der für den klinischen Einsatz notwendigen Robustheit und Genauigkeit ergeben. Die Individualität des Bildmaterials sowie die vielfach nicht mögliche Trennung zwischen Objekt und Hintergrund wirkt hier zusätzlich erschwerend. Der interdisziplinäre Charakter dieses Forschungsbereiches erfordert weiterhin intensive Kommunikation und Informationsaustausch zwischen den Disziplinen. Obwohl der Bereich Medizinische Bildverarbeitung in vielen Fachgesellschaften als Arbeitsgruppe etabliert ist, fehlte bislang ein gemeinsames Forum für Wissenschaftler, Hersteller und Anwender aus (Medizin-)Informatik, Natur- und Ingenieurwissenschaft, Medizin und (Biomedizin-)Technik.

Mit dem Workshop **Bildverarbeitung für die Medizin 1998**, der als gemeinsame Veranstaltung der auf Seite V genannten Organisationen durchgeführt wird, ist es erstmals gelungen, dieses Forum zu schaffen. Dies manifestiert sich durch das hohe Interesse, das der Veranstaltung entgegengebracht wurde. Knapp 120 Beiträge wurden auf unseren Call for Papers eingesandt und anonymisiert von jeweils zwei renommierten Wissenschaftlern (Programmkomitee siehe S. V) beurteilt. Anhand dieser Bewertung wurden 88 Beiträge für den Workshop ausgewählt. Diese werden als wissenschaftliche Vorträge (V), Poster- (P) und Systemdemonstrationen (S) präsentiert. Die Industrieausstellung zählt zur Zeit bereits 18 Firmen, die Ihre Aktivitäten in der medizinischen Bildverarbeitung auch in Industrievorträgen (I) präsentieren werden. Darüber hinaus ist es gelungen, Herrn Professor Robert M. Haralick von der University of Washington, Seattle, USA, für den Eröffnungsvortrag zu gewinnen. Als weiterer Schritt zur Etablierung dieses gemeinsamen Forums werden die Proceedings vom Springer-Verlag publiziert und sind damit auch nach dem Workshop dauerhaft erhältlich.

Wir freuen uns, daß dieser erste gemeinsame Workshop in Aachen stattfindet. Die Abteilung Medizinische Bildverarbeitung des Instituts für Medizinische Informatik der RWTH Aachen spiegelt die interdisziplinären Rahmenbedingungen dieser Wissenschaft exemplarisch wider. Zur Medizinischen Fakultät gehörend, forschen hier primär Informatiker und Ingenieure. Der anderswo oft schwierige Dialog mit den klinischen Partnern wird in Aachen durch die räumliche Integration in einem Gebäude, dem Universitätsklinikum, besonders gefördert. Auch der Workshop 1998 wird im Universitätsklinikum Aachen stattfinden.

Trotz allem soll der traditionelle Charakter eines Workshops mit guter Arbeitsatmosphäre erhalten bleiben. Nur der finanziellen Unterstützung der Firma Sun Microsystems, Ratingen, und der Industriepartner (siehe S. VI) ist es zu verdanken, daß die Teilnahmegebühren so niedrig gehalten werden konnten.

Ebenfalls gebührt unser Dank der Deutschen Gesellschaft für Medizinische Informatik, Biometrie und Epidemiologie (GMDS) und dem IEEE Joint Chapter Engineering in Medicine and Biology (IEEE German Section), die die Anreise von Herrn Professor Haralick finanziell unterstützt haben.

Die Herausgeber dieser Proceedings möchten es sich nicht nehmen lassen, allen, die zum Gelingen des Workshops beigetragen haben, ganz herzlichen Dank auszusprechen: den Autoren für die rechtzeitige und formgerechte Einsendung ihrer interessanten Beiträge, dem Programmkomitee für die gründliche und termingerechte Begutachtung, den Mitarbeitern des Instituts für Medizinische Informatik und den Ansprechpartnern der Verwaltung der Medizinischen Einrichtungen der RWTH Aachen für die tatkräftige Unterstützung bei der Organisation und Durchführung des Workshops. Herrn Jörg Schwarz, Sun Microsystems, danken wir für seine Beteiligung an der Organisation der Industrieausstellung und Herrn Christian Thies, Institut für Medizinische Informatik, u.a. für die Macro-Programmierung zur Erstellung der Proceedings.

Zum Abschluß möchten wir noch auf die Internet-Leitseite des Workshops hinweisen, von der aus alle Informationen zum Workshop abrufbar sind:

http://www.imib.rwth-aachen.de/www/bvm98

Allen Teilnehmerinnen und Teilnehmern wünschen wir auf dem ersten gemeinsamen Workshop **Bildverarbeitung für die Medizin 1998** einen fruchtbaren wissenschaftlichen Austausch und einen angenehmen Aufenthalt in der Kaiserstadt Aachen.

Aachen, im Februar 1998

Thomas Lehmann
Volker Metzler
Klaus Spitzer
Thomas Tolxdorff

Inhaltsverzeichnis

Eingeladener Vortrag

Wissenschaftliche Beiträge

Industriebeiträge

Automated Ventriculargram Boundary Delineation

Robert M. Haralick, Jasjit Suri, Florence Sheehan

University of Washington
Seattle, WA 98195

Abstract. Quantitative analysis of the left ventricle wall motion is important for the diagnosis of coronary heart disease. From wall motion, stroke volume, ejection fraction, and velocity of ventricular circumference can be estimated. These are helpful in identifying the state of diseased hearts.

This paper describes a left ventricle boundary delineation algorithm which operates on X-Ray image data sets (ventriculargrams) produced in a catheterization laboratory for patient cardiovascular assessment. On a data set of 377 patient studies, the algorithm was able to delineate the boundary for the left ventricle with an average error just over 2.4 mm relative to the gold standard of cardiologist hand traced boundaries.

1 Ventriculography

Contrast ventriculography is a procedure routinely performed in clinical practice during cardiac catheterization. Catheters are intravascularly inserted into the heart to inject a contrast dye so that the left ventricle may be more clearly images with X-Rays. The time sequence of such image frames is called a ventriculogram. They constitute a projection image sequence of the endocardial surface of the left ventricle chamber. These images are used to determine the endocardial boundary at the end diastole, when the heart is filled up with blood, and at the end systole, when the heart is at the end of the contraction phase during the cardiac cycle.

A typical set of the end diastole and the end systole frames is shown in fig. 1. The left image shows the time frame when the left ventricle is filled with blood while the right image shows the time frame when the left ventricle is at the end of the contraction phase. By manually tracing the contour or boundary of the endocardial surface of the heart at these two extremes in the cardiac cycle, a cardiologist can determine the size and function of the left ventricle and can diagnose certain abnormalities or defects in the heart.

2 Characterstics of the Cardiac Data Sets

2.1 Variability in the Cardiac Data Sets

The variability in the cardiac data sets is to the heart rate, size, shape, position, orientation, and cardiac diseases like: ischemic cardiomyopathy, hypertensive

Fig. 1. Typical end distole and end systole frames of a cardiac cycle. **Left**: End distole frame, **Right**: End systole frame.

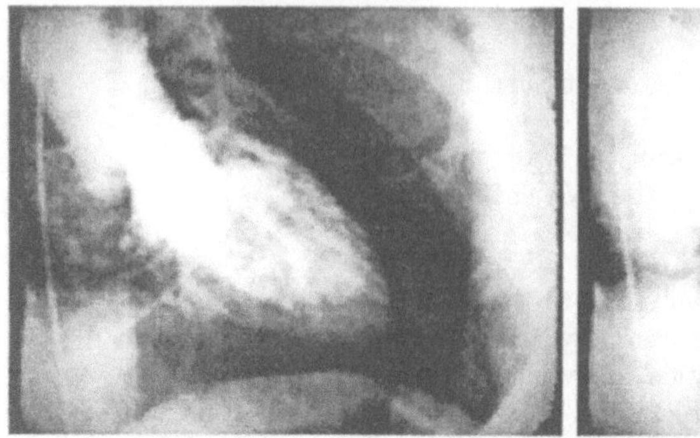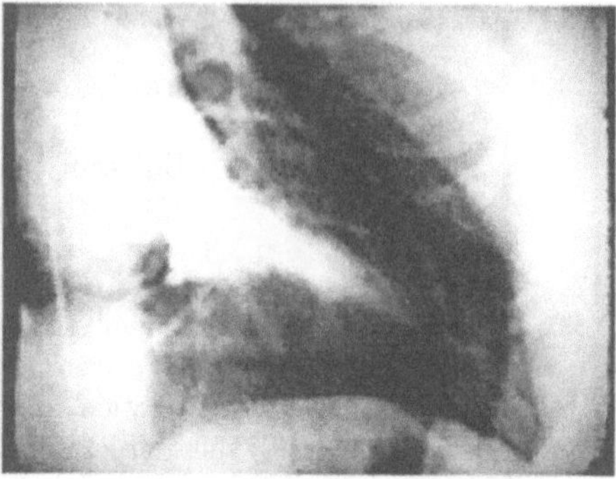

Fig. 2. Left: Position of catheter in the LV chamber. Also seen are the diaphragm and ribs. **Right**: Labelling of the LV parts: anterior wall, apex zone, inferior wall, aortic valve plane and the longitudinal axis.

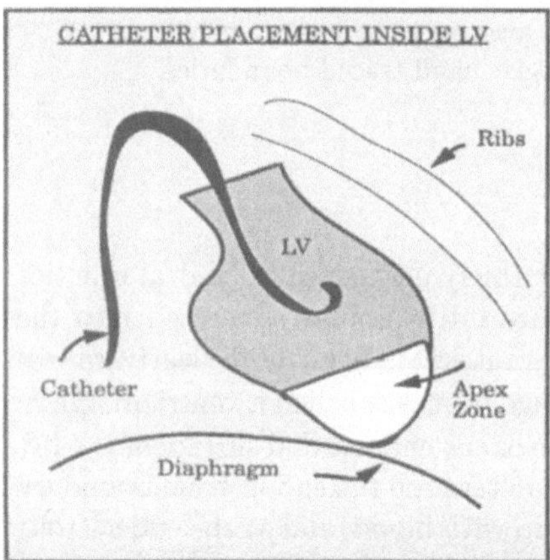

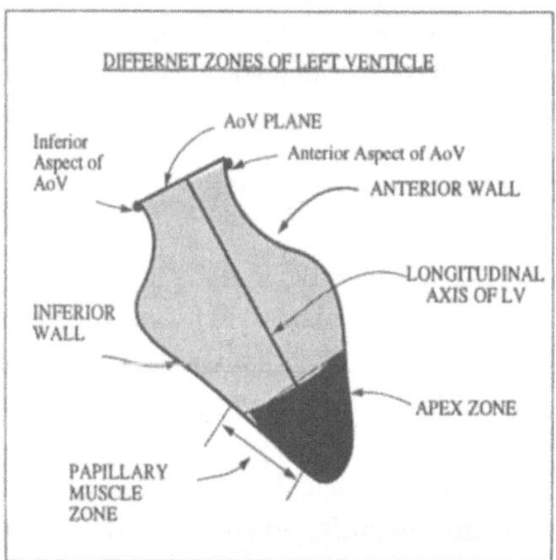

cardiomyopaothy, rheumatic heart disease, myocarditis, and congestive heart failure. Fig. 3 shows examples of the variability of the left ventricle shapes for the end diastole frame. Fig. 4 shows the variability of left ventricle shapes for the same studies as in fig. 3, but for the end systole frame. The bottom row shows two left ventricles having an altogether different orientation, position, size and shape for the end systole frame. The variability of left ventricle contrast during the systole cycle is shown in fig. 5.

One of the most serious shortcomings in these ventriculograms is the non-homogeneous mixing of the dye with the blood. This causes almost no propagation of the dye in the apical zone of the left ventricle chamber. Thus boundaries must be delineated in the apical zone where there may be no or little gray scale contrast across the boundary. The end systole apex position in end systole gray

Fig. 3. Demonstration of variability in the LV shapes in end diastole (ED) frame. LV image size: 384 x 512. **Top left:** LV has a bulge in the anterior wall. **Top right:** LVG has an almost horizontal inferior wall. **Bottom left:** The LV has a very different shape in the inferior wall zone. **Bottom right:** The LV is too tiny and bulge in the anterior wall. These different shapes demonstrate the large variability in cardiac data sets.

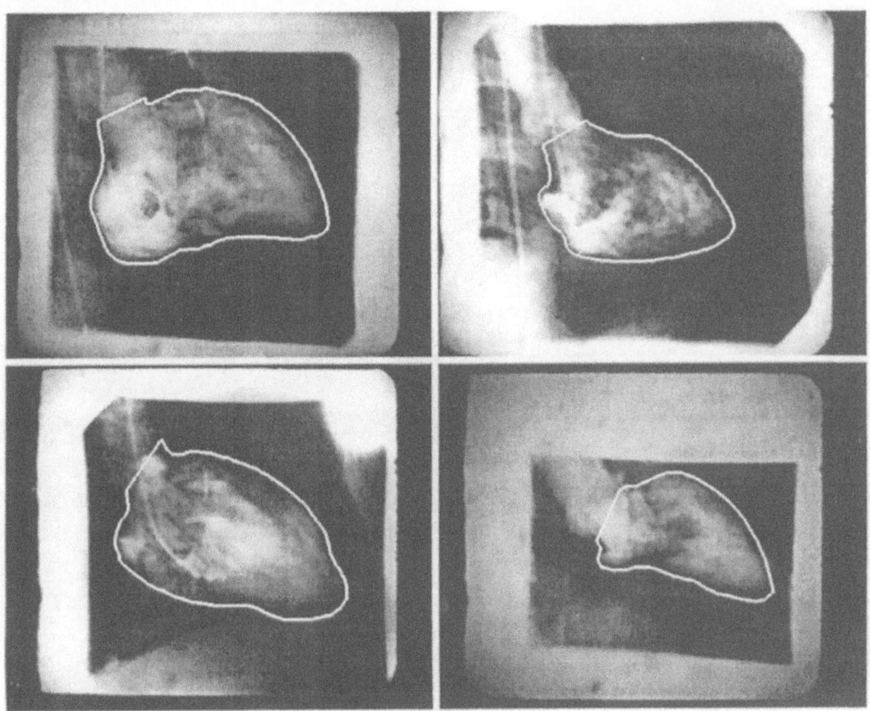

scale image is even harder to estimate compared to the end diastole apex position because the contrast level is further decreased in the apex zone in the end systole frame of the cardiac cycle.

3 Pre-Processing of Gray scale Cardiac Data

The pre-processing of the cardiac gray scale data consists of: (i) Morphological smoothing and (ii) Heart rate normalization.

3.1 Morphological smoothing

The first step is gray scale morphological smoothing which consists of a gray scale opening followed by a gray scale closing using a disk structuring element. Gray scale opening and closing [12] are defined in an analogous way to opening and closing in binary morphology. They have the similar properties. First, the definitions of gray scale dilation and erosion are defined followed by the gray scale opening and closing.

Fig. 4. ES frames for different patient studies showing the variability in the LV shape, size, position and orientation. LVG size: 384 x 512. **Top Left**: Bulge seen in the anterior wall and sharp bends in the inferior wall. **Top Right**: Bulge in the inferior wall. **Bottom Left**: Unusually large left ventricle for the ES frame. **Bottom Right**: Inferior wall deshaped like a cusp.

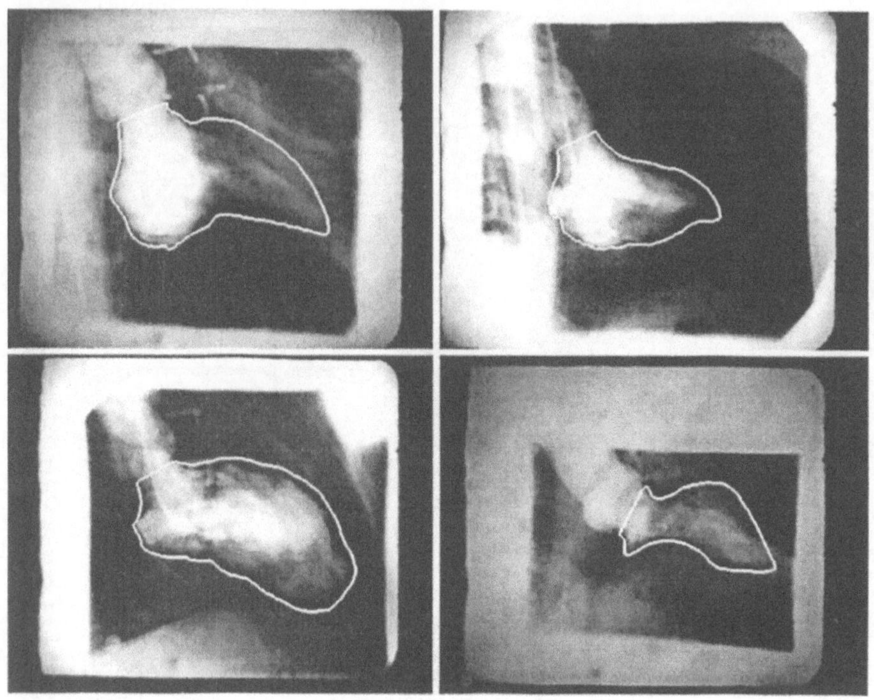

Dilation If f: F→E and k:K→E, the dilation of f by k is denoted by $f \oplus k$ and is define by:

$$f \oplus k = max_{z \in k}\{f(x - z) + k(z)|x - z \in F\} \tag{1}$$

Erosion If f: F→E and k:K→E, the erosion, $f \ominus k$ and is define by:

$$f \ominus k = min_{z \in k}\{f(x + z) - k(z)|z \in k\} \tag{2}$$

Opening If f: F→E and k:K→E, then the gray scale opening of f by a structuring element k is denoted by

$$f \circ k = (f \ominus k) \oplus k. \tag{3}$$

$$(f \circ k)(x) = max_{z \in k} \, min_{y \in k}\{f(x - z + y)\} \tag{4}$$

Fig. 5. Demonstration of the variability of the gray scale contrast data of a patient study during the systole cycle (contraction phase). Shown are the normalized frames of size 384 x 512 pixels. These images are obtained from the raw left ventricle images of size 480 x 512 after gray scale normalization, scaling, and morphological smoothing.

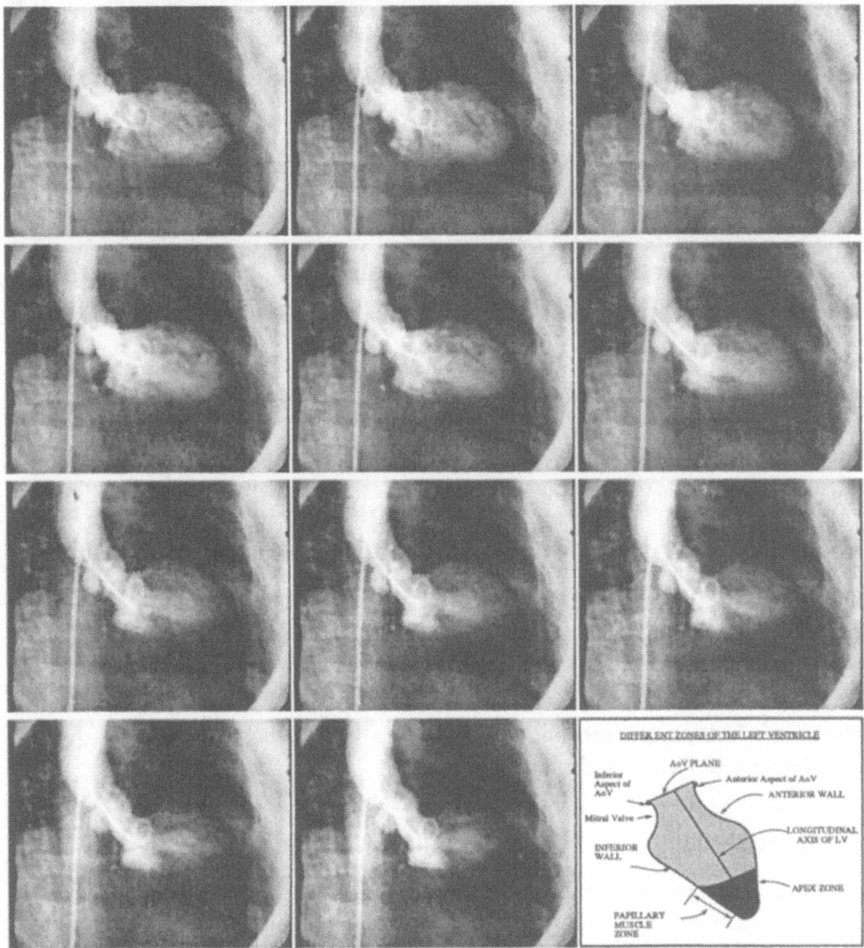

It can also be understood in terms of Umbras as:

$$f \ominus k = T[U[f] \ominus U[k]] \tag{5}$$

where, U[f] is the umbra of surface f, U[k] is the umbra of the surface k, and T is the transformation operator. Opening basically smooths contours, breaks isthmuses, eliminates small islands or peninsulas and eliminates sharp peaks.

Closing Closing basically smooths contours, fuses narrow breaks, fuses long bulfs, eliminates small holes and fills gaps. If f: F→E and k:K→E, then the gray

Fig. 6. Left: Anterior and inferior wall do not have uniform motion when moved from end diastole to end systole boundary. **Right**: Anterior wall has not moved much from end diastole to end systole boundary.

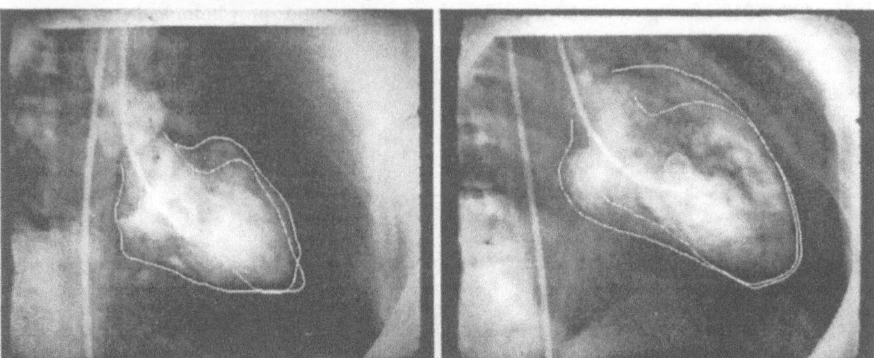

scale closing of f by a structuring element k is denoted by

$$f \bullet k = (f \oplus k) \ominus k. \tag{6}$$

This can also given in the discrete case as:

$$(f \bullet k)(x) = min_{z \in k}\, max_{y \in k}\{f(x + z - y)\} \tag{7}$$

If f: F→E and k:K→E, then $f \oplus k$ =F $\oplus$ K → E. It can also be understood in terms of Umbras as under:

$$f \ominus k = T[U[f] \ominus U[k]] \tag{8}$$

In terms of Umbras, the erosion of f by k is by taking the surface of the erosion of the Umbra of f by the Umbra of k.

3.2   Interpretation of the Opening and Closing

Opening and closing was explained by Sternberg [12] using a physical picture of the gray scale opening and closing of the rolling ball algorithm. In this algorithm, the closing of the gray scale image $a(x, y)$ by a spherical structuring element S is visualized in terms of the closing of the Umbra $U[a]$ by S. Imagine an extra terrestrial landscape of peaks and valleys and visualize a sphere which is free to move above the terrain surface but whose downward mobility is constrained by the surface. The closing is formed by the union of all translations of the sphere above and touching the gray scale surface. Sternberg calls it a rolling ball because those that touch the surface are said to be rolling on the surface. Closing a gray scale surface by dilating and then eroding by a spherical structuring elements rolls the ball. Gray scale opening by a spherical structuring element is visualized as a ball rolling along the underside of the gray level surface. The effect of the opening is opposite to that of closing. Ruts and pits are followed while peaks and ridges leave gaps in the coverage of the rolling ball.

3.3 Heart Rate Normalization

Stage two of the pre-processing consists of a gray scale heart normalization that normalizes the variable number of frames to a fixed number of frames (30). From the ground truth database the average ratio of the total frames in diastole cycle to the total number of frames in the cardiac cycle is:

$$r_d = \frac{n_{ED}}{n_{ED} + n_{ES}} \tag{9}$$

This ratio r_d is 0.4. Thus the systole cycle consists of 0.4 × 30=12 frames and the diastole cycle consists of 0.6 × 30=18 frames. The interpolation is made from the variable number of frames (F_v) to 30. If a patient study has F_v variable number of frames, then there are $0.4F_v$ frames in systole cycle and $0.6F_v$ frames in diastole cycle. Thus the interpolation is done from $0.4F_v$ to 12 frames for systole cycle and $0.6F_v$ frames to 18 frames in diastole cycle. First and the last frame's gray scale values are fixed thus interpolation is applied to $F_v - 2$ frames. Interpolation is done in the following way. A sequence of gray scale values at a fixed location throughout the cardiac cycle of F frames, $g_i, i = 1, \ldots, F$, is extracted. The number of frames in systole F_s and that in diastole F_d are $0.4F_v$ and $0.6F_v$. For the sequence of $F_s(F_d)$ frames, we interpolate it into a sequence of 12(18) frames. Let us assume F_i frames are interpolated into F_I. The last stage of the pre-processing consists of normalization of the gray scale intensities between 0 to 255.

4 Bayesian Approach to Pixel Classification

Lee et al. [1] developed a classical Bayesian classification framework for solving the left ventricle boundary detection problem. From the multiple LVG's throughout the cardiac cycle and the corresponding ground truth which are manually traced boundaries, the *a priori* probability for any position (x, y) being in any class c was estimated. This *a priori* probability is also made dependent of the user input of 3 points: the aortic valve plane (2 points) and the apex (1 point).

A pixel's class label c means that the pixel is in LV from the first frame to frame $(c-1)$ and out of LV from frame c to the end systolic frame in systole and *vice versa* in diastole. This class assignment strategy enables us to transform the classifier result to a sequence of 0's and 1's, which results in an LV region at each frame. Note, heart rate normalization was done to fix the length of the feature vector.

Lee made two assumptions in classifying the pixels from the multiple frames of the LVG. The first one is that the end-systolic frame number from a new patient's LVG is known prior to the classification step. This permitted Lee to deal with the frames in the systole cycle and those in diastole separately. Another assumption was with respect to the heart motion. The heart motion is mainly contracting in systole and expanding in diastole. This means that when we look at a pixel location throughout the cardiac cycle, there is at most one transition in

Fig. 7. From a binary sequence, class number is decided.

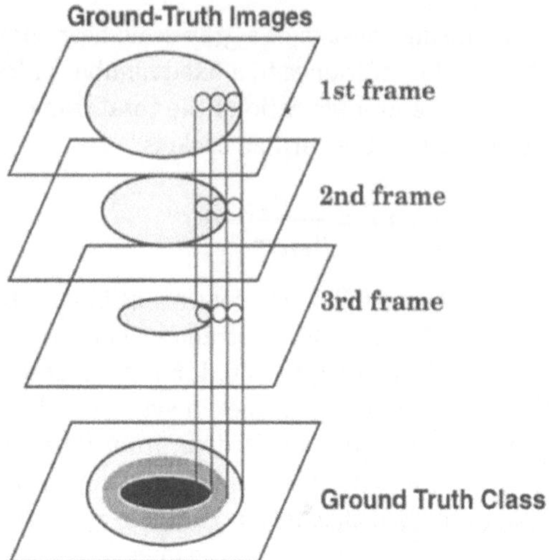

systole where the location is in left ventricle and then moves out of LV. Likewise there is at most one transition in diastole where the location out of LV moves inside LV.

4.1 Problem Statement

Under Lee's restricted motion assumptions, the problem statement can be formulated as a problem of maximizing the expected gain using a restricted set of classes.

Given F_s grey-scale images in systole, $G_i, i = 1, \ldots, F_s$,
Classify a pixel at location (x, y) and having gray values $(g_1, \ldots, g_{F_s})$ to class $c \in \{1, 2, \ldots, F_s, F_s + 1\}$ where c which maximizes

$$\sum_{c'} e(c, c') P(c'|X)$$

where $(g_1, \ldots, g_{F_s})$ is the feature vector X, $P(c|X) = P(X|c)P(c)/P(X)$ and $P(X|c)$ is class conditional probability and $P(c)$ is the *a priori* class probability which depends on image position.

4.2 Ground Truth Class Assignment

The ideal class assignment was determined from the physician's hand-drawn boundaries of the LV region in each frame. Filling the inside of these boundaries by pixel value "1" produces *LV regions*, $\bar{R}_f$, $f = 1, \ldots, F_s(F_d)$. A location in region $\bar{R}_f$ means that the location is in the LV at frame i. By stacking LV regions of the entire cardiac cycle, $\bar{R}'_f s$, we can look at them as 3 dimensional array

Table 1. Binary sequence pattern under the monotonic motion assumption.

frame	Diastole			
1	1 0 0 $\cdots$	0	0	0
2	1 1 0 $\cdots$	0	0	0
3	1 1 1 $\cdots$	0	0	0
$\vdots$		$\vdots$		
F_d	1 1 1 $\cdots$	1	0	0
F_d	1 1 1 $\cdots$	1	1	0
class number	1 2 3 $\cdots$	$F_d - 1$	F_d	$F_d + 1$

(a) Diastole.

frame	Systole			
1	0 1 1 $\cdots$	1	1	1
2	0 0 1 $\cdots$	1	1	1
3	0 0 0 $\cdots$	1	1	1
$\vdots$		$\vdots$		
$F_s - 1$	0 0 0 $\cdots$	0	1	1
F_s	0 0 0 $\cdots$	0	0	1
class number	1 2 3 $\cdots$	$F_s - 1$	F_s	$F_s + 1$

(b) Systole.

specified by frame number, row coordinate, and column coordinate, (f, x, y). For any location specified by (x, y), we can extract the sequence of 0's and 1's, from which the class number for that location can be estimated (see Figure 7).

In systole (diastole) of $F_s (F_d)$ frames, the number of all possible sequences is $2^{F_s} (2^{F_d})$, but that of realistically feasible sequences is far less. Under the assumption we made about the LV motion, contracting in systole and expanding in diastole, the ideal sequence has the following patterns (Table 1) and the number of cases is $F_s (F_d) + 1$.

But the ground truth sequences from the LV regions differ from the ideal ones in that they include multiple 1-0 transitions and 0-1 transitions. The ground truth class is, therefore, determined by a matched filter. From the sequence of 0's and 1's, $< b_1, b_2, \ldots, b_F >$, we determine its ground truth class by applying a matched filter with the kernel 11000 in systole and the kernel 00111 in diastole. These kernels were choosen based on the monotonic LV boundary motion assumption. Prior to the matched filter, a running average filter of length 5 is applied. The matched filter with the kernel picked the frame number at which the transition occurs. If there is more than one transition that occurs in the sequence, it picks the first one. If the sequence is all 1's (0's) in systole (diastole), the class number is $F_s (F_d) + 1$ and if the sequence is all 0's (1's), the class number is 1. Figure 8. shows Ground-truth class image for systole and for diastole.

4.3 Class To Sequence To LV Region Mapping

In the assignment of ground truth to each pixel location we convert the binary sequence to a class label. We also need its inverse operation which converts a class label into a sequence of 0's and 1's where 0 means out of LV and 1 means in LV. Under the monotonicity motion assumption, class c in systole means that the transition from 1 to 0 occurs at the c-th frame, *i.e.*, the location is in the region up to frame $c - 1$ and out of the region from frame c. The conversion of a pixel's class label c to the corresponding binary sequence $< b_1, \ldots, b_F >$ is accomplished by defining

$$\begin{cases} b_n = 1 \text{ if } n < c \\ b_n = 0 \text{ otherwise} \end{cases}$$

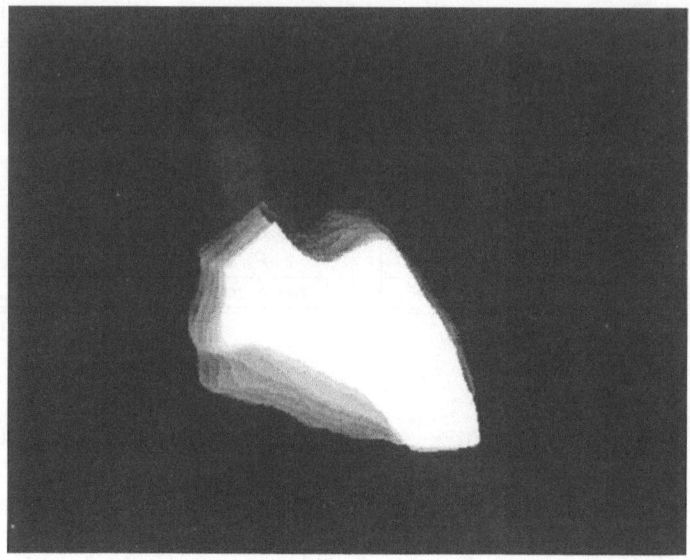

(a) Systole, class number increases from 1 to 13 as the pixel becomes brighter.

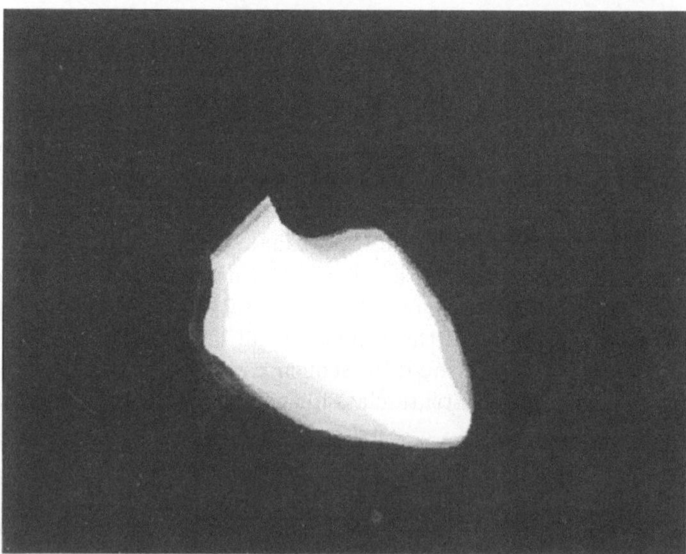

(b) Diastole, class number increases from 1 to 18 as the pixel becomes darker.

Fig. 8. Ground truth class images for systole and diastole. Class number represents the frame number of the pixel's transition from inside to outside (systole) of the heart and from outside to inside (diastole) due to the compression and the expansion.

Fig. 9. Conversion of class label to the corresponding binary sequence.

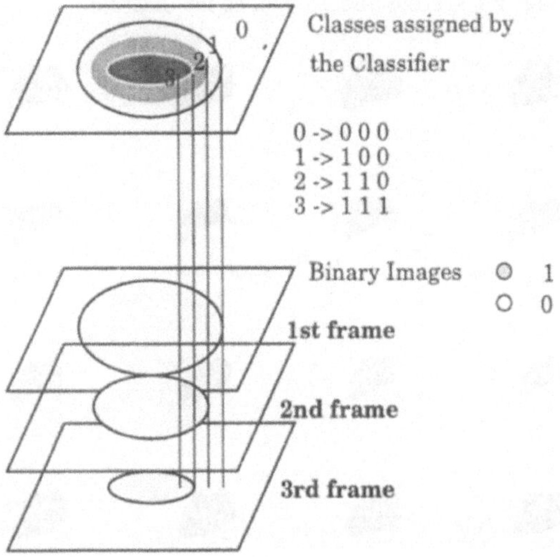

and is shown in Figure 9.

Elements of the sequences of all locations for a fixed frame tells us whether each location is in LV or out of LV. At each frame, the region made up of all the pixels in LV is called by *observed LV region R_i*, and is defined by

$$R_i = \{(x, y) \mid C(x, y) \geq c\}$$

where $c = 1, \ldots, F_s + 1$ and $C(x, y)$ denotes class label assigned to location (x, y). *Observed LV regions* are found for all frames simultaneously. Figure 10. is the multiband image generated from the ground truth class image of Figure 7.

4.4 Maximum Expected Economic Gain Classifier

Each pixel is specified by patient i, frame number f, x-coordinate x, and y-coordinate y. Its gray-value is $g(i, f, x, y)$. From the hand-drawn boundary associated with the LVG, we obtain the corresponding LV region by filling the inside of the boundary. The indicator function for the LV region is denoted by $r(i, f, x, y)$ and is defined by

$$r(i, f, x, y) = \begin{cases} 1 \text{ if } (i, f, x, y) \text{ is in LV Region} \\ 0 \text{ otherwise} \end{cases}$$

where $1 \leq i \leq F_p$, $1 \leq f \leq F$, $1 \leq x \leq IX$, and $1 \leq y \leq IY$. IX and IY are the number of rows and number of columns in the image. The ground truth class number $C(i, x, y)$ at location (x, y) for patient i is extracted from the sequence $< r(i, 1, x, y), \ldots, r(i, F_s, x, y) >$.

We initially assumed that the feature vector of patient i, $X(i, x, y)$, consisting of grey values at location (x, y) of all frames, $g(i, f, x, y)$, $f = 1, 2, \ldots, F_s$, follows

Fig. 10. Multiband images generated by class to sequence mapping from ground-truth class image. 12 frames for systole and 18 frames for diastole.

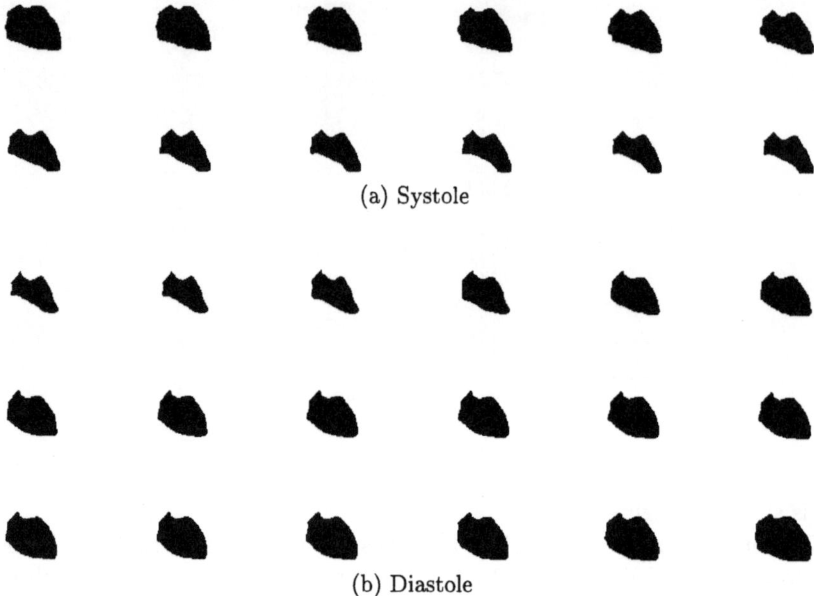

(a) Systole

(b) Diastole

a multi-variate normal distribution which is specified by

$$P(X|c) = P(X|\mu_c, \Sigma_c) = (2\pi)^{-\frac{F_s}{2}} |\Sigma_c|^{-\frac{1}{2}} \exp(-\frac{1}{2}(X - \mu_c)^t \Sigma_c^{-1} (X - \mu_c))$$

Then we refined this model by determining from the training data for each class c the histogram $h(*; c)$ of

$$(X - \mu_c)^t \Sigma_c^{-1} (X - \mu_c)$$

for all X in class c and used

$$P(c|x) = h((X - \mu_c)^t \Sigma_c^{-1} (X - \mu_c); c)$$

With this model, our problem statement becomes

For a given feature vector X find the class c which maximizes the expected gain

$$\sum_{c'} e(c, c') P(c'|X)$$

where $e(c, c')$ is the economic gain for assigning class c when class c' is the true class.

Parameter Estimation From the training data set, we can estimate the mean vector $\hat{\mu}_c$ and the covariance matrix $\hat{\Sigma}_c$ for each class. The estimated class mean and covariance matrix specify the class probability distribution $P(X|\hat{\mu}_c, \hat{\Sigma}_c)$. Mean vector and covariance matrix for class c are estimated by

$$\hat{\mu}_c = \frac{1}{\#L_c} \sum_{(i,x,y)\in L_c} X(i,x,y)$$

$$\hat{\Sigma}_c = \frac{1}{\#L_c - 1} \sum_{(i,x,y)\in L_c} \left(X(i,x,y) - \hat{\mu}_c\right)\left(X(i,x,y) - \hat{\mu}_c\right)^t$$

where

$$L_c = \{(i,x,y)|C(i,x,y) = c\}$$

In order to reduce the number of parameters to estimate, the pooled covariance matrix is used, which is estimated by

$$\hat{\Sigma} = \frac{\sum_{c=1}^{F_c} L_c \hat{\Sigma}_c}{\sum_{c=1}^{F_c} L_c}$$

Once a classified image is computed, it is spatially simplified and the boundary of the largest connected component on the simplified image is determined. We call this boundary the raw classified boundary. Fig. 11 shows a typical raw classification boundary for the end diastole and end systole frames of the cardiac cycle.

5 Systematic Error Cancellation

The raw boundaries obtained from the pixel classifier have significant error and much of the error in the inferior wall and apical zone is systematic and can be eliminated with a post-processing procedure that uses physician specified points for the aortic valve plane and the apex.

5.1 Calibration methodology

The systematic boundary error cancellation methodology is, in effect, a calibration procedure which calibrates out all systematic position, orientation, and shape errors of the raw classified boundaries. The calibration transformation is estimated using a database consisting of the ground truth boundaries and the corresponding raw boundaries generated by the classifier [1]. The cross-validation protocol for estimating the accuracy of the boundary error cancellation procedure takes a database of N patient studies and partitions it into K equal sized subsets. Then for all K *choose* L combinations, the transformation using L subsets is estimated. Now using the estimated transformation on the remaining $K - L$ subsets, the mean error of the transformed boundary is estimated.

Fig. 11. Results of the pixel classification algorithm over ED and ES frames of the cardiac cycle. **Top row**: End Systole (ES) frame showing very little dye in the apex zone of the left ventricle and the pixel classification boundary (the thin boundary line) falls short in the apical zone. Also seen is the over estimation of the inferior walls. Thicker boundaries are the boundaries drawn by the cardiologist. **Bottom row**: End-Diastole (ED) frame showing very little dye in the apex zone of the left ventricle and the pixel classification boundary (the thin boundary line) is under-estimated in the apex zone of the left ventricle. The thick boundary lines represent the boundary of the left ventricle as delineated by the cardiologist.

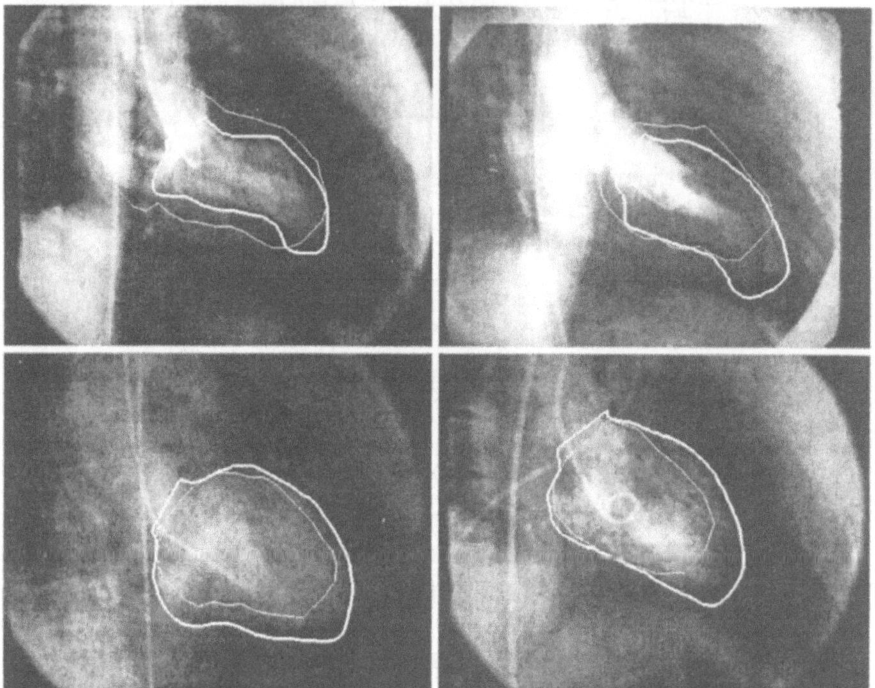

5.2 Sampling

The input raw and ground truth boundaries are initially in an irregularly spaced vertex polygon format with 100 vertices and unit dimensions in millimeters. The polygons are resampled and interpolated into into an appropriate number of equally spaced vertices before it undergoes the calibration procedure discussed below.

5.3 Performance and data analysis scheme

The error between a computed boundary and the ground truth boundary is defined as the average distance between each vertex of the computed boundary and the polygon of the ground truth boundary and the distance between each vertex of the ground truth boundary and the polygon of the computed boundary.

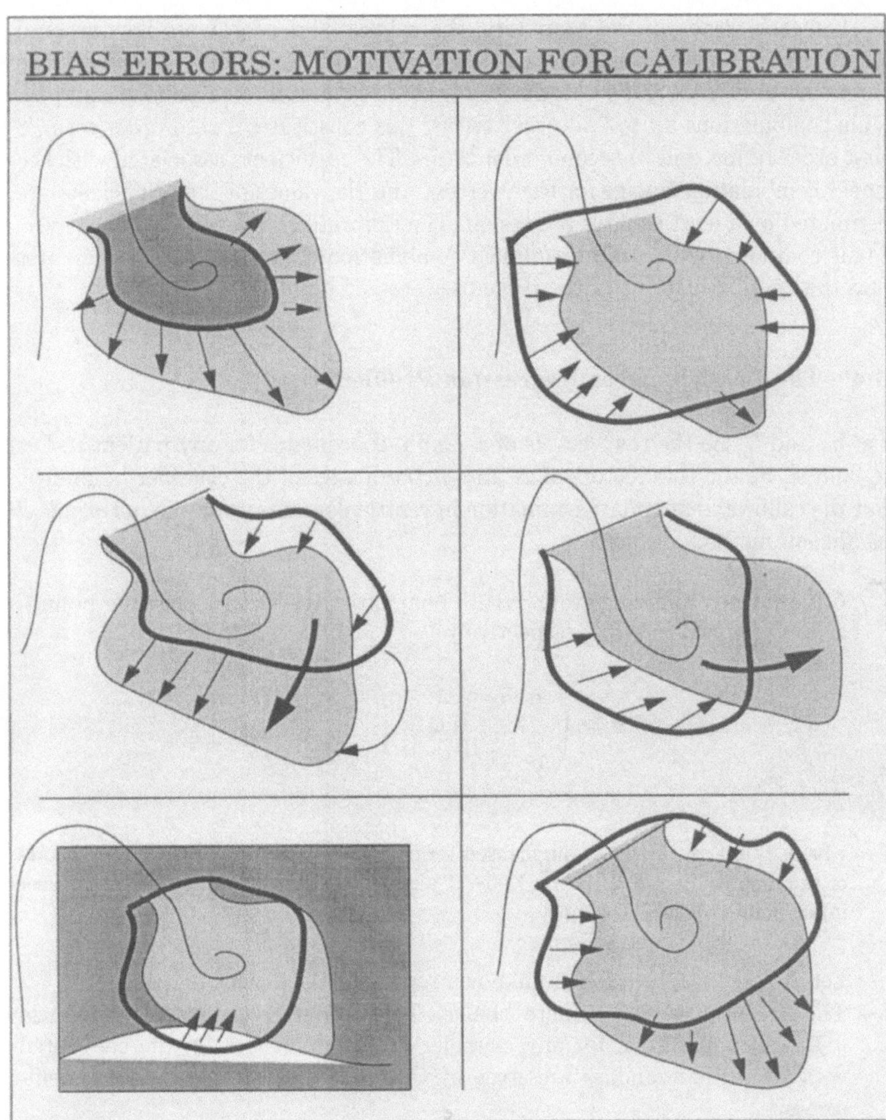

Fig. 12. Bias errors produced by the pixel classification system. **Top row**, left and right: classifier boundary inside and outside the ideal boundary. **Middle row**, left and right: classifier boundary towards the anterior and inferior wall. **Last row**, left: classifier boundary overlaps the diaphragm. **Last row, right**: classifier boundary outside the ideal boundary in top two-third region and under-estimated in the bottom one-third region.

For each vertex of the boundary, the calibrated x-coordinate is computed as the linear combination of raw x- *and* raw y-coordinates of the left ventricle boundary and the x and y coordinate of the three user entered points in all possible combinations up to 2nd order terms: this constitutes 1 zero order term, 6 first order terms, and 21 second order terms. The coefficients associated with the linear combination change for each vertex. And the values of the coefficients are estimated by a least squares regression. The calibrated y-coordinate of that vertex is computed with a *different* linear combination of raw x- *and* y-coordinates and the 2nd order terms of the three user-entered points.

5.4   The Least Squares Regression Problem Setup

Let g'_n and h'_n be the row vectors of x- and y-coordinates for any patient n. Let r'_n and s'_n be the row vectors of x- and y-coordinates of the classifier boundary. For the calibrated boundary estimation in ventriculograms using the *independent coefficient* method, we are:

- **Given**: Corresponding ground truth boundaries $\mathbf{R}$ $[N \times 2P]$, classifier boundaries $\mathbf{Q}$ $[N \times (2P + 28)]$ respectively:

$$\mathbf{R} = \begin{pmatrix} g'_1 \; h'_1 \\ \dots \\ g'_N \; h'_N \end{pmatrix} \quad \mathbf{Q} = \begin{pmatrix} r'_1 \; s'_1 \; t'_1 \\ \dots \\ r'_N \; s'_N \; t'_N \end{pmatrix}$$

  where, t'_1 are the 1+6+21 augmented terms coming from the 3 user input points of the first study and t'_N is the 1+6+21 augmented terms coming from the 3 user input points of the Nth study.

- Let $\mathbf{A}$ $[(2P + 28) \times 2P]$ be unknown regression coefficient matrix.
- The problem is to estimate the coefficient matrix $\mathbf{A}$ and to minimize $\| \mathbf{R} - \mathbf{Q}\,\mathbf{A} \|^2$. Then for any classifier boundary matrix $\mathbf{Q}$, the calibrated vertices of the boundary are given by $\mathbf{Q}\hat{\mathbf{A}}$, where $\hat{\mathbf{A}}$ is the estimated coefficients.

This problem is solved by the standard least squares solution.

Due to the finite number of our patient studies, 377, and the large number of coefficients being estimated, there is a relationship between the number of vertices we sample the polygon and the resulting mean and standard deviation of the boundary error on the test set. If we sample to many points, we in effect memorize the training data and performance on the test set will be poor. If we sample to few points, we do well in terms of generalizing but we incur a large error due to the coarse sampling. Therefore we optimize for the number of vertices. At the optimal values the mean boundary error is just more than 2.4 millimeters.

Fig. 13. Classifier vs. Estimated boundaries with gray scale in the back ground using the systematic error cancellation procedure patient name: **1017f**, **Thick LV contour** -Ground Truth, **Thin LV contour**-Classifier, and Estimated, **Upper**: (a1) Classifier ED frame boundary with ground truth. (a2) Calibrated ED frame boundary with ground truth. **Bottom**: (b1) Classifier ES frame boundary with ground truth. (b2) Calibrated ES frame boundary with ground truth. Mean end frame error ($\frac{ED+ES}{2}$) = 2.0 mm,

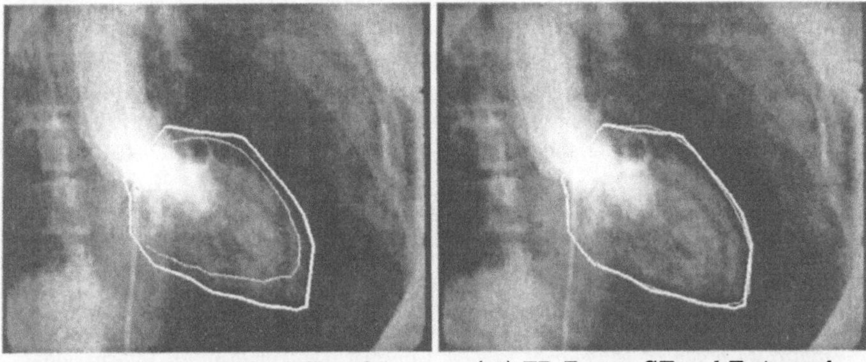

(a1) ED Frame: GT and Classifier   (a2) ED Frame: GT and Estimated

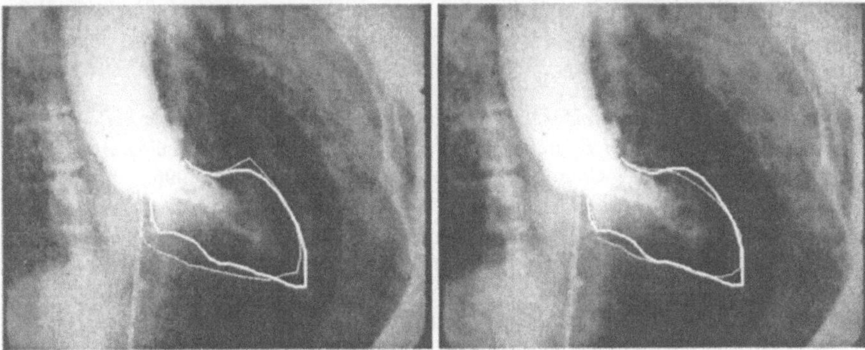

(b1) ES Frame: GT and Classifier   (b2) ES Frame: GT and Estimated

6 Future Work

We are currently examining the errors produced by the algorithm in an attempt to refine it to reduce the average error to less than 2mm. Then we will gather statistics on the ejection fraction estimates that are based on the automatic boundary delineation algorithm.

References

1. C. K. Lee, *Automated Boundary Tracing Using Temporal Information*, Ph.D Thesis, Department of Electrical Engineering, Universtiy of Washington, Seattle, 1994.

2. Helmut Wollschleger, Robert Wal Tenspiel, Ulrich Solzbach, Andreas M. Zeiher and Hangoerg Just, *Reliable Automatic Frame-By-Frame Contour Detection of Digitized LV Cine-Angiograms*, IEEE Computers in Cardiology, p353-p356, 1988.

3. Florence H. Sheehan, Robert M. Haralick, Jasjit S. Suri and Yong Shao, *Method for determining the contour of an In Vivo Organ Using Multiple Image Frames of the Organ*, Contents: (i) Aorta and the Aortic Valve Plane Estimation (ii) Left ventricle boundary estimation, Patent Submitted to University of Washington, Seattle, filed through Office of Technology Transfer (OTT), File Number 1221, August 1996.

4. Jasjit S. Suri, Robert M. Haralick and F. H. Sheehan, *Two Automatic Calibration Algorithms for Left Ventricle Boundary Estimation in X-ray Images*, Published in Proc. of IEEE Int. Conf. of Engineering in Medicine and Biology (EMBS), Amsterdam, The Netherlands, ISBN 90-9010005-9(CD-ROM) SOE 9609001, Oct 31 - Nov. 3, 1996.

5. Jasjit S. Suri, Robert M. Haralick and F. H. Sheehan, *Two Calibration Algorithms and Its Performance for Boundary Estimation of Left Ventricle in Noisy Ventriclograms*, Accepted for Jour. of IEEE Trans. in Bio Engineering, 1996, revision required.

6. Jasjit S. Suri and Robert M. Haralick, *Systematic Error Correction in automatically produced boundaries in Low Contrast Ventriculograms*, International Conference in Pattern Recognition, Austria, 1996.

7. Jasjit S. Suri, Robert M. Haralick and F. H. Sheehan, *Correction of Systematic Errors in Automatically Produced Boundaries from Low Contrast Ventriculograms*, Accepted (final submission) for Journal of IEEE Trans. in Medical Imaging, 1996.

8. Jasjit S. Suri, Robert M. Haralick and Florence H. Sheehan, *Accurate Left Ventricle Apex Position and Boundary Estimation From Noisy Ventriculograms*, Proceedings of the IEEE Computers in Cardiology, Indianapolis, 1996.

9. Jasjit S. Suri, Robert M. Haralick and F. H. Sheehan, *A General technique for automatic Left Ventricle Boundary Validation: Relation Between Cardioangiograms and Observed Boundary Errors*, Accepted for: Society for Computer Applications in Radiology (SCAR), Rochester, Minnesota, June 21-24, 1997.

10. Jasjit S. Suri, Robert M. Haralick and F. H. Sheehan, *Effect of Edge Detection, Pixel Classification, Classification-Edge Fusion Over LV Calibration, A two Stage Automatic system, 10th Scandinavian Conference on Image Analysis (SCIA '97)*, June 9-11, Finland, 1997.

11. Jasjit S. Suri, Robert M. Haralick and F. H. Sheehan, *Abstract: Accurate Left Ventricle Position and Boundary Estimation from Noisy Ventriculograms*, Computers in Cardiology 1996, Indianapolis, page 68, S52.1, Left Ventricular Wall Motion Track, Sep. 8-11, 1996, Indiana, USA.

12. Sternberg, *Grayscale Morphology*, Computer Vision, Graphics, Image Processing, 1985.

Robust Motion Vector Relaxation for X-Ray Fluoroscopy Using Generalized Gauss-Markov Random Fields

Til Aach and Dietmar Kunz

Philips Research Laboratories,
Weisshausstr. 2, D-52066 Aachen, Germany
Email: (aach/kunz)@pfa.research.philips.com

Abstract. We describe a Bayesian motion estimation algorithm which is part of a temporally recursive noise reduction filter for X-ray fluoroscopy images. Our algorithm draws its robustness against high quantum noise levels from a statistical regularization, where a priori expectations about the spatial and temporal smoothness of motion vector fields are modelled by generalized Gauss-Markov random fields. We show that by using generalized Gauss-Markov random fields both smoothness and motion edges can be captured, without the need to specify an often critical edge detection threshold. Instead, our algorithm controls edges by a single parameter by means of which the regularization can be tuned from a median-filter like behaviour to a linear-filter like one.

Keywords: fluoroscopy, image restoration, Bayesian motion estimation, generalized Gauss-Markov random fields, thresholdless edge model.

1   Introduction

We describe a robust X-ray fluoroscopy motion estimator which we use within a motion compensated temporally recursive noise reduction filter. Our estimation algorithm is well able to cope with the high noise levels in fluoroscopy (see Fig. 1), which are caused by the very low X-ray dose rates used in fluoroscopic imaging [1, 2].

Motion compensated temporal filters for usually only moderately noisy real world video sequences [3] are often based on the well known block matching algorithm for motion estimation, which, however, is very noise-sensitive. To make motion estimation robust against noise, we regularize the estimation problem by suitably formulated prior knowledge, namely by exploiting the expected smoothness in both space and time of 'true' motion vector fields. We express these prior expectations by generalized Gauss-Markov random fields applied within a Bayesian framework. The advantage of using generalized Gauss-Markov random fields is that, apart from smoothness, they can also describe motion edges without requiring explicit specification of edge detection thresholds. Edges are controlled by a single 'soft' parameter, by means of which the influence of regularization can be tuned from a median-filter like behaviour to a linear-filter like one.

2 Bayesian Motion Estimation

2.1 MAP-Approach

Let Y_n denote the n-th frame of the observed fluoroscopy sequence, with $y_n(k)$, $k = 1, \ldots, N$ being the grey level at pixel k, and N being the number of pixels in each frame. (For simplicity, we use a one-dimensional notation here). We seek motion vectors $v_n(k)$ such that for each pixel k, $k + v_n(k)$ is the corresponding location in the previous frame Y_{n-1}, with the motion vector matrix $v_n(k)$, $k = 1, \ldots, N$ forming the motion field V_n. Given the images Y_n and Y_{n-1} *and* the previous motion field estimate V_{n-1}, we intend to determine the motion field estimate $\hat{V}_n$ so that it obeys

$$\hat{V}_n = \arg\max_V p\left(V | Y_n, Y_{n-1}, \hat{V}_{n-1}\right) \; , \tag{1}$$

with $p(V|Y_n, Y_{n-1}, \hat{V}_{n-1})$ being the a posteriori probability density function (pdf) for a motion field V given the observations. With conditional statistical independence between (Y_n, Y_{n-1}) and $\hat{V}_{n-1}$, this can be rewritten to

$$\hat{V}_n = \arg\max_V \left[p\left(Y_n, Y_{n-1}|V\right) \cdot p\left(\hat{V}_{n-1}|V\right) \cdot p(V)\right] \; . \tag{2}$$

2.2 The Observation Model

To specify the likelihood term $p(Y_n, Y_{n-1}|V)$, we assume that temporal grey level changes are caused only by either motion or (quantum) noise (cf. [4]). As the influence of motion can be compensated by the *displaced* frame difference (DFD) $D(V_n) = \{d[k, v_n(k)]\}$, where $d[k, v_n(k)] = y_n(k) - y_{n-1}(k + v_n(k))$, what remains is modelling quantum noise. Approximating the Poissonian distribution of quantum noise by a Gaussian one with signal-dependent variance, we obtain

$$p\left(Y_n, Y_{n-1}|V\right) \propto \prod_{k=1}^{N} \frac{1}{\sqrt{4\pi\sigma^2(k)}} \cdot \exp\left\{-\frac{d^2(k, v(k))}{4\sigma^2(k)}\right\} \; , \tag{3}$$

where we also made the approximating assumption of spatially uncorrelated noise. The variable $\sigma^2(k)$ is the quantum noise variance at each pixel k. In the remainder of this paper, we assume that the quantum noise variance σ^2 as a function of intensity — and hence also as a function of location k — is known [2], either by being predicted from acquisition parameter settings of the system, or by estimation from the acquired images.

2.3 The Motion Field Model

We model $p(V)$ by a Markov random field, where statistical dependencies are described locally [5]. Invoking the Hammersly-Clifford theorem, this permits to write $p(V)$ as a Gibbs density, i.e. $p(V) \propto \exp\{-E(V)\}$, where $E(V)$ is an *energy* ascribed to a motion field. This density clearly favours low energies, hence $E(V)$

should be specified in such a way that it is low for smooth motion vector fields V. As a consequence of the Markovian assumption, this energy can be decomposed into a sum of local energy terms according to $E(V) = \sum_{k=1}^{N} E_L(k, V)$. Each local energy $E_L(k, V)$ depends only on the eight vectors adjacent to pixel k (2nd order Markov random field). To obtain a local energy which favours smooth vector fields, we penalize differences between neighbouring motion vectors by

$$E_L(k, V) = \lambda \cdot \sum_{l \in N_k} g_l \cdot \Delta_l^\nu(k) \ , \tag{4}$$

with $\Delta_l(k) = ||v(k) - v(l)||_2$. Our model views differences between $v(k)$ and its four diagonally adjacent neighbours as less severe than differences between $v(k)$ and its four nearest neighbours. This is expressed through the weights g_l, with $g_l = 1$ if $v(l)$ is horizontally or vertically adjacent to $v(k)$, and $g_l = 0.5$ for the diagonal neighbours of $v(k)$. The factor $\lambda > 0$ is a weighting parameter.

For exponent values $\nu > 1$, this model clearly discourages large differences between adjacent vectors, and hence encourages (locally) smooth motion fields. For $\nu = 2$, (4) is referred to as a Gauss-Markov random field ("quadratic regularization") [6]. While this model is quite common to describe smoothness, it inherently blurs abrupt transitions of motion occurring between neighbouring and differently moving objects. The reason for this is that motion edges correspond to relatively large values of $\Delta_l^2(k)$, which are governed by the quickly decaying tails of the (multidimensional) Gaussian density. To prevent such blurring, (4) can be replaced by

$$E_L(k, V) = \lambda \cdot \sum_{l \in N_k} g_l \cdot \min\left\{ \Delta_l^2(k), T \right\} \ , \tag{5}$$

which is quadratic if $\Delta_l^2(k)$ is smaller than the *edge detection threshold* T, and flat otherwise [7]. The necessity of having to specify this threshold, however, is of twofold disadvantage: firstly, it is often hard to find an appropriate threshold value to reliably detect edges of usually unknown magnitude. Furthermore, it is by no means certain that all edges can be captured by single threshold parameter. Also, (5) is not convex, which is disadvantageous for the maximization of (2).

These problems can be avoided by employing a density the tails of which do not fall off as rapidly as those of a quadratic Gaussian density. To achieve this, it suffices to *reduce* the exponent ν, what results in a *generalized* Gauss-Markov random field [6]. Reduction of ν corresponds to a gradual increase of the magnitude of the tails of the density function, what in turn makes edges more likely to occur. Eventually, for $\nu = 1$, a (multidimensional) Laplacian density is reached.

In temporal direction, we use a similar model. Assuming that each vector $\hat{v}_{n-1}(k)$ depends only on its successor $v(k)$, we have $p(\hat{v}_{n-1}(k)|V) = p(\hat{v}_{n-1}(k)|v(k))$. Assuming furthermore conditional statistical independence results in $p(\hat{V}_{n-1}|V) = \prod_{k=1}^{N} p[\hat{v}_{n-1}(k)|v(k)]$. Inserting the generalized Gaussian model yields

$$p[\hat{v}_{n-1}(k)|v(k)] \propto \exp\left\{ -\lambda' \cdot ||v(k) - \hat{v}_{n-1}(k)||_2^\nu \right\} \ . \tag{6}$$

3   The Estimation Algorithm

Inserting the derived expressions for $p(Y_n, Y_{n-1}|V)$, $p(\hat{V}_{n-1}|V)$ and $p(V)$ into (2), and taking the negative logarithm results in the following optimization criterion:

$$C(V|Y_n, Y_{n-1}, \hat{V}_{n-1}) = \sum_{k=1}^{N} \left[\frac{d^2(k, v(k))}{\sigma^2(k)} + \right. \tag{7}$$

$$\left. \lambda' \cdot ||v(k) - \hat{v}_{n-1}(k)||_2^\nu + \lambda \cdot \sum_{l \in N_k} g_l \cdot \Delta_l^\nu(k) \right] ,$$

where a factor of four was absorbed into λ and λ'. We minimize this criterion by a deterministic ICM-relaxation [5] on a blockwise basis, where each block comprises e.g. 16×16 pixels and counts as one macro-pixel. Initialization of the relaxation can for instance be done by full search block matching or by simply using the motion vector field for the previous frame. The initial estimate is then optimized by repeatedly scanning the image grid. For each block, the motion vector is tentatively replaced by the following candidates: each of its eight spatial neighbours, its temporal predecessor, the four vectors differing from the current one by half a pixel, and the average of all vectors in N_k weighted by g_l. For each of these candidates and the current vector, the optimization criterion is *locally* recomputed, and the candidate minimizing the criterion retained. In practice, this relaxation converges in only three iterations.

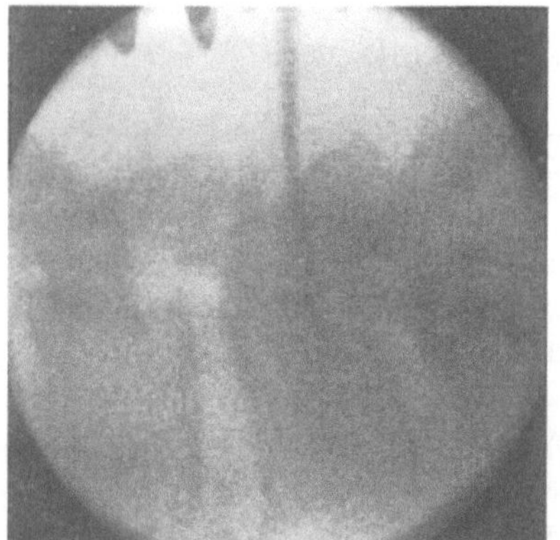 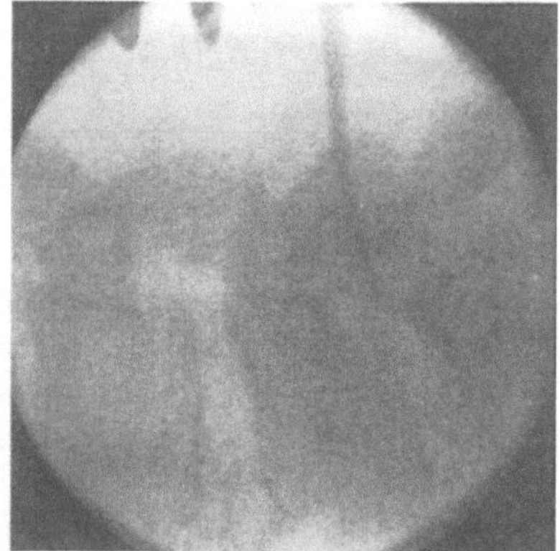

Fig. 1. Two subsequent fluoroscopy frames depicting vertebrae which remain almost still, whereas the surgical instrument in the upper image parts starts moving abruptly in horizontal direction.

Fig. 1 shows two subsequent frames of a noisy fluoroscopy sequence, between which the depicted surgical tool starts to move abruptly in horizontal direction. The motion field estimated by the Gaussian model ($\nu = 2$) is shown left in Fig. 2. Clearly, the motion of the tool is not captured due to edge blurring. This is quite different in the right hand side of Fig. 2, where the tool motion vectors are clearly delineated from the stationary background. Here, estimation was based on the generalized Gaussian model with $\nu = 1.3$.

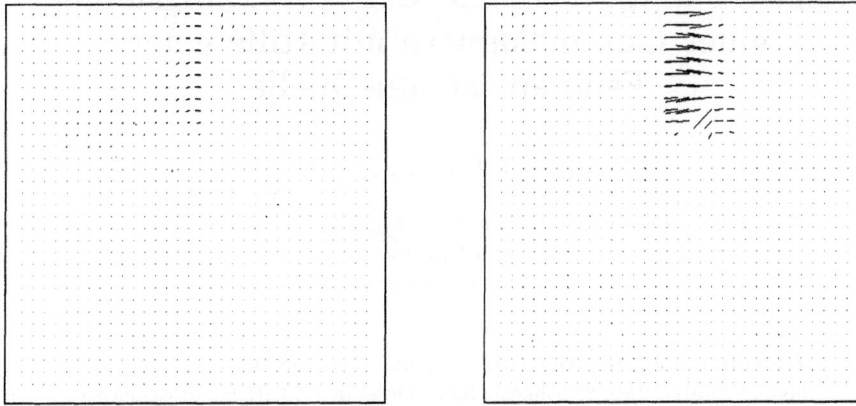

Fig. 2. *Left:* Motion vector field with $\nu = 2$, oversmoothing the motion of the tool. *Right:* Motion vector field with $\nu = 1.3$, where the motion of the tool is clearly reconstructed.

4 Conclusions

We have described a regularized motion estimator which is on the one hand able to cope with strong quantum noise levels, while on the other hand well reconstructing motion edges. No edge threshold is necessary, rather, edges are controlled by a single 'soft' parameter. In combination with a recursive noise reduction filter [3], significant noise reduction can be achieved without noticeably blurring objects.

An extended paper of this algorithm is to appear in a forthcoming issue of the Philips Journal of Research.

References

1. T. Aach, U. Schiebel, G. Spekowius, "Digital image acquisition and processing for medical x-ray imaging applications," Proc. ISEP-96, Cologne,Sept. 21–22, 82–90.
2. T. Aach, D. Kunz, "Spectral estimation filters for noise reduction in x-ray fluoroscopy imaging," Proc. EUSIPCO-96, Trieste, Sept. 10–13, 571–574.
3. E. Dubois, S. Sabri, "Noise reduction in image sequences using motion compensated temporal filtering," IEEE Trans. Comm. 32(7), 826–831, 1984.
4. T. Aach, A. Kaup, "Disparity-based segmentation of stereoscopic foreground / background image sequences," IEEE Trans. Comm. 42(2), 673–679, 1994.
5. J. Besag, "On the statistical analysis of dirty pictures," J. Roy. Stat. Soc. B 48(3), 259–302, 1986.
6. C. Bouman, K. Sauer, "A generalized gaussian image model for edge-preserving MAP-estimation," IEEE Trans. Im. Proc.2(3)296–310, 1993.
7. A. Blake, A. Zisserman, Visual Reconstruction. Cambridge, MIT Press, 1987.

Analyse und Korrektur der Abbildungsfehler einer Gammakamera mit Hilfe einer Feinnadelstrahl-Quelle

U.Engeland, T.Striker und H.Luig

Forschungsgruppe Medizinische Physik, Zentrum Radiologie
Abteilung Nuklearmedizin Universitätsklinikum Göttingen
Email: uengela@gwdg.de

Zusammenfassung. Die Abbildung mit einer Gammakamera zeigt Inhomogenitäten und Nichtlinearitäten. Diese in vielfältigen Ursachen zu suchenden Fehler werden in der Elektronik der Kamera mit Hilfe von Korrekturalgorithmen teilweise behoben. Die für die Korrekturalgorithmen notwendigen Daten werden durch die Abbildung ausgedehnter Phantome gewonnen.
Ziel der Entwicklung einer hochkollimierten Nadelstrahlquelle war es, eine genau definierte Quellsituation zu besitzen. Anhand der Bilddaten, gwonnen mit einer solchen parallel zur Kamera-Oberfläche verfahrbaren Feinnadelstrahlquelle, entwickeln wir einen neuen Korrekturalgorithmus, der eine genauere differentielle Analyse der Abbildungseigenschaften der Kamera und eine entsprechende Korrektur ermöglicht.
Die Ergebnisse der Studie zeigen sowohl in der experimentellen Situation als auch mit Hilfe von Monte-Carlo Simulationen sehr gute Erfolge bei der Korrektur der Abbildungsfehler.

Schlüsselwörter: Gammakamera, Phantom, Homogenität, Nichtlinearität

1   Einleitung

In der nuklearmedizinischen Diagnostik werden Bilder der räumlichen Verteilung mit Gammastrahlern markierter Substanzen (Radiopharmaka) im Patienten aufgenommen. In der Regel werden diese Bilder mit Hilfe einer Gammakamera erstellt (siehe z.B [1]). Allein aufgrund der Funktionsweise einer Gammakamera kommt es zu inhärenten Abbildungsfehlern [2]. In jedem modernen Kamera-System werden diese Fehler microprozessorgestüzt korrigiert [2, 3].

Ziel unserer Arbeit war es, diese Abbildungsfehler mit hoher räumlicher Auflösung zu analysieren und neue Korrekturverfahren zu entwickeln.

Zunächst beschreiben wir die Abbildungsfehler einer Gammakamera. Danach gehen wir auf eine Quellanordnung ein, die es uns ermöglicht, gezielt sehr kleine Areale der Detektionsfläche anzusprechen. So ist es möglich, den Zusammenhang zwischen dem Ort des Auftreffens eines γ-Quants auf den Detektor und dem ihm durch die Gammakamera zugewiesenen Ort genau zu bestimmen.

Mit Hilfe dieser Information definieren wir ein verzerrungsfreies Pixelraster. Aufgrund der Kenntnis der lokalen Abbildungseigenschaft der Kamera haben wir ein iteratives Korrekturverfahren entwickelt, das insbesondere lokale Asymmetrien der Systemfunktion berücksichtigt. Wir haben die Korrekturverfahren anhand einer Monte-Carlo-Simulation einer Gammakamera untersucht.

Für unsere Experimente wurde eine Gammakamera vom Typ Picker CX-250 compakt eingesetzt.

2 Abbildungseigenschaften der Gammakamera

Gammakameras besitzen eine inhärente Unschärfe, d.h. die auf den Detektor aufgetroffenen Quanten werden von der Kamera mit einer Verteilung, die eine Halbwertsbreite von 3-4 mm besitzt, lokalisiert. Da dieser Effekt in der stochastischen Natur der beteiligten physikalischen Prozesse im Detektorsystem liegt und somit nicht vermieden werden kann, betrachten wir ihn im folgenden nicht als Abbildungsfehler.

Die beiden wichtigsten Abbildungsfehler der Gammakamera sind Nichtlinearitäten in der Ortsbestimmung und eine örtlichen Variation in der Energiebestimmung. Außerdem kann es es räumliche Unterschiede der Sensitivität des Detektors geben, die zu Inhomogenitäten führen.

Die für die üblichen Korrekturverfahren notwendigen Daten werden anhand von Aufnahmen spezieller Quellverteilungen ermittelt, bei denen ausgedehnte Bereiche des Detektors gleichzeitig bestrahlt werden. Eine sichere Zuordnung zwischen dem Ort des Auftreffens eines Quants auf den Detektor und der durch die Kamera registrierten Position ist dabei nicht möglich.

3 Die Feinnadelstrahlquelle (FNSQ)

Um die Abbildungseigenschaften der Gammakamera differentiell analysieren zu können, haben wir eine Quelle entwickelt, die einen gut definierten, möglichst nadelförmigen Strahl liefert.

Die Quelle besteht aus einem System dreier, aus Blei gefertigter Blenden (siehe Abbildung 1). Sie wird mit einer wäßrigen Lösung von ^{99m}Tc befüllt.

Die Quelle kann mit Hilfe einer Mechanik punktgenau unter der Gammakamera positioniert werden.

4 Bestimmung der Pixel

Der Grundgedanke unseres Korrekturverfahrens ist es, mit Hilfe der Quelle ein verzerrungsfreies Pixelraster zu definieren. Eine Position der Quelle entspricht dabei genau dem Zentrum eines Pixels des Bildes. Mit einer Kamera des uns

Abb. 1. a Schnitt durch die FNSQ, alle Maße in mm. **b** Projektion des Histogramms einer Aufnahme der FNSQ parallel zur y-Richtung. Die Einheiten an der Abzisse entsprechen 1.1 mm, an der Ordinate sind Counts aufgetragen.

a   b

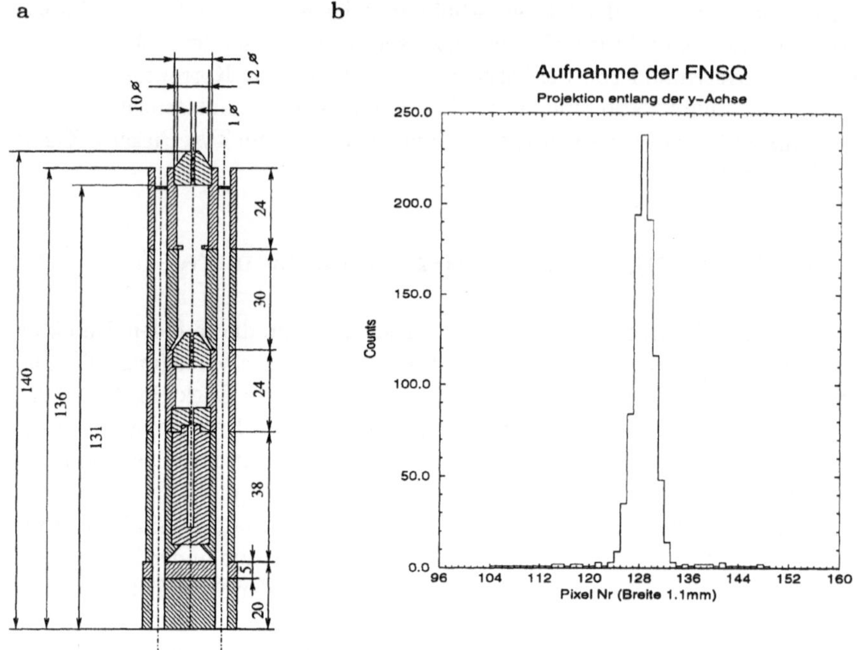

vorliegenden Typs werden Bilder mit maximal 256x256 Pixeln gemacht. Dementsprechend fahren wir mit der Quelle ein gleichmäßiges Raster aus 256x256 Positionen ab, wobei jeweils eine Aufnahme von einigen Sekunden gemacht wird.

Zu jeder Aufnahme wird mit Hilfe eines iterativen Algorithmus aus der Verteilung der "Bildorte" der registrierten Quanten der "repräsentative Bildort" bestimmt. Diese Punkte stellen die Mittelpunkte der zu definierenden Pixel dar. In Abbildung (2) **a** und **b** sind Beispiele gezeigt. Das Bild einer Position der FNSQ soll zunächst als symmetrisch angenommen werden. Die sich dadurch ergebenden Fehler werden im nächsten Abschnitt berücksichtigt. Zur Findung der repräsentativen Bildorte gehen wir folgendermaßen vor: Es wird zunächst ein dreidimensionales 128x128x4 Histogramm in x,y und Energiekoordinate gebildet und das Maximum gesucht. Um den Mittelpunkt der Koordinaten dieses Maximums wird ein Fenster gelegt, dessen Breite bzgl. des Ortes und der Energie so groß zu wählen ist, daß zum einen der überwiegende Anteil von γ-Quanten aus der FNSQ in diesem Bereich zu finden und zum anderen der Einfluß Hintergrundes so gering wie möglich ist. Aus den Quanten, die in diesem Fenster liegen, kann ein neuer Mittelpunkt berechnet werden. Um diesen wird erneut ein Fenster gelegt und die darin enthaltenen Quanten bestimmt aus denen wiederum ein neuer Mittelpunkt berechnet wird. Dies Verfahren wird in dem Moment abgebrochen, wo sich in zwei aufeinanderfolgenden Iterationsschritten keine wesentliche Änderung in den Koordinaten des Mittelpunkts ergeben hat.

Abb. 2. Nach unserem Verfahren bestimmte Mittelpunkte der Aufnahmen der FNSQ. Die FNSQ ist ein gleichmäßiges Raster mit Kantenlänge 1.1 mm abgefahren. **a**: Gleicher Maßstab auf x- und y-Achse. **b**: Zur Verdeutlichung der Abbildungsfehler ist der Maßstab in x-Richtung ein größerer Maßstab gewählt.(**a** stellt einen Ausschnitt aus **b** dar.).

a   b

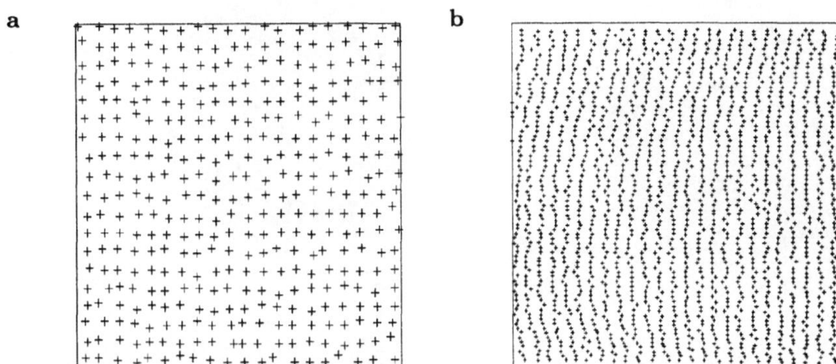

Diese Koordinaten werden der Position der FNSQ zugeordnet (Wichtig: Auch ein Mittelpunkt in der Energiekoordinate wird somit festgelegt.).

Die so bestimmten repräsentativen Bildorte haben sich als reproduzierbar erweisen. Die Abweichungen, die sich bei der Bestimmung der repräsentativen Bildorte mehrerer Aufnahmen der gleichen Quellposition ergeben, sind klein gegenüber der Kantenlänge des Rasters.

Zur Anwendung des obigen Verfahrens werden die registrierten Quanten einer Aufnahme in das Pixelraster eingeordnet. Die einem Quant zugewiesene Energie wird durch die Differenz des Mittelpunktes der Energie zum Sollwert korrigiert. (Dieses Verfahren läßt sich nur auf Aufnahmen anwenden, die mit dem gleichen Isotop wie in der FNSQ gemacht werden, in unserem Fall ^{99m}Tc.)

5 Berücksichtigung von Asymmetrien

Das Histogramm der Aufnahme in einer bestimmten Position der FNSQ liefert uns die Information, mit welcher Wahrscheinlichkeit ein γ-Quant einem bestimmten Pixel zugeordnet wird. Mit Hilfe dieser Information können wir das Bild berechenen, welches die Kamera aus einer vorgegebenen Verteilung von Auftrefforten auf den Detektor liefert. Betrachten wir das nach obigem Verfahren gewonnene Bild als erste Näherung für die Verteilung der Auftrefforte, können wir das zugehörige Gammakamera-Bild berechnen. Die Differenz aus beiden Bildern kann entsprechend der Abbildungscharakteristik umverteilt werden. Wir haben einen Algorithmus entwickelt, der diese Differenz iterativ minimiert. In Abbildung 3 ist das Ergebnis nach fünf Iterationsschritten (**b**) im Vergleich mit dem unkorrigierten Bild (**a**) dargestellt.

Abb. 3. Simulation der Aufnahme einer gitterförmigen Quellanordnung überlagert mit einer kreisförmigen, homogenen Quelle. **a** vor, **b** nach iterativer Korrektur.

a

b

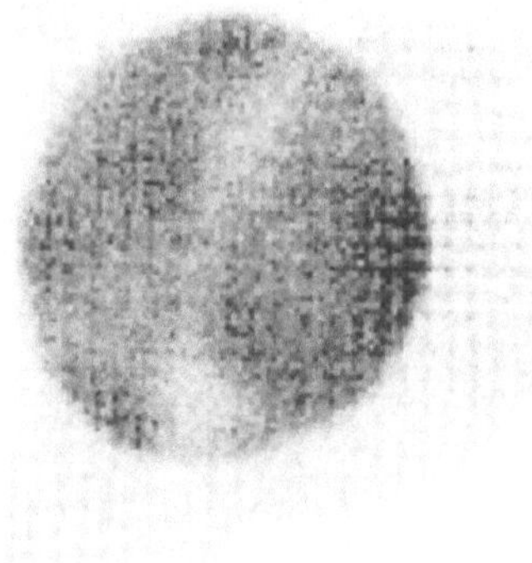

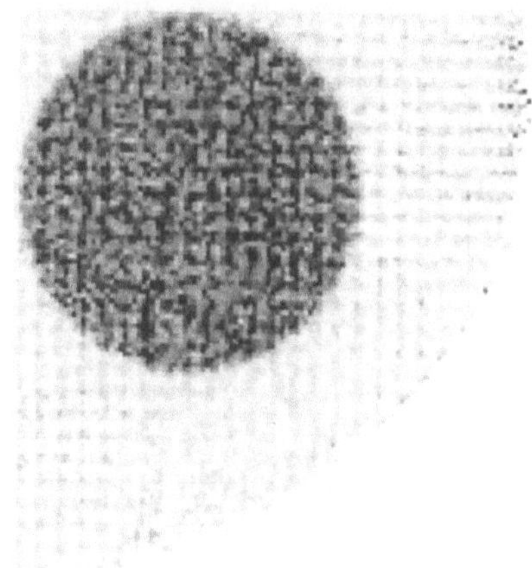

6 Diskussion

Einzelne Positionen der FNSQ liefern Daten über die Abbildungscharakteristik der Gammakamera an unterschiedlichen Orten, die eindeutig voneinander trennbar sind. Dies ist möglich, weil einzelne Positionen nacheinander angefahren werden und die Bilder verschiedener Positionen sich daher nicht überlagern können. So ist eine sehr feine Korrektur der Fehler der Abbildung durchführbar.

Wir nutzen die gewonnene Information in zwei Schritten. Zunächst sind wir in der Lage, ein verzerrungsfreies Pixelraster zu erzeugen und gleichen somit Nichtlinearitäten der Kamera aus. Im zweiten Schritt werden lokale Anisotropien mit Hilfe eines Iterativen Algorithmus berücksichtigt. Es ist möglich die Datenerhebung zu automatisieren. Ziel der Entwicklung ist ein System, das die Parameter der Korrektur ständig aktualisiert.

Literatur

1. Webb S: The Physics of Medical Imaging. Institut of Physics Publishing, Bristol and Philadelphia, 1988.
2. Sorensen JA and Phelps ME: Physics in Nuclear Medicine. Grune & Stratton, Orlando, 1987.
3. Simmons GH: The Scintillation Camera. The Soc. of Nucl.Med., New York, 1988.

Theoretische und experimentelle Untersuchung eines Verfahrens zur Schätzung von Attributen der Grauwertkanten in 2D CT/MR-Bildern

Alexander Hagemann, Karl Rohr und H. Siegfried Stiehl

Universität Hamburg, Fachbereich Informatik, AB KOGS
Vogt-Kölln-Strasse 30, D-22527 Hamburg
Email:hagemann@informatik.uni-hamburg.de

Zusammenfassung. Die Merkmale von Grauwertkanten in CT/MR-Bildern liefern wichtige Informationen für eine nachfolgende Bildanalyse. Basierend auf einem Modell für sigmoide Grauwertkanten existiert ein Verfahren zu deren Schätzung. Neben einer experimentellen und theoretischen Evaluierung der Leistungsfähigkeit dieses Verfahrens werden Erweiterungen zur Erkennung von Modellabweichungen sowie zur Ermittlung der lokalen Grauwertkantenkrümmung vorgestellt.

Schlüsselwörter: Kantendetektion, Skalenraum, Schätzung von Kantenattributen

1 Einleitung

Grauwertkanten definieren signifikante Bildstrukturen und stehen i.a. in direkter Beziehung zu physikalischen Objekten oder Phänomenen. Die Extraktion der Merkmale von Grauwertkanten, im folgenden als Attribute bezeichnet, liefert Informationen, die im Rahmen einer der Kantendetektion nachfolgenden medizinischen Bildanalyse wichtig sind. Beispielsweise können die Attribute als zusätzliche Information für landmarkenbasierte Registrierungsansätze dienen oder die Gruppierung unterstützen.

In dieser Arbeit wird die Leistungsfähigkeit eines differentiellen Skalenraumverfahrens untersucht, das sowohl die automatische Detektion der im Bild auftretenden Grauwertkanten als auch die Schätzung der jeweiligen Attribute Breite (d.h. Ausdehnung der Kontrastvariation in Gradientenrichtung), Kontrast und Orientierung erlaubt. Die Notwendigkeit eines Multiskalenansatzes ergibt sich dabei zwingend aus der Tatsache, daß entlang von Organkonturen i.a. verschieden skalierte Grauwertkanten auftreten, die für ihre optimale Detektion entsprechend skalierter Differentialoperatoren bedürfen.

2 Multiskalenkantenextraktion

Das Skalenraumverfahren von Back et al. [1] erlaubt, basierend auf der Fehlerintegralkurve als Kantenmodell, eine Schätzung der Attribute realer CT/MR-Grauwertkanten. Mittels eines über die Standardabweichung σ parametrisierbaren, normalisierten Differentialoperators $\nabla G(\sigma)$ wird ein Skalenraum über der Intensitätsfunktion I aufgebaut. Dabei definieren die Positionen der lokalen Maxima der Operatorantwort $M(x,\sigma) = I \otimes \nabla G(\sigma)$ auf verschiedenen

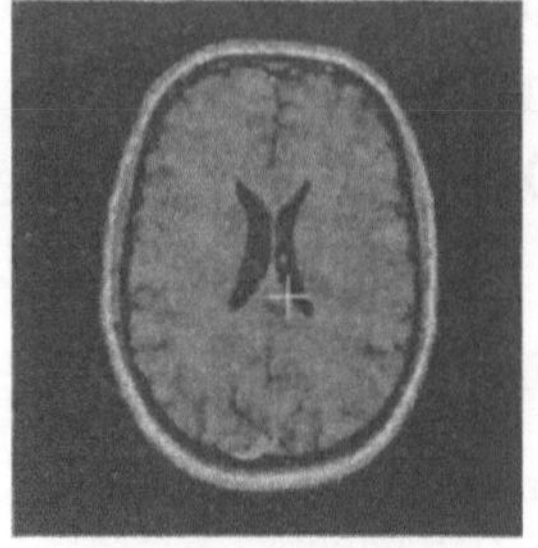

Abb. 1. MR-Bild

Abb. 2. Überlagertes
Kantenprofil aus Abb. 1

Skalen mögliche Grauwertkantenorte, von denen nur die nicht rauschinduzierten Antworten betrachtet werden.

Der Aufbau des diskreten Skalenraums erfolgt für jede Grauwertkante inkrementell durch Operatoren zunehmender Breite (wobei $\Delta\sigma = \sigma_{i+1} - \sigma_i$), bis das auf Basis der Modellfunktion entwickelte Abbruchkriterium für $\sigma_{i+1} > \sigma_i$,

$$\frac{M(x,\sigma_{i+1}) - M(x,\sigma_i)}{M(x,\sigma_i)} < \frac{\sigma_{i+1} - \sigma_i}{2\sigma_i}, \tag{1}$$

erstmalig erfüllt ist. Die dieses Kriterium erfüllende Skala wird als Maß für die Breite der Grauwertkante angesehen, deren Kontrast durch $c = \sqrt{2}M(x,\sigma_i)$ bestimmt werden kann. So werden bei einer Anwendung des Verfahrens auf Abb. 1 für die markierte Kante die Attributwerte $x = 138.1$, $y = 140.9$, Orientierung $144.6°$, Breite 0.73 und Kontrast 74.6 ermittelt, siehe auch Abb. 2 und [2].

3 Experimentelle Untersuchungen

Zur experimentellen Validierung des Verfahrens wurde der in [3] durchgeführte Vergleich zwischen Signaturverfahren [4] und Modellanpassungsverfahren [5] um das Verfahren [1] erweitert. Im Vordergrund der Untersuchung steht dabei die Genauigkeit der erreichten Ergebnisse für Kontrast- und Breitenschätzung.

3.1 Synthetisches Bildmaterial

Untersucht wurden synthetische Bilder mit sigmoiden Grauwertkanten der Breite $\tau_0 = 0.5, 1.0, 2.0, 5.0$ und Kontrast 84, welche sowohl unverrauscht, als auch mit überlagertem Gaußschen Rauschen ($\sigma_{\text{noise}} = 15, 30$) vorlagen. Bei den in Tab. 1 zusammengefaßten Ergebnissen weist das Verfahren von Back et al. [1] für $\tau_0 = 0.5$ bei zunehmendem Rauschen eine immer stärkere Abweichung auf. Die Ursache liegt in den zu geringen Abtastraten der Grauwertkante und des Differentialoperators. Die dadurch entstehenden Diskretisierungseffekte verfälschen die Operatorantworten, welche dann zu den beobachteten Abweichungen führen.

3.2 Reales Bildmaterial

Die Ergebnisse der Verfahren bei Anwendung auf die in Abb. 3 markierten Grauwertkanten sind in Tab. 2 zu finden. Trotz der unbekannten wahren Attributwerte können Aussagen bezüglich der Schätzgenauigkeit getroffen werden, indem entsprechend parametrisierte Fehlerintegralkurven den realen Grauwertkanten überlagert werden, siehe Abb. 4. Insgesamt liefert das Verfahren von Back et al. [1] gute Ergebnisse, wobei aufgrund der geringen Breite der Kante

	Breiten			Kontraste		
	$\sigma_{\text{noise}} = 0$	$\sigma_{\text{noise}} = 15$	$\sigma_{\text{noise}} = 30$	$\sigma_{\text{noise}} = 0$	$\sigma_{\text{noise}} = 15$	$\sigma_{\text{noise}} = 30$
Skalenraumverfahren						
$\tau_0 = 0.5$	0.69	0.75	1.06	87.8	86.1	97.4
$\tau_0 = 1.0$	1.02	1.13	1.34	83.8	84.5	94.0
$\tau_0 = 2.0$	2.01	1.91	1.85	83.8	83.2	84.3
$\tau_0 = 5.0$	5.00	5.07	5.16	83.6	84.4	85.8
Signaturverfahren						
$\tau_0 = 0.5$	0.50	0.66	0.86	83.9	84.9	84.3
$\tau_0 = 1.0$	0.99	0.90	1.02	83.9	84.3	85.4
$\tau_0 = 2.0$	2.00	1.92	1.71	84.1	84.3	84.0
$\tau_0 = 5.0$	4.87	3.85	3.24	82.3	74.1	73.0
Modellanpassungsverfahren						
$\tau_0 = 0.5$	0.50	0.49	0.47	84.0	84.0	84.1
$\tau_0 = 1.0$	0.98	1.01	1.07	84.0	84.2	84.7
$\tau_0 = 2.0$	2.01	2.03	2.03	84.2	84.4	84.7
$\tau_0 = 5.0$	4.92	4.89	5.15	82.9	82.7	86.9

Tabelle 1. Geschätzte Übergangsbreiten und Kontraste für synthetische Bilder

Nr. 2 Diskretisierungseffekte das dortige Ergebnis verfälschen. Für die Schattenkanten 5 und 6 ist durch Profilüberlagerung nicht zu entscheiden, ob das Verfahren [1] oder das Modellanpassungsverfahren [5] die besseren Ergebnisse liefert. Das Signaturverfahren [4] liefert bei beiden Kanten relativ schlechte Ergebnisse, siehe auch [3].

Abb. 3. Realbild

Kante	Skalenraumv.		Signaturv.		Modellanpassungsv.	
	τ	c	τ	c	τ	c
1	1.33	131.5	0.81	124.8	1.34	138.7
2	0.70	132.3	0.59	129.8	0.53	130.7
3	0.70	49.5	0.73	52.0	0.37	48.5
4	0.73	129.6	0.63	119.2	0.73	136.1
5	2.85	56.3	1.37	38.5	3.27	56.5
6	2.31	55.5	1.63	48.4	3.14	62.3
7	0.97	90.3	0.95	93.3	1.04	96.8
8	1.04	101.0	1.02	101.1	0.87	97.0

Tabelle 2. Ergebnisse der Verfahren für die in Abb. 3 markierten Grauwertkanten.

4 Theoretische Untersuchungen

4.1 Untersuchung des Einflusses der Skalenraumdiskretisierung

Die beim Verfahren [1] notwendige Diskretisierung des Skalenraums erlaubt nur dann eine exakte Schätzung der Breite τ, wenn diese einer der berechneten Ebenen σ_i des Skalenraums entspricht. Anderenfalls kann durch nähere Betrachtung des Abbruchkriteriums (1), das auf einem Vergleich der Tangentensteigung der Operatorantwort am Ort $\sigma = \tau$ mit der durch zwei Operatorantworten aufeinanderfolgender Skalen $\sigma_i < \sigma_{i+1}$ gebildeten Sekantensteigung beruht, die

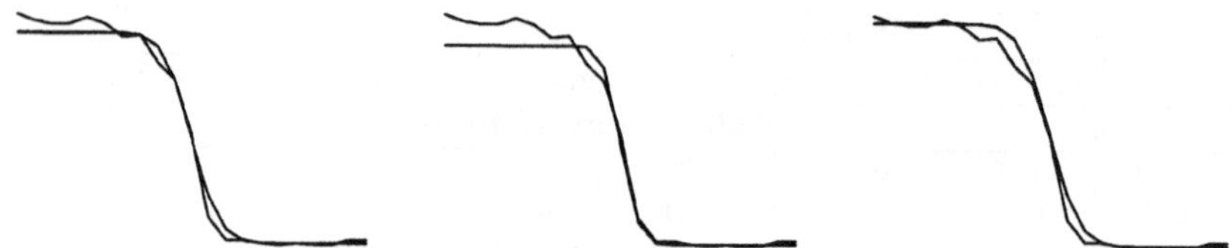

Abb. 4. Überlagertes Profil der Kante 1 aus Abb. 3 mit einer Fehlerintegralkurve, deren Parametrisierung durch das Skalenraumverfahren (links), das Signaturverfahren (mitte) bzw. das Modellanpassungsverfahren (rechts) ermittelt wurde.

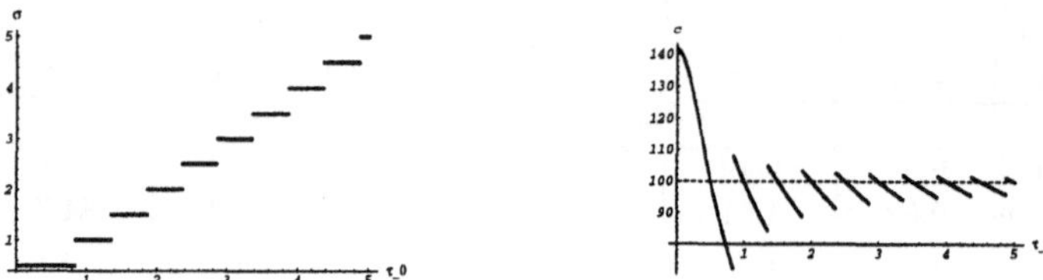

Abb. 5. Linke Seite: Durch das Abbruchkriterium (1) ermittelte Breiten $\sigma_i = \tau$ in Abhängigkeit von der realen Breite τ_0. Rechte Seite: Geschätzte Kontrastwerte für Fehlerintegralkurven unterschiedlicher Breiten τ_0, deren Kontrast $c_0 = 100$ beträgt (gestrichelte Linie).

das Verfahren terminierende Skala bestimmt werden. Dem *Mittelwertsatz der Differentialrechnung* entsprechend, existiert zu jeder Skala σ_i ein umgebendes Intervall von Breiten τ, durch deren Tangentensteigungen erstmalig das Abbruchkriterium erfüllt wird, siehe Abb. 5. Da die Kontrastschätzung unter der Annahme $\tau = \sigma_i$ durch $c = \sqrt{2}M(x,\sigma)$ erfolgt, setzt sich die Ungenauigkeit auch hier fort. Eine Verbesserung der Schätzung kann erreicht werden, indem nach Abbruch des Verfahrens die Breite aus dem Verhältnis t der zuletzt berechneten Operatorantworten über

$$\tau = \sigma_i\sigma_{i+1}\sqrt{\frac{1 - t^2}{t^2\sigma_{i+1}^2 - \sigma_i^2}} \tag{2}$$

bestimmt wird.

4.2 Erkennung von Modellabweichungen

Treten bei einer Grauwertkante Abweichungen von der zugrundeliegenden Modellfunktionen auf, entsprechen die Ergebnisse i.a. nicht den realen Werten. Da im Falle sigmoider Grauwertkanten deren Breite über Gl. (2) exakt bestimmt werden kann, erlaubt die Anwendung im Skalenraum, Modellabweichungen zu erkennen. Diese äußern sich dabei in einer Variation der Ergebnisse auf verschiedenen Skalen.

Aufgrund des durch Rauschen gestörten Verlaufs der Operatorantwort bezüglich σ ergeben sich i.a. auch für die korrekte Modellfunktion Variationen in den jeweils berechneten Breiten. Wie in Abb. 6 für zwei der getesteten Fälle dargestellt, ist bei der korrekten Modellfunktion die Variation der normierten Schätzergebnisse jedoch deutlich geringer als bei einem abweichenden Modell.

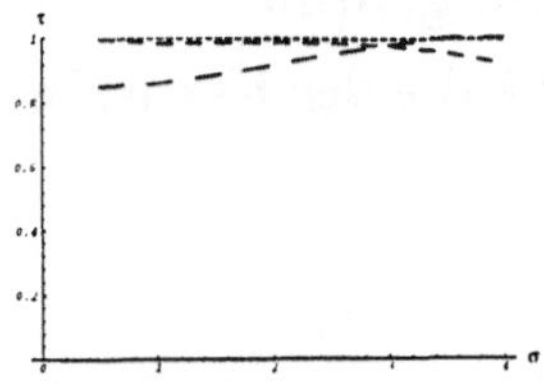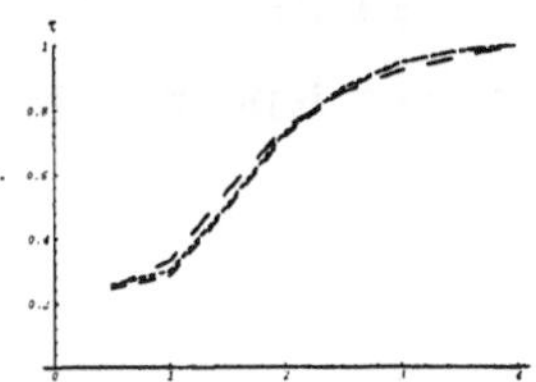

Abb. 6. Normierte Ergebnisse der Breitenschätzung (2) für aufeinanderfolgende Skalen. Die Standardabweichung des Gaußschen Rauschens betrug $\sigma_{noise} = 1.0$ (punktiert), 3.0 (gestrichelt) und 5.0 (längere Striche). Linke Seite: Fehlerintegralkurve. Rechte Seite: Modellabweichung

Die Erkennung von Modellabweichungen kann durch Einführung eines Schwellwertes erfolgen, welcher die maximale, rauschinduzierte Abweichung festlegt, die innerhalb der berechneten Breiten auftreten darf.

4.3 Krümmungschätzung

Durch Berechnung der zweiten Ableitung der Intensitätsfunktion senkrecht zur Gradientenrichtung kann die lokale Krümmung einer Grauwertkante über

$$
\kappa = \frac{\left(2\cos\phi\,\sin\phi\,\hat{G}_2^{45°} - \cos^2\phi\,\hat{G}_2^{0°} - \sin^2\phi\,\hat{G}_2^{90°}\right) \otimes I(x)}{M(x,\sigma)} \tag{3}
$$

bestimmt werden. Hier bezeichnen $\hat{G}_2^{0°}$ etc. die zur Berechnung der Richtungsableitung des Differentialoperators notwendigen Basisfilter.

5 Zusammenfassung

Grauwertkantenattribute liefern zusätzliche Informationen für die nachfolgende Bildanalyse. Wir haben ein differentielles Skalenraumverfahren zur Attributschätzung untersucht und Erweiterungen zur Detektion von Modellabweichungen sowie zur Krümmungsschätzung vorgestellt.

Literatur

1. S. Back, H. Neumann, H.S. Stiehl. On Scale-Space Edge Detection in Computed Tomograms. In H. Burkhard, K.-H. Höhne, B. Neumann (Hrsg) *Mustererkennung 1989*, Informatik Fachberichte 219, Seiten 216-223, Springer-Verlag Berlin, 1989.
2. G. Gabrielides, H. Neumann, H.S. Stiehl. Estimating Partial Volume Induced Local Blurring of Organ Contours in Computed Tomograms. Aus H.U. Lemke, M.L. Rhodes, C.C. Jaffe, R. Felix (Hrsg) *Computer Assisted Radiology*, Seiten 556-562, Springer-Verlag, 1991.
3. F. Bergholm, K. Rohr. A Comparsion between Two Approaches Applied for Estimating Diffuseness and Height of Step Edges. Computational Vision and Active Perception Laboratory (CVAP) 83, University of Stockholm, Schweden, 1991.
4. F. Bergholm, W. Zhang. An Extension of Marr's "Signature" Based Edge Classification. Aus *Proceedings of The 7th Scandinavian Conference on Image Analysis*, Aalborg, Seiten 435-443, 1991.
5. K. Rohr. Recognizing Corners by Fitting Parametric Models. Aus *International Journal of Computer Vision*, Vol. 9:3, Seiten 213-230, 1992.

Festkörper-Kernspintomographie
Darstellung von Knochenstrukturen mit Hilfe der Kernspintomographie

T. Oerther

Ruprecht-Karls-Universität Heidelberg
Fakultät für klinische Medizin Mannheim, 68135 Mannheim
EMAIL : oerther@fh-karlsruhe.de

D. Höpfel

Fachbereich Naturwissenschaften
Fachhochschule Karlsruhe / Hochschule für Technik, 76133 Karlsruhe
EMAIL : hoepfel@fh-karlsruhe.de

G. Rohr

Klinikum Bad Homburg V. a. H.
Innere Medizin II, 61348 Bad Homburg

Zusammenfassung. Die *Kernspintomographie* (MRT bzw. MRI von Magnetic Resonance Tomographie bzw. Imaging) hat sich heute zu einer Standardmethode für die Schnittbilddarstellung von Weichteilgewebe in der Medizin entwickelt. Erst mit speziellen Aufnahmemethoden, in diesem Fall der *Single-Point-Imaging-Sequenz* (SPI-Sequenz) ist Kernresonanzbildgebung mit Festkörpern möglich. Der Grund hierfür ist, daß die Relaxationszeit T2 bei Festkörpern sehr kurz ist, und mit der SPI-Sequenz MRT-Signale sehr schnell nach der Anregung aufgenommen werden können. Nachteil der SPI-Methode ist die lange Aufnahmedauer, weshalb sie in der Praxis momentan kaum zum Einsatz kommt. Die acquirierten Signale werden nach entsprechender Datenaufbereitung mit Hilfe einer 3D-Oberflächenrekonstruktion dargestellt und können aus beliebigen Positionen hinsichtlich Aufbau und Struktur beurteilt werde.

Schlüsselwörter: Kernspintomographie, Festkörper, Knochen, Osteoporose, Oberflächenrekonstruktion

1 Einleitung

In einem Zeitraum von 10 Jahren hat sich die Kernspintomographie zu einem Standardwerkzeug der Medizin entwickelt. Dies ist hauptsächlich durch den exzellenten Gewebekontrast bedingt, wodurch nichtinvasive Einblicke in den menschlichen Körper mit einer vorher nicht erreichbaren Qualität möglich werden. In biologischen Materialien stammt das MRT-Signal im allgemeinen von Protonen (Wasser, Fettgewebe), besser gesagt von beweglichen Protonen. Der Grund, warum Festkörper wie Knochen oder Sehnen in Standard MRT-Bildern nicht dargestellt werden können ist die stark eingeschränkte Beweglichkeit ihrer Protonen. Ausschlaggebend für den Signalbeitrag in MRT-Bildern sind zum einen die Quantität der Protonen, zum anderen sind es Relaxationsprozesse, definiert über die sogenannten Relaxationszeiten T1 und T2. Sie geben Auskunft darüber, wie lange ein bestimmtes Material ein Meßsignal liefert, welches einen Beitrag zum Gesamtsignal bringt. Ausschlaggebend für die Festkörpertomographie ist die T2-Relaxationszeit (Spin-Spin-Relaxation), die bei Festkörpern im Promille- bis Prozentbereich derer von Wasser liegt. Als Größenordnung kann hier der Bereich von 10µs bis einige hundert µs bei Festkörpern, und mehrere hundert ms bei Wasser genannt werden. Da für die in der Bildgebung notwendige Ortskodierung bereits eine Zeit von einigen Millisekunden benötigt wird, liefern Festkörper bei Standard MRT-Sequenzen keinen Signalbeitrag zu einem MRT-Bild.

2 Methode zur Festkörperdarstellung

Ein vielversprechender Ansatz zur Lösung dieses Problems wurde 1985 von S. Emid und J. Creyghton vorgestellt. Sie beschreiben die *Single-Point-Imaging Sequenz (SPI, oder auch Constant-Time-Imaging Sequenz -CTI-)* die prinzipiell darauf beruht, in allen 3 Raumrichtungen eine Phasenkodierung durchzuführen [1], d.h. sie benutzt keine Lese- oder Scheibengradienten und kann in jede bestehende Kernspintomographieanlage implementiert werden..

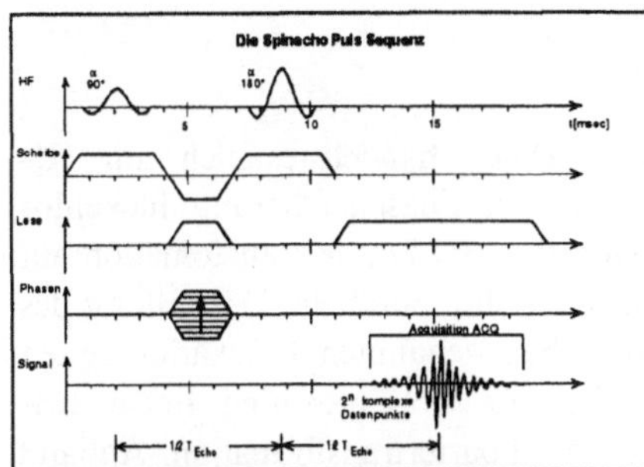
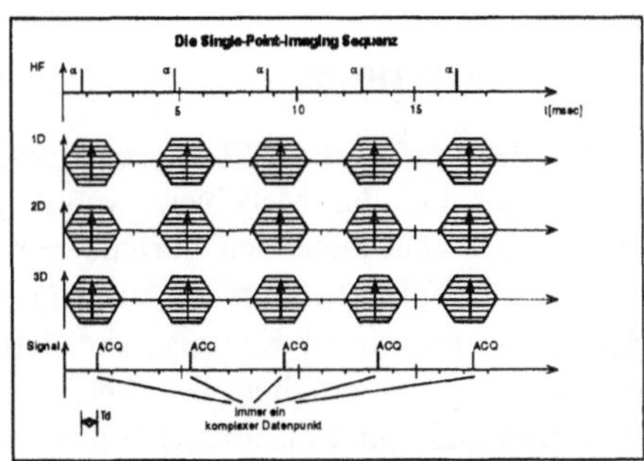

Abb. 1 : Darstellung der Spinecho- (links) und der SPI-Sequenz (rechts). Beide Sequenzen sind im gleichen zeitlichen Maßstab gezeichnet. Das erste Diagramm beider Skizzen zeigt die Anregung durch den HF-Impuls. Die folgenden drei Diagramme zeigen das Gradiententiming für die Phasen- bzw. Frequenzkodierung in allen drei Raumrichtungen. Das letzte Diagramm jeder Sequenz zeigt den chronologischen Ablauf der Signalacquisition.

2.1 Eigenschaften der SPI-Methode

Die Unterschiede zwischen der SPI-Methode und den Standard MRT-Sequenzen liegen darin, daß bei der SPI-Sequenz immer nur ein komplexer Datenpunkt pro Aufnahme acquiriert wird, während bei den Standardmethoden immer eine gesamte Zeile aufgenommen wird. Nach der Anregung werden bei der SPI-Sequenz keine Gradienten mehr geschaltet, wodurch Materialien untersucht werden können, deren *Relaxationszeiten* (genauer gesagt die Relaxationszeit T2) kleiner als die Gradientenschaltzeiten sind.

Es gibt mehrere Vorteile dieser Aufnahmemethode. Erstens kann dieser eine Punkt sehr schnell nach der Anregung acquiriert werden. Je nach gewünschter Auflösung und vorhandenem Gradientensystem können Zeiten unter 50µs erzielt werden, was Voraussetzung für die Festkörperanalyse ist. Zum zweiten ist die Zeit zwischen Anregung und Acqusition für jeden Signalpunkt gleich, wodurch die zeitliche Entwicklung der Magnetisierung keine Rolle mehr spielt. Dies bedeutet, daß *Chemical Shift-* und *Suszeptibilitätseffekte* eliminiert werden und keine *dipolaren oder quadrupolaren Störungen* auftreten [2].

Der große Nachteil der Methode liegt in der Aufnahmedauer. Im Gegensatz zu den frequenzkodierten Aufnahmemethoden wird pro Anregung nur ein komplexer Datenpunkt aufgenommen, d.h. für einen Schritt im frequenzkodierten Experiment muß bei der SPI-Methode n mal die Pulsfolge wiederholt werden (wobei n der Größe der gewünschten Bildmatrix in der ersten Dimension entspricht). Da es keinerlei Scheibengradienten gibt, handelt es sich um eine 3 dimensionale (3D) Aufnahmemethode wodurch die Phasencodierung der dritten Raumrichtung notwendig wird. Dies alles führt dazu, daß ein SPI-Experiment mehrere Stunden dauern kann, weshalb die Methode bislang auch keinen Einzug in der Praxis erlangt hat.

2.2 Bildverarbeitung

Bei den durch die SPI-Sequenz erhaltenen Daten handelt es sich um 3D-Datensätze, d.h. das Meßobjekt wurde mit Hilfe der Phasencodierung lückenlos „abgetastet". Dies bietet den Vorteil, sehr einfach eine 3D-Fouriertransfomation auf die Daten anzuwenden, um als Ausgangsinformation die räumliche Darstellung des Meßobjekts mit einem Kontrast, der durch die oben genannten Relaxationszeiten bestimmt wird, zu erhalten. Die Abbildung erfolgt auf 256 Graustufen, linear zwischen minimaler und maximaler Intensität nach der Fouriertransformation. Anhand eines Bildausschnitts werden nun die zwei Grauwertschwellen gesucht, die die Grenze von Meßobjekt zur Umgebung bilden. Anhand der erhaltenen Übergänge zwischen Umgebung (außerhalb der gefundenen Schwellen) und dem Meßobjekt kann nun nach Clusterbildung eine Oberflächenrekonstruktion des Meßobjekts durchgeführt werden. Ergebnisse solcher *Oberflächenrekonstruktionen* sind in Kapitel 3 zu sehen.

3 Experimente

3.1 Knochenexperimente

In Zusammenarbeit mit der Firma Bruker Analytische Meßtechnik und Bruker Medizintechnik in Karlsruhe wurden mehrere Messungen an Knochenproben von Rindern durchgeführt. Hierfür wurde aus einem Knochen mit Hilfe einer Stanze eine Probe von 4mm Durchmesser und 4mm Höhe gewonnen, die mit Hilfe von Perchlorethlyen auf chemischem Wege vom Fett (Knochenmark) getrennt wurde.

Als Meßsystem stand ein supraleitender 7 Tesla Magnet zur Verfügung, in deren Zentrum die Probe mit Hilfe eines Glasröhrchens fixiert wurde. Die zu Verfügung stehende Gradientstärke betrug 2 Tesla pro Meter. Das hohe Feld ist notwendig, da zur Auflösung der Knochentrabekelstruktur (Knochentrabekel : das Knochenbälkchen; phys. anat.: die sich rechtwinklig kreuzenden „Spannungslinien" als Ort großer Zug und Druckbelastung; im Knochen durch entsprechend ausgerichtete Spongiosazüge manifestiert [3]) eine Voxelgröße von wesentlich besser als 100µm Kantenlänge pro Voxel erzielt werden muß und das Meßsignal entsprechend klein ist. Geht man zu geringeren Feldstärken über, nimmt der Signal- zu Rauschabstand ab und muß entsprechend durch zusätzliche Signalmittelungen verbessert werden. Hierdurch wird jedoch die ohnehin sehr lange Meßzeit nochmals drastisch erhöht, da jede Verdopplung der Mittelungsanzahl eine Verdopplung der Meßzeit mit sich bringt.

Abb. 2 : Oberflächenrekonstruktion einer Knochenprobe aus einem Ochsenschwanz. Die Auflösung beträgt 78µm/Pixel in allen 3 Raumrichtungen, die Meßzeit betrug 20.38 Stunden mit einem 7 Tesla Magnetsystem. Zur Darstellung wurde die Oberfläche der Knochenprobe mit Hilfe einer tripolaren Interpolationsmethode berechnet.

Abb. 3 : 3D-Oberflächenrekonstruktion eines Legosteins. Die Auflösung beträgt hierbei 500µm/Pixel bei einer Dephasierungszeit TD von 150µsec und einer Matrix von 64 Punkten in allen 3 Raumrichtungen. Die Aufnahme wurde an einem resistiven Magneten mit 0.35 Tesla durchgeführt, die Aufnahmedauer betrug 104 Minuten.

3.2 Sonstige Festkörperexperimente

Natürlich können auch andere Arten von Festkörpern für die Tomographie mit Hilfe der SPI-Methode herangezogen werden. Hier seien vor allem Kunststoffe genannt, wofür als Beispiel in Abbildung 3 ein Legostein gezeigt ist, der mit einem resistiven 0.35 Tesla Magneten an der Fachhochschule Karlsruhe aufgenommen wurde. Aber auch andere Werkstoffe wie Holz, Gummi oder Verbundmaterialien aus mehreren Materialien können untersucht we rden.

Dieser Kunststoff kann sogar mit nichtferromagnetischem Metall zusammen als Meßobjekt dienen (mechanische Verbindungen). Dieses wird natürlich nicht abgebildet, jedoch kann der Kunststoff praktisch ohne Beeinträchtigung durch das Metall untersucht werden.

4 Aussichten

Mit Hilfe der SPI-Methode ergeben sich viele neue Einsatzmöglichkeiten für die Kernspintomographie. Besonders interessant ist die Knochenstrukturanalyse hinsichtlich der Dicke, Anzahl und Vernetzung der Trabekelstrukturen um Aussagen über die Knochenstabilität treffen zu können, und somit eine Diagnosemöglichkeit für die Osteoporose zu erhalten. Weiterhin können unter anderem Polymerisationsprozesse und zerstörungsfreie Festkörper- und Werkstoffprüfungen mit einer bislang nicht möglichen Auflösung realisiert werden.

5 Literatur

1. S. Emid und J. H. N. Creyghton: Physica B 128, 81, 1985.
2. S. Gravina und D. G. Cory: Sensitivity and Resolution of Constant-Time-Imaging, Journal of Magnetic Resonance, Series B 104, 53-64, 1994.
3. Roche Lexikon Medizin, Urban&Schwarzenberg Verlag, , 2.Auflage, S. 958, 1987.

zugänglich zu machen. Im folgenden wird ein Protokoll vorgeschlagen, welches sich insbesondere bei der Auswertung von Aktivierungsuntersuchungen mit der PET in Kombination mit einer Untersuchung desselben Patienten mit der MRT bewärht hat.

2 Methoden

2.1 Datenmaterial

Tomographische Daten liegen gewöhnlich als Bildmatrizen vor, bestehend aus 128x128 oder 256x256 Pixel, die übereinandergestapelt bei ca. 50 bis 160 Schichten (abhängig von der Schichtdicke) das gesamt menschliche Gehirn überdecken können. Für die vorliegenden Untersuchungen wurden PET-Daten benutzt, die von einem ECAT EXACT HR (CTI-Siemens, Knoxville, TN) stammen. Die Bilder wurden zu 47 Schichten mit 2 mm Pixelgröße in einer 128 x128 Pixelmatrix rekonstruiert bei einem Schichtabstand von 3.125 mm. Bis zu 12 aufeinanderfolgende Untersuchungen wurden zwecks Studium der Durchblutungssteigerung im Gehirn als Folge von Stimulation wie Wiederholung von Wörtern oder Bewegung der Finger durchgeführt. Jede Untersuchung dauerte 10 min, wodurch sich eine Gesamtlänge von 2 Std. ergibt. Trotz behutsamer Lagerung des Patientenkopfes in einer Kopfstütze kann eine Bewegung des Kopfes durch den Patienten nicht ausgeschlossen werden. Vielmehr ist anzunehmen, dass kleine Verschiebungen zwischen den einzelnen Untersuchungen auftreten. Als anatomisches Datenmaterial lagen MRT Daten desselben Patienten vor. Die Bilder, aufgenommen mit T1 gewichteten 3D FLASH Sequenz, wurden auf einem Siemens Impact (Siemens Medizinsysteme, Erlangen) erzeugt. Mit 64 Schichten bei einer Dicke von 2.5 mm wurde das gesamte Gehirn überdeckt. Die Pixelgröße lag bei 1.0 mm, die Bildmatrix war 256x256. Alle Daten standen digital zur Verfügung.

2.2 Bildabgleichverfahren

Um den vielfältigen Anforderungen des Bildabgleichs in der klinischen Forschung, der klinischen Routine und zunehmend auch in Praxen gerecht zu werden insbesondere was die Robustheit und Schnelligkeit angeht, wurde eine interaktive Bildabgleichsprozedur [1] mit automatisierten Optionen kombiniert, die den Benutzer darin unterstützt, einen optimierten Abgleich zu finden, nachdem er einen (gröberen) Vorabgleich erreicht hat. Ebenso hat er die Wahl, den Abgleich entweder gänzlich interaktiv oder auch vollständig automatisiert vorzunehmen. Die letzte Entscheidung, ob ein Bildabgleich zufiedenstellend verlaufen ist, liegt wiederum beim Arzt oder allgemeiner, beim Benutzer. Die eingesetzen Kriterien und Maße, die zur Prüfung des automatisierten Bildabgleichs ausgenutzt werden, haben sich in wissenschaftlichen Untersuchungen als sehr robust herausgestellt. Im einzelnen wird der Korrelationskoeffizient [2], die Varianz über ein Quotientenbild [3] und die Summe der absoluten Differenzen der entsprechenden Bilder [4] ausgenutzt. Eine direkte Kombination der einzelnen Maße, um zu einem Gesamtmaß und zu einer breiteren Anwendbarkeit zu gelangen, befindet sich noch in der Erprobungsphase.

2.3 Das Hybridverfahren

Vor dem eigentlichen Abgleichprozess wurden einige Voreinstellungen vorgenommen. So wurde interaktiv eine Schwelle definiert (gewöhnlich ca. 25 bis 30%), die darüber entschied, was für die Berechnung der Ähnlichkeitsmaße vom Bild berücksichtigt werden sollte. Der gleiche Schwellenwert wurde auch zur Definition der Kontur übernommen, welche bei der visuellen Prüfung zwischen der Referenzstudie und der zu transformierenden Studie ausgetauscht wird. Vor der Berechnung der pixelbezogenen Ähnlichkeitsmaße wurden die Bilder gefiltert. Für die recht verrauschten PET-Bilder aus den Aktivierungsuntersuchungen bot sich ein Mittelungsfilter mit einer Filtergröße von 5 Pixel an. Das Hybridverfahren ist so ausgelegt, dass jeder Bildabgleich nach der Wahl des Benutzers interaktiv oder automatisiert ablaufen kann. Es hat sich jedoch herausgestellt, dass für die Kombination PET und MRT (multi-modaler Bildabgleich) der interaktive Abgleich Vorteile hat. So fällt mit interaktiven Bildabgleich der sonst bei den z. Z. implementierten automatisierten Algorithmen notwendige (und sehr zeitaufwendige) Schritt des Entfernens der nicht zum Gehirn gehörenden Pixel in den MRT-Bilder weg. Wiederum hat sich gezeigt, dass eine Serie von PET-Untersuchungen (uni-modaler Bildabgleich), die sehr gleichartige Bilder ergeben, automatisiert abgeglichen werden kann. Ebenso ist es möglich bei sehr unterschiedlichen Lagen des Patientenkopfes relativ zum Koordinatensystem des Tomographen (z.B. bei Wiederholungsmessungen mit PET) einen groben Vorabgleich vorzunehmen und dann mit Hilfe der automatisierten Algorithmen den Abgleich zu optimieren.

2.4 Schichtauswahl, Optimierung der Transformationsparameter

Zunächst wurde eine Referenzstudie festgelegt, gemäß dieser die weiteren Studien ausgerichtet werden sollten. Die Ähnlichkeitsmaße wurden nicht für alle Daten, d.h. für all Schichten, sondern nur für eine Auswahl von drei orthogonalen Schichten (transaxial, koronar und Sagittal) berechnet, was eine erhebliche zeitliche Ersparnis bedeutet. Die Auswahl dieser Ansichten ist demnach für den Bildabgleich von besonderer Bedeutung, da insbesondere Randschichten, aber auch z.B. die mittlere sagittale Schicht von Partialvolumeneffekten beeinflußt sind und dadurch den Vergleich der Schichten erschwert.
Die Optimierung der Transformationsparameter ist als einfache Suche bei Variation der einzelnen aktuellen Transformationsparametern innerhalb vorgegebener Schranken ausgelegt. Die Suche schreitet immer in Richtung der größten Ähnlichkeit (definiert durch Maße, s.o.) voran. Die Schrittweite halbiert sich bei jedem Durchgang durch die 6 Parameter bis eine Schrittweite von 0.1 mm und 0.1° erreicht wird.

3 Resultate

3.1 Protokoll für das Hybridverfahren

Das folgende Protokoll erwies sich als optimal bei der Analyse von Aktivierungsstudien mit PET und dem Vergleich zu anatomischen Bildern aus der MRT:

- Definition der Filtergröße, Schwelle und Auswahl der drei orthogonalen Schichten
- Automatisierter Bildabgleich der individuellen PET-Untersuchungen, Speichern der Transformationsparameter
- Berechnung eines Mittelwertbildes über alle transformierten PET-Untersuchungen
- Interaktive Reorientierung der MR-Bilder in eine standartisierte Position (Linie zwischen Commissura anterior und posterior), interaktiver Abgleich des PET-Mittelwertbildes und die ausgerichteten MR-Bilder (MRT ist Referenz)
- Kombination der Transformationen aus dem automatisierten Abgleich der PET-Bilder und dem interaktiven Abgleich aus dem letzten Schritt (PET und MRT), um alle individuellen PET-Studien einzeln auf die AC-PC-ausgerichtete MRT-Studie zu transformieren.

Es muss betont werden, dass die Kombination der Transformationen ohne Zwischenschritt formuliert ist, so dass keine wiederholte Interpolation erforderlich ist und damit die Qualität der Daten (Kontrast, Auflösung) nicht unnötig reduziert wird.

3.2 Wahl der Parameter, Zeitlicher Bedarf

Als wichtige Standardparameter beim Abgleich der hier verwendeten Daten ergaben sich für den automatisierten Abgleich der PET-Daten: Mittelungfilter mit Filtergröße von 5 Pixel, Schwelle: 25 - 30 % vom Maximalwert. Höhere Schwellwerte führten nicht zu zufriedenstellenden Ergebnissen, da zu wenig markante Strukturen in den Bildern übrig blieben. Ein Vergrößern des Filterkernes zeigte ebenso keine Verbesserung in den Ähnlichkeitsmaßen, da mit stärker gefilterten Bilder auch die Sensitivität auf kleinere Verschiebungen und Rotationen sinkt.

Der zeitliche Bedarf hängt zwangsläufig von der Kapazität des Rechnersystems ab. Auf einer SUN UltraSparc 1 mit 200 MHz liegt der Bedarf für den Abgleich mit dem Hybridverfahren bei ca. 10 min. Eingeschlossen sind dabei alle obenerwähnten Schritte und zusätzlich eine abschließende visuelle Kontrolle.

4 Diskussion

Ein Hybridverfahren zum Abgleich medizinischer Schnittbilder wurde entwickelt, welches sowohl die Vorzüge des automatiserten Abgleichs mit denen des visuell - interaktiven verbindet. Rechenaufwendige Schritte lassen sich computergestützt bewältigen, wogegen der Abgleich komplexer Bildinhalte wie beim Vergleich von PET und MRT durch die visuelle Kontrolle bevorzugt ist. Ferner wird die Zahl der Interpolationen auf ein Minimum reduziert.

5 Literatur

1. Pietrzyk U, Herholz K, Fink G, et al : An interactive technique for three-dimensional image registration: validation for PET, SPECT, MRI and CT brain studies. J Nucl Med, 35:2011-2018,1994.
2. Anderson JLR: A rapid and accurate method to align PET scans utilizing image edge information. J Nucl Med, 36:657-669,1995.
3. Woods RP, Cherry SR, Mazziotta JC: Rapid automated algorithm for aligning and resliceing PET images. J Comput Assist Tumorgr, 16:620-633, 1992.
4. Svedlow M, McGillem CD, Anuta PE: Image registration: Similarity measure and processing method comparisons. IEEE Trans Aeros Elec Syst, 14:141-149,1978.

Automatische Augenstellungsbestimmung in Infrarot-Videobild-Sequenzen

Rainer Schian[*], Jean-Cyriaque Barry[◇], Uwe Pongs[+], Lutz Priese[*]

[*] Labor Bilderkennen, Universität Koblenz-Landau, Rheinau 1, 56075 Koblenz
[◇] Universitäts-Augenklinik, Sektion Motilitätsstörungen, Schleichstraße 12, 72076 Tübingen
[+] Medizinische Fakultät der RWTH Aachen, Pauwelsstr. 30, 52057 Aachen

Zusammenfassung In diesem Artikel soll ein Verfahren vorgestellt werden, mit dem genau, robust und schnell die Augenstellung beider Augen einer Person objektiv bestimmt werden kann, um eine dynamische Schielwinkelmessung durchzuführen. Das Verfahren wird erfolgreich in der Augenheilkunde eingesetzt.

1 Einleitung

Während bei Eye-Tracking-Systemen der Schwerpunkt in der sehr schnellen Berechnung der Blickrichtung in weiten Bereichen liegt [5], liegt in unserer Anwendung der Schwerpunkt auf der exakten Bestimmung der Blickrichtung, um Augenfehlstellungen bei Säuglingen und Kleinkindern im Bereich von wenigen Grad (Mikrostrabismus) sicher diagnostizieren zu können [1][2][3].

Mit Hilfe von Hochleistungs-Infrarot-Leuchtdioden werden Lichtspiegelungen an bzw. in den Augen, die sog. Purkinje-Reflexe, erzeugt und die beiden Augen jeweils mit einer infrarotempfindlichen Videokamera mit einer Auflösung von 768 × 512 Pixeln aufgenommen. Aus den relativen Positionen der Purkinje-Reflexe erster Ordnung (an der Hornhautoberfläche reflektiertes Licht) und vierter Ordnung (eine punktförmige Reflexion des Lichts an der Linsenrückseite) läßt sich die optische Achse und damit die Augenstellung des Auges berechnen. Aus dem Mittelpunkt des Hornhautrandes bzw. der Pupille und den Purkinje-Reflexen erster Ordnung läßt sich ebenfalls (jedoch nicht so exakt) die Augenstellung bestimmen.

Dazu ist eine echtzeitnahe und robuste Bildauswertung zur dynamischen Schielwinkelmessung für Bildfolgen mit bis zu 5 Bildpaaren pro Sekunde auf einem PC entwickelt worden, die im folgenden beschrieben werden soll. Diese gliedert sich in die Bestimmung der „Region of Interest", Form- und Lagebestimmung der Pupille, der Lagebestimmung der Iris sowie der Bestimmung der Mittelpunkte der Purkinje-Reflexe erster und vierter Ordnung.

2.1 Bestimmung der „Region of Interest" (RoI)

Bei der Auswertung von Bildfolgen kann die Tatsache ausgenutzt werden, daß die Lage der Pupille sich in zwei aufeinanderfolgenden Bildern meist nur geringfügig ändert. Daher wird nicht das gesamte Bild, sondern nur der Bildteil, der die vorherige Pupille enthält, mit dem in [6] beschriebenen GSC (Grey Structure Code) segmentiert. Wenn in dem segmentierten Bildausschnitt kein Kandidat für eine Pupille gefunden wird, wird das gesamte Bild erneut segmentiert. Genauso wird das gesamte Bild segmentiert, wenn im vorherigen Bild keine Pupille gefunden wurde.

Nach der, evtl. zweimaligen, Segmentierung des Bildes wird dasjenige Segment ausgewählt, das am ehesten zum Attribut „sehr dunkle, kompakte Kreisfläche" paßt. Die Pupille wird durch dieses Segment - stark unterabgetastet - beschrieben. Aus diesem Segment wird ein rechteckiger Bildausschnitt (RoI) bestimmt, der die Pupille vollständig und auch Teile der Iris enthält, um eine stabile und robuste Erkennung der Pupille und der Purkinje-Reflexe zu erzielen und den Rechenaufwand möglichst gering zu halten.

Mit einem Schwellwert, der aus den Grauwerten des Pupillensegmentes berechnet wird, wird das Originalbild innerhalb der RoI binarisiert und mittels der morphologischen Standardoperationen Dilatation und Erosion [4] geglättet. Das so berechnete Binärbild wird im folgenden mit „Pupillenmaske" bezeichnet.

Wenn in der in 2.2 beschriebenen Mittelpunkt- und Formbestimmung der Pupille nicht alle 16 Randpunkte bestimmt werden konnten, dann besteht die Möglichkeit, daß eine deutliche Lageveränderung der Pupille die Ursache ist. In diesem Fall ist ein Rand der Pupille abgeschnitten. Wenn zusätzlich weitere Randpunkte fehlen oder fehlerhaft sind, kann die genaue Lage der Pupille nicht bestimmt werden. Deshalb werden die vorhandenen Randpunkte durch einen (wesentlich robuster bestimmbaren) Kreis approximiert und damit die RoI und die Pupillenmaske neu berechnet.

2.2 Mittelpunkt- und Formbestimmung der Pupille Teil 1

In der Praxis ist die Pupille häufig teilüberdeckt, etwa durch Brillenspiegelungen oder das Lid. Die Umrandung der Pupille kann als (mathematische) Kurve in einer zweidimensionalen Ebene aufgefaßt werden. Sie sollte recht genau die meisten Pupillen beschreiben, aber gleichzeitig nicht zu viele Freiheitsgrade besitzen, um effizient berechenbar zu sein. Dafür hat sich die Ellipse bewährt. Der Mittelpunkt der Ellipse, die die sichtbare Pupille beschreibt, ist damit gleichzeitig der Mittel- bzw. Schwerpunkt der unverdeckten Pupille. Ausführlich wird die Approximation der Pupille durch eine Ellipse in [7] beschrieben. Grob gliedert sie sich in drei Teile:

1. Aus der Pupillenmaske werden bis zu 16 Randpunkte der Pupille bestimmt.
2. Mit Hilfe des Newtonverfahrens wird im $\mathrm{I\!R}^5$ eine Ellipse bestimmt, die die Randpunkte möglichst gut, d.h. quadratminimal, approximiert.
3. Es werden iterativ Randpunkte weggelassen, die mit hoher Wahrscheinlichkeit nicht zum Rand der Pupille gehören und die verbleibenden erneut durch eine Ellipse approximiert, bis die mittlere Abweichung der approximierten Randpunkte von der Ellipse klein genug ist.

2.3 Mittelpunkt- und Formbestimmung der Pupille Teil 2

Die Wahl der zu approximierenden Koordinaten hat einen sehr großen Einfluß auf die Güte des Approximationsergebnisses. Ohne Vorwissen über die Lage der Pupille lassen sich jedoch Koordinaten, die nicht den Pupille-Iris Übergang beschreiben, kaum von denen unterscheiden, die zwar den korrekten Übergang beschreiben, aber nicht dem Modell Ellipse entsprechen. Mit dem ersten Teil der Pupillenbestimmung ist die Lage der Pupille bekannt. Ausgehend von dem Mittelpunkt der Pupille wird in 24 Strahlen im Bereich des erwarteten Pupillenrandes nach einem Pupille-Iris Übergang im Originalbild gesucht und so neue Koordinaten bestimmt.

Da in einem recht begrenzten Bereich nach den Übergängen gesucht wird, führen Artefakte wie Brillenspiegelungen und Verdeckungen durchs Lid nicht zu fehlerhaften, sondern nur zu fehlenden Koordinaten, d.h. (nahezu) alle Koordinaten liegen auf dem äußeren Rand der Pupille. Diese lassen sich mit einem, ähnlich dem in [8] beschriebenen, adaptiven Verfahren durch eine Ellipse approximieren. Dazu werden folgende Schritte iteriert, bis der gewichtete, mittlere Abstand der Koordinaten von der Ellipse in zwei aufeinanderfolgenden Iterationschritten sich nicht mehr nennenswert ändert.

1. Es wird eine quadratminimale Ellipse berechnet, wobei jede Koordinate gewichtet wird. Das initiale Gewicht für jede Koordinate ist 1.
2. Der gewichtete, mittlere Abstand der Koordinaten von der Ellipse wird für das oben genannte Abbruchkriterium berechnet.
3. Für jede Koordinate wird der (ungewichtete) Abstand zur Ellipse berechnet. Ebenso die Varianz und der Mittelwert aller Abstände. Das Gewicht für jede Koordinate wird in Abhängigkeit des Abstandes dieser Koordinate von der Ellipse zum Mittelwert der Abstände, normiert mit der Varianz, neu berechnet. Dabei erhalten stark abweichende Koordinaten sehr kleine Gewichte und beeinflussen damit die Ellipsenapproximation nur minimal.

2.4 Mittelpunkt- und Formbestimmung der Iris

Die Beschreibung der Iris erfolgt im Gegensatz zur Pupille nicht durch eine Ellipse sondern durch einen robuster berechenbaren Kreis, da die Iris in den meisten Bildern durch die Augenlider teilweise verdeckt und der kontrastarme Übergang Iris-Sklera (Augenweiß) variabel und kaum genau definierbar ist.

Auf 24 Strahlen, die ihren Ursprung im Mittelpunkt der Pupille haben und maximal 40 Grad von der waagerechten abweichen, wird der Iris-Sclera Übergang bestimmt, indem in der stark geglätteten Folge von Grauwerten der maximale Gradient berechnet und der entsprechende Punkt als Rand zurückgegeben wird. Da deutlich vom mittleren Abstand der Randpunkte zum Mittelpunkt der Pupille abweichende Punkte nicht den Iris-Sclera Übergang sondern Übergänge zu Störungen wie Lid oder Brillenspiegelungen beschreiben, werden sie weggelassen. Die restlichen Randpunkte werden, analog zur Pupillenapproximation Teil 1, durch einen Kreis approximiert. Ausführlich wird dies in [6] beschrieben.

Die Bestimmung der Iris-Sclera Übergänge durch den maximalen Gradienten ist nicht für alle Bilder geeignet, z.B. ist der Gradient an einem Kontaktlinsenrand oft größer als am Irisrand. Deshalb wird, wenn die Möglichkeit der fehlerhaften Bestimmung des Iris-Kreises besteht, die obige Berechnung des Iris-Kreises mit einem anderen Kriterium für einen Iris-Sclera Übergang wiederholt. Als Kriterium dient dabei das Modell der Arcus-Tangens- Funktion. Es wird jeder Helligkeitsübergang (in einem Intervall von 20 Pixeln) mit dem Funktionsgraphen der Arcus-Tangens-Funktion verglichen und die Punkte mit der besten Übereinstimmung als Iris-Randpunkte deklariert.

Das zweite Verfahren ist, im Gegensatz zum ersten, robust gegenüber kontrastreichen Störungen, liefert dennoch häufiger falsche Ergebnisse, wenn der Irisrand nicht genau dem Modell entspricht. Deshalb wird anhand der Genauigkeit der Approximation der Punkte durch den Kreis und dem Abstand des Iris- und des Pupillenmittelpunktes entschieden, ob das erste oder zweite Verfahren die „richtige" Beschreibung der Größe und Lage der Iris liefert.

2.5 Bestimmung der Purkinje-Reflexe

Für die Detektion der Purkinje-Reflexe erster Ordnung (1. Purkinjebilder) und vierter Ordnung (4. Purkinjebilder) werden Filter verwendet, die dort einen hohen Filterwert ergeben, wo sich ein heller Kreis bzw. Punkt auf dunklem Grund befindet. Die Koordinaten, die einen maximalen Filterwert haben, entsprechen den Mittelpunkten der Reflexe. Um die Lage der Reflexe exakt, d.h. Subpixelgenau, zu beschreiben, erfolgt eine in [6] beschriebene Interpolation.

Für die Lagebestimmung der 1. Purkinjebilder wird ein Filter mit einer 19×19 Filtermatrix eingesetzt. Um den Rechenaufwand gering zu halten, ist die zu filternde Fläche möglichst klein zu wählen. Wenn sich die Lage der Pupille im Bild nicht geändert hat, dann braucht auch nur das Gebiet, in dem die Reflexe im letzten Bild vorkamen, gefiltert zu werden. Wenn sich die Lage der Pupille in Bezug auf das letzte Bild geändert hat, sind zwei Fälle zu unterscheiden: Entweder hat sich die Augenstellung geändert, dann ändert sich die Lage der 1. Purkinjebilder nicht, oder das gesamte Auge ist (z.B. wegen Kamerabewegung) verschoben, dann entspricht der Verschiebungsvektor der Pupillen dem der Reflexe. Es wird daher derjenige rechteckige Bildausschnitt gefiltert, der beide Gebiete enthält.

Bei den 4. Purkinjebildern kann die zu filternde Fläche über die Symmetrieeigenschaften des Reflexmusters eingeschränkt werden. Die 4. Purkinjebilder lassen sich als Punktspiegelung der 1. Purkinjebilder durch ein Symmetriezentrum darstellen, wobei der Abstand der 4. Purkinjebilder zum Symmetriezentrum gegenüber dem der 1. Purkinjebilder im Durchschnitt um den Faktor 0.762 verkürzt ist. Der Mittelpunkt der Iris bzw. der Pupille ist ein guter Schätzwert für das Symmetriezentrum. Um alle Bereiche abzudecken, werden die „Erwartungsgebiete" der 4. Purkinjebilder mit beiden Schätzwerten berechnet und die „Vereinigungsfläche" gefiltert. Bereiche außerhalb der Pupille bleiben unberücksichtigt, da 4. Purkinjebilder nur innerhalb der Pupille vorkommen.

3. Ergebnisse

Die vorgestellten Algorithmen laufen stabil und brauchen auf einem PC mit Pentium Pro Prozessor, 200 MHz, durchschnittlich zusammen etwa 90 Millisekunden pro Bild (Auge), d.h. eine Sequenzauswertung ist mit etwa 5 Bildpaaren pro Sekunde möglich. Um die Güte der vom Programm gefundenen Koordinaten beurteilen zu können, wurden in Testbildern die Daten von Hand erfaßt. Die Abweichung bei den Purkinje-Reflexen und der Pupille ist nur selten über 1 Pixel (im euklidischen Abstand), häufig jedoch unter einem halben Pixel. Bei der Iris liegt das gros der Abweichungen zwischen 1 und 2 Pixeln, wobei eine Streuung von bis zu 2 Pixeln auch bei der Handerfassung der Iris von verschiedenen Personen auftritt und fehlerhaft vom Programm bestimmte Koordinaten meist in Y-Richtung abweichen, also bei der Schielwinkelmessung unerheblich sind. Damit erreicht dieses Verfahren die Güte von menschlichen Messungen.

Alle obigen Angaben beziehen sich auf einen Testset von 771 Bildern, der überproportional viele Bilder mit Artefakten (Brillenspiegelungen, Linsentrübungen, etc.) enthält. Auch die Sequenztests wurden auf diesem Testset durchgeführt, obwohl alle Bilder als Einzelbilder von 42 Personen mit verschiedenen Blickrichtungen aufgenommen wurden. Doch damit entspricht dies einem schlecht fixierendem Patienten bei gleichzeitig unruhiger Kamerahaltung.

Literatur

1. J. C. Barry, R. Effert, M. Reim, D. Meyer-Ebrecht, *Computaional Principles In Purkinje I and IV Reflection Pattern Evaluation for the Assessment of Ocular Alignment*, Invest Ophthalmol Vis Sci. 1994;35:4205-4218
2. J. C. Barry, R. Effert, A. Kaupp, A. Burhoff, *Measurement of Ocular Alignment With Photographic Purkinje I and IV Reflection Pattern Evaluation*, Invest Ophthalmol Vis Sci. 1994;35:4219-4235
3. J. C. Barry, R. Effert, A. Kaupp, M. Kleine, M. Reim, *Computergestützte Messung von Augenfehlstellungen bei Säuglingen und Kleinkindern mit Hilfe des digitalen Purkinje-Reflexmuster-Verfahrens*, Springer-Verlag Ophthalmologe 1994 91:51-61
4. R. M. Haralick, L. G. Shapiro, *Computer and Robot Vision*, Addison Wesley Publishing Company, 1992
5. H. Klingpohr, T. Block, R.-R. Grigat, *Ein echtzeitfähiges System zur Erkennung der Blickrichtung des menschlichen Auges*, Tagungsband 19. DAGM-Symposium, Braunschweig 15.-17. September 1997, S. 191-198, erschienen im Springer-Verlag
6. R. Schian, J. C. Barry, U. Pongs, L. Priese, *Detektion von Purkinje-Reflexen in Infrarot-Videobildern*, Tagungsband zum 5. Freiburger Workshop 10.-11. März 1997, S. 192-196
7. R. Schian, L. Priese, *Automatische Lagebestimmung von Pupillen in der Medizinischen Datenverarbeitung*, Tagungsband 19. DAGM-Symposium, Braunschweig 15.-17. September 1997, S. 568-579, erschienen im Springer-Verlag
8. H. Suesse, K. Voss, *Adaptive Ausgleichsrechnung und Ausreißerproblematik für die digitale Bildverarbeitung*, Tagungsband 15. DAGM-Symposium, Lübeck 27.-29. September 1993, S. 600-607, erschienen im Springer-Verlag

Kantenerhaltende Glättung von Volumendaten bei sehr geringem Signal-Rausch-Verhältnis

Volker Aurich, Eva Mühlhaus und Sven Grundmann

Abteilung für Informatik des Mathematischen Instituts der
Heinrich-Heine-Universität Düsseldorf, Universitätsstraße 1, 40225 Düsseldorf
Email: aurich@cs.uni-duesseldorf.de

Zusammenfassung. Es wird ein massiv parallisierbares Verfahren beschrieben, das in einem Signal Feinstruktur wie z.B. Rauschen eliminiert, dabei aber die gröberen Strukturen gut erhält. Die Wertänderungen der zu entfernenden Feinstruktur dürfen in derselben Größenordnung wie die der zu erhaltenden gröberen Struktur sein.

Schlüsselwörter: Kantenerhaltende Glättung, nichtlineare Filter.

1 Problemstellung

Gegeben sei eine einzige Realisierung f eines verrauschten dreidimensionalen Signals f_{ori}, das bis auf einige Sprungstellen, die sog. Kanten, nur langsam variiert. Hat das Rauschen den Erwartungswert Null, so ist die beste Schätzung von f_{ori} auf Basis von f eine lokale Mittelung, die nicht über die Kanten hinweggreift. Weil man aber nicht a priori die Kanten kennt, benötigt man Verfahren, die simultan Rauschen glätten und Kanten erhalten. Sie sind notwendigerweise nichtlinear. Das im folgenden vorgestellte Verfahren beruht auf einer Folge sorgsam aufeinander abgestimmter, weicher Schwellwertentscheidungen.

2 Das nichtlineare Gaußfilter

Bei hohem Signal-Rausch-Verhältnis kann man das Rauschen reduzieren, ohne die Kanten zu verschmieren, indem man ein lineares Glättungsfilter so modifiert, daß in den Mittelwert an einer Stelle p nur die Werte $f(q)$ an Nachbarstellen q eingehen, die von $f(p)$ höchstens um eine vorgegebene Schranke abweichen. Anschaulich bedeutet dies, daß nur die Punkte $(q, f(q))$ des Signalgraphen gemittelt werden, die sich innerhalb eines in $(p, f(p))$ zentrierten Fensters befinden. In Abbildung 1 sind zwei solche Datenfenster an den Signalsprungstellen 64 und 320 eingezeichnet. Solche Filteroperationen sind als robuste Schätzer in der Statistik bekannt.

Weil das Rauschen in Anwendungen oft glockenförmige Verteilungen hat, ersetzen wir die harte Auswahl der zu mittelnden Werte durch eine weichere Entscheidung, indem wir sowohl in Orts- wie in Werterichtung statt durch ein Fenster durch Gauß-förmige Gewichtsverteilungen abschneiden. Dadurch ergibt sich das folgende nichtlineare Gaußfilter; es liefert an der Stelle p bei Eingabe des Signals f den Ausgangswert

$$NLG_{\sigma,\zeta}f(p) = \frac{1}{N} \sum_q g_\sigma(\|q - p\|)\, g_\zeta(|f(q) - f(p)|)\, f(q)$$

Dabei sind $g_\lambda(t) = \exp(-\frac{t^2}{2\lambda^2})$ die unnormierte Gaußfunktion mit Streuung λ und $N = \sum_q g_\sigma(\|q - p\|)\, g_\zeta(|f(q) - f(p)|)$ ein Faktor zur Normierung des Gesamtgewichts auf 1.

Die Breite der Gaußglocke g_ζ in Werterichtung sollte einerseits groß sein, damit das Rauschen sicher eingefangen wird, andererseits jedoch klein sein, damit die Kanten nicht verschmiert werden. Diese gegensätzlichen Kriterien lassen sich nur bei hohem Signal-Rausch-Abstand erfüllen, wie z.B. in Abbildung 1 bei den beiden hohen Sprüngen rechts; die niedrigen Sprünge links werden verschmiert. Diesem Dilemma kann man durch eine geeignete Hintereinanderschaltung mehrerer nichtlinearer Gaußfilter entkommen.

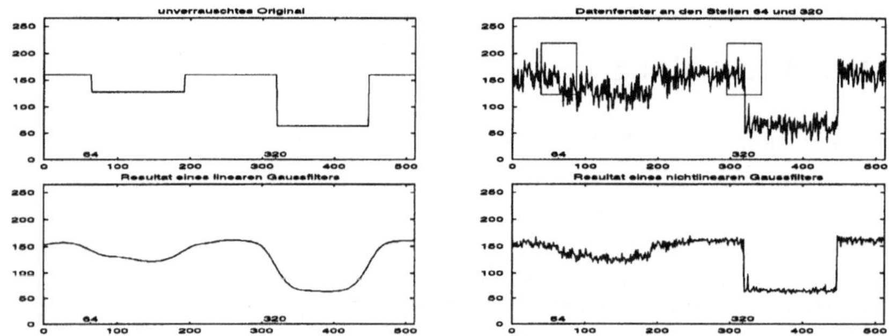

Abb. 1. Filterung eines 1-dimensionalen Signals

3 Die nichtlineare Gaußfilterkette

In einer Kette nichtlinearer Gaußfilter $f_{aus} = NLG_{\sigma_k,\zeta_k} \circ \ldots \circ NLG_{\sigma_1,\zeta_1}(f)$ sollte einerseits jeder Filterschritt das Rauschen um einen vorgegebenen Faktor α reduzieren, andererseits sollten die Kanten möglichst wenig verschmiert werden. Dazu müssen die Werte der ζ_j fallen und die der σ_j wachsen. In Abbildung 2 wird dies für ein eindimensionales Signal demonstriert, indem an den Sprungstellen 64 und 320 (harte) Fenster eingezeichnet sind, deren Breite und Höhe den Werten von σ und ζ der folgenden Filterstufe entspricht. In [3] wird gezeigt, daß die optimale Parameterwahl dimensionsabhängig ist; für dreidimensionale Signale ergibt sich $\zeta_{j+1} = \frac{1}{\alpha}\, \zeta_j$ und $\sigma_{j+1} = \sqrt[3]{\alpha^2}\, \sigma_j$. Kanten, die in den ersten Filterschritte verschmiert wurden, können sich in den nachfolgenden wieder aufrichten ([2]). In der Praxis sind Filterketten aus drei bis fünf Stufen ausreichend; denn dann ist der Parameter ζ bereits so klein, daß weitere Filterstufen fast keine Veränderung mehr bewirken. Das Ausgangssignal f_{aus} einer solchen Filterkette ist stückweise nahezu konstant, und die Kanten sind leicht detektierbar. Daher liegt es nahe, einen weiteren modifizierten Filterschritt anzuhängen, bei dem die Filtergewichte wie bisher aus f_{aus} berechnet werden, jedoch nicht die Werte von f_{aus}, sondern die des ursprünglichen Eingangssignals f gemittelt werden ([1]).

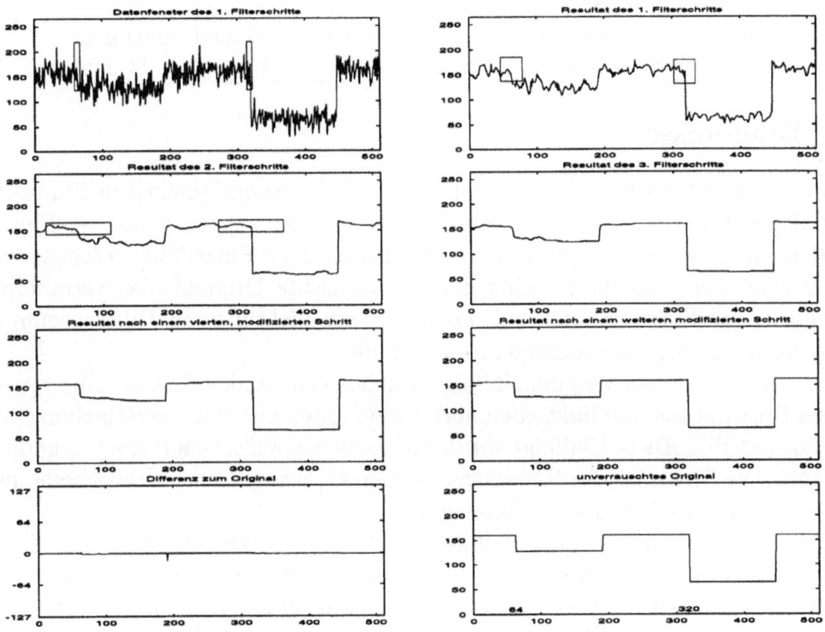

Abb. 2. Mehrstufige Filterung eines 1-dimensionalen Signals

4 Implementierung

Bei der praktischen Implementierung erstrecken sich die Summen nicht über den gesamten Definitionsbereich, sondern lediglich über eine kleinere Quaderumgebung des jeweiligen Punktes p, außerhalb derer die Gaußgewichte klein sind. Eine Kantenlänge von $\lambda\sigma_j$ mit $\lambda \geq 6$ reicht aus. Die Rechenzeit wird erheblich verkürzt, wenn λ von etwa 6 in der ersten Filterstufe bis auf 2 in der letzten Stufe abnimmt; die Filterergebnisse werden dadurch nicht nennenswert beeinflußt.

In jedem Filterschritt sind nur einfache lokale Operationen auszuführen; Zwischenresultate werden nur nach jedem Filterschritt ausgetauscht. Jeder Filterschritt ist auf einfachste Weise parallelisierbar, indem jede Recheneinheit das Ergebnis in einem Bereich (z.B. einem Streifen) des Definitionsbereichs ausrechnet. Zwar müssen die einzelnen Filterschritte einer Kette nacheinander ausgeführt werden; weil aber die Filterketten in der Praxis nicht sehr lang sind und nur Zwischenergebnisse benachbarter Bereiche ausgetauscht werden müssen, werden bei größeren Datenmengen durch die Parallelisierung der einzelnen Filterschritte erhebliche Geschwindigkeitssteigerungen erzielt. Zur Demonstration wurde die Filterkette mit PVM auf einem Netz unterschiedlicher SparcWorkstations verteilt. Die folgende Tabelle enthält die Rechenzeiten für die Glättung einer Bildfolge aus 64 Bildern mit einer 5-stufigen Filterkette.

		1 Rechner	8 Rechner	16 Rechner	32 Rechner
Größe	128×128	7:40 min	1:50 min	1:50 min	1:10 min
der	256×256	33 min	7.5 min	4 min	3:00 min
Einzelbilder	512×512	2:20 h	28 min	16 min	11 min

5 Ergebnisse

Anhand zweier synthetischen Bildfolgen soll die Leistungsfähigkeit nichtlinearer Gaußfilterketten demonstriert werden. Beide Folgen bestehen aus 64 Einzelbildern. In den Abbildungen 3 und 4 werden typische Einzelbilder gezeigt, und zwar sind von links nach rechts das unverrauschte Original, das verrauschte Original, das Filterergebnis und das mit einem nichtlinearen Differenzenfilter ([2]) lokal binärisierte Filterergebnis abgebildet.

1. Beispiel: In der Originalbildfolge wandert eine dunkle Kreisscheibe von 10 Pixel Durchmesser von links oben nach rechts unten mit einer Verschiebung von 1 Pixel pro Bild. Diese Bildfolge wurde mit weißem Gaußschem Rauschen additiv gestört. Die Streuung des Rauschens beträgt 48, während die Kreisscheibe nur 32 Grauwerte dunkler als der Hintergrund ist.

2. Beispiel: In der Originalbildfolge wandert ein dunkles Quadrat mit 4 Pixel Kantenlänge von links oben nach rechts unten mit einer Verschiebung von 1 Pixel pro Bild. Ein weiteres Quadrat rechts unten verändert seine Position nicht, ist aber nur immer 8 Bilder lang vorhanden. Die Bilder dieser Folge wurden mit weißem Gaußschen Rauschen additiv gestört. Die Streuung des Rauschens ist genauso groß wie die Grauwertdifferenz der Quadrate zum Hintergrund. In Abbildung 5 sind links die dunklen Voxel der unverrauschten Originalbildfolge räumlich dargestellt und rechts die im binärisierten Filterergebnis. Die falsch detektierten Voxel liegen alle am Rand des Datenvolumens, wo die dreidimensionalen Umgebungen, über die beim Filtern gemittelt wird, kleiner sind und daher die Mittelwerte mit geringerer Wahrscheinlichkeit gute Schätzungen des Originalsignals sind.

Literatur

1. V. Aurich, J. Weule: Non-Linear Gaussian Filters Performing Edge Preserving Diffusion. Proceedings 17. DAGM Symposium über Mustererkennung, Springer 538–545, 1995.
2. J. Weule: Iteration nichtlinearer Gauß-Filter in der Bildverarbeitung. Dissertation. Universität Düsseldorf, 1994.
3. E. Mühlhaus: Die sprungerhaltende Glättung verrauschter, harmonischer Schwingungen. Dissertation (eingereicht). Universität Düsseldorf, 1997.

Abb. 3. Bild Nummer 16 in Beispiel 1

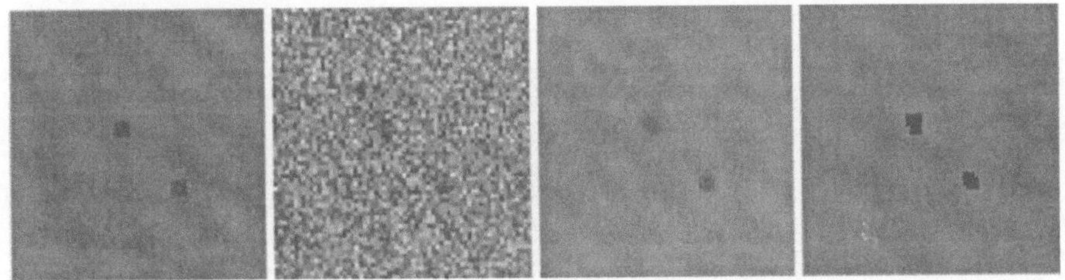

Abb. 4. Bild Nummer 33 in Beispiel 2

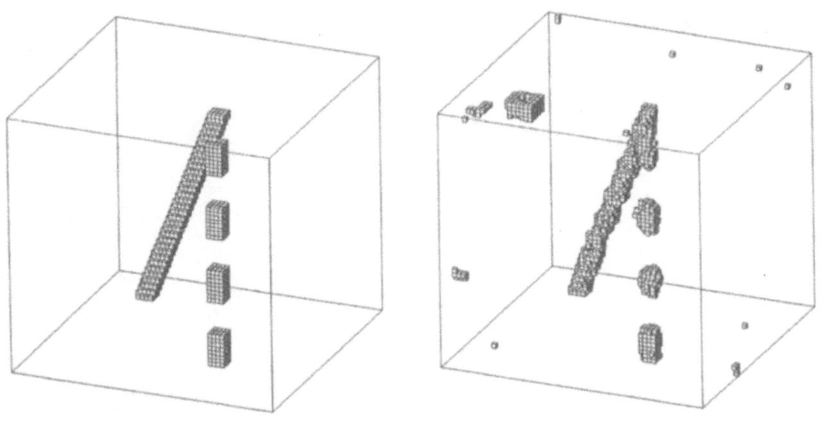

Abb. 5. Unverrauschte Originalstruktur und Filterergebnis für Beispiel 2

- Nichtperiodische, kleine Körperbewegungen (< 2−4mm Auslenkung) werden durch Registration in der Zeitreihe eliminiert.

- Einzelne Zeitschritte mit großen Körperbewegungen innerhalb der Meßperiode eines Zeitschrittes ("verwischte Schichten") werden aufgrund ihrer anderen Intensitätscharakteristik detektiert und von der weiteren Verarbeitung ausgeschlossen.

- Schwankungen in der Langzeitstabilität des Scanners äußern sich u.a. in einer Schwankung der mittleren Intensität eines gegebenen Voxels in der Zeitreihe. Diese Grundline kann durch eine Tiefpaßfilterung geschätzt und vom Eingangssignal subtrahiert werden. Hierdurch wird auch das anatomische (T2-gewichtete) Bild von den funktionellen Informationen getrennt.

- Der Großteil der heutigen fMR-Studien wendet ein single- bzw. embedded-single-trial-Design an und besitzt damit eine im Vergleich zum Blockdesign relative hochfrequente (Quasi-)periodizität der Stimulation. Mithilfe von entsprechend angepaßten Bandpaßfiltern lassen sich Rauschen und periodische Artefakte (Pulsationen, Atmung) breitbandig abtrennen.

Eine Vorverarbeitungskette für fMR-Rohdaten, die an diesen Ansatzpunkten angreift, soll nun algorithmisch kurz skizziert und mit ihren Ergebnissen exemplarisch dargestellt werden.

3 Algorithmen

Die fMRI-Rohdaten werden einer Sequenz von vier Vorverarbeitungsschritten unterworfen:

- *Artefaktdetektion.* Jede Schicht wird in Vordergrund (Gehirn) und Hintergrund segmentiert. Die Intensität und ihre Varianz werden in beiden Regionen berechnet und in der Zeitreihe klassifiziert. Zeitschritte mit groben Körperbewegungen und Magnetisierungsartefakten (die zu einer veränderten Intensitätscharakteristik des Vordergrundes führen) fallen als Außenseiter heraus und werden von der weiteren Verarbeitung ausgeschlossen.

- *Bewegungskorrektur.* Kleine und physiologische Bewegungen (< 2 − 4mm) werden durch eine Registrationsprozedur in der Zeitreihe korrigiert. Auf eine Referenzschicht werden alle folgenden Zeitschritte linear transformiert, wobei als Zielfunktion die Kreuzkorrelation zwischen homotopen Schichten zweier Zeitschritte maximiert wird.

- *Grundlinienkorrektur.* Die langsame fluktuierende Grundlinie wird durch einen FIR-Tiefpaßfilter rekonstruiert. Das Resultat wird vom Eingangssignal abgezogen, so daß effektiv eine Hochpaßfilterung erzielt wird.

- *Signalrestauration.* In den verbleibenden Daten liegt neben der funktionellen Aktivierung und in der Regel höherfrequenten, nicht mit den Experiment korrelierten Signalvariationen noch ein breitbandiger Rauschanteil vor. Im einfachsten Fall kann das funktionelle Signal durch ein FIR-Tiefpaßfilter extrahiert werden. Einen deutlichen Vorteil bietet die Signalrekonstruktion

durch ein raum-zeitliches Markov-Feld, das eine kantenerhaltende Glättung
durchführt.

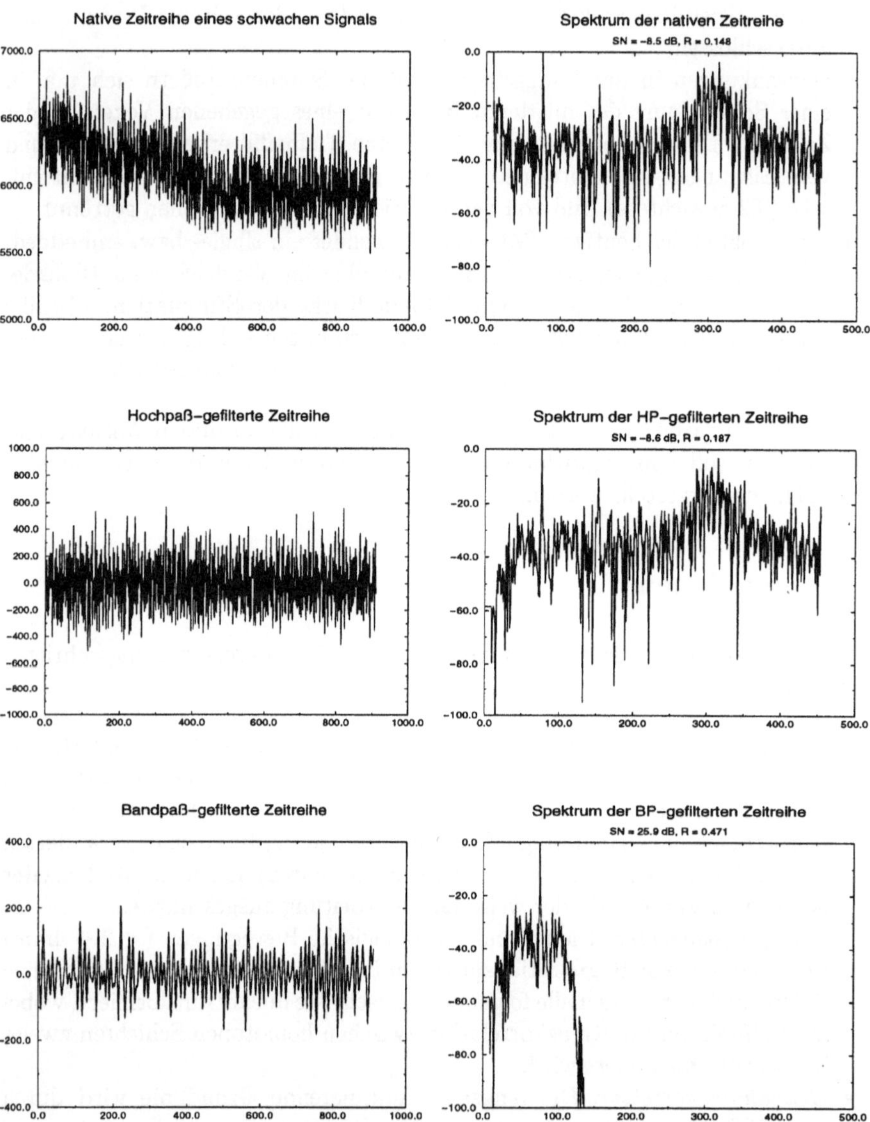

Abb. 1. Zeitreihen (links) und Spektren (rechts) eines Voxels mit schwacher funktioneller Aktivierung in nativer Form, nach Grundlinienkorrektur bzw. nach Bandpaßfilterung. Für die Spektren wurden zusätzlich das Signal-Rausch-Verhältnis (SN) und
die Pearson-Korrelation (R) mit dem Stimulus (als box-car-waveform) angegeben.

An diese Vorverarbeitung schließt sich die statistische Auswertung an, um signifikant mit dem experimentellen Design verknüpfte Signalschwankungen zu detektieren, die als funktionelle Aktivierungen interpretiert werden können. Das Ziel der Vorverarbeitung, die Rekonstruktion des funktionellen Signals, wird in der Teststatistik durch eine deutliche Steigerung der Korrelation und ein wesentlich verbessertes Signal-Rausch-Verhältnis wiedergegeben. Letztendlich führt dies zu einer geringeren Anzahl an falsch positiv detektierten Voxel.

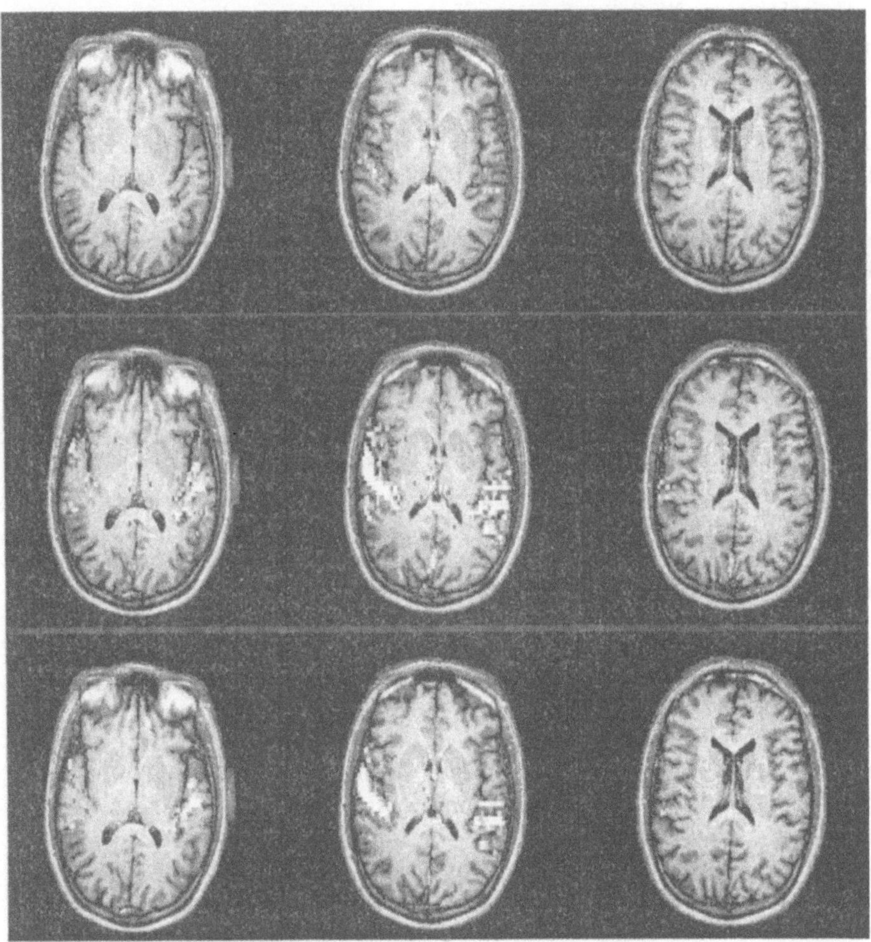

Abb. 2. Auswertung eines fMR-Experimentes zur auditorischen Sprachverarbeitung. In Vergleich sind die Auswertung des nativen Datensatzes, nach Bandpaßfilterung, und nach Bildrekonstruktion mithilfe eines Markov-Feldes dargestellt. Zur Detektion der aktivierten Regionen wurde die Pearson-Korrelation mit einer um 4s verschobenen box-car-waveform gerechnet, anschließend z-transformiert und auf Signifikanz getestet. Die z-Skala reicht von 12 (!) bis 24.

4 Anwendungsbeispiel

Im Rahmen einer fMR-Studie zur auditorischen Sprachverarbeitung wurden
alle 2s 4 Schichten mit 128x64 Voxeln (Auflösung 1.9x3.8x5mm) gemessen. Die
Präsentation eines Satzes dauert etwa 6s (3 Zeitschritte), gefolgt von einer Ruhe-
phase von 18s (9 Zeitschritte). 76 Durchläufe (912 Zeitschritte) wurden in einem
halbstündigen Experiment aufgenommen. Ein einzelner Datensatz wurde ausgewählt, um exemplarisch den Nutzen der Vorverarbeitung zu demonstrieren.

In *Abb. 1* ist die Zeitreihe eines Voxels im Thalamus dargestellt. Die konventionelle Auswertung ergibt eine schwache, aber signifikante Aktivierung (z-
score 2.5). Jeweils in der linken Spalte ist die Zeitreihe, rechts das zugehörige
Spektrum dargestellt. Die obere Zeile stellt das native (ungefilterte) Signal,
die mittlere nach Grundlinienfilterung, die untere nach Bandpaßfilterung dar.
In der oberen Zeile deutlich erkennbar sind die Grundlinienschwankungen, die
sich nicht durch ein einfaches (lineares) Modell erklären lassen, aber nach Filterung weitgehend eliminiert sind, ohne die Signalstärke zu mindern. Eine starke
Begrenzung des Spektrums führt zu einer deutlichen Verbesserung des Signal-
Rausch-Verhältnisses und läßt die funktionellen Antworten je Durchlauf einzeln
hervortreten.

Abb. 2 zeigt die Ergebnisse der statistischen Auswertung des Sprachexperi-
mentes. Deutlich erkennbar ist der Gewinn in der z-Statistik nach der Grundlinienkorrektur: im auditorischen Kortex werden z-scores über 20 gefunden. Allerdings variiert die Teststatistik durch die Anwendung eines rein zeitlichen Filters
von Voxel zu Voxel. Bei Signalrekonstruktion mit einem Markov-Feld treten diese
Schwankungen nicht auf. Durch Simulationen mit artifiziell aufmodulierten Sig-
nalen läßt sich nachweisen, daß die Rekonstruktionsleistung des Markov-Feldes
dem eines optimal angepaßten Bandpaßfilters ebenbürtig ist.

5 Zusammenfassung

Ziel der Vorverarbeitung von fMR-Daten ist die Trennung des funktionellen Signals von den begleitenden Meßartefakten. Die beschriebene Vorarbeitung erleichtert und verbessert die Voraussetzungen für die nachgeschaltete statistische
Auswertung. Hieraus resultiert eine höhere Empfindlichkeit und eine bessere
Charakterisierung einer aktivierten Region (in Ausdehnung und Aktivations-
stärke) bei einer gleichzeitigen Minimierung falsch positiv detektierter Voxel.
Durch Elimination von Grundlinienschwankungen im Rahmen dieser Vorverarbeitung wird zudem ein Vergleich von Testblöcken ermöglicht, die einige Minuten
auseinanderliegen oder in getrennten Scans aufgenommen wurden.

Aufgrund dieser Vorteile hat sich Vorverarbeitung von fMR-Daten innerhalb
kurzer Zeit als Standard in unserem Labor etablieren können.

Literaturreferenzen können von den Autoren zur Verfügung gestellt werden.

Erste klinische Untersuchungen mit einem mechanischen Finite-Elemente-Modell des menschlichen Kopfes

Ulrich Hartmann, Frithjof Kruggel

Max-Planck-Institut für neuropsychologische Forschung
Inselstraße 22-26, 04103 Leipzig
Email: {hartmann, kruggel}@cns.mpg.de

Zusammenfassung. Das Verständnis der mechanischen Folgen externer und interner Krafteinwirkungen auf den Kopf ist von hoher klinischer Relevanz und kann Einfluß auf die Wahl der Therapieform nehmen. Wir benutzen die Finite-Elemente-Methode (FEM), um computerbasiert mechanische Einwirkungen auf das System Kopf zu modellieren. Mit unserem räumlich hochaufgelösten FE-Modell des menschlichen Kopfes sind wir in der Lage, Simulationsrechnungen durchzuführen, die auf individuellen dreidimensionalen MRT-Datensätzen basieren. Wir präsentieren zwei FE-Analysemethoden unterschiedlicher Zielrichtung, deren Ergebnisse mit experimentell ermittelten Daten verglichen werden. Mit der dynamischen FE-Analyse wird das Coup-Contrecoup-Phänomen untersucht; die Eigenschwingungsanalyse des Kopfes kann als Ansatz zur Erklärung von Verletzungsmechanismen wie z.B. der diffusen axonalen Gehirnschädigung (DAI) genutzt werden.

Schlüsselwörter: Finite Elemente, Biomechanik des Kopfes

1 Einleitung

Die Methode der finiten Elemente (FEM), die zur Lösung partieller Differentialgleichungen auf komplexen Geometrien dient, wird in letzter Zeit zunehmend zur Beantwortung medizinischer Fragestellungen auch im Bereich der Neurowissenschaften herangezogen. Die Methode der finiten Elemente wird angewandt um

- elektromagnetische Quellen im Gehirn zu lokalisieren [1],
- neurochirurgische Eingriffe zu planen [2] und
- die biomechanische Systemantwort infolge von externen Kräften (z.B. Unfallsituationen) [3] und intrakraniellen Massenveränderungen(z.B. Tumorwachstum) zu modellieren.

Eine kurze Zusammenstellung und kritische Würdigung der FE-Modelle, die zur Untersuchung neuromechanischer Fragestellungen erstellt wurden, findet man in [4]. Im Vergleich mit den dort zitierten Arbeiten weist unser Modell folgende Vorteile auf:

- Die Geometrie unseres Modells basiert auf *individuellen* MRT-Datensätzen
  des Kopfes. Dadurch werden Langzeitstudien am Patienten möglich, die
  dessen individuelle neuroanatomische Verhältnisse (z.B. Krankheitsprozesse)
  berücksichtigen. Im Gegensatz dazu basiert die Geometriebeschreibung beste-
  hender Modelle auf einer Durchschnittsform des menschlichen Kopfes.
- Die Anzahl der finiten Elemente, mit denen unsere Simulationen durchgeführt werden, ist bis zu zehnmal so hoch wie die bisher verwendeten Ele-
  mentanzahlen. Dadurch werden die der FE-Methode inhärenten Diskretisier-
  ungsfehler minimiert und die Finite-Elemente-Repräsentation anatomischer
  Objekte wird detailliert und realitätsnäher.
- Mittels einer modalen FE-Analyse gewinnen wir wichtige Einblicke in das
  Schwingungsverhalten des mechanischen Systems. In Zusammenhang mit
  Kopfmodellen ist diese Analysemethode unseres Wissens bisher nur für ein
  Modell durchgeführt worden [5].

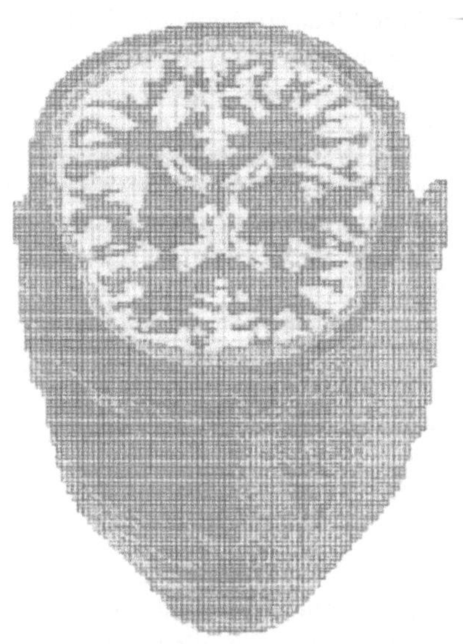

Abb. 1. Finite-Elemente-Repräsentation des Kopfes.

2 Modellierung

Grundlage der Geometriebeschreibung unseres Modells sind 3D MRT-Datensätze
des Kopfes. Die Vorverarbeitung (Interpolation, Segmentation) dieser Datensätze
dient dem Ziel, bestimmten neuroanatomischen Strukturen auf der Basis der
Grauwerte ihrer Voxel Materialeigenschaften zuzuweisen. Diese Vorgehensweise
ist ausführlich in [4] beschrieben. Ausgehend vom vorverarbeiteten Datensatz
kann mithilfe unseres Netzgenerators [6] der Kopf als Verbund finiter Elemente
dargestellt werden. Die in Kapitel 3 präsentierten Simulationsergebnisse sind
alle mit Würfelnetzen von 2 mm und 3 mm Kantenlänge durchgeführt worden.

Einen Durchschnitt durch ein solches Würfelnetz mit 2 mm Kantenauflösung, das zwischen fünf Materialien unterscheidet, zeigt Abb. 1.

Das Materialverhalten wird mithilfe von zwei Parametern beschrieben, dem Elastizitätsmodul E und der Poissonschen Zahl ν. Tab. 1 gibt eine Übersicht über die verwendeten Materialparameter. Alle in unserem Modell auftretenden Gewebetypen werden als sogenannte St. Venant-Kirchhoff Materialien interpretiert, bei denen auch für relativ große Deformationen lineares Verhalten postuliert wird. Interessiert man sich für die zeitliche Entwicklung der Deformationen U

Struktur	E [MPa]	ν	ρ [kg/m^3]
Kopfhaut	16.70	0.42	1200
Schädel	6500.00	0.22	1420
Weisse Gehirnsubstanz	0.12	0.499	1040
Graue Gehirnsubstanz	0.075	0.499	1040
Ventrikel	0.075	0.4995	1045

Tabelle 1. Materialparameter

infolge einer Krafteinwirkung, ist eine dynamische FE-Analyse durchzuführen. Das Gleichungssystem

$$M\ddot{U}(t_i) + C\dot{U}(t_i) + KU(t_i) = F(t_i) \tag{1}$$

wird mit der Methode von Newmark für eine bestimmte Anzahl von Zeitschritten gelöst. In Gleichung (1) steht M für die Massenmatrix des Systems, C repräsentiert die Rayleigh-Dämpfungsmatrix und K ist die Steifigkeitsmatrix. Bei der modalen Analyse wird das generalisierte Eigenproblem

$$KU_i = \lambda_i MU_i \tag{2}$$

für den gewünschten Eigenwertbereich mit der Lanczos-Methode [7] gelöst. Ergebnis einer derartigen Analyse sind Eigenfrequenzen ($f_i = \sqrt{\lambda_i}/2\pi$) mit den zugehörigen Eigenvektoren U_i.

3 Erste klinisch-relevante Simulationen

In unserer ersten klinischen Simulation analysierten wir das Coup-Contrecoup-Phänomen. Ist der gesamte Kopf Gegenstand einer Beschleunigung infolge einer lokalisiert einwirkenden Kraft, stößt das Gehirn aufgrund seiner Trägheit gegen die Schädelkalotte. In der dem Stoßbereich gegenüberliegenden Kopfregion kommt es aufgrund des sich einstellenden Unterdrucks zu einer Saugwirkung. Mit der Durchführung einer dynamischen FE-Analyse können intrakranielle Druckänderungen, die sich infolge einer dem Kopf auferlegten Beschleunigung entwickeln, in hoher Zeitauflösung studiert werden. Von Experimenten mit Kadavern [8], deren Köpfe definierten Stößen ausgesetzt wurden, kennt man die daraus resultierenden Druckveränderungen an vier verschiedenen Orten des Gehirns. Wir modellierten eines dieser Experimente, indem wir einen der in [8] beschriebenen Kraftverläufe auf unser Modell übertrugen. Abb. 2 zeigt anhand eines Schnittes durch den Kopf die Entwicklung der berechneten Druckverteilung infolge eines im Stirnbereich applizierten Kraftverlaufs. Die weitgehende Übereinstimmung der experimentell bestimmten mit den berechneten Druckentwicklungen zeigt, daß unser Modell qualitativ und quanititativ gültige Aussagen liefert.

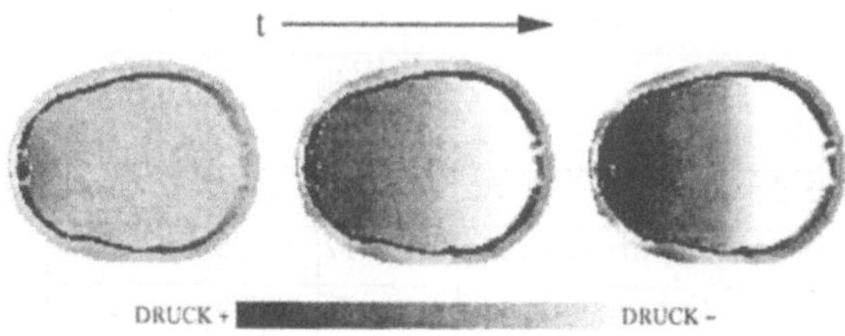

Abb. 2. Intrakranielle Druckveränderungen beim Coup-Contrecoup-Phänomen.

Als eine zweite Möglichkeit, die Eignung unseres Modells für klinische Studien zu prüfen, haben wir eine modale FE-Analyse durchgeführt, die Eigenfrequenzen f_i und zugehörige Eigenvektoren U_i des Kopfes liefert. Abb. 3 zeigt das Ergebnis einer modalen Analyse, bei der der Eigenvektor U_{min} zur niedrig-

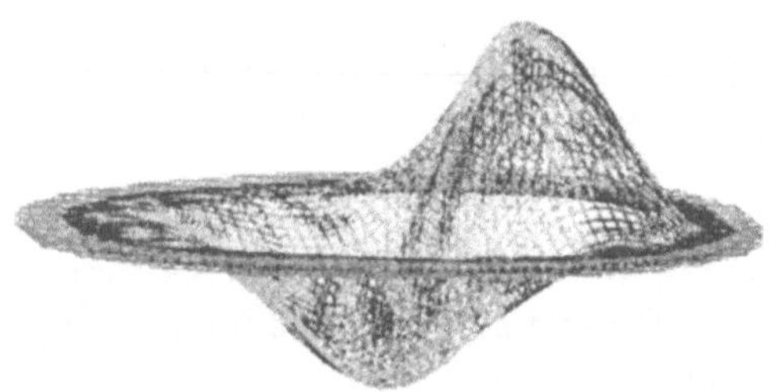

Abb. 3. Darstellung des Eigenvektors U_{min} zur niedrigsten Eigenfrequenz $f_{min}=77$ Hz.

sten Eigenfrequenz f_{min} bestimmt wurde. Aus Gründen der Anschaulichkeit ist nur ein Schnitt durch das FE-Kopfmodell (siehe Abb. 1) dargestellt und die entsprechenden Komponenten des Eigenvektors sind mit dem Faktor 50 multipliziert. Als zugehörige Eigenfrequenz liefert der Algorithmus einen Wert von $f_{min} = 77$ Hz. Untersuchungen mit Probanden [5] bestätigen die Existenz einer Eigenfrequenz des menschlichen Kopfes im Bereich von 100 Hz, bei der das Gehirn relativ zum Schädel schwingt.

Die modale Analyse dient uns über dieses erste Ergebnis hinaus als Konzept zum besseren Verständnis von Verletzungsmechanismen. Kommt es zu Anregungen des Kopfes, die im Frequenzbereich einer Eigenschwingung liegen, kann dies zu großen Schwingungsamplituden und damit zu schweren Gewebsverletzungen führen. Somit könnte die Kenntnis des Schwingungsverhaltens des Gehirns zum Verständnis des Pathomechanismus der diffusen axonalen Gehirnschädigung (DAI) beitragen, die die Folge eines abrupten Abbremsens des Kopfes (z.B. bei schweren Auffahrunfällen) ist. Hier treten regelmäßige Muster von Gewebszerreißungen im Gehirn auf, die einen Zusammenhang zwischen Orten von Schwingungsknoten und Gewebsverletzungen vermuten lassen. Wir präsentieren Eigenschwingungen aus dem mittleren Wertebereich des gesamten Frequenzspektrums mit einer Wellenlänge von ungefähr 5 cm, die als Ursache solcher Zerreißungsmuster in Frage kommen.

Die obigen Simulationsrechnungen zeigen, daß unser Modell mit klinischen Erfahrungen im Einklang steht und ermutigen uns, weitere Pathomechanismen wie z.B. das Wachstum von Tumoren, zu untersuchen.

Literatur

1. Yan Y, Nunez RL, Hart RT: Finite element model of the human head: scalp potentials due to dipole sources. Medical and Biological Engineering and Computing: 475-481, 1991.
2. Koch RM, Gross MH, Carls FR, von Buren DF, Fankhauser G, Parish YIH: Simulating facial surgery using finite element models. Computer Graphics Proceedings, Annual Conference Series: 412-428, 1996.
3. Hartmann U, Kruggel F: Ein virtueller Dummy zur Simulation des Schädel-Hirn-Traumas, Spektrum der Wissenschaft (9), 96-98, 1997.
4. Hartmann U, Kruggel F: Ein mechanisches dreidimensionales Finite-Elemente-Modell des menschlichen Gehirns, In: Arnolds B, Müller H, Saupe D und Tolxdorff T (Hrsg.): Digitale Bildverarbeitung in der Medizin: 219-224, 1997.
5. Willinger R, Taleb L, Kopp CM: Modal and temporal analysis of head mathematical models. Journal of Neurotrauma 12: 743-754, 1995.
6. Hartmann U, Kruggel F: A fast algorithm for generating large tetrahedral 3D finite element meshes from magnetic resonance tomograms Technical Report, MPI-CNS 1997.
7. Lehoucq RB, Sorensen DC, Yang C: Arpack's User Guide: Solution of large scale eigenvalue problems by implicitly restarted Arnoldi methods. *http://www.caam.rice.edu/kristyn/parpack_home.html*, 1996.
8. Nahum AM, Smith R, Ward CC: Intracranial pressure dynamics during head impact, Proc. of 21st Stapp Car Crash Conference: 339-366, 1977.

PROSTATE ULTRASOUND IMAGES PROCESSING

Daniela Crivianu-Gaita[1], Fl. Miclea[2], A. Gaspar[3], St. Holban[4], G. Muntean[4]

1 - Dept. of Computer, County Hospital of Timisoara, Romania
2 - Urology Clinic, University of Medicine and Pharmacy Timisoara, Romania
3 - Soft-nrg Company, Timisoara, Romania
4 - Dept. of Computer Science, The Technical University, Timisoara, Romania
E-mail: crivianu@mail.dnttm.ro

Abstract. The purpose of this paper is to present a software package for the handling and management of prostate transabdominal ultrasound images. The software package can be used to detect men's prostate in transabdominal ultrasound images, to build a 3D model for the detected object, to represent the 3D model obtained, to calculate prostate's volume and to classify the prostate transabdominal ultrasound images acquired. The software system can be used in hospitals which do not have either CAT scanners or NMR/MRI equipment (the majority of Romanian hospitals). It provides these hospitals with a tool enabling a more accurate diagnosis, which in turn improves the efficiency of the hospital, saves money, and has a profound psychological benefit on the well-being of the patient.

Keywords: ultrasound, prostate, 3D reconstruction, classification.

1 Introduction

It is known that in the gastrointestinal and genitourinary systems, the image processing has mostly been focused on computed tomography images or magnetic resonance images [1], three-dimensional ultrasound imaging being still in a research phase [1]. This is due both to technical problems of data acquisition, and theoretical and practical problems of how to render the complex information contained in ultrasound data onto a display [2].

We developed and implemented a software package which is dealing with prostate transabdominal ultrasound images. The software package allows to acquire images from a 3.5 MHz ultrasound equipment for different incidences, to filter the images, to detect the prostate in the 2D images acquired, to build the 3D model of the prostate, to represent the 3D model in different ways, to compute its volume. Also the software presents information about an image, information which can be used to classify the image in one of the following classes: normal and pathologic. For pathological images a second classification will be made, trying to differentiate between benign and malignant lesions.

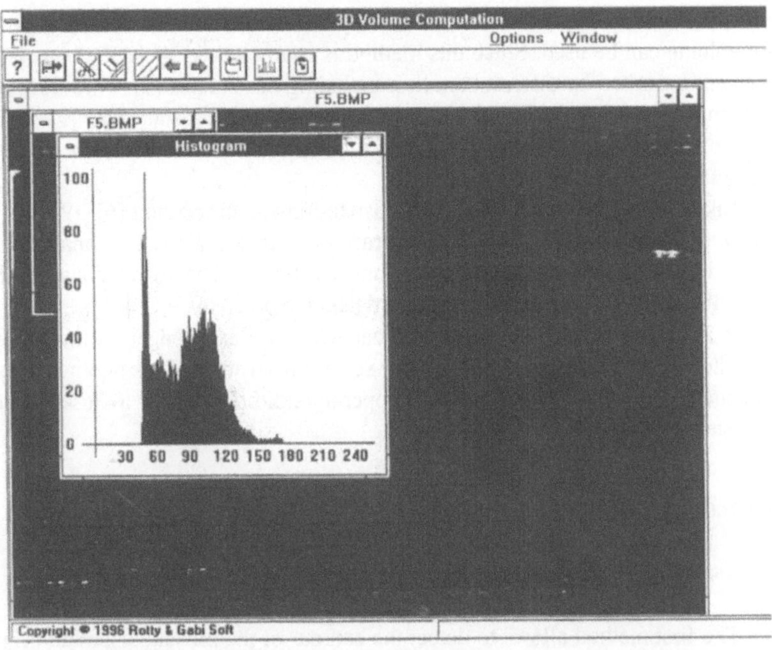

Fig. 1. Histogram of a prostate transabdominal ultrasound image.

2 Medical Preliminaries

Diseases of the prostate gland are common in adult and elderly men, and primary care physicians as well as urologists are frequently consulted for treatment of prostate problems [3]. Correct diagnosis of a prostate disorder cannot be made solely by assessing symptoms, however, as the symptoms of the most common disorders - prostatitis, benign prostatic hyperplasia (BHP), and prostatic adenocarcinoma - are similar and include both irritative and obstructive voiding problems [4]. Because of this, the most important task of the physicians is the early detection of prostate cancer.

Evaluation of prostate volume is very important in the diagnosis of prostatic cancer [5]. Also, for the patients with benign prostate hyperplasia, the selection of an operative procedure is influenced by the size of the prostate as estimated preoperatively. So it is necessary to compute the prostate's volume with an error as small as possible.

3 Technical Preliminaries

Prostate size is reliably measured using ultrasound - either suprapubic, transurethral, or transrectal - and ultrasound is the imaging of choice in most men with BPH [6]. The role of ultrasound is further enhanced by its relatively low cost and its lack of side effects, such as contrast reactions and radiation exposure. In the case of Urology

Clinic of the County Hospital of Timisoara only the transabdominal evaluation of the prostate volume can be used. Since this method is characterised by lack of precision - as it was demonstrated by different studies, including our studies [7] - we developed different image processing algorithms in order to estimate prostate size [7] and the efficiency of bladder emptying [8], and also in order to evaluate the upper tracts and exclude cancer.

Like the majority of studies on ultrasound image processing [6], [9], we first established the characteristics of prostate ultrasound images. We started analysing the histograms of a large test-set of ultrasound images (fig. 1). The conclusions [7] show that image thresholding could not be used to detect the prostate.

It is known that the common approach for localising edges in images is to associate them with the zero crossing of the second derivative of a smoothed version of the image [10]. But we found that these operators did not deliver a closed contour of the prostate's image.

4 3D reconstruction of prostate

We have developed and implemented two methods for the 3D reconstruction of the prostate.

The first method allows to detect the contour of the prostate using an original algorithm [7]. The prostate is then extracted from the image by a region-growing algorithm. The central point of the prostate is used afterwards as the reference point in the criterion of acceptance used, and it is also used in the algorithm of region-growing, as the starting point.

In general, in order to perform a 3D reconstruction of medical images it is necessary to obtain several images from predetermined positions [1] or to use continuous data acquisition [11]. For the Urology Clinic of the County Hospital of Timisoara it was impossible to apply such methods. So, we designed a method of 3D reconstruction of the objects using 2 orthogonal sections: one is the transversal incidence and the other is the sagittal incidence.

In the second method proposed [8], we used the circular filter, the grey level selection and an algorithm for eliminating the multiple points. We obtained then a set of "depth curves" which describes the 3D image of the prostate.

The next step was to represent the 3D model of the prostate. If the efforts are focused to the clinical usefulness of the application (choosing the method of resolving prostate adenoma) it is possible to select a depth algorithm in order to present the 3D object [7]. If the physician needs precious information about the shape of the prostate (especially in the case of prostatic cancer), he can choose the wireframe representation (fig. 2) [8]. The 3D representation of the prostate can be rotated by the user, being possible to show the asymmetrical regions of the prostate.

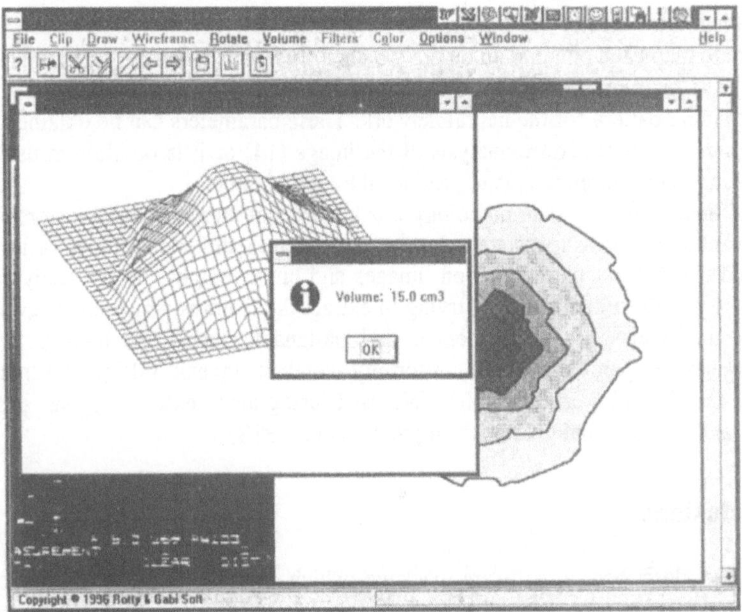

Fig. 2. The wireframe representation of 3D prostate's model.

5 Automatic classification of prostate ultrasound images

It is known that the success of an automatic classification system depends on careful selection of the disease and images. That is the reason why all the images were acquired from the same ultrasound equipment (an Alloka 3.5 MHz) and the examinations were performed by the same experienced sonographers. It was demonstrated that even with these restrictions, it is possible to use artificial neural networks to aid the diagnostic process [12].

At the beginning 60 patients with well defined diagnoses were investigated by ultrasound examination. 20 patients had normal prostate, 20 had benign prostate hyperplasia and 20 presented cancer tumours. For each patient two significant transabdominal ultrasound images were acquired: one from the sagittal incidence and the other from the transversal incidence.

Each original image was transformed into a 640x480 bitmap array quantified on 256 grey levels. Using the mouse the user has to specify a rectangular region for clipping. The chosen region (containing the prostate) is clipped and a new, smaller bitmap is created, a bitmap which will be the source for the next processing stages.

In order to remove noise, the next step was the filtering of the reduced image. We have tried different types of filters, finally choosing the circular filter [8], which non-uniformly illuminates the chosen region (the prostate).

In the papers dedicated to this field of automatic classification of images, there are several approaches. It is possible to select several training areas from identifiable malignant tissue in the data set [13]. Also it is possible to reduce the image to a set of vectors where each member of the set contains information about some salient attributes of the image. The neural network then will take these vectors and learn to map each one into an output which corresponds to a classification [12].

The main problem remains the choosing of significant parameters which will form a training pattern for the neural network. These parameters can be obtained from a histogram and from texture analysis of the image [14] or it is possible to use edge detection and area computations to produce the set of vectors.

Since in the prostate pathology it is known that there are three factors which are relevant in diagnosis (prostate volume, obstruction factor, and irritative factor), we combined the features extracted from images and clinical signs. So we analysed the images for the 60 studied patients, trying to extract the features which are relevant for the three finally classes: normal, benign, and malignant. During this analysis, several image-processing parameters (like uniformity, contrast, inverse differential moment, entropy, correlation) were calculated. We used histograms, texture analysis, prostate volume, and international prostatic symptoms score (IPSS).

6 Conclusions

This paper described a software package which can be used to obtain a 3D representation of prostate from transabdominal ultrasound images and also to obtain an automated classification of transabdominal ultrasound prostate images. With the help of image processing, tissue characterisation was performed to predict the probability of the presence of malignant prostate tumours. The software system developed has proved its usefulness especially in early detection of prostate cancer.

The program was written in C++ (Borland implementation) and data processing was performed on a Pentium 166 MHz computer. The application was implemented and it is used in the present in the Urology Clinic of Timisoara.

Our study proved that it is not always necessary to use advanced mathematical techniques or sophisticated hardware equipment in order to obtain good results in increasing the quality of medical process.

It is known that the most suitable imaging modality for studying prostate tumours is transrectal ultrasonography. But there are several hospital which do not have such equipment and primary care physicians, who have often to solve prostate problems, do not have all transrectal ultrasound equipment. At the same time, transrectal ultrasonography does have some drawbacks, including cost, inability to detect cancer in the transition zone or in those area that appear isoechoic, and with high sensitivity or low specificity for hyperechoic areas.

In this way, a software system for automatic classification of transabdominal ultrasound prostate images, can be a useful alternative to transrectal ultrasonography.

References

1. Zonneveld FW, Fukata K: A Decade of Clinical Three-Dimensional Imaging: A review. Part 2: Clinical Applications. Yearbook of Medical Informatics, 386-401, 1995.
2. Gardner JE et al.: Techniques for 3D Volume Imaging with Ultrasound. In CAR'91 Proceedings of the International Symposium (Eds: HU Lemke), Springer-Verlag, Berlin, 837, 1991.

3. Parkin DM, Stjenward J, Muir CS: Estimates of the worldwide frequency of twelve major cancers. Bull. WHO, 62:163-182, 1984.
4. Ware JL: Prostate cancer progression. Implications of histopathology. Amer. J. Path., 145: 983-990, 1994.
5. Graham SD Jr. - Editor: Urologic Oncology. Raven Press, New York, 1986.
6. De la Rosette J et al.: Automated Analysis and Interpretation of Transrectal Ultrasonography Images in Patients with Prostatitis. European Urology (Eds: CC Schulmam), Karger, 47-53, January 1995.
7. Crivianu-Gaita D et al: 3D reconstruction of prostate from ultrasound images. International Journal of Medical Informatics, 45:43-51, June 1997.
8. Crivianu-Gaita D et al: 3D reconstruction of objects from ultrasound images: possibilities and limits. Conference Proceedings of HC'97 (Current Perspectives in Healthcare Computing) (Eds: Richards B), Weybridge: BJHC, 149-156, 1997.
9. Kratzik C. et al.: Texture Analysis - A New Method of Differentiating Prostatic Carcinoma from Prostatic Hypertrophie. Urological Research, Springer, 395-397, 1988.
10. Huttunen O. et al.: Segmentation System for Medical Images. CAR'91 Proceedings of the International Symposium (Eds: HU Lemke), Springer-Verlag, Berlin, 612-617, 1991.
11. Englmeier K-H et al.: Segmentation and Three dimensional Visualisation of Spiral-CT-Scans of the Abdomen. MIE'94 Proceedings (Eds: P Barahona), 585-589, 1994.
12. Buller D, Buller A, Innocent PR, Pawlak W: Determining and Classifying the region of interest in ultrasound images of the breast using neural networks. Artificial Intelligence in Medicine, 8(1): 53-66, 1996.
13. Hanka R, Harte TP, Dixon AK, Lomas DJ, Britton PD: Neural networks in the interpretation of contrast-enhanced magnetic resonance images of the breast. Conference Proceedings of HC'96 (Current Perspectives in Health Computing) (Eds: Richards B), Weybridge: BJHC, 275-283, 1996.
14. Cavouras D, Kandarakis I, Theotokas I et al: Computer Image Analysis of Ultrasound Images for discriminating and Grading Liver Parenchyma Disease Employing a Hierarchical Decision Tree Scheme and the Multilayer Perceptron Neural Network Classifier. Conference Proceedings of MIE'97 (Eds: Pappas C, Maglaveras N, Scherrer JR), IOS Press, 522-526, 1997.

Lokal-trilineare Bewegungskorrektur in der MR-Mammographie

Harald Fischer, Claudia Ehritt-Braun, Matthias Otte*, Jürgen Hennig,
Thomas Mergner*

Röntgendiagnostik, Neurologie*
Universitätsklinik Freiburg, 79106 Freiburg
Email: fischerh@nz160.ukl.uni-freiburg.de

Zusammenfassung: Kontrastmittel-gestützte MR-Mammographie wird zur Diagnose von Mammakarzinomen in Fällen unklarer Aussagen von Ultraschall und Röntgenuntersuchung auf Grund seiner hohen Spezifität herangezogen. Die einzelnen Volumen können auf Grund der benötigten Datenakquisitionsdauer nicht unter Atemanhalten aufgenommen werden, sondern bei normaler Lungenaktivität. Dies kann zu starken lokalen Bewegungsartefakten führen, welche zu Fehldiagnose oder Unbefundbarkeit der Daten führen kann. Es soll hier ein Verfahren zur Korrektur dieser artefaktbehafteten Daten vorgestellt werden.

Schlüsselwörter: MR-Mammographie, Bewegungskorrektur, Kontrastmittel

1 Einleitung

In der Kontrastmittel-gestützten MR-Mammographie werden mehrere Volumen der weiblichen Brust nach Injektion des Kontrastmittels Gadolinium-DTPA akquiriert. Malignes Gewebe zeichnet sich durch einen schnellen und starken Kontrastmittel (KM) Anstieg aus, welches durch eine starke Intensitätssteigerung der entsprechenden Voxel beobachtet werden kann. Ein Intensitätsanstieg von über 70-80 % zwischen Pre-KM und erstem Post-KM ist ein deutliches Indiz für eine maligne Gewebsveränderung. Sehr ähnliche Intensitätsveränderungen können durch Bewegungsartefakte [1-4] – speziell durch Atmung – hervorgerufen werden, auf Grund der großen Intensitätsunterschiede von Fettgewebe und Parenchym.

In der medizinischen Diagnostik muß nun zwischen bewegungsbedingter und KM-bedingter Kontrastveränderung getrennt werden. Typischerweise wird dies durch medizinisches Wissen wie anatomische Lage der entsprechenden Pixel und Informationen aus bisherigen Befunden der Patientin ermittelt. Hier kann eine automatische Bewegungskorrektur die Genauigkeit bei der Tumorerkennung erhöhen, sowie eine automatische Auswertung der Daten ermöglichen.

Global arbeitende Bewegungskorrekturalgorithmen welche typischerweise bei der Registrierung des Kopfes verwendet werden und die lediglich globale Rotationen, Translationen und u.U. affine Verzerrungen zulassen, können für die MR-Mammographie auf Grund des weichen Gewebes nicht verwendet werden. Das Modell eines Starren Körpers kann hier nicht angenommen werden. Hier werden Verfahren nötig, die lokale Verzerrungen korrigieren können [5].

2 Methodik

Bei der Bewegungskorrektur wird jedes akquirierte Volumen auf ein Referenzvolumen der aufgenommenen Serie registriert, typischerweise auf das Nativvolumen oder auf das erstes Post-KM Volumen. Jedes Post-KM Volumen ist in gleich große Subvolumen unterteilt. Jedes Subvolumen wird auf das Referenzvolumen mit einer eigenen Transformationsvorschrift abgebildet. Die Transformation aller Volumen unterliegt der Randbedingung eines stetigen Übergangs an den Grenzen der Subvolumen. Damit ist die Gesamttransformation als Spline beschrieben. Zur schnellen Bewegungskorrektur werden trilineare Bezier Splines verwendet, die ein effizientes Resampling der Daten im Optimierungsprozess erlauben. Die Ähnlichkeit der Volumen wird direkt aus den Voxelintensitäten mit dem linearen oder dem Entropie basierten Korrelationskoeffizienten [6] ermittelt. Die optimale Abbildung wird mit Hilfe einer iterativen Optimierung gefunden.

3 Resultate

Das zugrunde gelegte Datenmaterial besteht aus klinischen Mammographien mit vornehmlich 5 Post-KM Volumen mit jeweils 40 axialen Schichten. Die Registrierung jedes Post-KM Volumens benötigt ca. 10 Minuten auf einer SGI Indigo Workstation. Die Ergebnisse wurden durch Bildung und Vergleich von Differenzbildern aus Nativaufnahmen und Post-KM Aufnahmen überprüft (*Abb. 2*), wie in der Diagnostik üblich. Ferner wurden für den bewegungskorrigierten und nicht korrigierten Fall Bilder berechnet, bei denen alle Pixel selektiert werden, die in allen Post-KM Aufnahmen eine Intensität größer als 80 % bezogen auf das Nativbild zeigen (*Abb. 1*).

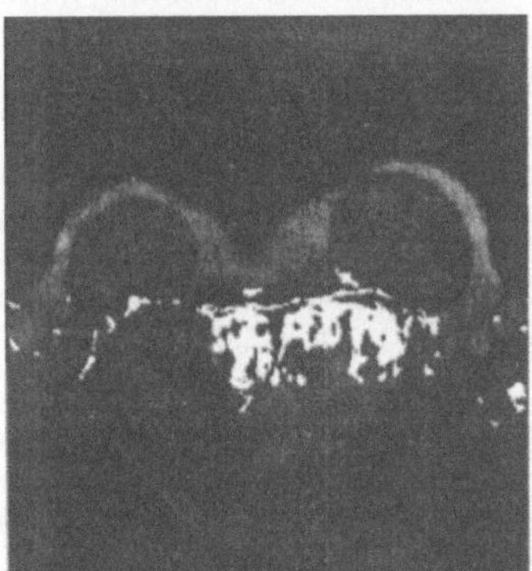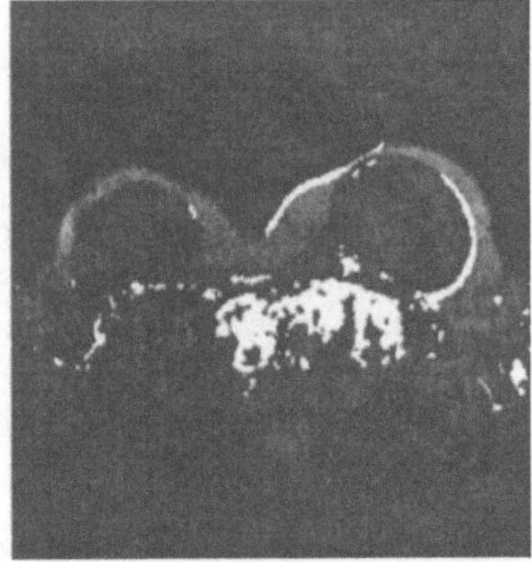

Abb. 1. Korrekturergebnisse der Daten einer Patientin mit beidseitigen Implantaten gezeigt an einer anatomischen Schicht bei korrigierten (links) und nicht korrigierten (rechts) Daten. Pixel mit einem Intensitätsanstieg von über 80 % sind im Nativbild weiß markiert.

Abb. 2. Daten einer Patientin mit positivem Befund. Differenzbilder vor (links) und nach (rechts) Bewegungskorrektur.

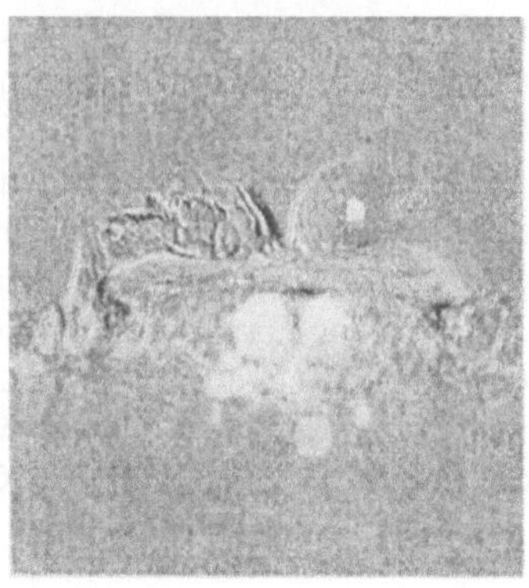 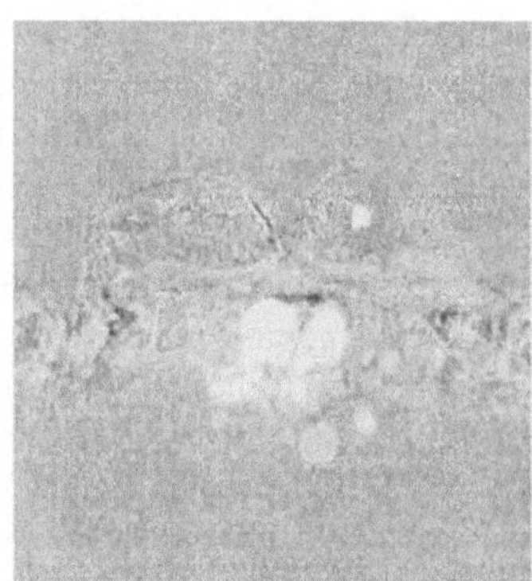

4 Diskussion

Lokal-trilineare Transformationen können lokale Bewegungsartefakte, wie sie bei der MR-Mammographie auftreten, korrigieren. Sie können effizient implementiert werden und benötigen keine Benutzerinteraktionen. Sie stellen somit einen vielversprechenden Ansatz zur Verbesserung der MR-Mammographie Diagnose dar und sind Voraussetzung für eine Automatisierung der Analyse.

Literatur

1. Zuo CS, Jiang A, Buff BL, Mahon TG, Wong TZ: Automatic Motion Correction for Breast MR Imaging. Radiology, **198**: 903-906, 1996.
2. Beier J, Büge T, Oellinger H, Fleck E, Felix R: MR-Mammography based Perfusion Analysis – A 3D Extension. CAR 97: 105-110, 1997.
3. Clair C, Verdenet J, Le Mouel A, Cardot JC, Kastler B: MR Mammography using Karhunen-Loeve-Transformation: a method for optimizing signal to noise and display kinetic of contrast media uptake. CAR 97: 970, 1997.
4. Pedevilla M, Stollberger R, Bammer R, Schmidt F, Wach P, Ebner F: Improving the Diagnostic Reliability of Dynamic MR-Mammography – ROI vs. Pixel-by-Pixel Evaluation. CAR 97: 117-122, 1997.
5. Otte M, Schreiber A, Büchert M, Schmider K, Hennig J, Mergner T, Lücking CH. 5th SMR Meeting: 2018, 1997.
6. Press, W.H., Flannery, B.P., Teukolsky, S.A., Vetterling, W.T: Numerical Recipes in C, The Art of Scientific Computing. Cambridge University Press, 1994.

Dynamic X-Ray Imaging System based on an all-solid-state Detector

N.Jung[1], F.Busse[1], N.Conrads[1], H.Meulenbrugge[2], W.Rütten[1], H.Stouten[2], H.Wieczorek[1]

Philips Research Laboratories, 52066 Aachen, Germany [1]
Philips Medical Systems, 5680 DA Best, The Netherlands [2]
Email: jung@pfa.research.philips.com

Abstract. New digital detector systems based on all-solid-state large area electronics offer a number of advantages for the user, like no image distortions, flat and light weight housing, no veiling glare, and large dynamic range. On the other hand, they require a dedicated image preprocessing to exploit their full image quality. In this paper we address design concepts, performance characterization and resulting image preprocessing aspects of our experimental detector system. The system comprises the detector frontend and a realtime image preprocessing unit with an interface to a commercial digital video system. It is intended for clinical evaluation of this new technology.

Keywords: dynamic x-ray imaging system, all-solid-state x-ray detectors, large area thin film electronics, realtime image processing

1 Introduction

Due to the progress in the field of large area thin film technology a first generation of novel medical x-ray detector systems based on all-solid-state devices is close to market introduction. We have made investigations to a 20 x 20cm^2 detector setup with 1k^2 pixels of 200μm running at up to 30 frames/s [1]. These values come close to the needs of a real product and allow first clinical evaluations in a number of application areas. In this paper we address design, performance and image preprocessing issues of such a novel detector system. The technology chosen offers the possibility of a large detection area in combination with a large dynamic range. Image sizes beyond 40 x 40cm^2 and pixel pitches down to 100μm are within reach. Furthermore the detectors do not show the artifacts found in state-of-the-art systems like geometric distortion, vignetting and veiling glare. In addition, they offer a superior Detective Quantum Efficiency, leaving room for image enhancements. With these properties a single detector system promises the realization of a flat and thin x-ray imaging detector that combines the capabilities for a full size high quality radiography and those for a low dose fluoroscopy system. Systems based on the new detector technology can be considered as a milestone on the track to the digital hospital.

2 Description of the experimental detector system

The experimental system was developed in order to exploit the maximum image quality that could be derived with the thin-film technology. Therefore, we created a very flexible setup based on first principles that can be used for a reproducible performance optimization process. The system comprises the modules shown in Fig. 1:

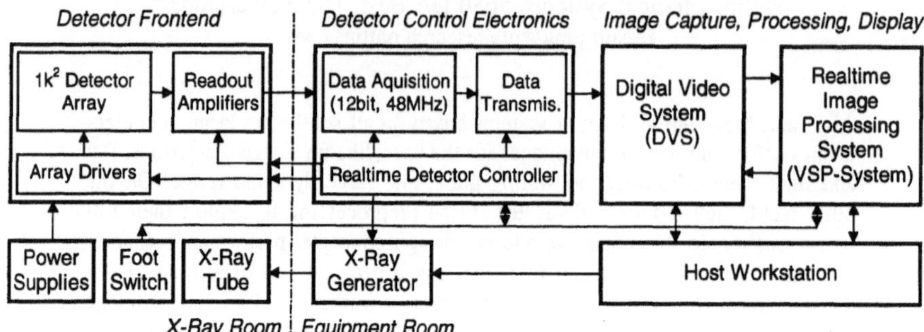

Fig. 1: Experimental x-ray system for first clinical applications

The imaging system is split into two physically separated parts: frontend related components placed in the x-ray room and system control, image acquisition and image processing related parts placed in the equipment room. The whole imaging chain is controlled via a host software running on a Unix workstation. The image sequences are acquired by the DVS and in realtime preprocessed by the Video Signal Processor system (VSP-system). The workstation does image analysis, however, in off-line mode.

The detector is read out by means of charge sensitive amplifiers. The output signals of these amplifiers are digitized by A/D converters with an amplitude resolution of 12bit. Subsequently the image data are multiplexed to a single progressive scan data stream and sent to the DVS at a burst data rate of up to 48Mwords/s.

The DVS allows the recording, archiving and displaying of the generated video sequences. Further it relaxes the input data bursts, transfers the raw images to the VSP system and reads the processed data back. This modality does not replace the entire functionality of a commercial x-ray imaging system, but showed to be sufficient for the clinical investigations.

The VSP system consists of a VME-rack with a 68k control processor board, two VSP boards, two SDRAM memory boards and two I/O boards for interfacing to the DVS. The realtime image processing is carried out by means of the two VSP boards, based on the Video Signal Processor chip (VSP-2 chip). The memory boards, 32Mwords each, are used for realtime storage, e.g. of the correction images. The realtime processor system is capable of processing up to 25 images of $1k^2$ pixels per second at a sustained data rate of about 27 MWords/s. The Philips VSP-2 chip is a general-purpose realtime programmable video processor, designed for high performance by using a number of parallel operating pipeline processors and a switch matrix for flexible signal routing. The chip is 12 bit oriented and is running at a clock rate of 54MHz. It has 12 arithmetic logic elements, 4 x 2k dual ported memory and 6 buffer and in- and output elements. The VSP-2 chip contains 1.15 M transistors and is programmable by means of powerful graphical programming tools. Twelve of these VSP chips, configured on the two boards, have been used to realize the corrections. The realtime processing is done frame-synchronously. The total image delay by the preprocessing is less then 0.5 ms.

3 Detector frontend

We applied an approach with an array of photodiodes, Thin-Film-Transistors (TFT) and a scintillator layer on top as the most promising choice. The general architecture of the detector frontend is shown in Fig. 2:

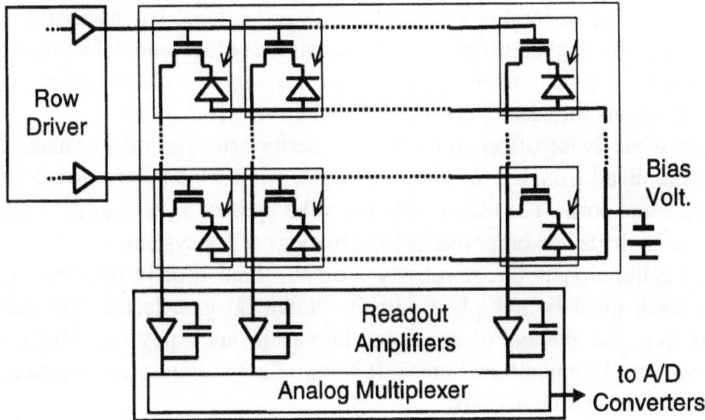

Fig. 2: Schematic of the 2D image sensor

In this architecture all pixels of an entire line are read out simultaneously. The maximum readout speed of the configuration is characterized by the time constant according to $\tau = C_P \times R_{TFTon}$ where C_P denotes the storage capacitance of the pixel photodiode and R_{TFTon} denotes the resistance of the TFT in on-mode.

Our sensor plate is a custom specific development from the Xerox Palo-Alto-Research Center [2]. A dedicated amorphous silicon process for detectors is applied. The top side of the detector plate is covered by an x-ray sensitive CsI:Tl screen which was evaporated directly to the sensor plate. The applied evaporation process guarantees a good trade-off between spatial resolution and x-ray sensitivity.

4 Image quality evaluation

The measured modulation transfer function amounts to MTF(1lp/mm) $\approx$ 50%. It drops to 18% at 2lp/mm. The Nyqusit frequency is 2.5lp/mm. The detector offers an average electrical signal size of 1750e⁻/nGy with respect to incident x-ray dose. The total measured electronic noise amounts to $N_{EI} \approx 1200e^-$. Hence, the system yields an S/N-ratio of $S/N_{EI} \approx 23.3$ dB at 10nGy dose and the 200µm pixel size.

We calculated the detective quantum efficiency DQE(f) from the MTF(f) and noise measurements. For high doses we get a value DQE(0lp/mm)≈ 5% at 500nGy. It drops to DQE(1lp/mm)≈52%. We consider these values appreciably high. At lower exposure doses the DQE declines due to the increasing influence of the electronic noise. If we take a value DQE(0)=50% as limit, the detector allows quantum limited operation down to a dose of about 4nGy/exposure [3].

5   Image data preprocessing

Different to CCD cameras, the thin-film detectors do not offer image data that can be used without prior conditioning. This preprocessing comprises several basic corrections and associated calibrations of detector imperfections, but no image enhancements. We basically applied offset correction, gain correction and defect interpolation. All fixed pattern noise is removed by this preprocessing. The procedures require dedicated correction sets for each operation mode of the detector system.

As first step a pixelwise offset subtraction is performed. The offset values for each pixel are determined from averaged dark images, so that the subtraction does not introduce additional noise. The offset table has to be updated in regular intervals during operation due to drifts and other thermal fluctuations of the system.

The second calibration is the sensitivity normalization, usually referred to as gain correction. Each pixel is multiplied with its individual gain factor. The factors are determined from the average of equal and homogeneous exposures. This correction also does not introduce additional noise. It is important to notice that the gain showed to be stable over long time periods.

The last procedure is the defect interpolation. Every pixel that showed unusual behavior is marked in a defect map and is replaced in the final images by the interpolation of its neighbors values in either direction. Unusual behavior in first instance means completely insensitive pixels, but also too large or too low offset, more than 25% sensitivity deviation from the average sensitivity and too large noise caused by instability. With these criteria we typically find 0.3% isolated pixel defects and 1-2 broken lines in the current detectors. Only simple interpolation, referencing two suitable neighbors, is applied. Higher order interpolations yielded substitute values for the defect pixels with lower noise. This lower noise can be recognized and is disturbing. The histogram of a dark image roughly shows a Gaussian-like shape. The values can amount to about 25% of the dynamic range in the highest sensitivity mode. At lower sensitivities the offset distribution becomes relatively smaller. Thus, the quality of the offset calibration is most demanding in the highest sensitivity setting. A detailed analysis shows, that major contributions to the offset values are caused by the preamplifier. The sensitivity variations from pixel to pixel over the total image can amount up to 20%. The named dispersions are not critical, but they limit the available dynamic range in the highest sensitivity mode to about 75% of the possible range. The use of an A/D converter with more than 12 bit resolution would be advantageous.

The term "memory effect" describes a residual image due to charge that is trapped in the photodiodes of the detector after an exposure. The charge release time constants amount up to several seconds. With our array we find about 1.3% residual signal after

1s and still 0.3% after 10s. This means that the memory effect is relevant for mixed mode operation where a low dose fluoroscopy sequence immediately follows after a high dose exposure. According to our current knowledge, the only option for a removal of the after-images is an adequate digital image processing. For this experimental clinical demonstrator a first simple version of memory-effect correction is implemented in order to be able to study the impact of the effects during clinical practice. The correction method is only suited for pulsed fluoroscopy. It is based on dark frames taken in between exposed frames. As a consequence the effective frame speed is halved i.e. from 25 images/s to 12.5 images/s with every other frame exposed. The unexposed images contain the residual signal due to the memory-effect. The correction is done by real-time subtraction of this previous unexposed image from the next exposed image. The method works well, however, it introduces additional noise.

After all corrections have been carried out, the mean pixel value in a region of interest (ROI) is calculated. This mean value is used to do realtime image normalization by scaling the image data to a certain mean level, independent of the applied dose. The normalization is done by multiplying all pixel values with the calculated scaling factor. The mean value in the ROI is also used to generate a control signal to the X-ray generator for dose control during pulsed fluoroscopy mode.

6 Summary

We have described our experimental x-ray system based on a photodiode-TFT matrix detector with $1k^2$ pixels running at 25 images/s. The results show that the enormous potential of the thin-film technology in fact can be exploited in a technical system matched to the medical application. The new detector systems offer the required performance to replace today's film and image-intensifier-camera based systems in all practical cases. In many aspects they do not only offer the replacement, but real system improvements become possible e.g. all kinds of fixed pattern noise can be removed for the first time. The digital detector is an important base for extended digital image processing functionality. Interactive image enhancements will allow the radiologist to match the image presentation to the individual needs exploiting the full potential given by the detector.

7 Literature

1. Bruijns AJC, Alving PL, Luijendijk JA, Meulenbrugge HM, Stouten JJ, Jung N, Baker EL, Bury R, Cowen AR: Technical and clinical results of an experimental flat dynamic x-ray detector based system with online corrections. SPIE Medical Imaging 1998: Physics of Medical Imaging, 3336, 1998.
2. Street RA, Fujieda I, Weisfield R, Nelson S, Nylen P: Large area 2-dimensional a-Si:H imaging arrays, Mat. Res. Soc. Symp. Proc. 258: 1145-1150, 1992.
3. Jung N, Alving PL, Busse F, Conrads N, Meulenbrugge HM, Rütten W, Schiebel U, Weibrecht M, Wieczorek H: Dynamic X-Ray Imaging System based on an Amorphous Silicon Thin-Film Array. SPIE Medical Imaging 1998: Physics of Medical Imaging, 3336, 1998.

Gewebedifferenzierung in sonographischen Aufnahmen der Haut

Regina Pohle und Jens Ulrich

Institut für Simulation und Graphik und Universitätsklinik für Dermatologie
Otto-von-Guericke-Universität, 39016 Magdeburg
Email: regina@isg.cs.uni-magdeburg.de

Zusammenfassung. In dem Beitrag wird ein System vorgestellt, welches den Arzt bei der Auswertung von Ultraschallbildern der Haut unterstützen soll. Dazu wurden zuerst Segmentierungsverfahren entwickelt. Sie erlaubten eine möglichst automatische Detektion der interessierenden Objekte. Anschließend erfolgte die Berechnung einer Vielzahl von Textur- und Formmerkmalen für jeden segmentierten Bereich, von denen dann für die verschiedenen Unterscheidungsaufgaben eine optimale Untermenge ausgewählt wurde. Die bisher erzielten Ergebnisse werden dargestellt und Verbesserungsmöglichkeiten werden diskutiert.

Schlüsselwörter: Texturanalyse, Gewebedifferenzierung, Klassifikation

1 Einleitung

Auf dem Gebiet der Auswertung von sonographischen Aufnahmen dominieren derzeit noch manuelle Verfahren, bei denen anhand von immer wiederkehrenden sonographischen Mustern eine Beschreibung und Grobklassifizierung der Tumore bzw. Lymphknoten vorgenommen wird. Diese Methode erfordert ein aufwendiges Untersuchertraining und ist subjektiv geprägt. Aus diesem Grund wird seit mehr als einem Jahrzehnt wissenschaftlich daran gearbeitet, die Aussagen von Ultraschallbildern durch computergestützte Systeme zu erhöhen [1]. Bei dem im folgenden vorgestellten Programmsystem soll der subjektiv empfundene Bildeindruck, der größtenteils vom Erfahrungsschatz des Untersuchers bestimmt wird, durch reproduzierbare Methoden der Bildanalyse objektiviert werden.

2 Bildmaterial

In unsere Untersuchungen wurden sowohl 7,5-MHz- als auch 20-MHz-Sonogramme (Abb. 1) einbezogen. Beide Sonogrammtypen wiesen aufgrund der, bei den Ultraschallaufnahmen der Haut auftretenden, sehr geringen Impedanzunterschiede oft nur schwache Grauwertkontraste innerhalb der Hautregion auf.

Neben dieser Gemeinsamkeit waren bei der Auswertung auch einige Unterschiede zwischen den beiden Bildtypen zu berücksichtigen. So bewirkte die unterschiedliche Schallfrequenz sowohl eine unterschiedliche laterale und axiale Auflösung der Bilder

Abb. 1: Ultraschallbild von einem Hauttumor bei einer Schallfrequenz von 7,5 MHz (a) und von 20 MHz (b) sowie Bilder von einem unspezifischen Lymphknoten (c) und einem spezifischen Lymphknoten (d), beide mit 7,5 MHz geschallt.

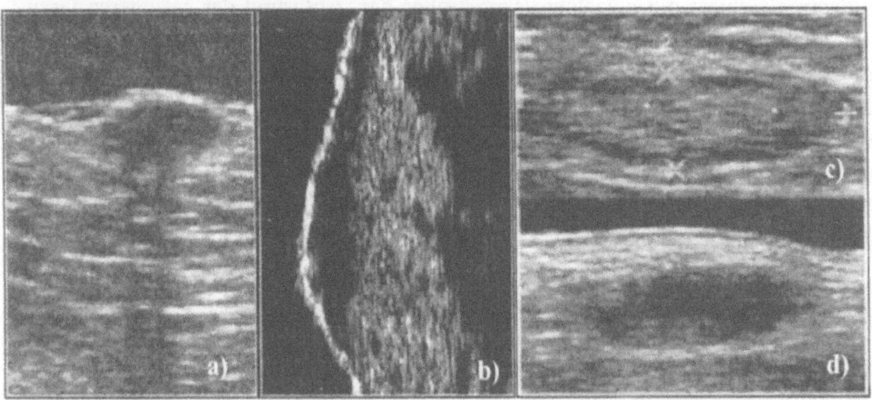

als auch Unterschiede im typischen Specklerauschen, welches durch Überlagerungs- und Auslöschungserscheinungen der Ultraschallwellen hervorgerufen wird.

Bei der Wahl der Bildverarbeitungsalgorithmen spielte weiterhin das mögliche Auftreten von Störungen (Tabelle1) eine wesentliche Rolle. Diese erschwerten durch das Verursachen echofreier Bereiche eine Abgrenzung der Tumorregion.

3 Segmentierung der Hauttumore

Zur Minderung der Rauscheinflüsse erfolgte zu Beginn eine Medianfilterung der Bilder. Bei der sich anschließenden Segmentierung wurden in Abhängigkeit von den typischen Bildeigenschaften zwei verschiedene Verfahren angewandt.

Störung	Ursache	Merkmal
Schallschatten	stark reflektierende oder stark absorbierende Grenzflächen	echofreier Streifen
Mehrfachechos	große Impedanzsprünge	mehrfache Echos im gleichen Abstand
Streuung der Signale	Unebenheiten oder ungünstige Einstrahlwinkel bewirken, daß die Signalantwort nicht zum Empfänger gelangt	Unterbrechungen des Signals in schräg aufsteigenden und abfallenden Bereichen
Artefakte	Haare oder Luftblasen in der Wasservorlaufstecke	echoreiche Anzeigen vor Beginn der eigentliche Hautoberfläche

Tabelle 1. Ursache und charakteristisches Erscheinungsbild möglicher Störungen im Sonogramm

3.1 Segmentierung mittels Multi-Schwellwertverfahren

Die untersuchten Hauttumore stellten sich im 7,5-MHz-Ultraschallbild zumeist als reflexarme Gebiete mit einzelnen Binnenechos dar. Aufgrund der geringeren Grauwerte der Tumorregion im Vergleich zum umgebenden Gewebe wurde zur Segmentierung ein Multi-Schwellwertverfahren eingesetzt. Dabei erfolgte nach Markierung der Tumorposition eine iterative Binarisierung mit anschließender Berechnung der konvexen Hüllfläche des Tumors. Überschritt das Verhältnis zweier aufeinanderfolgender Flächen einen vorgegebenen Wert, brach der Algorithmus ab. Diese Bedingung wurde deswegen gewählt, um zu gewährleisten, daß nicht infolge von Signalstreuungen und Schallschatten Gebiete außerhalb des Tumors erfaßt werden.

3.2 Segmentierung mittels aktiver Konturen

Die Segmentierung der Tumore in den hochfrequenten Aufnahmen wurde infolge der sich häufig ergebenden stark strukturierten Begrenzungsechos in zwei Schritten durchgeführt. Im ersten Schritt erfolgte die Detektion der Hautoberfläche, welche auf einer Schwellwertentscheidung mit nachfolgender Störungsbeseitigung basierte und zur Definition der Abbruchbedingung bei der eigentlichen Segmentierung genutzt wurde. Die anschließend eingesetzten aktiven Konturen werden in der Literatur als erfolgversprechende Möglichkeit zur Erkennung von schlecht abgegrenzten Bildteilen beschrieben und wurden schon mehrfach zur Segmentierung in Ultraschallbildern genutzt [2, 3]. Die Energiefunktion der Kurve, welche im Rahmen der Segmentierung minimiert werden soll, ist eine Kombination aus definierten inneren und äußeren Kräften und hängt von der Gestalt und der Lage des zu segmentierenden Objekts im Bild ab. Wird die Position der aktiven Kontur über Fourier-Deskriptoren definiert als v(s)=(x(s),y(s)), wobei x(s) und y(s) die x, y-Koordinaten entlang der Kontur sind und s $\in$ [0, 1], so läßt sich die Energiefunktion angeben als

$$E_{Kurve} = \int_0^1 E_{intern}(v(s)) + E_{Bild}(v(s)) + E_{extern}(v(s)) ds. \tag{1}$$

Die innere Energie der Kurve E_{intern} stellt die Glattheit der Kontur sicher. Durch die Bildkräfte E_{Bild} und durch die externen Kräfte E_{extern}, welche vom Nutzer definiert werden, erfolgt eine Anziehung zu wesentlichen Bildmerkmalen. Im realisierten Ansatz wurde davon ausgegangen, daß durch den Nutzer drei Punkte angegeben werden, die innerhalb des Tumors liegen. Diese wurden dann vom Programm in die mögliche Maximalposition verschoben. Bei dem anschließenden iterativen Algorithmus erfolgte, wie in Abb. 2 zu erkennen ist, jeweils zwischen zwei Punkten das Einfügen neuer Stützpunkte, die dann verschoben wurden. Zum Aufweiten der Kontur diente ein Schwellwertoperator. Um zu verhindern, daß die Kontur aus dem Tumor

Abb. 2: Iterationsschritte zur Segmentierung des Tumors

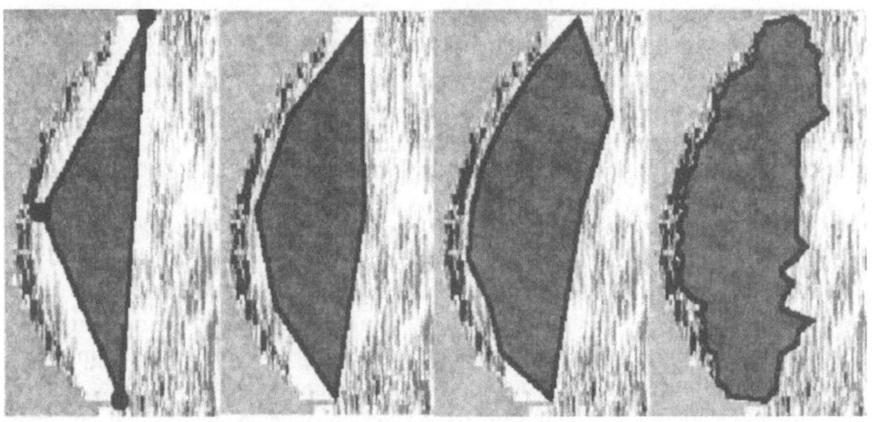

herauswuchs, wurden als äußere Kriterien der Abstand der Punkte untereinander sowie die Lage der Wasservorlaufstrecke eingeführt.

3.3 Merkmale zur Gewebedifferenzierung

Zur Beschreibung der detektierten Gewebestrukturen wurden 41 Merkmale herangezogen. Diese orientierten sich an den bei der manuellen Sonogrammauswertung genutzten Kriterien, wie z.B. seitliche und tiefe Begrenzung des Tumors, Form, Abgrenzbarkeit zum umliegenden Gewebe und Echomorphologie. Die berechneten Merkmale lassen sich zu folgenden Gruppen zusammenfassen: Merkmale der Form und Kontur, Merkmale der Statistik 1. und 2. Ordnung, Merkmale zum Vergleich mit der Nachbarregion und Merkmale zur Beschreibung der Binnenechos. Besonders letztere spielten auch bei der Charakterisierung der Lymphknoten in Ultraschallbildern eine wichtige Rolle.

Im Gegensatz zu den Untersuchungen bei den 7,5-MHz-Aufnahmen konnten in den 20-MHz-Aufnahmen kaum Texturen wahrgenommen werden. Deshalb ergaben sich für die einzelnen untersuchten Tumoren auch nur signifikante Unterschiede bei den Form- und Konturmerkmalen. Anhand dieser Kenngrößen war eine Zuordnung zu den verschiedenen Hauttumorarten nicht möglich.

3.4 Merkmalsauswahl und Klassifikation

Anhand von Trainingsdaten erfolgte die Auswahl der optimalen Merkmale mittels Evolutionsstrategie. Diese wurde schon für andere Problemstellungen erfolgreich zur Reduktion der Merkmalsanzahl [4, 5] eingesetzt. Bei dem erstellten Programm wurde von einer Populationsgröße von 200 Individuen ausgegangen, wobei ein Individuum einem String entsprach, in dem die Verwendung der einzelnen Kenngrößen zur Klassifizierung durch die Werte 0 oder 1 codiert war. An der so erzeugten Population wurden im Rahmen der Optimierungsstrategie verschiedene Manipulationen, die der Natur entlehnt sind, ausgeführt.

Ein großer Vorteil der Evolutionsstrategien ist deren Verzicht auf jegliche Hilfs-
informationen. Der Übergang zu immer besseren Strukturen erfolgt bei diesem Opti-
mierungsschema einzig und allein durch die Werte, die als individuelle Strings codiert sind, so daß es dadurch sehr allgemein und leicht auf verschiedene Problemstellungen zu übertragen ist. Als Klassifikator wurde bei dem vorgestellten Ergebnissen ein Minimum-Distance-Klassifikator verwendet.

4 Ergebnisse und Ausblick

Von den insgesamt 253 untersuchten 7,5-MHz-Sonogrammen konnten mit der vorgeschlagenen Methode 76 % der 186 Hauttumore mit relativ scharfer Begrenzung und
55 % der 67 Tumore mit unscharfer Begrenzung richtig automatisch segmentiert
werden. Bei den untersuchten 50 hochfrequenten Sonogrammen lieferte das implementierte Segmentierungsverfahren für ca. 85 % der Bilder Konturen, die mit dem
visuellen Eindruck übereinstimmten. Bei den restlichen Bildern mußte aufgrund des
Auftretens von extremen Schallschatten, Schallunterbrechungen und sehr starken
Binnenechos eine manuelle Markierung vorgenommen werden.

Die Differenzierung zwischen drei wichtigen Hauttumorarten (Basaliom, Karzi-
nom, malignes Melanom) wurde anhand der 7,5-MHz-Sonogramme untersucht. Hier
wurde eine Klassifikationsrate von 71 % erreicht.

Gegenwärtig wird an der Übertragung der Erkenntnisse auf die Gewebedifferenzierung von Lymphknoten gearbeitet. Erste Untersuchungen lieferten für
die Unterscheidung zwischen unspezifischen und spezifischen Lymphknotenschwel-
lungen ein Klassifikationsergebnis von 73 %.

Die Einführung weiterer Merkmale, speziell auch aus der Analyse von duplexso-
nographischen Bildern der Lymphknoten, soll im Hinblick auf eine mögliche Verbesserung der Ergebnisse überprüft werden.

5 Literatur

1. Delorme S, Zuna I: Quantitative Auswerteverfahren in der B-Bild- und Farbdopplersono-
   graphie, Ultraschall Klin Prax 10, 50-61, 1995.
2. Sonka M, Hlavac V, Boyle R: Image processing, Analysis and Machine Vision.Chapman
   & Hall Computing, London, 1. Auflage 1993.
3. Chalana V, Linker DT, Haynor DR, Kim Y: A multiple active contour model for cardiac
   boundary detection in echocardiographic sequences, IEEE Trans. on Medical Imaging
   15:290-298, 1996.
4. Pohle R: Segmentierung und Klassifikation von Schweißnahtfehlern in radioskopischen
   Aufnahmen. Otto-von-Guericke-Universität, Dissertation, 1995.
5. Pohle R, Rohden L v Fischer D: Skeletal muscle sonography using texture analysis. in
   Medical Imaging 1997: Image Processing, Kenneth M. Hanson (Editor), Proceedings of
   SPIE Vol. 3034, 772-778 (1997).

Verbesserung der Dynamik und Ortsauflösung in der Ultraschalldiagnostik durch die Kombination kodierter Anregung und tiefenangepaßter Mismatched-Filterung

K. Eck, A. R. Brenner, W. Wilhelm, T. G. Noll

Lehrstuhl für Allgemeine Elektrotechnik und Datenverarbeitungssysteme
Schinkelstraße 2, 52062 Aachen
Email: eck@eecs.rwth-aachen.de

Zusammenfassung. Durch Verwendung kodierter Signale kann die Abbildungstiefe und der Signal-Rausch-Abstand von Ultraschallaufnahmen erheblich gesteigert werden. Nachteilig wirkt sich dabei vor allem bei der Aufnahme dämpfenden Gewebes die mit der Tiefe sinkende Dynamik und Ortsauflösung auf die Bildqualität aus. Mit Hilfe des hier vorgestellten Pulskompressionsverfahrens der tiefenangepaßten Mismatched-Filterung können Dynamik und Ortsauflösung der Abbildung über weite Tiefenbereiche erhalten werden. Der Erfolg des Verfahrens wird durch Simulationen und Experimente bestätigt. Eine Flächenabschätzung für einen Echtzeit-Pulskompressor mit nachladbaren Koeffizienten in 0.5 μm CMOS-Technologie bei einer Taktfrequenz von 200 MHz wird vorgestellt.

Schlüsselwörter: Ultraschall, Kodierte Anregung, Mismatched-Filterung

1 Einleitung

Mit Hilfe von Ultraschall gewonnene Bilder der medizinischen Diagnostik weisen im Vergleich zu Bildern anderer Modalitäten einen geringen Signal-Rausch-Abstand und eine für viele Anwendungen unzureichende Ortsauflösung auf. Eine Steigerung der Bildqualität durch Erhöhung der verwendeten Amplitude ist auf Grund der damit verbundenen erhöhten Belastung des Patienten nicht möglich [1]. Diese Einschränkung kann durch die Verwendung zeitlich ausgedehnter Signale umgangen werden. Die aus dem Gewebe empfangenen Signale müssen in diesem Fall vor der Verwendung zur Bildrekonstruktion komprimiert werden [2][3]. Die Kompression durch Korrelation mit dem ausgesendeten Signal (Matched-Filterung) führt hierbei zu Ergebnissen mit schlechter Dynamik und Ortsauflösung [4]. Durch Anpassung des Filters an das Übertragungssystem (tiefenangepaßte Mismatched-Filterung) kann die Dynamik und Ortsauflösung erheblich gesteigert werden [5].

2 Methoden

2.1 Modellierung des Systems

Die Modellierung des Abbildungssystems ist in Abb. 1 skizziert: Ein Sendesignal $s(t)$ wird über einen Kanal mit der Übertragungsfunktion $H(f, z, \alpha_0)$ bestehend aus dem Transducer mit der Übertragungsfunktion $H_t(f)$ und dem Medium mit der Übertragungsfunktion $H_m(f, z, \alpha_0)$ übertragen. Zum Echosignal wird weißes Rauschen $n(t)$ addiert. Um das resultierende Signal $x(t)$ zu einem kurzen Signal $y(t)$ zu komprimie-

Abb. 1. Modellierung des Systems

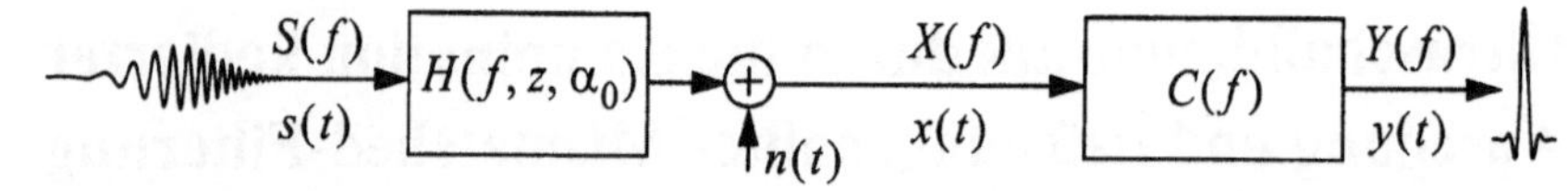

ren, wird anschließend eine Faltung mit einem Filter der Stoßantwort $c(t)$ mit dem Amplitudenspektrum $|C(f)|$ vorgenommen. Die Übertragungsfunktion des dämpfenden Gewebes [1] hat bei konstanter Schallgeschwindigkeit v in Abhängigkeit vom Dämpfungskoeffizienten α_0 für einen Reflektor in der Tiefe z die Form

$$H_m(f, z, \alpha_0) = \exp\left\{-2z\left[\alpha_0 \cdot f + j\frac{2\pi f}{v}\right]\right\}. \tag{1}$$

2.2 Qualitätsmaßzahlen des Kompressionsergebnisses

Die Abbildungsqualität von Ultraschallbildern wird wie folgt quantitativ erfaßt: Der *Signal-Rausch-Abstand* (SNR) ist der logarithmische Abstand des Hauptmaximums des Echos eines punktförmigen Reflektors vom Erwartungswert der Rauschleistung. Die *Dynamik* wird als logarithmischer Abstand des Hauptmaximums zum höchsten Nebenmaximum angegeben. Die *Hauptmaximumbreite,* gemessen auf einer angegebenen Höhe relativ zum Hauptmaximum, gibt die Ortsauflösung des Abbildungssystems an. Das *Kontrastverhältnis* der Abbildung eines Reflektors ist das Verhältnis der Energie des gesamten Signals zur Summe der Energie der Nebenmaxima.

2.3 Matched-Filterung und Mismatched-Filterung

Die Pulskompression kann im einfachsten Fall durch eine Korrelation des Echosignals mit dem Sendesignal $(C(f) = S^*(f))$ durchgeführt werden. Durch eine Mismatched-Filterung mit einem Filter der Übertragungsfunktion $C(f) \neq S^*(f)$ kann das Amplitudenspektrum des komprimierten Echosignals in einer Weise modifiziert werden, daß die Stoßantwort $y(t)$ eine für die Bildgebung geeignete, kompakte Form mit hoher Dynamik aufweist. Der damit verbundene Verlust an SNR gegenüber dem theoretischen Optimum berechnet sich als Filtereffizienz η zu

$$\eta = \frac{\left(\int |X(f)C(f)|df\right)^2}{\left(\int |X(f)|^2 df \cdot \int |C(f)|^2 df\right)}. \tag{2}$$

Bei der Wahl der Form des Amplitudenspektrums $|Y(f)|$ kann mit Hilfe des in [6] erstmals im Zusammenhang mit Ultraschallsignalen vorgestellten Algorithmus für eine gewünschte Hauptmaximumbreite das Amplitudenspektrum bestimmt werden, welches das beste erreichbare Kontrastverhältnis aufweist [5].

2.4 Synthese tiefenabhängiger Mismatched-Filter

Gegeben ist eine zeitdiskrete Stoßantwort x_k der Länge L und ein angestrebtes Ergebnis der Pulskompression $\tilde{y}_k$ der Länge $L+N$-1. Gesucht wird nun das Mismatched-Filter c_k der Länge N, durch das die Vorgabe $\tilde{y}_k$ im Sinne der kleinsten Fehlerquadrate bestmöglich angenähert wird.

Mit den Abkürzungen $a_{ij} = \sum_{k=0}^{N+L-2} x_{k-i} \cdot x_{k-j}$ und $r_j = \sum_{k=0}^{N+L-2} \tilde{y}_k \cdot x_{k-j}$ $\qquad$ (3)

und durch Einführung der $N \times N$ Matrix $A = (a_{ij})$ sowie der Vektoren $c = (c_0, c_1, ..., c_{N-1})^T$ und $r = (r_0, r_1, ..., r_{N-1})^T$ ergeben sich die Koeffizienten c_j des Mismatched-Filters als Lösung des linearen Gleichungssystems $A \cdot c = r$.

Das Vorliegen einer Dämpfung nach (1) führt im Fall der Kompression des gesamten Signals mit einem festen Mismatched-Filter zu einer Verformung des Amplitudenspektrums $|Y(f)|$ über der Tiefe z mit der Folge eines Dynamikverlustes durch das Ansteigen der Nebenmaxima. Durch die abnehmende Korrelation zwischen $|C(f)|$ und $|X(f)|$ sinkt zusätzlich die Filtereffizienz η und damit das SNR von $y(t)$ gemäß (2). Durch eine tiefenabhängige Anpassung von $c(t)$ mit dem Ziel der Maximierung von $\eta(z)$ können die Dynamik und das SNR über weite Bereiche nahezu konstant gehalten werden.

2.5 Auswirkung von Dämpfungsfehlschätzungen

Die Berechnung des Mismatched-Filters setzt eine Schätzung der vorliegenden Dämpfung voraus. Unter der Voraussetzung, daß das Amplitudenspektrum $\tilde{Y}(f)$ der angestrebten Systemstoßantwort $\tilde{y}(t)$ symmetrisch ist, einen linearen Phasenverlauf aufweist und daß eine Dämpfung nach (1) vorliegt, kann gezeigt werden, daß sich Über - und Unterschätzungen des Dämpfungskoeffizienten identisch auf die Einhüllende der Systemstoßantwort $y(t)$ auswirken. In Abhängigkeit von der Stärke der Fehlschätzung zeigt $y(t)$ gegenüber $\tilde{y}(t)$ eine verringerte Dynamik und ein verringertes SNR.

3 Ergebnisse

Die in Simulation und Experiment verwendeten nichtlinear frequenzmodulierten Chirpsignale haben eine Länge von 20.48 µs und Grenzfrequenzen von 2.5 MHz und 5 MHz. Die Hüllkurve des Chirpsignals ist konstant bis auf die ersten und letzten 0.5 µs des Signals, die jeweils mit einem einseitigen Hanning-Fenster gewichtet sind. Bei dem verwendeten und simulierten Transducer handelt es sich um ein Pie-Medical CA80 Curved-Array mit 56% relativer Bandbreite. Bei dem in den Experimenten verwendeten Probekörper handelt es sich um das Modell 539 (gewebenachbildendes Phantom mit Nylonfäden) des Herstellers ATS Laboratories.

3.1 Simulation

Für die Simulationen wird ein Dämpfungskoeffizient von $\alpha_0 = 0.5$ dB / (MHz cm) angenommen. Typische Dämpfungswerte im menschlichen Körper sind für Blut 0.2 dB / (MHz cm), für Muskelgewebe 1.5 bis 2.5 dB / (MHz cm) und für Lebergewebe 0.5 bis 0.9 dB / (MHz cm).

Abb. 2 a) zeigt, daß die Pulskompression durch Matched-Filterung hohe Nebenmaxima erzeugt, die zu einer Beschränkung der Dynamik auf ca. 15 dB führen. Darüber hinaus sinkt das SNR bis zur Tiefe von 24 cm um ca. 6 dB. Demgegenüber zeigt das Ergebnis der tiefenangepaßten Mismatched-Filterung eine konstante Dynamik von

Abb. 2. Pulskompression durch a) Matched-Filterung, und b) durch tiefenangepaßte Mismatched-Filterung für verschiedene Tiefen des Reflektors im dämpfenden Gewebe. Die fett gedruckten Linien zeigen die Einbußen an SNR gegenüber dem theoretischen Optimum.

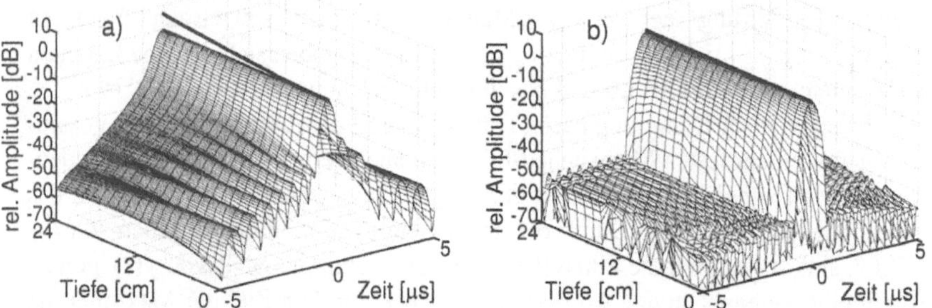

50 dB und einen SNR-Verlust von < 0.6 dB über der gesamten Abbildungstiefe (Abb. 2 b). Die Hauptmaximumbreite steigt bei beiden Kompressionsverfahren auf Grund des durch die Dämpfung verursachten Bandbreitenverlustes um ca. 50% an.

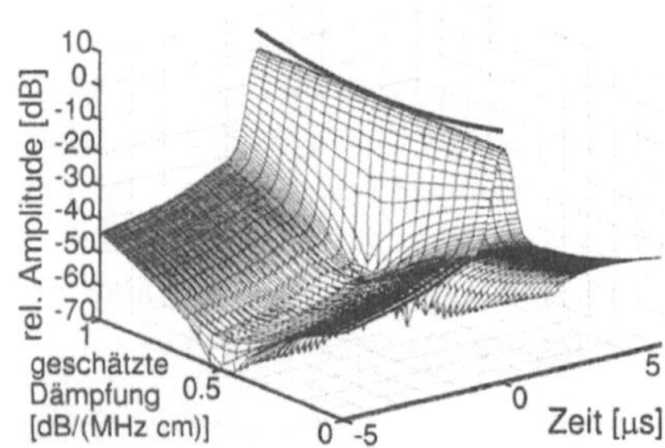

Abb. 3. Verlust an Dynamik und SNR für eine Abweichung der angenommenen von der tatsächlichen Dämpfung um +5 bis -5 dB/MHz. Die fett gedruckte Linie zeigt den Verlust an SNR gegenüber dem Fall einer korrekten Annahme der vorliegenden Dämpfung.

Der Berechnung von tiefenabhängigen Mismatched-Filtern muß eine Schätzung oder Annahme des Dämpfungskoeffizienten α_0 vorangehen. Bei der Schätzung des Dämpfungskoeffizienten aus A-Scans liegt der relative Fehler bei Anwendung von Fourier-Methoden unter 20% [7]. Eine fehlerhafte Schätzung von α_0 verursacht einen Verlust an SNR und Dynamik (Abb. 3). Im Fall einer Schätzung von $\alpha_0 = 1$ dB / (MHz cm) statt der vorliegenden 0.5 dB / (MHz cm) (d.h. mit einem relativer Fehler von 100 %) sinkt bei der Abbildung eines Reflektors in der Entfernung $z = 5$ cm die Dynamik auf ca. 25 dB, die Breite des Hauptmaximums oberhalb von -25 dB steigt um 10% und das SNR verringert sich um 6 dB. Auch im Fall einer fehlerhaften Schätzung des vorliegenden Dämpfungskoeffizienten ist damit die tiefenabhängige Mismatched-Filterung der Matched-Filterung hinsichtlich des SNR gleichwertig und hinsichtlich der Dynamik überlegen.

3.2 Experiment

Abb. 4 zeigt B-Scans des Probekörpers. Durch die Mismatched-Filter-Pulskompression (Abb. 4 b) wurde eine deutliche Steigerung der axialen Auflösung gegenüber der Matched-Filter-Pulskompression (Abb. 4 a) erreicht. Die durch den Algorithmus angestrebte Absenkung der Nebenmaxima auf eine Höhe von -50 dB ist im B-Scan nicht sichtbar, da die Reflektoren im verwendeten Probekörper in eine Masse mit Mikrostreuern eingebettet sind. Diese nicht einzeln auflösbaren Reflektoren verursachen das beobachtete Specklemuster auf einer Höhe von -20 dB unter den Hauptmaxima.

Abb. 4. B-Scans eines Probekörpers. a) Matched-Filterung, b) Mismatched-Filterung. Angegeben ist der Abstand des Reflektors zur Transduceroberfläche.

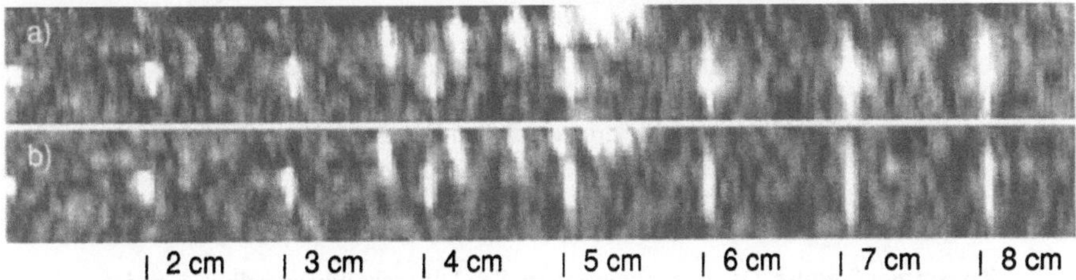

4 VLSI-Implementierung

Eine Full-Custom VLSI-Implementierung der tiefenabhängigen Mismatched-Filterung für eine Abtastrate von 14 MSa/s und eine Filterlänge von 512 Koeffizienten in 0.5 μm CMOS-Technologie bei 200 MHz unter Anwendung von Mehrfachnutzungsstrategien [8] führt zu einer Fläche von 9 mm^2. Eine Implementierung mit Hilfe von Standardzellen würde 5-6 mal soviel Fläche benötigen.

5 Zusammenfassung

Die Bildqualität von Ultraschallaufnahmen wird durch die tiefen- und frequenzabhängige Dämpfung organischen Gewebes beeinträchtigt. Durch die Kombination von kodierter Anregung und tiefenangepaßter Mismatched-Filterung ist es möglich, tiefe Objektbereiche ohne sichtbare Einbußen an axialer Auflösung abzubilden. Das Verfahren erweist sich als robust gegenüber einer fehlerhaften Schätzung der vorliegenden Dämpfung. Eine VLSI-Implementierung der tiefenabhängigen Mismatched-Filterung ist zum heutigen Zeitpunkt technisch und ökonomisch möglich.

6 Literatur

1. Rao NAHK: Investigation of a pulse compression technique for medical ultrasound: a simulation study. Medical & Biological Engineering & Computing, 32:181-188, 1994.

2. O'Donnell M: Coded excitation system for improving the penetration of real-time phased-array imaging systems. IEEE Trans. UFFC, 39(3): 341-351, 1992.

3. Bressmer H, Joppek C, Pfau R, Faust U: Pulskompression in handelsüblichen Ultraschall B-Bildsystemen. Biomedizinische Technik, Ergänzungsband, 41:170-171, 1996.

4. Pollakowski M, Ermert H: Chirp signal matching and signal power optimization in pulse-echo mode ultrasonic nondestructive testing. IEEE Trans. UFFC, 41(5): 655-659, 1994.

5. Brenner AR, Eck K, Wilhelm W, Noll TG: Improved resolution and dynamic range in medical ultrasonic imaging using depth-dependent mismatched filtering. IEEE Proc. UFFC Symp., 1997, in Druck.

6. Adams JW: A new optimal window. IEEE Trans. Sig. Proc., 39(8):1753-1769, 1991.

7. Baldeweck T, Laugier P, Herment A, Berger G: Application of autoregressive spectral analysis for ultrasound attenuation: interest in highly attenuating medium. IEEE Proc. UFFC Symp., 1181-1186, 1993.

8. Wilhelm W, Noll TG: A new mapping technique for automated design of highly efficient multiplexed FIR digital filters. IEEE Proc. ISCAS, 2252-2256, 1997.

Tiefenangepaßte Filterung für das Puls-Echo-Verfahren in der Ultraschalldiagnostik

R. Schwann, K. Eck, A. R. Brenner, T. G. Noll

Lehrstuhl für Allgemeine Elektrotechnik und Datenverarbeitungssysteme
Schinkelstraße 2, 52062 Aachen
Email: schwann@eecs.rwth-aachen.de

Zusammenfassung. Das in der konventionellen Ultraschalldiagnostik verwendete Puls-Echo-Verfahren hängt in seiner Abbildungsqualität maßgeblich vom ausgesendeten Signal ab. Beeinträchtigt wird die Ortsauflösung des Systems vom Übertragungsverhalten des Transducers und des Gewebes. Mit einer geeigneten Filterung der von den Transducerelementen empfangenen Hochfrequenzdaten wird sowohl das Nachschwingen der Wandlerelemente kompensiert, als auch der Einfluß der frequenzabhängigen Dämpfung berücksichtigt. Damit kann die Pulsdauer der aus dem Gewebe empfangenen Echos reduziert werden. Eine Filterimplementierung als zusätzliche Hardwarekomponente ermöglicht den Einsatz bei der Echtzeit-Bildgebung in kommerziellen Ultraschallgeräten. Der erforderliche Aufwand wird für Systeme mit und ohne digitaler Strahlschwenkung abgeschätzt.

Schlüsselwörter: Medizinelektronik, Ultraschall, Dämpfung, FIR-Filterung

1 Einleitung

Die Signalform eines im Puls-Echo-Betriebes empfangenen Ultraschall-Pulses wird im wesentlichen vom mechanischen Verhalten des verwendeten Transducers bestimmt. Bei der Anregung mit einem nadelförmigen elektrischen Signal wird eine hohe Ortsauflösung durch das Aussenden eines breitbandigen, im Zeitbereich kurzen Pulses erzielt. Beim Empfang wird das akustische Echo in ein elektrisches Signal gewandelt und kann als Stoßantwort gemessen werden. Um ein Nachschwingen zu vermeiden, ist die Rückseite der Transducerelemente idealerweise reflexionsfrei abzuschließen [1]. Durch eine mechanische Bedämpfung der Transducerelemente ist es zwar möglich, das Nachschwingen zu reduzieren, ein optimal kurzer Echopuls ist auf diesem Weg jedoch nicht zu realisieren (Abb. 1). Ein dem elektrischen Echosignal nachgeschaltetes Filter kann das Amplitudenspektrum und den Phasenverlauf derart beeinflussen, daß am Filterausgang ein nachschwingungsfreies Echosignal anliegt.

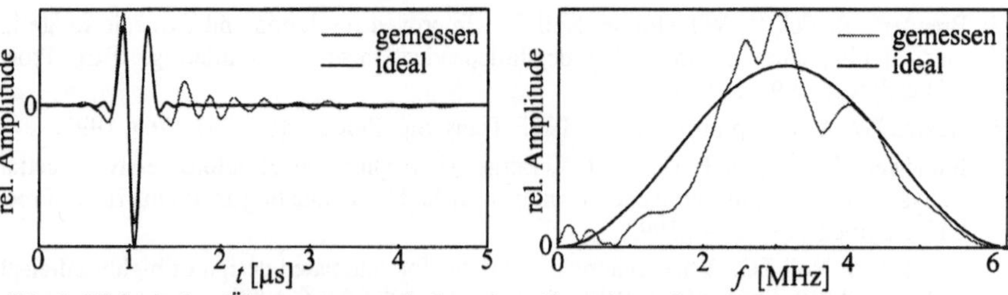

Abb. 1. Elektrisches Übertragungsverhalten eines Transducerelementes: dargestellt sind die Stoßantwort (links) und das Betragsspektrum (rechts).

Die Pulsform der empfangenen Echos wird durch eine tiefen- und frequenzabhängige Dämpfung im biologischen Gewebe beeinträchtigt [2, 3]. Auswirkungen dieser Dämpfung sind eine generelle Verminderung der Echoamplituden und eine asymmetrische Verformung des Amplitudenspektrums. Daraus resultiert eine Reduzierung der Bandbreite sowie eine Senkung der Mittenfrequenz des Echosignals. Die sinkende Bandbreite und die Verformung des Amplitudenspektrums verursachen einen Verlust an Ortsauflösung in den rekonstruierten Ultraschallbildern.

2 Modellbildung

Die Strecke vom elektrischen Sendesignal bis hin zum elektrischen Echosignal läßt sich als linear zeitinvariantes System darstellen, wenn man die dämpfende Eigenschaft des Gewebes als Eigenschaft der darin enthaltenen Reflektoren auffaßt (Abb. 2). Bei festem Sendesignal ist die elektrisch-akustische Wandlung und damit der in die Echostrecke eingebrachte Anregungspuls bei jedem Meßvorgang gleich. Bei der akustisch-elektrischen Empfangswandlung wird davon ausgegangen, daß das Übertragungsverhalten nicht von der Echoamplitude abhängt.

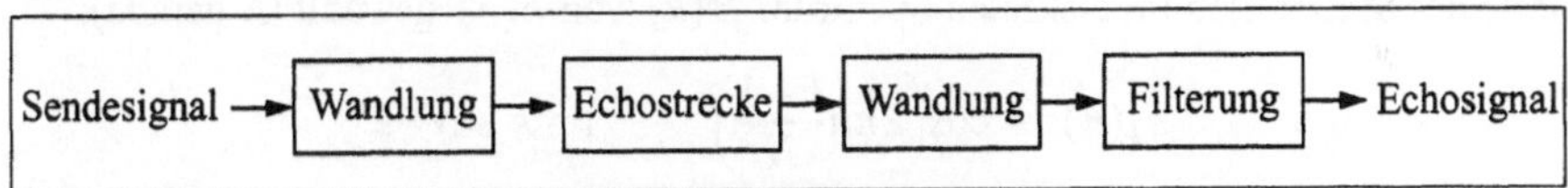

Abb. 2. Meßstrecke als linear zeitinvariante Übertragungskette

Für den Entwurf des Empfangsfilters wird eine Messung vorgenommen, bei der die Echostrecke ein reines Verzögerungsglied darstellt. Dazu wird in einem Wassertank das Echo eines einzelnen, möglichst punktförmigen Reflektors aufgenommen. Nach der A/D-Wandlung steht für den Filterentwurf ein zeitdiskretes Signal $s(n)$ zur Verfügung. Üblicherweise wird als Empfangsfilter ein an den Transducer angepaßter Bandpaß verwendet, der den Rauschanteil im Nutzsignal auf den Frequenzbereich des Echos beschränkt. Das beste Signal-Rauschverhältnis zum Zeitpunkt des Echomaximums bietet dabei das konjugierte Filter mit der Stoßantwort $h(n) = s(-n)$. Damit liegt das Faltungsergebnis $w(n)$ der Empfangsfilterung und die Abbildungseigenschaft des Systems fest. Ein schmales Hauptmaximum bei hoher Bilddynamik wird normalerweise nicht erreicht. Eine inverse Filterung wie die Wiener-Filterung kann bei sichtbarer Auflösungserhöhung in der Ultraschallanwendung nicht gleichzeitig eine hohe Bilddynamik und ein hohes Signal-Rauschverhältnis erreichen.

Ein optimaler Kompromiß zwischen dem Empfangsrauschen, der Bilddynamik und der Echopulsbreite läßt sich mit der Vorgabe von $w(n)$ als diskrete Fouriertransformierte einer reell symmetrischen Fensterfunktion $W(k)$ nach [4] erzielen. Die Anpassung der Bandbreite B und der Mittenfrequenz f_0 der Fensterfunktion ergibt sich aus der Maximierung des Signal-Rauschverhältnisses am Filterausgang [5]. Mit den kontinuierlichen Spektren $S(f)$ und $W(f)$ gilt:

$$\frac{1}{B^2} \cdot \int_{f_0 - B/2}^{f_0 + B/2} \frac{\left| W\left(\frac{f - f_0}{B}\right) \right|^2}{|S(f)|^2} \, df \overset{!}{=} \min \tag{1}$$

2.1 Filtersynthese

Mit der Vorgabe der diskreten Zeitfunktion $w(n)$ als Faltungsergebnis wird ein Empfangsfilter $h(n)$ der Länge $n = 1...N$ gesucht, dessen Faltung mit einem gegebenen Signal $s(n)$ die Vorgabe annähert:

$$s(n)*h(n) \overset{!}{=} w(n) \tag{2}$$

Sei $a_k(n)$ ein Satz orthogonaler Musterfunktionen der Länge N, dann ist $b_k(n) = s(n)*a_k(n)$ die jeweilige Faltung mit $s(n)$. Für skalare Konstanten λ_k gilt mit der Superposition der Faltung:

$$s(n)*[\lambda_1 a_1(n) + ... + \lambda_N a_N(n)] = \lambda_1 b_1(n) + ... + \lambda_N b_N(n) \tag{3}$$

Wählt man zeitverschobene Einheitsimpulse $a_k(n) = \delta(n-k)$ als Musterfunktionen, dann ist $b_k(n) = s(n-k)$. Für $k = 1...N$ ist die Anzahl der Freiheitsgrade beim Filterentwurf gleich N. Die λ_k entsprechen hierbei den Abtastpunkten von $h(n)$.

Um bei der Berechnung von $h(n)$ eine Kontrolle über die untere und obere Grenzfrequenz zu haben, werden die Musterfunktionen $a_k(n)$ als diskrete Fouriertransformierte der Stützstellen im diskreten Spektrum $H(k)$ von $h(n)$ gewählt (N gerade):

$$a_k(n) = \cos\left(2\pi n\frac{k-1}{N}\right) \qquad 1 \le k \le N/2$$

$$a_k(n) = \sin\left(2\pi n\frac{k-N/2}{N}\right) \qquad N/2 + 1 \le k \le N \tag{4}$$

Der Frequenzbereich von $h(n)$ wird eingeschränkt, indem nur diejenigen Musterfunktionen $a_k(n)$ verwendet werden, die den Frequenzbereich von $w(n)$ abdecken. Eine Apodisierung der Ränder der Musterfunktionen verbessert die Übereinstimmung von $H(k)$ mit der kontinuierlichen, aperiodischen Fouriertransformierten $H(f)$. Als Abweichung von der Vorgabe $w(n)$ wird die Summe der Quadrate des Differenzsignals zwischen dem Faltungsergebnis und der Vorgabefunktion definiert:

$$Q = |\lambda_1 b_1(n) + ... + \lambda_N b_N(n) - w(n)|^2 \tag{5}$$

Mit der Distributivität des Skalarproduktes ($\bullet$) folgt für das Minimum von Q:

$$\frac{\partial Q}{\partial \lambda_k} = -2w(n) \bullet b_k(n) + 2\sum_{m=1}^{N} \lambda_m \cdot b_k(n) \bullet b_m(n) \overset{!}{=} 0 \tag{6}$$

Da $w(n)$ und die Faltungen $b_k(n)$ bekannt sind, kann mit (6) ein lineares Gleichungssystem zur Bestimmung der λ_k aufgestellt werden. Mit den Gleichungen (2, 3) geben die λ_k das gesuchte Filter $h(n)$ als Stoßantwort des FIR-Empfangsfilters.

2.2 Dämpfung

Beim Empfang des Echos eines Reflektors in der Tiefe z bewirkt die frequenzabhängige Gewebedämpfung eine Filterung des Echosignals $s_d(n)$, die sich näherungsweise als nullphasige Multiplikation des Amplitudenspektrums in der Form

$$S_d(f) = S(f) \cdot e^{-2z \cdot \alpha_0 \cdot f} \tag{7}$$

darstellen läßt. Die exponentielle Dämpfungsfunktion nimmt einen konstanten Dämpfungskoeffizienten α_0 an, der üblicherweise in dB / (cm MHz) angegeben wird. Mit größerer Tiefe z sinken nach (7) die Mittenfrequenz und die Bandbreite von $S_d(f)$. Entsprechend Gleichung (1) ändert sich damit die optimale Vorgabefunktion $w(n)$ für die Filterberechnung. Bei der Konstruktion einer gedämpften Stoßantwort wird der gemessene Phasenverlauf von $s(n)$ beibehalten.

3   Experiment

Abb. 3 zeigt links einen Schnitt durch den äußeren schrägen, inneren schrägen und den queren Bauchmuskel beim Schwein. Es sind als Gefäßimitation zwei wassergefüllte Plastikröhrchen eingebracht worden. Die Datenaufnahme erfolgte mit einem Scanner vom Typ Color Flow 350 der Fa. Pie Medical und einem Linear-Array mit einer Mittenfrequenz von 7.5 MHz. Zur Schätzung der frequenz- und tiefenabhängigen Dämpfung wurde das Betragsspektrum über 114 Einzellinien des Ultraschallbildes für Abschnitte von je 4 mm Tiefe gemittelt. Um aus den Betragsspektren die gedämpften Stoßantworten zu bestimmen, wurden diese als minimalphasig angenommen [6].

Das Ergebnis einer tiefenangepaßten Filterung ist in Abb. 3 auf der rechten Seite dargestellt. Die Erhöhung der Ortsauflösung und des Signal-Rausch- bzw. des Kontrastverhältnisses ist mit zunehmender Tiefe gut zu erkennen.

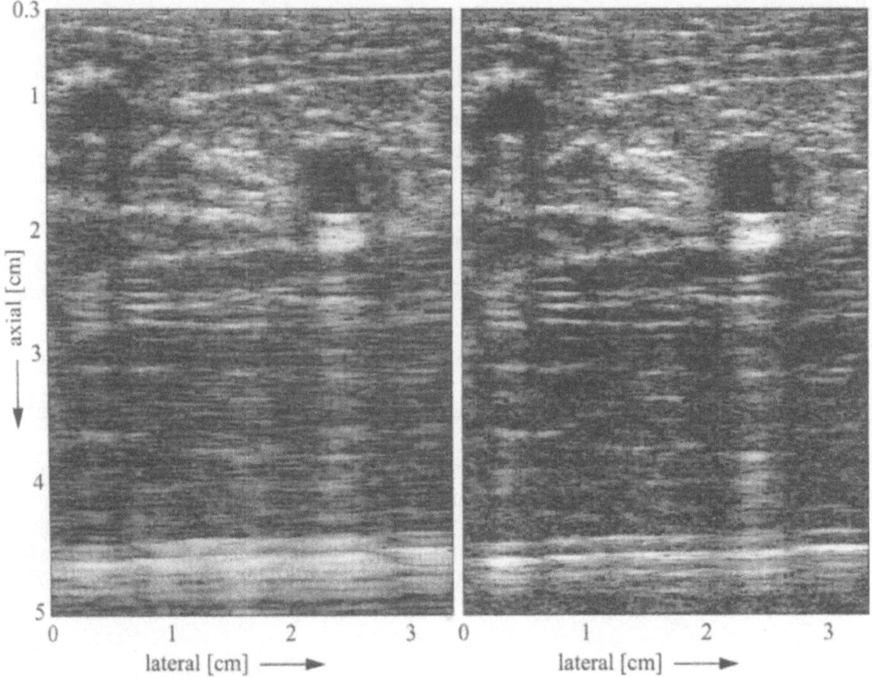

Abb. 3. Aufnahme der Bauchmuskulatur beim Schwein:
Links das Bild vor, rechts nach der tiefenangepaßten Filterung.
Der Dynamikbereich der Grauwerte beträgt jeweils 45 dB.

4 Realisierung in Hardware

Die Implementierung in einem Ultraschallgerät setzt die A/D-Wandlung des empfangsverstärkten HF-Signals vor der Demodulation voraus. Dazu ist ein steilflankiger, analoger Tiefpaß vor dem A/D-Wandler erforderlich. Die anschließende FIR-Filterung kann mit der Parallelschaltung moderner, handelsüblicher Signalprozessoren erfolgen. Für die tiefenangepaßte Filterung der Meßdaten werden bei einer Abtastrate von 30 MSa/s von dem in [7] besprochenen Typ neun Stück für ein Filter mit 96 Koeffizienten benötigt.

Bei Systemen mit digitaler Strahlschwenkung sind die HF-Empfangsdaten bereits digital für eine FIR-Filterung verfügbar. Wird für die digitale Strahlschwenkung ein dedizierter Chip entworfen, so kann das FIR-Filter auf dem Chip integriert werden: Mit der in [8] vorgestellten Strategie der Mehrfachnutzung beträgt der zusätzliche Flächenaufwand für ein FIR-Filter mit 96 nachladbaren Koeffizienten bei 30 MSa/s in 0.5 µm CMOS Technologie nur ca. 3.7 mm^2.

5 Zusammenfassung

Die Bildrekonstruktion aus experimentell gewonnenen Daten zeigt den Nutzen eines tiefenabhängig einstellbaren FIR-Filters. Neben anderen Maßnahmen [9] kann dies ein Beitrag zur Steigerung der Bildqualität in der medizinischen Ultraschalldiagnostik sein. Eine Implementierung als zusätzliche Komponente in Ultraschallgeräten mit digitaler Strahlschwenkung ist mit geringem Aufwand realisierbar.

6 Literatur

1. Kuttruff H: Physik und Technik des Ultraschalls. Hirzel Verlag, Stuttgart, 1988.
2. Rao NAHK: Investigation of a pulse compression technique for medical ultrasound: a simulation study. Medical & Biological Engineering & Computing, 32:181-188, 1994.
3. Macovski A: Medical Imaging Systems. Prentice-Hall, USA, 1983.
4. Adams JW: A new optimal window. IEEE Trans. Sig. Proc., 39(8): 1753-1769, 1991.
5. Brenner AR, Eck K, Wilhelm W, Noll TG: Improved resolution and dynamic range in medical ultrasonic imaging using depth-dependent mismatched filtering. IEEE Proc. UFFC Symp., 1997, in Druck.
6. Jensen JA, Leeman S: Non-Parametric Estimation of Ultrasound Pulses. IEEE Trans. Biomed. Eng., 41(10): 929-936, 1994.
7. Texas Instruments Semiconductors: Digital Signal Processor TMS320C62x Assembly Benchmarks, 1997.
8. Wilhelm W, Noll TG: A new mapping technique for automated design of highly efficient multiplexed FIR digital filters. IEEE Proc. ISCAS, 2252-2256, 1997.
9. Eck K, Brenner AR, Wilhelm W, Noll TG: Verbesserung der Ortsauflösung in der Ultraschalldiagnostik durch die Kombination kodierter Anregung und tiefenangepaßter Mismatched-Filterung. Bildverarbeitung für die Medizin, Klinikum der RWTH Aachen, 1998, in diesem Tagungsband.

Evaluierung der Detektionsleistung von 3D-Operatoren zur Ermittlung anatomischer Landmarken in tomographischen Bildern

Thomas Hartkens, Karl Rohr, H.-Siegfried Stiehl

Arbeitsbereich Kognitive Systeme, Fachbereich Informatik, Universität Hamburg
Vogt-Kölln-Str. 30, D-22527 Hamburg
{hartkens, rohr, stiehl}@informatik.uni-hamburg.de

Zusammenfassung Während die Leistungsfähigkeit von 2D-Operatoren zur Detektion von Punktlandmarken in 2D tomographischen Bildern bereits untersucht wurde (z.B. [10]), sind Untersuchungen bzgl. der Detektionsleistung von 3D-Operatoren kaum bekannt. In dieser Arbeit werden neun verschiedene 3D-Differentialoperatoren dahingehend untersucht, ob und inwieweit sie geeignet sind, Landmarken in 3D-Bildern zu detektieren. Dazu verwenden wir Maße, die unterschiedliche Aspekte der Detektionsleistung der Operatoren widerspiegeln.

Schlüsselwörter: 3D-Differentialoperatoren, Detektionsleistung, anatomische Landmarken, Bildregistrierung

1 Motivation und Einleitung

In Hinblick auf eine punktbasierte Registrierung ist die Detektion korrespondierender Punkte notwendig. In dieser Arbeit werden korrespondierende Punkte in 3D MR- und CT-Bildern, d.h. Landmarken, durch 3D-Differentialoperatoren ermittelt ([9]). Als Landmarken dienen ausgezeichnete Punkte, an denen die Oberflächen von anatomischen Strukturen (z.B. das Ventrikelsystem des menschlichen Gehirns) stark gekrümmt sind. Wir gehen davon aus, daß zuvor eine interessierende Region (ROI), in der eine Landmarke zu finden ist, von dem Benutzer vorgegeben wurde.

Wir untersuchen in dieser Arbeit 3D-Operatoren, (a) ob sie grundsätzlich geeignet sind, korrespondierende Punkte in tomographischen Bilder zu ermitteln und (b) wie gut sie die vorgegebenen Landmarken detektieren. Dazu wenden wir die in Tabelle 1 aufgeführten Operatoren sowohl auf synthetische als auch tomographische Bilder an und berechnen aus den Detektionen anhand der in Abschnitt 2 vorgeschlagenen Maße die Detektionsleistung der Operatoren.

2 Maße für die Detektionsleistung

Um die Operatoren miteinander vergleichen zu können, legen wir geeignete Maße für die Detektionsleistung fest. Dabei betrachten wir zwei unterschiedliche Aspekte der Detektionsleistung:

Ansatz „mittlere Krümmung" [4] [6] [11] [13] [14]

- $k_{mittlere\,Kruemmung} = \dfrac{1}{2|\nabla g|^3}\left[g_x^2(g_{yy}+g_{zz}) + g_y^2(g_{xx}+g_{zz}) + g_z^2(g_{xx}+g_{yy}) \right.$
$\left. -2(g_x g_y g_{xy} + g_x g_z g_{xz} + g_y g_z g_{yz}) \right]$
- $k_{KitchenRosenfeld3D} = k_{mittlere\,Kruemmung} \cdot 2|\nabla g|$
- $k_{Blom3D} = k_{mittlere\,Kruemmung} \cdot 2|\nabla g|^3 \quad \text{mit } \nabla g = (g_x, g_y, g_z)^T$

Ansatz „Gaußkrümmung" [2] [6] [14]

- $k_{Gausskruemmung} = \dfrac{1}{|\nabla g|^4}\left[g_x^2 \cdot (g_{yy}g_{zz} - g_{yz}^2) + 2g_y g_z \cdot (g_{xz}g_{xy} - g_{xx}g_{yz}) \right.$
$+ g_y^2 \cdot (g_{xx}g_{zz} - g_{xz}^2) + 2g_x g_z \cdot (g_{yz}g_{xy} - g_{yy}g_{xz})$
$\left. + g_z^2 \cdot (g_{xx}g_{yy} - g_{xy}^2) + 2g_x g_y \cdot (g_{xz}g_{yz} - g_{zz}g_{xy}) \right]$
- $k_{Gausskruemmung*Grad^4} = k_{Gausskruemmung} \cdot |\nabla g|^4$

Ansatz „Förstner/Rohr" [7] [12] [13]

- $k_{V1} = \dfrac{det(\underline{C})}{trace(\underline{C})} \cdot$
- $k_{Rohr3D} = det(\underline{C})$
- $k_{Foerstner3D} = \dfrac{1}{trace(\underline{C}^{-1})} = \dfrac{det(C)}{trace(\underline{C}^{adj.})} \quad \text{mit } \underline{C} = \overline{\nabla g(\nabla g)^T}$

Ansatz „Beaudet" [3]

- $k_{Beaudet3D} = det(H_g) \qquad\qquad H_g \text{ Hesse-Matrix}$

Tabelle 1: 3D-Differentialoperatoren *Die Operatoren berechnen aus den ersten bzw. ersten und zweiten partiellen Ableitungen der Bildfunktion für jeden Punkt des Bildes ein Maß für die Krümmung der Strukturen im Bild. Die Operatoren lassen sich in vier Gruppen einteilen, entsprechend vier unterschiedlichen Ansätzen für die Berechnung des Maßes. Innerhalb der Gruppen unterscheiden sich die Operatoren z.B. durch eine unterschiedliche Gewichtung durch den Gradienten der Grauwertfunktion. Einige Operatoren sind Erweiterungen von sogenannten Eckenoperatoren für 2D-Bilder. Wir bezeichnen diese Operatoren mit dem Namen der ursprünglichen Autoren und dem Suffix „3D".*

Anzahl korrespondierender Punkte

Eine wichtige Eigenschaft der Operatoren ist es, korrespondierende Punkte in zwei Bildern zu detektieren. Nach [7] sollten diese Punkte u.a. invariant gegenüber Verzerrungen und stabil bzgl. Rauschen sein. Wir untersuchen diese Eigenschaften, in dem wir die 3D-Bilder algorithmisch verformen bzw. mit Gauß-Rauschen überlagern und automatisch die Anzahl korrespondierender Punkte ermitteln (siehe auch [10] für 2D Bilder).

Klassische Detektionsleistung

Die in der Vergangenheit vorgeschlagenen Maße zur Beurteilung der Detektionsleistung von Operatoren (siehe z.B. [1], [8], [15], [16]) bezogen sich zumeist auf die Detektion von Grauwertkanten. Wir übertragen diese Maße auf die Detektion von Punktlandmarken und fassen die Maße unter dem Begriff „klassische Detektionsleistung" zusammen.

Nach Anwendung der Operatoren und Auswertung der Ergebnisse erhalten wir folgende Größen: Anzahl aller Detektionen (n_d), Anzahl der Detektionen, die die Landmarken korrekt detektieren, d.h. innerhalb eines Detektionsgebiets (z.B. $7 \times 7 \times 7$ Voxel) einer Landmarke liegen ($n_{d,in}$) und Anzahl der mindestens einmal detektierten Landmarken ($n_{l,detect}$), wobei n_l die Anzahl der Landmarken ist. Drei Ausdrücke beschreiben die Detektionsleistung der Operatoren: der

Anteil der Detektionen, die die Landmarke korrekt detektieren (P_{in}), der Anteil der detektierten Landmarken (P_{detect}) und die durchschnittliche Anzahl der Mehrfach-Detektionen pro Landmarke ($P_{multiple}$):

$$P_{in} = \frac{n_{d,in}}{n_d} \qquad P_{detect} = \frac{n_{l,detect}}{n_l} \qquad P_{multiple} = \frac{n_{d,in}}{n_l}$$

3 Versuchsparameter und -durchführung

In die Untersuchung wurden die Extremalwerte der Operatorantworten nur dann einbezogen, wenn sie größer als ein bestimmter Schwellenwert sind. Dieser Schwellenwert ergibt sich prozentual aus allen Operatorantworten, in unserem Fall 1% des größten Operatorbetrags. Es werden 22 synthetische und 43 tomographische Teil-Bilder verwendet. Die 3D synthetischen Bilder bestehen aus Tetraeder (Öffnungswinkel α =30, 40, 50, 60, 70, 80 und 90), Ellipsoiden (Halbachsenlänge a =8, 9, 10, 11, 12, 13, 14, 15 und 16, $b = 8$, $c = 40$) und hyperbolischen Paraboloiden (Parameter $(a, b) = (1, 1)$, $(2, 2)$, $(3, 3)$, $(1, 2)$, $(1, 3)$ und $(2, 3)$) und werden mit einer Gaußfunktion der Standardabweichung $\sigma = 0.7$ geglättet. In vier 3D MR-Bildern und einem 3D CT-Bild schneiden wir an 10 verschiedenen Landmarke jeweils einen Ausschnitt der Größe $40 \times 40 \times 40$ aus und betrachten diesen Bildausschnitt als ein einzelnes Bild, in dem genau eine Landmarke zu detektieren ist.

Wir untersuchen die Stabilität der Operatoren bzgl. Deformationen, indem wir die Bilder dreimal algorithmisch mittels einer elastischen Transformation (siehe [5]) deformieren und die Anzahl korrespondierender Punkte in allen Bildern automatisch ermitteln. In der Untersuchung der Stabilität bzgl. Rauschen gehen wir entsprechend vor und überlagern die Bilder zusätzlich dreimal mit Gauß-Rauschen unterschiedlicher Stärke. Da die Operatoren unterschiedlich viele Detektionen liefern, teilen wir die Anzahl korrespondierender Punkte durch die Gesamtzahl der Detektionen und erhalten so den Anteil korrespondierender Punkte. Wir berechnen jeweils getrennt für die Tetraeder, die Ellipsoide, die hyperbolischen Paraboloide, die MR- und CT-Bilder den Mittelwert der Ergebnisse (als Beispiel für die hyperbolischen Paraboloide siehe Abb. 1 links). Aufgrund der unterschiedlichen Rauschstufen und Deformationen erhalten wir insgesamt 154 synthetische und 301 tomographische Bilder in diesem Teil der Untersuchung.

Zur Untersuchung der klassischen Detektionsleistung ermitteln wir aus den Detektionen der Operatoren die Werte für P_{in}, P_{detect} und $P_{multiple}$ und mitteln diese Werte entsprechend der Untersuchung bzgl. der Anzahl korrespondierender Punkte (für die MR-Bilder siehe Abb. 1 rechts). Die Landmarke gilt dabei als detektiert, wenn mindestens eine Detektion innerhalb des Detektionsgebiets (Größe $7 \times 7 \times 7$) der Landmarke liegt. Die synthetischen Bilder werden zusätzlich mit 10 unterschiedlichen Rauschstufen ($\sigma_n^2 = $ 0.6, 1, 2, 4, 8, ,10, 50, 100, 500, 1000) überlagert und die Mittelwerte in Abhängigkeit vom Rauschen in Diagrammen aufgetragen (ohne Abbildung). Damit werden in diesem Teil der Untersuchung insgesamt 242 synthetische und 43 tomographische Bilder verwendet.

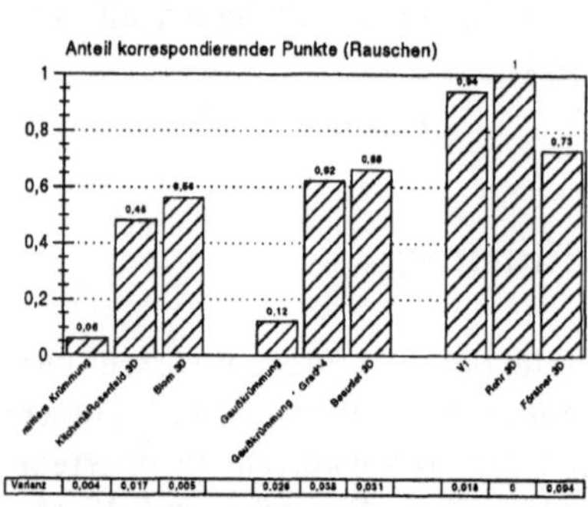

Varianz	0,004	0,017	0,005		0,026	0,038	0,031		0,018	0	0,094

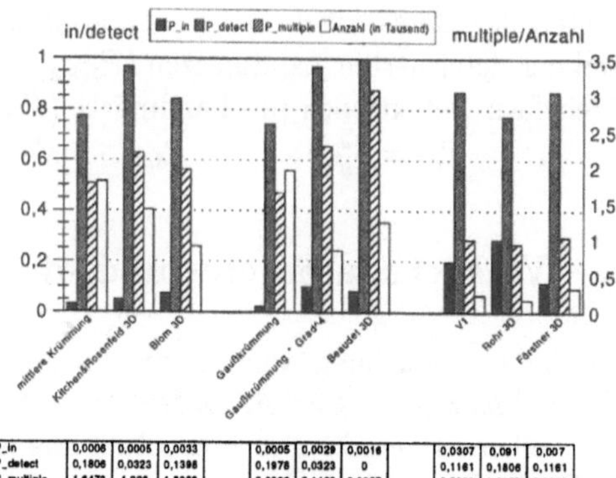

P_in	0,0006	0,0005	0,0033		0,0005	0,0029	0,0016		0,0307	0,091	0,007
P_detect	0,1806	0,0323	0,1398		0,1978	0,0323	0		0,1161	0,1806	0,1161
P_multiple	1,6473	1,228	1,8989		2,8366	2,1462	0,9957		0,3333	0,3957	0,2989

Abbildung 1: Zwei von insgesamt 66 ausgewerteten Diagrammen *Für das Diagramm links wurden die synthetischen Bilder des hyperbolischen Paraboloids dreimal unterschiedlich stark verrauscht und der Anteil korrespondierender Punkte in den Bildern ermittelt. In dem Diagramm ist für jeden Operator der Mittelwert dieser Bilder angegeben. Die rechte Abbildung zeigt die Mittelwerte der Maße der klassischen Detektionsleistung in den MR-Bildern. Außerdem ist die Anzahl aller Detektionen in den Bildern, über die gemittelt wurde, angegeben. Unter den Diagrammen sind die Varianzen der Mittelwerte aufgeführt.*

4 Ergebnisse und Zusammenfassung

1. Die Operatoren des Ansatzes „Förstner/Rohr" reagieren am stabilsten auf Rauschen und liefern daher signifikant weniger Detektionen als die Operatoren der Ansätze „mittlere Krümmung" und „Gaußkrümmung". Die Operatoren des Ansatzes „Förstner/Rohr" detektieren dabei den größten Teil der Landmarken (in MR-Bildern über 70%), wodurch sie i.a. einen höheren Anteil korrekter Detektionen liefern.

2. Vergleicht man die Operatoren des Ansatzes „Förstner/Rohr" miteinander, so reagiert i.a. der Operator *Förstner3D* am empfindlichsten auf starkes Rauschen im Bild und liefert daher im Vergleich zu den Operatoren *V1* und *Rohr3D* insbesondere in den tomographischen Bildern einen geringeren Anteil korrespondierender Punkte.

3. Die Multiplikation mit dem Betrag des Grauwertgradienten beim Ansatz „mittlere Kümmung" und „Gaußkrümmung" verbessert die Ergebnisse (vgl. [10]). Die Operatoren *Blom3D* und *Gaußkrümmung*Grad^4* ermitteln sowohl in den deformierten als auch in den verrauschten Bildern einen größeren Anteil korrespondierender Punkte als die Operatoren *mittlere Krümmung* und *Gaußkrümmung*. Der Operator *Blom3D* liefert bessere Ergebnisse als der Operator *Kitchen&Rosenfeld3D*.

4. Der Operator *Beaudet3D* ergibt in der gesamten Untersuchung schlechtere Ergebnisse als die Operatoren des Ansatzes „Förstner/Rohr".

Die Untersuchung hat gezeigt, daß insbesondere die Operatoren des Ansatzes „Förstner/Rohr" geeignet sind korrespondierende Punkte zu liefern und die vorgegebenen Landmarken zu detektieren. Für die MR- und CT-Bilder ergab der Operator *Rohr3D* bessere Ergebnisse als der Operator *Förstner3D*.

Danksagung

Diese Arbeit enstand im Rahmen des von den Philips Forschungslaboratorien Hamburg finanzierten Projektes IMAGINE.

Literatur

1. I.E. ABDOU, W.K. PRATT, "Quantitative Design and Evaluation of Enhancement/Thresholding Edge Detectors", *Proceedings of the IEEE,* Vol. 67, No. 5, S. 753-763, May 1979
2. W. BEIL, K. ROHR, H.S. STIEHL , "Investigation of Approaches for the Localization of Anatomical Landmarks in 3D Medical Images", *Proc. Computer Assisted Radiology and Surgery (CAR'97),* Seite 265-270, Juni 1997
3. P. R. BEAUDET, "Rotationally invariant image operators ", *Proc. Intern. Conf. Pattern Recognition, Kyoto, Japan,* 579-583, Nov. 1978
4. J. BLOM, B.M. TER HAAR ROMENY, J.J. KOENDERINK, "Affine invariant corner detection", *zur Veröffentlichung eingereicht,*
5. F.L. BOOKSTEIN, "Principal Warps: Thin-Plate Splines and the Decomposition of Deformations", *IEEE Transaction on Pattern Analysis and Maschine Intelligence,* Vol. 2, Seite 567-585, June 1987
6. L.M.J. FLORACK, B.M. TER HAAR ROMENY, J.J. KOENDERINK AND M.A. VIERGEVER, "General intensity tranformations and differential invariants", *J. Mathematical Imaging and Vision ,* Vol. 4, Seite 171-187, 1994
7. W. FÖRSTNER, "A Feature based correspondence algorithmus for imaging matching", *Int. Arch. Photogramm. Remote Sensing,* Vol. 26, S. 150-166, 1986
8. J.R. FRAM, E.S. DEUTSCH, "On the Quantitative Evaluation of Edge Detection Schemes and Their Comparison with Human Performance", *IEEE Transactions on Computers,* Vol. 24, No.6, Seite 616-628, June 1975
9. S. FRANTZ, K. ROHR, H.-S. STIEHL, "On the Localization of 3D anatomical point-landmarks in medical imagery using multi-step differential approaches ", *Proc. 19. DAGM-Symposium Mustererkennung, Braunschweig/Germany, Springer-Verlag Berlin Heidelberg,* Seite 340-347, Sept. 1997
10. T. HARTKENS, K. ROHR, H.-S. STIEHL, "Evaluierung von Differentialoperatoren zur Detektion charakteristischer Punkte in tomographischen Bildern", *Proc. 18. DAGM-Symposium Mustererkennung, Heidelberg/Germany, Springer-Verlag Berlin Heidelberg,* Seite 637-644, Sept. 1996
11. L. KITCHEN, A. ROSENFELD, "Gray-level corner detection", *Patt. Recog. Lett.,* Vol. 1, S. 95-102, 1982
12. K. ROHR, "Untersuchung von grauwertabhängigen Transformationen zur Ermittlung des optischen Flusses in Bildfolgen", *Diplomarbeit, Institut für Nachrichtensysteme, Universität Karlsruhe,* Germany 1987
13. K. ROHR, "On 3D differential operators for detecting point landmarks", *Image and Vision Computing,* Vol. 15, 219-233, 1997
14. J.-P. THIRION, A. GOURDON, "Computing the Differential Characteristics of Isointensity Surfaces", *Computer Vision and Image Understanding,* Vol. 61, 190-202, 1995
15. S. VENKATESH, L.J. KITCHEN, "Edge Evaluation Using Necessary Components", *CVGIP:Graphical Models and Image Processing,* Vol. 54, No.1, Seite 23-30, Jan. 1992
16. O.A. ZUNIGA, R.M. HARALICK, "Corner Detection using the Facet Model", *Proc. IEEE Computer Vision and Pattern Recognition,* Seite 30-37, 1983

TRANSFORMER
Ein Software-System zur Registrierung medizinischer Bilddaten

Matthias Otte

Arbeitsgruppe Neurobildverarbeitung,
Neurologische Universitätsklinik Freiburg, 79106 Freiburg
Email: otte@sun1.ukl.uni-freiburg.de

Zusammenfassung. In diesem Beitrag wird das Software-System TRANSFORMER vorgestellt, daß für den räumlichen Abgleich medizinischer Schichtbildaufnahmen entwickelt wurde. In TRANS-FORMER sind manuelle, semi-automatische und automatische Registrierungsverfahren implementiert, die eine Bearbeitung verschiedener Registrierungsprobleme erlauben. Abhängig von der Beschaffenheit des zur Verfügung stehenden Datenmaterials und der speziellen Aufgabenstellung können mehr oder weniger komplexe Transformationen berechnet werden, die eine geometrische Zuordnung in einem gemeinsamen Koordinatensystem erlauben. Zur Überprüfung der Registrierungsergebnisse werden verschiedene visuelle und statistische Werkzeuge zur Verfügung gestellt.

Schlüsselwörter: Elastische Registrierung, Bézier-Splines, Multimodale Visualisierung, Digitale Atlanten, Neuronavigation

1 Einleitung

Bei vielen Anwendungen der medizinischen Bildverarbeitung ist es wünschenswert, Bildinformationen von verschiedenen Modalitäten, von verschiedenen Zeitpunkten oder von verschiedenen Personen gemeinsam auswerten zu können. Abhänging von der Beschaffenheit des zur Verfügung stehenden Datenmaterials und der spezifischen Aufgabenstellung müssen hierzu mehr oder weniger komplexe Registrierungsverfahren eingesetzt werden, mit deren Hilfe die zu untersuchenden Daten möglichst exakt in ein gemeinsames Koordinatensystem transformiert werden können. Insbesondere zur Erforschung der Strukturen und Funktionen des Gehirns wurden in den vergangenen Jahren verschiedene Methoden wie MRT, fMRT, EEG, etc. entwickelt, die häufig erst in geeigneter Kombination verwertbare Aussagen liefern. Auch die Ordnung und Archivierung der mit diesen Verfahren gewonnenen Daten wird auf Grund der anfallenden Datenflut immer mehr zu einer Notwendigkeit. Hierzu können die Ergebnisse in ein standardisiertes Koordinatensystem transformiert werden, wo sie mit vorausgegangenen Untersuchungen und Vorwissen aus digitalen Atlanten verglichen werden können und so zu einem immer besseren Verständnis der neurofunktionalen

Zusammenhänge beitragen. Da bei dieser Transformation auch lokale interindividuelle Abweichungen berücksichtigt werden müssen, sind die Anforderungen an die Registrierung hier besonders groß. Wichtig ist hier auch die theoretischen und rechentechnischen Grenzen der zur Verfügung stehenden Verfahren zu erkennen und zu berücksichtigen, da die gewonnenen Ergebnisse sonst eher zu einer Verwischung als zu einer Klärung von Struktur-Funktionsbeziehungen führen [1, 2]. Hohe Anforderungen an Registrierungsverfahren ergeben sich auch bei Anwendungen aus dem Bereich der Neurochirurgie. Mit dem Ziel, die Ergebnisse neurochirurgischer Eingriffe zu verbessern wird immer häufiger versucht, Computer zur Unterstützung der Operationsplanung, seit einiger Zeit auch zur Neuronavigation während der Operation, einzusetzen [3, 4]. Der Einsatz der bisher in diesem Bereich entwickelten Systeme erweist sich in der Praxis allerdings häufig noch als problematisch, da die lokalen Bwegungen von Gehirnstrukturen, die nach der Öffnung der Schädeldecke z.B. durch den Abfluß von Liquorflüssigkeit hervorgerufen werden, noch nicht hinreichend berücksichtigt werden können. Neue Möglichkeiten ergeben sich hier durch intraoperative MR-Aufnahmen, die mit preoperativen Bilddaten registriert werden können und damit die Integration von Ergebnissen aus der preoperativen Funktionsdiagnostik erleichtern.

In dem Software-System TRANSFORMER (Abbildung 1) sind verschiedene Registrierungsverfahren implementiert, die eine Bearbeitung der beschriebenen Registrierungsprobleme erlauben. Abhängig von der Beschaffenheit des zur Verfügung stehenden Datenmaterials und der speziellen Aufgabenstellung können mehr oder weniger komplexe Transformationen berechnet werden, die eine geometrische Zuordnung in einem gemeinsamen Koordinatensystem erlauben. Zur Überprüfung der Registrierungsergebnisse werden verschiedene visuelle und statistische Werkzeuge zur Verfügung gestellt.

2 Manuelle Registrierung

Bei der manuellen Registrierung werden zwei Datensätze unter visueller Kontrolle geometrisch zur Deckung gebracht. Mit der Anwendung elementarer Transformationen (Translation, Rotation und Skalierung) wird die räumliche Lage der beiden Datensätze zueinander solange verändert, bis eine hinreichend gute Übereinstimmung der Daten erreicht ist [5]. Eine manuelle Registrierung von Datensätzen wird häufig als erste Näherung für automatische oder semiautomatische Verfahren eingesetzt. Die Qualität der Registrierungsergebnisse hängt bei manuellen Verfahren sehr stark von der Erfahrung des Anwenders ab. In der Praxis gibt es jedoch immer noch zahlreiche Anwendungsbeispiele, bei denen eine rein manuelle Registrierung mit den heute verfügbaren automatischen Verfahren nicht weiter verbessert werden kann.

3 Semi-automatische Registrierung

Bei semi-automatischen Registrierungsverfahren werden die Transformationen mit Hilfe korrespondierender Landmarken berechnet. Hierbei werden

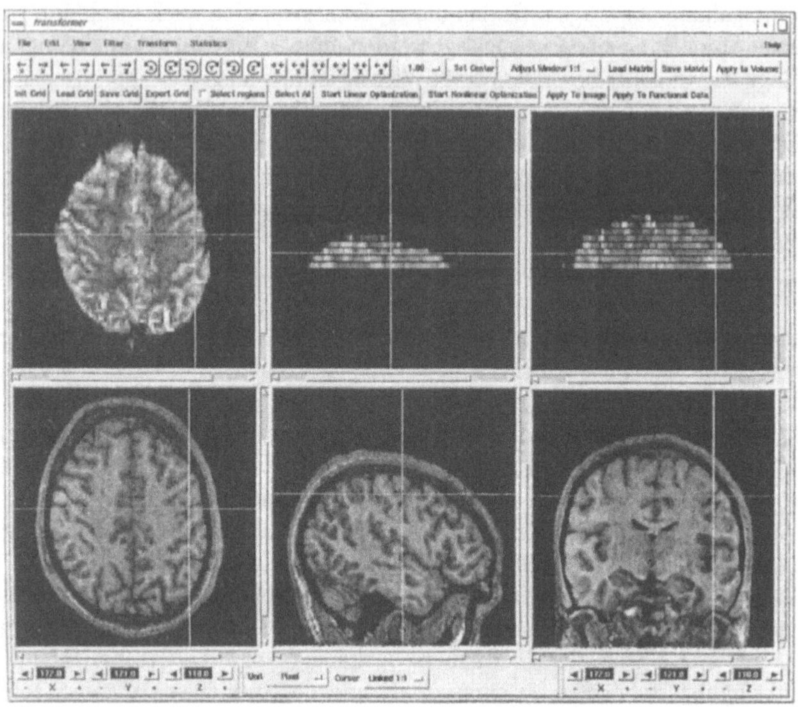

Abb. 1. Bedieneroberfläche von TRANSFORMER

zunächst einzelne Landmarken in den Datensätzen interaktiv markiert. Über geeignete Interpolations- oder Approximationsverfahren können dann die Transformationsparameter automatisch berechnet werden. In TRANSFORMER sind affine und elastische Transformationen in 2D und 3D, sowie ein elastisches Morphingverfahren zur Interpolation von Schnittbildern implementiert. Die Transformationen werden an Hand einer vorgegebenen Liste mit korrespondierenden Kontrollpunkten berechnet. Eine affine Approximation der Kontrollpunkte wird mit einem Standardverfahren berechnet [6], zur elastischen Interpolation wurde eine Schnittstelle zu einem externen Software-System zur elastischen Deformation von Volumendaten implementiert. Das in diesem System implementierte Verfahren benutzt zur Interpolation der vorgegebenen Kontrollpunkte radiale Basisfunktionen wie z.B. Hardy's Multiquadriken [7]. Neuere Entwicklungen bei semi-automatischen Verfahren werden u.a. in [8], [9] und [10] beschrieben.

Wenn einzelne Landmarken in den Datensätzen punktgenau detektiert werden können, sind semi-automatische Verfahren zuverlässig und sehr effizient (z.B. bei Verwendung künstlicher Marker). Ein anderer Anwendungsbereich sind Registrierungsprobleme bei denen eine Zuordnung grundsätzlich nur an Hand einzelner weniger Strukturen vorgenommen werden kann (z.B. beim Abgleich individueller Datensätze mit digitalisierten Buchatlanten).

4 Automatische Registrierung

Die in TRANSFORMER implementierten automatischen Verfahren benutzen voxelbasierte Ähnlichkeitsmaße (Linearer- und Entropie-Korrelationskoeffizient [11, 6]) und iterative Optimierungsverfahren um die gesuchten Transformationsparameter zu bestimmen. Auch hier werden affine und elastische Transformationen in 2D und 3D unterstützt. Die elastischen Transformationen werden durch trilineare Bézier-Splines beschrieben. Splinefunktionen in Bézier-Darstellung zeichnen sich durch einige günstige geometrische Eigenschaften aus, die sie zu idealen Kandidaten zur Beschreibung von geometrischen Transformationen auf Bilddaten machen. Die vielleicht wichtigste Eigenschaft bei der Verwendung in elastischen Registrierungsverfahren sind die Möglichkeiten zur Entwicklung schneller inkrementeller Resamplingalgorithmen. Eine trilineare Splinetransformation mit über 250.000 Kontrollparametern kann beinahe ebenso schnell wie eine einfache affine Abbildung auf Volumendaten angewendet werden. Mit Hilfe des Unterteilungsalgorithmus von de Casteljau kann ein Bézier-Volumenelement in acht Teilsegmente aufgeteilt werden. Bézier-Splines sind daher besonders geeignet zur Implementierung von hierarchischen Verfahren. Bei fortgesetzter Unterteilung kann eine vorgegebene Transformation mit beliebiger Genauigkeit approximiert werden.

Eine besondere Schwierigkeit bei elastischen Registrierungsverfahren ergibt sich aus der Forderung nach der Existenz der Umkehrabbildung. Für Bézier-Volumenelemente können einfache Kriterien direkt aus den Kontrollparametern abgeleitet werden, die die Existenz der Umkehrabbildung für das gesamte Volumenelement garantieren. Die Umkehrabbildung kann zwar selbst für trilineare Splines nicht mehr explizit angegeben werden, das zu lösende Gleichungssystem ist aber numerisch stabil und kann für einzelne isolierte Punkte auch hinreichend schnell mit Standardverfahren gelöst werden. Zur Anwendung der Umkehrabbildung auf den gesamten Datensatz ist es sinnvoller ein inkrementelles Vorwärtsresampling [12] zu verwenden, bei dem zunächst die ursprüngliche Transformation auf jeweils acht benachbarte Voxel angewendet wird. Das von den acht Bildvoxeln gebildete Hexaeder wird dann, ähnlich wie beim Gouraud-Shading-Algorithmus [13], interpoliert.

Bei der Verwendung lokaler Registrierungsverfahren muß berücksichtigt werden, daß eine Zuordnung korrespondierender Strukturen nicht in allen Bildbereichen eindeutig aus den Bildpunkten rekonstruiert werden kann (Korrespondenzproblem). Insbesondere bei schlechter Datenqualität ist daher eine sorgfältige Vorverarbeitung der Daten erforderlich, bei der die Regionen in den Bilddaten markiert werden, die hinreichend kontrastreich sind und damit bei der Registrierung zur Berechnung der Ähnlichkeit zwischen den Datensätzen verwendet werden können. In TRANSFORMER erlaubt eine Maskierung der Daten eine selektive Auswahl von Bildbereichen. Nur markierte Bildpunkte werden bei der Registrierung berücksichtigt. Neben einer Verbesserung der Registrierungsergebnisse führt die damit verbundene Datenreduktion gleichzeitig zu einer erheblichen Verkürzung der benötigten Rechenzeit.

Über ein Elastizitätsmodell kann die maximale Deformation der Transformationen in den Bildbereichen beschränkt werden, wo eine eindeutige Zuordnung korrespondierender Strukturen nicht exakt genug aus den Bilddaten rekonstruiert werden kann. Bei einem Bézier-Volumenelement kann die Deformation auf Grund der geometrischen Eigenschaften der Bézier-Darstellung vollständig aus den Abständen zwischen den Kontrollparametern berechnet werden. Das Lösen aufwendiger Differentialgleichungen ist daher für eine Beschränkung der maximalen Deformation nicht notwendig.

5 Implementierung

Das Software-System TRANSFORMER wurde in C auf einer SGI Indigo^2 entwickelt. Für die Programmierung der grafischen Bedieneroberfläche wurde das X-Window System und OSF/Motif eingesetzt. Die spezielle Graphikhardware des Rechners wurde nicht genutzt, so daß eine Portierung auf andere UNIX-Plattformen ohne Schwierigkeiten durchgeführt werden kann. Das Laufzeitverhalten der einzelnen Registrierungsverfahren ist schwierig abzuschätzen, da die jeweils benötigte Rechenzeit sehr stark von der Qualität und der maximalen Deformation der Daten abhängt. Das in TRANSFORMER implementierte elastische Registrierungsverfahren ist aber immerhin noch so schnell, daß ein lokal verzerrter Volumendatensatz mit einer $256 \times 256 \times 256$ Bildmatrix und einer lokalen Verzerrung von bis zu $15mm$ in weniger als 60 min. mit Subvoxelgenauigkeit korrigiert werden kann.

6 Ergebnisse

Die Zuverlässigkeit der implementierten Verfahren wurde an verschiedenen simulierten Daten überprüft. Simulierte Testdatensätze wurden mit dem oben beschriebenen semi-automatischen Deformationsverfahren generiert, wobei die korrespondierenden Landmarken (unter der Nebenbedingung eine maximale Abweichung von $14mm$ nicht zu überschreiten) mit einem Zufallsgenerator erzeugt wurden. Bei einem hochaufgelösten T_1-gewichteten anatomischen MR-Datensatz des Gehirns mit $1 \times 1 \times 1mm$ isotropen Voxeln konnten die so simulierten Verzerrungen mit dem automatischen Registrierungsverfahren vollständig rekonstruiert werden. Bei insgesamt 10 Testdatensätzen war der mittlere Registrierungsfehler kleiner als $0.1mm$, der maximale Fehler lag zwischen $0.18mm$ und $0.89mm$.

Bei einer zweiten Versuchsreihe wurde ein verzerrter T_2^*-gewichteter Volumendatensatz (mit bewußt schlechterer Datenqualität) mit dem unverzerrten T_1-gewichteten Datensatz registriert. Da beide Datensätze von der "Simulated Brain Database" (SBD) [14, 15] zur Verfügung gestellt wurden, war es möglich die Verschiebungsvektoren der simulierten Verzerrungen auch zwischen den unterschiedlichen Sequenzen exakt zu bestimmen, was auch hier eine genaue Abschätzung des Registrierungsfehlers ermöglichte. Auch hier wurde das Registrierungsergebnis an 10 künstlich verzerrten Datensätzen überprüft. Der mittlere Fehler betrug hier $0.6mm$, der maximale Fehler lag zwischen $1.5mm$ und $3.4mm$.

In Anwendungen mit realen Bilddaten wird TRANSFORMER bisher zur Registrierung von funktionellen und anatomischen MR-Bilddaten, zur geometrischen Normalisierung von anatomischen und funktionellen Daten bezüglich Talairachkoordinaten und zur elastische Bewegungskorrektur bei MR-Mammographien eingesetzt. Weitere Anwendungen sind möglich.

Literatur

1. Kruggel F, von Cramon DY: Perspektiven technischer Untersuchungsverfahren in der Neuropsychologie. Zeitschrift für Neuropsychologie, 5(2):91–100, 1994.
2. Kruggel F: Multimodale Registrierung – Algorithmen und Applikationen. Tagungsband zum 5. Freiburger Workshop, Digitale Bildverarbeitung in der Medizin:139–145, 1997.
3. Peters T, Davey B, Munger P, Comeau R, Evans A, Olivier A: Three-Dimensional Multimodal Image-Guidance for Neurosurgery. IEEE Trans. on Medical Imaging 15(2):121–128, 1996.
4. Grimson WEL, Ettinger GJ, White SJ, Lozano-Pérez T, Wells WM, Kikinis R: An Automatic Registration Method for Frameless Stereotaxy, Image Guided Surgery, and Enhanced Reality Visualisation. IEEE Trans. on Medical Imaging 15(2):129–140, 1996.
5. Pietrzyk U, Herholz K, Heiss WD: Three-dimensional Alignment of Functional and Morphological Tomograms. J. Comput. Assist. Tomogr. 14:51–59, 1990.
6. Press WH, Flannery BP, Teukolsky SA, Vetterling WT: Numerical Recipes in C, Cambridge University Press, 1988.
7. Ruprecht D, Müller H: Image Warping with Scattered Data interpolation. IEEE Comput. Graphics and Application 15:37–43, 1995.
8. Ruprecht D, Müller H: A framework for scattered data interpolation. in Goebel M, Müller, Urban B, eds.: Visualization in Scientific Computing. Springer-Verlag, Wien, 1995.
9. Rohr K, Stiehl HS, Sprengel R, Beil W, Buzug TM, Weese J, Kuhn MH: Landmark-based elastic Matching of Tomographic Images. Tagungsband zum 5. Freiburger Workshop, Digitale Bildverarbeitung in der Medizin:139–145, 1997.
10. Thompson P, Toga AW: A Surface-Based Technique for Warping Tree-Dimensional Images of the Brain. IEEE Trans. on Medical Imaging 15(4):402–417, 1996.
11. Astola J, Virtanen I: Entropy correlation coefficient, a measure of statistical dependence for categorized data. in Proc. Univ. Vaasa, Discussion Papers 44, Finland, 1982.
12. Wolberg G: Digital Image Warping. IEEE Computer Society Press, 1990.
13. Gouraud H: Continous Shading of Curved Surfaces. IEEE Trans Computers 20(6):623–628, 1971.
14. Kwan R, Evans AC, Pike GB: An Extensible MRI Simulator for Post-Processing Evaluation. Visualization in Biomedical Computing (VBC'96). Lecture Notes in Computer Science 1131:135–140, Springer-Verlag, 1996.
15. Kwan R, Evans AC, Pike GB: fMRI Simulation for Quantitative Evaluation of Analysis Methods. Proc. Third International Conference on Functional Mapping of the Human Brain, NeuroImage 5(4):449, 1997.

Neuronavigation und Elektrophysiologie

Intraoperative anatomische Darstellung funktioneller Regionen des sensomotorischen Kortex

Gabriele A. Krombach[1], Uwe Spetzger[1], Veit Rohde[1], Wilhelm Küker[2],
Claudia Zacharias[2], Joachim M. Gilsbach[1]

[1]Neurochirurgische Klinik, [2]Abteilung für Neuroradiologie
Rheinisch-Westfälische Technische Hochschule (RWTH), 52057 Aachen
Email: g.krombach@usa.net

Zusammenfassung. Die Operation cerebraler Läsionen im Bereich der Zentralregion erfordert intraoperativ eine exakte anatomische Orientierung und die
Kenntnis der individuellen Lage funktionell wichtiger Regionen, um operati-
onsbedingte motorische Defizite zu vermeiden. Wir kombinierten bei 29 Patienten die intraoperative Neuronavigation, mit der Phasenumkehr somatosensorisch evozierter Potentiale und der elektrischen Stimulation des Kortex. Durch
dieses Vorgehen gelang die Orientierung in der individuellen Anatomie, die
Identifikation funktioneller motorischer Areale, ihre anatomische Darstellung
und die Evaluation ihrer Lage in Bezug auf die Läsion.

Schlüsselwörter: Computer-assisted Surgery, Neuronavigation, Phasenumkehr, Elektrostimulation

1 Einleitung

Seit der Einführung von Computertomographie und Magnetresonanztomographie in
die Routinediagnostik gelingt es, kleine Tumoren, die noch keine oder nur geringe
neurologische Defizite ausgelöst haben zu erkennen. Damit ist die Möglichkeit einer
frühen Operation verbunden, die dem Patienten die Entwicklung ausgeprägter Symptome und folgender Komplikationen ersparen kann. Die intraoperative Orientierung
ist jedoch durch den Mangel an anatomischen Landmarken, insbesondere bei Läsionen, die in der Tiefe des Gehirns liegen und von gesundem Gewebe bedeckt werden
schwierig. Die Einführung der Computer-Assisted-Surgery erlaubte erstmals eine
interaktive Orientierung anhand eines CT- oder MRT-Datensatzes intraoperativ am
Patienten. Operationen im Bereich des sensomotorischen Kortex erfordern darüber
hinaus die Kenntnis der individuellen Lage funktionell wichtiger Regionen und ihrer
Relation zu der Läsion, um dieses Gewebe schonen zu können. Durch die mehrkana-
lige Ableitung somatosensorisch evozierter Potentiale (SSEP) von der Hirnoberfläche
kann der Sulkus centralis lokalisiert werden. Mittels der elektrischen Stimulation des
Motorkortex werden anschließend funktionelle Regionen identifiziert. Die Neuronavigation kann diese Areale in der individuellen Anatomie darstellen und ermöglicht
so die Beurteilung ihrer Lage in Bezug auf die Läsion.

2 Material und Methoden

2.1 Patienten

29 Patienten mit Läsionen in der Zentralregion (m: 16; w: 13, mittleres Alter: 59 Jahre, 22-78; 9 Meningeome, 9 Metastasen, 7 Gliome, 3 Kavernome, 1 Hamartom) wurden unter Anwendung der Neuronavigation und der Mappingtechniken operiert. Die Eingriffe wurden bei Vollnarkose, ohne Muskelrelaxation durchgeführt.

2.2 Neuronavigation

Das EasyGuide Neuro (Philips Medical Systems, Best, Niederlande) stellt ein interaktives Navigationssystem zur Orientierung bei neurochirurgischen Operationen dar. Das Gerät besteht aus einer mobilen UNIX 4.0 Workstation und einem optischen, mit Infrarotlicht arbeitendem Meßsystem aus zwei am Operationstisch fixierten Kameras und einem mit Leuchtdioden ausgestatteten Zeigeinstrument. Präoperativ werden 5-8 kontrastmittelhaltige Hydrogelmarkierungen auf der Kopfhaut des Patienten fixiert und ein MRT durchgeführt. In diesem 3-D Datensatz werden die Marker an der Workstation identifiziert und unmittelbar vor der Operation auf dem fixierten Kopf des Patienten mit dem Zeigeinstrument registriert. Nach dieser Kalibrierung superpositioniert das System die Lage des Zeigeinstruments und das Volumenmodel. Die Darstellung des Zeigers in Relation zum Operationsfeld ermöglicht nun die genaue Orientierung: Tief liegende intracerebrale Prozesse können auf die Oberfläche projeziert werden, so daß der optimale Zugangsweg am Kopf des Patienten geplant werden kann. Intraoperativ ist es jederzeit möglich, die Position des Instrumentes in der realen Anatomie in den Bilddaten anzuzeigen, und sich so immer wieder erneut zu orientieren [1]. Mittels des Navigationssystems wurde die exakte Planung der Kraniotomie und die Lokalisation der Läsion durchgeführt.

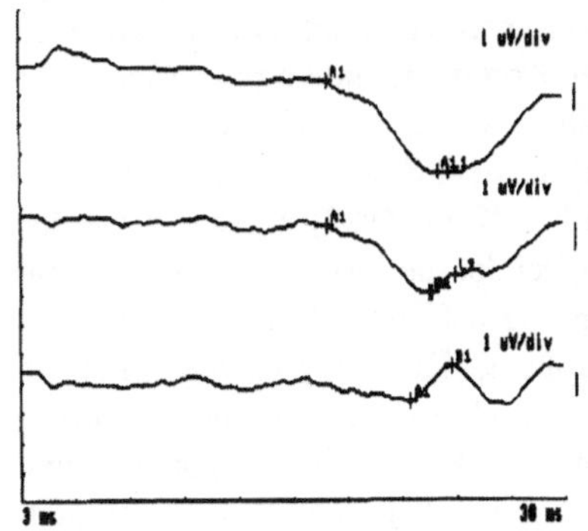
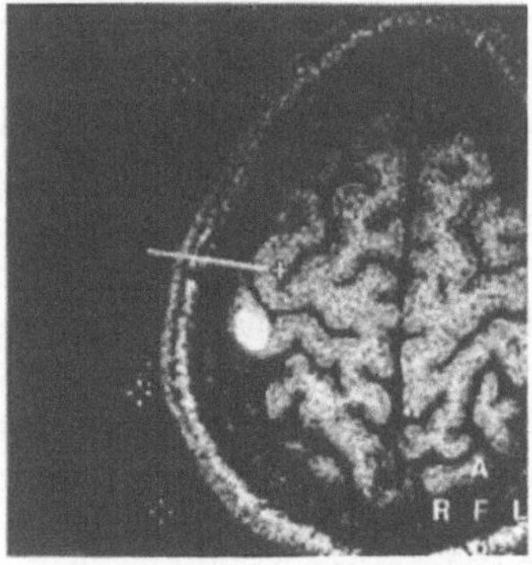

Abbildung 1. links: drei-kanalige Ableitung der SSEP Phasenumkehr; rechts: Position des ersten Kanals der Streifenelektrode mittels des Navigationssystems angezeigt.

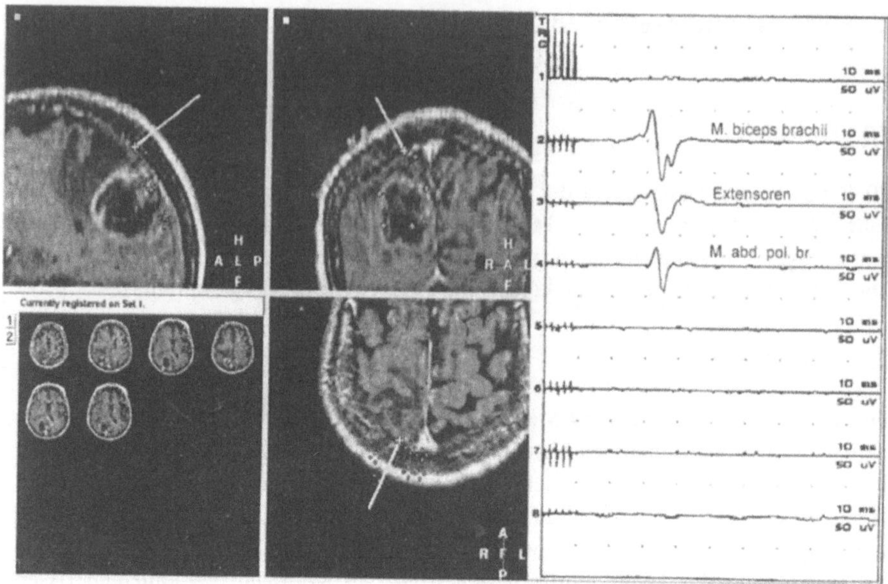

Abbildung 2. Kortikale Stimulation. links: Lage der Stimulationselektrode, rechts: Muskel-summenaktionspotentiale

2.3 Elektrophysiologie

Nach der Durchführung der Trepanation wurden somatosensorisch evozierte Potentiale (SSEP) vom Kortex abgeleitet um den Sulcus centralis anhand der Phasenumkehr zu identifizieren [2]. Hierfür wurde der kontralaterale N. medianus am Handgelenk elektrisch stimuliert und die Potentiale mit einer parallel zur Mittellinie auf den Kortex aufgelegten 4-kanaligen Streifenelektrode (Add-Tech, Medical Instrument Cooperation, Racine, WI, USA) aufgenommen. Die Referenzelektrode lag bei Fpz (Internationales 10-20 Schema). Für jede Ableitung wurden simultan aus 3 Kanälen 200 Sweeps gemittelt. Vom primären sensorischen Kortex, der im Gyrus postcentralis liegt, kann ein negatives Potential mit einer Latenz von 20 ms abgeleitet werden, während vom primären motorischen Kortex, der vor dem Sulcus centralis im Gyrus präcentralis liegt, eine positive Potentialantwort bei 22 ms (P22) registriert werden kann (Abb. 1). Die Position der Streifenelektrode, bei der die Phasenumkehr ableitbar war, wurde mit den Navigationssystem angezeigt, so daß der Sulcus centralis auch auf dem MRT identifiziert werden konnte. Die Größe der Kraniotomie wurde nicht an die Größe der Elektrode angepaßt, sondern nur so groß gewählt, wie für die Entfernung der Läsion unabdingbar, um nicht unnötig gesundes Gewebe zu exponieren und hierdurch zu gefährden. War die Ableitung der Phasenumkehr aus diesen operationstechnischen Gründen nicht möglich, stellte die Stimulation des Kortex den ersten Schritt dar.

Mittels einer auf den Kortex aufgelegten Plättchenelektrode wurde ein monopolarer anodischer Reiztrain von 5 Impulsen (500 Hz) apliziert. Die Kathode war bei Fpz fixiert. Die Ableitung erfolgte über subdermale Nadelelektroden, die nach der Belly-Tendon Methode über 8 Zielmuskeln plaziert worden waren. Standardisiert wurden jeweils 4 Muskeln der kontralateralen oberen und unteren Extremität herangezogen, oder andere, in Abhängigkeit von den präoperativen Symptomen ausgewählt. Die Potentiale wurden mittels eines elektrophysiologischen Meßsystems (Viking IV, Nicolet Biomedical Instruments, Madison, WI, USA) aufgezeichnet (Filter: 30-3000 Hz, Empfindlichkeit 10 µV/Division). An dem Ort der besten P22 der Phasenumkehr wurde mit der Stimulation begonnen. Die Stimulusstärke wurde schrittweise erhöht, bis Potentiale aufgetreten sind oder die Grenze von 25 mA erreicht worden war [3]. Konnten motorisch evozierte Potentiale (MEPs) ausgelöst werden, wurde die Lage der Stimulationselektrode mittels des Navigationssystems evaluiert (Abb. 2). Die funktionell wichtigen Areale wurden so in Relation zu der Läsion auf dem Bildschirm des Navigationssystems dargestellt. Der Chirurg konnte nun den sichersten Zugang zu der Läsion wählen. Mußte eine Läsion in unmittelbarer Nähe zum primären Motorkortex reseziert werden, wurden die MEPs permanent gemonitort.

3 Ergebnisse

Bei 12 (12/15) Patienten konnte die Phasenumkehr abgeleitet und der Sulcus centralis mittels des Neuronavigationssystems dargestellt werden (Abb. 1). Bei 25 der insgesamt 29 Patienten führte die kortikale Stimulation zur Auslösung reproduzierbarer MEPs.. Einer der Patient, bei den die kortikale Stimulation keine Potentialantworten hervorgerufen hat, hatte ebenfalls keine ableitbaren SSEPs. Das MRT zeigte ein ausgeprägtes Ödem des Gewebes; präoperativ bestand jedoch nur eine leichte Hemiparese. Bei dem zweiten Patienten war nur die Phasenumkehr ableitbar; der Motorkortex war durch die Läsion nach rostral und unten verdrängt worden und zunächst nicht zugänglich. Bei den beiden weiteren Patienten, zeigte die Navigation, daß der Motorkortex nicht durch die Trepanation freigelegt worden war

Bei den 23 Patienten mit erfolgreich ausgelösten MEPs konnte der sensomotorische Kortex durch den Einsatz der Mappingtechniken und der Navigation identifiziert werden. Bei Aufnahme hatten 16 der 29 Patienten ein motorisches Defizit. Neun Patienten gaben Krampfanfälle und 3 Kopfschmerzen als einzige Symptome an. Unmittelbar postoperativ hatte nur einer der 12 Patienten ohne präoperatives motorisches Defizit eine Armschwäche, die sich jedoch nach drei Tagen vollständig zurückgebildet hatte. Von den 15 Patienten mit präoperativen motorischen Defiziten blieben acht postoperativ unverändert. Bei vier Patienten verbesserten sich die motorischen Fähigkeiten. Drei hatten zunächst verstärkte Lähmungen, die sich jedoch in zwei Fällen zurückbildeten und nur bei einem Patienten bestehenblieben.

Zusammenfassend verbesserte sich die Motorik bei 4 Patienten und blieb bei 10 präoperativ symptomatischen Patienten unverändert und bei den 12 motorisch asymptomatischen Patienten erhalten. Nur ein Patient erlitt ein operationsbedingtes bleibendes Defizit.

4 Diskussion

In dieser Studie wurden erstmals Neuronavigation, SSEP Phasenumkehr und die elektrische Stimulation des Gehirns kombiniert. In vorausgehenden Untersuchungen stellte Fiersching et al. den Sulcus centralis mittels der Phasenumkehr dar und benutzte Ultraschall zur Lokalisation der Läsion [4]. Mit dieser Technik können jedoch motorische Areale des Kortex nicht identifiziert und dargestellt werden. Reinhardt et al. setzte bei 2 Patienten Neuronavigation und kortikale Stimulation ein [5]. Er beurteilte diese Technik als wertvolle Hilfe, um die komplette Resektion maligner Tumoren zu erreichen, erachtete den technischen Aufwand jedoch als zu hoch für den Einsatz bei allen Operationen im Bereich der Zentralregion.

Die Phasenumkehr erlaubt die sichere und exakte Identifikation des Sulcus centralis. Der Einsatz dieser Methode reduziert die für das gesamte Mapping der Zentralregion benötigte Zeit, da die kortikale Stimulation gezielter vorgenommen werden kann. Um über die Identifikation funktioneller Regionen hinaus ihre Konstellation zu der Läsion darstellen zu können, ist der Einsatz eines bildgebenden Verfahrens unabdingbar. Die Neuronavigation bietet eine millimetergenaue Orientierung in Echtzeit und bildet das Kortexrelief anhand von MRT-Daten detailliert ab. Die identifizierten funktionellen Regionen können in der individuellen Anatomie in Relation zu der Läsion dargestellt werden, so daß der Chirurg eine umfassende Kenntnis der Topographie und Funktion des Gewebes erhält. Die Methode stellt ein ausgezeichnetes Werkzeug dar, wenn die komplette Resektion maligner Tumoren erzielt werden soll. In der Zentralregion ist eine Orientierung allein anhand von anatomischen Landmarken nicht hinreichend. Läsion und assoziiertes Ödem können die anatomischen Strukturen auf unvorhersehbare Weise verlagern.

Die geschilderte Methode ist technisch aufwendig und erfordert speziell ausgebildetes Personal. Sind diese Voraussetzungen jedoch erfüllt, beträgt der intraoperative Zeitaufwand nur 15 Minuten. Das funktionelle Outcome dieser Serie war so überzeugend, daß wir die Technik als Routine bei allen Operationen im Bereich der Zentralregion einsetzen.

5 Literatur

1. Laborde G, Gilsbach JM, Harders A: Computer assisted lokalizer for planning of surgery and intraoperative orientation. Acta Neurochir (Wien), 119:116-170, 1992.
2. Woolsey CN, Erickson TC, Gilson WE: Lokalization in somatic sensory and motor areas of human cerebral cortex as determined by direct recording of evoked potentials and electrical stimulation. J Neurosurg, 51: 476-506, 1979.
3. Taniguchi M, Cedzich C, Schramm J: Modification of cortical stimulation for motor evoked potentials under general anesthesia. Neurosurg, 32:219-226, 1993.
4. Fiersching R, Klug K, Börner U: Lesions of the sensorimotor region: somatosensory evoked potentials and ultrasound guided surgery. Acta Neurochi (Wien), 118:87-90,1992.
5. Reinhardt HF, Trippel M, Westermann B, Horstmann GA, Grazl O: Computer assisted brain surgery for small lesions in the central sensorimotor region. Acta Neurochi (Wien), 138:200-205, 1996.

Konzept zur Modellierung und funktionellen Simulation von Strukturen in der Biomedizin

Andres Kriete

Institut für Anatomie und Zellbiologie
Bildverarbeitungslabor, Uni-Klinikum , Aulweg 123, 35385 Giessen
Email: andres.kriete@anatomie.med.uni-giessen.de

Zusammenfassung. Computergestützte Repräsentationen biologischer Organe, Gewebe und Zellen können zum besseren strukturellen und funktionellen Verständnis beitragen. Zur Strukturierung des Arbeitsablaufs von funktionellen Simulationen wird ein Konzept vorgestellt, welches am Beispiel des Organs der Lunge erläutert wird. Dabei wird durch Kombination der Daten aus verschiedenen 3D bildgebenden Modalitäten, der Extraktion und fraktalen Modellierung typischer Merkmale zunächst ein exaktes strukturelles System auf der Basis finiter Elemente gewonnen. Durch iterative CFD-Berechnungen werden dann Massentransportgleichungen gelöst und visualisiert, die den Gastransport beschreiben.

Schlüsselwörter: Modellbildung, FEM, funktionelle Simulation, CFD

1   Einleitung

Neben rein mathematischen Modellbildungen, die primär auf die Repräsentation des strukturellen Aufbaus abzielen, gewinnen diejenigen Simulationen an Bedeutung, die versuchen, dynamisch-funktionelle Eigenschaften biologischer Strukturen auf der Basis der Physik zu beschreiben [1]. Dazu gehören unter anderem elektrophysiologische, kinematische, elastomechanische oder thermische Prozesse. Zu berücksichtigen dabei ist, daß gerade bei funktionellen Aspekten die strukturelle Hierarchie biologischer Strukturen Einfluß auf die Funktion hat.

Es ist also in der Regel nicht ausreichend und abweichend von dem bisherigen Einsatz der Bildanalyse, mit nur einem Abbildungsmasstab oder festen Bildelementen (Pixel,Voxel) zu arbeiten. Vielmehr muß das System auflösungsunabhängig in Elemente zerlegt werden, die eine physikalisch-numerische Berechnung zulassen. Im gleichen Moment macht jedoch die Berücksichtigung mehrerer Ebenen ein Modell zunehmend komplexer. Es ist daher vorher genau zu definieren, welche strukturellen Ebenen und funktionellen Eigenschaften der Strukturen in Kauf genommen werden müssen, um ein bestimmtes Ziel zu erreichen. Um den Arbeitsablauf und Datenfluß zu beschreiben, wird ein Konzept zur strukturellen und funktionellen Repräsentation biologischer Strukturen vorgestellt und dieses exemplarisch auf den Bronchialbaum der Lunge angewandt.

2 Integratives Konzept

Das Konzept, welches den Arbeitsablauf und Datenfluß zur funktionellen Simulation beschreibt, ist im Überblick in Abbildung 1 gezeigt. Es beinhaltet als wesentliche Charakteristika:

- eine Rückkopplungsschleife
- eine strukturell-dynamische Modellierung mit einer Finite-Elemente- Methode, die hierarchisch und auflösungsunabhängig ist und
- eine funktionelle Simulation durch computergestützte Physik mit nachgeschalteter Visualisierung.

Die Integration des Hilfsmittels Simulation in den Modellbildungsprozess biologischer Strukturen kann als Regelkreis beschrieben werden. Dabei geht man davon aus, das zunächst die Ziele bezüglich der Simulation definiert sind. Durch eine Quantifizierung gewonnener morphologischer Daten und Modellierung kombiniert mit computergrafischer Visualisierung wird ein strukturelles Simulationsmodell aufgebaut. Die Morphologie wird auflösungsunabhängig als Finite-Elemente-Modell angelegt, da dies eine wichtige Voraussetzung dafür ist, funktionelle Simulationen zu berechnen.

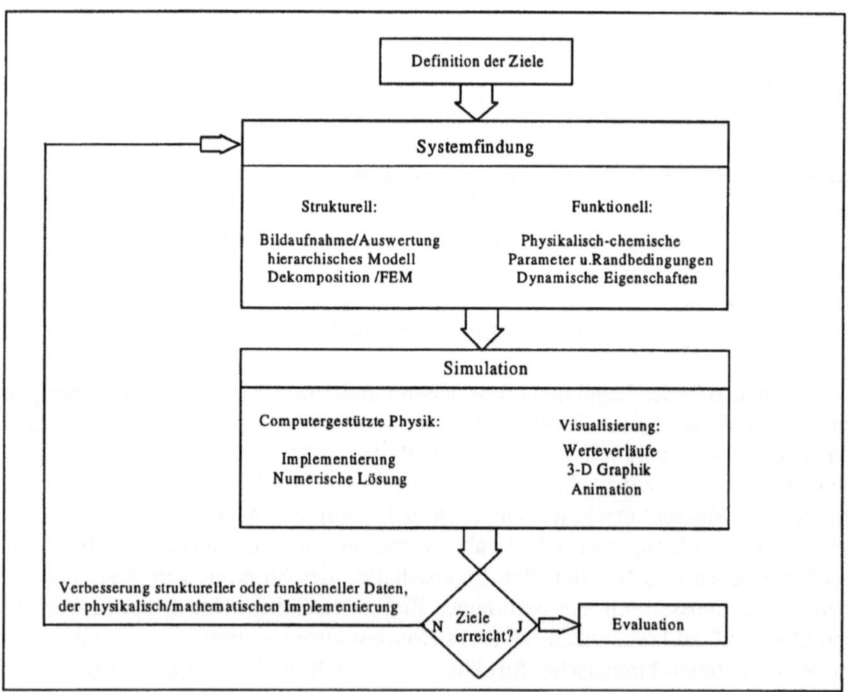

Abb.1: Arbeitsablauf und Datenfluß zur funktionellen Simulation

Zusammen mit den strukturell-dynamische Eigenschaften, den physikalisch-chemischen Parametern und funktionellen Randbedingungen ergibt sich das System. Dieses stellt dann den Input für die eigentliche funktionelle Simulation dar. Die Ergebnisse lassen Folgerungen für das reale System (Organ) zu. Wenn die Ziele nicht erreicht sind, muß erneut der Modellbildungsprozess durchlaufen werden.

3 Modellbildung und Simulation des Bronchialbaums

Das oben vorgestellte Konzept soll im folgenden für das Organ Lunge exemplarisch angewandt werden. Bezüglich der Lunge von Säugetieren wurde gezeigt, daß der Bronchialbaum entsprechend seiner Hierarchie als konduktiver und respiratorischer Teil modelliert werden muß [2,3]. Der konduktive Teil beinhaltet die Luftröhre und die angeschlossen Bronchien und Bronchiolen. In diesen Teilen wird Luft nur transportiert. Im respiratorischen Teil findet der Gasaustausch in den einzelnen Lungenbläschen oder Alveolen statt, die größere respiratorische Einheiten oder Acini bilden. Diese zwei Ebenen der biologischen Hierarchie, die des Organs und Gewebes, müssen betrachtet werden, wenn der Gastransport in der Lunge funktionell untersucht werden soll.

3.1 Modellierung des Bronchialbaums

Zur strukturellen, geometrischen Modellbildung des respiratorischen Teils der Lunge werden bei kleineren Säugerlungen Plastik-Ausgußmodelle untersucht, die die Hohlräume wiedergeben. Bei der menschlichen Lunge können neben Ausgussmodellen auch HRCT-Serien benutzt werden. Nach der Auswertung dieser Daten bzgl. Selbstähnlichkeit und Symmetrie erfolgt eine geometrische Simulation mittels fraktaler Grafik. Das Modell besteht dabei aus 4000 (Ratte/Maus) bis 700000 (Mensch) einzelnen Segmenten (Röhren zwischen Bifurkationen), die als finite Elemente oder Volumina aufgefaßt werden können.

Die Anzahl der respiratorischen Einheiten, ca. 3000 bei Ratte und Maus, 50000 beim Menschen, macht es notwendig, einige Acini exakt zu untersuchen um dann die typischen Merkmale zu modellieren. Neben der konfokalen Mikroskopie kommen Serienschnitttechniken oder Micro-CT zum Einsatz. [4].

Die so gewonnen Volumendaten werden mit speziellen 3-D Bildverarbeitungstools ausgewertet, einschließlich Segmentierung und dem Tracen des Verzweigungsmusters. Projeziert man das Verzweigungsmuster zweidimensional und analysiert den Zuwachs des Volumens, so ergibt sich eine Normalverteilung. Diese Normalverteilung, bezüglich Varianz und Mittelwert abhängig von der Größe der respiratorischen Einheiten, läßt sich trotz des unregelmässigen Aufbaus der Acini gut für eine strukturelles Modell verwenden [4].

3.2 Funktionelle CFD-Simulation mit finiten Volumina

Eine Dekomposition in einzelne Volumina ist durch das Modell von einzelnen Bronchial-Segmenten bereits vorgegeben, eine weitere Dekomposition ist bei dieser Anwendung, im Vergleich zum menschlichen Rachenraum, nicht notwendig [5]. Der Gastransport kann physikalisch durch Massentransport ausgedrückt werden, der aus den drei Anteilen Konvektion, Diffusion und Gasaufnahme besteht.

Für jedes einzelne Segment des Bronchialbaums, welches ein finites Volumen umschreibt, läßt sich eine solche Massentransportgleichung postulieren. Die Gleichungen können durch partielle Differentialgleichungen ausgedrückt werden, die analytisch jedoch nicht lösbar sind. Statt dessen findet neben der schon vorgenommen Aufteilung in finite Volumina auch eine zeitliche Aufteilung des Atemzuges statt[3].

Die Atemamplitude wird in Einzelschritte (>5000) unterteilt und die Gleichungen dann iterativ gelöst (Gauss-Seidel Iteration). Die sich aus dieser CFD-Berechnung ergebenden zugehörigen Gaskonzentration werden innerhalb der 3-D Modells computergrafisch und farbkodiert visualisiert. Die besondere Eigenschaft dieses Modells der Computerlunge ist es, daß für jeden beliebigen Teil des Bronchialbaums Gaskonzentrationen abgelesen werden können. Damit ist eine digitale Dosimetrie realisierbar.

4 Diskussion

Es wurde ein Konzept für computergestützte Repräsentationen biologischer Systeme bezüglich ihrer Struktur und Funktion vorgestellt. Am Beispiel des Organs der Lunge wurde exemplarisch gezeigt, wie durch Kombination der Daten aus verschiedenen 3D bildgebenden Modalitäten, der Extraktion und fraktalen Modellierung typischer Merkmale zunächst ein exaktes strukturelles Modell gewonnen werden kann. Bisherige Modelle gehen entweder von einem idealisierten, regelmäßig-dichotomischen Verzweigungsmuster des Bronchialbaums aus [6,7] oder untersuchen nur funktionelle Teilaspekte [8]. Aus solchen Modellen lassen sich daher nur in beschränkten Umfang Aussagen zur Gesamtfunktionalität der Lunge ableiten.

Die strukturell-geometrischen Untersuchungen ergaben Aufschluß über die Selbstähnlichkeit und Symmetrien im Bronchialbaum. So wurde herausgefunden, daß die Struktur des konduktiven Teil des Bronchialbaums abhängig vom Lungenflügel ist und sich von proximal (innen) nach distal (außen) von monopodial (asymmetrisch) nach dichotom (symmetrisch) ändert. Bisherige Modelle gehen von regelmäßgen Verzweigungsmustern aus [7]. Das Verzweigungsmuster in den respiratorischen Einheiten ist unregelmäßig, die Durchmessersummen sind aber normalverteilt. Damit ist eine geometrische Modellierbarkeit dieser Struktur gegeben.

Durch Dekomposition des Bronchialbaums in finite Volumina können Computational Fluid Dynamics (CFD) - Berechnungen durchgeführt werden. Dazu werden Massentransportgleichungen iterativ gelöst und Gaskonzentrationen visualisiert, die den Lufttransport in der Lunge beschreiben. Jede Atmungsamplitude führt zu einem typischen Konzentrationsverteilungsmuster innerhalb des Bronchialbaums, dieses kann visualisiert oder numerisch angezeigt werden. Die Struktur des Bronchialbaums hat dabei eindeutig einen Einfluss auf die Funktion: Jeder Acinus erhält zwar seinen gleichen Anteil an Ventilation, aber die effektive Ventilation (Sauerstoffversorgung) ist von der Lage des Acinus in der Lunge abhängig.

Das entwickelte Konzept, gekennzeichnet durch Auflösungsunabhängigkeit, finite Elemente und iterativer Simulationsrechnung, ist nicht nur für die Lunge, sondern prinzipiell auch für andere Organsysteme oder zelluläre Strukturen anwendbar. Von besonderem Interesse ist dabei das Studium der Wechselwirkung zwischen Form und Funktion.

Literatur

1. Hersh, J.S.: A survey of modeling representations and their application to biomedical visualization and simulation. Conf. Proc. VBC 1990, IEEE Comp.Society Press, pp 432-441, 1990.
2. Kriete,A.: Hierarchical data representation of lung to model morphology and function. in: (Eds. Höhne,K.-H., Kikinis, R).: Visualization in Biomedical Computing. Springer, NY, pp 399-404, 1996.
3. Kriete,A.: Form and function of mammalian lung: analysis by scientific computing. in press for Advances in Anatomy, Embryology and Cell Biology, Springer -Verlag, Berlin, 1998.
4. Kriete,A.: Microscopical quantification and functional simulation of pulmonary respiratory units. SPIE Conf.Proc.,Vol. 2655, pp 234-244, 1996.
5. Davidson,L.,Nielson,P.: Calculation of 2-D airflow in facial regions and nasal cavaties using an unstructured finite volume solver. Conf. on Finite Volume Methods, ISSN 1395-7953 R 9539, Dec. 1995.
6. Talhami,H.:L-Systems for three-dimensional anatomical modelling: towards a virtual laboratory in anatomy, in: (Eds.)Höhne,K.-H., Kikinis,R.: Visualization in Biomedical Computing, Springer, NY, pp 393-398, 1996.
7. Weibel, E.R.: Morphometry of the human lung. Springer, Berlin, 1963
8. Mercer, R.R., Anjivel,S., Miller,F.J., Crapo,J.D.: Inhomogenity of ventilatory unit volume an ist effects on reactive gas uptake. J.Appl.Physiol. 70,5, pp 2193-2205, 1991.

Operatoren zur deskriptiven und modellbasierten unscharfen Wissensbeschreibung in der medizinischen Bildverarbeitung

Jens Hiltner

Universität Dortmund
Fachbereich Informatik, Lehrstuhl I
Otto-Hahn-Str. 16, 44227 Dortmund
Email: hiltner@ls1.informatik.uni-dortmund.de

Zusammenfassung: Der Bereich der medizinischen Bildverarbeitung gewinnt zunehmend an Bedeutung, insbesondere bedingt durch die fortschreitende Entwicklung moderner bildgebender Verfahren und der weiten Verfügbarkeit entsprechender Aufnahmegeräte. Trotz wachsender Bildqualität können die Bilddaten verschiedenste Arten von Unsicherheiten enthalten, die bei einer computer-unterstützten Auswertung geeignet berücksichtigt werden müssen. In diesem Beitrag wird der Umgang mit den in Bilddaten auftretenden Unsicherheiten behandelt. Berücksichtigung findet dabei unter anderem die sogenannte interindividuelle Variabilität. Zur Segmentierung und Erkennung von Objekten trotz vorkommender Unsicherheiten werden neu entwickelte Lösungsansätze vorgestellt und diskutiert.

Schlüsselwörter: Medizinische Bildverarbeitung, MRT-Analyse, Fuzzy-Logik, Klassifikation, Wissensbeschreibung

1 Einleitung

In der modernen medizinischen Bildgebung treten viele interessante Fragestellungen im Bereich der automatisierten Strukturerkennung und Bildanalyse auf. Deren zentrale Bedeutung wird durch die Tatsache deutlich, daß die gefundenen Daten eine existentielle Grundlage für viele Diagnosen bilden. In den letzten Jahren haben sich durch die bildgebenden Verfahren in der Medizin gerade im Bereich der Invivo-Untersuchungen sehr gute Fortschritte gezeigt. Bei der Bildanalyse handelt sich um ein aktuelles Forschungsgebiet, bei dem noch viele Fragen offen sind [7, 8, 10, 13]. Beispielsweise treten in medizinischen Bilddaten verschiedene Arten von Unsicherheiten auf. Als erstes sei hier die interindividuelle Variabilität in den Aufnahmen genannt. So beinhaltet beispielsweise ein volumen-orientiertes Magnet-Resonanz-Tomogramm (MRT) verschiedener menschlicher (gesunder) Köpfe jeweils die gleichen Strukturen. Trotzdem unterscheiden sich diese teilweise sehr deutlich in Form, Lage und Größe voneinander (vgl. Abb. 1). Ein System zur automatischen Erkennung dieser Organ-Strukturen muß demzufolge in der Lage sein, solche Variabilitäten sowohl zu erkennen als auch zu handhaben, was die Entwicklung verschiedener speziell darauf abgestimmter Operatoren erfordert.

Abb. 1. Beispiel für die Variabilitäten menschlicher Köpfe (jeweils mittlere MRT-Schicht)

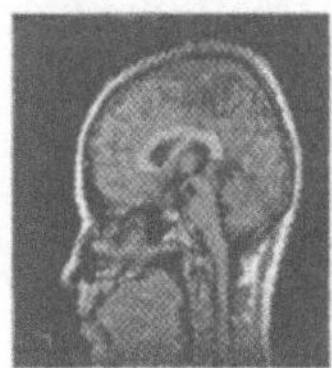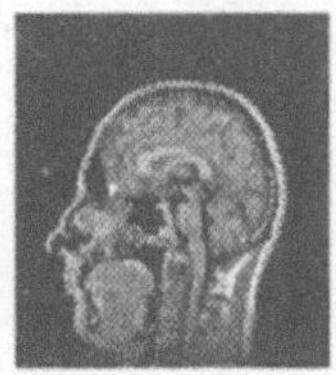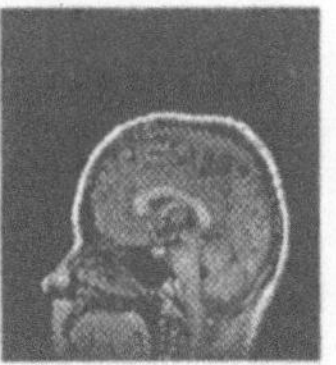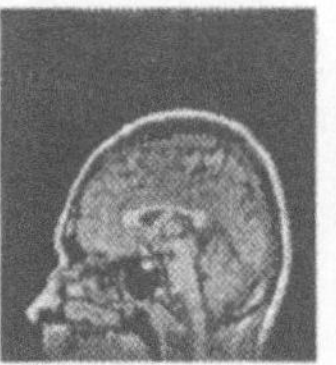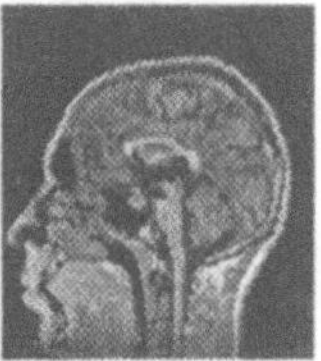

Weiterhin treten Ungenauigkeiten in den Bilddaten durch unterschiedliche Artefakttypen auf. So existieren z.B. Bewegungsartefakte, die dadurch entstehen, daß sich der Patient während der doch recht langen Aufnahmezeit bewegt. Darüber hinaus sind Bilddaten aufnahmebedingt häufig verrauscht oder unscharf. Für die Modellierung dieser Unsicherheiten zur Segmentierung und Erkennung von Bildobjekten hat sich die unscharfe Logik in den letzten Jahren als sehr nützlich erwiesen [3, 4, 5, 9, 11, 13]. In diesem Beitrag soll im folgenden eine Möglichkeit zur Verarbeitung der Variabilitäten mit Hilfe der Fuzzy-Logik vorgestellt werden. Mit dieser Technik ist es möglich, gesuchte Strukturen auf eine intuitivere Weise zu beschreiben und sich somit der natürlichen Vorgehensweise des Mediziners anzunähern. So kann beispielsweise der Hirnstamm als längliches Organ beschrieben werden, welches unter dem Großhirn liegt, nach unten hin schmaler wird und zudem einen hohen Grad an Homogenität besitzt. All diese Begriffe beschreiben Eigenschaften, die nicht exakt durch eine quantitative Anzahl von Pixeln oder Voxeln definiert werden können und sich somit nur schwer durch klassische mathematische Methoden ausdrücken lassen.

Trotz dieser Beschreibungsmöglichkeiten hat sich in den Wissensakquisitionssitzungen mit den Medizinern gezeigt, daß häufig eine deskriptive Beschreibung der gesuchten Objekte allein nicht ausreicht bzw. möglich ist. Hier ist es für den Experten leichter, das Objekt zu skizzieren, um die verbale Beschreibung zu ergänzen. Eine solche Skizze kann jedoch nicht absolut behandelt werden, sie beschreibt nur das schematische Aussehen der gesuchten Struktur, eine geeignete Flexibilität der Operatoren, die mit solchen Skizzen arbeiten, muß also gewährleistet sein, was wiederum durch den Einsatz von Fuzzy-Methoden erreicht werden kann.

2 Arten der Wissensbeschreibung

Deskriptive Beschreibungen werden schon länger und mit gutem Erfolg mittels unscharfer Eigenschaften modelliert und deshalb hier nicht sehr ausführlich beschrieben. Mehr Informationen kann der interessierte Leser in [2, 3, 4, 5] nachlesen.

2.1 Deskriptive Beschreibung

Die Beschreibung von Eigenschaften gesuchter Objekte lassen sich in vielen Fällen unscharf durchführen. Dies macht natürlich nur dort Sinn, wo auch derartige Unsicherheiten auftreten. Allgemein werden die Eigenschaften durch linguistische Variablen, welche die Eigenschaft selbst beschreiben, bezeichnet und mit linguistischen Termen belegt. Als Beispiel sei hier die linguistische Variable *Größe* genannt, die etwa mit den linguistischen Termen *klein, mittel, groß* belegt werden kann. Wie die Terme interpretiert werden sollen, wird in den Fuzzy-Mengen definiert (vgl. Abb. 2).

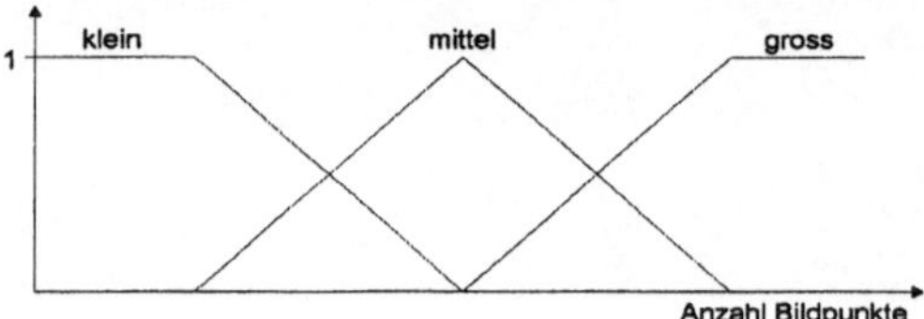

Abb. 2. Beispiel für Fuzzy-Mengen für die Eigenschaft *Größe*

Unscharfe Eigenschaften dienen zur Beschreibung der gesuchten Strukturen und werden zur Identifizierung gefundener Segmente herangezogen. Die Beschreibung selbst wird in einer unscharfen Wissensbasis abgelegt. Für scharfe Zahlenwerte (etwa die Anzahl der Bildpunkte eines Segmentes, vgl. Abb. 2) werden dann die Zugehörigkeiten zu den Fuzzy-Mengen ermittelt, mit denen in einem nachfolgenden Schritt weiter gerechnet werden kann. Nach Betrachtung verschiedener unscharfer Eigenschaften wird anschließend das Segment als das Objekt identifiziert, bei dem die Beschreibung am besten mit dem Inhalt der Wissensbasis übereinstimmt. Folgende Eigenschaften (mit entsprechenden umgangssprachlichen Beschreibungen) werden u.a. zur Identifizierung herangezogen: *Größe, Helligkeit, Formeigenschaften, Lage, Orientierung* und *Textur*.

2.2 Modellbasierte Beschreibung

Unter einer modellbasierten Beschreibung soll hier die Beschreibung von in Skizzen vorgegebenen Strukturen verstanden werden. Dazu muß eine geeignete Repräsentationsform gefunden werden, die auch die Behandlung von Variabilitäten zuläßt. Durch die Verwendung von unscharfen Kanten (vgl. Abb. 3) kann ein gewisser Grad an Flexibilität gewonnen werden [1, 3, 6]. Ausgehend von der Kontur der Skizze wird ein unscharfer Rand mit sinkenden Zugehörigkeitswerten aus dem Einheitsintervall definiert, dessen Breite über einen Parameter δ eingestellt werden kann. Die Wahl von δ soll objektabhängig erfolgen und muß experimentell festgelegt werden. Dazu werden aus einer größeren Anzahl segmentierter Datensätze die Variabilitäten zwischen den einzelnen Strukturen ausgewertet und in die Berechnung der Breite δ mit einbezogen.

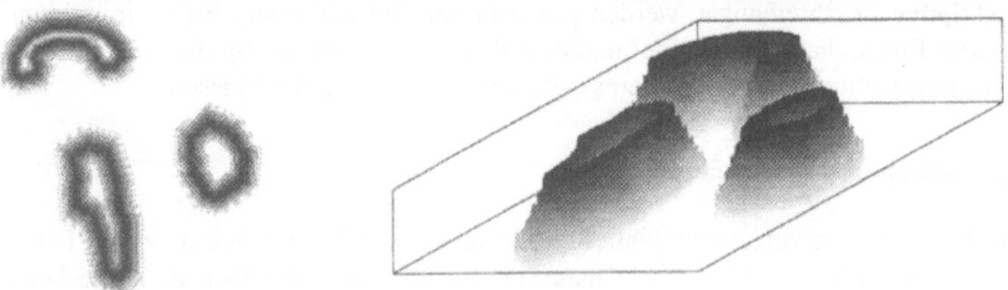

Abb. 3. Schematische Darstellung von unscharfen Referenzobjekten (Auf- und Seitenansicht)

Um die Erkennung bzw. den Vergleich von gefundenen mit dem vorgegebenen Segment zu erleichtern, werden beide Strukturen an ihrer Hauptachse ausgerichtet und bzgl. der Kopfgröße normiert. Die Normierung ist aufgrund der unterschiedlich großen Köpfe notwendig (vgl. Abb. 1). Der Grad der Zugehörigkeit des gefundenen Segmentes zum gesuchten Objekt wird durch die Zugehörigkeitswerte des unscharfen Referenzobjektes bestimmt, wobei derzeit noch verschiedene Möglichkeiten der Bestimmung überprüft werden (denkbar sind u.a. Minimum, Maximum oder Durchschnitt).

Falls keine zufriedenstellenden Ergebnisse bei einem Vergleich des gefundenen Segmentes mit allen möglichen in der Wissensbasis definierten Objekten erreicht werden, werden Fuzzy-Regeln (vgl. Abb. 4) zur Modifikation des Referenzobjektes herangezogen. Diese können z.B. das Objekt stauchen, strecken oder auch gezielt deformieren.

```
WENN SollObj=lang UND IstObj=kurz   DANN Strecken = pos_viel
WENN SollObj=lang UND IstObj=mittel DANN Strecken = pos_mittel
WENN SollObj=kurz UND IstObj=mittel DANN Strecken = neg_mittel
```

Abb. 4. Drei Beispielregeln mit unscharfen Begriffen

Die Regeln können aus der deskriptiven Beschreibung des Objektes gewonnen werden, falls bis auf die Formeigenschaften das gefundene Segment schon klassifiziert wurde und mit der Formänderung eine Bestätigung erreicht werden soll. Andererseits wirken diese Modifikationen sich negativ auf den Zugehörigkeitsgrad aus, um extreme Änderungen und somit falsche Klassifikationen zu vermeiden.

2.3 Kombination beider Methoden

Sinnvoll erscheint die Kombination beider Verfahren (deskriptive und modellbasierte Beschreibung) für bestimmte Problembereiche, wo ein deskriptiver Ansatz allein nicht ausreicht. Dieses unterschiedliche Vorgehen erlaubt eine gegenseitige Kontrollinstanz für das jeweils komplementäre Verfahren, so daß eine deutlich verbesserte Qualität und somit Sicherheit erwartet werden kann, was die Akzeptanz seitens der Anwender erhöht.

Dieser Vorteil muß durch erhöhten Rechenaufwand und auch von einer im Vorfeld aufwendigeren Wissensakquisition erkauft werden. Da aber gerade im Bereich medizinischer Bilddaten der gesundheitliche Aspekt des Patienten im Vordergrund steht, ist dieser Mehrpreis als gering einzustufen. Weiterhin tritt aufgrund schnell steigender Rechnerleistungen dieser Mehraufwand zumindest in der Nutzungsphase des Systems in den Hintergrund.

3 Zusammenfassung und Ausblick

In diesem Beitrag wurden nach einer anfänglichen Erläuterung der Problematik bei der Strukturerkennung in medizinischen Bilddaten zwei verschiedene Arten der unscharfen Wissensdarstellung aufgezeigt. Schließlich wurde eine Kombination beider Verfahren kurz diskutiert.

Derzeit werden die Operatoren in einem Baukasten [12] implementiert und getestet. Dies hat den Vorteil der schnellen Überprüfbarkeit in einem Rahmen, der zudem weitere Bildverarbeitungsmethoden umfaßt. Das Ziel dieses Projektes liegt in einem Gesamtsystem, welches es dem Anwender erlaubt, sein Expertenwissen auf eine ihm verständliche Weise zu integrieren. Dazu soll er das Wissen in unterschiedlichen, sich ergänzenden Formen definieren können. Neben der umgangssprachlichen Eigenschaftsbeschreibungen ist beabsichtigt, dem Experten die Möglichkeiten zu geben, in intuitiver Form Skizzen und Modelle zu definieren. Dazu sind Editoren zu entwerfen, die den Inhalt geeignet für die unscharfe Wissensbasis aufbereiten.

Neben den Fuzzy-Methoden sollen noch weitere Methoden aus dem Bereich der *Computational Intelligence* genutzt werden [3], um die Ergebnisqualität und somit die Akzeptanz zu erhöhen, aber auch um mühsame Optimierungen (etwa der Fuzzy-Mengen oder des Parameters δ, vgl. Abschnitt 2) zu automatisieren.

4 Literatur

1. Han J.H, Koczy L.T, Poston T: Fuzzy-Hough Transform. Pattern Recognition Letters, Vol. 15, pp. 649-658, 1994.
2. Hiltner J, Jäger M, Meyer zu Bexten E, Tresp C, Fathi M: Analyse medizinischer Bilddaten mit Hilfe unscharfen Wissens. Digitale Bildverarbeitung in der Medizin. Tagungsband zum 5. Freiburger Workshop. Universität Freiburg, 1. Auflage, 1997.
3. Hiltner J: Einsatz von Methoden der Computational Intelligence in der digitalen Bildverarbeitung. 17. Workshop Interdisziplinäre Methoden in der Informatik. Forschungsbericht, Universität Dortmund, 1998.
4. Hiltner J: Formbeschreibungen in der Bildverarbeitung. 16. Workshop Interdisziplinäre Methoden in der Informatik. Forschungsbericht Nr. 639, Universität Dortmund, 1997.
5. Jäger M, Moser M: Ein Modellentwurf zur wissensbasierten Analyse von 3D-Bildern unter Berücksichtigung von Unsicherheiten. Diplomarbeit am Fachbereich Informatik, Lehrstuhl I, Universität Dortmund, 1996.
6. Kim Y. T, Han J.H: A Fuzzy Approach to Edge Detection and Representation. Fuzz-IEEE 97, pp. 69-74, 1997.
7. Lehmann T, Oberschelp W, Pelikan E, Repges R: Bildverarbeitung für die Medizin. Grundlagen, Modelle, Methoden, Anwendungen. Springer-Verlag, Berlin, 1. Auflage 1997.
8. Lehmann T, Scholl I, Spitzer K (Hrsg.): Bildverarbeitung für die Medizin. Algorithmen, Systeme, Anwendungen. Proceedings des Aachener Workshops. Verlag der Augustinus Buchhandlung, Aachen, 1. Auflage, 1996.
9. Menhardt W: Unscharfe Mengen (Fuzzy Sets) zur Behandlung von Unsicherheit in der Bildanalyse. Dissertation, Universität Hamburg, 1990.
10. Meyer zu Bexten E, u.a.: Bedeutung und Perspektiven der medizinischen Bildverarbeitung. 3. Anwendersymposium "Aktuelle Entwicklungen und Realisierungen der Bildverarbeitung", Aachen, 1997.
11. Pedrycz W: Fuzzy Sets in Pattern Recognition: Methodology and Methods. Pattern Recognition, Vol. 23, No. 1/2, pp. 121-146, 1990.
12. Projektgruppe Bambus: Baukasten für die Analyse und Modellierung von Bildobjekten aufgrund unscharfen Wissens. Endbericht der Projektgruppe 294, Universität Dortmund, 1997.
13. Tizhoosh H.R: Fuzzy-Bildverarbeitung. Einführung in Theorie und Praxis. Springer-Verlag, Berlin, 1. Auflage 1997.

Virtuelle Endoskopien aus CT- und MR-Datensätzen
Alternative Visualisierung hochaufgelöster Schnittbildserien

A.P. Wunderlich, T. Fleiter, A.J. Aschoff, R. Sokiranski, H.-J. Brambs

Abteilung Radiologie I
Universitätsklinikum Ulm, 89070 Ulm
Email: arthur.wunderlich@medizin.uni-ulm.de

Zusammenfassung. Die heute verfügbare hohe Rechen- und Grafikleistung
moderner Grafik-Workstations ermöglicht dreidimensionale Oberflächenrekonstruktionen aus Schittbild-Datensätzen in so kurzer Zeit, daß eine interaktive Visualisierung ohne Probleme möglich ist. Darüberhinaus erlaubt entsprechende Software, nicht nur die Außenansicht der Strukturen darzustellen,
sondern den Beobachter- bzw. Kamera-Standort im Sinne einer Endoskopie in
das rekonstruierte Objekt hinein zu verlagern. Ausgangsmaterial hierfür sind
die digitalen Bilder hochauflösender Schnittbildverfahren. Vorgestellt werden
einige Ansätze zur Rekonstruktion von Spiral-CT- und 3D-MR-Studien.

Schlüsselwörter: Spiral-CT, 3D-MR, 3D-Rekonstruktion, virtuelle Endoskopie

1 Einleitung

In diesem Jahrzehnt gab es entscheidende Verbesserungen der Schnittbild-Methoden
Computer-Tomographie (CT) und Magnetresonanz-Tomographie (MR). Dies war
zum einen die Spiral-CT [1], die Anfang der 90er Jahre Eingang in die klinische
Routine fand, zum anderen bei der MR ein Fortschritt in der Technik der Gradien-
tenspulen und -verstärker mit der Option ultraschneller 3D-Gradientenecho-
Sequenzen [2]. Mit beiden Techniken können heute ganze Volumina in weniger als
30 sec. Aufnahmezeit, d.h. innerhalb eines Atemstillstands, abgebildet werden. Dies
eröffnet neue Perspektiven für das schon vor etlichen Jahren etablierte Verfahren der
dreidimensionalen (3D-) Rekonstruktion [3], das anfangs auf Strukturen wie Schädel
und Skelett beschränkt war, die nicht der Atemverschiebung unterliegen.

Die Möglichkeiten zur 3D-Rekonstruktion von z.B. Blutgefäßen, Organen oder
der Trachea aus Datensätzen schnittbildgebender Verfahren wurden schon früh erkannt und genutzt [4,5], seit einiger Zeit sind sie Gegenstand klinischer Studien [6].
Durch die Fortschritte in Computerleistung und Software konnte in jüngster Zeit ein
wichtiger Schritt in bezug auf die Rekonstruktion selbst vollzogen werden: wurden
bisher vornehmlich statische Bilder als Ergebnis oftmals minutenlanger Rechnungen
zur Diagnose herangezogen, rückt nun vermehrt die interaktive Auseinandersetzung
mit dem Datensatz in den Vordergrund. Darüberhinaus erlaubt eine entsprechend
flexible Software nicht nur die Visualisierung der Oberfläche von außen, sondern

auch endoskopieartige Ansichten durch die Wahl entsprechender Kamerakoordinaten innerhalb der Strukturen.

Die Anwendung dieses Verfahrens, der virtuellen Endsokopie (VE), auf CT- und MR-Datensätze bei verschiedenen Fragestellungen als Querschnitt durch die Arbeit unserer Abteilung auf diesem Gebiet [7,8] ist Gegenstand des vorliegenden Beitrags.

2 Methodik

Voraussetzung für gute VE-Rekonstruktionen ist neben der guten Ortsauflösung ein hohes Kontrast-Rausch-Verhältnis (contrast-to-noise ratio, CNR). Diesen prinzipiell gegensätzlichen Forderungen wurde durch entsprechende Untersuchungstechnik, teils mit Kontrastmittel (KM), Rechnung getragen.

2.1 CT-Untersuchung

Mit einem CT Twin (Elscint Corp., Haifa, Israel) wurden im Doppelhelix-Modus bei einer primären Kollimation von 2 x 2,5 mm Schnittbilder mit einer effektiven Schichtdicke von 3,2 mm bei einem Inkrement von 1,6 mm berechnet. Die Auflösung in Schichtebene betrug 0,8 mm.

Eine KM-Gabe war bei der VE-Bonchoskopie, der Nasen-Nebenhöhlen-(NNH)-VE oder der VE-Laryngoskopie nicht erforderlich. Für die VE-Angioskopie wurde jodhaltiges, nichtionisches KM über eine Kubitalvene appliziert, der CT-Scan erfolgte mit kurzem (20 s für arterielle Gefäße) bzw. mittlerem Delay (40 s für Venen). Dieselbe Kontrastierung kam für die Cystoskopie zur Anwendung, hier wurde jedoch zwischen KM-Gabe und CT-Datenaquisition 10 bis 15 Minuten gewartet. Patienten für die VE-Coloskopie wurden ab 2 h vor Untersuchungsbeginn oral mittels Gastrografin kontrastiert, unmittelbar vor der Untersuchung zusätzlich noch rektal.

2.2 MR-Untersuchung

Am MR Vision (Siemens AG, Erlangen) wurden MRCP-(MR-Cholangio-Pankreaticographie)-Untersuchungen mit einer HASTE-Sequenz (TE/TR 60/2000 ms, Ortsauflösung 1,6 x 1,6 x 3,6 mm) durchgeführt. Wegen des hohen Kontrasts zwischen freier Flüssigkeit und Gewebe war keine KM-Gabe erforderlich.

Für alle anderen VE-Anwendungen wurde mit einer 3D-Gradientenecho-Sequenz bei TE/TR/FA von 1,5 ms/4,5 ms/20 ° und einer Ortsauflösung von 1,4 x 1,4 x 2 mm gearbeitet. Die Kontrastierung erfolgte mittels Gd-DTPA, für die Angioskopien intravenös, für die Duodeno- und Coloskopien über eine Magensonde.

2.3 Rekonstruktion

Die Schnittbilder wurden auf den Modalitäten in das DICOM-Format konvertiert und mittels Netzwerk auf Nachverarbeitungssysteme überspielt. Ein erster Schritt ist die Beschränkung auf wesentliche Strukturen. In einem 3D-Editor wurde auf den primären Bildern sowie auf sekundär berechneten Schnittbildern in den zwei fehlenden orthogonalen Richtungen das Datenvolumen eingegrenzt. Hier erfolgte auch die Umwandlung von DICOM in das Silicon Graphics (SGI)-eigene Standardformat.

Auf einer SGI O2 Workstation (SGI, Mountain View, Kalifornien) wurde mit der Explorer-Software (Numerical Algorithms Group, Downers Grove, Illinois) aus den mittels Schwellwert klassifizierten Daten eine Oberfläche berechnet, wobei auf jede Manipulation (z.B. Glättung) verzichtet wurde. Diese Oberflächendaten wurden dann über ein spezielles Software-Modul interaktiv visualisiert. Die Video-Optionen der Workstation erlauben es, die 3D-Animation direkt in eine digitale Videodatei mitzuschneiden und ggf. zur Demonstration auf ein Videoband zu überspielen.

3 Ergebnisse

Die VE-Rekonstruktionen leben von der interaktiven Auseinandersetzung mit dem Datensatz. Im Internet kann man dies auf der VRML-Seite unserer Abteilung unter der Adresse http://www.uni-ulm.de/klinik/radklinik/rad1/vrml online nachvollziehen. Im Rahmen des vorliegenden Beitrags soll anhand einiger Bildbeispiele ein Eindruck der vielfältigen Möglichkeiten der VE vermittelt werden.

3.1 CT

Bei der Bronchoskopie (Abb. 1) fanden wir sehr gute Übereinstimmung zwischen VE und konventioneller Endoskopie, ebenso bei der NNH-Endoskopie sowie der Laryngoskopie. Auch Details, wie z.B. dünne Septen in der NNH-Endoskopie, kommen gut zur Darstellung.

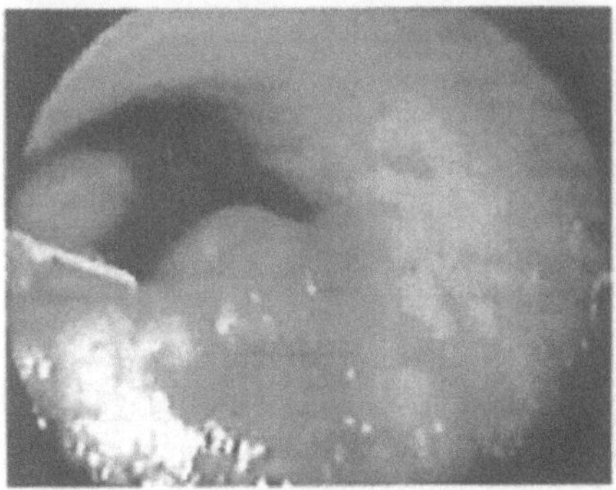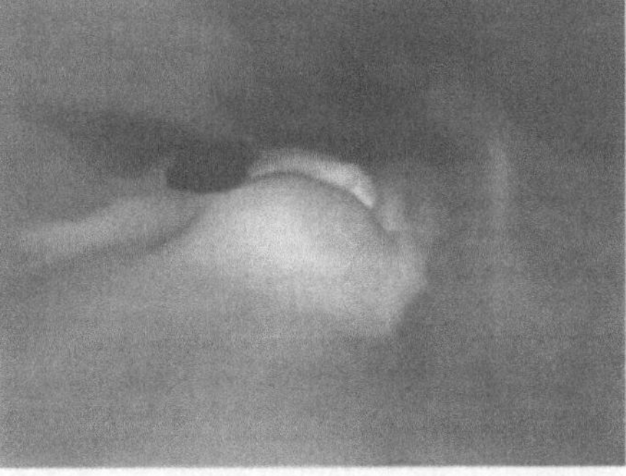

Abb. 1. Bronchoskopie (links) und virtuelle Bronchoskopie (rechts) eines Patienten mit Bronchial-CA-Rezidiv. Deutlich erkennt man in beiden Modalitäten die Verengung der Trachea sowie die polypartige Ausstülpung des Tumors nach distal.

Wegen des erforderlichen CNR ist die VE-Angioskopie hauptsächlich auf Arterien beschränkt. Große Gefäße (> 3 mm) stellen sich sehr gut und artefaktfrei dar, kleinere Gefäße nur, wenn sie in Richtung der Körper-Längsachse verlaufen. Die Visualisierung senkrecht zur Tischvorschubrichtung liegender Arterien ist stark abhängig vom Schwellwert und daher oft suboptimal. Eine Ausnahme bilden die Hirngefäße: wegen ihrer geringen Ausdehnung in Scanrichtung wurde mit einer primären Kollimation von 2 x 0,5 mm gearbeitet und damit gute Ergebnisse erzielt.

Die VR-Cystoskopie zeigte ebenfalls größtenteils gute Ergebnisse. Lediglich bei unbeweglichen Patienten war wegen Sedimentation des KM in der Blase nicht die gesamte Blasenwand beurteilbar. Der Vergleich mit der optischen Cystoskopie zeigte eine gute Übereinstimmung der beiden Verfahren.

In unserem Ansatz zur VE-Coloskopie erzielten wir gute Darstellungen der Darmwand einschließlich pathologischer Veränderungen.

3.2 MR

Die VE-MRCP zeigt die Gallenblase sowie die Gallenwege mit vielen Details. Konkremente in der Gallenblase erscheinen in den Schnittbildern signalarm und werden damit in der VE sichtbar (Abb. 2). Verzweigungen der Gallengänge bis zur zweiten oder dritten Ordnung sind jedoch nur bei Dilatation derselben gut darzustellen. Aus diesem Grund sind Gallengang-Stenosen der VE kaum zugänglich.

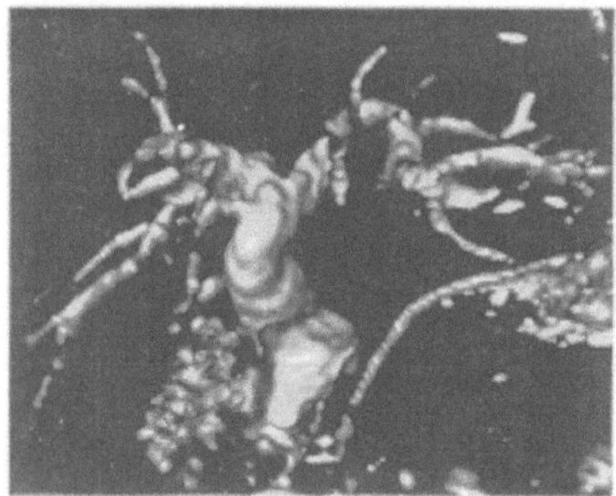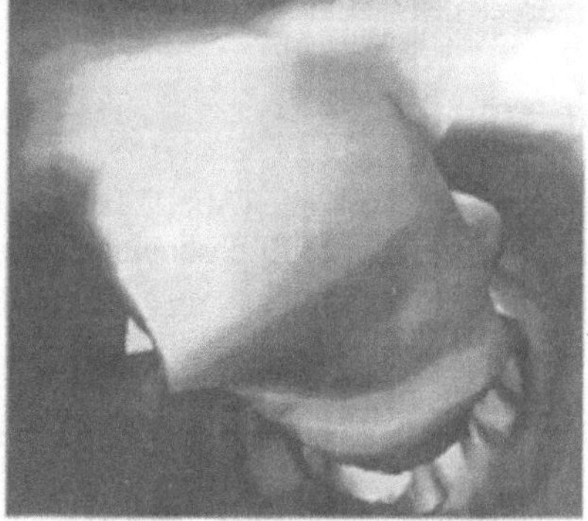

Abb. 2. 3D-Rekonstruktion des biliären Systems (links) sowie VE-Innenansicht der Gallenblase (rechts) mit einem Konkrement. Das an der Gallenblasenwand anliegende Konkrement scheint mit dieser verschmolzen. - Die Artefakte von retroperitonealem Fett (linkes Bild, untere Hälfte) haben keinen nennenswerten Einfluß auf die interaktive Bildberechnungsrate.

Aufgrund der hervorragenden Qualität der CE-MRA bilden diese ein ausgezeichnetes Ausgangsmaterial für VE-Rekonstruktionen. Die Ortsauflösung kann isotrop gewählt bzw. die primäre Schnittführung dem Gefäßverlauf angepaßt werden, so daß auch kleine Gefäße bis hinab zu etwa 1 mm Durchmesser gut visualisierbar sind. Wie bei der CT ist man in der Praxis auf VE-Angioskopien von Arterien beschränkt.

Bei der VE-MR-Duodeno- bzw. -Coloskopie kann unter Umständen nicht das gesamte Duodenum bzw. Colon innerhalb eines Atemstillstands mit optimaler Auflösung abgebildet werden. Dann muß entweder das Scanvolumen reduziert oder eine verminderte Ortsauflösung in Kauf genommen werden. In letzterem Fall können Details verlorengehen.

4 Diskussion

Das CT als historisch wichtige Modalität hat zwei Vorteile: hohe räumliche Auflösung und gutes CNR. Letzteres trifft aufgrund des Dichteunterschieds zwischen Luft und Gewebe besonders auf VE-Broncho-, -Laryngo- und -NNH-Endoskopie zu. Dies dürfte die Ursache dafür sein, daß mit der Bronchoskopie die Geschichte der VE begann [9]. Auch bei den anderen beschriebenen Anwendungen erreicht man durch Kontrastierung ohne weiteres ein gutes CNR. Lediglich die Cystoskopien zeigen wegen der Absorption der Röntgenstrahlen durch die Beckenknochen erhöhtes Rauschen und daher fallweise suboptimale Oberfächen.

Im MR ist von vornherein der Kompromiß zwischen CNR und räumlicher Auflösung zu optimieren. Bei der MRCP gelingt dies aufgrund des hohen Signals der HASTE-Sequenz ohne weitere Maßnahmen. Durch die Kontrastmittelgabe sind auch die übrigen Verfahren mit gutem Ergebnis möglich.

Mit Hilfe der interaktiven Manipulation lassen sich Endoskopien für Planungs- und Schulungszwecke simulieren. In Zukunft können wahrscheinlich diagnostische Endoskopien sukzessive durch die neue Technik abgelöst werden. Vorteile sind kürzere Untersuchungsdauer, praktisch auf null reduziertes Patientenrisiko sowie die Erweiterung der Betrachtungsmöglichkeiten.

5 Literatur

1. Kalender WA, Seissler W, Klotz E, Vock P: Spiral volumetric CT with single-breath-hold technique, continuous transport, and continuous scanner rotation. Radiology, 176(1):181-183, 1990.
2. Leung DA, McKinnon GC, Davis CP, Pfammatter T, Krestin GP, Debatin JF: Breath-hold, contrast-enhanced, three-dimensional MR angiography. Radiology, 200(2):569-571, 1996.
3. Marsh JL, Vannier MW: Surface imaging from computerized tomographic scans. Surgery, 94:159-165, 1983.
4. Gmeinwieser J, Wunderlich AP, Gerhardt P, Strotzer M: Dreidimensionale Rekonstruktion von atemverschieblichen Organen und Gefäßstrukturen aus Spiral-CT-Datensätzen. Röntgenpraxis, 44:2-8, 1991.
5. Wunderlich AP, Strotzer M, Gmeinwieser J, Gerhardt P: Colour-coded 3D-reconstruction of abdominal organs and vessels. In: Lemke HU, Rhodes ML, Jaffe CC, Felix R (Hrsg.): Computer Assisted Radiology 1991. Springer-Verlag, Berlin, 187-193, 1991.
6. Zeiberg AS, Silverman PM, Sessions RB, Troost TR, Davros WJ, Zeman RK: Helical (spiral) CT of the upper airway with three-dimensional imaging: technique and clinical assessment. AJR Am. J. Roentgenol., 166(2):293-299, 1996.
7. Fleiter T, Merkle EM, Aschoff AJ, Lang G, Stein M, Görich J, Liewald F, Rilinger N, Sokiranski R: Comparison of real-time virtual and fiberoptic bronchoscopy in patients with bronchial carcinoma: opportunities and limitations. AJR Am. J. Roentgenol., 196:1591-1595, 1997
8. Merkle EM, Fleiter T, Wunderlich A, Rilinger N, Gorich J, Sokiranski R: Virtuelle Zystoskopie aus Spiral-CT-Datensätzen. Röfo Fortschr. Röntgenstr., 165(6):582-585, 1996
9. Summers RM, Feng DH, Holland SM, Sneller MC, Shelhamer JH: Virtual bronchoscopy: segmentation method for real-time display. Radiology, 200(3):857-862, 1996.

Beurteilung des präoperativen Brain shift mit Hilfe des Neuronavigationssystems EasyGuide Neuro

Marcus H. T. Reinges, Hong-Ha Nguyen, Uwe Spetzger, Wilhelm Küker[*],
Joachim M. Gilsbach

Neurochirurgische Universitätsklinik und [*]Abteilung Neuroradiologie
Rheinisch-Westfälische Technische Hochschule (RWTH), 52057 Aachen

Zusammenfassung: Brain shift, d.h. die Verschiebung des Gehirns gegenüber seiner knöchernen Umhüllung, führt zu Einschränkungen der Verläßlichkeit beim intraoperativen Einsatz der heute gebräuchlichen Neuronavigationssysteme. Bei 12 Patienten wurde untersucht, ob unterschiedliche Kopfpositionen während der präoperativen Bilddatenerfassung für die intraoperative Neuronavigation einen ähnlichen Einfluß auf die intraoperative Verläßlichkeit des Navigationssystems haben, d.h., ob auch schon vor Eröffnung der Dura eine relevante, gravitationsabhängige Verschiebung des Gehirns auftritt. Die erhaltenen Ergebnisse sprechen dafür, daß die Kopfposition während der Bilddatenerfassung keinen wesentlichen Einfluß auf die intraoperative Verläßlichkeit der Neuronavigation hat. Jedoch sind zur Beurteilung des Problems des Brain shift weitere, insbesondere intraoperative, Untersuchungen nötig.

Schlüsselwörter: Neuronavigation, Brain shift, minimal invasive Neurochirurgie, digitale Bildverarbeitung

1 Einleitung

Ungenauigkeit aufgrund intraoperativer Gewebeverschiebungen durch Hirnödem, Liquorverlust und Tumorhöhlung ist eines der wichtigsten Defizite der heute gebräuchlichen Neuronavigationssysteme, welche i.d.R. mit präoperativ erhobenen Bilddatensätzen arbeiten [1-11]. Diesem intraoperativen Brain shift wird in jüngster Zeit experimentell mit der Anpassung der präoperativ erhobenen Daten an die tatsächliche intraoperative Situation mit Hilfe intraoperativer Datenaquirierung zu begegnen versucht [3].

Inwieweit aber auch schon präoperativ bzw. vor Eröffnung der Dura ein Brain shift existiert und von klinischer Bedeutung ist, war unklar. Erklärbar wäre ein präoperativer Brain shift beispielsweise durch Unterschiede der Kopfposition der Patienten während der präoperativen Bilddatenerfassung und der später im OP in Narkose herbeigeführten Lagerung des Kopfes mit konsekutiver, gravitationsabhängiger Lageveränderung des Gehirns in seiner knöchernen Umhüllung oder eine ventilationsbedingte intraoperative Hirnvolumenänderung [7].

Ziel der vorliegenden Untersuchung war es, zu beurteilen, ob die Kopfposition während der präoperativen Erfassung der für die intraoperative Neuronavigation benötigten Bilddaten einen bedeutsamen Einfluß auf die spätere intraoperative Genauigkeit und Verläßlichkeit des Neuronavigationssystems hat.

2 Patienten und Methode

In der Zeit zwischen Juni 1996 und Januar 1998 wurden 12 Patienten (m:w = 7:5; Durchschnittsalter 47 [23 - 70] Jahre) mit unterschiedlichen intrakraniellen Tumoren auf einen eventuellen präoperativen Brainshift untersucht.

Als Referenzpunkte wurden vor der MR-tomographischen Datenaquirierung jeweils 12 kontrastmittelhaltige Marker (fiducial marker) auf den Köpfen der Patienten fixiert. Die Datenaquirierung selbst erfolgte jeweils mit den für das Neuronavigationssystem EasyGuide Neuro (Philips Medical Systems, Best, The Netherlands) gebräuchlichen Meßparametern mit dem 0,5T MR-Tomographen Gyroscan T5 (Philips Medical Systems, Best, The Netherlands) in Rückenlage mittels Kopfspule: 3D scan mode, fast field echo, TE: 4,5ms, TR: 30ms, FOV: 240mm, Flipwinkel: 30°, Schichtdicke: 3mm, 256*256 Bildmatrix.

Für jeden Patienten wurden unmittelbar nacheinander zwei kernspintomographische Datenerfassungen mit jeweils unterschiedlicher Kopfposition durchgeführt: einmal in neutraler Kopfposition und einmal in annähernd der für eine pterionale Kraniotomie benutzten Kopfposition, d.h. um jeweils etwa 45° retroflektierter und rotierter und um etwa 30° zur ipsilateralen Schulter abduzierter Kopf.

Für beide Datensätze wurden daraufhin mit Hilfe des Neuronavigationssystems EasyGuide Neuro bei einer virtuellen Pointer-Verlängerung von 10-15mm, um Haut- und Kalottendicke auszugleichen, und bei senkrechtem Aufsetzen des Pointers auf die Kopfhaut, um Meßungenauigkeiten aufgrund der Pointer-Verlängerung zu vermeiden, der Sulcus centralis, die Fissura Sylvii und die Sulci temporales superior und inferior beidseits auf die Kopfhaut gezeichnet (Abb. 1). Anschließend wurden etwaige Unterschiede der auf diese Weise mit beiden Datensätzen erhaltenen Linien ermittelt und Abweichungen entsprechender Punkte beider Datensätze mit Hilfe des Navigationssystems berechnet.

Für alle Patienten, bei denen im Rahmen der nachfolgenden operativen Therapie eine entsprechend lokalisierte Kraniotomie durchgeführt wurde, wurde zudem die Lage der erhaltenen Linien mit der intraoperativen tatsächlichen Lage der entsprechenden Sulci verglichen.

3 Ergebnisse

Bei allen untersuchten 12 Patienten war die Übertragung des Sulcusreliefs aus dem MR-Datensatz auf die Kopfhaut schnell und einfach möglich (Abb. 2).

Die exakte Positionierung der erhaltenen Linien konnte bei allen Patienten, bei denen im Rahmen der nachfolgenden operativen Therapie eine entsprechende Kraniotomie durchgeführt wurde, für den Bereich der Kraniotomie mit einer Abweichung von maximal 1,0mm bestätigt werden.

Der Vergleich der mit beiden Datensätzen unabhängig voneinander erhaltenen Linien auf der Kopfhaut zeigte in allen Fällen eine Abweichung von unter 1,0mm.

4 Diskussion

Die erhaltenen Ergebnisse sprechen dafür, daß bei noch verschlossener Dura kein lageabhängiger Brain shift auftritt, welcher für die Verläßlichkeit der heute gebräuchlichen Navigationssysteme von Bedeutung ist. Die Kopfposition während der Datenerfassung scheint für die spätere Verläßlichkeit der Navigation nicht von entscheidender Bedeutung zu sein. Es ist somit nicht notwendig, die Datenaquirierung in annähernd der Kopfposition durchzuführen, in der später operiert werden soll. Dies hat entscheidende Vorteile sowohl in der Simplizität und Standardisierbarkeit, als auch in der für den Patienten erhöhten Bequemlichkeit der präoperativen Datenerfassung in Neutralposition des Kopfes verglichen mit der später im OP in Narkose hergestellten Kopfposition, z.B. der oben beschriebenen Kopflagerung für eine pterionale Kraniotomie.

Natürlich muß berücksichtigt werden, daß die bisher untersuchte Fallzahl sehr gering ist, und daß weitere, insbesondere auch intraoperative, Untersuchungen folgen müssen. Zudem sind die bisherigen Untersuchungen nur an Patienten mit normaler Weite der äußeren Liquorräume durchgeführt worden. Es müssen somit auch noch analoge Untersuchungen bei Patienten folgen, deren äußere Liquorräume erweitert sind, beispielsweise Patienten mit fortgeschrittener Hirnatrophie oder mit Arachnoidalzysten. Auch die Bedeutung einer subduralen Flüssigkeitskollektion - z.B. eines chronischen Subduralhämatoms - oder eines postoperativen Pneumatocephalus bedarf noch weiterer Untersuchungen hinsichtlich der Verläßlichkeit der Neuronavigationssysteme und eines - in diesen Fällen sicher nicht auszuschließenden - präoperativen, positionsabhängigen Brain shift.

5 Schlußfolgerung

Das Problem des Brain shift scheint - mit Ausnahme der bisher nicht beurteilbaren Patienten mit Erweiterung der äußeren Liquorräume und intrakranieller Luftansmmlung - für die intraoperative Verläßlichkeit der heute üblichen Neuronavigationssysteme nicht relevant zu sein. Hingegen ist eine Verschiebung des Gehirns gegenüber seiner knöchernen Umhüllung nach Eröffnung der Dura ein ernstzunehmendes Problem, welches man in Zukunft vielleicht durch intraoperative Anpassung der präoperativ erfaßten MR- oder CT-Bilddaten mittels intraoperativer Bildgebung wird lösen können. Solange solche Möglichkeiten jedoch noch nicht für die klinische Routine verfügbar sind, sollte man sich in unsicheren Fällen nicht auf die virtuelle Realität des Neuronavigationssystems verlassen, sondern bei bekannt hohem Shiftrisiko zusätzlich konventionelle Methoden, beispielsweise die intraoperative Sonographie, nutzen.

Abb. 1 Photographie des Bildschirms des Neuronavigationssystems EasyGuide Neuro (Philips, Best, the Netherlands) während der Übertragung des Sulkusreliefs eines Patienten auf die Kopfhaut mit einer virtuellen Pointer-Verlängerung von 15mm. Die Position der virtuell verlängerten Pointer-Spitze wird auf der sagittalen, coronaren und axialen Schnittebene im vorab aquirierten kernspintomographischen Bilddatensatz dargestellt. Hier: Fissura Sylvii. Die sagittalen und coronaren Schittbilder wurden aus dem Datansatz der axialen Schnittbilder rekonstruiert und sind daher in der Bildauflösung etwas reduziert.

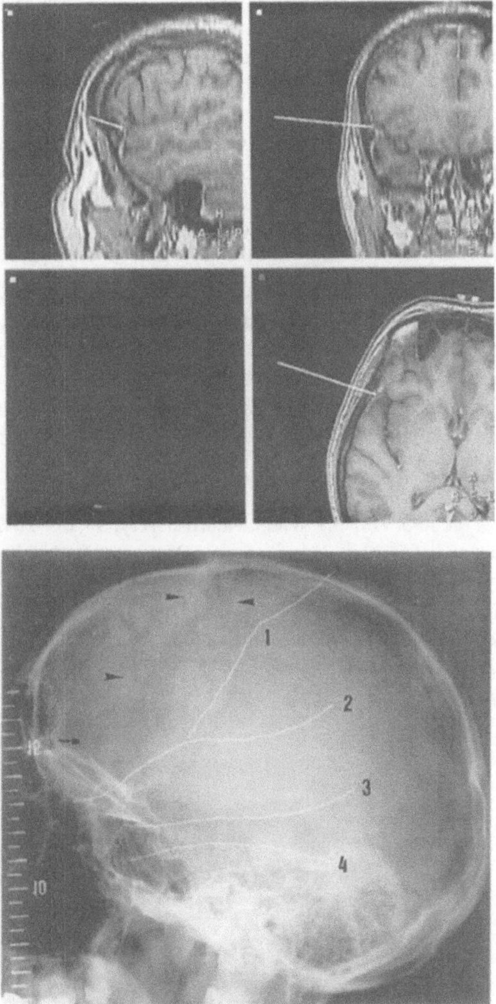

Abb. 2 Röntgenbild in lateralem Strahlengang bei einem 32-jährigen Patienten. Präoperativ wurden mit Hilfe des Neuronavigationssystems EasyGuide Neuro für 2 Datensätze mit unterschiedlicher Kopfposition der Sulcus centralis (1), die Fissura Sylvii (2) und die Sulci temporales superior (3) und inferior (4) röntgenpositiv auf die Kopfhaut übertragen. Abweichungen > 1,0mm fanden sich beim Vergleich der mit beiden Datensätzen erhaltenen Linien nicht. Pfeilspitzen: Coronarnaht.

6 Literatur

1. Buchholz R, Sturm C, Henderson J: Detection of Brain Shift with an Image Guided Ultrasound Device. Acta Neurochir (Wien), 138:627, 1996.
2. Golfinos JG, Fitzpatrick BC, Smith LR, Spetzler RF: Clinical use of a frameless stereotactic arm: results of 325 cases. J Neurosurg 83:197-205, 1995.
3. Hata N, Dohi T, Iseki H, Takakura K: Development of a Frameless and Armless Stereotactic Neuronavigation System with Ultrasonographic Registration. Neurosurgery, 41:608-614, 1997.
4. Kaus M, Steinmeier R, Sporer T, Ganslandt O, Fahlbusch R: Technical Accuracy of a Neuronavigation System Measured with a High-precision Mechanical Micromanipulator. Neurosurgery, 41:1431-1437, 1997.
5. Koivukangas J, Louhisalmi Y, Alakuijala J, Oikarinen J: Ultrasound-controlled neuronavigator-guided brain surgery. J Neurosurg, 79:36-42, 1993.
6. Laborde G, Gilsbach J, Harders A, Klimek L, Moesges R, Krybus W: Computer Assisted Localizer for Planning of Surgery and Intra-Operative Orientation. Acta Neurochir (Wien), 119:166-170, 1992.
7. Reinges MHT, Nguyen H, Spetzger U, Rohde V, Küker W, Thron A, Gilsbach JM: Significance of Pre- and Intraoperative Brain-Shift in Neuronavigation. In: Hütter B-O, Gilsbach J-M (Eds.): Neuropsychology in Neurosurgery, Psychiatry and Neurology. Verlag der Augustinus Buchhandlung, Aachen, pp. 154-155, 1997.
8. Reinges MHT, Krombach G, Nguyen H, Spetzger U, Küker W, Thron A, Gilsbach JM: Assessment of intraoperative brain tissue movements by frameless neuronavigation. Comp Aid Surg (Suppl.), 1997.
9. Sipos EP, Tebo SA, Zinreich SJ, Long DM, Brem H: In Vivo Accuracy Testing and Clinical Experience with the ISG Viewing Wand. Neurosurgery, 39:194-204, 1996.
10. Spetzger U, Laborde G, Gilsbach JM: Frameless Neuronavigation in Modern Neurosurgery. Minim Invas Neurosurg, 38:163-166, 1995.
11. Zinreich SJ, Tebo SA, Long DM, Brem H, Mattox DE, Loury ME, Vander Kolk CA, Koch WM, Kennedy DW, Bryan RN: Frameless Stereotaxic Integration of CT Imaging Data: Accuracy and Initial Applications. Radiology 188:735-742, 1993.

3D-Darstellung der inneren Struktur des Zellkerns - Rekonstruktion und Modelle zur Zellfunktion

A. Bischoff, R. Bracht, D. Komitowski

Abteilung Histodiagnostik, Deutsches Krebsforschungszentrum Heidelberg
Im Neuenheimer Feld 280, 69120 Heidelberg
e-mail: A.Bischoff@DKFZ-Heidelberg.de

Zusammenfassung. Molekularbiologische Methoden erlauben heute, durch Anfärbung von spezifischen DNS-Bereichen der Chromosomen, die inneren Struktur von Zellkernen durch eine dreidimensionale Rasterung mit dem Konfokalen-Fluoreszenz-Scanning-Mikroskop darzustellen. Zur quantitativen Untersuchungen der Morphologie der Zellkerne wird die Kernoberfläche mit Hilfe von Kugelflächenfunktionen modelliert, was zum einen zur Beschreibung der Form, zum anderen zur Definition eines kerneigenen Koordinatensystems führt. Zur Ermittlung der räumlichen Verteilung markierter DNS-Sequenzen, wie z.B. Kinetochoren, Centromere, Nukleoli u.a., wird die Pyramid-Linking-Segmentierung benutzt. Mit zwei Parametern, dem Abstand der segmentierten Region zum Zellkernrand bzw. zum Zellkernmittelpunkt, wird die Verteilung von Kinetochoren innerhalb des Zellkernes untersucht.

Schlüsselwörter: 3D-Visualisierung, Zellkernstruktur, Konfokale-Fluoreszenz-Scanning-Mikroskopie, Kugelflächenfunktionen, Pyramid-Linking-Segmentierung

1 Einleitung

Die moderne Forschung liefert Beweise dafür, daß die räumliche Organisation des Genoms Aufschlüsse über die Grundmechanismen der Tumorentstehung zuläßt. Ziel der vorliegenden Arbeit ist die 3D-Visualisierung und die Beschreibung der Verteilung definierter Zellkernstrukturen in Lymphozyten von Tumorpatienten, bei denen eine chromosomale Instabilität nachgewiesen wurde. Es werden hierbei nicht nur Chromosomen oder Teilbereiche von Chromosomen untersucht, sondern auch Kinetochoren, Centromere, Nukleoli und Genprodukte wie DNA-Polymerase oder Ki67-Proteine. Um tumorbedingte Abweichungen in der Genomorganisation zu erfassen, wurden Modellvorstellungen über die innere Struktur der Lymphozytenkerne bei gesunden Personen und Tumorpatienten zugrunde gelegt.

2 Material und Methode

Für die Untersuchungen werden unbehandelte Patienten mit urologischen Tumoren, vorwiegend Harnblasenkarzinome, herangezogen. Ein Patient, bei dem noch keine Krebskrankheit nachgewiesen ist, kann bereits Träger von chromosomalen- oder Genveränderungen sein, die eine neoplastische Transformation auslösen können. Auf diese Art und Weise wäre es möglich, Risikogruppen frühzeitig zu erkennen.

In Zusammenarbeit mit der Urologischen Universitätsklinik Heidelberg erhalten wir von den entsprechenden Patienten eine Blutprobe. Aus der Blutprobe werden die Lymphozyten isoliert und innerhalb des Zellkernes werden die Kinetochoren mit einem Antikörper, der speziell an die Centromere Proteine A, B und C (CENP-A, CENP-B, CENP-C) bindet, markiert. Im nächsten Schritt wird der Antikörper mit einem Sekundärantikörper, der mit dem Fluoreszensfarbstoff Flourescein-Iso-ThioCyanat (FITC) beladen ist, markiert. Der Zellkern wird mit Propidiumjodid (PI) gegengefärbt. Man erhält somit Zellkerne, die mit PI angefärbt sind und idealerweise innerhalb des Zellkerns 46 markierte Regionen, die die Kinetochoren repräsentieren.

Mit Hilfe eines Konfokalen-Fluoreszenz-Scanning-Mikroskops werden ca. 80 optische Schnitte durch den Zellkern gelegt. Die insgesamt ca. 10 MByte Daten pro Zellkern werden mit einer Workstation (SGI Indy) ausgewertet. Als Basis für die quantitative Untersuchungen und Beschreibung der Morphologie der Zellkerne dient die Modellierung der Kernoberfläche, die zum einen zur Beschreibung der Form führt, zum anderen zur Definition eines kerneigenen Koordinatensystems. Dieses Koordinatensystem erleichtert die Parametrisierung der räumlichen Verteilung markierter DNS-Sequenzen. In einem weiteren Schritt ist mit geeigneten Segmentierungsmethoden die räumliche Organisation von Kernkompartimenten, wie z.B. Kinetochoren zu bestimmen.

Eine Möglichkeit der Beschreibung der Zellkernform stellt das Ellipsoidmodell dar. In der Praxis erweist sich dieses Modell als wenig geeignet, da die Kerne der Tumorzellen sehr irregulär sind. Sie weisen Eindellungen oder Ausstülpungen auf und lassen sich mit Kugel- bzw. Ellipsoidmodellen nicht ausreichend beschreiben. Zur Beschreibung der Zellkernform wurden daher Kugelflächenfunktionen, die in der Physik als Lösungen der quantenmechanischen Gleichungen für rotationssymmetrische Systeme bekannt sind gewählt. Sie beschreiben beispielsweise die Form der Atomorbitale. Da ihr Funktionensystem vollständig ist, kann jede beliebige Form mit Hilfe einer Summe von Kugelflächenfunktionen Y_l^m dargestellt werden. Es ergibt sich eine Gleichung für die Oberflächenpunkte in Kugelkoordinaten r, t, p:

$$r = \sum_{l=0}^{L} \sum_{m=-l}^{l} a_{lm} Y_l^m(t, p)$$

die Vorfaktoren a der Funktion Y kennzeichnen die Form der Objekte. In ihnen manifestieren sich vorhandene Symmetrien des Objekts.

Diese Gleichung gilt im objekteigenen Koordinatensystem, dem sogenannten Eigensystem. Da die Objekte beliebig im Raum verschoben und gedreht erscheinen können, ist es erforderlich, das Eigensystem zu bestimmen. Die Transformation vom Koordinatensystem des Beobachters zum Eigensystem des Objekts wird allgemein beschrieben durch die Vektorgleichung:

$$\mathbf{X}' = A\mathbf{x} + \mathbf{v}$$

A = Matrix der Drehung, $\mathbf{v}$ = Verschiebungsvektor

Dieses Verfahren wird verwendet, um Zellkerne von beliebiger Form zu modellieren. Man erhält die Modellfunktion für die Oberfläche eines Zellkerns als eine Funktion $M(a_{lm}, r', \phi', \theta')$ mit den Entwicklungskoeffizienten a_{lm} der Funktionen $Y_l^m(\phi', \theta')$ in Kugelkoordinaten r', ϕ', θ' der Oberflächenpunkte, gültig im Eigensystem des Zellkerns. Zur Beschreibung eines Objekts, dessen Oberflächenpunkte bekannt sind, müssen die freien Parameter der Modellfunktion bestimmt werden. Es werden diejenigen Werte der Parameter berechnet, für die sich die minimale Abweichung der Modellfunktion von den gemessenen Daten ergibt, auch als Least-Squares-Ansatz bezeichnet.

$$\sum_O \left| D_O - M_O(a_i, A, \mathbf{v}) \right|^2 \longrightarrow Min$$

D bezeichnet die gemessenen Daten,
M die Modellfunktion in Abhängigkeit ihrer freien Parameter a, A, $\mathbf{v}$

Da die Modellfunktion nichtlinear von den Parametern A und $\mathbf{v}$ abhängt, kann die Lösung nur iterativ ausgehend von einer ersten Schätzung gewonnen werden.

Verwendet wird die Standardmethode nach Levenberg-Marquardt. Erste Schätzungen für die Verschiebung des Eigensystems ist der Objektschwerpunkt, während die Drehung des Eigensystems bezüglich des Koordinatensystems des Beobachters aus der Lage der Hauptträgheitsachsen des Objekts bestimmt wird.

Im nächsten Schritt wird das Datenmaterial des 2. Kanals durch entsprechende Segmentierungsverfahren ausgewertet. Zur Ermittlung der räumlichen Verteilung markierter DNS-Sequenzen, wie z.B. Kinetochoren, Centromere, Nukleoli oder Genprodukte, wie DNA-Polymerase oder Ki 67-Proteine, wurden verschiedene Segmentierungsverfahren wie Schwellwert-, Cluster- oder Pyramid-Linking-Segmentierung verwendet. Vergleiche zwischen punkt- und regionenorientierter Segmentierung ergab, daß die Pyramid-Linking-Segmentierung hierbei die besten Ergebnisse lieferte. Bei diesem Verfahren handelt es sich um ein regionenorientiertes Verfahren, bei der ein Pixel einem Objekt zugeordnet wird, unabhängig davon, was mit den Nachbarpixeln geschieht. Damit können, losgelöst vom eigentlichen Objekt, einzelne isolierte Punkte oder Regionen entstehen. Ein entscheidender Gesichtspunkt der Segmentierung ist jedoch, daß ein Objekt zusammenhängend sein muß.

Als Startpunkt für die Pyramid-Linking-Segmentierung dient die unterste Gauß-pyramide eines Bildes. Hierbei werden die Grauwerte der benachbarten Pixeln gemittelt und zu einem Bildpunkt auf der nächsthöheren Pyramidenebene zusam-mengefaßt. Dies entspricht einer Glättungsoperation mit einem Rechteckfilter. Da jeder Bildpunkt einen Beitrag zu mehreren Bildpunkten auf der nächst-höheren Ebene leistet, ist zu entscheiden, zu welchem er wahrscheinlich gehört. Die Entscheidung fällt durch Vergleich der Grauwerte und Wahl des am nächsten liegenden Bildpunktes. Dieses Verfahren wird für alle Ebenen der Pyramide durchgeführt. Die erhaltene Datenstruktur wird in der Informatik als Baum be-zeichnt. Diese ermittelte Baumstruktur ist der zentrale Punkt, um eine Verbind-ungsstruktur in der Pyramide zu schaffen mit dem Ziel, eindeutige Verbindungen zwischen den Bildpunkten der verschiedenen Ebenen herzustellen, sogenannte Vater-Sohn-Verbindungen. Dabei wird der Sohnknoten mit dem Vaterknoten verbunden, dessen Grauwert minimal abweicht. Dieses Vorgehen wird in folgen-den Schritten iterativ wiederholt, bis ein stabiles Ergebnis erreicht wurde:

1. Berechnung der Bildpyramide unter Berücksichtigung der in der vorigen Ite-ration geschaffenen Verbindungen.
2. Erstellung der Vater-Sohn-Verbindungen durch das Prinzip minimaler Grau-wertabweichung.
3. Abbruch der Iteration wenn das Ergebnis stabil bleibt, d.h. die Verbindungen der vorigen Iteration erhalten bleiben.

Nach Abschluß der Iteration entsteht eine sogenannte Baumstruktur, in der die Bildpunkte der verschiedenen Pyramidenebenen miteinander verknüpft sind. Ausgehend von der höchsten Ebene können nun die verschiedenen Bildregionen durch Propagation durch die Baumstruktur getrennt werden.
Für die Untersuchungen werden 2 Parameter berücksichtigt:

1. Abstand der segmentierten Region zum Zellkernrand, hier als Randstand bezeichnet.
2. Abstand der segmentierten Region zum Zellkernmittelpunkt, hier als radiale Distanz bezeichnet.

Zur Verifizierung der gefundenen Ergebnisse wurde der Kolmogorov-Smirnov-Anpassungstest verwendet, mit dessen Hilfe überprüft werden kann, ob gewisse Unterschiede zwischen zwei Verteilungsfunktionen signifigant sind oder nicht.

3 Ergebnisse

Erste Ergebnisse zeigen die Eignung des Verfahrens zur Klassifizierung von Zell-kernen und zur Charakterisierung der räumlichen Genomorganisation, beson-ders bei unregelmäßig geformten Zellkernen des Tumorgewebes. Es konnte mit Hilfe dieses Testes gezeigt werden daß es bei gesunden Personen innerhalb eines Signifikanzniveaus von +5% und -5% eine Gleichverteilung der Kinetochoren innnerhalb des Zellkernes gibt. Untersuchungen mit Patientenblut haben gezeigt, daß die Zellkerne sehr unterschiedlich geformt sind und die Gleichverteilung der Kinetochoren sehr stark schwankt. Um hier genauere Aussagen machen zu können, sind noch weitere Messungen notwendig.

Eine hierarchische Wasserscheidentransformation für die Spotdetektion in 2D Gelelektrophorese-Bildern

S. Wegner, A. Sahlström, K.-P. Pleißner, H. Oswald, E. Fleck

Deutsches Herzzentrum Berlin und
Virchow-Klinikum der Humboldt-Universität Berlin,
Augustenburger Platz 1, D-13353 Berlin, Germany

Zusammenfassung Eine hierarchische Wasserscheidentransformation (WST) zur Spotdetektion in 2D Gelelektrophorese-Bildern wird beschrieben. Die WST wird auf dem Gradientenbild durchgeführt und resultiert folglich in Regionen mit unterschiedlicher Krümmung. Da sich Spots durch eine konvexe Krümmung auszeichnen, können Spotregionen sofort im Ergebnis der WST lokalisiert werden. Weil jedoch Spots durch mehrere Regionen charakterisiert sein können, müssen diese Teilspotregionen noch zusammengefaßt werden.

1 EINLEITUNG

Ein wichtige Voraussetzung für molekularbiologische Untersuchungen auf Protein-ebene ist das Detektieren von Proteinspots in 2D Gelelektrophorese-Bildern. Da in diesen Gelbildern oftmals mehr als 1000 Spots gefunden werden müssen, sollte für ein effizientes und reproduzierbares Ergebnis eine automatische Bildanalyse durchgeführt werden. In der Literatur wird hierfür eine markerbasierte Wasserscheidentransformation (WST) beschrieben [3]. In diesem Verfahren wird aufgrund von a priori Wissen zuerst eine grobe Segmentierung durchgeführt, um sogenannte Marker zu bestimmen, auf denen dann die Anwendung der WST beruht. Im Gegensatz dazu verwenden wir eine hierarchische WST. Diese WST wird ohne vorherige Bestimmung von Markern angewandt und die entstandenen Regionen werden aufgrund bildbasierter Kriterien analysiert. Die WST wird direkt auf dem Gradientenbild durchgeführt, so daß Regionen mit konkaver und konvexer Krümmung voneinander getrennt werden. Da sich Proteinspots durch eine konvexe Krümmung auszeichnen, können nun Spotregionen sofort im Ergebnis der WST lokalisiert werden.

Zuerst beschreiben wird das Prinzip der WST. Die dabei entstehenden Spotregionen werden durch ein Preprocessing und eine Merkmalsanalyse lokalisiert. Durch diese beiden Schritte werden alle Spotregionen gefunden. Da jedoch Spots auch durch mehrere Regionen charakterisiert sein können, müssen diese Teilspotregionen noch zusammengefaßt werden.

2 SEGMENTIERUNG MIT DER WST

Um die WST als Segmentierungsverfahren anwenden zu können, wird das Gradientenbild als Grauwertgebirge interpretiert, indem jeder Gradientenwert als entsprechende Erhebung repräsentiert wird. Dabei wird angenommen, daß Regionen im Bild durch einen geringen Kontrast und folglich durch niedrige Gradienten, die Täler, charakterisiert werden; während hohe Gradienten, die Berggrate bzw. Wasserscheiden, auf starke, kontrastreiche Konturen im Grauwertbild zurückzuführen sind.

Für die Bestimmung von Wasserscheiden im Gradientenbild wird die topographische Oberfläche mit Wasser, das aus verschiedenen Quellen kommt, geflutet [1]. Beginnend mit den kleinsten regionalen Minima, füllen sich die Täler des Gradientengebirges mit Wasser und bilden Regionen. Wasserscheidendämme werden an solchen Stellen errichtet, an denen Regionen zusammenfließen würden. Am Ende dieses Flutungsprozesses begrenzen diese Wasserscheiden bzw. Konturen die einzelnen, jeweils durch ein Minimum entstandenen Regionen (Abb. 1).

Die WST ergibt ein Mosaikbild mit gut lokalisierten, geschlossenen Grenzen, das jedoch stark übersegmentiert ist, d.h. neben den relevanten Regionengrenzen werden auch Grenzen gefunden, die hauptsächlich auf Bildrauschen zurückzuführen sind. In diesem Ergebnis müssen nun die Regionen gefunden werden, die einem Spot entsprechen.

3 LOKALISIEREN VON SPOTREGIONEN

Im Mosaikbild wird aufgrund der starken Übersegmentierung nicht jeder Spot als eine einzelne Region erkannt. In vielen Fällen setzt sich ein Spot noch aus mehreren Teilregionen zusammen. Es müssen folglich zwei unterschiedliche Arten von Regionen lokalisiert werden (Abb. 2):
1. Die Region entspricht bereits dem vollständigen Spot.
2. Die Region beschreibt nur einen Teil des Spots.
Diese Spot- bzw. Teilspotregionen werden nun durch zwei Schritte bestimmt: einem Preprocessing und einer Merkmalsanalyse bzw. Krümmungsuntersuchung.

Im ersten Preprocessing-Schritt wird die Anzahl der möglichen Spotregionen durch einfache Schwellwertkriterien reduziert, indem a priori Wissen verwendet wird, daß es sich bei Spots um dunkle Flecken auf hellem Hintergrund handelt.

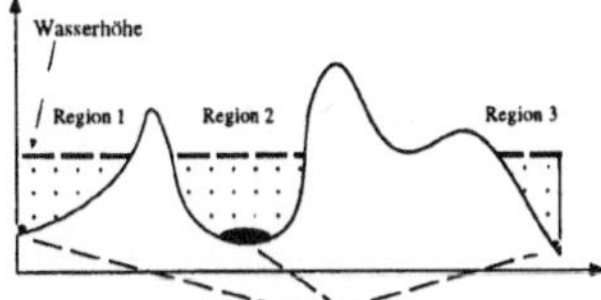

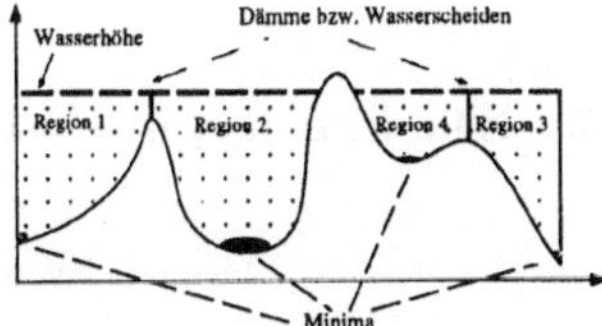

Abb. 1. Prinzip des Flutungsalgorithmus (1D).

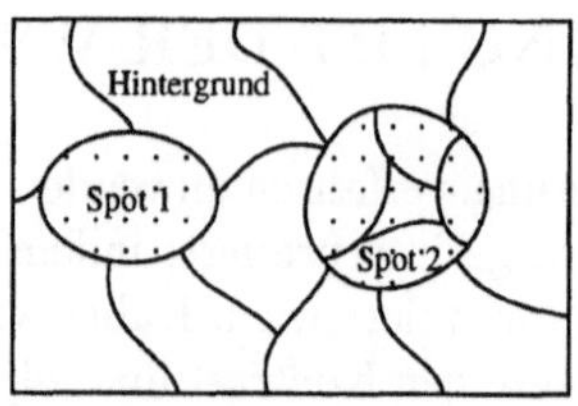

Abb. 2. Mosaikbild mit den zu lokalisierenden Spottypen. Spot 1 wird bereits durch eine Region separiert, Spot 2 besteht noch aus mehreren Regionen.

Jede Region wird im Mosaikbild zusätzlich durch ein Merkmal repräsentiert. Im folgenden wird als Merkmal der Mittelwert der Grauwerte der Region im Gelbild verwendet. Die verwendeten Schwellwerte werden in Abhängigkeit von den Grauwerten im aktuellen Gelbild bestimmt.

Das erste Kriterium basiert auf der Annahme, daß ein Spot durch signifikant höhere Grauwerte im Gelbild dargestellt wird. Jede mögliche Spot- bzw. Teilspotregion grenzt an eine Hintergrundregionen mit deutlich niedrigerem Grauwert. Folglich kann es sich nur dann um eine Spot- bzw. Teilspotregion handeln, wenn eine Nachbarregion mit wesentlich niedrigeren Grauwerten vorhanden ist. Für alle weitere Betrachtungen sei:

- N_r die Anzahl der Regionen im Mosaikbild
- r_i, i = 1, ..., N_r, die jeweilige Region
- $Neighbor_{r_i}$ die Nachbarregionen einer Region r_i
- μ_{r_i} der Mittelwert der Grauwerte einer Region r_i

Kriterium 1: Der Abstand $D(r_i)$ einer Region r_i, i = 1, ...,N_r, zu seinen Nachbarregionen wird gegeben durch :

$$D(r_i) = inf\left\{d_{ij} = \mu_{r_i} - \mu_{r_j} : \forall j \in Neighbor_{r_i}\right\} \qquad \forall i = 1, ..., N_r \qquad (1)$$

Eine mögliche Spot- bzw. Teilspotregion ist eine Region r_i, wenn

$$D(r_i) > T_1, \tag{2}$$

wobei der Schwellwert T_1 aufgrund von 20% aller Grauwerte im Gelbild bestimmt wird.

Die oben gemachte Annahme ist jedoch nicht für alle Teilspotregionen erfüllt. Hierbei handelt es sich oftmals um Teilspots, die sich in der Mitte eines Spots befinden (siehe die mittlere Region von Spot 2 in Abb. 2). Der mittlere Grauwert solcher Regionen ist jedoch immer sehr hoch. Hieraus ergibt sich das zweite Kriterium.

Kriterium 2: Eine Region r_i ist ein Kandidat für eine Spot- bzw. Teilspotregion, wenn

$$\mu_{r_i} > T_2, \tag{3}$$

wobei T_2 sich durch 80% aller auftretenden Grauwerte im Gelbild ergibt.

Obwohl durch die obigen Kriterien die Anzahl der möglichen Spotregionen erheblich reduziert wird, sind diese nicht spezifisch genug, um nur Spotkandidaten zu finden. Im zweiten Schritt wird nun als ein signifikantes Spotmerkmal die Krümmung einer Region bestimmt.

Wird ein Gelbild als topographische Oberfläche betrachtet, zeichnen sich Spots durch eine konvexe Krümmung aus. Diese Eigenschaft gilt ebenfalls für Teilspotregionen. Da die WST auf der ersten Ableitung ausgeführt wird, werden bereits Regionen mit konvexer und konkaver Krümmung separiert.

Krümmungskriterium: Die Krümmung einer Region r_i, i=1,..., N_r, wird beschrieben durch:

$$C_{r_i} = \sum_{j=1}^{N_{r_i}} f''(p_{ij}), \qquad (4)$$

wobei p_{ij}, j $= 1, ...,N_{r_i}$ die Pixel einer Region r_i sind und f'' die zweite Ableitung des Bildes ist. Eine mögliche Spotregion bzw. Teilspotregion ist eine Region r_i, wenn

$$C_{r_i} > 0. \qquad (5)$$

Es verbleiben nur solche Regionen, die einem Spot oder einem Teilspot entsprechen. Nur diese Teilspotregionen müssen noch zusammengefaßt werden.

4 ZUSAMMENFASSEN VON TEILSPOTREGIONEN

Das Zusammenfassen von Teilspotregionen basiert auf zwei Eigenschaften von Spots:

    1) Ein Spot sollte ungefähr eine elliptische Form haben.

    2) Grenzen zwei Spots aneinander, ist die lokale Krümmung entlang ihrer Grenze konkav.

Da jede dieser beiden Eigenschaften nicht für alle Regionen hinreichend genug bestimmt werden kann, wird hier die Kombination beider Kriterien betrachtet.

Um die Ähnlichkeit einer Region zu einer Ellipse beurteilen zu können, wird eine Ellipse anhand des umschreibenden Rechtecks der Region konstruiert. Dann wird mit dem χ^2-Test beurteilt, inwieweit die Region der konstruierten Ellipse ähnelt. Eine Region sollte mit einer Nachbarregion zusammengefaßt werden, wenn die Ähnlichkeit der einzelnen Regionen zu einer Ellipse kleiner ist als die Ähnlichkeit der zusammengefaßten Region zu einer Ellipse.

Für die Bestimmung der lokalen Krümmung zwischen zwei Regionen wird entlang der Wasserscheidenlinie zwischen diesen Regionen die zweite Ableitung bestimmt. Die Richtung ergibt sich hierbei aufgrund einer Linie, die zwischen den Schwerpunkten der Regionen bestimmt wird. Teilspotregionen eines Spots zeichnen sich durch eine lokale positive Krümmung um die Wasserscheidenlinie aus. Ist die lokale Krümmung entlang der Wasserscheidenlinie hingegen konkav, handelt es sich um zwei getrennte Spots, die folglich nicht zusammengefaßt werden sollten.

Abb. 3. Ergebnis der Spotdetektion.

5 ERGEBNISSE UND DISKUSSION

Die Spotdetektion mit der WST wurde anhand von mehreren Gelbildern für Herzproteine getestet. Nach der Anwendung der WST ist das Ergebnis zunächst sehr stark übersegmentiert, so daß sehr viele Spots durch mehrere Teilregionen beschrieben werden. Diese müssen entsprechend zusammengefaßt werden. Ein Ergebnis einer Spotdetektion zeigt Abb. 3. In den getesteten Gelbildern wird der überwiegende Teil der Spots gefunden. Zu Problemen kann es jedoch bei gesättigten Spots oder aufgrund von Bildstörungen durch Streifen kommen. Der Vergleich mit der Spotdetektion eines Gelanalysesystems (PDQUEST [2]) zeigte, daß mit dem hier vorgestellten Verfahren wesentlich mehr Spots gefunden werden konnten. Besonders deutlich waren die Unterschiede in Gelbildern mit geringem Grauwertumfang zu sehen, bei denen das PDQUEST-System nur sehr wenige Spots separieren konnte. Ein weiterer Vorteil des beschriebenen Verfahrens ist, daß auch überlappende Spot, die vielfach auftreten, gefunden und voneinander getrennt werden können.

References

1. L. Vincent, P. Soille : Watersheds in Digital Spaces: An Efficient Algorithm Based on Immersion Simulation. IEEE Transactions on Pattern Analysis and Machine Intelligence, Vol.13, No.6, (1991) 583–598
2. P.J. Collins, S.H. Blose: Todays densitometer- Multi-application densitometry for biotechnology. Biotech Forum Europe, International Journal Biotechnology, Vol.9 (1992) 202-205
3. F. Meyer, S. Beucher: Morphological Segmentation. Journal of Visual Communication and Image Representation, Vol. 1, No. 1, (1990) 21-46

Elastic registration of medical images using finite element meshes

Hartwig Grabowski

Institute of Real-Time Computer Systems & Robotics, University of Karlsruhe,
D-76128 Karlsruhe, Germany.
Email: grabow@ira.uka.de

Summary. In this paper a new method for elastic registration of medical images is presented. The method uses corresponding regions of gray values, which are segmented interactively. The deformation part is based on finite element meshes generated from the segmented regions. During the deformation process, the similarity between the deformed mesh and the target image is measured and the 'intensity' of the deformation is controlled.

Keywords: Mesh generation, deformable model, elastic matching

1 Introduction

The registration of volumetric medical images obtained from different imaging devices, e.g. from CT and MRT, is an important task for neurosurgery and radiotherapy. In order to achieve better accuracy, the registration has to be a non-rigid one, because MR images can be geometrically distorted up to 5 mm [1].

Strongly related with the problem of distortion is the so called atlas-matching problem, where the patient data set has to be registered with an electronic atlas. Again, non-rigid registration is necessary to individualize the electronic atlas and to obtain sufficient accuracy.

2 Principle approach

Therefore, we developed a new method for deforming medical images, which is based on finite element meshes. For simplicity, we assume that one image remains rigid, while the other image has to be warped toward the rigid one. In the following context, the rigid image will be defined as $R(x)$ and the image that will be deformed as $T(x)$. Our approach can be divided into the following four parts:

1. Both images are divided into N corresponding regions. As a result, we obtain a set of regions R_i and T_i ($i = 1..N$) which represent three-dimensional domains. Since R_i and T_i are corresponding domains, our goal is to deform T_i, so that it becomes R_i.

2. For performing the deformation, the regions T_i are transformed into a finite element mesh, which serves as a deformable model.

3. The generated model is warped towards the rigid image $R(x)$. In the first warping step, high similarity is achieved. In the second relaxation step, the 'strength' of the deformation is reduced. Warping and relaxation steps are performed several times to obtain high similarity with low 'amount' of deformation.

4. The deformed model is transformed into a volumetric image by resampling the generated mesh. To avoid aliasing an oversampling is performed.

3 Segmentation of corresponding regions

For finding corresponding segments, region growing is a useful approach. The image can be segmented by placing a 'seed' point within the interior of a homogeneous region and 'growing' out to the grayscale-bounded and connected border of that region. It should be noticed that the segmented regions do not have to represent anatomic structures. It must only be guaranteed, that the segmented regions R_i and T_i are corresponding in a certain way.

If the two images $R(x)$ and $T(x)$ are of the same modality, defining corresponding regions is easy, cause the thresholds of the gray values of two corresponding regions are the same in both images. Figure 1 illustrates the result of the seed-point segmentation. The images show one slice of a series of MR-scans of a patient lying in two different positions (right, left). The cross-hair indicates the position of a seed-point. The colored areas show the two segmented regions. Corresponding regions have been segmented with the same thresholds and seed-points. Obviously, they do not represent any existing anatomic structure.

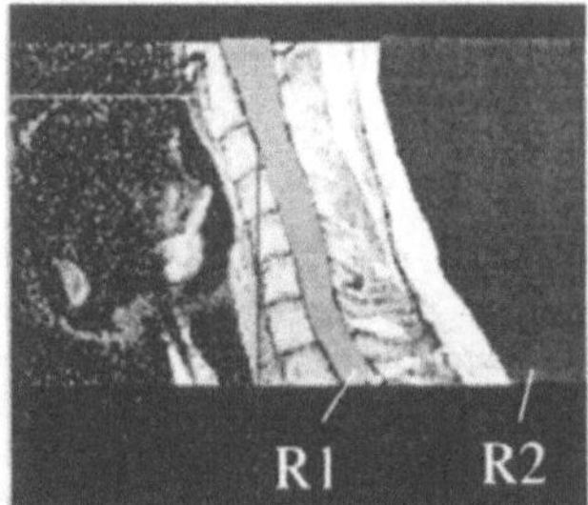

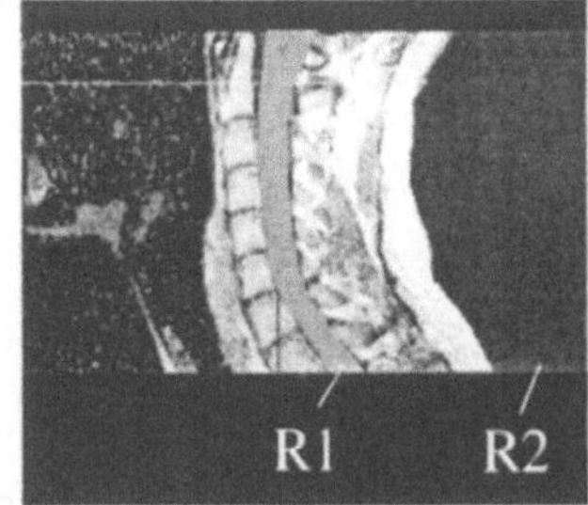

Fig. 1: Two MR images of the same patient lying in different positions.

4 Generating deformable models

1. Since the volumetric image is divided into different homogenous regions, each of this regions will be replaced by a finite element mesh consisting of tetrahedral elements. For mesh generation [2], a set of points lying on the surface of the regions is created, which is then triangulated with by the Delaunay triangulation. With a classification step, the obtained tetrahedras a classified corre-

sponding to the segmented regions. Figure 2, left, presents the obtained set of points from the regions of shown in Figure 1. Figure 2, middle, presents reduced set of contour points and Figure 2, right, shows the obtained classified sets of tetrahedras.

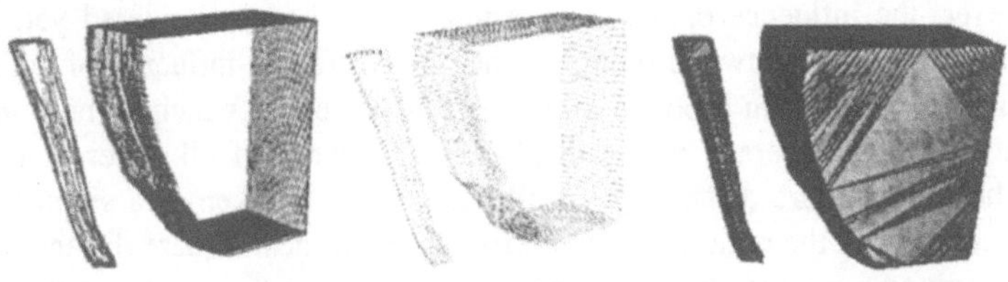

Fig. 2: The generated set of points (left) is reduced (middle) and triangulated (right).

5 Deforming meshes

With the mesh generation, the voxel based representation of the template image $T(x)$ is transformed into a tetrahedral based representation. This tetrahedral based representation is now deformed towards the rigid image $R(x)$. Therefore, the nodes n_i of the mesh have to be moved towards a specified direction. For simplicity, we assume that both images $T(x)$ and $R(x)$ are globally aligned and equally scaled.

Since R_i and T_i are corresponding regions and each node of the mesh lies on the surface of a region T_i, its new position has to be somewhere on the surface S_i of the region R_i. Additionally, we assume that taking the shortest line between the actual position of a node and its target surface is an intelligent guess for determining the displacement vector of a node. But calculating the shortest line between each node and its target surface is very time consuming. Therefore, we use the concept of the distance transformation [3], which serves as a potential field. Each node is attracted by the potential field D_i of its target surface S_i. Figure 3 presents the distance maps of the two segmented regions R_1 and R_2.

Fig.3: The distance map of the segmented regions R_1 (left) and R_2 (right).

5.1 Forward warping

After the surface S_i and its distance transformation $D_i(x)$ have been calculated for each region R_i, the iterative deformation process can be carried out: For each node n, its position $p(n)$ in the distance map is determined. Since the negative gradient $g_i(n) = -$ grad $D_i (p(n))$ represents a vector with a direction towards the surface S_i, this direction is a good estimation for the direction of the displacement vector. The length of the vector can be estimated directly form the distance map, since an entry $d_i(n)$ in the map represents the length of the shortest line between its position and the surface.

However, the influence of only one region R_i has been considered yet, but normally one node is part of two or more regions. Therefore, the influence of the different regions has to be taken in account. Since there is no region which is more important than the others, the average of the displacement vectors of all different regions is taken. The mean square distance m_i of all nodes in D_i is taken as a similarity measurement concerning the region R_i. The maximum of all mean square distances over all different regions $a = max(\ m_i\ )$ is the criterion for aborting the iteration process.

5.2 Relaxation

Even if matches with high accuracy can be obtained with the straight forward warping approach, the question for measuring the 'mass' of deformation still remains open. To measure a deformation, we have to introduce some methods of the theory of elastic deformations.

As the displacement at each point x inside a tetrahedra T is know through the displacement vectors of the nodes (we assume a linear form function), we are now able to evaluate the distortion tensor $v_{ij}(x)$ inside T. Cause geometric interpretation of $v_{ij}(x)$ is very complex, it is helpful to determine the eigenvectors a_i and eigenvalues e_i of v_{ij} which are called principal axes a_i and principal extensions e_i of the medium T at x. With the help of the principal extensions, we determine the relative change k_i of length along the principal axes a_i ($k_i = sqrt(1+2e_i)$).

With the help of the values k_i , we are able to derive a measurement for the 'mass' of a deformation: The quantity q of the deformation is minimal if no deformation occurred $(k_i = 1)$ and the quantity increases the more k_i differs from one. Therefore, a rough estimation of the quantity of the deformation of a tetrahedra can obtained with $q_T = $ abs$(\ 1 - 1/k_i\ )$: The lowest quantity is $q_T = 0$ and the highrt the quantity the bigger becomes q_T. Then the 'mass' q_m of the total deformation can be estimated by sum of the quantity values of each tetrahedra.

In order to reduce the 'mass' of the deformation, we now expand the compressed tetrahedras and compress the expanded. Therefore, we determine the three vectors rv_i with the direction equal to that of the three principal axis a_i. If the tetrahedra is compressed $(k_i < 1)$, the vector points away from the center of gravity g_T of the tetrahedra, otherwise it points towards g_T. Then, the nodes of the tetrahedra are moved into the direction of the vectors rv_i and the deformation of the tetrahedra is reduced.

This 'relaxation displacement vector' is calculated for each node of a tetrahedra. Since one node shares multiple tetrahedras the resultant displacement vector $d(n)$ of node n is obtained by averaging over the displacement vectors $d_T(n)$ of all tetrahedras T of the mesh which belong to node n.

6 Resampling of volumetric images

After the mesh M has been deformed, a deformed volumetric image $T'(x)$ has to be generated. First, the size of the target image T' has to be defined. In order to avoid undersampling in regions of compression, the resolution of the target image T' should be higher than the one of the original image T. However, if the compression is too large, two or more gray values have to be stored in one single voxel. Then the average gray value of them is taken. At regions of decompression, a tri-linear interpolation of the original gray-values can be used to obtain smooth results. Figure 3 shows the re-sampled image $T'(x)$ (left) and the target image $R(x)$ (right).

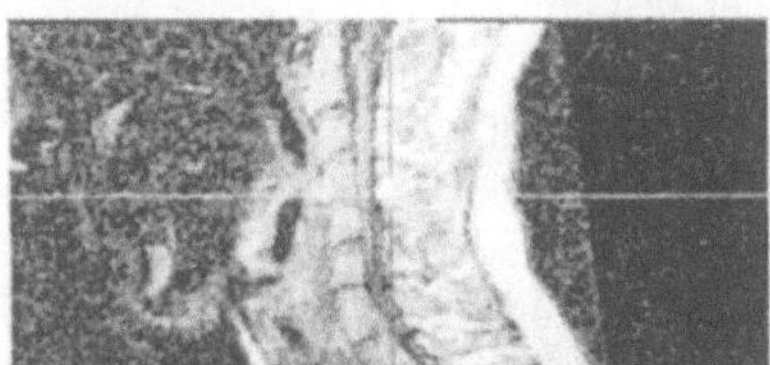 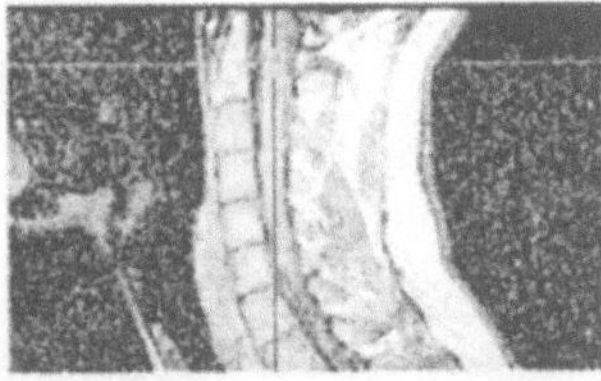

Fig. 3: The deformed image $T'(x)$ (left) and its target image $R(x)$ (right).

7 Summary

We presented a method of deforming volumetric images based on finite element meshes. Two main procedures have been introduced: the warping step and the relaxation step. With alternating use of these two steps, an elastic matching of two images can be obtained. The use of meshes relieves the problem of finding corresponding structures, since corresponding regions can be segmented with less interaction.

8 Acknowledgment

This research was performed at the Institute of Real-Time Computer Systems and Robotics, Prof. Dr.-Ing. U. Rembold, Prof. Dr.-Ing. H. Wörn, Prof. Dr.-Ing. R. Dillmann, Faculty of Computer Science, University of Karlsruhe, Germany. The work is being funded by the 'Sonderforschungsbereich Informationstechnik in der Medizin - Rechner- und sensorgestütze Chirurgie' of the Deutsche Forschungsgemeinschaft.

9 References

1. C. R. Maurer, G. B. Aboutanos, B. M. Dawant, S. Gadamsetty, R. A. Margolin, R. J. Maciunas, J. M. Fitzpatrick. Effect on Geometrical Distorsion Correction in MR on Image Registration Accuracy. Jounral of Computer Assisted Tomography, 20(4):666-679, 1996
2. H. Grabowski, C. Burghart, Generating finite element meshes from Volumetric Medical Images, Proceedings of the IARP 2nd Workshop on Medical Robotics, Heidelberg, Germany, 1997
3. Per-Erik Danielsson. Euclidean Distance Mapping. Computer Graphics and image processing 14, pp. 227-248, 1980

Einsatz von steuerbaren Filtern zur modellbasierten Segmentation von Fundusphotographien

B. Kochner[1], D. Schuhmann[1], M. Michaelis[1], M. Obermaier[2],
T. Bek[3], G. Mann[1], K.-H. Englmeier[1]

[1]GSF-Institut für Medizinische Informatik und Systemforschung,
85764 Neuherberg
Email: kochner@gsf.de
[2]Augenklinik rechts der Isar, 81675 München
[3]Aarhus University Hospital, DK-8000 Aarhus C

Zusammenfassung. Bildverarbeitungsmethoden zur automatischen Analyse von Fundusphotographien hinsichtlich der Entdeckung und Quantifizierung von diabetischer Retinopathie werden entwickelt. Die zentrale Aufgabe dieser Methoden ist die Segmentation der Papille und des Gefäßbaumes. Dadurch sollen einerseits pathologische Veränderungen am Verlauf und der Kontur von Gefäßästen erkannt und andererseits Läsionen auf dem restlichen Augenhintergrund durch einfache Bildverarbeitungsverfahren lokalisiert werden. Die Segmentation der Papille erfolgt durch ein hierarchisches Filterschema unter Berücksichtigung ihrer Lage und Form. Die Gefäße werden durch ein dreistufiges Verfahren extrahiert: 1) Tracken des Gefäßverlaufes, 2) Ermittlung der Gefäßkontur und 3) Identifikation von Gefäßverzweigungen. Alle Verfahren basieren auf steuerbaren Filtern.

Schlüsselwörter: Steuerbare Filter, Fundusphotographie, Gefäßsegmentation, Diabetische Retinopathie

1 Einleitung

Diabetische Retinopathie (DR) repräsentiert die führende Ursache für Erblindung in der westlichen Welt. Gefäßveränderungen, wie Mikroaneurysmen, perlschnurartige Veränderungen der Venen und Neovaskularisationen, zusammen mit Läsionen, wie Hämorrhagien und Exsudaten, sind Symptome dieser Erkrankung. In der klinischen Routine erfolgt die Beurteilung der krankhaften Veränderungen qualitativ durch direkte Untersuchung (Ophthalmoskopie) oder semiquantitativ durch Analyse photographischer Aufnahmen des Fundus (Fundusphotographien).

Das Ziel der im Rahmen des EU-geförderten OPHTEL-Projektes zu entwickelnden Bildverarbeitungsmethoden [1] ist die Quantifizierung der qualitativen Daten. Die Ergebnisse können durch einen wissensbasierten Monitor [2] ausgewertet und im Zusammenhang mit anderen Informationen, z.B. Patientendaten, interpretiert werden, um die Kontrolle von Diabetespatienten hinsichtlich der Entwicklung und des Verlaufs von diabetischer Retinopathie zu verbessern.

Zur computergestützten Bearbeitung von Fundusaufnahmen und insbesondere zur Segmentation [3, 4] und Analyse der retinalen Gefäße wurden unterschiedliche Methoden entwickelt. Jedem automatischen Bildverarbeitungsverfahren stellt sich das Problem der Farbunterschiede innerhalb eines Bildes durch die inhomogene Beleuchtung des Augenhintergrundes und der Farbunterschiede zwischen verschiedenen Bildern. Außerdem ist die Bildqualität, wie Kontrast und Helligkeit, nicht standardisiert.

Beste Segmentationsergebnisse werden beim Einsatz von kontinuierlich skalierten und orientierten gaussförmigen Filtermasken erwartet. Der Einsatz eines solch flexiblen Filterschemas ermöglicht detaillierte Beschreibungen der Bildinhalte, muß jedoch sorgfältig implementiert werden, da der Rechenaufwand mit der Zahl variierender Parameter dramatisch ansteigt. Im folgenden wird ein modellbasierter Ansatz zur Segmentation der Papille, des Gefäßbaumes und der Exsudate in Fundusphotographien präsentiert, der auf steuerbaren Filtern [5] basiert.

2 Material und Methoden

2.1 Bildmaterial

Die vorliegenden Fundusphotographien (41) wurden folgendermaßen klassifiziert: keine DR (1), milde nicht-proliferative DR (22), moderate nicht-proliferative DR (11), pre-proliferative DR (5), proliferative DR (2). Die Aufnahmen wurden durch eine 60° Funduskamera erfaßt und in 24 Bit Bilder (RGB) digitalisiert. Die Auflösung beträgt ca. 600 x 500 Pixel. Da sowohl die retinalen Gefäße als auch die Papille und die relevanten pathologischen Veränderungen (Exsudate) im grünen Farbkanal am besten repräsentiert sind, wird dieser im folgenden wie ein Grauwertbild behandelt.

2.2 Steuerbare Filter

Um detaillierte Informationen über die Bildinhalte zu erhalten, werden gaussförmige Filterkerne verwendet, die in der Skalierung (σ), der Aspect-Ratio (ϵ) und der Orientierung (ψ) variiert werden. Die Filterantworten der Gausskerne 1. Ordnung werden als $F_1(x, \sigma, \epsilon, \psi)$ und die der Gausskerne 2. Ordnung als $F_2(x, \sigma, \epsilon, \psi)$ bezeichnet. Um dieses flexible Filterschema effizient zu implementieren, wird die Methode der steuerbaren Filter verwendet [5]: Mit Hilfe von Linearkombinationen der Basisfunktionen A_m werden die kontinuierlichen Filterantworten $F_\alpha(x)$ in der Form

$$\hat{F}_\alpha(x) = \sum b_m(\alpha) A_m(x) \tag{1}$$

approximiert, d.h. das Bild wird nur mit den A_m gefiltert. α bezeichnet den Steuerparameter (z.B. σ) und $b_m(\alpha)$ die Koeffizienten der Interpolationsfunktion.

2.3 Algorithmen

Papille Die Papille ist eine kreisförmige Struktur, die durch hohe Grauwerte charakerisiert ist. Die Hauptgefäßäste treten durch die Papille ins Auge und verlaufen dann auf einem ellipsenförmigen Weg. Gaussfilter 1. Ordnung in verschiedenen Orientierungen und Schwellwertverfahren werden dazu verwendet, die Kanten der Hauptgefäßäste zu extrahieren. Aus diesen Punkten wird mit Hilfe einer Hough-Transformation eine Ellipse berechnet. Die erwartete Position der Papille liegt auf einem der beiden Ellipsenbögen. Ein hierarchisches Filterschema basierend auf steuerbaren Filtern 1. Ordnung wird dazu verwendet, die exakte Lage und Größe der Papille zu ermitteln: Im ersten Schritt werden die Filterantworten an diskreten Punkten um jeden erwarteten Papillenmittelpunkt ausgewertet, um nicht in Frage kommende Punkte sofort auszuschließen. Im zweiten Schritt werden die Filterantworten auf gesamten Kreisen um jeden noch möglichen Papillenmittelpunkt analysiert: Der Mittelpunkt und Radius des Kreises mit dem maximalen Gradienten identifiziert die Papille.

Gefäße Die retinalen Gefäße sind linienförmige Strukturen, deren Profil durch eine Gausskurve approximiert werden kann. Um Durchmesser- und Richtungsdaten der einzelnen Gefäßsegmente zu erhalten, wird ein Tracking durchgeführt (Abb. 1). Im i. Schritt, beginnend beim Gefäßpunkt x_i wird der Punkt x_{i+1} in einem Abstand λ gesucht. ϕ_i bezeichnet die aktuelle Gefäßrichtung und r_i den aktuellen Gefäßradius. $\check{x}_{i+1} = x_i + X(\lambda, \check{\phi}_i)$ ist ein Vorschlag für den nächsten Gefäßpunkt, wobei $\check{\phi}_i = \phi_i + \theta, \theta \in [\pm\alpha/2]$. An den Punkten $\check{x}_{i+1}$ wird die maximale Antwort der rotierten und skalierten Linienfilter

$$\rho_2(\check{x}_{i+1}) = \max_{\sigma,\psi}\{F_2(\check{x}_{i+1}, \sigma, \psi)\} \tag{2}$$

bestimmt, wobei $\psi = \check{\phi}_i + \theta, \theta \in [\pm\beta/2]$. $\check{x}_{i+1}^{max}$ bezeichnet die Positionen der maximalen Linienfilterantworten, die eine vordefinierte Grenze überschreiten.

Zusätzlich zu den Filterantworten muß die Grauwertinformation untersucht werden, um über den nächsten Gefäßpunkt $x_{i+1} = x_{i+1}^{max}$ entscheiden zu können. Dies kann auf zwei Arten erfolgen: Das *local threshold tracking* verwendet die Grauwertinformation des bereits getrackten Gefäßes, indem es prüft, wie weit der Grauwert des nächsten Gefäßpunktes von denen der vorigen Punkte abweicht. Das *greyvalue minimum tracking* sucht zusätzlich noch nach den Grauwertminima, um den nächsten Gefäßpunkt zu identifizieren.

Die Gefäßkontur wird folgendermaßen ermittelt: Beginnend beim Mittelpunkt x_i werden die Punkte $\check{x}_{i+1,l} = x_i + X(\lambda, \phi_{i,l})$ auf der linken Scanlinie mit $\phi_{i,l} = \phi_i + \pi/2$ (rechte Seite analog) vertikal zu der aktuellen Ausbreitungsrichtung ϕ_i analysiert ($\lambda = 1, \ldots, \lambda_{max}$). Die angewendeten Kantenfilterkerne sind in der Richtung $\psi = \phi_i + \theta, \theta \in [\pm\gamma/2]$ orientiert, d.h. sie variieren parallel zur Mittellinie. Der linke Konturpunkt wird berechnet, indem nach der maximalen Filterantwort

$$x_{i+1,l}^{max} = \max_{\psi,\lambda}\{\rho_1(\check{x}_{i+1,l})\} \tag{3}$$

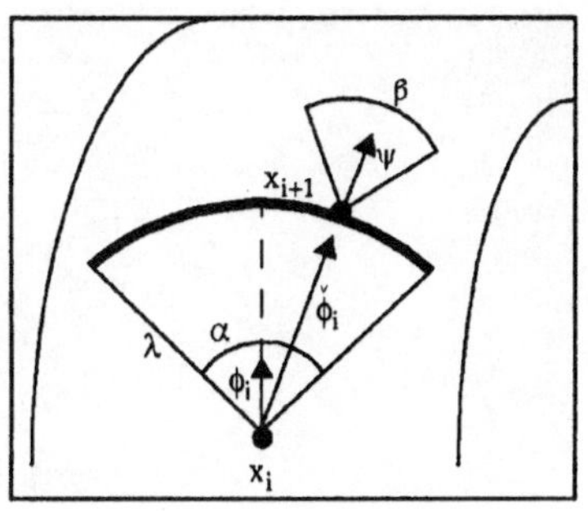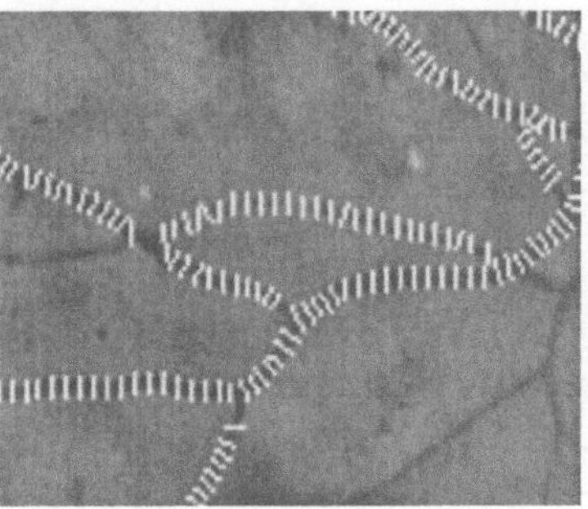

Abb. 1. (a) Tracking-Verfahren; (b) Segmentierte Gefäße

auf der linken Seite gesucht wird.

Abzweigende Gefäße werden anhand der bereits erläuterten local threshold oder greyvalue minimum Regeln bestimmt. Dafür werden Linienfilterkerne, die nahezu orthogonal zur Gefäßrichtung ausgerichtet sind, in einer Distanz λ links und rechts des Gefäßes eingesetzt.

Exsudate Nachdem die Papillenregion und die extrahierten Gefäße auf dem Fundusbild ausgeblendet sind, kann der Rest der Retina im Hinblick auf andere Läsionen untersucht werden. Exsudate zeichnen sich durch hohe Grauwerte und relativ scharfe Kanten zur Umgebung aus. Für ihre Segmentation wird zunächst eine Histogrammanalyse durchgeführt, wobei ein Schwellwert ermittelt wird, der die 5% höchsten Grauwerte im Grünkanal extrahiert. Dieser Schwellwert wird so angewendet, daß er vom Bildzentrum zur Peripherie exponentiell ansteigt. Liegt die Anzahl der markierten Pixel unter einer vordefinierten Grenze, wird das Verfahren mit einem niedrigen Zentralschwellwert wiederholt. An jedem markierten Pixel selbst und in der Umgebung wird die Kanteninformation analysiert. Als Exsudate klassifizierte Pixel müssen eine Mindestanzahl an Pixeln mit ausreichender Filterantwort in der Umgebung vorweisen.

3 Ergebnis und Diskussion

In Abb. 2 ist ein Ergebnis der Papillen-, Gefäß- und Exsudatextraktion abgebildet. Durch die Verwendung von Modellwissen über die Lage, die Form und die Grauwerte der Papille ist ihre Segmentation robust gegen auf der einen Seite Läsionen im Bild und auf der anderen Seite Variationen in den Papilleneigenschaften. Anfangspunkte der Gefäße werden automatisch an der Papille detektiert.

Für das Tracking der Gefäße werden die Filterantworten kontinuierlich skalierter und rotierter Gausskerne 2. Ordnung richtungsorientiert ausgewertet. Zusätzlich wird die Grauwertinformation in der lokalen Umgebung berücksichtigt. Das *greyvalue minimum* Tracking liefert in der Regel die besseren Ergeb-

148

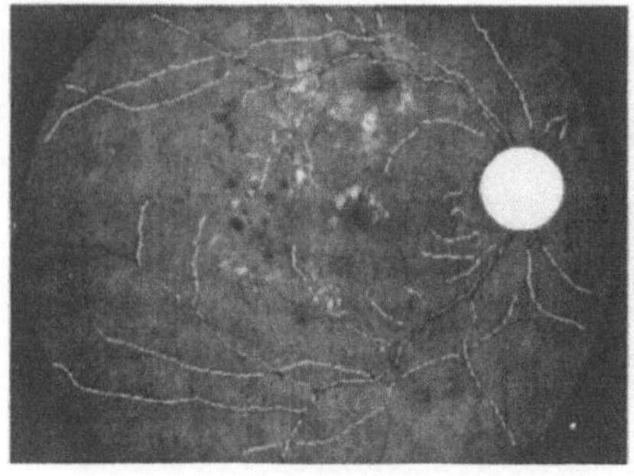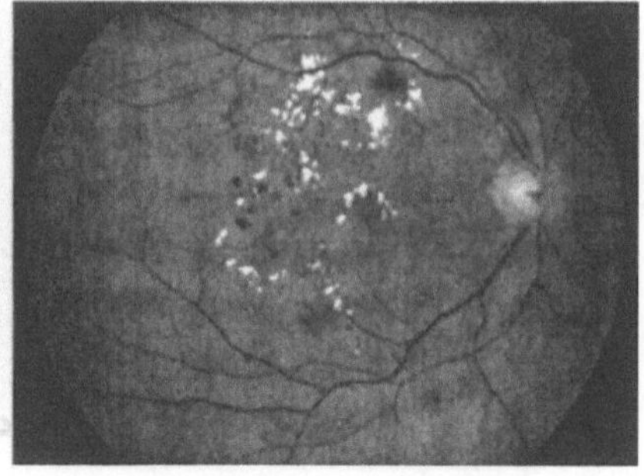

Abb. 2. Segmentationsergebnis (a) Gefäßbaum; (b) Exsudate

nisse, insbesondere wenn die Fundusaufnahme pathologische Veränderungen aufweist, da die Gefäßmittellinie durch die zusätzliche Suche nach dem Grauwertminimum präziser verfolgt wird. Segmentationsfehler können jedoch auftreten, wenn der Gefäßkontrast zu niedrig, das Gefäß zu schmal ist oder wenn große Läsionen das Gefäß überlagern. Einige dieser Probleme können dadurch gemindert werden, daß die Suche nach dem nächsten Gefäßpunkt in einem vergrößerten Abstand λ wiederholt wird. Die Bestimmung der Gefäßbreite erfolgt durch die Auswertung der Antworten der kontinuierlich rotierten Gaussfilter 1. Ordnung auf beiden Seiten der Gefäßmittellinie. Dies kann aus denselben Gründen, wie beim Tracking bereits aufgeführt, problematisch sein. Außerdem ist eine ausreichende Auflösung des Bildes und die korrekte Feststellung der Gefäßrichtung eine Grundvoraussetzung für diesen Schritt.

Nach dem Ausblenden der Papillenregion und der segmentierten Gefäße kann der restliche Augenhintergrund hinsichtlich anderer pathologischer Veränderungen untersucht werden. Die extrahierten Läsionen werden durch Parameter, wie Abstand zur Papille oder Fläche, quantifiziert.

Literatur

1. Kochner B, et al: An Image Processing System for Analysing Color Fundus Photographs with Regard to Diabetic Retinopathy. Klin. Monatsblätter für Augenheilkunde, 211(Suppl. 5):11, 1997.
2. Wegner A, et al: Knowledge-Based Monitoring of Glaucoma and Diabetic Retinopathy by Means of Fuzzy Rules, Neural Nets and Image Processing Methods. Proc. of the Int. Congress on Computer Integrated Surgery, P03-069, 1997.
3. Chaudhuri S, Chatterjee S, Katz NP, Nelson MR, Goldbaum MH: Detection of Blood Vessels in Retinal Images Using Two-Dimensional Matched Filters. IEEE Transactions on Medical Imaging, 8:263–269, 1989.
4. Tamura S, Okamoto Y, Yanashima K: Zero-Crossing Interval Correction in Tracing Eye-Fundus Blood Vessels. Pattern Recognition, 21:227–233, 1988.
5. Michaelis M: Low Level Image Processing Using Steerable Filters. Dissertation, Technische Fakultät der Christian-Albrechts-Universität Kiel, 1995.

Entwicklung eines klinischen Demonstrators für die computerunterstützte Orthopädische Chirurgie mit CT-Bildbasierten Individualschablonen

F. Portheine[1], K. Radermacher[1], A. Zimolong[1], M. Anton[2], H.-W. Staudte[2], G. Rau[1]

[1]Institut für Biomedizinische Technik an der RWTH, Pauwelsstr. 20, 52074 Aachen
[2]Abt. für Orthopädische Chirurgie, Kreiskrankenhaus Marienhöhe Würselen,
D-52146 Würselen
Email: portheine@hia.rwth-aachen.de

Zusammenfassung. Bei der Planung von Eingriffen in der orthopädischen Chirurgie kann der Orthopäde auf eine Vielzahl von bildgebenden Verfahren zurückgreifen, wie z.B. CT, MR, Ultraschall und Röntgenaufnahmen. Die jüngsten Entwicklungen im Bereich der computerunterstützten Chirurgie bieten verschiedene Lösungsansätze, um die hohe geometrische Genauigkeit der präoperativen Bildgebung und Planung für eine ebenso präzise intraoperative Ausführung zu nutzen. Am Helmholtz-Institut wurde dafür das Prinzip der Individualschablonen entwickelt. Hierbei werden individuell angepaßte Schablonen auf Basis von CT-Daten präoperativ gefertigt, die intraoperativ eine präzise Werkzeugführung für die geplanten Knochenbearbeitung darstellen. Die Realisierbarkeit des Konzeptes für verschiedene chirurgische Anwendungen wurde bereits in Laboruntersuchungen sowie in klinischen Applikationen demonstriert. Im folgenden werden Aspekte der Entwicklung eines integrierten klinischen Demonstrators zur chirurgischen Planung und Fertigung von Individualschablonen für periacetabuläre Umstellungsosteotomien dargestellt.

Schlüsselwörter: Individualschablonen, präoperative Planung, ergonomisches Systemdesign

1 Einleitung

Individualschablonen sind auf Basis von CT-Daten präoperativ erstellte Werkzeugführungen, die die räumliche Beziehung zwischen Werkzeug und Knochen über eine definierte Kontaktfläche zwischen Werkzeugführung und Knochen herstellen. Intraoperativ läßt sich die Referenzierung manuell gesteuert über taktiles und visuelles Feedback durch formschlüssiges Aufsetzen auf den Knochen erreichen [1][2][3].

Im Rahmen des EU Projektes IGOS (Image Guided Orthopedic Surgery „IGOS", HC1026HC, Telematics Application Program) wird ein integrierter klinischer Demonstrator entwickelt, der Engpässe und Möglichkeiten eines klinischen Einsatzes von Individualschablonen für eine periacetabuläre Umstellungsosteotomie nach Tönnis aufzeigen soll [4].

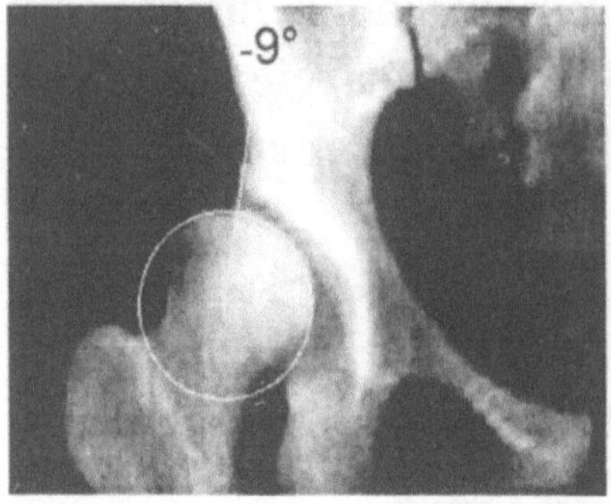
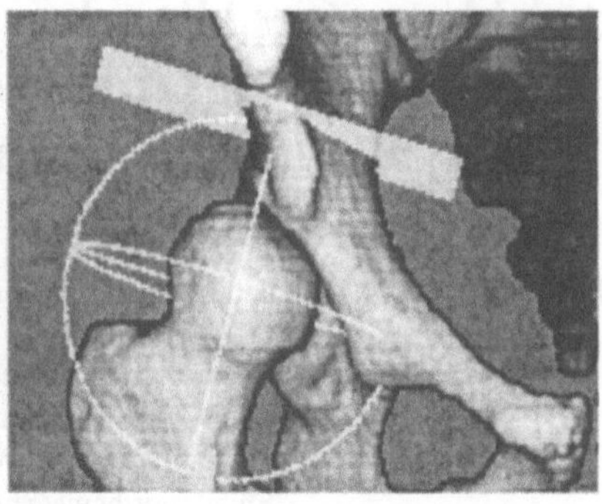

Abb. 1 Bestimmung des LCE-Winkels am künstlichen Röntgenbild

Abb. 2 Definition der Schnittebene für die Osteotomie des Darmbeins

2 Entwicklung eines computerunterstützten Operationsplanungssystemes

Der Demonstrator besteht aus einem computerunterstützten Bildverarbeitungssystem, das auf Basis von CT-Daten eine 3D Operationsplanung mit anschließender Fertigung von Individualschablonen ermöglicht [5].

Die Planungsplattform besteht aus handelsüblichen Komponenten, einer standard PC-Hardware (Pentium 133MHz++) sowie einer kleinen Kompaktfräseinheit. Bei der Realisierung des Benutzerinterfaces wurden die Gestaltungsrichtlinien der ISO 9241 berücksichtigt, sowie die Vorstellungen und Wünsche der Orthopäden als spätere Nutzer integriert. Durch die benutzerorientierte Dialoggestaltung des Planungssystems, die sich an der Terminologie des Benutzers und dem konventionellen Planungsablauf orientiert, kann das System mit geringem Schulungsaufwand eingesetzt werden. Die gesamte Schnittplanungssequenz wird dabei in die Teilbereiche Diagnose, Planung der Knochenmanipulationen, Simulation der Operation und Schablonenherstellung unterteilt.

2.1 Diagnose

Bei der computerunterstützten Diagnose werden die aus der konventionellen Operationsplanung bekannten operationsspezifischen Parameter bestimmt. Die für die Bekkenosteotomie üblichen Parameter ACE- und LCE- Winkel werden konventionell an Röntgenbildern ermittelt. Diese Integralprojektionsaufnahmen werden aus dem CT-Datensatz mittels speziell entwickelten Algorithmen erzeugt (Abb.1). Die Differenz der pathologischen Werte zu den aus der Literatur bekannten anatomischen Werten von LCE und ACE Winkel läßt einen direkten Rückschluß auf die nötige Korrektur der dysplastischen Hüftpfanne zu. Eine höhere Genauigkeit verspricht jedoch ein Ermitteln der nötigen Korrekturwerte anhand einer 3D-Simulation der Operation.

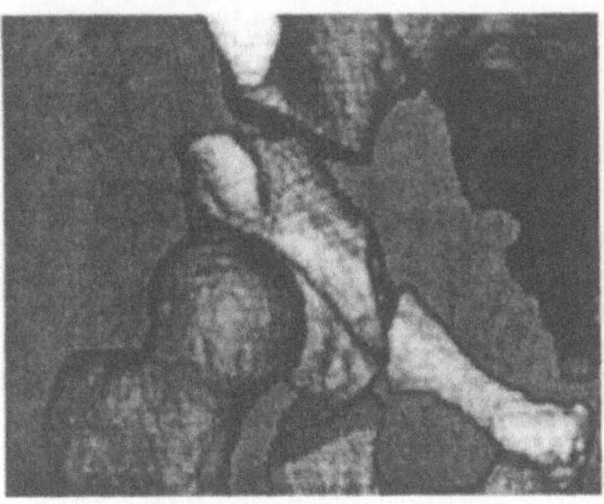

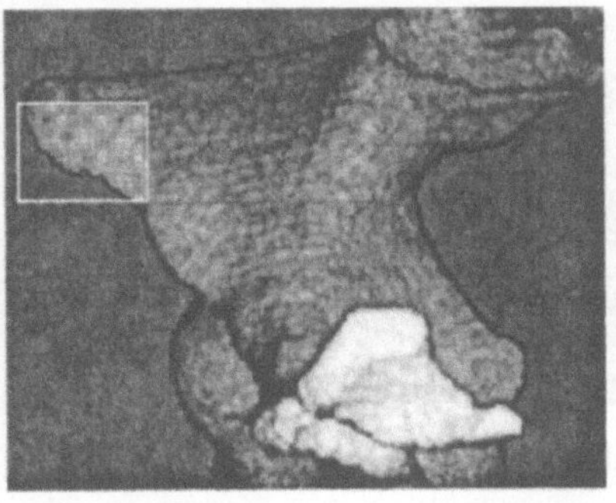

Abb. 3 Simulation der Triple-Becken-Osteotomie

Abb. 4 Definition der Kontaktfläche für die Individualschablone

2.2 Planung der Osteotomien

Für die Planung der Osteotomien stellt das System dem Benutzer eine 3D Rekonstruktion der Knochenstruktur zur Verfügung, an der die Schnitte geplant werden. Die Definition der Schnittebenen ist durch medizinische Randbedingungen bestimmt. Einerseits birgt ein geringer Abstand der Osteotomie zur Hüftpfanne ein höheres Risiko einer avaskulären Nekrose, andererseits kann durch ein zu großes Acetabulum Fragment die freie Rotation behindert werden. Um diese Randbedingungen zu erfüllen, stellt das System eine Sicherheitskugel um den Femurkopf dar, an dem die Schnittebene tangential anliegt (Abb.2). Zur Definition der Schnittebene wird der Radius der Sicherheitskugel variiert und die Ebene um die sagitale und transversale Achse rotiert. Der Verlauf des Schnittes kann an einem Grauwertbild, welches die den Schnitt umgebenden Weichteile darstellt, überprüft werden.

2.3 Simulation der Knochenmanipulation

Um den Schnittverlauf der drei geplanten Osteotomien sowie die Mobilisierung und die intraoperativ notwendige Korrektur zu überprüfen, führt das System automatisch die geplanten Osteotomien durch, um das Acetabulum zu mobilisieren. Für die vollständige Mobilisierung des Acetabulums ist neben der Durchführung der Osteotomien die Trennung des Femurkopfes von der Hüftpfanne notwendig. Bei dysplastischen Hüftpfannen ist der Gelenkspalt durch die Auflösung der CT-Scanner nicht zwangsläufig auf den Tomogrammen sichtbar, so daß eine Trennung des Femurkopfes über eine Konturverfolgung nicht möglich ist. Hierfür wurden Algorithmen entwickelt, die in den Originalschichtbildern einen virtuellen Schnitt zwischen Femurkopf und Acetabulum durchführen und somit eine Trennung von Femur und Acetablum in den Tomogrammen ermöglichen. Die segmentierten Knochenstrukturen werden anschließend getrennt zu 3D Modellen rekonstruiert.

Abb. 5 Kompaktfräseinheit   **Abb. 6** Individualschablone

Durch die vollständige Mobilisierung des acetabularen Fragmentes ist der Benutzer in der Lage, die Rotation des Fragmentes durchzuführen und somit zu überprüfen, ob die geplante Schnittführung die erforderliche Umstellung ermöglicht (Abb.3). Des weiteren läßt sich auf diese Weise feststellen, in wie weit das Fragment gedreht werden muß, um eine gute Überdachung des Femurkopfes zu erreichen. Unterstützt wird der Chirurg dabei durch eine automatische Bestimmung der ACE- und LCE-Winkel, womit eine quantitative Aussage über die intraoperativ notwendige Korrektur möglich wird.

2.4 Schablonendefinition

Die Definition und Herstellung der Individualschablonen stellen den abschließenden Schritt der präoperativen Planung dar. Vom Arzt wird ein Schablonenrohling durch Auswahl aus einer Liste vorgegebener Rohling ausgewählt. Die Aufsatzrichtung der Schablone ergibt sich aus dem gewählten Operationszugang, wobei sie jedoch zusätzlich parallel zum Schnittverlauf verschoben werden kann. Während auf diese Weise die Kontaktfläche selektiert wird, stellt sich das Knochenmodell senkrecht zur Aufsatzrichtung dar, und der resultierende Kontaktbereich wird berechnet und angezeigt (Abb. 4).

Die für die Herstellung der Individualschablonen benötigten NC-Fräsfiles werden automatisch nach der Auswahl der Kontaktflächen generiert und auf einer angeschlossenen Kompaktfräseinheit zur Ausführung gebracht (Abb. 5).

2.5 Intraoperativer Einsatz

Die Individualschablonen sind autoclavierbar und können mit dem übrigen Operationsbesteck zur Operation bereitgestellt werden (Abb.6). Intraoperativ läßt sich die Referenzierung durch formschlüssiges Aufsetzen der Individualschablone auf den Knochen erreichen. Die aufgesetzte Schablone wird mit einem Fixierungsnagel gegen Verrutschen gesichert und dient der Werkzeugführung. Die Position der aufgesetzten Individualschablonen kann durch intraoperative Röntgenaufnahmen verifiziert werden. Bei klinischen Versuchen mit Individualschablonen konnten wir neben einer Verkleinerung des Zugangsweges, eine Verkürzung der Operationsdauer sowie eine Verringerung der Durchleuchtungszeiten feststellen.

3 Zusammenfassung und Ausblick

Anhand der 3D präoperativen Planung auf Basis von CT-Daten kann sich der Benutzer über die Möglichkeiten der konventionellen Operationsplanung hinaus, ein mentales Modell der vorliegenden biomechanischen Verhältnisse bilden. Des weiteren erlaubt dies eine exakte Planung der Knochenbearbeitung, wie z.B. von Osteotomien. Durch eine Simulationsumgebung können die geplanten Knochenmanipulationen durchgeführt werden und ein erster Eindruck der Auswirkungen vermittelt werden. Darüber hinaus bietet sich eine auf 3D Daten gestützte Korrekturplanung an. In Verbindung mit dem Prinzip der Individualschablonen steht ein intuitiv zu gebrauchendes und den ursprünglichen Arbeitsprozeß unterstützendes Hilfsmittel zur Verfügung, welches eine exakte intraoperative Umsetzung der präoperativ Planung ermöglicht.

Im Rahmen des IGOS II Projektes wird das Planungssystem derzeit um ein Planungsmodul für das Setzen von Pedikelschrauben bei Skolioseoperationen erweitert.

4 Literatur

1. Radermacher, K., Staudte, H.-W., Rau, G.: Computer Assisted Orthopaedic Surgery by Means of Individual Templates - Aspects and Analysis of Potential Applications. DiGioia III, A. et al. (eds.): Medical Robotics and Computer Assisted Surgery, Carnegie Mellon University Pittsburgh, 1995, pp.451-463
2. Radermacher, K., Staudte, H.-W., Rau, G.: Computer Assisted Orthopedic Surgery By Means of Individual Templates. Proc.3rd European Conference on Engineering an Medicine, 1995, p.348
3. Radermacher, K., Rau, G., Staudte, H.-W.: Computer Integrated Orthopedic Surgery - Connection of Planning and Execution in Surgical Interventions. in: Taylor,R., Lavallée, St., Burdea, G., Moesges, R. (eds.): Computer Integrated Surgery, MIT-Press, Cambridge, MA, 1996, pp.451-463
4. Tönnis, D., A. Arnig, M. Bloch, A. Heinecke, K. Kalchschmidt, (1994): Triple Pelvic Osteotomy. J. of Ped. Orthopeadic Part B, Vol.3, No.1, pp. 54-67
5. Portheine, F.,Radermacher,K., Zimolong, A., Anton,M. ,Eichhorn, Ch., Staudte, H.-W., Rau, G.: Development of a clinical demonstrator for computer assisted orthopedic surgery with CT-image based individual templates - in: Lemke, Vannier, Inamura (eds.): Computer Assisted Radiology and Surgery, Elsevier, 1997, pp. 944 - 949

Analyse von Fundusbildern zur Bewertung des Erfolges von Operationen bei Macula pucker

Chr. Roßmanith[1], O. Huwendiek[2], H. Handels[1], W. Brockmann[2], A. Hager[3],
H. Laqua[3], E. Maehle[2], S.J. Pöppl[1]

Institute für Medizinische Informatik[1] und Technische Informatik[2],
Klinik für Augenheilkunde[3],
Medizinische Universität zu Lübeck, Ratzeburger Allee 160, 23564 Lübeck
Email: rossmani@medinf.mu-luebeck.de

Zusammenfassung. Dieser Beitrag präsentiert ein Verfahren zur Segmentierung und Ausrichtung von Fundusbildern, die bei Macula pucker Patienten zur Dokumentation des Operationserfolges aufgenommen wurden. Bei diesen Patienten hat sich eine kontraktionsfähige, epiretinale Membran am hinteren Augenpol gebildet, die zu Verziehungen der Netzhaut führt. Die Segmentierung erfolgt durch ein Template Matching Verfahren auf Grauwertgradienten prä- und postoperativer Fundusbilder. Nach der Markierung korrespondierender Gefäßabschnitte werden durch ein Ausrichtungsverfahren dann unter der Berücksichtigung, daß sich die Lage der Gefäße durch die Operation verändert haben kann, optimale Transformationsparameter bestimmt. Dies ermöglicht quantitative Analysen der Veränderungen der Gefäßverläufe.

Schlüsselwörter: Fundusbild, Registrierung, Segmentierung, Bildanalyse

1 Einleitung

Im Mittelpunkt des Beitrages stehen Methoden zur Analyse und Vermessung von Augenhintergrundbildern, die zur objektivierten Beurteilung des Erfolges von Augenoperationen bei Macula pucker entwickelt wurden. Bei den erkrankten Personen hat sich eine kontraktionsfähige, epiretinale Membran am hinteren Augenpol gebildet, die zu Verziehungen der Netzhaut führt. Diese Kontraktion kann zu einer Herabsetzung der zentralen Sehschärfe und Verzerrungen bei der visuellen Wahrnehmung (Metamorphopsien) führen. Bei ausgeprägten Beschwerden ist eine chirurgische Entfernung der Membran über eine Parsplana-Vitrektomie möglich, wodurch es in den meisten Fällen zu einer deutlichen Reduktion der Metamorphopsien kommt. Der Effekt dieser operativen Membranentfernung soll durch Vergleich der prä- und postoperativen Verziehung der inneren Netzhautschichten untersucht werden.

Ansätze zur computergestützten Analyse der retinalen Morphologie wurden beispielsweise in [1] vorgestellt. Bei dem hier vorgestellten Ansatz werden die retinalen Gefäße als Marker genutzt, um das Ausmaß der retinalen Verziehung zu bestimmen, die entweder durch einen typischen korkenzieherartigen oder besonders gestreckten Verlauf der Netzhautgefäße deutlich wird. Als Ausgangsbasis dienen prä- und postoperativ erstellte Farbbilder des Augenhintergrundes. Diese werden auf eine Photo CD übertragen und stehen somit für eine digitale Verarbeitung zur Verfügung.

2 Ausrichtung

Die visuelle Beurteilung der Gefäßbewegungen wird wesentlich erleichtert, wenn prä- und postoperatives Bild in einer Animation in raschem Wechsel gezeigt werden, statt sie nebeneinander zu präsentieren. Um nur die durch die Entfernung der Membran verursachten Gefäßbewegungen darzustellen, ist es notwendig, zunächst durch Anwendung von Registrierungsverfahren eine Ausrichtung der Bilder durchzuführen. Bei der gesuchten Transformation muß berücksichtigt werden, daß die Gefäßveränderungen in den nicht ausgerichteten Bildern zum einem auf unterschiedliche Aufnahmebedingungen und zum anderen auf Gefäßbewegungen zurückzuführen sind.

Nur für die Papille kann angenommen werden, daß sie durch die Entfernung der Membran keine Lageveränderung erfahren hat. Daher werden zunächst die Papillen in beiden Bildern durch eine Translation zur Deckung gebracht und anschließend die optimalen Parameter für eine Rotation und eine zentrische Streckung ermittelt.

Es bezeichnen τ und τ' die Translationen, die die Papillen zur Deckung bringen und sie in den Ursprung des Koordinatensystems überführen. Ferner bezeichnen p_i Punkte aus dem Referenzbild und p_i' Punkte aus dem auszurichtenden Bild. Ihre Bestimmung wird in Abschnitt 4 beschrieben. Nach der Translation erhält man

$$q_i = p_i - \tau \qquad \text{und} \qquad q_i' = p_i' - \tau' \tag{1}$$

Für korrespondierende Punktepaare (q_i, q_i'), $i = 1, \ldots, M$, gilt nun:

$$
\begin{aligned}
q_i' &= \underbrace{\begin{pmatrix} \cos\alpha & -\sin\alpha \\ \sin\alpha & \cos\alpha \end{pmatrix}}_{M_\alpha} \cdot q_i + t_i \\
&= \begin{pmatrix} a & -\sqrt{1-a^2} \\ \sqrt{1-a^2} & a \end{pmatrix} \cdot q_i + t_i \qquad (\text{mit } a = \cos\alpha)
\end{aligned}
\tag{2}
$$

d.h. ein Teil der Abweichung zwischen $q_i = (x_i, y_i)$ und $q_i' = (x_i', y_i')$ läßt sich durch eine Rotation beschreiben und es verbleibt ein Anteil, der die Skalierung sowie die Gefäßbewegung repräsentiert. Der Winkel α ergibt sich aus der Bedingung, daß der Translationsanteil minimiert wird, d.h.

$$f(a) := \sum |t_i|^2 \overset{!}{=} \min \quad \Leftrightarrow \quad f'(a) = 0 \wedge f''(a) > 0.$$

Die eindeutige Lösung für a lautet:

$$a = \sqrt{\frac{A^2}{A^2 + B^2}} \tag{3}$$

$$A := \sum_i (x_i x_i' + y_i y_i') \quad B := \sum_i (x_i y_i' - x_i' y_i).$$

Somit erhält man

$$r_i = q_i \quad \text{und} \quad r_i' = M_\alpha \cdot q_i' \tag{4}$$

Mit einem analogen Ansatz erhält man für den Skalierungsfaktor σ:

$$\sigma = \frac{1}{M} \sum_i \frac{r_i \cdot r_i'}{|r_i^2|} \tag{5}$$

und insgesamt für die gesuchte Transformation

$$s_i = r_i \quad \text{und} \quad s_i' = \sigma \cdot r_i' \tag{6}$$

3 Segmentierung

Das Ziel der Segmentierung besteht in der Extraktion der Mittellinien der Gefäße. Sie erfolgt im Grünkanal I_g eines Fundusbildes I_{rgb}, da die Gefäße hier am kontrastreichsten dargestellt werden. Abb. 1 zeigt links den Grünkanal eines

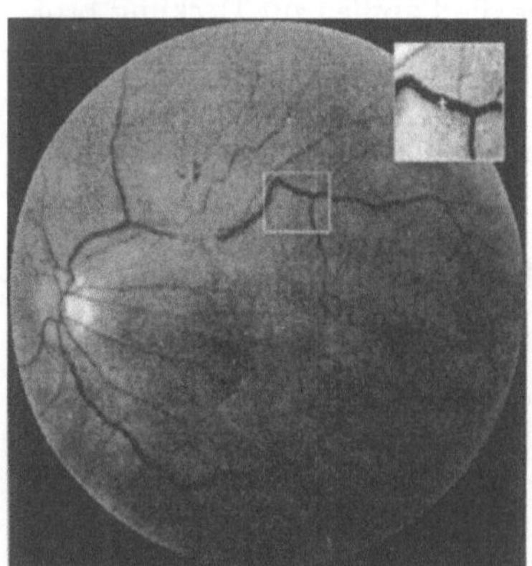
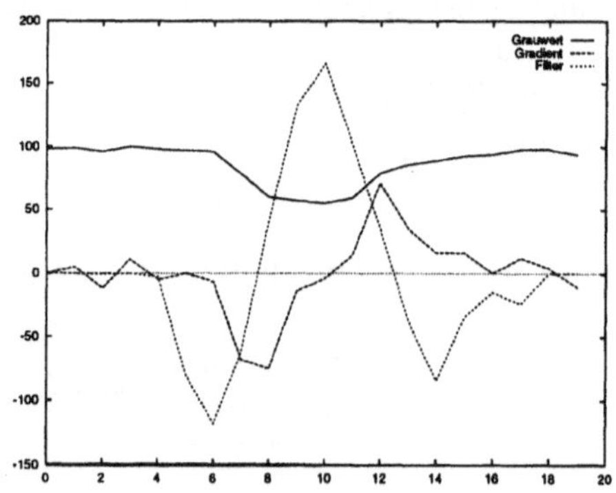

Abb. 1. Grünkanal eines Fundusbildes *(links)*. Vertikales Grauwertprofil durch den im linken Bild markierten Punkt (durchgezogen), Gradientenverlauf (gestrichelt), Filterantwort (gepunktet).

Fundusbildes und rechts das Grauwertprofil entlang einer vertikalen Linie, die ein Gefäß orthogonal zu seiner Verlaufsrichtung schneidet. Gestrichelt ist der Gradient dieses Grauwertprofils dargestellt. Punkte auf den Gefäßmittellinien zeichnen sich durch ein lokales Minimum im Intensitätsverlauf und somit durch einen

Nulldurchgang im Gradientenverlauf aus, wobei ein Vorzeichenwechsel von $+$ nach $-$ erfolgen muß. Der Gradientenverlauf ähnelt in seiner Form der Funktion $sin(x)$ im Intervall $-\frac{\pi}{2} \leq x \leq \frac{\pi}{2}$. Dies motiviert den Einsatz der diskretisierten sin-Funktion als Template S in einem Template-Matching Verfahren [2] zur Detektion von Punkten auf der Mittellinie. Ein binäres Linienbild L wird aus I_g wie folgt generiert:

1. Berechne mit Hilfe des Sobeloperators [3] Gradientenbilder $I_{grad_{\alpha_i}}$ für die Richtungen $\alpha_i = 0°, 45°, 90°, 135°$.

2. Falte $I_{grad_{\alpha_i}}$ nacheinander mit Templates S_k der Breite $k = 3, 5, 9$, um Gefäße unterschiedlicher Breite detektieren zu können: $I_{grad_{\alpha_i},k} = I_{grad_{\alpha_i}} * S_k$. Es hat sich herausgestellt, daß es genügt, diese Templatebreiten zu berücksichtigen.

3. Bestimme für jeden Bildpunkt (x, y) und für jede Templatebreite k die Richtung α_0, für die $I_{grad_{\alpha_i},k}$ maximal wird. Erzeuge für jede Templatebreite ein Maximumsbild m_k nach folgender Vorschrift:

$$m_k(x, y) := \begin{cases} I_{grad_{\alpha_0},k}(x, y) & : \quad I_{grad_{\alpha_0},k}(x, y) \text{ ist lok. Maximum} \\ & \qquad \text{in Richtung } \alpha_0 \\ 0 & : \quad \text{sonst} \end{cases}$$

Durch die Bedingung *lok. Maximum* wird m_k für Punkte neben der Mittellinie zu 0 gesetzt, so daß die Binarisierung im nächsten Schritt ein Bild liefert, daß weitgehend ein Pixel breite Linien enthält.

4. Bilde $m(x, y) = \max_k m_k(x, y)$ und setze

$$L(x, y) := \begin{cases} 1 & : \quad m(x, y) > \theta \\ 0 & : \quad \text{sonst} \end{cases}$$

Die Binarisierung bezüglich des Schwellwertes $\theta > 0$ bewirkt insbesondere, daß im Hintergrund detektierte Punkte eliminiert werden. Abb. 2 zeigt den Grünkanal I_g eines Fundusbildes, dem ausgewählte Teilsegmente des skelettierten Linienbildes L überlagert wurden.

Das so erhaltene Binärbild wird skelettiert [4].

4 Quantitative Analyse

Die quantitative Analyse verfolgt das Ziel, ein Maß für den Grad der durch die Operation bewirkte Änderung der Gefäßverläufe zu finden. Ausgangspunkt bilden die in den prä- und postoperativen Linienbildern durch die Augenärztin markierten Gefäßabschnitte mit korrespondierenden Anfangs- und Endpunkten. Korrespondierende Endpunkte der Gefäßabschnitte sind geeignete Kandidaten p_i, p'_i für die Bestimmung des Rotationswinkels α und des Skalierungsfaktors σ. In Abb. 2 (links) sind die ausgerichteten Gefäßabschnitte gemeinsam dem postoperativen Bild überlagert dargestellt. Für die quantitative Beschreibung der Gefäßbewegungen wird für jedes Segmentpaar punktweise die euklidische

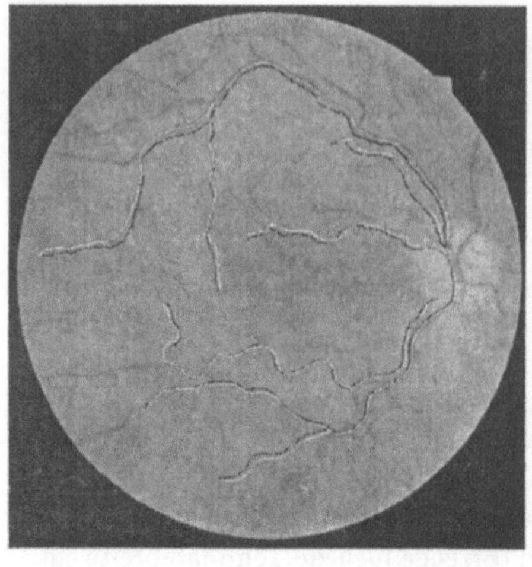

Abb. 2. *Links:* Ausgerichtete prä- und postoperative Gefäßsegmente (dunkel/hell) wurden dem postoperativen Bild gemeinsam überlagert. *Rechts:* Darstellung der punktweisen euklidischen Distanz zwischen korrespondieren Segmenten kodiert auf einer Grauwertskala. Große Distanzen sind dunkel, kleine hell dargestellt.

Distanz zwischen den Segmenten berechnet. Um zu gewährleisten, daß beide Segmente dieselbe Anzahl von Punkten enthalten, wird das Kürzere zuvor linear interpoliert und neu abgetastet. In Abb. 2 werden rechts die so bestimmten Distanzen auf einer Grauwertskala visualisiert.

In nächsten Arbeitsschritten wird untersucht, inwieweit die Transformation zur Ausrichtung auch bei stärker abweichenden Aufnahmewinkeln hinreichend durch Translation, Rotation und Skalierung modelliert werden kann.

Literatur

1. A. Kaupp, A. Dölemeyer, R. Schlösser, R. Wilzeck, S. Wolf: Automatische Analyse der retinalen Morphologie mit einem hierarchischen Bildverarbeitungsansatz. Mustererkennung 1994, 91ff.
2. M. Sonka, V. Hlavac, R. Boyle: Image Processing, Analysis and Machine Vision, Chapman & Hall, 1993.
3. R.C. Gonzalez, P. Wintz: Digital Image Processing, 2nd edition. Addison-Wesley, 1987.
4. P.Zamperoni: Methoden der digitalen Bildsignalverarbeitung, Vieweg, 2. Auflage, 1991.

Bestimmung und Visualisierung von aktivierten Hirnregionen aus fMRT-Daten

Ch. Hahn[1], H. Handels[1], M.F. Nitschke[2], U.H. Melchert[3], S.J. Pöppl[1]

Institute für [1]Medizinische Informatik, [2]Neurologie, [3]Radiologie,
Medizinische Universität Lübeck, Ratzeburger Allee 160, D 23538 Lübeck
hahn@medinf.mu-luebeck.de

Zusammenfassung: Mit der funktionellen Magnetresonanztomographie fMRT kann neuronale Aktivierung des menschlichen Gehirns erfaßt werden. Zu deren Visualisierung ist die Klassifikation aktivierter und nicht-aktivierter Voxel anhand der gemessenen zeitlichen Signalverläufe erforderlich. Hierzu werden verschiedene Merkmalsextraktions- und Segmentierungsverfahren systematisch untersucht, anhand von Simulationsdaten optimiert und schließlich auf klinische Daten angewendet.

Schlüsselwörter: fMRT, Signalanalyse, Segmentierung

1 Einleitung

Mit der funktionellen Magnetresonanztomographie fMRT hat sich der Untersuchung des menschlichen Gehirns in den letzten Jahren eine nicht-invasive Methode eröffnet, die sich durch hohe räumliche und zeitliche Auflösung, direkte anatomische Zuordnung und breite Verfügbarkeit auszeichnet [1, 2]. Bei einer fMRT-Untersuchung wird eine Bildfolge einer oder mehrerer kranieller Schichten generiert, während die untersuchte Person eine zeitliche Abfolge von Ruhe- und Stimulationsphasen (sog. OFF- und ON-Phasen), in denen z.B. externe Reize präsentiert werden, durchläuft (Abb. 1).

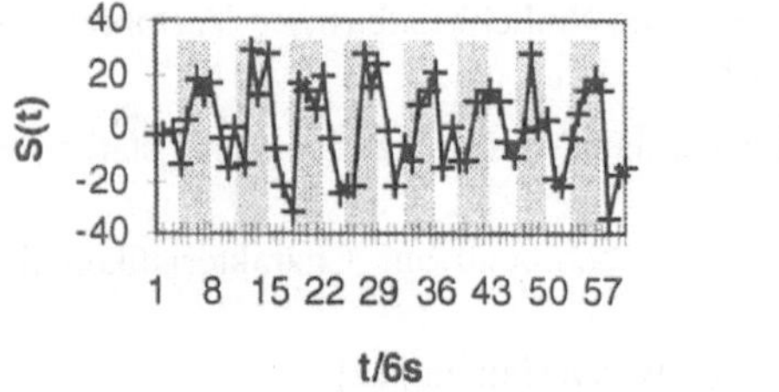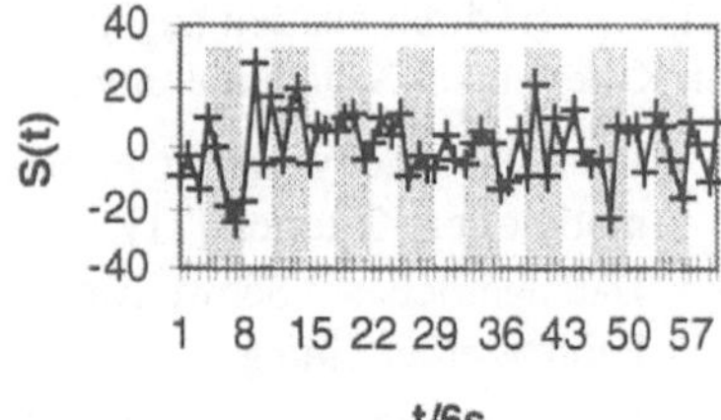

Abb. 1: Beispielhafte Signalkurven aktive Region (links) inaktive Region (rechts) mit Stimulationsphasen im Experiment grau hinterlegt

2 Merkmalsextraktion

Merkmalsextraktionsverfahren in der fMRT sollen anhand der voxelbezogenen Signalverläufe die Bestimmung von Sekundärmerkmalen zur Charakterisierung der aktivierungsbedingten zeitlichen Signaländerungen erlauben. Gegenübergestellt werden:

- Subtraktionsverfahren zur Prüfung der Differenz der Mittelwerte von ON- und OFF-Phasen [3]
- Studentscher t-Test zur Prüfung unterschiedlicher Mittelwerte in ON- und OFF-Phasen [4]
- Lineare Korrelationsanalyse zwischen Signalvektoren und einen den Experimentverlauf beschreibenden Referenzvektor [5]
- Kolmogorov-Smirnov-Test zum Vergleich der empirischen Verteilungsfunktionen der aus ON- und OFF-Phasen gebildeten Stichproben [6]
- Rang-Korrelationskoeffizient Kendall's τ zwischen Signal- und Referenzvektor [7, 8]
- Wilcoxon-Rangsummen-Test zur verteilungsfreien Prüfung der Differenz der Mittelwerte von ON- und OFF-Phasen [9]
- Autokorrelationsanalyse zur Bestimmung von Periode und Phase periodischer Stimulationsparadigmen [10]
- Euklidischer Abstand zwischen a) Signal- und Referenzvektor und b) deren Autokorrelationsfunktionen

Die für jeden Bildpunkt berechneten Parameter lassen sich in sog. Parameterkarten zusammenfassen, die nachfolgend segmentiert werden können.

3 Segmentierung

Die Segmentierung hat zum Ziel, in einem Parameterbild aktivierte Regionen von nicht aktivierten zu separieren. Bei aktivierten Regionen wird davon ausgegangen, daß sie a) zusammenhängend sind; b) aus mehr als einem Bildpunkt bestehen; c) die Ränder einen fließenden Übergang zur nicht aktivierten Umgebung bilden. Neben Schwellwertverfahren werden aus diesem Grunde ähnlichkeitsbasierte Verfahren mit lokalen Kriterien zur Segmentierung betrachtet:

- Interaktive Schwellwertverfahren beruhend auf subjektiven und statistisch motivierten Kriterien [11]
- Datengetriebene Schwellwertverfahren beruhend auf Charakteristiken der Parameterverteilung
- Histogrammbasierte optimale Schwellwertverfahren [12]
- Bereichswachstumsverfahren [13] mit Punkten höherer Aktivierungswahrscheinlichkeit als Saatpunkte und lokal relaxierter Aktivierunsschwelle
- Probabilistische Relaxation [14] zur iterativen Modifikation der Klassenzugehörigkeitswahrscheinlichkeiten aufgrund lokaler Kontextinformation [15, 8]

4 Ergebnisse

Da physiologische Reaktionen auf Stimulationsparadigmen nicht deterministisch sind und somit an gemessenen Datensätzen keine Validierung möglich ist, werden simulierte fMR-Datensätze zur systematischen Untersuchung und Bewertung der Auswerteverfahren herangezogen [16]. Die Bestimmung der Sensitivität der einzelnen Merkmalsextraktionsverfahren erfolgt nach Segmentierung mit dem Bereichswachstumsverfahren, dessen Homogenitätskriterium anhand eines „gutartigen" simulierten Datensatzes so optimiert ist, daß keine falsch positiven Zuordnungen auftreten (Abb. 2).

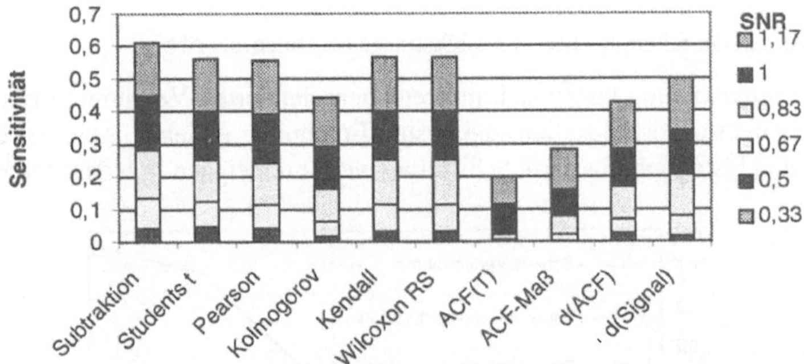

Abb. 2: Sensitivität der auf Simulationsdaten mit unterschiedlichen Signal-Rausch-Verhältnissen angewendeten Merkmalsextraktionsverfahren; Spezifität=1

Die Gegenüberstellung zeigt, daß verteilungsfreie Verfahren, insbesondere die Berechnung des Rangkorrelationskoeffizienten Kendall's τ, bei vergleichbarer Sensitivität eine höhere Spezifität besitzen. Abb. 3 und Abb. 4 verdeutlichen dies an Simulationsdaten mit stimuluskorrelierten Artefakten.

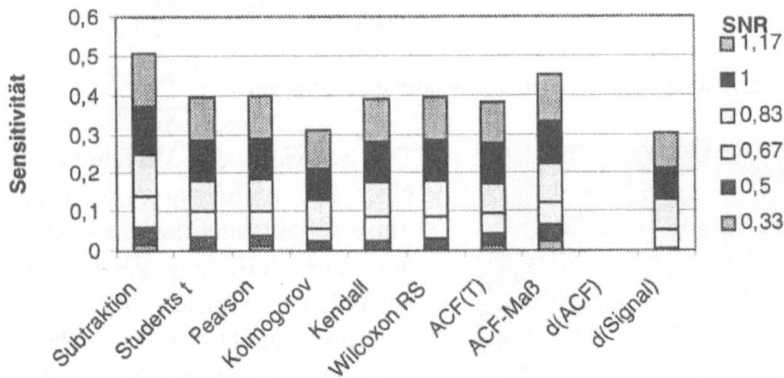

Abb. 3: Sensitivität der Merkmalsextraktionsverfahren bei Simulationsdatensatz mit stimuluskorrelierten Bewegungsartefakten; Segmentierungsparameter wie in Abb. 2; Spezifität≠1 (Abb. 4)

Parametrische Verfahren zeigen sich empfindlicher gegenüber Abweichungen von den Modellannahmen, was z.B. wenig robuste Ergebnisse mit Autokorrelations- und Abstandsmaßen zeigen.

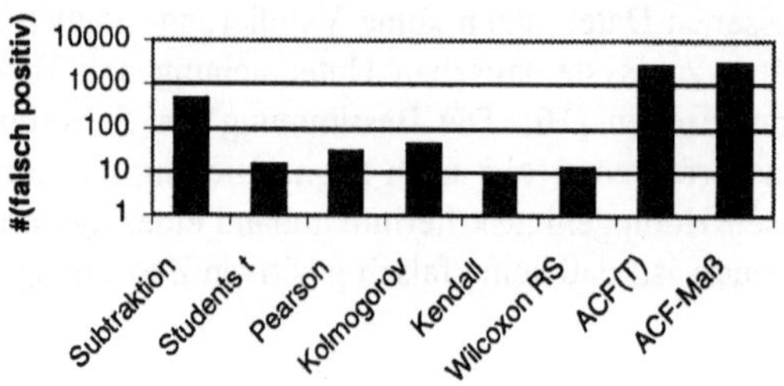

Abb. 4: Anzahl der falsch-positiven Klassifikationen bei Daten aus Abb. 3

Bei der Segmentierung lassen sich mit regionenorientierten Verfahren, insbesondere der probabilistischen Relaxation, die besten Ergebnisse erzielen (Abb. 5). Datengetriebene und histogrammbasierte Schwellwertverfahren eignen sich dagegen nicht.

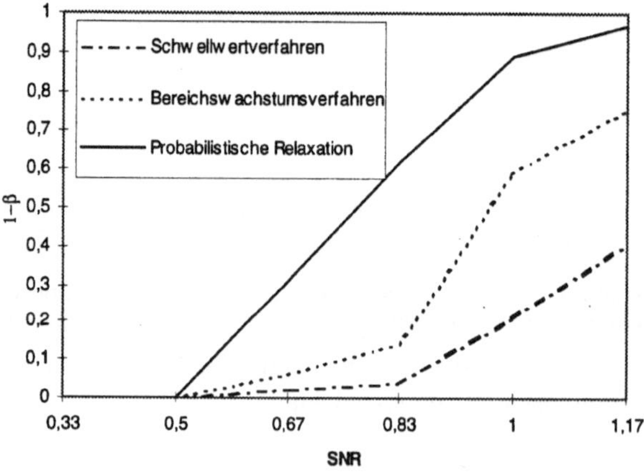

Abb. 5: Sensitivität der untersuchten Segmentierungsverfahren

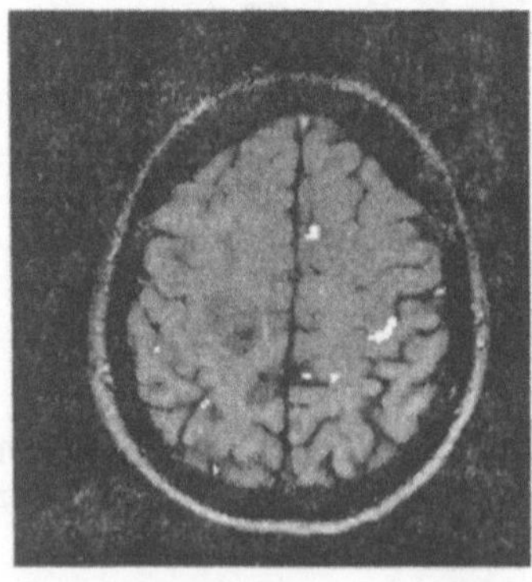

Abb. 6: FMR-Bild Tumorpatient

Die entwickelten Verfahren wurden in einer mit AVS/Express entwickelten Benutzerschnittstelle den medizinischen Partnern zur Verfügung gestellt und werden sowohl auf klinisch relevante als auch forschungsorientierte Fragestellungen angewendet. Schwerpunkte sind dabei die neurochirurgische OP-Planung und Kleinhirnuntersuchungen mit unterschiedlichen Stimulationsparadigmen [17]. Abb. 6 zeigt ein typisches Aktivierungsbild eines mit fMRT untersuchten Tumorpatienten.

5 Literatur

[1]   J. Frahm, H. Bruhn, K.D. Merboldt, W. Hänicke, *Dynamic MR Imaging of Human Brain Oxygenation during Rest and Photic Stimulation*, JMRI, 2, 501-505, 1992

[2]   K.K. Kwong, J.W. Belliveau, D.A. Chesler, I.E. Goldberg, R.M. Weisskoff, B.P. Poncelet, D.N. Kennedy, B.E. Hoppel, M.S. Cohen, R. Turner, H.M. Cheng, T.J. Brady, B.R. Rosen, *Dynamic magnetic resonance imaging of human brain activity during primary sensory stimulation*, Proc. Natl. Acad. Sci. USA 89, 5675-5679, 1992

[3]   D. Le Bihan, R. Turner, T.A. Zeffiro, C.A. Cuenod, P. Jezzard, V. Bonnerot, *Activation of human primary visual cortex during visual recall: A magnetic resonance imaging study*, Proc. Natl. Acad. Sci. Neurobiology, Vol. 90, 11802-11805, 12/1993

[4]   J. Hartung, *Lehr- und Handbuch der angewandten Statistik*, Oldenbourg 1993

[5]   P.A. Bandettini, A. Jesmanowicz, E.C. Wong, J.S. Hyde, *Processing Strategies for Time-Course Data Sets in Functional MRI of the Human Brain*, MRM 30, 161-173, 1993

[6]   G.E. Noether, *Elements of Nonparametric Statistics*, Wiley, 1967

[7]   W.J. Conover, *Practical Nonparametric Statistics*, Wiley 1980

[8]   C. Hahn, H. Handels, M.F. Nitschke, U.H. Melchert, S.J. Pöppl, *Probabilistische Relaxation zur Segmentierung aktivierter Hirnregionen in fMRT-Daten*, in Mustererkennung 1997, Informatik aktuell, eds. E. Paulus, F.M. Wahl, 323-330, Springer, 1997

[9]   J.L. Devore, *Probability and Statistics for Engineering and the Sciences*, Wadsworth California, 1982

[10]   A.-L- Paradis, J.-F. Mangin, V. Cornilleau-Pérès, I. Bloch, V. Frouin, D. Le Bihan, *Detection of Periodic Temporal Responses in fMRI*, NeuroImage 5, 469, 1997

[11]   R. Turner, K. Friston, J. Ashburner, O. Josephs, A. Howseman: *Analysis of fMRI Data Using the General Linear Statistical Model*, NeuroImage 3, 102, 1996

[12]   R.M. Haralick, L.G. Shapiro, *Computer and Robot Vision Volume 1*, Addison-Wesley, 1992

[13]   R.C. Gonzalez, P. Wintz, *Digital Image Processing*, 2nd Edition, Addison-Wesley, 1987

[14]   A. Rosenfeld, A.C. Kak, *Digital Picture Processing*, 2nd Edition, Volume 2, Academic Press, 1982

[15]   C. Hahn, U.H. Melchert, K. Wessel, H. Handels, S.J. Pöppl, *Segmentation of Parametric Maps by Probabilistic Relaxation*, NeuroImage 5, 471

[16]   D. Ekatodramis, G. Szekely, E. Martin, G. Gerig, *A Simulation Environment for Validation and Comparison of Evaluation Procedures*, NeuroImage 3, 57, 1996

[17]   M.F. Nitschke, U.H. Melchert, C.J. Hahn, H. Handels, P. Trillenberg, K. Wessel, *High and Low Frequency Movements Activate Distinct Areas within the Human Anterior Cerebellum: A High-Resolution Functional MRI Study*, NeuroImage 5, 261, 1997

Segmentation of MR images with B-spline snakes: A multi-resolution approach using the distance transformation for model forces

T. Stammberger[1,2], S. Rudert[1], M. Michaelis[3], M. Reiser[2], K.-H. Englmeier[1]

[1] GSF - Institut für Medizinische Informatik und Systemforschung,
Ingolstädter Landstr. 1, 85764 Oberschleißheim, Germany
Email: stamm@gsf.de
[2] Institut für Radiologische Diagnostik, LMU, 81377 München
[3] Plettac Electronics, 90766 Fürth

Abstract A B-spline snake algorithm is proposed for the segmentation of the knee joint cartilage from MR images. A first guess of the contour is provided interactively and is transformed into a B-spline representation. Image forces attract the B-spline curve towards the real cartilage boundaries. In addition, model forces based on a distance transformation are introduced in order to guide the evolution of the contour in those parts of the image that show no significant features. The total energy of the B-spline curve is minimized within a multiple scale approach. The algorithm turned out to be more accurate as the manual delineation of cartilage boundaries from medical experts.

Keywords: segmentation, deformable contours, B-spline snakes, MR imaging, cartilage

1   Introduction

Many quantitative medical image analysis applications, like the measurement of anatomical structures, require prior segmentation of the organ from the surrounding tissue. Our special interest is the segmentation of the knee joint cartilage from magnetic resonance images (MR) for 3D visualization [1], volume and thickness measurements [2, 3], and tracking of the cartilage surfaces in compression experiments [4].

Since the manual delineation of the cartilage boundaries is tedious and time consuming, a lot of effort has been devoted to automate this processing step [5]. The seminal work of Kass et al. [6] inspired many promising approaches to find boundaries in medical images by the use of deformable contour models [7] or B-spline snakes [8, 9]. Both concepts have proven to be suitable for matching an initial contour to smooth object boundaries in noisy images such as the cartilage in MR images. These boundaries can *not* be detected by simple low level features like edges alone. The power of the method lies in the combination of *external image forces* that are based on low level features and attract the initial contour towards the object boundaries, and of *internal forces* that preserve the shape of the contour. In the B-spline snakes approach no explicit internal energy term is required since the B-spline represantation implies the smoothness of the contour.

In addition to the external image forces, we have introduced so-called *model forces* that measure the similarity of the contour to a given model using the Euclidean distance transformation (EDT) [10, 3]. In contrast to other model based approaches [5] where the movements of the contour are restricted within fixed limits implied by the model, the EDT permits to influence and guide the adaption process of the contour in a continuous and smooth way. The initial contour is either provided by user interaction or another initial guess taken for instance from a training set or a geometric model of the cartilage.

In this work we propose an energy-minimizing deformable contour algorithm for the segmentation of the cartilage from MR images. 3D segmentation is achieved by subsequently projecting the 2D contours to the following image slice. The performance of the algorithm is compared to manual segmentation from experienced physicians.

2 Segmentation method

The first step of the segmentation process is the transformation of the initial contour into a B-spline representation. Then the external image and model energy associated with the B-spline curve is minimized subsequently on different filter scales.

2.1 B-spline contour representation (internal energy)

A B-spline of order k is a C^{k-2} continuous parametric curve that depends only on a number of *control points* $v_1, \ldots, v_N \in \mathrm{I\!R}^2$. The B-spline curve is defined as

$$x(u) = \sum_{i=1}^{N} v_i B_i^k(u) \tag{1}$$

where $B_i^k(u)$ are the polynomial *blending functions* (of order k), u is the curve parameter and $x(u) = (x(u), y(u))$ [11].

Due to the following properties B-spline curves are an appropriate curve representation for deformable contour segmentation: (i) The smoothness of the curve corresponding to the internal energy of the contour can be adjusted by the number of control points. (ii) The blending functions $B_i^k(u)$ have only local support, i.e. varying the position of one control point only affects a small part of the curve.

In our algorithm the initial contour is transformed into a B-spline representation by sampling the contour with regard to a curvature measure in a way that the more a curve segment varies the more control points are inserted up to a user defined maximal number. These sampled contour points are taken as control points that are iteratively adjusted until the B-spline fits the initial contour.

2.2 External energy

There are two external forces in this algorithm: image forces E_I, and model forces E_M. The total energy E is then given as a weighted sum of the image and model forces $E = \alpha E_I + (1 - \alpha)E_M$ where α is a heuristic parameter depending on the object to be segmented and the image contrast.

Image forces The contour is attracted to the edges of the object that are measured by the gradient of the image intensity $I(x, y)$. We estimate the strength of the gradient $\|\nabla I(x, y)\| = \sqrt{I_x^2 + I_y^2}$ by convolving the image data with Gaussian derivative filters $I_x(x, y) = I * g_x$ and $I_y(x, y) = I * g_y$ with $g_x(x, y) = -\frac{x}{2\pi\sigma^4} e^{-\frac{x^2+y^2}{2\sigma^2}}$, etc., where σ is the scale of the filter [12]. Then the gradient magnitude is integrated along the B-spline curve yielding a measure E_I how well the contour fits to the image evidence (L is the length of the curve):

$$E_I = -\frac{1}{L} \int_u \|\nabla I(x(u), y(u))\| du \tag{2}$$

Model forces We introduce a model energy to force the contour to be in accordance with a model of the object geometry. This is particularly important in images or image regions with no significant edges. The model can either result from a training set, an analytical object description, or - as in our case - from an initial guess provided by the user.

A distance map $D(x, y)$ of the model boundary is created [10, 3] assigning to every pixel of the map the Euclidean distance to the closest boundary point. The energy E_M is then defined as the sum of the distance values in the map along the B-spline curve:

$$E_M = \frac{1}{L} \int_u D(x(u), y(u)) du \tag{3}$$

This is equivalent to the mean distance between the B-spline curve and the model contour which determins the similarity of the contour with the model.

2.3 Hierarchical minimization

The B-spline curve and hence the total energy E only depends on the positions of the control points v_i ($2N$ degrees of freedom). Therefore, the problem of finding the best match of the contour with the image evidence can be stated as a minimization of the total energy over the $2N$-dimensional space of all control point configurations: $E = E(v_1, \ldots, v_N) \overset{!}{=} \min$.

The minimization is performed in the scale space, starting at a corse filter scale σ and reducing the scale by a factor 2 in each step. The optimal contour of one level is taken as initial contour for the next detailed level, while minimizing the energy function on each level using the gradient descent optimization method.

2.4 Extention to 3D segmentation

The segmented boundary in one slice is used as initial contour for the following image of the 3D volume sequence thus providing a full 3D segmentation of the cartilage. This simple and straight forward approach shows still satisfying results since the shape of the cartilage does not change dramatically from slice to slice in transverse or sagittal imaging planes.

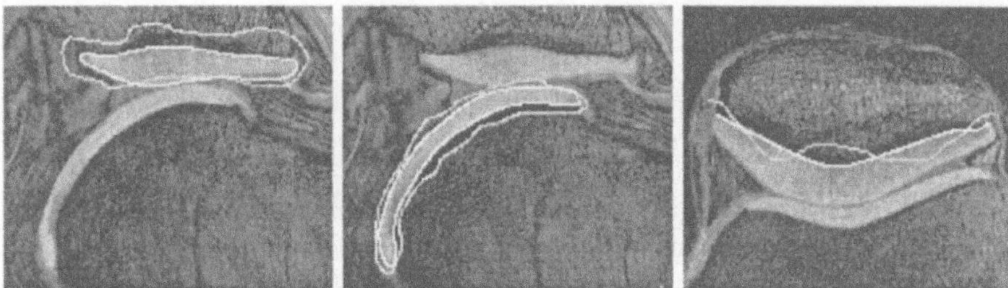

Figure1. Due to the hierarchical minimization even bad initial contours (gray lines) can be attracted to the required object (bright lines) (patella (left) and femur (middle) cartilage). The algorithm handles both open and closed contours (right: bone-catilage interface).

3   Results and discussion

The algorithm is currently employed in several clinical studies [2, 3, 4]. The correct performance is controlled visually by medical experts whereas only in few cases interaction is required to improve the segmentation results.

We compared our method to the manual segmentation of experienced physicians. The same object was segmented eight times while systematically excluding one and calculating the mean Euclidean distance to the seven remaining segmentation results. The average of theses experiments was taken as a measure giving an upper bound for the reproducibility of the segmentation method. In this way the segmentation results of eight medical experts were compared to that of our algorithm with eight randomly chosen start contours. For both, an open and a closed object boundary (Fig. 1), the snake segmentation (0.22 and 0.18 pixel) was more than twice as precise as the manual one (0.48 and 0.43 pixel). This means that the snake segmentation is is not only faster but particularly more reproducible than the manual segmentation even though it is not fully automatic.

Moreover, in comparison to feature based algorithms (e.g. region growing) that had also been tested in the scope of our clinical studies the snake approach proved to be more suitable for the segmentation of smooth objects in noisy MR images.

In practice, three filter scales σ with a minimal scale of about one pixel turns out to be a good compromise between time performance and robustness for the hierarchical minimization scheme. The largest filter scale serves for the coarse matching whereas the lowest scale permits to delineate the exact shape of the cartilage. This ensures that even if the first contour guess is far away from the cartilage boundary the snake still 'feels' the image forces since their range is limited by the filter scale (Fig. 1).

The adaption of the snake to a given model can be achieved by superimposing model forces to the image forces. In regions with insufficient image features, they prevent the contour from random movements or attraction to nearby objects (Fig. 2).

In contrast to other deformable contour approaches [5] our algorithm is able to perform the energy minimization in real-time on a SGI workstation. This

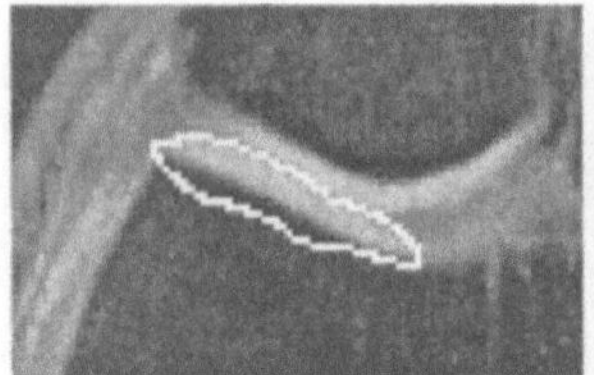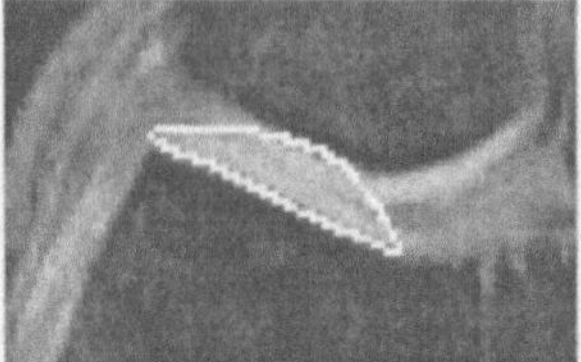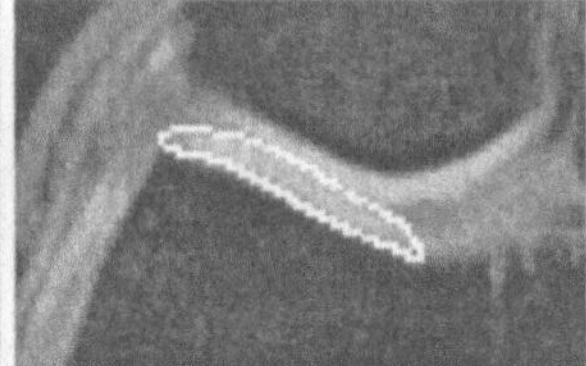

Figure2. The influence of model forces. Segmentation of the femur cartilage without (middle) and with (right) model forces starting from the same initial contour (left) (10 control points). With model forces the snake is correctly matched to the femur boundary (right).

is due to the efficient contour representation as B-spline curve. Therefore the proposed method is not only useful for a quasi-automatic segmentation procedure but also a powerful tool in assisting the interactive segmentation of a large variety of image objects.

References

1. Englmeier KH, et al.: Hybrid rendering of multidimensional image data. Meth Inform Med, 36:1–10, 1997.
2. Eckstein F, et al.: Determination of knee joint cartilage thickness using three dimensional magnetic resonance chondro-crassometry (3D MR-CCM). Magn Reson Med, 36:256–265, 1996.
3. Stammberger T, et al.: Determination of 3D cartilage thickness data from MR imaging - computational method and reproducibility in the living. Magn Reson Med, submitted.
4. Herberhold C, et al.: A MR-based technique for quantifying the deformation of articular cartilage during mechanical loading in an intact cadaver joint. Magn Reson Med, in press.
5. Solloway S, et al.: The use of active shape models for making thickness measurements of articular cartilage from MR images. Magn Reson Med, 37:943–952, 1997.
6. Kass M, et al.: Snakes: Active contour models. Int J Comput Vision, 1(4):321–331, 1988.
7. McInerney T, Terzopoulos D: Deformable models in medical image analysis: A survey. Medical Image Analysis, 1(2):91–108, 1996.
8. Menet S, et al.: Active contour models: Overview, implementation and applications. Int Conf. Systems, Man, and Cybernetics, 212:194–199, 1990.
9. Leitner F, et al.: From splines and snakes to Snakes Splines. Geometric Reasoning: From Perception to Action, LNCS, Springer-Verlag, 264–281, 1993.
10. Borgefors G: Distance transformations in digital images. Comp. Vision, Graphics and Image Proc., 34:344–371, 1986.
11. Mortenson M: Geometric modeling. Wiley, New York, 1985.
12. Stammberger T, et al.: A hierarchical filter scheme for efficient corner detection. Computer Analysis of Images and Patterns, LNCS 1296, Springer Verlag, Proceedings of CAIP'97, Kiel 215–222, 1997.

Contour tracking on sequences of ventriculographic images: a comparison between gradient of Gaussian and first order absolute moment.

V. Gemignani (1), M. Demi (1)(2), A. Benassi (1)

(1) CNR Institute of Clinical Phyisiology, v. Savi 8, 56100 Pisa, Italy
(2) Esaote SpA, Florence, Italy
Email: gemi@po.ifc.pi.cnr.it

Abstract. In this paper the properties of both the GoG and FOAM operators, as well as the results obtained with their respective localization procedures, are compared. FOAM (first order absolute moment) and GoG (gradient of Gaussian) filters are used to enhance the discontinuities between the gray levels of the different structures of the images. The contour we are tracking is then localized through the filtered images by starting from an approximate contour. Results of the two automatic contour tracking procedures are presented on sequences of ventriculographic and synthetic images.

Keywords: edge detection, contour tracking, ventriculography.

1 Introduction

Adequate procedures to detect contours automatically are particularly needed when processing sequences of cardiovascular images. In this field the number of images to be processed is, in general, so large that a manual tracing phase proves unacceptable. A contour detection algorithm usually requires two steps; first the discontinuities between the gray levels of the different structures of the images are enhanced by means of a filtering process, and second the points of the contour we are looking for are localized through the filtered images. First and second order derivatives are widely used to enhance the gray level discontinuities while a low pass prefilter is introduced to cope with noise. The gradient of Gaussian (GoG) is the first order derivative operator most frequently used in literature to enhance the luminance variations with a ridge. However, a similar ridge map can be provided by a filter which is obtained from the generalization of the first order absolute moment (FOAM). Unlike the GoG filter, the FOAM filter provides ridges at both edges and lines and gives rise to local maxima of the ridges at line endings, corners and junctions [1]. In this work the properties of the two GoG and FOAM operators, as well as the results obtained with their respective localization procedures, are compared.

2 The Contour Tracking Approach

When an approximate contour C_a is traced manually by an operator on the first frame of the sequence, the "true" contours C_i can be estimated from C_a as follows:

I. The images are processed by means of a two-dimensional operator giving a null result on homogeneous regions and a ridge at the gray level discontinuities. In the representations so obtained (edge maps) the contours C_i are the top lines of the ridges.

II. Every point of C_a is brought to the top of the respective ridge along a computed direction.

III. Let the sample rate of the temporal sequence be high enough to allow the true contour C_i to lie within the $(i+1)^{th}$ ridge. Thus, when the C_1 contour is determined it can be used as the starting contour to determine contour C_2 on the next frame and so on.

3 The filtering process

Let $f(x,y)$ be the gray level map of an image and let Θ be a circular domain, the generalized first order absolute moment is computed as follows:

$$e(x,y) = \iint_{\Theta} |f_1(x,y) - f_2(x-\tau_x, y-\tau_y)| g_3(\tau_x,\tau_y) d\tau_x d\tau_y$$

$$f_1(x,y) = f(x,y) * g_1(x,y) \qquad f_2(x,y) = f(x,y) * g_2(x,y)$$

(1)

where three Gaussians with unitary integral are adopted for the functions $g_1(x,y)$, $g_2(x,y)$ and $g_3(x,y)$.

Let us associate every point of the domain Θ to a mass $m(\tau_x,\tau_y)$ so that:

$$m(\tau_x,\tau_y) = |f_1(x,y) - f_2(x-\tau_x, y-\tau_y)| g_3(\tau_x,\tau_y)$$

(2)

We will call the mass center of the function $m(\tau_x,\tau_y)$ "center of mass of the first order absolute moment". The center of mass of the first order absolute moment is obtained by computing the vector $\mathbf{b}(x,y)$:

$$\mathbf{b}(x,y) = \frac{1}{e(x,y)} \iint_{\Theta} \tau |f_1(x,y) - f_2(x-\tau_x, y-\tau_y)| g_3(\tau_x,\tau_y) d\tau_x d\tau_y$$

(3)

where τ is the vector with τ_x,τ_y components. While function $e(x,y)$ provides the ridge map of the image, vector $\mathbf{b}$ provides the direction of the path which joins every point of the starting contour to the nearest point of the ridge top [2].

The amplitude of the gradient of Gaussian is computed as follows:

$$h(x,y) = \left[\frac{\partial}{\partial x} [f(x,y) * g_3(x,y)] \right]^2 + \left[\frac{\partial}{\partial y} [f(x,y) * g_3(x,y)] \right]^2$$

(4)

While function h(x,y) provides the ridge map, the gradient $\mathbf{v}$ of the ridge map provides the direction of the path which joins every point of the starting contour to the nearest point of the ridge top [3].

4 Comparison between GoG and FOAM

The localization procedures take every single point of an approximate contour to the top of the ridges provided by the GoG and FOAM filters. The final contour is obtained by computing the values of the ridge maps along the path given by vector $\mathbf{v}$ and $\mathbf{b}$ respectively, until a local maximum is reached. The path length is bounded to the radius r of the circular domain Θ. In order to evaluate only the properties and drawbacks of using the two ridge maps, no additional regularization criteria were used, except for the low pass filters of the GoG and FOAM operators.

	GoG			FOAM $\sigma1=2$ $\sigma2=0.67$			FOAM $\sigma1=2.67$ $\sigma2=1.33$		
Δ	PRM1	PRM2	PRM3	PRM1	PRM2	PRM3	PRM1	PRM2	PRM3
0	100	100	77	100	100	91	100	100	93
1	100	100	92	100	100	99	100	100	98
2	100	100	93	100	100	99	100	100	98
3	100	100	95	100	100	100	100	100	99
4	100	100	95	100	100	100	100	100	100
5	100	100	75	100	100	82	100	100	86
6	100	100	45	100	100	61	100	100	69
7	100	96	28	100	100	55	100	100	64
8	95	78	13	98	98	48	100	100	56
9	82	40	6	91	91	36	98	98	46
10	57	18	2	76	74	23	90	90	29
11	38	8	2	53	47	14	70	69	18

Table 1. The percentage of points of the starting contour which reach the discontinuity versus the distance of the starting contour from the discontinuity. The size of both operators is $\sigma_3=3$ pixel.

Let Δ be the distance between the starting contour and a straight step discontinuity; in Table 1 three parameters relating to the robustness of the automatic contour tracking procedures are reported:
I. PRM1: Percentage of points of the starting contour which reach the discontinuity; the path direction is chosen perpendicularly to the discontinuity.
II. PRM2: Percentage of points of the starting contour which reach the discontinuity; the path direction is computed.
III. PRM3: Percentage of points of the starting contour which reach the nearest point of the discontinuity; the path direction is computed.
PRM1 reveals only those errors due to the presence of spurious local maxima of the ridge profile. If Δ is small with respect to the size of the operator, then no errors arise in the localization process: gaussian filters regularize both operators well enough and there are no spurious local maxima close to the discontinuity. As Δ increases, PRM1 decreases due to the presence of spurious local maxima which are far from the

discontinuity. Table 1 shows that when the path direction is given, both GoG and FOAM operators behave in the same way.

PRM2 highlights both spurius local maxima and wrong path direction. While PRM2 is lower than PRM1 if a GoG operator is used, no significant differences between the two parameters are present if FOAM is adopted. Therefore, the computation of the center of mass of the FOAM is more robust to noise than the computation of the gradient of the GoG map. In figure 1 the results of the procedure applied on a synthetic image are presented: localization is better if FOAM operator is used.

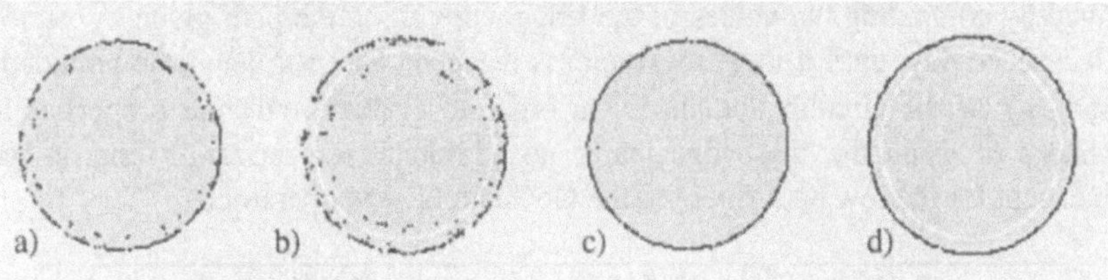

Figure 1. The test image is a step discontinuity of 20 affected by additive Gaussian noise with $\sigma=10$. The starting contour is the white inner circular contour ($\Delta=8$ pixels). In a),b) the GoG filter is used; in c),d) the FOAM filter is used. In a),c) the final contour is shown; in b),d) the ending points of the paths $r\cdot\mathbf{v}/|\mathbf{v}|$ and $r\cdot\mathbf{b}/|\mathbf{b}|$, respectively, are shown.

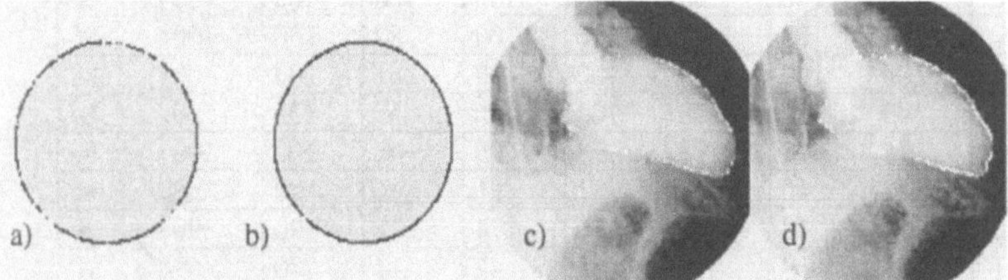

Figure 2. The final contours on sequences of synthetic and ventriculigraphics images using GoG a),c) and FOAM b),d).

PRM3 highlights mainly localization errors which arise when the approximate contour is close to the discontinuity. The amplitude of vector $\mathbf{v}$ is small on the top of the ridge (very close to the discontinuity). Therefore, errors arise in computation of the direction because of the presence of noise. The amplitude of vector $\mathbf{b}$ is also small when points near the discontinuity are considered. However, as regards FOAM, a simple rule can be applied to the localization procedure i.e. "if the distance from the starting point to the center of mass is less then 1 pixel than the final point is the same as the starting point". If this rule is applied than PRM3 is approximately equal to 100% when $\Delta=0$. The same rule cannot be applied when using GoG because the amplitude of vector $\mathbf{v}$ is small both at the top of the ridge and on the two tails of the ridge. In sequences where discontinuities move very slowly this error gives rise to a movement of the points along the contour itself. In figure 2-a),b) the effect of this error in a synthetic sequence is presented; the contour we are searching for does not move and the images of the sequence differ only according to the noise added. Let the approximate starting contour be the true contour itself, it can be observed that some of the points move leaving gaps in the final contour. In figure 2-c),d) automatic contour tracking on 10 frames of a ventriculographic sequence where motion is slow is presented.

5 Conclusion and results

Sequences of images of left ventricles, recorded in low dose digital angiography, were used to test the localization procedures. Figure 3 shows the results provided by the automatic contour tracking procedure over a 28 frame sequence when the FOAM filter is used. The approximate starting contour is a polygonal line and it is traced manually on the first frame of the sequence. When FOAM was used, localization performances increased and only a few points shifted along the contour. The better performance of the localization procedure was mainly due to the better results obtained in the computation of the path direction. When contrast material decreases, failure to localize some points of the contour occurs. In order to deal with this kind of error additional constraints must be added to regularize the localization procedure [4].

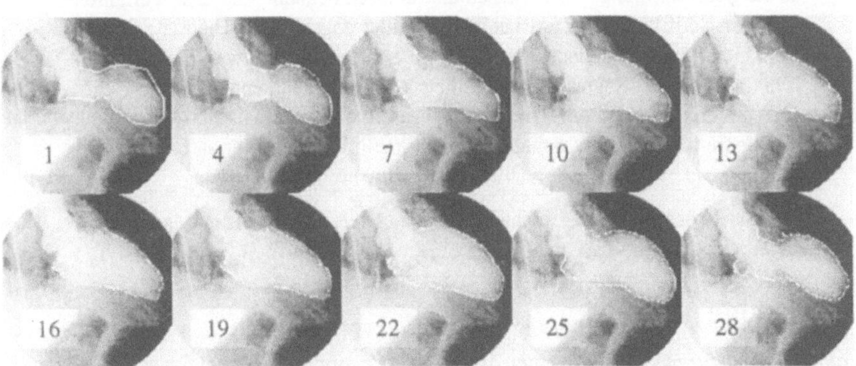

Figure 3. Results of the automatic contour tracking procedure over a sequence of 28 ventriculographics images.

References

1. M. Demi, M. Paterni, The first order absolute moment in low-level image processing, *DSP97,* 1997, pp. 511-514.
2. M.Paterni, M.Demi, C.Morizzo, M.Kozakova, C.Palombo, The First Order Absolute Moment in Contour Tracking, *Proc. Computers in Cardiology*, 1997, pp. 545-548
3. D.Marr, Vision, *Freeman*, New York 1982.
4. M.Bertero, T.A.Poggio, Ill-Posed Problems in Early Vision, *Proceeding of the IEEE*, vol. 76, n. 8, August 1988.

Unüberwachte Bildsegmentierung durch die Adaption geometrischer Objekte mit einem Evolutionsalgorithmus

H. Brinck[1], R. Grebe[2], J. Krone[3], V. Metzler[4]

[1]Fachhochschule Gelsenkirchen, [2]Universite de Compiegne, France
[3]Märkische Fachhochschule Iserlohn
[4]Institut für Medizinische Informatik der RWTH Aachen

Email: krone@mfh-iserlohn.de

Zusammenfassung. Die automatische Segmentierung ist aufgrund der Komplexität der zu analysierenden Strukturen eines der größten Probleme bei der Verarbeitung medizinischer Bilder. Dieser Beitrag stellt ein neues Segmentierungsverfahren vor, das auf einem evolutionären Algorithmus, also auf einer stochastischen Optimierungsmethode basiert. Ausgehend von elementaren, geometrischen Objekten wird dabei das zu segmentierende Zielbild iterativ rekonstruiert. Dadurch erhält man inplizit eine Segmentierung des Zielbildes, da die Segmentierungen der Elementarstrukturen bekannt sind. Das Verfahren wird zur Verifikation auf artifizielle Testbilder angewendet. Hierbei zeigt ein Vergleich mit verschiedenen Schwellwertverfahren einen etwa zwei- bis dreifach geringeren Segmentierungsfehler. Die Gefäßerkennung auf radio-angiographischen Bildern wird exemplarisch als medizinische Anwendung demonstriert. Eine wissensbasierte und pixelorientierte Variante des Algorithmus wird ebenfalls vorgestellt und experimentell verifiziert.

Schlüsselwörter: Unüberwachte Bildsegmentierung, Evolutionsalgorithmus, Gefäßerkennung

1 Einleitung

Evolutionsalgorithmen stellen einen interessanten, methodischen Ansatz in der medizinischen Bildverarbeitung dar [Bri96]. Hier wird ein Segmentierungsverfahren vorgestellt, welches auf der evolutionären Modifikation geometrischer Objekte basiert. Ausgangspunkt des evolutionären Bildsegmentierungsalgorithmus sind bereits vorsegmentierte Bilder, welche die sogenannte „Grundpopulation" bilden. Diese Grundpopulation besteht aus elementaren, geometrischen Objekten wie z.B. Rechtecke, Liniensegmente, etc., deren Segmentierungen bereits bekannt sind. Ein Zielbild, das mit dieser Methode automatisch segmentiert werden soll, wird durch die evolutionären Operatoren *Reproduktion*, *Mutation* und *Selektion* aus der Grundpopulation schrittweise rekonstruiert und „lernt" dadurch seine Segmentierung. Angewandt wird das Verfahren auf radio-angiographische Bilder, deren Segmentierung eine anspruchsvolle algorithmische Aufgabe darstellen [All97,Döl97]. Ein verwandter Ansatz, welcher eine Wissensbasis mit kompletten vorsegmentierten Beispielbildern verwendet, basiert auf der pixelweisen Rekombination des Zielbildes [Met97]. Dieser kann auch bei medizinischen Bildern eingesetzt werden, die nicht durch synthetisierbare Elementarstrukturen modelliert werden können.

2 Methode

Aufgabe des hier vorgestellten Algorithmus ist die unüberwachte Segmentierung eines Zielbildes, welches aus der selben Bilddomäne stammt wie die vorsegmentierten Bilder der Grundpopulation. Das Prinzip des Algorithmus besteht darin, das Zielbild aus den vorhandenen Bildern der Grundpopulation mittels evolutionärer Operatoren zu rekonstruieren. Diese spezialisierten Manipulationsoperationen sind so gewählt, daß sie sich gleichermaßen auf die Grauwerte und die Segmentierung (Label) der Bilder beziehen. Das Verfahren erzeugt also sukzessive neue Grauwertmatrizen und deren Segmentierungen, wobei sich die Grauwerte immer stärker denen des Zielbildes annähern. Der eigentliche Antrieb der evolutionären Optimierung ist der Selektionsdruck, der durch eine Fitneßfunktion aufgebaut wird. In diesem Ansatz repräsentiert die Fitneß die Ähnlichkeit zweier Grauwertbilder. Dies wird über die Euklid'sche Distanz zwischen einer Bildmatrix der Population und dem Zielbild realisiert. Im Laufe der evolutionären Anpassung haben also solche Individuen (Segmentierungen) hohe Reproduktionswahrscheinlichkeiten, die möglichst gut an das Zielbild angepaßt sind. Damit wird erreicht, daß durch die Rekonstruktion des Zielbildes automatisch dessen Segmentierung generiert wird. Die Segmentierungsqualität kann allerdings nicht Bestandteil der Fitneßfunktion sein, da die optimale Segmentierung natürlich nicht bekannt ist. Daraus ergibt sich, daß die Operatoren die in der Grundpopulation vorhandene Korrelation zwischen Grauwerten und Regionenindizes (Label) nicht zerstören darf. Das folgende Schema veranschaulicht das Prinzip der evolutionären Segmentierung.

Vorbedingungen:

Segmentierte Beispieldatensätze als Grundpopulation
Definition der Fitneßfunktion als Grauwertabstand zum Zielbild

Iteration:

Auswahl von Partnern in der Nachbarschaft
Rekombination und Vererbung der Segmentierung an die Nachkommen
Mutation der Nachkommen
Selektion in Abhängigkeit von der Fitneß

Abbruchkriterium:

Rekonstruktion des Zielbildes, bzw. maximale Iterationszahl

Nachkommen entstehen durch die geeignete Rekombination der Grauwert- und Segmentierungsinformation des Elternpaares. Die Mutation wird in diesem Zusammenhang durch lokale Verschiebungsoperationen von kleinem Betrag realisiert. Um die Korrelation nicht zu zerstören werden also lediglich Grauwert/Label-Paare aus der lokalen Umgebung des zu mutierenden Pixels kopiert und ersetzt. Die Selektion wählt die Individuen mit hoher Fitneß als Eltern der nächsten Generation aus. Alle Operationen ermöglichen eine Übertragung der Segmentierung auf das manipulierte Bild. Dieses erbt durch seine evolutionäre Rekonstruktion eine Segmentierung, die aus den Segmentierungen der Grundpopulation ebenso kombiniert wurde wie das Grauwertbild aus den Grauwertbildern der Grundpopulation.

3 Experimentelle Ergebnisse

Zur Verifikation des Algorithmus wird ein einfaches Experiment durchgeführt, bei dem Rechtecke auf 8x8 Testbildern segmentiert werden. Hierbei sind die Grauwerte des Vorder- und des Hintergrundes um die Mittelwerte 0.3 bzw. 0.7 normalverteilt und mit unterschiedlichen Standardabweichungen gestreut. Im direkten Vergleich der Segmentierungsergebnisse mit zwei verschiedenen Schwellwertverfahren ergibt sich eine zwei- bis dreifach bessere Segmentierungsleistung bei Verwendung des Evolutionsalgorithmus (siehe Tabelle 1). Das einfachste Schwellwertverfahren ist die Anwendung eines konstanten Schwellwertes von 0.5, seine Ergebnisse sind in der zweiten Spalte aufgeführt. Das dynamische Schwellwertverfahren verwendet für jedes Pixel den optimalen Schwellwert, welcher aufgrund der bekannten Verteilungen a-priori errechnet werden kann. Die in Tabelle 1 präsentierten Daten sind Mittelwerte von jeweils 1000 Testläufen mit zufällig erzeugten Testbildern.

Fehlerrate (in %)			
Standardabw.	statische Schwelle	dynamische Schwelle	Evolutionsalgo.
0.1	15.938	11.034	5.458
0.09	13.247	9.358	4.283
0.08	10.606	7.594	3.333
0.07	7.639	5.742	2.330
0.06	4.777	3.566	1.561
0.05	2.327	1.922	0.758
0.04	0.734	0.550	0.220
mean:	7.895	5.681	2.563

Tabelle 1: *Ein Vergleich der Segmentierungsergebnisse des Evolutionsalgorithmus mit einem statischen bzw. dynamischen Schwellwertverfahren ergibt dessen eindeutige Überlegenheit. Die Ergebnisse der evolutionären Segmentierung fallen um den Faktor zwei bis drei besser aus.*

Die Vorteile des evolutionären Algorithmus werden noch deutlicher, wenn man nach dem besten der drei untersuchten Verfahren fragt. Der beste Algorithmus ist in über 90 % der 1000 Testläufe der evolutionäre Algorithmus.

3.1 Wissensbasierte Segmentierung

Bei der wissensbasierten Segmentierung besteht die Grundpopulation aus mehreren vorsegmentierten Beispielbildern, die dem zu segmentierenden Zielbild ähnlich sind. Aus den Bildern der Grundpopulation wird das Zielbild mit spezialisierten evolutionären Operatoren pixelweise rekonstruiert. Dabei entsteht implizit eine Segmentierung des Zielbildes. In Abbildung 1 werden Bilder der Größe 64x64 Pixel mit fünf verschiedenen Segmenten untersucht. Die abgebildeten vier Bilder zeigen das Zielbild und dessen optimale Segmentierung (obere Zeile), sowie das Rekonstruktionsergebnis und dessen Segmentierung (untere Zeile). Der Segmentierungsfehler kann als pixelweiser Unterschied zwischen der optimalen Segmentierung (oben rechts) und dem errechneten Ergebnis (unten rechts) angegeben werden. Das Diagramm veranschaulicht die exponentielle Konvergenz des Algorithmus durch den zeitlichen Verlauf des Segmentierungsfehlers.

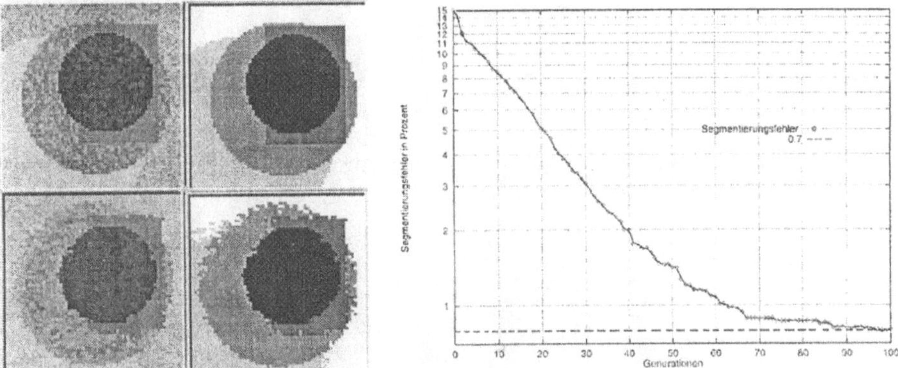

Abbildung 1: *Die vier Bilder zeigen das Zielbild und die optimale Segmentierung (obere Zeile), sowie dessen Rekonstruktion und die zugehörige Segmentierung als Ergebnis (untere Zeile). Die exponentielle Konvergenz des Algorithmus ergibt sich aus dem qualitativ linearen Abfall des Segmentierungsfehlers bei logarithmisierter y-Achse.*

Der pixelorientierte Evolutionsalgorithmus hat sich bei der Segmentierung physiologischer Bilder, wie z.B. NMR Sequenzen des menschlichen Gehirns, bereits bewährt. Hierbei werden die evolutionären Operatoren gezielt funktionell eingeschränkt, wodurch eine Reduktion des Suchraums und damit auch der Rechenzeit erreicht wird. Durch die Definition bestimmter Constraints bei der Manipulation, wie z.B. Topologieinvarianz und Minimierung von Konturkrümmungen, werden fehlerhafte Segmentierungen weitestgehend vermieden [Met98].

3.2 Medizinische Anwendung

Eine häufige Anwendung in der medizinischen Bildverarbeitung ist die Segmentierung radio-angigraphischer Bilddaten. In [All97] und [Döl97] wurde dieses Problem bereits untersucht. Hierbei ist das Ziel die automatische Segmentierung des zweidimensionalen Gefäßskeletts. Das Zielbild (Abb.2, links) wird hierzu in Ausschnitte der Größe 32x32 Pixel zerlegt, die unabhängig voneinander segmentiert werden. Die Grundpopulation besteht in diesem Fall aus mehreren tausend Liniensegmenten. Experimentelle Testergebnisse sind in Abbildung 2 dokumentiert. Neben dem Zielbild sind die Zwischenergebnisse der Iterationsstufen 1, 2, 5, 10 und 20 dargestellt. Das Endergebnis der Segmentierung ist das äußerst rechte Bild in der unteren Zeile. Bei der Segmentierung können außer den eindeutigen Klassenindizes 0 (Gefäß) und 1 (Gewebe) auch Werte zwischen 0 und 1 entstehen. Die endgültige Segmentierung erhält man aus den dargestellten Bildern nach einer entsprechenden Binarisierung. Die erzielten Ergebnisse sind denen herkömmlicher Schwellwertverfahren deutlich überlegen. Abbildung 2 veranschaulicht zusätzlich den Fortschritt der Ergebnisse während der evolutionären Adaption der Population an das Zielbild.

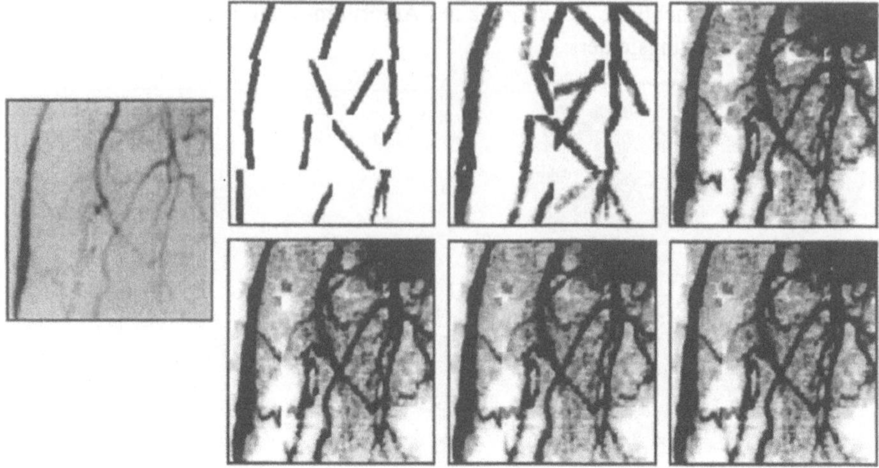

Abbildung 2: *Dargestellt ist das zu segmentierende Zielbild, sowie die Zwischenergebnisse der Iterationsstufen 1, 2, 5, 10, 20 und das Endergebnis nach 34 Iterationen.*

4 Ausblick

Die evolutionäre Segmentierung hat sich bei medizinischen Anwendungen bereits bewährt. Dennoch sind vielfältige qualitäts- und effizienzsteigernde Erweiterungen denkbar. Da die Individuen eines evolutionären Algorithmus autonom sind und mit der Selektion eine übergeordnete Kontrolle existiert, bietet sich die Paralellisierung des Problems an. Eine erste Parallelisierung führte zu akzeptablen speed-up-Werten. Evolutionsalgorithmisch ist die Einführung intelligenter Fitneßfunktionen, die wichtige Bereiche des Bildes stärker berücksichtigen, sicher geboten. Ein daraus resultierender spezifischer Selektionsdruck würde zu einer mehr zielgerichteten Segmentierung führen. Insgesamt stellt der präsentierte Algorithmus eine neue lernende Segmentierungstechnik dar, deren Lösungspotential noch ausgebaut werden kann.

Literatur

[Bri96] H. Brinck, R. Kottenhoff, J.Krone, C. Strättgen, *Evolutionsalgorithmen in der medizinischen Bildverarbeitung*, Bildverarbeitung für die Medizin, Tagungsband des Aachener Workshops 1996, S. 152-157.

[All97] M. Allelein, H. Brinck, C. Bucker, J.Krone, *Segmentation of radio-angigraphic images*, Proc. of CAR 97, Elviser, 1997, S. 152-157.

[Döl97] M. Döllner, J.Krone, U. Lehmann und V. Twer, *Gefäßsegmentierung mit Fuzzy- und Standardmethoden*, Biomedizinische Technik, Vol. 42, Supp. 2, 1997, S. 451-452.

[Met97] V. Metzler, R. Vandenhouten, J.Krone, R. Grebe, *Wissensbasierte Bildsegmentierung mittels stochastischer Optimierung*, Digitale Bildverarbeitung in der Medizin, Tagungsband des 5. Freiburger Workshops, 1997, S. 75-80.

[Met98] V. Metzler, R. Vandenhouten, J. Krone, R. Grebe, *Unsupervised Image Segmentation by Stochastic Reconstruction*, SPIE Symposium on Medical Imaging, Procs SPIE, Vol. 3338, 1998, in press

Computer Aided Diagnosis of Bone Lesions in the Facial Skeleton

Wolfgang Sörgel[1,2], Sabine Girod[2], Martin Szummer[3] and Bernd Girod[1]

[1]Lehrstuhl für Nachrichtentechnik I, Universität Erlangen-Nürnberg, 91058 Erlangen
[2] Klinik und Poliklinik für Mund-,Kiefer-,Gesichtschirurgie, 91054 Erlangen
[3] M.I.T. Media Lab, Cambridge MA 02139, USA. **
{wsoergel,girod,szummer}@nt.e-technik.uni-erlangen.de

Abstract. We present a system for computer aided diagnosis of bone tumors in the facial skeleton. There are many different lesions with radiographic manifestation in the jaws. Our system helps performing the differential diagnosis of these. The input is a digitized orthopantomograph (OPG) in which the user marks the position of the lesion with a single mouse click. An active contour model then automatically finds the boundaries of the lesion. Gray-level histograms, MRSAR texture features and Gabor filter features are computed for the lesion region. These features are then combined and used to query a database containing expert-diagnosed reference cases. The result is a number of similar cases, with tumor position marked and with available expert annotations. We show good agreement between our results and differential diagnosis given by humans. The system is also a suitable tool for training and education.

Keywords: Computer aided diagnosis, content based image retrieval

1   Introduction

Bone tumors in the maxilla and mandible are relatively rare. The clinical symptoms are usually unspecific and therefore most of the tumors are discovered accidentally during routine radiological exams. The differential diagnosis of bone tumors in the jaws is difficult and can be based on the radiologic findings, e.g. the structure of the tumor region in the x-ray, defined or diffuse margins, presence or absence of teeth and localization of the lesion. Traditionally a printed tumor atlas [1] is used to compare the images and narrow down possible differential diagnoses. A system for computer-aided diagnosis of these lesions, based on characterization of the findings by the user and the use of Bayes rule to find a probability for each disease has also been devised [2]. In contrast to those approaches requiring the user to interpret the image, in our system the images are analyzed and features characterizing the lesions are computed. Based on these features a database containing expert diagnosed reference cases is queried for the cases most similar to the one presented. It is then the responsibility of the user to interpret the results and decide on necessary therapeutic measures, we do *not* attempt to classify a case or even give a computer diagnosis.

** M. Szummer contributed to this project as a visiting scientist supported by the Graduiertenkolleg 3-D Image Analysis and Synthesis.

2 Database

At the moment our database contains 236 cases from 20 different disease classes. Of these cases 161 were taken from the DOESAK (Deutsch-OEsterreichisch-Schweizerischer Arbeitskreis für Tumoren im Mund-Kiefer- und Gesichtsbereich) central registry of bone tumors in Basel, Switzerland, the rest are local cases from Erlangen. At least one OPG is stored for each case. The images were digitized at 150 dpi and normalized at 256 gray levels. Precomputed features for queries and tumor localization information are stored. Age and sex prevalence for the different diseases is also available in addition to the data of individual cases. Combination of databases, addition of new cases, manual browsing and restriction of the search is possible as well as remote access over the Internet.

3 Identification of Lesion Boundaries

After a new image is digitized the boundaries of a present lesion must be outlined. In our current implementation we rely on the user to find the lesion and point to it with the cursor. The subsequent outlining is automatic and usually requires no additional user interaction. Based on user input the contour boundaries are outlined using active contour models. Since lesion appearance is not uniform and the margins are often very diffuse, we use an energy formulation which is partly based on the image properties in a small circle around the initialization point to get a region based active contour model [3, 4]. While the contour converges, the region around each of its points is compared to the initial region, based on the result from filtering operations to indicate texture and gray-level properties. As long as there is similarity, given by a Mahalanobis measure, the contour expands rapidly, otherwise it stops.

We use three regions for image analysis: rectangular regions inscribed in and bounding the contour and the polygonally bounded region of the lesion itself.

4 Features for Database Query

Using this segmentation, features for database query are computed. The first, most important group of features is based on the image gray level. Further features are derived from the lesion contour and additional patient information.

The brightness of a lesion is a significant radiologic feature which we analyze using histograms to obtain a quantification of whether a lesion is radiopaque or radiolucent, and whether it is more uniformly colored or has flecks.

Different texture metrics are employed to assess the radiologic microstructure of the lesion bone tissue. Texture analysis is a powerful tool which has been successfully used in different content-based image query systems [5, 6] and has been proposed for identification and comparison of bone lesions in radiologic images [7]. It is also well-known that a single metric is not suitable for all queries, this was confirmed by early experiments. We thus apply several different metrics. The segmented image regions are first preprocessed by unsharp masking with a large median filter to remove low frequency disturbances and enhance the microstructure. The following algorithms have been chosen for feature computation:

- An autoregressive texture model (MRSAR) [8] with three resolution levels and four neighbors at each level. This metric is well suited to recover fine grainy structures and, applied to the lesion bounding region, indicates the presence of teeth around a lesion quite well.
- A texture description based on filtering with Gabor filters at different scales and orientations [9]. The metric derived from the energy of the filter output in the different bands identifies line-like structures especially well.

Each of these features is directly compared to the corresponding feature for each case in the database, using the Euclidean metric, Mahalanobis distance or undirected divergence.

Besides the above image derived features we also use the age and the sex of a patient to find similar images in a query. Since these features are only relevant for certain diseases, a probability density for each disease class has been estimated using 2744 cases from the DOESAK central registry as a statistical basis. The feature distance is then the joint conditional probability density function of the presented case and the database case under the hypothesis they are both from the same class as the database case.

To finally query the database we must combine the multiple features into a single similarity measure for each case. We use a weighted rank-order combination of the features. Specifically, the database cases are sorted according to ascending distance for each feature. The rank numbers are then weighted by a feature weighting and summed up to give an overall measure of similarity for each database case. To gain robustness, the most poorly matching features for a given case are discarded.

The best matches are then presented to the user. Tumors are marked and all available annotations are displayed. The user can now view these images, retrieve more images which are similar to returned ones or perform a new query with changed parameters or a restricted database.

5   Example Queries

We show two example queries using our system. For case A we used an image of a 81-year-old female patient who was diagnosed with a kerato cyst of fairly typical appearance. The following features were used in the query: gray-level histogram (inscribed rectangle and polygonal region), MRSAR and Gabor filter based texture (inscribed and bounding rectangles), age and sex of the patient, contour aspect ratio and smoothness. Figure 1 shows the image and the best returned matches, Table 1 summarizes the results. All results returned for example case A, with exception of the fourth match, are either the correct diagnosis or relevant differential diagnoses. As a second example case B we used an osteogenic tumor,

Fig. 1. Example Results: Reference case A (Kerato Cyst) on top with the three best matches shown left to right below. The lesions are marked.

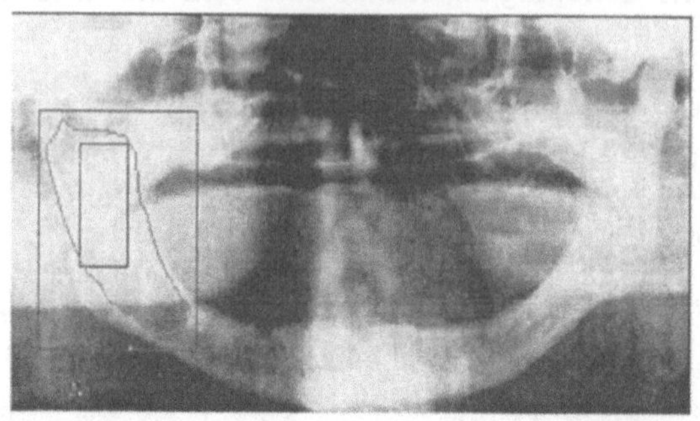

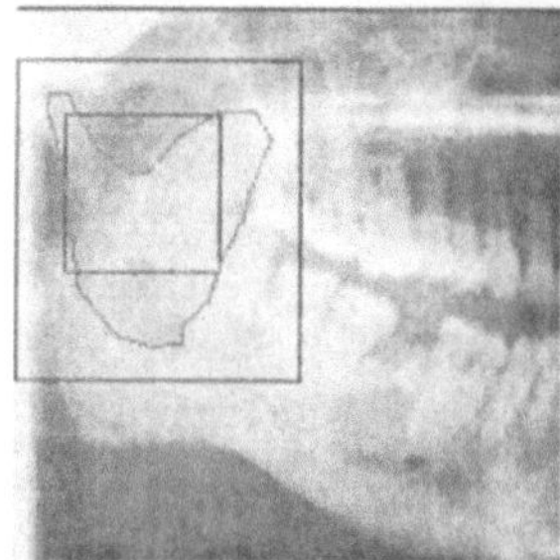 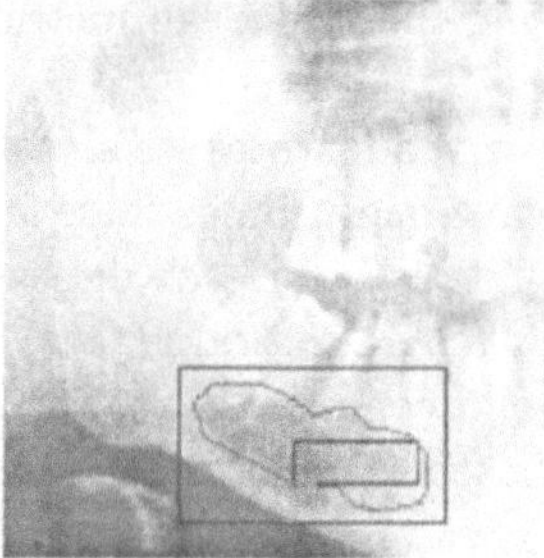 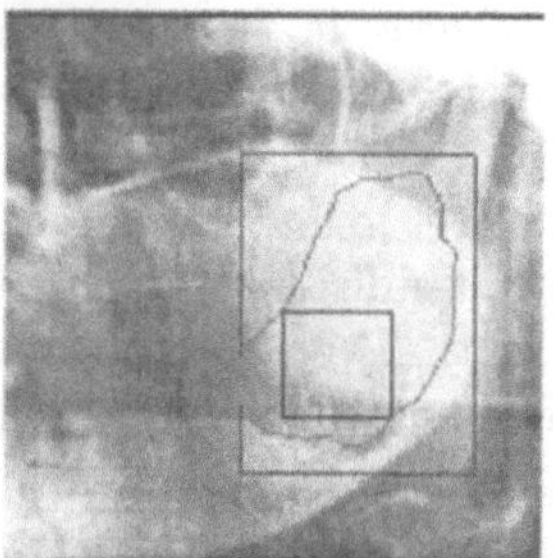

an osteoma, diagnosed in 28-year-old female as reference, results are also shown in Table 1. Again, all cases with exception of one (sixth match, a fairly atypical giant cell granuloma) are correct or relevant. More results, including images, can be found in the WWW at `http://www.nt.e-technik.uni-erlangen.de/~wsoergel/diagnosis/`. In general, we found that the system returns visually similar cases to the query case, and most of them are also diagnostically relevant.

6 Conclusions and Future Work

We have presented a system for computer aided diagnosis of bone lesions in the jaw, based on image analysis and content-based query of a database. A lesion in a digitized radiograph of the jaw is marked and then outlined by a region-based active contour model. Then gray level, texture and other features are computed for the suspicious region. Based on these features a database with expert diagnosed bone cancer cases is queried for similar cases. The returned matches have been found to be a valuable aid in giving a differential diagnosis. Currently we are evaluating additional features, e.g. considering form and location of the tumors. Clinical evaluation of the system also plays an important role in the project, as well as expanding our database.

Table 1. Results returned for example queries.

Case	Disease	Age	Sex	Case	Disease	Age	Sex
A	Kerato Cyst	81	female	B	Osteoma	28	female
1.	Pseudo Cyst	41	male	1.	Osteoma	36	female
2.	Kerato Cyst	46	male	2.	Osteoma	51	female
3.	Ameloblastoma	65	female	3.	Osteosarcoma	28	male
4.	Fibroma	17	female	4.	Compound Odontoma	12	female
5.	Kerato Cyst	25	female	5.	Compound Odontoma	54	male
6.	Kerato Cyst	54	male	6.	Giant Cell Granuloma	26	female

7 Acknowledgments

We acknowledge the support of Friatec AG, Mannheim for this project. We would also like to express our gratitude towards Dr. Jundt at Kantonshospital in Basel, Switzerland for providing us with images from the DOESAK central registry of bone tumors maintained at his institute.

References

1. J. Prein, W. Remagen, B. Speissl, and E. Uehlinger. *Atlas of Tumors of the Facial Skeleton.* Springer Verlag, 1996.
2. S.C. White. Computer-aided differential diagnosis of oral radiographic lesions. *Dentomaxillofacial Radiology*, 18(5):53 – 59, May 1989.
3. S. C. Zhu and A. L. Yuille. Region competition: Unifying snakes, region growing and Bayes/MDL for multi-band image segmentation. *IEEE Transactions on Pattern Analysis and Machine Intelligence*, 18(9):884 – 901, September 1996.
4. J. Ivins and J. Porril. Active region models for segmenting medical images. In *Proc. ICIP'94*, volume 2, pages 377 – 386, 1994.
5. A. Pentland, R. Picard, and S. Sclaroff. Photobook: Tools for content-base manipulation of image databases. In *Proc. SPIE*, volume 2185, pages 34 – 47, San Jose, CA, February 1994.
6. J. R. Smith and S.-F. Chang. Local color and texture extraction and spatial query. In *Proc. International Conference on Image Processing*, Lausanne, Switzerland, September 1996.
7. F. Weiler, E. Pelikan, T. Nobis, T. Tolxdorff, and K. Bohndorf. Texturbasierte Extraktion medizinischer Merkmale aus Filmröntgenbildern. In S.J. Pöppl and H. Handels, editors, *Mustererkennung 1993*, Berlin, 1993. Springer.
8. J. Mao and A. K. Jain. Texture classification and segmentation using multiresolution simultaneous autoregressive models. *Pattern Recognition*, 25(2):173 – 188, 1992.
9. B. S. Manjunath and Y. W. Ma. Texture features for browsing and retrieval of image data. *IEEE Transactions on Pattern Analysis and Machine Intelligence (PAMI)*, 18(8):837 – 841, August 1996.

Eine modulare Architektur zur Vereinfachung der Entwicklung klinischer Bildverarbeitungssysteme

Athanasios M. Demiris, Carlos E. Cardenas S.,
Manuela H. Makabe, Hans-Peter Meinzer

Abt. für Medizinische und Biologische Informatik
Deutsches Krebsforschungszentrum
INF 280, 69120 Heidelberg
Email: A.M.Demiris@dkfz-heidelberg.de

Zusammenfassung. Das Problem der Bearbeitung medizinischen Bildmaterials in der klinischen Routine wurde bisher systemtheoretisch auf zwei Arten angegangen. Die eine Lösung sieht ein monolithisches System vor, das mit einem Maximum an Funktionalität ausgestattet ist. Die andere dagegen besteht aus mehreren kleineren Systemeinheiten, welche spezialisierte Teilaufgaben in der klinischen Bildverarbeitung angehen, wie z.B. Volumenmessung in der Leberchirurgie, Flußmessungen in der Herzchirurgie und zahlreiche andere. Diese kleineren Systeme können dann in ein sog. Host-System eingebettet werden und koexistieren. Für die Unterstützung der Entwicklung der modularen und konfigurierbaren Systeme der zweiten Gruppe stellen wir eine Architektur vor. Wir erläutern die Gründe für die Einführung einer derartigen Architektur, die Aktivitäten des Bildverarbeiters, die diese Architektur unterstützen soll, ihre Komponenten, und abschließend eine mögliche Implementierung in Form von objektorientierten Frameworks.

Schlüsselwörter: objektorientierte Frameworks, Entwicklungswerkeuze, Bildverarbeitungsalgorithmen Repository, Parametrisierung

1 Einleitung

Die Bildverarbeitung hat ihren Weg in viele Anwendungsdomänen gefunden. In einigen dieser Domänen soll ihre Einführung nicht nur eine Erweiterung, sondern auch eine Beschleunigung der Aktivitäten darstellen. Damit ist die zusätzliche Auseinandersetzung der Anwender mit Bildverarbeitungsinternas ausgeschlossen. Das gilt insbesondere für die klinische Bildverarbeitung.

Ein Problem der klinischen Bildverarbeitung ist die Vielfalt der Aufgaben, die damit angesprochen werden können. Dieses wird in vielen Systemen mit einem Maximum an verfügbaren Algorithmen versucht zu lösen. Somit entstehen oft Systeme, welche primär technische und weniger medizinische Kenntnisse erfordern und damit niedrige Akzeptanz erzielen. Eine zweite Lösung ist die komponentenbasierte Entwicklung mehrerer Teillösungen, die anschießend kombiniert werden können.

In unserer Arbeitsgruppe wurde aufgrund der Vielfalt der klinischen Einsatzgebiete die zweite Lösung bevorzugt. Diese Lösung bedeutet das Entwickeln einer dedizierten Applikation für jede neue klinische Fragestellung. Es ist deshalb wünschenswert,

Aufgaben, die eine schnelle Reaktion auf eine neue Anforderung verzögern können, zu vereinfachen. Als zeitaufwendige Aufgaben erweisen sich das Vertraut machen mit neuem Bildmaterial, die Selektion der adäquaten Bildverarbeitungsalgorithmen, die richtige Parametrisierung derselben, die Evaluation ihrer Wirkung und die Erstellung einer graphischen Benutzungsschnittstelle sowohl zum Testen als auch zum Integrieren in die klinische Routine. Zusätzlich sollte diese Architektur alle Komponenten, die von mehreren Systemen benutzt werden können, identifizieren und zur Verfügung stellen, wie z.B. das Laden und Anzeigen der Bilder. Um die Zeit von der Anforderung zum fertigen, klinisch einsetzbaren System zu reduzieren, haben wir eine Architektur entworfen, die diesen Problemen durch Modularität, Erweiterbarkeit und Anpassungsfähigkeit entgegentritt.

2 Methoden und Vorgehen

Das Szenario, welches unterstützt werden soll, ist in Abbildung 1 gezeigt. Der medizinische Endanwender kontaktiert den Systementwickler mit den Anforderungen ①. Dieser sucht nach existierenden Komponenten, die für die Lösung gut geeignet sind ②. Diese Komponenten sind in einem Datenbanksystem gespeichert und werden aus diesem geladen ③. Bei Bedarf werden für selektierte repräsentative Bilder Parametereinstellungen vom System vorgeschlagen ④.

Wird ein Algorithmus für ein neues Teilproblem der Bildverarbeitung entwickelt, so kann dieser in das Repository aufgenommen werden. Um seine formale Dokumentation, und damit ein schnelleres Auffinden, zu gewährleisten,   werden vom Ent-

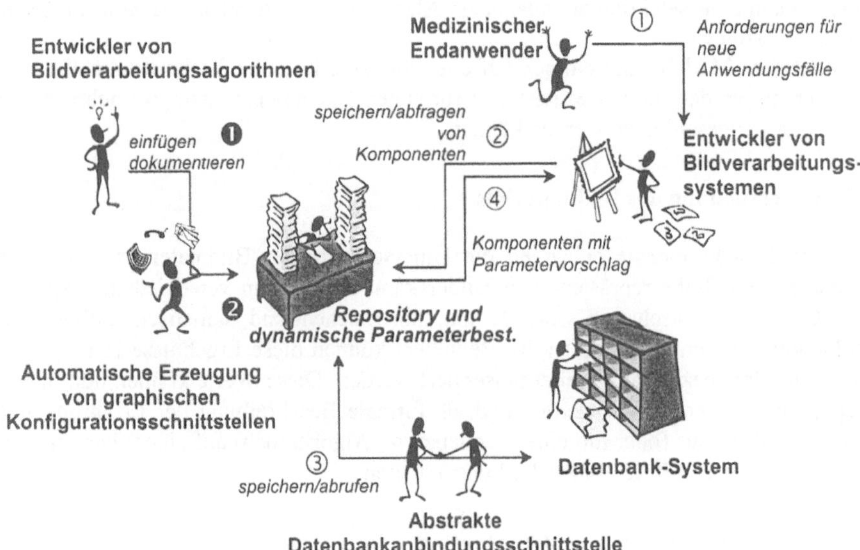

Abb. 1 Übersicht der Abläufe für die Erstellung eines neuen Bildverarbeitungssystems (Schritte ①, ②, ③, ④) und der Erweiterung des Algorithmen-Repository (Schritte ❶, ❷).

wickler zusätzliche Informationen, die im Repository-Modell enthalten sind, einge-geben ❶. Optional kann eine graphische Konfigurationsschnittstelle zum interaktiven Einstellen der Parameter automatisch erzeugt werden und im Repository aufgenom-men werden ❷. Dann kann der neue Algorithmus (oder die neue Sequenz von Algo-rithmen) als eine vollständige, wiederverwendbare Komponente bezeichnet werden. Im Folgenden werden die Komponenten, die diese Aktivitäten unterstützen sollen, im Einzelnen beschrieben.

2.1 Algorithmen-Repository

Die Wiederverwendung von Software auf der Basis von Programmiersprachen bein-haltet noch den Nachteil, daß die am besten geeigneten wiederzuverwendenden Komponenten nicht leicht zu finden sind. Aus diesem Grund ist eine Strukturierung und das Versehen der Software-Module mit zusätzlicher Information nötig. Die Lö-sung für dieses Problem ist ein Repository. Existierende Ansätze sind in der Regel entweder zu kompliziert, da sie domänenübergreifend sein sollen [1], oder zu einge-schränkt, weil sie plattformgebunden sind [2].

Aus diesem Grund haben wir ein Repository unter Berücksichtigung existierender Standards, wie CDIF (Computer Aided Software Engineering Data Interchange For-mat) [3], speziell für die klinische Bildverarbeitung entwickelt. Zunächst wurde eine allgemeine Beschreibung für medizinische Bildverarbeitungsalgorithmen entworfen und implementiert. Diese stellt eine Spezialisierung bekannter Beschreibungsmodelle für allgemeine Algorithmen dar, wie sie z.B. in vielen objektorientierten Program-miersprachen zu finden sind [4], [5], [6] oder in CDIF modelliert wurden. Zusätzlich sind die Strukturen für das Ablegen des notwendigen medizinischen Wissens model-liert. So kann die Selektion der adäquaten Algorithmen auch anhand nicht technischer Kriterien erfolgen.

Das gesamte Modell kann einfach auf eine abstrakte Datenbankschnittstelle abgebil-det werden, so daß die am weitesten verbreiteten Datenbanken zum Aufnehmen des Repository angeschlossen werden können.

2.2 Untersuchung des Bildmaterials

Die zweite Komponente behandelt die Untersuchung des Bildmaterials. Nach der Eingabe einer Reihe repräsentativer Bilder kann das System verschiedene Aspekte, wie Grauwerteigenschaften, -profile u.ä, untersuchen und statistisch aufbereiten. Abhängig von den Kenntnissen des Benutzers können diese Ergebnisse in ihrer Ge-samtheit oder speziell aufbereitet präsentiert werden. Diese Werte können nun in das Repository aufgenommen werden und als formale Beschreibung der Erfahrung mit einem Algorithmus (oder mit einer Sequenz von Algorithmen) auf einem bestimmten Bildmaterial (z.B. CTAP Bilder der Leber) dienen.

2.3 Vorparametrisierung und Evaluation

Die dritte Komponente übernimmt die optimale Parameter-Einstellung der selektier-ten Algorithmen in Bezug auf das Bildmaterial. Aus den errechneten Eigenschaften der Bilder kann ein initialer Parametersatz für einen Algorithmus bestimmt und anschließend dessen Wirkung mit diesen Parametern evaluiert werden.

Die Evaluation erfolgt mit Hilfe einer Fuzzy-Logik-basierten Steuerung und kann allerdings nur dann eingesetzt werden, wenn statistische Werte über die Kategorie vom aktuell vorliegenden Bildmaterial vorhanden sind, die als Richtwerte dienen. Wenn die Evaluation schlecht ausfällt, werden die Werte angepaßt und ein neuer Versuch erfolgt.

Zur Evaluation von Segmentierungsalgorithmen stehen momentan folgende Möglichkeiten zur Verfügung: relative Größe des segmentierten Objekts zu einem einfach zu detektierenden Objekt in der selben anatomischen Umgebung, Schwerpunktlage, Ausbreitung des Objekts, Richtung des Trägheittensors, Zusammenhang (grauwertbasiert), Homogenität.

2.4 Automatische Erzeugung von graphischen Konfigurationsschnittstellen

Die vierte Komponente stellt aufgrund der Algorithmusschnittstelle (Signatur) automatisch graphische Benutzungselemente zur Verfügung, um die Algorithmen zu testen und anschließend in eine übergeordnete Applikation zu integrieren. Die Parametertypen werden herangezogen, um für jeden Parameter ein dediziertes, adäquates Element zu erzeugen. Die Algorithmen können momentan in C oder C++ implementiert sein und die Datentypen des in unserer Abteilung verwendeten Bildformats einsetzen. Sowohl die Erweiterung auf andere Implementierungssprachen der Algorithmen als auch zusätzlich definierte Datentypen lassen sich durch leichte Modifikationen der Komponente erreichen. Um eine größere Flexibilität zu gewährleisten, basierte der Entwurf dieser Komponente auf dem MVC-Konzept, welches die eigentliche Applikation von der graphischen Benutzungsschnittstelle trennt [7].

Das Aussehen der graphischen Elemente kann von der Host-Applikation festgelegt werden, indem diese einen Satz von solchen, an sie angepassten Elementen zur Verfügung stellt. Alternativ ist es möglich, ein von der Komponente angebotenes Aussehen zu wählen. Die Gestaltung der Komponenten erfolgte nach Regeln der kognitiven Ergonomie in der medizinischen Informations- und Bildverarbeitung [8], [9].

2.5 Eine mögliche Implementierung mit objektorientierten Frameworks

Die Beschreibung der einzelnen Komponenten der hier vorgestellten Architektur soll flexibel gehalten werden und konfigurierbar sein. Da objektorientierte Frameworks diese Bedingungen optimal erfüllen, scheint ihre Verwendung am besten geeignet zu sein [10], [11]. Aus diesem Grund haben wir für jede Komponente jeweils ein Framework implementiert. Somit lassen sich alle Einzelteile getrennt voneinander modifizieren und an andere Umgebungen anpassen. In ihrer Gesamtheit bleiben sie trotzdem funktionstüchtig.

3 Diskussion und Ausblick

Die Komponenten der hier beschriebenen Architektur sind in unterschiedlichen Ausbaustufen implementiert und die erste Machbarkeitsstudie ist erfolgreich abgeschlossen. Das Repository ist bereits modelliert und in der Programmiersprache Smalltalk implementiert. Eine Portierung nach Java ist bereits angelaufen. Eine Reihe von Algorithmen zur Vorparametrisierung und Evaluation wird an Einzelfällen getestet. Bislang haben wir uns auf die Bildgebungsmodalitäten MR und CT und die anatomischen Regionen Abdomen und Herz konzentriert. Die automatische Erzeugung von graphischen Konfigurationsschnittstellen ist in ihrer ersten Phase abgeschlossen. Eine Ansammlung von statistischen Auswertungsalgorithmen wird mit dem Repository gekoppelt, um sie über Begriffe der Bildverarbeitung anzusteuern.

Da eines der Ziele die Erweiterbarkeit war, haben wir die Komponenten als objektorientierte Frameworks umgesetzt. Noch fehlende Elemente können deswegen einfach hinzugefügt werden. Um eine Verteilung zu gewährleisten, werden einige der Komponenten mit CORBA-Funktionalität ausgestattet [12]. Eine größere Studie, die den eigentlichen Zeitgewinn nach Einsatz der hier beschriebenen Architektur untersucht, ist geplant. Der routinemässige Einsatz sollte in den nächsten Monaten stattfinden.

4 Literatur

1. Unisys Corp. Universal Repository Information Model Technical Overview. Doc. Nr. 86002094, 1996.
2. Bernstein PA, Sanders P, Harry B, Shutt D, Zander J: The Microsoft Repository. Proceedings of the 23rd VLDB Conference, Athens Greece, 1997.
3. EIA/IS-106: CDIF CASE Data Interchange Format - Overview. Released as Interim Standard.
4. Goldberg A, Robson D: Smalltalk-80 The Interactive Programming Environment. Addison-Wesley, Reading MA, 2. Auflage 1989.
5. Grand M, Knudsen J: Java Fundamental Classes Reference. O'Reilly & Assoc., Sebastopol CA, 1997.
6. Cattell RGG (Ed): The Object Database Standard: ODMG-93 Release 1.1. Morgan Kaufmann Publishers, 1994.
7. Rumbaugh J: Modeling Models and Viewing Views: A Look at the Model-View-Controller Framework. Journal of Object-Oriented Programming, 7(2):14-20, 1994.
8. Borälv E, Göransson B, Olsson E, Sandblad B: Usability and Efficiency: the HELIOS Approach to Development of User Interfaces. Computer Methods and Programs in Biomedicine, 45(Suppl.):47-64, 1994.
9. Demiris AM, Meinzer HP: Cognition Based Development and Evaluation of Ergonomic User Interfaces for Medical Image Processing and Archiving Systems. Medical Informatics, in print.
10. Lewis T (Ed): Object-oriented application frameworks. Manning Publications, Greenwich, 1995.
11. Taligent Inc.: Leveraging Object-Oriented Frameworks. Taligent Inc., Cupertino CA, 1993.
12. Object Management Group, Inc.: Common Object Request Broker Architecture and Specification, CORBA Revision 2. Framingham, Massachusetts, 1995.

Ein System zur automatischen Generierung graphischer Benutzungsschnittstellen für Bildverarbeitungsalgorithmen

Carlos E. Cárdenas S., Athanasios M. Demiris,
Manuela H. Makabe, Hans-Peter Meinzer

Abt. für Medizinische und Biologische Informatik
Deutsches Krebsforschungszentrum
INF 280, 69120 Heidelberg
Email: C.Cardenas@dkfz-heidelberg.de

Zusammenfassung. Seit Anfang der achtziger Jahre ist eine große Anzahl von Tools für die Entwicklung graphischer Benutzungsschnittstellen (GUI) auf unterschiedlichen Abstraktionsebenen entstanden. Einige dieser Tools zwingen den Entwickler sich mit unnötig vielen Details auseinanderzusetzen. Andere Tools lassen dem Benutzer keine Flexibilität oder sind so komplex, daß dadurch die Arbeit nicht erleichtert wird. Mit Hilfe von Generierungssystemen erreicht man eine Senkung der Entwicklungszeiten und Kosten. Wir stellen eine generische Architektur vor, die eine weitestgehende Automatisierung des Generierungsprozeßes graphischer Benutzungsschnittstellen für Bildverarbeitungsalgorithmen erlaubt. Dabei werden keine zusätzlichen Anforderungen an den Benutzer gestellt.

Schlüsselwörter: Generierungssystem, Benutzungsschnittstellen, Bildverarbeitungsalgorithmen, Frameworks

1 Einleitung

Zur Unterstützung der Mediziner bei der Interpretation tomographischer Schichtbildserien, wie MR oder CT, ist es notwendig, Bildverarbeitungsalgorithmen zu erstellen. Das effektive Entwickeln eines neuen Bildverarbeitungsalgorithmus, das Testen und dessen Einsatz wird durch die entsprechende Benutzungsschnittstelle unterstützt. Außerdem erlaubt eine Benutzungsschnittstelle die interaktive Bedienung und Parametrisierung der Algorithmen.

Die Entwicklung einer graphischen Benutzungsschnittstelle (GUI), welche einfach zu bedienen ist, und außerdem die Anforderungen des Benutzers erfüllt, ist sehr oft ein langwieriger und komplexer Prozeß. Im Durchschnitt besteht der Code einer Applikation zu 48% aus einem "User Interface"-spezifischen Teil, und über 50% der Zeit bei der Implementierung eines Systems verbringt man mit dem User Interface [1].

2 State-of-the-Art

In den letzten Jahren wurden verschiedene Ansätze eingesetzt, um den Aufwand für die Erzeugung von GUIs zu verringern. Dabei werden Ansätze, wie das "Model-Based Interface" Paradigma verwendet [2], welches die Zentralisierung aller nötigen Informationen ermöglicht, um mit Hilfe bestimmter Regeln den statischen Teil des GUIs ohne konventionelle Programmierung und ohne Interface Entwicklungsumgebung realisieren zu können. Die für die vollständige Generierung des GUIs fehlenden Informationen werden durch punktuelles Eingreifen des Benutzers gewonnen.

Bei der Verwendung dieses Ansatzes kann der dynamische Teil des GUIs nicht automatisch generiert werden, er muß statt dessen getrennt definiert werden. Der Interaktionsfluß (dynamischer Teil) zwischen den graphischen Elementen wird normalerweise mit graphischen Editoren oder auch mit der Einführung von "pre-" und "postconditions" durchgeführt. Die Trennung des Generierungsprozeßes in zwei Teile ist ein großer Nachteil, weil die Konsistenz der Elemente dadurch gefährdet ist. Je höher die Anzahl der graphischen Komponenten ist, desto größer ist die Gefahr der Inkompatibilität zwischen den Teilen. Es entstehen außerdem sehr komplexe Systeme, weil die Anforderungen an den Anwender ständig anwachsen. Die Modelle, welche solchen Systemen zugrunde liegen, sind eher an die Generierungskomponente des jeweiligen Systems angepaßt, und weniger an den Anwender. Innerhalb der Tätigkeiten, welche der Anwender erledigen muß, zählt zwar nicht die Syntax von graphischen Bibliotheken, jedoch muß er sich mit deklarativen Modellen, deren Aufgabe die Erzeugung der verschiedenen Modell-Mechanismen ist, auseinandersetzen.

3 Methode und Vorgehensweise

In der hier vorgestellten Arbeit wurde ein System entworfen und implementiert, welches die Erzeugung graphischer Benutzungsschnittstellen für Bildverarbeitungsalgorithmen so weit wie möglich automatisiert. Alle nötigen Informationen für die Generierung des GUIs werden anhand der Datenstrukturen gewonnen, welche der Bildverarbeiter in seinem Arbeitsfeld verwendet. Neben anderen Eigenschaften sollte das System anpassungsfähig, benutzerfreundlich und erweiterbar sein.

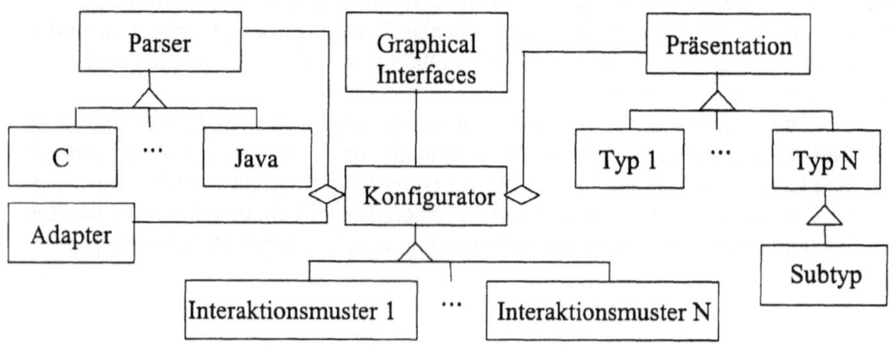

Abb. 1: Klassenstrukturdiagramm des Generierungssystems [3].

Mit dem in dieser Arbeit verwendeten Ansatz ist für die Generierung des GUIs kein Dialogmodell erforderlich, d.h. der Bildverarbeiter braucht, im Gegensatz zu existierenden Ansätzen, weder eine zusätzliche Beschreibung zu erzeugen, noch deklarative Modelle für die Generierung zu erstellen. Das System erzeugt nämlich anhand einer programmatischen Schnittstelle des jeweiligen Algorithmus (Signatur) die entsprechenden Präsentationselemente. Bei der Generierung des GUIs wird sowohl der statische, als auch der dynamische Teil erzeugt. Diese Zusammensetzung der Generierung der statischen und der dynamischen Teile des GUIs wurde durch den Entwurf und die Implementierung der graphischen Komponenten als selbständige Elemente mit lokaler Verantwortung erreicht. Die erstellte graphische Benutzungsschnittstelle bietet verschiedene Interaktionsmuster an. Es ist somit möglich festzulegen, wie die Informationen, welche der Algorithmus für seine Funktionalität braucht, gewonnen werden. Diese können z.B. aus dem Eingabebild durch einen Mausklick gewonnen werden. Das System erlaubt auch die Kombination von mehreren Bildern als Eingabe. Die Ergebnisse, die durch die Ausführung der Algorithmen erzielt werden, können gespeichert und durch andere Algorithmen weiterverarbeitet werden. Die einzelnen Komponenten des Frameworks wurden mit objektorientierten Konzepten nach dem Model View Controller-Paradigma (MVC) implementiert. Der Einsatz objektorientierter Konzepte erfolgte so, daß sowohl ein eigenständiges System zum Testen von Bildverarbeitungsalgorithmen, als auch eine Komponente eines übergeordneten Systems generiert werden können.

4 Das Generierungssystem

Das gesamte System (Generierungssystem) ist eine mehrstufige Umsetzung des MVC-Modells, d.h. anhand verschiedener Modelle (Algorithmen), werden verschiedene Views (statisches GUI), mit ihren ensprechenden Controllern (GUI Interaktion) generiert. Das System ist als ein sog. objektorientiertes Framework implementiert. Es besteht aus vier Modulen. Diese Module wurden durch die Zusammensetzung verschiedener Klassen, im Sinne der objektorientierten Technologie, implementiert (siehe Abb. 1).

1. Das *Konfigurator-Modul* ist das Modul, welches sowohl die Kommunikation der Komponenten des Generierungssystems miteinander erlaubt, als auch ihre Ansteuerung durchführt. In diesem Modul werden die sog. Interaktionsmuster als Untermodule implementiert. Das Generierungssystem bietet insgesamt drei Interaktionsmuster. Das erste Interaktionsmuster wird für die Bildverarbeitungsalgorithmen verwendet, bei denen die Eingabeparameter die Werte sind, welche der Benutzer in die generierten graphischen Komponenten eintragen wird. Das zweite Interaktionsmuster bietet für die Einstellung der Parameterwerte zusätzlich die Möglichkeit, Werte aus dem Eingabebild zu lesen, z.B. das Lesen der Position eines Mausklicks. Das dritte Interaktionsmuster bietet für die Parametrisierung der Algorithmen zusätzlich zu den Parameterwerten die Möglichkeit, mehrere Eingabebilder zu verwenden.
2. Das *Parser-Modul* hat die Aufgabe, die Signatur der Bildverarbeitungsalgorithmen zu identifizieren. Dafür wird einfach der Dateiname des entsprechenden Algorithmus eingegeben.

3. Das *Präsentationsmodul* enthält eine Reihe von Klassen und Subklassen, welche als Präsentationselemente für bestimmte Datentypen verwendet werden. Anhand dieser Klassen werden die graphischen Komponenten generiert. Diese lassen sich einfach durch andere ersetzen oder erweitern. Hierdurch können auch unterschiedliche Plattformen unterstützt werden.

4. Das *Graphical Interfaces-Modul* ist die Schnittstelle zwischen dem Framework und dem Benutzer oder einem anderen System (siehe Abb. 3).

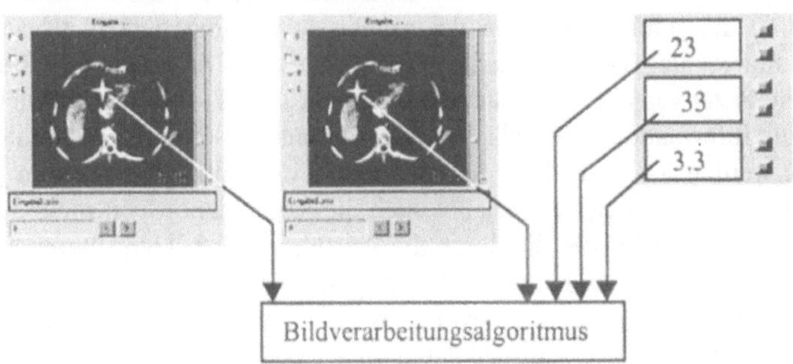

Abb. 2: Im dritten Interaktionsmuster lassen sich Informationen aus mehreren Bildern mit den Einträgen in die entsprechenden Elemente kombinieren und als Parameterliste für die Ansteuerung der Algorithmen einsetzen.

Die Struktur der einzelnen Komponenten wurde nach verschiedenen "Design Patterns" implementiert [4]. Durch den Einsatz der objektorientierten Konzepte bei der Implementierung des Systems, war es möglich ein System zu erstellen, welches ohne Änderung des bestehenden Codes einfach zu erweitern ist. Der Austausch der Komponenten ist auch problemlos realisierbar. Man ist in der Lage, das System als eine "stand-alone" Applikation zu verwenden (Black Box Framework), um kleine prototypische GUIs zu erzeugen oder auch als Teilkomponente von größeren Systemen z.B für die schnellere Erzeugung von "Plug-ins". Es ist außerdem möglich, das System mit einem Algorithmen-Repository zu verbinden. Dadurch kann es zum Bestandteil einer übergeordneten Architektur zur Vereinfachung der Entwicklung klinischer Bildverarbeitungssysteme werden.

Ein wichtiger Bestandteil des Frameworks ist die Dokumentation. Diese wurde in mit einem "Top Down"-Verfahren entlang verschiedener Abtraktionsebenen des Systems durchgeführt, um die Komplexität der Beschreibung des Systems zu bewältigen und die Wiederverwendung auf verschiedenen Ebenen zu ermöglichen. Die Darstellung wurde mit Hilfe der verschiedenen Diagramme der "Unified Modelling Language" Notation realisiert [3].

5 Diskusion und Ausblick

Das Generierungssystem beschränkt sich zur Zeit auf Bildverarbeitungsalgorithmen, welche in den Programmiersprachen C oder C++ geschrieben sind. Durch die Erweiterung des Parser-Moduls, anhand vorhandener Komponenten, ist man in der Lage die Funktionalität des Systems für andere Programmiersprachen zu implementieren.

Das Generierungssystem ist auf UNIX-Plattformen verfügbar. Seine Verfügbarkeit auf anderen Plattformen ist durch die Erweiterung der graphischen Elemente möglich. Dabei wird der GUI-Elemente-Pool des Systems mit neuen Komponenten unter Motif, TeleUSE, MFC, etc. erweitert.

Die generierten GUIs verfügen über 2D-Interaktions-Elemente, um die Parametereinstellungen des Bildverarbeitungsalgorithmus zu ermöglichen. Eine denkbare Erweiterung ist die Erzeugung einer neuen Klasse, welche die 3D-Interaktion ermöglicht.

Das Framework wird zur Zeit in der Abteilung für Medizinische und Biologische Informatik am Deutschen Krebsforschungszentrum auf verschiedenen Bildverarbeitungsfunktionen getestet und unabhängig von der Anzahl der Parameter, dem Typ der Bilddaten, der Dimension und der Art der Algorithmen (kantenorientiert, regionenbasiert) eingesetzt. Als nächster Schritt wird die Verbindung des Systems mit einer modularen Architektur zur Vereinfachung der Entwicklung klinischer Bildverarbeitungssysteme durchgeführt [5]. Für die Realisierung dieser Verbindung ist weder eine Erweiterung noch eine Änderung des Generierungssystems erforderlich.

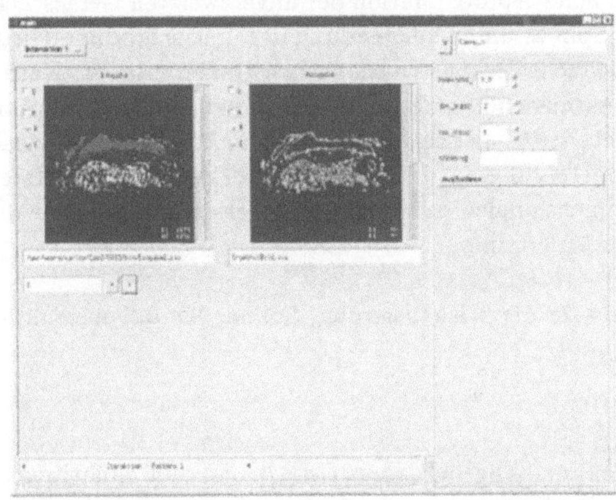

Abb. 3: Die generierte graphische Benutzugsschnittstelle für unsere Implementierung des Canny-Filters anhand der C-Quelldatei.

6 Literatur

1. Myers BA, Roson MB: Survey on the User Interface Programming. ACM CHI'92 Conference Proceedings, New York, 1992.
2. Puerta AR: A Model-Based Interface Development Environment. IEEE Software, 14(4):40-47, 1997.
3. Fowler M, Scott K: UML Distilled - Applying the Standard Object ModelingLanguage. Addison-Wesley, Reading MA, 1997.
4. Gamma E, Helm R, Johnson R, Vlissides J: Design Patterns: Elements of Reusable Object-Oriented Software. Addison-Wesley, New York, 1994.
5. Demiris AM, Cardenas CES, Makabe MH, Meinzer HP: An Architecture for Implementing Customizable Medical Image Processing Systems. Akzeptiert als Vortrag in MedInfo '98, Korea.

3D–Rekonstruktion von Blutgefäßen mit polynomialen und rationalen Splinefunktionen aus segmentierten MRA Datensätzen

Dr. Alexander Zimmermann

Universität Passau
94030 Passau
Email: Alexander.Zimmermann@fmi.uni-passau.de

Zusammenfassung In dieser Arbeit wird ein Verfahren zur 3D–Rekonstruktion von Blutgefäßen aus Magnet–Resonanz–Angiographie (MRA) Datensätzen vorgestellt. Grundlage des Rekonstruktionsprozesses bildet eine Segmentierung der Blutgefäße, die eine Liste von Gefäßquerschnitten in beliebiger Raumrichtung liefert. Der erste Schritt der Rekonstruktion besteht in einer Approximation der unverzweigten Gefäßstücke mit polynomialen Splines unter Verwendung der Tensorprodukt–Gitter–Technik, die sehr schnelle Rekonstruktionsalgorithmen erlaubt. Nach der Einteilung in verschiedene Strukturklassen erfolgt die Rekonstruktion der Verzweigungen, wobei hier rationale Splinefunktionen zum Einsatz kommen. Als Ergebnis steht eine glatte, aus Splines zusammengesetzte Oberfläche im Dreidimensionalen zur Verfügung, die weitergehende diagnostische Möglichkeiten eröffnet.

Schlüsselwörter: Visualisierung, Spline, 3D–Rekonstruktion, MRA

1   Einleitung

Die Magnetresonanz–Angiographie (MRA) ist ein nichtinvasives bildgebendes Verfahren, das mit Hilfe spezieller Pulssequenzen dreidimensionale Datensätze erzeugt, in denen sich bewegende Materie (Wasserstoffkerne) hell und stehendes Gewebe dunkler dargestellt wird, wodurch im wesentlichen das strömende Blut zu sehen ist. Die Standardmethode zur Darstellung der so erzeugten 3D–Bilddaten ist die Maximum–Intensitäts–Projektion (MIP). Diese weist jedoch einige Nachteile auf, wie fehlender räumlicher Eindruck, unklare Gefäßgrenzen und erschwerte Sichtbarkeit kleinerer Gefäße. Deswegen wurde das Projekt ANGIO gemeinsam vom Unternehmensbereich medizinische Technik der Firma Siemens AG, dem Institut für MR-Tomographie Passau und dem Bayerischen Forschungszentrum für Wissensbasierte Systeme (FORWISS) ins Leben gerufen. In diesem Projekt wurden Techniken zur Segmentierung und Rekonstruktion von Blutgefäßen entwickelt und in ein Gesamtsystem integriert, das die Nachteile des MIP ausgleichen soll. Das System besteht grundsätzlich aus zwei Teilen: Segmentierung und Rekonstruktion.

Die Segmentierung der der Blutgefäße liefert einen Konturgraph, der eine Art Drahtgittermodel des Gefäßes darstellt und alle relevanten Daten enthält, wie die Lage und Richtung des Gefäßes sowie den Gefäßrand, beschrieben durch eine Liste von Randkonturen. Einzelheiten zur Segmentierung finden sich in [1].

Zur Rekonstruktion werden Tensorprodukte von polynomialen Splinefunktionen [2] verwendet, die folgende Eigenschaften aufweisen:

- Die Glätte bzw. Differenzierbarkeitsordnung der Oberfläche kann über die Knotenpunkte sowohl lokal als auch global sehr einfach kontrolliert werden.
- Glatte Randanschlüsse lassen sich leicht, d.h. durch lineare Nebenbedingungen einbringen.
- Die Passung von Kurven oder kleinen Oberflächenstücken kann sehr effizient und schnell durchgeführt werden.

Für die vorliegende Rekonstruktionsaufgabe hat sich die Quadratmittelabweichung als Maß zur Gütebewertung der Approximation bewährt, da isolierte Fehlinterpretationen der Vorbearbeitung sich nicht störend auf die gesamte Passung auswirken und das Resultat effizient mit Hilfe der Verfahren zur Lösung linearer Ausgleichsprobleme berechnet werden kann.

2 Rekonstruktion unverzweigter Gefäße

Der erste Schritt der Rekonstruktion und 3D–Visualisierung besteht in einer Approximation der unverzweigten Gefäßstücke. Hierbei wird jedes Stück einzeln mit Hilfe eines Tensorprodukts von parabolischen Splinefunktionen approximiert, die zusätzlich in Gefäßumlaufsrichtung zyklisch zusammengesetzt wurden. Bildlich gesprochen wird ein Blatt Papier zusammengerollt, zu einem Zylinder verklebt und verformt, um die Gefäßränder möglichst gut anzunähern.

2.1 Knotenpunktwahl und Parametrisierung

Wesentlich für diesen Rekonstruktionsschritt ist die Wahl der Knotenpunkte des Splines und die Parametrisierung, d.h. die Zuordnung der Datenpunkte zu Punkten im Definitionsraum des Splines. Durch einen benutzergegebenen Parameter, kann die gewünschte Glätte der Approximation vorgegeben werden. Aus diesem Parameter und der Länge des unverzweigten Gefäßstücks bestimmt sich die Anzahl der Knotenpunkte in Gefäßfortschrittsrichtung. Aus der Maximalzahl der Randpunkte eines Querschnitts ergibt sich die Anzahl der Knotenpunkte in Gefäßumlaufsrichtung. Letztere werden äquidistant gesetzt, um eine möglichst rotationsinvariante Approximation zu gewährleisten. In Gefäßfortschrittsrichtung erfolgt die Wahl der Knotenpunkte dagegen abhängig vom Abstand der Querschnittsmittelpunkte und von der Dichte der vorliegenden Querschnitte, da ein gleichbleibendes Verhältnis von Datenpunkten zu Knotenpunkten die Passung stabilisiert.

Die Parametrisierung in Gefäßfortschrittsrichtung erfolgt für alle Punkte eines Querschnitts durch Projektion des Mittelpunkts auf die zuerst berechnete Gefäßzentrale, die als Splinekurve kodiert ist. In Gefäßumlaufsrichtung wird chordal parametrisiert, d.h. gemäß der Weglänge des Randpolygons. Hierbei werden aber nicht die Originalrandpunkte zur Passung herangezogen, sondern das Randpolygon äquidistant abgetastet, um neue Datenpunkte zu generieren. Durch dieses Vorgehen ist es möglich, statt einer Passung im vollen Tensorproduktraum die Tensorprodukt–Gitter–Approximation [3] zu verwenden, die eine erhebliche Beschleunigung der Berechnung bewirkt. Beispielsweise reduziert sich die Rechenzeit auf einer SPARCstation 20 für lange unverzweigte Stücke (z.B. Carotis interna) von 101.96 auf 0.15 Sekunden und für kurze Stücke von 0.12 auf 0.02 Sekunden. Besonderes zu achten ist auf die Synchronisation des Parametrisierungsnullpunkts zwischen den Querschnitten, um eine Verdrillung der Rekonstruktion zu vermeiden, die zu künstlichen Gefäßverengungen führen würde und damit zu einer falschen Gefäßdarstellung.

3 Rekonstruktion der Verzweigungen

Der anschließende Schritt ist die Approximation der Verzweigungen. Hierbei ist eine Klassifikation der Verzweigungen wichtig. Die Einteilung erfolgt in folgender Weise:

- *Steckverzweigung*: liegt vor, wenn ein kleines Gefäß von einem großen abzweigt und ist daran erkennbar, daß die Gefäßquerschnittsfläche eines abzweigenden Astes dieselbe Größe aufweist wie der Hauptast, der zweite abzweigende Ast dagegen wesentlich kleiner ist.
- *Überblendverzweigung*: alle drei Äste weisen etwa dieselbe Gefäßquerschnittsfläche aus.
- *Große Verzweigung*: der Hauptast hat eine signifikant größere Gefäßquerschnittsfläche, als die beiden anderen Äste, die ihrerseits dieselbe Fläche aufweisen.
- *Mehrfachverzweigung*: es sind mehr als drei Äste beteiligt.

Jede dieser Verzweigungsklassen kann nun mit Hilfe adäquater Modelle approximiert werden. Bei der Steckverzweigung, kann das durchgehende größere Gefäß als unverzweigt behandelt werden. Das kleine wird in dieses Stück seitlich "hineingesteckt". Die Überblendverzweigung wird rekonstruiert, indem vom Hauptast aus zwei glatt anschließende kurze unverzweigte Stücke zu jedem abzweigenden Ast berechnet und diese beiden Stücke gleichzeitig visualisiert werden. In einer Mehrfachverzweigung müssen, beim kleinsten Ast beginnend, solange Abzweigungen als Steck- oder Überblendverzweigung klassifiziert werden, bis nur noch drei Äste zur abschließenden Klassifikation übrig bleiben. Die Großen Verzweigungen können mit einer besonderen Art von rationalen Splinefunktionen approximiert werden, den Variable–Knoten–Splines [4].

3.1 Variable–Knoten–Splines

Diese stellen eine Erweiterung der Tensorproduktsplines dar. Hierbei werden die Knotenpunkte durch Knotenpunktfunktionen ersetzt. Die Knotenpunkte für einen Spline in einer Variable definieren sich als Funktion in der jeweils anderen Variable. Das bewirkt wesentlich flexiblere Modellierungseigenschaften, da nun eine Anpassung an die gegebenen Datenpunkte sowie eine Änderung der Glattheitsbedingungen innerhalb einer Splinefunktion entlang bestimmter Kurven möglich ist. Der Nachteil dieser "hochgradig nicht–automatischen Methode, die mehr für den erfahrenen Benutzer geeignet ist" (Zitat [4]) ist, daß eine Vielzahl neuer Gestaltungsparameter, d.h. jede einzelne Knotenpunktfunktion, zu kontrollieren sind. Dazu wurde ein parametrisierter Knotenpunktfunktionsentwurf entwickelt, der durch die folgenden Kenngrößen an die gegebene Eingabedatenmenge angepaßt werden kann: Anzahl der Knotenpunkte im Hauptgefäß und den Nebenästen bzw. vor und nach der Verzweigung, sowie der Höhe des Jochpunkts. Dieser Entwurf erlaubt es die Splinefunktion von der verzweigten Seite her "einzuschneiden" um zwei ausgehende Gefäße und ein Hauptgefäß in einem einzigen Stück zu modellieren. Durch spezielle Bedingungen kann dabei der Hauptast und jeder der Nebenäste zyklisch fortgesetzt werden.

Die Parametrisierung erfolgt in Gefäßumlaufsrichtung wiederum chordal und in Gefäßfortschrittsrichtung durch Projektion jedes einzelnen Datenpunktes auf die entsprechende der zwei konkurrierenden Gefäßzentralen. Folgendes Vorgehen hat sich bewährt um die Approximation optimal zu unterstützen: aus den beteiligten bereits rekonstruierten unverzweigten Gefäßstücken werden die Parameter für den Knotenpunktfunktionsentwurf extrahiert. Danach werden diese Rekonstruktionen zurückgeschnitten und die Verzweigungsrekonstruktion glatt daran angeschlossen. Desweiteren werden alle Datenpunkte der zurückgeschnitten Teile in die Approximation der Verzweigung mit eingebracht. Dabei werden die Parametrisierung der beteiligten Äste und der Verzweigung synchronisiert. Leider ist in dieser Situation aber keine schnelle Tensorprodukt–Gitter–Approximation mehr möglich.

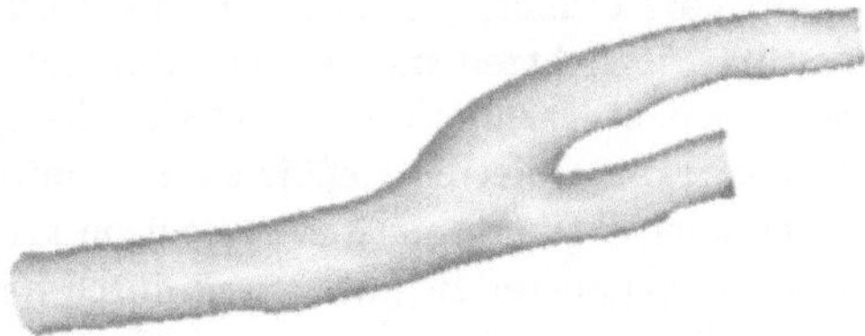

Abbildung1. Rekonstruktion einer Verzweigung

4 Ergebnisse

Zur Visualisierung werden die approximierten Splinefunktionen triangularisiert und mit Hilfe eines Gradientenschattierungsverfahrens dargestellt. Abbildung 1 zeigt die Rekonstruktion einer Verzweigung mit Hilfe eines Variable–Knoten–Splines. In Abbildung 2 ist ein kompletter Gefäßbaum eines menschlichen Kopfes als Konturgraph und dessen Rekonstruktion zu sehen.

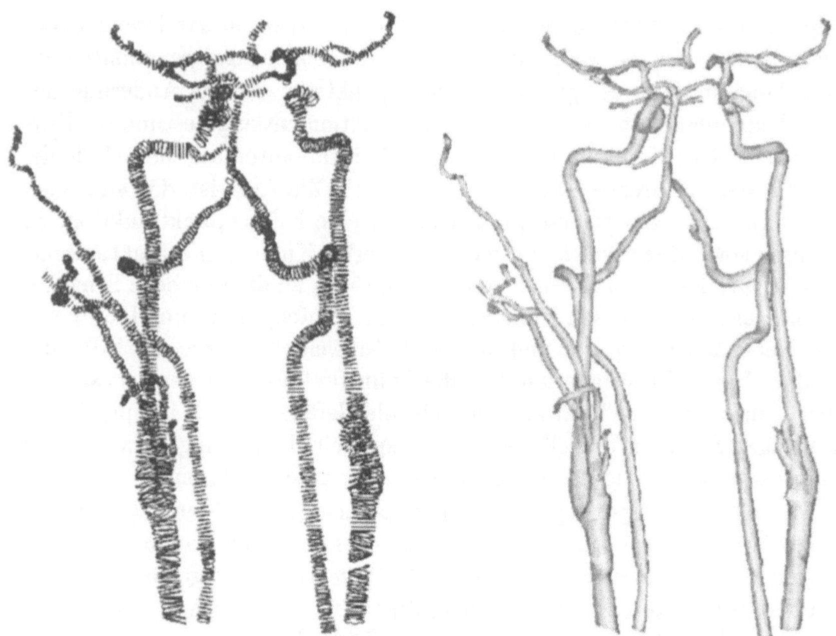

Abbildung 2. Konturgraph (links) und Rekonstruktion (rechts) des kompletten Gefäßsystems eines menschlichen Kopfes

Diese Darstellung des Gefäßsystems hat gegenüber dem MIP folgende Vorteile: die Gefäßgrenzen (gegeben durch die Blutflußoberflächen) sind klar erkennbar, umgebendes Gewebe kann aus der Visualisierung ausgebelendet werden und die Gefäße werden räumlich korrekt wiedergegeben. Desweiteren können die Gefäße an einem Grafik–Arbeitsplatzrechner, der diese Art der Visualisierung bereits hardwaremäßig unterstützt, in Echtzeit manipuliert, d.h. beliebig gedreht, vergrößert und verkleinert werden. Darüberhinaus läßt sich die Querschnittsfläche und der Durchmesser der rekonstruierten Gefäße exakt ermitteln um z.B. Stenosegrade zu bestimmen oder eine automatische Selektion kritischer Stellen im Gefäßsystem zu liefern, die genauerer Begutachtung durch den Arzt bedürfen. Mit Hilfe von 3D–Druck–Techniken kann sogar ein Modell des Gefäßsystems gefertigt und dem Mediziner zur Ansicht bereitgestellt werden.

Literatur

1. Koller, Walter: Segmentierung und Diagnose von Gefäßen mit Atlasunterstüzung. VDI-Verlag, Düsseldorf, 1997.
2. Dierckx, Paul: Curve and Surface Fitting with Splines. Oxford University Press Inc., 1993
3. Zimmermann, Alexander: Parametrisierungs- und Lokalisierungstechniken in der Spline-Oberflächenapproximation. Shaker-Verlag, Aachen, 1997.
4. Hayes, J. G.: New shapes from bicibuc splines. NPL Report NAC (58), 1974.

Echtzeit 3D I/O für netzwerkorientierte Anwendungen der Volumenvisualisierung

Achim Mayer, Harald Evers, Hans-Peter Meinzer

Abteilung Medizinische und Biologische Informatik/ H0100,
Deutsches Krebsforschungszentrum (DKFZ)
Im Neuenheimer Feld 280, 69120 Heidelberg
E-mail: A.Mayer@DKFZ-Heidelberg.de

Zusammenfassung: Diese Arbeit beschreibt Ansätze, die es erlauben, Anwendungen basierend auf rechenaufwendigen, jedoch qualitativ hochwertigen, Volumenvisualisierungen interaktiv bedienbar zu machen. Die Volumenvisualisierung und die volumenorientierte Bildverarbeitung kann in einem Netzwerk auf einen zentralen, leistungsfähigen Rechner ausgelagert werden. Der Benutzer kann auf einer Viewing-Station mit den Visualisierungen im dreidimensionalen Raum interagieren, wobei sich mehrere solcher Clients die Resourcen des Servers teilen können. Ein hybrider Volumenvisualisierungsansatz erlaubt die Integration von oberflächen- und volumenorientierten Objektmodellen.

Schlüsselwörter: Hybride Visualisierung, 3D I/O, Client/Server.

1 Einleitung

Dreidimensionale bildgebende Verfahren wie z.B. CT, MR oder 3D-Ultraschall finden zunehmend Verwendung in der medizinischen Diagnostik. Der Nutzen dieser Verfahren beruht wesentlich auf den gelieferten Informationen über Lage, Größe und Form von Strukturen. Diese Parameter sind wertvoll für das Auffinden und die Beurteilung pathologischer Veränderungen.

Die Extraktion der für eine Fragestellung relevanten Informationen aus den Schichtbildern erfordert jedoch ein hohes Maß an Erfahrung und Aufmerksamkeit des Betrachters. Die für die Beurteilung eventuell notwendige Rekonstruktion der dreidimensionalen Form und Lage der Objekte obliegt dabei dem räumlichen Vorstellungsvermögen des Mediziners. Die Analyse mit Methoden der digitalen Bildverarbeitung kann den Mediziner unterstützen, indem relevante Informationen vorselektiert und visuell aufbereitet werden. Das Ziel unserer Arbeitet ist es, Methoden der dreidimensionalen Bildanalyse und Präsentation für das klinische Umfeld anwendbar zu machen.

Insbesondere die dreidimensionale Visualisierung hat sich als sehr hilfreich erwiesen, um ein räumliches Objekt schnell zu erfassen. Im Gensatz zu Schnittbildern sind solche Ansichten auch für den Laien verständlich, wodurch die Kommunikation zwischen Arzt und Patient sowie die interdisziplinäre Zusammenarbeit in der Forschung verbessert werden kann.

Eine wesentliches Hindernis für die erfolgreiche Integration von dreidimensionalen Verarbeitungs- und Präsentationsmethoden besteht in der Antwortzeit des Systems. Wir unterscheiden explizit zwischen der Berechnung und der Präsentation der Ergebnisse. Dadurch kann für jede der Aufgaben eine geeignete und leistungsfähige Rechnerplattform eingesetzt werden.

2   Client/Server-Interface

Wir haben ein Client/Server-Interface entwickelt, das speziell darauf zugeschnitten ist, mehreren Clients über ein Netzwerk effizient die Ressourcen eines Rechenservers zur Verfügung zu stellen. Das besondere Augenmerk dieser Entwicklung lag darauf, die wiederholte Übertragung von Volumendaten über das Netzwerk zu vermeiden. Der Server generiert zu diesem Zweck abstrakte Bilddaten-Handles, welche der Client verwendet, um die Verarbeitung eines Datensatzes anzustoßen

Eine Verarbeitungsanforderung liefert als Ergebnis wieder ein Handle zurück. Die wiederholte Übertragung von Volumendaten wird somit vermieden. Hinter diesem Ansatz steht die Beobachtung, daß die Beurteilung von Zwischenergebnissen typischerweise anhand ausgewählter 2D-Schnitte eines Volumens oder einer zu diesem Zweck erzeugten 3D-Visualisierung stattfindet. Der dabei anfallende Datenverkehr kann auch auf den derzeit typischen LANs , welche eine verhältnismäßig geringe Bandbreite besitzen, mit zufriedenstellenden Antwortzeiten bewältigt werden.

3   Darstellung der Bilddaten auf der Viewing-Station

Auf der Viewing-Station wird das Mensch-Maschine Interface implementiert. Wir beschreiben im folgenden Ansätze, mithilfe derer ein interaktives Arbeiten mit Volumenvisualisierungen ermöglicht wird.

Wir präsentieren hier eine Methode, die es erlaubt, graphische Elemente wie z.B. Pointer oder virtuelle Operationsinstrumente in Echtzeit innerhalb einer Visualisierung von Volumendaten zu bewegen. Eine Volumenvisualisierung kann ohne den Umweg über die Erstellung eines Oberflächenmodells direkt aus den Daten erzeugt werden. Das verwendete Verfahren ist eine Weiterentwicklung des Heidelberger Raytracing Modells [4]. Der Vorteil direkter Volumenvisualisierung liegt zum einen in der exakten und detailreichen Darstellung auch kleinster Strukturen, andererseits ist keine aufwendige Extraktion eines Oberflächenmodells notwendig. Die Berechnung einer neuen Ansicht dauert jedoch ca. 0.5 bis 3 Sekunden für einen üblichen Datensatz. Mäßig komplexe Oberflächenmodelle können hingegen auf entsprechender graphischer Spezialhardware in Echtzeit berechnet werden.

Wir integrieren die Ansätze der direkten Volumenvisualierung und der Oberflächenmodelle im Rahmen der standardisierten Graphikbibliothek OpenGL. Das Prinzip der Integration beruht auf dem "Z-Buffer Merging" [1], wobei die Möglichkeiten der visuellen Effekte bei sich gegenseitig durchdringenden Objekten im Vergleich zu allgemeineren Ansätzen, wie z.B. dem "Ray-Merging" [2], begrenzt sind. Das Modell ist ausreichend für die Erstellung von Applikationen, in denen es darauf ankommt, einzelne oder wenige Objekte relativ zueinander in einer Szene zu positionieren.

Die Integration der beiden Objektmodelle geschieht unter Ausnutzung des Z-Puffer Mechanismus der OpenGL Rendering-Pipeline. Die Volumenvisualisierungen werden getrennt berechnet, gegebenenfalls auf einem Rechner mit einem oder mehreren leistungsfähigen Prozessoren. Die Tiefendaten aus dieser Berechnung werden entsprechend den Datenformaten und der Visualisierungsparameter der Oberflächenvisualisierung konvertiert und zusammmen mit dem eigentlichen Bild in die Rendering-Pipeline geladen [5]. Die Oberflächenelemente werden dann als OpenGL Graphikprimitive gerendert, wobei der Z-Puffer Test dafür sorgt, daß Verdeckungen richtig dargestellt werden.

Die Leistungsfähigkeit dieses Ansatzes in Bezug auf die erreichbaren Bildwiederholraten wird durch zwei Faktoren bestimmt. Die Geschwindigkeit der Volumenvisualisierung ist ausschlaggebend dafür, ob Objekte, die mit dieser Methode dargestellt werden, direkt manipuliert, z.B. gedreht, werden können. Die speziellen Graphikleistungen des Rechners, auf dem die eigentliche Integration stattfindet, ist ausschlaggebend dafür, wie schnell die Oberflächenelemente berechnet werden können und wie schnell die Tiefendaten in die OpenGL Umgebung geladen werden. Die Geschwindigkeit der volumenorientierten Bildgenerierung ist derzeit nur in sehr begrenztem Maße ausreichend für die direkte Manipulation. Ausgehend von einer statischen Ansicht auf die Volumenelemente können diese jedoch auf leistungsfähigen Graphikrechnern in Echtzeit mit Oberflächenelementen in einer hybriden Visualisierung integriert werden. Auf dieser Basis können sehr flexible Interaktionsmodelle implementiert werden.

Für den Fall, daß die Oberflächenobjekte einfach aufgebaut sind, kann das beschriebene Verfahren optimiert werden. Als "einfach" bezeichnen wir in diesem Zusammenhang solche Objekte, für die es mit vertretbarem Aufwand möglich ist, die konstituierenden Graphikprimitive des Objekts (typischerweise Dreiecke) zu sortieren. OpenGL erlaubt es, das Schreiben des Z-Buffers während der Scan-Konvertierung der Objekte abzuschalten. Der generelle Mechanismus für die korrekte Darstellung von Verdeckungen ist damit außer Kraft gesetzt. Der Test bezüglich der bereits geschriebenen Tiefenwerte wird jedoch weiterhin durchgeführt, d.h. bereits mit Tiefenwerten geschriebene Strukturen werden bzgl. potentieller Verdeckungen korrekt dargestellt. Die Darstellung der neuen Strukturen ist jedoch genau dann fehlerhaft, wenn Graphikprimitive die weiter im Hintergrund projiziert werden sollten in der Reihenfolge nach solchen dargestellt werden, die diese eigentlich verdecken sollten. Es gibt prinzipiell zwei Methoden mithilfe derer auch bei abgeschaltetem Schreiben der Z-Werte eine korrekte Darstellung gewährleistet werden kann. Die

Graphikprimitive können, abhängig von dem aktuellen Blickwinkel, von hinten nach vorne sortiert und projiziert werden (back to front rendering). Sind die Objekte von streng konvexer Form, so können alternativ auch die rückwärtigen Flächen mithilfe des "backface culling"-Mechanismus ausgeblendet werden. Dazu ist es notwendig, daß die Orientierung der Flächen (Innenfläche/Aussenfläche) definiert ist.

Der Vorteil der beschriebenen Vorgehensweisen liegt darin, daß die Tiefenwerte aus der Volumenvisualisierung nur einmal in die OpenGL-Umgebung geschrieben werden müssen, anstatt bei jedem Bildaufbau von neuem. Der Effekt ist ein deutlich beschleunigter Bildaufbau, da das Laden der Tiefenwerte verhältnismäßig aufwendig ist. Einfache graphische Elemente wie z.B. Schnittebenen oder linienorientierte Hilfselemente können leicht auf diese Weise mit der Volumendarstellung integriert werden. Die Performance ist dann sogar auf leistungsschwächeren Systemen (z.B. PCs ohne speziellen Graphikbeschleuniger) ausreichend.

Komplexe Objekte, also solche, die nicht konvex sind oder für die korrekte Reihenfolge der Graphikprimitive nicht ohne weiteres zu ermitteln ist, erfordern es, daß die Tiefenwerte aus der Volumenvisualisierung beim Aufbau jedes neuen Bildes in die OpenGL-Umgebung geschrieben werden. Unsere Erfahrungen haben gezeigt, daß die Performance in diesem Fall sehr stark von der Implementierung der OpenGL Bibliothek abhängig ist (alternative Implementierungen auf ein und demselben Rechner können deutlich unterschiedlich in der Leistung sein). Der limitierende Faktor ist hier insbesondere die Größe des Tiefenpuffers.

4 Eingabegeräte

Die Realisation echtzeitfähiger Graphik ist nur eine der notwendigen Voraussetzungen für die Erstellung interaktiver dreidimensionaler Modelle. Die möglichst intuitive Steuerung der graphischen Elemente mit geeigneten Eingabegeräten ist ebenso wichtig für Benutzbarkeit und Akzeptanz eines Systems. Wir haben eine Reihe von kommerziell verfügbaren Eingabegeräten in unser System integriert. Im folgenden beschreiben wir eine Auswahl, sowie deren Eignung für bestimmte Interaktionen.

Die 3D-Maus (Spacemouse) ist ein relatives Eingabegerät, das die gleichzeitige Manipulation aller sechs Freiheitsgrade erlaubt. Mit etwas Übung können mit der 3D-Maus Objekte flüssig im Raum orientiert werden. Das Interaktionsmodell erzeugt einen ähnlichen Eindruck, wie wenn man ein Objekt in der Hand hält und es vor dem Auge bewegt. Die präzise Handhabung von virtuellen Werkzeugen ist mit diesem Gerät jedoch aufgrund der relativen Bewegungsangabe schwierig. Versuchsreihen mit mehreren Probanden haben gezeigt, daß diese deutlich länger brauchen, um einen Punkt exakt anzufahren, als mit absoluten Eingabegeräten.

Geräte, die es erlauben, einen Stift absolut in einem *dreidimensionalen* Raum zu positionieren gibt es in verschiedenen Ausführungen (3D stylus). Abhängig davon, ob lediglich die Spitze des Stiftes, oder zusätzlich dessen Orientierung gemessen wird, besitzen diese Eingabegeräte vier bzw. sechs Freiheitsgrade. Die Stiftform und die Beweglichkeit im Raum erlauben die schnelle und intuitive Lokalisation von

Punkten in einer dreidimensionalen Szene. Das Interaktionsmodell entspricht der Führung eines Werkzeugs, z.B. eines Skalpells. Ein Nachteil liegt jedoch darin, daß der Stift frei im Raum gehalten wird, wodurch die Position verwackelt werden kann und der Benutzer evtl. vorzeitig ermüdet.

5 Ergebnisse und Diskussion

Mit den beschriebenen Visualisierungstechniken können Pointer oder virtuelle Werkzeuge interaktiv in der dreidimensionalen hybriden Szene bewegt werden. Diese können verwendet werden, um die Tiefeninformation der Szene besser zu ergründen, Strecken und Flächen im Volumen zu vermessen bzw. Objekte im Raum gezielt auszuwählen. Außerdem können graphische Hilfselemente integriert werden, die es erlauben, z.B. die Orientierung einer neuen Ansicht auf das Volumenmodell zu spezifizieren sowie mithilfe halbtransparenter Schnittflächen Relationen zwischen konventioneller Schnittbildpräsentation und Projektionen herzustellen.

Der Ansatz des Client/Server Computing erlaubt es, auf leistungsfähige Rechner im Netzwerk zuzugreifen und deren Ressourcen für mehrere Clients zur Verfügung zu stellen, wodurch Kosten gespart werden können.

Auf der Basis der präsentierten Methoden wurden bereits Applikationen für klinische Anwendungen sowie für Bildverarbeiter implementiert und mit Erfolg getestet [3,5]. Wir sind der Auffassung, daß die Verfügbarkeit von Volumen-Visualisierungsmethoden sowie deren Bedienbarkeit entscheidend verbessert wurde und somit neue Anwendungsgebiete erschlossen werden können.

Literatur

1. Kaufmann A, Cohen D, Yagel R, Intermixing Suface and Volume Rendering. In: Höhne KH, Fuchs H, Pizer SM (eds.): 3D Imaging in Medicine: Algorithms, Systems, Applications. NATO Advanced Workshop on 3D-Imaging in Medicine, NATO Advanced Series F, Computer and Systems Science, Vol. F60, pp. 217-227, 1990.
2. Levoy M: A Hybrid Raytracer for Rendering Polygon and Volume Data. IEEE Computer Graphics & Applications, 8(5), pp. 33-40, 1990.
3. Makabe MH, Glombitza G, Mayer A, Meinzer HP, Lederer W, Schneider S, Wradzidlo W: Interpretation Support of Contrast-Enhanced MR Mammography by Image Processing. Proceedings Computer Assisted Radiology '95, Berlin, Germany, S. 254-259, Juni 1995.
4. Meinzer HP, Meetz K, Scheppelmann D, Engelmann U, Baur HJ: The Heidelberg Raytracing Model. IEEE Computer Graphics & Applications, S. 34-43, November 1991.
5. Wolsiffer K: Entwurf und Realisierung eines interaktiven VR-basierten Tools zur Segmentierung und Visualisierung medizinischer Volumendaten. Technical Report Nr. 90, Abteilung Medizinische und Biologische Informatik/ H0100, Deutsches Krebsforschungszentrum, 1996.

Efficient Representation of Cortical Convolutions for the Analysis of Brain Surface Topology

Peter Hastreiter, Christof Rezk–Salama, Günther Greiner, Thomas Ertl

Computer Graphics Group (IMMD IX),
Friedrich Alexander University of Erlangen–Nuremberg,
Am Weichselgarten 9, 91058 Erlangen, Germany
Email: {hastreiter}@informatik.uni-erlangen.de

Abstract Various time efficient procedures were developed allowing to calculate planar representations of the brain in MR and CT clearly conveying the whole surface topology. For the comparison of the provided techniques we present additional complex functionality for the transformation of cortical convolutions between different representations after extracting and marking them manually or automatically. This includes re–projection to the original volume data in order to compare our approach to results obtained with direct volume rendering. Considering brain information exclusively, and ensuring a standardized orientation for the inter–patient comparison different segmentation and registration procedures are provided for the pre–processing. All implementation was integrated in a flexible and modular extensible platform allowing for convenient manipulation and visualization.

Keywords: cortical convolutions, visualization, segmentation, registration

1 Introduction

Medical image data from different 3D modalities like MR, CT and PET provide excellent representation of various parameters of the brain. Using anatomical and functional information brain areas are localized and related to specific functionality. Since most of these areas are part of the cerebral cortex which contains the gray brain matter, the efficient anatomical localization and meaningful visualization of the cortical convolutions is fundamental for analyzing morphological and functional information of the brain. In neuro–science it allows to examine physiological processes. In medicine it allows to understand the source and the effect of diseases if the affected convolutions and their related brain functions are identified. Additionally, the analysis of the topology and the size of convolutions can be used for a comparison of the left and the right hemisphere of the same individual or for a comparison of corresponding convolutions of different individuals.

Using tomographic slice images exclusively it is impossible to identify specific convolutions exactly. Therefore, contour lines are extracted in [1] using a 2D segmentation technique in order to reconstruct the brain surface. However, in case of volume rendering, the inspection of the whole brain surface is affected by the curvature of the cerebral cortex. Consequently, a planar representation was suggested in [2] using interior and exterior forces of a complex 3D network that models the brain surface. In order to prevent distortions which are caused by the projection, the network is appropriately cut open. Applying a similar approach according to [3], these irregularities are avoided by mapping the brain surface onto a sphere. Contrary to these time consuming techniques a more practical approach is presented in [4]. Based on dynamic programming and a slice oriented erosion procedure the relative brain surface is obtain which allows for fast visualization of the cortical convolutions in views of standardized orientation. Aiming at an intra– and inter–patient comparison of the brain hemispheres, we propose different approaches which allow for fast visualization of planar representations.

2   Segmentation and Registration

The calculation of the planar representations requires the segmentation of the brain volume. Two different approaches of volume growing are provided. Using a straight forward technique all voxels with gray values between a lower and a higher threshold are selected. Starting from a specific seed point within a user–defined volume of interest, they form a single coherent volume. Alternatively, a more sophisticated technique using a statistical process of voxel grouping [5], transforms the original image to a new gray value distribution. This allows for easy detection of the desired object by interactive thresholding. Ensuring an optimal segmentation, a diversity of tools is provided for user interaction. Finally, a registration procedure based on the a principal–axis method is applied in order to obtain a standardized orientation for the comparison of the left and the right hemisphere of the same or of different data sets [6].

3   Planar Representations

The principle idea of the presented approach is to unfold the brain surface in order to convey the cortical convolutions (gyri and sulci) simultaneously. Therefore, the global shape of the brain is transformed to an elementary geometric object while the local depth information of its surface is mapped to respective intensity values. Although a more complex geometry provides a better approximation, spheres and ellipsoids proved to be sufficient, and they are more convenient for the further processing. In particular, they are less time consuming with respect to the calculation of surface normals.

In order to extract the depth information the segmented brain surface is covered with a smooth envelop by closing its valleys with a small spherical filter. The surface normals of the geometric object then determine the direction of rays which are used to measure the distance between the envelop and the actual brain surface. After normalizing and applying a user–defined color look–up table the obtained values result in an image of the cortical convolutions on the surface of the geometric object. The final mapping to a planar representation inevitably causes distortions. Their location vary considerably depending on the applied technique.

If a *stereo-scopic spherical projection* is used both hemispheres are mapped separately. Linear rays are cast from the center of projection which transform every surface point directly onto the target plane. Starting from its center, which is mapped accurately, the distortion increases radially. Alternatively, a spherical parameterization allows to roll a sphere by 2π along a specified equator. In order to map the surface points to the plane it is additionally rolled $\pi/2$ perpendicular to the direction of the equator for every step. Distortions affiliated with this approach increase proportional to the distance from the equator.

Using *parallel projection* the surface is mapped onto opposite planes of a enclosing bounding–box. Since it does not aim at mapping the whole surface to a planar representation, there are only perspective distortions.

The *cylindrical projection* requires to project the depth information radially onto the surface of a cylinder object containing the brain. Similar to the unrolled spherical approach the geometric object is rotated by 2π around the longitudinal axis. The resulting images then show the whole brain surface topology since the information of the cylinder surface easily maps to the plane. Again, perspective distortions increase in directions perpendicular to the rotation axis.

4   Analysis of Cortical Convolutions

All methods provided for the segmentation, registration and visualization are combined in *SegMed* which represents a modularly extensible platform for the manipulation of medical image data based on *X/Motif* , *C++* and *OpenGL*. In order to allow for intra– or inter–patient comparison it provides multiple projections of one or more brain volumes with standardized orientation (see section 2). For a fast and convenient localization of cortical convolutions there is an extensive functionality of manual editing tools and a variety of adapted algorithms for automatic skeletonizing.

If manual identification of the cortical convolutions is selected it is possible to insert and manipulate an arbitrary number of vertices which are linearly connected. During the course of the analysis the resulting polygons are transformed on–the–fly between all planar representations. Optionally, they are re–projected to the original volume data in order to allow for a visualization with indirect and direct volume rendering. In order to obtain the center–lines automatically, different adapted thinning procedures [7, 8, 9] are provided. Since the quality of the results is related to the amount of noise inherent to the input images, a median filter is applied initially.

5   Results and Discussion

In order to obtain a comprehensive understanding of the cortical convolutions efficient techniques are provided which transform the whole brain surface to a concatenated planar representation. As an advantage of our approach related distortions are compensated using different projection techniques simultaneously presented in multiple windows with standardized orientation (Figure 1). They are interconnected with an extensive functionality for the localization of the gyri and sulci which encourages the intra– and inter–patient comparison. Aiming at practical applications efficiency is an important issue. Therefore, spheres, ellipsoids and cylinders were considered exclusively which allow for a fast calculation of the surface normals. The development of a fully automatic and fast segmentation procedure was beyond the scope of this work. Hence, manual correction is still necessary at this stage.

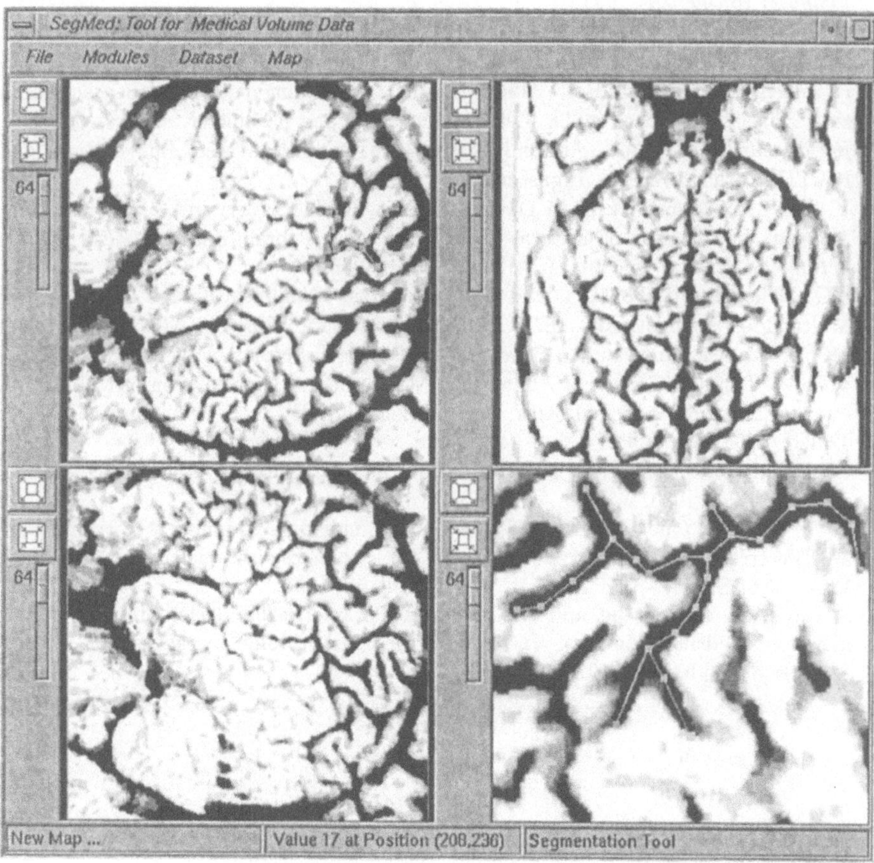

Figure1. Projection of brain: (left column) stereo–scopic spherical showing both hemispheres — (right column) unrolled spherical of front and back including manually inserted markers (right bottom) used for the identification of convolutions .

6 Conclusion

Several approaches are proposed which efficiently produce planar representations of the brain surface allowing for a convenient analysis of the cortical convolutions. For the evaluation of the available modules in practice they are transferred to a clinical environment in the near future. Further developments will mainly focus on accelerating the segmentation procedure required for the delineation of the brain volume.

References

1. H. Sherk. Flattening the Cerebral Cortex by Computer. *Journal of Neuroscience Methods*, 18:255–267, 1995.
2. G.J. Carman, H.A. Drury, and D.C. VanEssen. Computational Methods for Reconstructing and Unfolding the Cerebral Cortex. *Cerebral Cortex*, 5:506–517, 1995.
3. H. Zilken, H. Hallig, and H.W. Müller-Gärtner. Abbildung der Gehirnoberfläche auf eine sphärische Fläche. In Th. Lehman, I. Scholl, and K. Spitzer, editors, *Bildver. für die Med.: Alg., Sys., Anwend.*, pages 131–136. Inst. f. Med. Inf. u. Biom. d. RWTH, Aachen, Verl. d. Augustinus Buchh., 1996.
4. Y. Ge, J.M. Fitzpatrick, D.M Dawant, J. Bao, R.M. Kessler, and R.A. Margolin. Accurate Localization of Cortical Convolutions in MR brain images. *IEEE Transactions on Medical Imaging*, 15:418–428, Aug. 1996.
5. S.G. Dellepiane, f. Fontana, and G.L. Vernazza. Nonlinear Image Labeling for Multivalued Segmentation. *IEEE Trans. on Img. Proc.*, 5(3):429–446, March 1996.
6. l.K. Arata, A.P. Dhawan, J.P.Broderick, M.F. Gaskil-Shipley, A.V. Levy, and N.D. Volkow. Three–Dimensional Anatomical Model–Based Segmentation of MR Brain Images Through Principal Axis Registration. *IEEE Trans. on Biomed. Eng.*, 42(11):1069–1078, 1995.
7. C. Arcelli, L. Cordella, and S. Levialdi. More about Thinning Algorithm. *Electr. Let.*, 16:51–53, 1980.
8. R.W. Zhou, C. Quek, and G.S. Ng. A Novel Single-pass Thinning Algorithm and an Effective Set of Performance Criteria. In *Pat. Recogn. Let.*, volume 16, pages 1267–1275. Elsevier Sc. Pub. B.V., North-Holland, 1995.
9. S. Riazanoff, B. Cervelle, and J. Chorowicz. Parametrisable Skeletonization of Binary and Multilevel Images. In *Pat. Recogn. Let.*, volume 11, pages 1267–1275. Elsevier Sc. Pub. B.V., North-Holland, 1990.

Segmentierung medizinischer Bilddaten unter Verwendung eines automatisch generierten patientenspezifischen Gewebemodells und Superquadriken

Catherina Burghart, Arno Pernozzoli, Jörg Raczkowsky,

Ulrich Rembold, Heinz Wörn

Institut für Prozeßrechentechnik und Robotik
Universität Karlsruhe
76128 Karlsruhe
e_mail: burghart@ira.uka.de

Zusammenfassung. Im folgenden Artikel wird ein von uns entwickelter wissenbasierter Ansatz zur Segmentierung medizinischer Bilddaten beschrieben. Mit einem automatisch erstellten, aufnahmespezifischen Gewebemodell wird die Nutzung von Information über die Grauwertverteilung im inneren der zu segmentierenden anatomischen Strukturen ermöglicht. Das Gewebemodell unterstützt die Schätzung von Lage, Orientierung und Form der in einer Wissensbasis modellierten Strukturen. Die geometrische Modellierung anatomischer Strukturen wird mit Hilfe von verformbaren Superquadriken realisiert. Eine genaue Anpassung an die Umrisse der zu segmentierenden Objekte wird durch aktive Konturen erreicht. Mit Hilfe dieses mehrstufigen Verfahrens ist die genaue Segmentierung anatomischer Strukturen mit geringem zeitlichen Aufwand, ohne Benutzerinteraktion möglich.

Schlüsselwörter: Wissensbasierte Segmentierung, Superquadriken, Gewebemodell.

1 Einleitung

Der von uns entwickelte Ansatz basiert auf einem mehrstufigen Prozeß, welches eine Vorverarbeitung der zugrundeliegenden Tomographieaufnahme (CT,MRT) sowie die automatische Berechnung eines Gewebemodells und die Anpassung geometrischer Modelle an die gesuchten anatomischen Strukturen einschließt. Die Glättung mittels eines kantenerhaltenden Filters und die Extraktion der Bildkanten für die drei Hauptebenen der Tomogrammaufnahme bilden zusammen den Vorverarbeitungsschritt. Die so gewonnenen Daten werden der zweiten Prozeßstufe übergeben, welche die automatische Berechnung des aufnahmespezifischen Gewebemodells und die Anpassung der geometrischen Modelle mittels eines genetischen Optimierungsalgorithmus beinhaltet.

2 Berechnung des Gewebemodells

Homogene Bildbereiche in CT- und MRT-Aufnahmen charakterisieren die für die Segmentierung interessanten anatomischen Strukturen. Durch eine Analyse dieser

Bereiche kann ein Gewebemodell gewonnen werden, welches den darauffolgenden Schätzprozeß für Lage, Orientierung und Form der gesuchten anatomischen Struktur unterstützt.

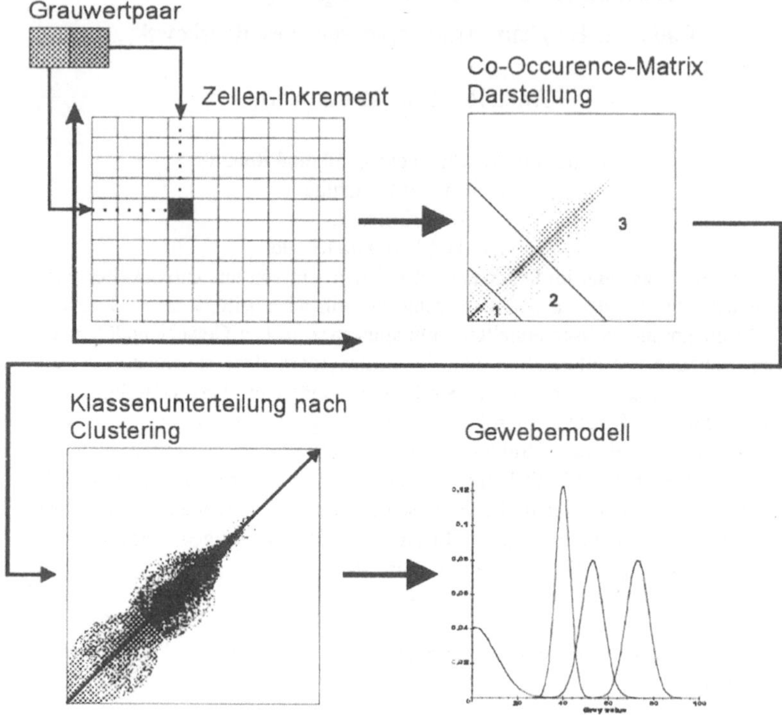

Abb. 1: Der Prozeß zur Berechnung des Gewebemodells.

Die Häufigkeit des Auftretens einer Grauwertkombination bezüglich einer direkten Nachbarschaftsrelation (8er Umgebung) in der gegebenen Aufnahme wird in die Grauwertübergangsmatrix (*cooccurrence*-Matrix) eingetragen [1]. Nachdem dieser Schritt für alle Bildpunkte stattgefunden hat, wird ein häufigkeitsbasiertes Clustering-Verfahren unter Vorgabe der Anzahl an Gewebeklassen auf die zuvor berechnete Grauwertübergangsmatrix angewendet. Betrachtet man die Projektion der erhaltenen Klassenunterteilung (Abb. 1) auf der Hauptdiagonalen der *cooccurrence*-Matrix, so erhält man den Mittelwert und die Varianz des Grauwerts für die unterschiedlichen Gewebeklassen. Daraus läßt sich nun ein Modell für die statistische Verteilung von Grauwerten in homogenen Bildbereichen gewinnen, welches charakteristisch für die in der Aufnahme auftretenden Gewebearten ist. Dieser Prozeßschritt findet ohne Interaktion mit dem Benutzer statt. Lediglich die Anzahl der erwarteten Gewebearten muß als a-priori-Wissen eingebracht werden.

3 Modellierung und Erkennung anatomischer Strukturen

Die gesuchten anatomischen Strukturen werden mit Hilfe von verformbaren Superquadriken [2] (Abb. 2) modelliert. Grenzwerte für Lage, Orientierung und die Verformungsparameter der geometrischen Modelle, sowie die erwartete Gewebeklasse werden einer Wissensbasis entnommen. Jedes Modell wird nun gezielt im Bild gesucht. Ein genetischer Optimierungsalgorithmus wird zur Anpassung der Superquadrikmodelle an die gegebenen Bildkanten verwendet. Im Unterschied zu bisherigen Verfahren nutzen wir zur Anpassung allerdings auch die Information über die Grauwertverteilung im inneren der zu segmentierenden Objekte. Das zuvor berechnete Gewebemodell hilft hierbei zu überprüfen, inwieweit die in der Wissensbasis vorgegebene Gewebeklasse der Grauwertverteilung in der durch die Superquadrik eingeschlossenen Region entspricht. Diese Verfahrensweise führt zu weitaus besseren Schätzungen der Modellpositionen und zu niedrigeren Ausführungszeiten im Vergleich zu Verfahren, die lediglich eine Anpassung an Regionenkonturen vornehmen.

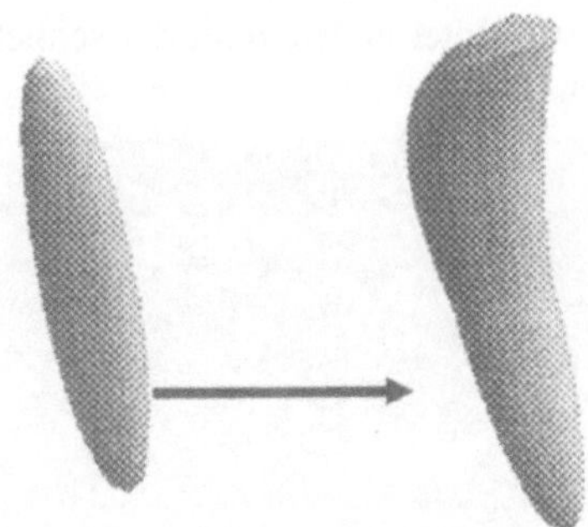

Abb. 2: Verformung einer ellipsoidförmigen Superquadrik

Leider können verformbare Superquadriken die Form einer anatomischen Struktur nur grob approximieren, so daß ein weiterer Schritt zur genauen Formanpassung notwendig ist. Hierzu werden aktive Konturen (*Snakes*) [3] verwendet. Die Anpassung an Bildkanten durch Snakes gehört inzwischen zu den Standardverfahren in der 2D-Bilderkennung, zum Beispiel beim Lippenlesen (Abb. 3).

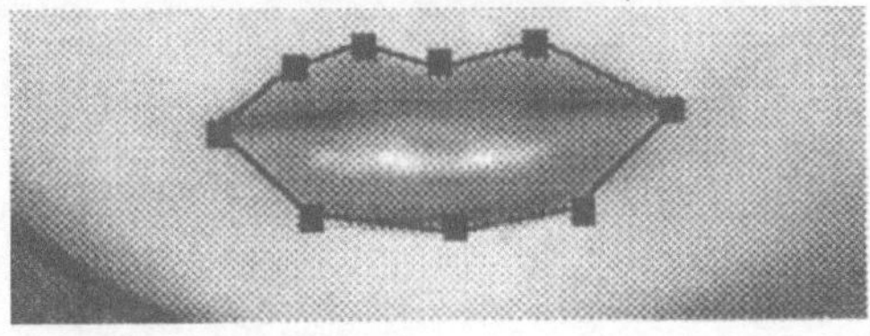

Abb. 3: Unterstützung von Spracherkennung durch Lippenlesen, ein typisches Anwendungsgebiet für aktive Konturen.

Aus der zuvor angepaßten Superquadrik werden entsprechend der Schichten im Tomogramm Schnitte berechnet, die als Initialisierung für eine aktive Kontur interpretiert werden können. Die Anpassung der aktiven Kontur findet durch die Minimierung einer Energiefunktion statt, die sich aus der Summe einer internen und einer externen Energiekomponente zusammensetzt. Die externe Energiekomponente erreicht in der Nähe von Bildkanten ein niedriges Niveau. Die interne Energiekomponente beschreibt die lokale Krümmung an den Stützstellen der aktiven Kontur. Die Minimierung der Energiefunktion einer Snake sorgt also für eine Anpassung der Kontur an die vorliegenden Bildkanten und verhindert scharfe Richtungswechsel im Konturenverlauf.

4 Ergebnisse

Wir haben ein allgemein formuliertes Modell des Hirnstamms mit Übergang zum Pons sowie ein einfaches Modell für das Auge mit unterschiedlichen MRT-Aufnahmen getestet. Die Segmentierung war in allen Fällen erfolgreich und führte zu äußerst präzisen Ergebnissen. Die Ausführungszeiten lagen bei einer SGI-Onyx unterhalb von 3 Minuten, was unter anderem an der schnellen Berechnung der Superquadrikmodelle [4] liegt.

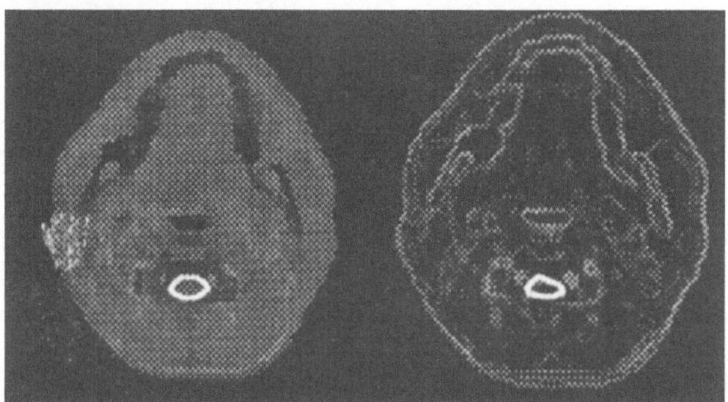

Abb. 4: Segmentierungsergebnis für den unteren Teil des Hirnstamms.

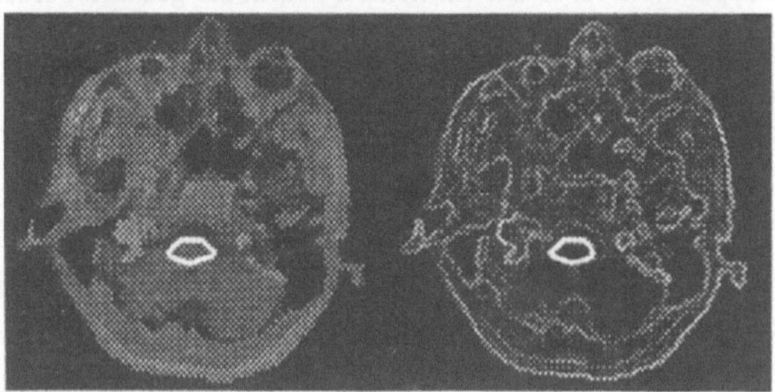

Abb. 5: Segmentierungsergebnis für den oberen Teil des Hirnstamms.

Die Verwendung des automatisch berechneten Gewebemodells führte im Vergleich zu einer rein kantenorientierten Modellanpassung zu weitaus besseren Ergebnissen (Abb. 4 und 5 links). Der genaue Formschluß wurde durch die Snake-Anpassung erreicht (Abb. 4 und 5 rechts).

5 Fazit

Das Ziel, anatomische Strukturen in MRT-Aufnahmen ohne Benutzerinteraktion zu erkennen und zu klassifizieren, wurde erreicht. Die Verwendung von Information über die Grauwertverteilung innerhalb der zu klassifizierenden Strukturen konnte durch die automatische Berechnung eines Gewebemodells erreicht werden. Verformbare Superquadriken wurden als Modell zur Anpassung an die gegebenen Aufnahmen mit Erfolg angewendet. Eine manuelle Unterstützung des Segmentierungsprozesses war nicht notwendig.

Derzeit wird an einer Weiterentwicklung des Verfahrens im Hinblick auf die Erkennung weiterer anatomischer Strukturen sowie an einer besseren Visualisierung der Segmentierungsergebnisse gearbeitet. Weiter sollen die Anwendung dieses Verfahrens auf Ultraschallaufnahmen sowie die Segmentierung pathologischer MRT erprobt werden.

6 Literatur

1. Haberäcker P.: Praxis der digitalen Bildverarbeitung und Mustererkennung. Carl Hanser Verlag, München, Wien, 1995.
2. Barr A.: Superquadrics and Angle Preserving Transformations. IEEE Comp. Graph. Appl., 1:11-23, January 1981.
3. Kaas M., Witkin A., Terzopoulos D.: Snakes: Active Contour Models. IEEE Trans. PAMI, 259-268, 1987.
4. Barr A., Franklin R.: Faster Calculation of Superquadric Shapes, IEEE Comp. Graph. Appl., 1:41, July 1981.

Similarity-Based Image Segmentation
Determination of Brain/Liquor Ratio by Alzheimer Dementia

Petra Perner

Institut für Bildverarbeitung und angewandte Informatik e.V.
Arno-Nitzsche-Str. 45, 04277 Leipzig
Email: ibaiperner@aol.com

Abstract. In the paper, we propose a similarity based image segmentation method, which takes the non-image information and the image characteristics and selects among a set of cases the case, which fits best to the current case. The segmentation parameters associated to the close case are applied to the segmentation unit and taken for segmentation of the current case. By taking into account the non-image and image information we break down our complex solution space to a subspace of relevant cases where the variation among the cases is limited. We use our approach for determination of brain/liquor ratio in CT-images. This parameter is used for diagnosis of Alzheimer disease.

Keywords: Image Segmentation, CT Image Analysis, Similarity-Based Image Segmentation, Alzheimer Demenz

1 Introduction

The complexity of the brain CT-scans is due to partial volume effects, which disturb the edges and produce contrast degradation by spatial averaging, and to the typical problems such as patient movements, beam hardening, and reconstruction artefacts. These image characteristics are responsible for the over- and undersegemented results observed when unsupervised segmentation is applied.

There are several methods for segmenting x-ray CT images recently reported in the literature: template matching [1], region oriented segmentation[2], knowledge based labeling [3], and edge-based segmentation and labeling[4].

In the paper, we propose a similarity based segmentation method, which takes the non-image information and the image characteristics and selects among a large set of cases the case, which fits best to the current case. The segmentation parameters associated to the close case are applied to the segmentation unit and taken for segmentation of the current case. By taking into account the non-image and image information we break down our complex solution space to a subspace of relevant cases where the variation among the cases is limited. We use the proposed method for labeling brain and liquor areas in CT slices. Based on this we calculate brain/liquor ration which is a parameter to determine the degree of degenerative brain disease [5].

2 The overall architecture

An overview about the architecture of the segmentation unit shows Figure 1.

A new image, which has been taken by a CT image acquisition unit, should be segmented and labeled for further calculation of brain/liquor ratio. In the following we will understand for segmentation: the definition of regions based on constant local image features, and for labeling: the classification of regions into the object classes: brain and liquor.

In the case base, there are stored formerly processed cases by their original CT images and their non-image information. The task is now to find the best segmentation for the current image by looking up the case base for similar cases. Similarity determination should be done in two phases: first it is asked for cases having similar non-image information and second among the resulting subset of close cases it is asked for the case having an image with similar image characteristics like the current case. Since also in the second step more than one case could be selected the evaluation unit will take the case with the highest similarity score. In case there are two or more cases with the same similarity score the first appeared case will be taken. After the closest case has been chosen, the image segmentation parameter associated with the selected case will be given to the image segmentation unit and the current image will be segmented.

In a further step, the area for brain and liquor will be calculated in the 2D image and after all slices for one medical treatment have been processed, the volume of brain and liquor will be calculated based on these information. The resulting brain/liquor ratio makes up the final result for the diagnosis of degenerative brain diseases and for the control of the progress of the disease [5].

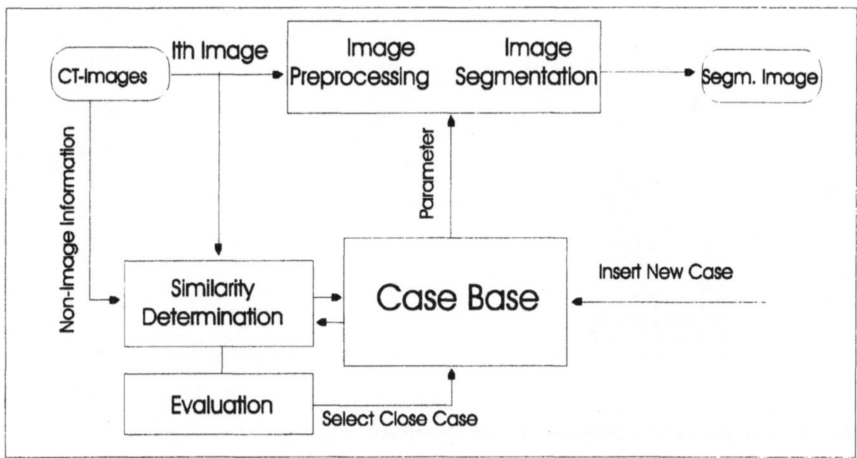

Fig. 1 Overall Architecture of Similarity Based Image Segmentation Unit

3 Case Structure and Case Base

A case consists of: the non-image information, the CT images itself, and segmentation parameter (see Sect. 4). The non-image informations are: a) Measurement parameters like e.g. slice thickness, b) Patent Specific Parameter (Age, Sex ...), c) Parameter and Information about the image processing of the acquired image done with CT-scanner, and d) slice number.

4 Segmentation Algorithm

The gray level histogram is calculated from the original image. This histogram is smoothed by some numerical functions and heuristic rules[6][7][8] to find the cutpoints for the liquor and brain gray level area. The parameters of the function and rules are stored with the cases and given to the segmentation unit if the associated case is selected.

The following steps are performed: The histogram is smoothed by a numerical function. There are two parameter to select, the complexity of the interpolation function and the interpolation width. Then the histogram is segmented into intervals such that each begins with a valley, contains a peak and ends with a valley. The peak to shoulder ratio of each interval is tested first: An interval is merged with the neighbor sharing the higher of its two shoulders if the ratio of peak height to the height of it's higher shoulder, is greater than or equal to a threshold. Finally, the number of the remaining intervals is compared to a predefined number of intervals. If more than this have survived, the intervals with the highest peaks are selected. The number of intervals depends on the number of classes the image should be segmented. The cutpoints are calculated and then applied to the image. Fig. 2 shows a histogram for an original image and also the histogram after it was processed by the algorithm. The original image and the resulting labeled images are shown in Fig. 3.

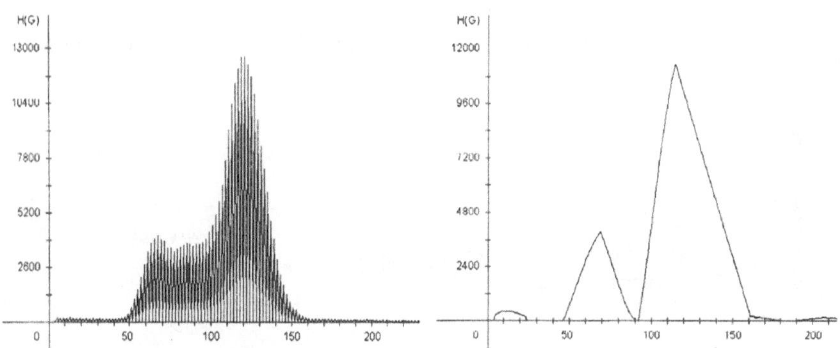

Fig. 2 Histogram of a CT-Image and refined Histogram

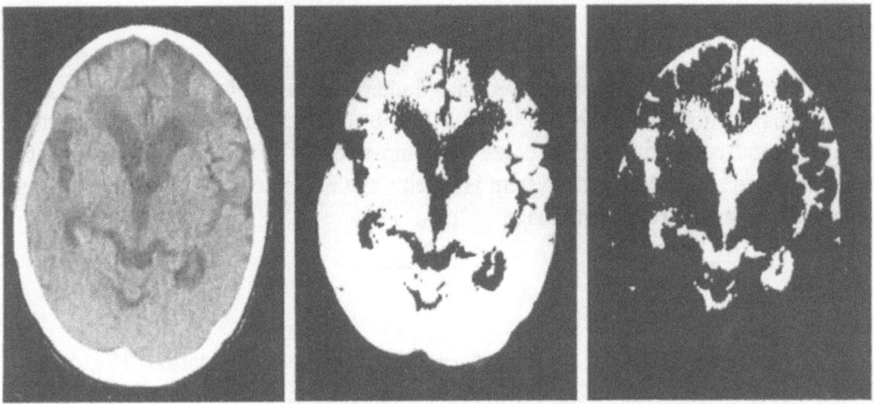

Fig. 3 Original Image, Labeled Images for Brain, and Labeled Image for Liquor

5 Similarity Determination

5.1 Similarity Measure for Non-Image Information

We use Tversky's similarity measure for the non-image information [9]. The similarity between a Case C_i and a new case b presented to the system is:

$$S(C_i, b) = \frac{|C_i|}{\alpha|A| + \beta|D| + \gamma|M|}$$

(1)

$$\alpha = 1, \beta, \gamma = \frac{1}{2}$$

where $|C_i|$ is the set of attributes in case C_i, A is the set of corresponding attributes in case C_i and b, D is the set of attributes having different values, and M is the set of attributes having missing values.

5.2 Similarity Measure for Image Information

Determination of similarity is done with an algorithm proposed by Zamperoni et. al [10]. The input to the algorithm are the two images that should be compared. According to the specified distance function the proximity matrix is calculated for one pixel at position r,s in image A to the pixel at the same position in image B and to surrounding pixel within the window size. The same is done for the pixel at position r,s in image B. Then, clustering is performed based on that matrix in order to get the minimum distance among the compared pixel. Afterwards, the average of both values is calculated. This repeats until all pixels of both images are processed. Then from the average minimal pixel distance the distance value for the whole image is calculated and this value is given to the output.

6 Results

The evaluation of our approach showed that similarity measure for comparing images and non-image information worked very well. The selected parameters for segmentation give good result for similar cases. A comparison of the automatic labeling to human labeling showed that the system is much more accurate. It is hard for a human to label all the small areas in an image.

7 Conclusion

We have presented a concept for a similarity based image segmentation. The system performs image segmentation by looking up a case base for similar formerly processed images and takes the segmentation parameters associated to the similar image in order to do segmentation of the current image. The results show the feasibility of the approach and that the results are better than human labeling. Further work will be done to evaluate the approach on a large set of cases and to compare it to other methods. The described architecture doesn't include evaluation of segmentation, updating of case base and case learning. This is left for further work.

References

1. R. Bajcsy, „Multiresolution elastic matching", Comput. Vision, Graphics, Image Processing, vol. 46-1, pp.1-21, 1989S.
2. Dellepiane et al., „Model generation and model matching of real images by a fuzzy approach", Pattern Recognition, vol. 25, no.2, pp 115-137, 1992C.
3. Li et al., „ Knowledge based classification and tissue labeling of MR images of human brain", IEEE Trans. Med. Imag., vol. 12, no.4, pp. 740-749, 1993
4. D.N. Kennedy et al., „Automatic segmentation and volumetric calculations in nuclear magnetic resonance imaging", IEEE Trans. Med. Imag., vol. 8, no.1, pp. 1-7, 1989
5. Bettin, J. Dietrich, C. Dannenberg, H. Barthel, D. Zedlick, K. Jobst, W.H. Knapp, "Früherkennung von Hirnleistungstörungen – Vergleich linearer und volumetrischer Parameter (CT) mit Ergebnissen der Perfusions-SPET," 78. Deutscher Röntgenkongreß Wiesbaden 1997
6. R. Ohlander, K. Price, and D.R. Reddy, "Picture Segmentation using recursive region splitting method," Comput. Graphics and Image Processing, 8: 313-333, 1978
7. C.H. Lee, "Recursive region splitting at the hierarchical scope views," Computer Vision Graphics, and Image Processing, 33, 237-259, 1986
8. P. Perner, Similarity-Based Image Segmentation, IBaI Report 1996 ISSN 1431-2360
9. A. Tversky, „Feature of Similarity", Psychological Review, vol. 84, No. 4, pp. 327-350, 1977
10. Zamperoni and V. Starovoitov, „How dissimilar are two gray-scale images", In Proc. of 17. DAGM Symposium 1995,Springer Verlag, pp.448-455S.

Funktionale Kernspintomographie
Sliding-Window Echtzeit-Korrelationsanalyse

Daniel Gembris[1], John G. Taylor[1,2], Stefan Schor[1], Dieter Suter[3] und Stefan Posse[1]

[1] Institut für Medizin,
Forschungszentrum Jülich, D-52425 Jülich
[2] Department of Mathematics, Kings College, London
[3] Institut für Physik, Universität Dortmund
Email: d.gembris@fz-juelich.de

Zusammenfassung. In dieser Arbeit werden Korrelations-Algorithmen vorgestellt, die die Erstellung funktionaler Karten des Gehirns aus Kernspintomographie(MR)-Daten in Echtzeit während eines laufenden Scan-Vorgangs erlauben. Ausgehend von einem Optimierungsproblem werden Formeln für die Berechnung von Korrelationskoeffizienten zwischen den Zeitreihen der MR-Datensätze und Modell-Zeitreihen hergeleitet. Die Formeln unterstützen "Detrending", das heißt die Unterdrückung von nicht-stimulus induzierten Signaländerungen, wie zum Beispiel Drifts. Mathematisch wird dies durch die Subtraktion einer Linear-Kombination von Basis-Vektoren erreicht. Bei den vorgestellten Algorithmen, die in unserer FIRE-Software (Functional Imaging in REal-time) implementiert wurden, läßt sich die Korrelationsberechnung auf die N letzten Datensätze beschränken, wobei $N <$ Anzahl der aufgenommenen Datensätze ist (Sliding-Window-Technik).

Schlüsselwörter: fMRI, Echtzeit, Korrelation, Sliding-Window-Technik

1 Einleitung

Anfang der 90-iger Jahre wurde der sogenannte *BOLD* (Bood Oxygen Level Dependent contrast)-Effekt entdeckt [1], der die Grundlage für die funktionale MR-Bildgebung (fMRI: functional Magnetic Resonance Imaging) ist. Die Aktivierung von Gehirnarealen in Protonen-MR-Bildern führt zu einer lokalen Intensitätszunahme in der Größenordnung von bis zu 10%. Der Grund dafür ist die Abnahme der Deoxyhämoglobin- und eine Zunahme der Oxyhämoglobin-Konzentration in aktivierten Arealen aufgrund der stark zunehmenden regionalen Durchblutung. Oxyhämoglobin ist weniger paramagnetisch als Deoxyhämoglobin und führt zu einer verringerten Relaxation der Kernmagnetisierung, die von den Wasserstoffkernen des Wassermoleküle herrührt. Die robustesten BOLD-Signale gibt es bei Aktivierung des visuellen oder des Motorcortex. Eine der standardmäßig für funktionale Bildgebung eingesetzte Pulssequenz ist *EPI* (Echo-Planar-Imaging), die für die Aufnahme eines 64×64-Schichtbildes eine Zeit von weniger als 100ms benötigt. FMRI-Experimente werden durch *Paradigmata* beschrieben, die den Zeitverlauf der Stimulation/Aktivierung definieren. Meistens finden einfache On/Off(Box-car)-Paradigmata Verwendung. Für die Verarbeitung von fMRI-Datensätzen existiert für PCs und Workstations bereits eine Vielzahl von Programmen, wie z.B. SPM, Stimulate oder AFNI [4]. Diese lassen sich aufgrund langer Rechenzeiten in der Regel nur als *Post-Processing*-Werkzeuge einsetzen. Programme zur Auswertung in Echtzeit, d.h. während der Zeitspanne zwischen zwei Messungen, befinden sich erst in der Erprobungsphase. Der primäre Vorteil der Echtzeitverarbeitung ist die Steigerung der Effizienz bei der Durchführung von Messungen. Bislang kann man eine Messung erst Minuten bis Stunden nach ihrer Beendigung bewerten, je nach Grad der Nachverarbeitung. Falls z.B. Meßparameter nicht korrekt eingestellt waren oder der Proband nicht ruhig genug im Scanner gelegen hat, muß eventuell die gesamte Messung und Auswertung wiederholt werden. Zu den führenden Arbeitsgruppen im Bereich der Echtzeitverarbeitung zählt die um Robert Cox [3] und die in Pittsburgh [5]. Letztere verwendet einen Parallelrechner vom Typ Cray-T3E.

Im Abschnitt 2 werden die mathematischen Grundlagen unserer Echtzeit-Korrelations-Algorithmen besprochen. Diese beherrschen "Detrending", also die Reduktion von Störanteilen, und die "Sliding-Window"-Technik. Die Summe aller Störanteile ist eine Linearkombination von Detrending-Vektoren. Die Detrending-Vektoren können entweder vordefiniert (z.B. polynomiale Zeitreihen) oder aus den Meßwerten spezieller Sensoren für Atmung, Herzschlag, Probandenbewegung etc. generiert werden.

Unseres Wissens nach wird die "Sliding-Window-Technik" von dem in [3] von Cox vorgeschlagenen Algorithmus nicht unterstützt. Die Anwendung der Sliding-Window-Technik ermöglicht erst eine Korrelationsberechnung, bei der die Korrelationskoeffizienten im Verlauf der Messung eine konstante Sensitivität gegenüber Änderungen des Signal-Verlaufs nach einem Stimulus haben. Abschnitt 3 beschreibt das von uns entwickelte FIRE (Functional Imaging in REaltime)-Softwarepaket, in das unser Algorithmus integriert wurde.

2 Theorie

In [2] wurden einige grundlegenden Methoden zur Auswertung von fMRI-Daten beschrieben. Sie zählen ebenso, wie die hier vorgestellten Verfahren, zur *Single-Voxel*-Analyse. Das Problem der Detektion neuronaler Aktivierung wird dabei auf den Vergleich der gemessenen Zeitreihe eines Voxels mit einer Modellzeitreihe reduziert. Eine wohletablierte Methode für den Vergleich ist die Berechnung des Korrelationskoeffizientens beider Zeitreihen. Es könnten auch die Fourier-Spektren der Zeitreihen miteinander korreliert werden. Diese rechenaufwendigere Variante findet selten Anwendung, da aus ihr, wie in [2] gezeigt, keine bessere Hervorhebung aktiver Areale resultiert. Mit statistischen Tests, wie z.B. dem t-Test, kann überprüft werden, ob die berechneten Korrelationswerte statistisch signifikant von null verschieden sind. Anstelle der Korrelationswerte selbst, kann auch der Grad der statistischen Signifikanz (p-Wert) als Maß für die neuronale Aktivierung gewählt werden. Als Vorverarbeitungsschritte sind eine räumliche und zeitliche Glättung der Ausgangsdaten möglich. Davon wird in unserer FIRE-Software aber kein Gebrauch gemacht. Mit "Detrending" wird versucht, Störanteile in den gemessenen Zeitreihen zu unterdrücken. Für die bildliche Darstellung wird üblicherweise ein Thresholding der Aktivierungswerte durchgeführt. Die so erhaltene funktionale Information kann dann einem anatomischen MR-Datensatz überlagert werden. Der von Cox et. al. [3] vorgeschlagene Algorithmus für Echtzeit-fMRI basiert ebenfalls auf der Berechnung von Korrelationskoeffizienten. Die Besonderheit ist, daß die Berechnung iterativ erfolgt, damit der Rechenaufwand für jeden Zeitschritt gleich bleibt. Bevor wir unsere Methodik vorstellen, wird zum besseren Verständnis zunächst die herkömmliche Definition der Korrelation angegeben.

2.1 Konventionelle Korrelation

Der Korrelationskoeffizient ρ zwischen zwei Vektoren $\mathbf{x}$ und $\mathbf{r}$ ist definiert als:

$$\rho = \frac{(\mathbf{x} - \bar{x}\mathbf{1})^T \cdot (\mathbf{r} - \bar{r}\mathbf{1})}{|\mathbf{x} - \bar{x}\mathbf{1}| \, |\mathbf{r} - \bar{r}\mathbf{1}|} \tag{1}$$

Die Vektoren seien N-dimensional, wobei N die Anzahl der Zeitpunkte ist. Der Referenzvektor $\mathbf{r}$ beinhaltet die Modell-Zeitreihe. Von den Komponenten des Meß- und Referenzvektors wird der Mittelwert aller Komponenten des jeweiligen Vektors subtrahiert, um den Einfluß unterschiedlicher Basislinien-Verschiebungen auf die Korrelationsergebnisse zu beseitigen. "Detrending", das im nächsten Abschnitt eingeführt wird, ist eine Verallgemeinerung dieser Subtraktion.

2.2 Korrelation mit Detrending

Die Definition des Korrelationskoeffizienten wird ausgehend von Gleichung (1) wie folgt erweitert:

$$\rho = \frac{\mathbf{x}_S^T \mathbf{r}_S}{|\mathbf{x}_S| \, |\mathbf{r}_S|} \tag{2}$$

$$\mathbf{x}_S = \mathbf{x} - \sum_{i=0}^{L-1} \gamma_i \mathbf{s}_i \tag{3}$$

$$\mathbf{r}_S = \mathbf{r} - \sum_{i=0}^{L-1} \delta_i \mathbf{s}_i \tag{4}$$

Sowohl $\mathbf{x}$ als auch $\mathbf{r}$ wird in die Summe zweier Vektoren zerlegt. Einer liegt in der Hyperebene, die durch die L Detrending-Vektoren $\mathbf{s}_i$ aufgespannt wird; der andere, $\mathbf{x}_S$ bzw. $\mathbf{r}_S$, ist orthogonal zu dieser Hyperebene, so daß

$$(\mathbf{x_S}^T \cdot \mathbf{s_i}) = (\mathbf{r_S}^T \cdot \mathbf{s_i}) = 0 \tag{5}$$

für jedes i. Die Detrending-Matrix S beinhaltet die s_i als Spaltenvektoren; die Vektoren γ und δ, zusammengesetzt aus den Detrending-Koeffizienten γ_i und δ_i, erhält man durch Lösen der linearen Gleichungssysteme

$$(S^T S)\,\gamma = S^T\mathbf{x} \tag{6}$$

$$(S^T S)\,\delta = S^T\mathbf{r} \tag{7}$$

mit $\gamma = (\gamma_1\gamma_2..\gamma_L)^T$ und $\delta = (\delta_1\delta_2..\delta_L)^T$. Der Ausgangspunkt für die mathematische Herleitung unserer Formeln ist die Minimierung der quadratischen Formen

$$|\mathbf{x} - \alpha\mathbf{r} - S\gamma|^2 \quad \text{und} \quad |\mathbf{r} - S\delta|^2 \;. \tag{8}$$

Minimierung bezüglich α, δ und γ ergibt die Gleichungen (6), (7) und den optimalen Wert für α, welcher sich als mit dem Korrelations-Koeffizienten ρ eng verwandt erweist:

$$\rho = \alpha\,|\mathbf{r}_S|\,/\,|\mathbf{x}_S| \tag{9}$$

Basierend auf diesen Gleichungen kann der nächste Schritt in der Entwicklung unseres Verfahrens erfolgen.

2.3 Iterative Berechnung

Durch Einsetzen von (3) und (4) in (2) und Ausmultiplizieren erhält man einen Ausdruck für ρ, der auschließlich aus iterativ berechenbaren Unterausdrücken besteht und somit in jedem Zeitschritt effizient neu berechnet werden kann:

$$\rho = \frac{\mathbf{xr} - \sum_i \delta_i\mathbf{xs_i}}{\sqrt{h_1 h_2}} \tag{10}$$

$$h_1 = \mathbf{x}^2 - 2\sum_i \gamma_i\mathbf{xs_i} + 2\sum_{i>j} \gamma_i\gamma_j\mathbf{s_i s_j} + \sum_i \gamma_i^2\mathbf{s_i}^2 \tag{11}$$

$$h_2 = \mathbf{r}^2 - 2\sum_i \delta_i\mathbf{rs_i} + 2\sum_{i>j} \delta_i\delta_j\mathbf{s_i s_j} + \sum_i \delta_i^2\mathbf{s_i}^2 \tag{12}$$

Für den Spezial-Fall eines einzigen Detrending-Vektors mit konstanten Elementen (konventionelle Korrelation) vereinfacht sich die Gleichung für ρ zu:

$$\rho = \frac{\sum_i x_{i,k,l}r_i - \bar{r}N\bar{x}_{k,l}}{\sqrt{\sum_i r_i^2 - \bar{r}^2 N}\sqrt{\sum_i x_i^2 - \bar{x}^2 N}} \tag{13}$$

Hierbei geben k und l die Koordinaten des Punktes an, dessen Zeitreihe in die Korrelationberechnung eingeht. Für alle Produkte in (10)-(13) werden Hilfsvariablen definiert, die in jedem Zeitschritt zu aktualisieren sind. Die Art der Aktualisierung ist mit der Anwendung *Sliding-Window-Technik* verknüpft, die einen N MR-Datensätze umfassenden Buffer-Speicher erfordert. In der ersten, der *Akkumulationsphase*, wird der Buffer sukzessiv gefüllt. Dabei wird zu den Hilfsvariablen jeweils ein Wert hinzuaddiert. In der zweiten Phase, der Phase des "stationären Gleichgewichts", überschreibt der jeweils neueste Datensatz den ältesten Datensatz im Buffer. Zu den Hilfsvariablen werden nun nicht nur Werte hinzuaddiert, sondern auch subtrahiert. Die Umsetzung der Korrelationsberechnung ist Thema des letzten Abschnitts.

3 Implementierung

Die Implementation des vorgestellten Sliding-Window-Korrelations-Algorithmus' ist Bestandteil des FIRE (Functional Imaging in REal time)-Softwarepakets, das von zwei der Autoren entwickelt wurde (Stefan Schor und Daniel Gembris). Sämtliche Programme des Pakets sind in C++ geschrieben und erfordern ein UNIX-System. Die Entwicklung erfolgte hauptsächlich unter Solaris bzw. SunOS; für andere Unix-Derivate sind Anpassungen in unterschiedlichen Ausmaßen erforderlich. Auf einer "Sun ULTRA 1"-Workstation (143 MHz) können in einer Sekunde maximal zwei MR-Bilder mit einer Matrix von 64×64 Bildpunkten verarbeitet werden (das schließt die Skalierung der anatomischen und funktionalen Bilder auf eine Auflösung von 256×256 mittels bilinearer Interpolation ein).

Die Implementierung unseres Algorithmus wurde mit dem Korrelations-Modul des AFNI-Softwarepakets [4], welches laut Programmbeschreibung auf dem in [3] beschriebenen Algorithmus basiert, bezüglich der Verarbeitungsgeschwindigkeit verglichen. Für die Phase der kumulativen Korrrelationsberechnung wurde eine ungefähre Übereinstimmung der Rechenzeiten festgestellt.

Wir danken der Europäischen Union die diese Arbeit durch den BioMed grant PL 950870 in Teilen unterstützt hat.

Literatur

1. Ogawa S, Lee TM, Kay AR, Tank DW: Brain magnetic resonance imaging with contrast dependent on blood oxygenation. Proc.Natl.Acad.Sci.USA Vol. 87, pp. 9868-9872, 1990.
2. Bandettini PA, Jesmanowicz A, Wong EC, Hyde JS: Processing Strategies for Time-Course Data Sets in Functional MRI of the Human Brain. Mag. Reson. Med., 30:131–176, 1993.
3. Cox RW, Jesmanowicz A, Hyde JS: Real-Time Functional Magnetic Resonance Imaging. Magn. Reson. Med., 33, 230–236, 1995.
4. Cox, RW: AFNI: software for analysis and visualization of functional magnetic resonance neuroimages. Comput. Biomed. Res., 29, 162–173, 1996.
5. Voyvodic JT: Real-Time fMRI Paradigm Control Software For Integrating Stimulus Presentation, Behavioral and Physiological Monitoring, and Statistical Analysis. ISMRM 1996, 1835.
6. Shewchuk JR: An Introduction to the Conjugated Gradient Method Without the Agonizing Pain. FTP: REPORTS.ADM.CS.CMU.EDU (IP: 128.2.222.79) 1994/CMU-CS-94-125.ps.

Mammalyzer II

A Decision Support System for Early Detection of Breast Cancer in Contrast-Enhanced MRI

Dirk Krechel[1], Felix Hess[1], Ralf Comes[1]
Aldo v.Wangenheim[2], Klaus Blasinger[3]

[1]Arbeitsgruppe Expertensysteme, Universität Kaiserslautern,
Postfach 3049, 67653 Kaiserslautern
Email: {krechel,hess,comes}@informatik.uni-kl.de
[2]Department of Computer Sciences, Universidade Federal de Santa Caterina,
88049-900 Florianpolis - S.C., Brazil
Email: awangenh@inf.ufsc.br
[3]Radiologische Gemeinschaftpraxis Dr. Buddenbrock, Dr. Blasinger, Dr.Benz
Kaiserstr. 20, 55116 Mainz

Abstract. We present an integrated system for the automatic analysis of MRI-breast images towards the early detection of breast cancer. The system operates on taken images using the method of dynamic contrast-enhanced MRI. Suspicious breast lesions are automatically marked with colours, thus directing the physician's attention towards the critical regions. The medical support system is based on image-matching algorithms using self organizing maps (SOM) and Monte Carlo methods, which enables the system to work properly even with image sequences that are strongly deformed by the patients breathing movements. The system is tested on real patient data and is now being refined in cooperation with Dr. Buddenbrock, Dr Blasinger, Dr. Benz hospital for Radiology and Nuclear Medicine, Mainz.

Keywords: MR-Mammography, Configuration, Motion Artifacts, Monte Carlo Methods, Tumor Detection

1 Introduction

The MAMMALYZER II presents a diagnosis supporting image processing system which preprocesses dynamic MR-Mammographs (MRM) for easier and less erroneous analyses by the medical practitioner. The breast images are provided by a special MRI sequence which is based on the work of [1], [2]. It uses the property that malignant tumors need a much higher perfusion than healthy tissue. Making use of a contrast-agent such as GDTA, the need for higher perfusion results in a faster accumulation of contrast agent in those areas. A comparison of the observed signal-increase ratios between different MRM-volumes gives an indication on the healthiness of the shown tissue. During the patient's examination several MR volumes of the breast are taken, one of which is a reference volume (native) containing no contrast agent. A cancerous region can then be defined as an image region showing a significant signal increase, which is a relative increase of more than 90% during the first minute. This threshold is stated according to the publications of both representative authors [1], [2]. An appropriate method for analyzing the signal increase is the Kelcz criterion [6], which is based on a histogram analysis over more time steps (we, however, use 10 steps in our protocol).

For medical practitioners the analysis of MR images is a tiring and errorprone process, since a complete examination with an up-to-date MR scanner creates up to 160 image slices per examination(10 frames with 16 slices). An automation greatly reduces the workload and thus errors of medical staff. When designing a system for achieving this, two main problems occur. On the one hand there were disparities between native and GDTA volumes caused by the patient's breathing and other movements. On the other hand the problem of noisy input images arises. A proper and careful decision procedure is needed to differentiate between increases of signal intensity triggered by noise and tissue dislocations (motion artifacts) and increases that are triggered by an accumulation of contrast agent in the related breast region. Both of them were not adequately addressed in research performed up to present. Related work in the field has been done by [3], who restricted her approach to the analysis of images that do not show any motion artifacts.

2 AI Methods

The first prototype of MAMMALYZER [4] was structured as a pipeline of different image-processing filters controlled by a graphical user interface. This pipeline can be interactively controlled by the physician, who chooses one of two processing pipes. One for fast results and one for a more accurate analysis.

A problem of the first prototype was, that most of the parameters for both matching and marking modules depend on image characteristics such as TE, TR, slice thickness, field of view, and image resolution and also on the extent of motion artifacts. A set of standard parameters was developed that works stable with the standard MRM sequences of the 1.0 T scanner of the former partner hospital in Kaiserslautern. These parameters have to be modified if one uses images from another scanner or images with another acquisition protocol. For this reason, the analysis sequences are modeled under the knowledge-based image analysis system Cyclops [5], developed at the University of Kaiserslautern, that uses AI techniques of configuration and planning to choose optimal image operator sequences and parameter sets for the analysis of given images based on image parameters, coded knowledge and already acquired image analysis results. The aim of modeling the MRM analysis [8] under this expert system is to automatically use the results of a previous calculation of MRM-inter-volume disparities and knowledge about interrelations between image parameters and module parameters for choosing optimal analysis sequences and module parameters. Thus, users do not have to perform the task of choosing between different analysis sequences and lots of parameters, since the sequence is automatically chosen and

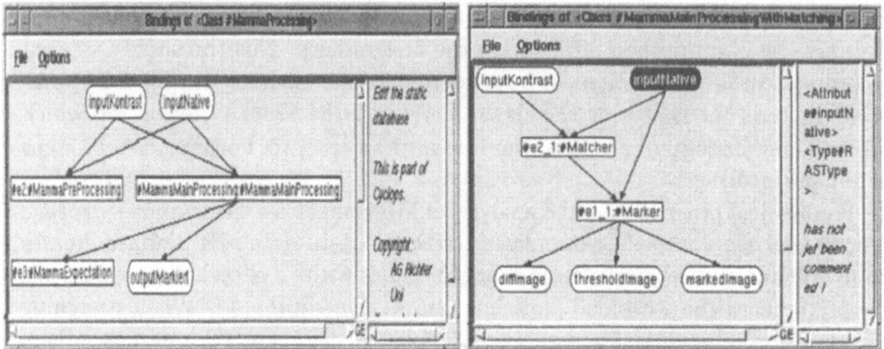

Fig. 1. Complete model of the MR-Mammography analysis process (left), decomposition of the Mamma main process into abstract image operators (right).

parameterized by Cyclops which communicates with **MAMMALYZER II**.
Figure 1 left shows the complete Mamma analysis process. The system automatically recognizes the type of sequence and chooses appropriate image operators and parameters (right). After execution of the configured pipeline an expectation matching module controls the process results and decides whether they have an acceptable quality or pipeline parts must be changed. With the aid of a TMS-structure only the responsible operators, and those operators using their results, must be refined.

3 Volume Processing Methods

3.1 Suppression of Motion Artifacts

The procedure of applying a redistortion process, i.e. the suppression of motion artifacts by comparing two subsequently measured MR-volumes V_1 and V_2, is to determine the proper voxel correspondance of every voxel $v \in V_1$ in V_2. Without loss of generalization, this process can be broken down to pictures (here volume slices), and therefore will be investigated in the following.

For every pixel $p_{xy} := (x, y)$ of picture $P_1 := \{(x, y) | x \in \mathbb{N}, y \in \mathbb{N}\}$, it is necessary to determine the corresponding pixel $p_{x'y'}$ in picture P_2. As consequence, the set $M := \{D_{xy} = (d_x(x, y), d_y(x, y)) | (x, y) \in P_1\}$, denoted as distortion map, delivers for every pixel $p_{xy} \in P_1$ the disparity D_{xy} towards picture P_2, if $d_x(x, y) = (x - x')$ and $d_y(x, y) = (y - y')$ holds for every corresponding pixel pair $p_{xy} \in P_1$ and $p_{x'y'} \in P_2$.

Speaking of pixel intensities $I_P(x, y)$ of pixel $p_{xy} \in P$, one can derive a redistorted picture $R = P_1$ out of P_2 for every pixel $p_{xy} \in P_1$ by means of

$$I_R(x, y) := I_{P_2}(x + d_x(x, y), y + d_y(x, y)) \ , \ (d_x(x, y), d_y(x, y)) \in M \qquad (1)$$

Thus, $I_R(x, y)$ denotes the proper pixel intensity of pixel $p_{xy} \in P_2$. Now, the correspondence problem reduces to finding the redistortion map M and therefore determining the disparity D_{xy} of every pixel in $P1$.

Our approach makes use of the least square error calculation of picture windows in P_1 and P_2. Given a pixel $p_{xy} \in P_1$ to be further invesigated, the native window in P_1 having a certain scale is centered at p_{xy} while the test window in P_2 of the same scale is moved around p_{xy}. Looking at the square error calculation of both windows (see equation 2), a least square error occurs where both windows fit best with respect to their respective pixel intensities.

In short, given a native window $NW := \{(x', y')|x' \in [x - c_x; x + c_x], y' \in [y - c_y; y + c_y]\}$ and an error window $EW := \{(x', y')|x' \in [-e_x; e_x], y' \in [-e_y; e_y]\}$ with widths and heights $c_x, c_y, e_x,$ and e_y, one can derive the least square error disparity $D_{xy} = (d_x(x, y), d_y(x, y))$ of pixel p_{xy} by

$$D_{xy} = \arg \min_{(x',y') \in CW} \sqrt{\sum_{(x'',y'') \in EW} (I_{P_1}(x + x'', y + y'') - I_{P_2}(x' + x'', y' + y''))^2}$$

$$(2)$$

Due to the large-scale nature of motion artifacts in MR-Mammographies (large tissue structures are moved with slight increases in resulting disparities), it is in terms of computational efforts suitable to apply a Monte-Carlo method for determining M. This means, only a fraction of pixels $p_{xy} \in P_1$ containing tissue information are processed in the above described way, and those left aside gain their disparity D_{xy} by an approximation process.

3.2 Improved Visualization

Due to a better image understanding using three dimensional volume representation methods, we implemented a ray-tracing operator generating pixel intensity based volume visualizations. By applying alpha buffering, breast tissue can be made translucent giving an insight view towards segmentated tumors. Furthermore, the application of stereoscopic imaging using LCD-shutter glasses gives the medical staff a better impression of the localization and topology of suspicious breast regions and tumors (see Fig. 2 right for details).

4 Discussion and Future Work

With the presented knowledge-based expert system MAMMALYZER II it is possible to automatically process different MR acquistions and protocols by means of adapted operator configurations and parameterizations. We introduced a Monte-Carlo based alternative to the SOM-matching with a better calculation performance. MAMMALYZER II reduces workload of medical staff when dealing with the time consuming choice of image processing sequences and supports them with a realistic visualization of suspicious breast regions. In the near future, the system will learn the combination of image parameter and operator sequence choices and shall apply and adapt this knowledge to unknown cases.

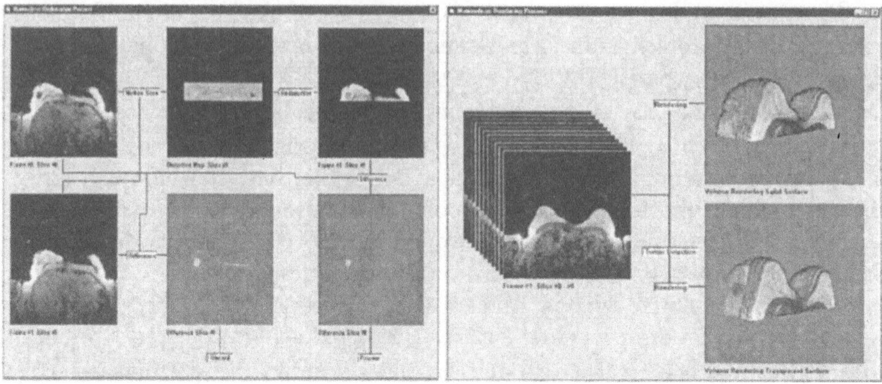

Fig. 2. Redistortion process (left) and improved visualization (right). While a pixelwise calculation of differences between two pictures (upper left and lower left, left figure) leads to a noised signal (lower middle, left), the Monte-Carlo based method creates a better difference picture (lower right, left). Applying a ray tracer using raw MR-volume information helps the physician gain a better understanding of position and type of suspicious breast regions (right figure).

References

1. Heywang-Köbrunner, Sylvia: Contrast- Enhanced MRI of the Breast. Kärger/ Schering, Basel, 1990.
2. Kaiser, Werner, Diedrich, Reiser, Krebs: Moderne Diagnostik der Mamma. Geburts- u. Frauenheilkunde, 1993.
3. Makabe M., Glomitza G., Mayer A., Meinzer H.P., Lederer W.,Schneider S., Wrazidlo W.: Interpretation Support of Contrast-Enhanced MR-Mammography by Image Processing, CAR 1995
4. Huwer S., v.Wangenheim A.: MAMMALYZER: An Approach for Automatic Detection of Breast Cancer by Analyzing Contrast-Enhanced MRI-Mammographs. AIM- 96 - Symposium on Artificial Intelligence in Medicine, Stanford, 1996.
5. v. Wangenheim A.: Cyclops: Ein Konfigurationsansatz zur Integration hybrider Systeme am Beispiel der Bildauswertung. Diss., Universität Kaiserslautern, 1996
6. Kelcz F., Giles E., Santry, Cron G., Mongin S.: Application of a Quantitative Model to Differentiate Benign from Malignant Breast Lesions Detected by Dynamic, Gd-enhanced MRI. JMRI September/October 1996
7. Huwer S., Rahmel J., v.Wangenheim A.: Data-Driven Registration for Local Deformations. Pattern Recognition Letters. North-Holland, 1995
8. Comes R.: Konzeption und Implementierung einer bildauswertungsorientierten Konfigurationswissensbasis. Diplomarbeit, Universität Kaiserslautern, 1997
9. Haralick, Robert M., Shapiro L.: Computer and Robot Vision II, Addison Wesley, 1993
10. Goshtasby A., Turner D., Ackerman L.: Matching of tomographic slices for interpolation. IEEE Transact. on Med. Imag. Vol.11, 1992

Waveletbasierte Rauschreduktion in medizinischen Ultraschalldaten

H. Mehldau, D. Zerfowski, A. Klappenecker

Universität Karlsruhe, IAKS, D-76128 Karlsruhe
Email: mehldau@ira.uka.de, zerfowsk@ira.uka.de, klappi@ira.uka.de

Zusammenfassung. Von Donoho und Johnstone wurde ein waveletbasiertes Verfahren zur Rauschreduktion entwickelt. Dieses Verfahren beruht auf der Annahme, daß signalunabhängiges Rauschen vorliegt. Medizinische Ultraschalldaten sind jedoch mit signalabhängigem Rauschen behaftet. In diesem Artikel werden zwei Ansätze vorgestellt, die das Vefahren von Donoho und Johnstone an das signalabhängige Rauschmodell anpassen.

Schlüsselwörter: Rauschminderumg, Wavelets, Ultraschall.

1 Einleitung

Ultraschallbilder weisen ein typisches, signalabhängiges Rauschen auf. In [1] wird dieses Rauschmodell durch

$$x = s + \sqrt{s}\,\eta,\tag{1}$$

angegeben. Hierbei bezeichnen x das verrauschte, s das unverrauschte Signal und $\eta \sim N(0, \sigma^2)$ einen unkorrelierten, weißen, Gaußschen Rauschprozess. Die meisten Rauschreduktionsverfahren setzen jedoch ein signalunabhängiges, additives Rauschmodell voraus. Insbesondere die waveletbasierten Verfahren, wie z.B. das Waveletreduktionsverfahren nach Donoho et al.[2] („Wavelet Shrinkage"), beruhen auf diesem einfachen Rauschmodell.

2 Orthonormale Wavelettransformation

Eine Orthonormalbasis des Hilbertraumes $L^2(\mathbb{R})$ von der Form

$$\Psi_{j,k}(x) = 2^{-j/2}\Psi(2^{-j}x - k), \qquad j, k \in \mathbf{Z},$$

wird Waveletbasis genannt. Wir nehmen stets an, daß das Wavelet Ψ kompakten Träger besitzt. Eine solche Waveletbasis läßt sich mit Hilfe einer Multiskalenanalyse konstruieren [3]. Insbesondere gibt es eine Folge von Approximationsräumen

$$\{0\} \subset \cdots \subset V_2 \subset V_1 \subset V_0 \subset V_{-1} \subset V_{-2} \subset \cdots \subset L^2(\mathbb{R}),\tag{2}$$

wobei der Teilraum V_j durch eine Orthonormalbasis $\Phi_{j,k}(x) = 2^{-j/2}\Phi(2^{-j}x - k)$, $k \in \mathbf{Z}$, aufgespannt wird. Die Funktion Φ wird Skalierungsfunktion genannt.

Das orthogonale Komplement W_j eines „gröberen"Approximationsraumes V_j im nächst „feineren" Approximationsraum V_{j-1} wird als Detailraum bezeichnet. Der Raum W_j wird durch die Wavelets $\Psi_{j,k}$, $k \in \mathbf{Z}$, aufgespannt [4]. Hat man ein Signal f aus dem Approximationsraum V_J vorliegen, so läßt es sich zerlegen in

$$f = \sum_{k \in \mathbf{Z}} v_{j_0,k} \Phi_{j_0,k} + \sum_{j=J+1}^{j_0} \sum_{k \in \mathbf{Z}} w_{j,k} \Psi_{j,k}, \tag{3}$$

mit den Skalarprodukten $v_{j_0,k} := \langle \Phi_{j_0,k} \mid f \rangle$ und $w_{j,k} := \langle \Psi_{j,k} \mid f \rangle$.

Die Waveletkoeffizienten $w_{j,k}$ und die Approximationskoeffizienten $v_{j_0,k}$ lassen sich aus den Koeffizienten $v_{J,k}$ mit dem schnellen Algorithmus von Mallat [5] berechnen. Die Erweiterung der Wavelettransformation auf zwei (und mehr) Dimensionen gelingt durch die Bildung von Tensorprodukten [4].

3 Waveletreduktion

In der Wavelettransformation eines Signals sind im allgemeinen nur wenige Koeffizienten $w_{j,k}$ ungleich Null und tragen somit zum Signal bei. Betrachten wir ein additives Rauschmodell auf den Waveletkoeffizienten einer Skala J

$$\omega_{J,k} := w_{J,k} + \eta_{J,k}, \tag{4}$$

mit den $\eta_{J,k} \sim N(0,\sigma^2)$ unabhängig verteilt. Bei einer orthonormalen Waveletbasis ergibt sich für die nächst gröberen $(J+1)$ (und alle weiteren) Skalen ebenfalls ein additives Rauschmodell. Die dabei auftretenden Rauschterme $\eta_{j,k}$ sind unabhängig und $N(0,\sigma^2)$ verteilt.

Das von Donoho und Johnstone in einer Reihe von Artikeln [2, 6, 7] vorgestellte Waveletreduktionsverfahren schätzt die Stärke des Rauschens auf den Waveletkoeffizienten. Um diesen additiven Rauschanteil von den Koeffizienten wieder zu entfernen, wird ein Schwellwert τ berechnet und dieser mit dem Schwellwertoperator

$$\delta_\tau(x) := \mathrm{sgn}(x)(x-\tau)_+ \quad \text{mit } (t)_+ := \begin{cases} t & t > 0, \\ 0 & \text{sonst}, \end{cases} \tag{5}$$

subtrahiert. Für die Berechnung des Schwellwertes τ gibt es eine Reihe von Ansätzen [6, 7, 8]. Hier wurde die in [6] vorgestellte hybride Methode aus den Schwellwertfunltionen VisuShrink und SUREShrink verwendet.

Durch die signalabhängige Varianz des Rauschens eignet sich das Waveletreduktionsverfahren nur bedingt für Ultraschalldaten.

4 Partitionierte Waveletreduktion

Dieses Verfahren beruht auf der Annahme, daß bei dem Rauschmodell (1) in Bereichen fast gleicher Signalamplitude ein nahezu signalunabhängiges Rauschmodell vorliegt. Zur Schätzung dieser Bereiche h_i wird der Approximationsraum verwendet. Die Schätzung der Rauschvarianz über diese Bereiche ist aber lokal sehr grob. Deshalb wird sie nur für die auf der gröbsten Skala liegenden Detailräume verwendet, da diese die gleiche lokale Auflösung besitzen. Danach wird rekonstruiert und das Verfahren erneut angewandt.

Wir betrachten den eindimensinalen Fall. Sei $s \in V_J$ das unverrauschte Signal mit kompaktem Träger. Das verrauschte Signal $x = s + \sqrt{s}\,\eta$, mit $\eta \sim N(0, \sigma^2)$, hat ebenfalls kompakten Träger. Die $\nu_{j_0,k}$ und $\omega_{j,k}$ seien die Approximations- bzw. Waveletkoeffizienten von x gemäß einer Waveletzerlegung (3) bis zu einem Approximationsraum V_{j_0}. Hiervon ausgehend wird folgender Algorithmus angewandt:

Eingabe: $(\nu_{j_0,k})_{k \in \mathbf{Z}}$, $(\omega_{j,k})_{k \in \mathbf{Z}}$ $j_0 > j > J$ (Waveletzerlegung von x)
Ausgabe: $\hat{\nu}_{J,k}$ (Approximationskoeffizienten von $\hat{x}$)

$\quad (\hat{\nu}_{j_0,k})_{k \in \mathbf{Z}} := (\nu_{j_0,k})_{k \in \mathbf{Z}}$ (Initialisierung).
$\quad j := j_0.$
$\quad$ Solange $j > J$:
$\qquad \hat{\nu}_{\max} := \max_{k \in \mathbf{Z}}(\hat{\nu}_{j,k});\ \hat{\nu}_{\min} := \min_{k \in \mathbf{Z}}(\hat{\nu}_{j,k})$
$\qquad$ Partitioniere $[\hat{\nu}_{\min}; \hat{\nu}_{\max}]$ in r Intensitätsintervalle $(\lambda_{j,i})_{i=1}^{r}$.
$\qquad$ Teile die Indizes in Klassen $h_i := \{k \in \mathbf{Z} \mid \hat{\nu}_{j,k} \in \lambda_{j,i}\}$ ein.
$\qquad$ Für $i := 1 \ldots r$:
$\qquad\qquad$ Bestimme für die Waveletkoeffizienten $(\omega_{j,k})$ mit $k \in h_i$
$\qquad\qquad$ einen Schwellwert τ (wie beim Waveletreduktionsverfahren).
$\qquad\qquad \hat{\omega}_{j,k} := \delta_\tau(\omega_{j,k})$ für alle $k \in \mathbf{Z}$.
$\qquad$ Aus $(\hat{\nu}_{j,k})_{k \in \mathbf{Z}}$ und $(\hat{\omega}_{j,k})_{k \in \mathbf{Z}}$ rekonstruiere $(\hat{\nu}_{j-1,k})_{k \in \mathbf{Z}}$.
$\qquad j := j - 1$

Um eine Schätzung für Bereiche gleicher Signalamplitude zu erhalten, wird der Wertebereich der $(\hat{\nu}_{j,k})_{k \in \mathbf{Z}}$ in Intervalle partitioniert. Alle $(\hat{\nu}_{j,k})_{k \in \mathbf{Z}}$, die in einem Intervall λ_i liegen, werden über die Indexmenge h_i zusammengefaßt. Für die zugehörigen Waveletkoeffizienten $(\omega_{j,k})_{k \in h_i}$ der untersten Skala wird dann wie beim Waveletreduktionsverfahren die Varianz des Rauschens geschätzt, ein Schwellwert berechnet und der entsprechende Schwellwertoperator auf die Koeffizienten angewandt. Die unterste Skala wird rekonstruiert und das Verfahren für die nächste Skala mit dem neuen, rauschgeminderten Approximationsraum fortgesetzt.

Die Partitionierung des Wertebereichs durch Intervalle muß nicht notwendigerweise äquidistant sein. Nichtlineare Partitionierungen mit quadratisch oder exponentiell wachsender Intervallänge haben sich als vorteilhaft erwiesen. Desweiteren hat sich gezeigt, daß ein kleine Anzahl an Intervallen ($r < 15$) völlig ausreichend ist.

5 Homomorphe Waveletreduktion

Ein verbreitetes Verfahren zur Reduktion von signalabhängigem Rauschen, insbesondere von multiplikativem Rauschen, ist die homomorphe Filterung [9]. Dabei wird die Rauschminderung nach einer Transformation vom signalabhängigen in ein signalunabhängiges Rauschmodell durchgeführt. Anschließend wird eine Rücktransformation in das ursprüngliche Rauschmodell vorgenommen.

Für das allgemeine signalabhängige Rauschmodell

$$x = t(s) + r(s)\,\eta, \quad \eta \sim N(0, \sigma^2) \tag{6}$$

ist also eine Funktion g von der Form $g(x) = u(s) + N(\eta)$ für zwei Funktionen u, N gesucht, um eine additive Verknüpfung von Signal und Rauschen zu erhalten. Hierzu betrachtet man die Taylor-Entwicklung von g um $t(s)$. Für das multiplikative Rauschmodell konvergiert diese Entwicklung gegen $g(x) = \ln(x)$. In anderen Fällen kann nur eine Näherung vorgenommen werden, indem die Terme ab dem zweiten Glied vernachlässigt werden. Für das vorliegende Rauschmodell (Gleichung 1) ergibt sich

$$g(x) = g(s + \sqrt{s}\,\eta) \approx g(s) + g'(s)\sqrt{s}\,\eta. \tag{7}$$

Um hieraus ein signalunabhängiges Rauschmodell zu erhalten, muß gelten, daß $g'(s)\sqrt{s} = 1$ ist. Also ist $g(x) = 2\sqrt{x}$. Desweiteren ist die Rücktransformation f zu berechnen. Für sie soll $f(g(s)) = s$ gelten, damit ist $f(x) = x^2/4$.

Beim homomorphen Waveletreduktionsverfahren wird das verrauschte Signal x punktweise mit g transformiert, und auf den transformierten Daten das Waveletreduktionsverfahren durchgeführt. Die so erhaltenen, rauschgeminderten Daten werden durch f zurücktransformiert.

6 Erste Ergebnisse

Beide Verfahren wurden in das am IAKS entwickelte Bildverarbeitungssystem TomAS [10] integriert. Die Tests wurden auf einem Referenzbild (Abb. 1) durchgeführt, das nachträglich gemäß (1) mit verschiedenen Rauschstärken verrauscht wurde. Zum Vergleich wurden ein 5×5 Medianfilter als Standardverfahren für signalabhängiges Rauschen und das oben beschriebene Waveletreduktionsverfahren herangezogen. Alle waveletbasierten Verfahren benutzen die D6-Waveletbasis [4]. Das partitionierte Waveletreduktionsverfahren verwendet eine exponentielle Partitionierung und $r = 11$ Intervalle. Gemessen wurde der Signal-Rauschabstand (PSNR) (s. Tabelle 1).

Alle waveletbasierten Verfahren erreichen bessere Werte als der Medianfilter, wobei das partitionierende Verfahren konsistent die besten Werte erzielt.

PSNR	verrauscht	Median	Wavlt.red.	Part. WR	Hom. WR
$\sigma = 2$	20,1767	25,0815	27,0483	27,3058	26,9185
$\sigma = 5$	12,2179	21,3248	21,9540	22,6113	21,5863
$\sigma = 10$	6,1973	16,8339	18,1395	19,2719	17,4770

Tabelle 1. PSNR-Messung anhand eines Referenzbildes. Ergebnisse verschiedener Rauschreduktionsverfahren, Alle Angaben in dB.

Abb. 1. Beispiele für Rauschreduktionsverfahren (von links nach rechts): Referenzbild, verrauschtes Bild ($\sigma = 5$), Median, Waveletreduktion, partitionierte Waveletreduktion, homomorphe Waveletreduktion

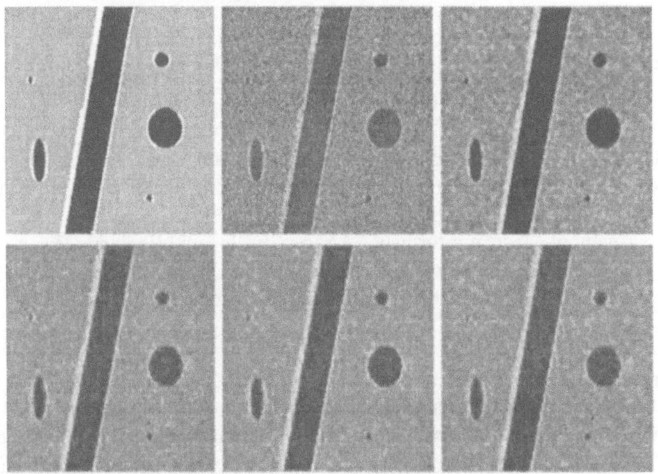

Danksagung. Wir danken der Deutschen Forschungsgemeinschaft für die Unterstützung durch den Sonderforschungsbereich SFB 414 „Informationstechnik in der Medizin – Rechner und sensorgestützte Chirurgie" (Teilprojekt Q1).

Literatur

1. T. Loupas, W. N. McDicken, and P. L. Allan. An adaptive weighted median filter for speckle suppression in medical ultrasonic images. *IEEE Trans. on Circuits and Systems*, 36(1):129–135, Januar 1989.
2. D. L. Donoho et al. Wavelet shrinkage: Asymptopia? *J. Roy. Stat. Soc.*, 57:301–369, 1995.
3. G. Gripenberg. A necessary and sufficient condition for the existence of a father wavelet. *Studia Math.*, 114(3):207–226, 1995.
4. A. Louis, P. Maaß, and A. Rieder. *Wavelets - Theorie und Anwendugen*. Teubner, 1994.
5. S. Mallat. A theory for multiresolution signal decomposition: the wavelet representation. *IEEE Trans. Pattern Anal. Mach. Intell.*, 11(7):674–693, Juli 1989.
6. D. L. Donoho and I. M. Johnstone. Adapting to unknown smoothness via wavelet shrinkage. *Journal of the Am. Stat. Association*, 90:1200–1224, 1995.
7. D. L. Donoho and I. M. Johnstone. Ideal spatial adaption by wavelet shrinkage. *Biometrika*, 81(3):425–455, 1994.
8. M. Hilton and T. Ogden. Data analytic threshold selection in 2D signal de-noising. *IEEE Trans. on Signal Processing*, 45(2):496–500, 1997.
9. I. Pitas and A. N. Venetsanopoulos. *Nonlinear Digital Filters*. Kluwer Academic Publishers, 1991.
10. D. Zerfowski, T. Rohlfing, U. Mende, and Th. Beth. TomAS – Tomographic Algorithms and Ultrasound Simulation. In Lemke (Hrsg.), *CAR'97*, Seite 1017. Elsevier Science, 1997.

OP 2000 and MedSeC
A Concept to Extend the DICOM Standard to Include Digital Stereoscopic Video Sequences

G. Bellaire[1], D. Steines[1], G. Graschew[1], A. Thiel[2], J. Bernarding[2], T. Tolxdorff[2], P. M. Schlag[1]

[1] Surgical Research Unit OP 2000, Robert Rössle Klinik am Max-Delbrück-Centrum für Molekulare Medizin, Universitätsklinikum Charité, Medizinische Fakultät der Humboldt Universität zu Berlin,
[2] Department of Medical Informatics, University Hospital Benjamin Franklin, Free University of Berlin
Email: bellaire@rrk-berlin.de

Abstract. We present a concept for a medical video server extended by a DICOM interface. DICOM conform security mechanisms will be integrated to enable secure Internet access. Especially *d*igital *s*tereoscopic *v*ideo *s*equences (DSVS) that are relevant for surgery should be examined regarding clip length necessary for diagnosis and documentation and clip size manageable with today's hardware. Methods for DSVS compression are described, implemented and tested. DSVS are provided by a stereoscopic surgery microscope and a stereo video camera.

Keywords: Video Server, DICOM, Compression of Stereoscopic Video, MPEG-2

1 Introduction

The Surgical Research Unit OP 2000 at the Robert-Rössle-Klinik, Humboldt University Berlin, and the Department of Medical Informatics of the University Hospital Benjamin Franklin are developing a video server that integrates security mechanisms, digital monoscopic and *d*igital *s*tereoscopic *v*ideo *s*equences (DSVS) into the DICOM standard. The use of public networks such as the internet for transmission of personal patient data must be in accordance with local legislation concerning data security and integrity. The tremendous amount of data with approximately 30 MB/s for each channel can only be handled with video compression and high speed hard disk systems. The MPEG-2 encoding method should be appropriate for video compression. However real-time coding requires specialized hardware, leading to a reduction of the data stream to 6 MBit/s. To significantly reduce the data and to facilitate image management we take advantage of redundant information especially in stereoscopic video sequences.

2 MedSEC and Mallinckrodt CTN-DICOM Server

The typical heterogeneous hardware and software infrastructure within a hospital requires a standardized data exchange format and a protocol as provided by the

DICOM standard in Medicine. Unfortunately, DICOM does not yet include inherent data security concepts. This aggravates the security problem, since the use of standardized protocols and formats weakens the data security: once an intruder has gained access to the data, no special knowledge or software is required to decipher image and patient data. Due to differing national data security regulations, the connection of hospitals to public networks may vary between full connection, restricted access via firewalls, and total isolation. For a university hospital offering special medical services and international research activities, total isolation would be counterproductive and is therefore usually not supported.

The experience in transfer of medical data exposes an additional problem: the compliance of medical users requires high-speed transfer methods, especially for the exchange of image data. This restrictive condition renders time-consuming encryption methods impractical for daily use.

Goal of the MedSeC project is therefore the evaluation of a secure high speed transfer of huge amounts of data within the local high-speed network that links project partners. To investigate different speed-optimized data security concepts, we constructed a scenario with users in- and outside a hospital. To account for the heterogeneous hard- and software infrastructure, the distributed medical services had to use the DICOM 3.0 standard. For the data management (encryption, database management, data transfer activities etc.) a platform-independent user interface had to be developed.

In order to develop a server security concept that permits the storage of video data, mechanisms for the coding of video-specific data into the DICOM object are needed. This concept must also integrate a security mechanism. The structure of DICOM allows the definition of additional data elements in new data groups. These so-called "private" groups have the sole restriction that they must use odd group number. We have developed a toolkit that easily allows to modify the publicly accessible DICOM software by the Mallinckrodt Institute of Radiology [2].

3　Video Server Concept

The video server concept consists of two main components: a specialized *video file server* (VFS) on the one hand, and an object-relational *database management system* (DBMS) on the other. The DBMS is responsible for the registration and administration of video sequences stored by the VFS. This allows the integration of broadcast-quality (stereoscopic) video into a multimedia patient record in such a way that the access to information as well as specific attributes of the video data are handled by the DBMS together with other patient data. Specific attributes can be time and date of video capture, keywords describing the examination and content of the sequence, or selected frames for content based retrieval of sequences.

The VFS captures and stores video data. It communicates with the DBMS via a special interface that is realized as an extension to the latter [3]. The DBMS receives the information necessary to register newly recorded sequences from the VFS.

Client access to video data uses database requests that are forwarded to the VFS, which returns a handle to the client via the database server. Using this handle, the client now has direct access to the sequence from the VFS.

4 Compression of Stereoscopic Video

To optimize patient documentation and diagnosis the question of the adequate clip size (storage space, access time) has to be solved. The parameters determining the clip size are clip length, image resolution, frame rate and compression scheme. In the following we describe theory and first results of the compression of stereoscopic video sequences.

4.1 Theory of Video Compression using the Epipolar Constraint

Compression schemes for digital video sequences that exploit the correlation between temporally adjacent frames (e.g. MPEG [5]), suggest the exploitation of spatially adjacent still frames (i.e. left-right stereoscopic image pairs).

Three kinds of redundancies can be exploited to compress DSVS [8]. The first two have no specific relation to stereoscopy. The third takes advantage of the camera geometry, which is used to capture real live DSVS, or the geometrical constraints, which are implemented to generate stereoscopic visualizations of 3-D computer graphics (e.g. for medical video conferences [1,7]).

- Spatial correlation: Still-image compression is often based on internal predictability, meaning neighboring pixels are most likely identical or nearly identical.
- Temporal correlation: Frames in a sequence imply a frame-to-frame predictability.
- Epipolar constraint: The left/right frames of a stereoscopic image pair contain similar image areas. The known camera geometry (epipolar lines) permits efficient coding using disparity predictability.

The disparity denotes the relative offset between corresponding points in a stereoscopic image pair. [8,10,11] use variations of the basic disparity-based approach for the coding of DSVS. In a *standard camera configuration* (SCC, parallel epipolar lines and complanar image planes), the disparity search can be performed in a single horizontal image line [4]. An image pair can be synthesized given one image and a low resolution map of the disparity of the image pairs. *Disparity map* entries (DMEs) can be represented by few bits.

- Suppose an image (true color) represented in YCbCr-4:2:0 color space (as we use in our experiments) is coded with 12 Bits/Pixel,
- suppose the disparity does not vary significantly over eight pixels and
- suppose the horizontal disparity can be coded with 5 Bits/DME (vertical disparity with 3 Bits/DME). Depending on the underlying geometry a disparity vector consists of one (SCC) or two components.

That implies net compression factors of 58% (SCC) / 30% (one component / two components). The main disadvantage of the mentioned approach is the missing representation of occlusions.

4.2 MPEG-2 Using the Epipolar Constraint

The methods of the MPEG-2 video compression standard [5] can be adapted for stereoscopic video in the following way: The same algorithms applied in the computation of motion prediction may be used for perspective redundancies between corresponding frames in the two channels. However, in contrast to motion prediction the search space for this disparity prediction is very limited, which will reduce encoding time. The reason for this is the missing vertical offset (using SCC for imaging) and the fact that the horizontal offset can be estimated beforehand from the distance between the two lenses and the focal distance. Taking channel 1 as the main channel and encoding it in the usual manner, the frames of channel 2 can be compressed as p-frames referencing the nearest preceding i- or p-frame of channel 1. Depending on the predetermined order of p- and b-frames in the first channel, this results in the sequences shown in Figure 1.

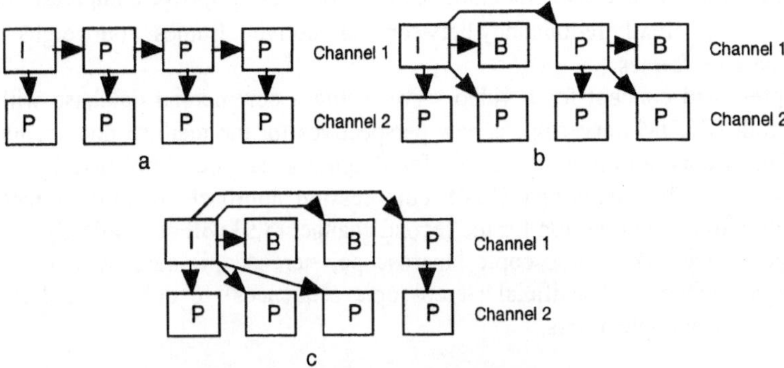

Figure 1: Coding sequence depending on channel 1 frame order;
a) IPPPP...   b) IBPBPBPBPB   c) IBBPBBPBBP

4.3 Experiments and Results

Some basic tests were carried out in order to determine the most appropriate method for compression of stereoscopic video. The reference MPEG-2 encoder from the University of California (Berkeley) [6] was customized to handle stereoscopic video as described in the preceding subsection. The horizontal search width for disparity prediction was used as a parameter for the experiments, whereas the vertical search width was set to zero pixels.

Seq Ch1	HSW 10 pix			HSW 30 pix			Separate compression		
	Time	Size	Ratio	Time	Size	Ratio	Time	Size	Ratio
IPPPP...	560	4710	61%	590	4812	60%	954	586	95%
IBPBP...	490	831	93%	522	836	93%	842	586	95%
IBBPBB...	473	481	96%	503	481	96%	800	586	95%

Table 1: Compression time [sec], size of compressed stereoscopic video [KB], and compression ratio depending on channel 1 frame order; HSW: Horizontal search width

A short sequence of 10 frames per channel of a phantom object (high contrast in shape and color) was captured from a Leica WILD M680 stereoscopic surgical microscope (2x 3 CCD ½'' Camera KC233, Ikegami) on a Silicon Graphics Onyx RE II workstation equipped with two Sirius video boards. The uncompressed sequence with 720x576 pixels resolution and YCbCr-4:2:0 color format was approx. 11.9 MB in size.

Encoding time and size of compressed stereoscopic video data were measured on the Onyx (using 1 R4400 CPU) and compared to the separate compression of each channel in the conventional way. The results for the microscope sequence are shown in Table 1. Captures from another stereoscopic device (room camera Ikegami LH33, 6 CCD ¾'') showed similar results.

5 Conclusion and Outlook

The results show that making use of redundancy in stereo image pairs can reduce encoding time up to 60%. This method, however, does not improve compression ratio (up to 96%). Apparently redundancy between consecutive frames outweighs that between parallel frames.

The presented concept for a video server using a commercial database with the Mallinckrodt DICOM Server opens new perspectives for the medical documentation. The *offline* second opinion procedure for diagnosis can be simplified by secure internet access. The mentioned DSVS compression approach as well as methods using highly lossy compression for the second channel [8,9] will be medically verified (by image sources like stereoscopic laparoscope, stereoscopic surgical microscope, stereoscopic camera and artificial stereoscopic sequences) to define standards for DVSV in surgical applications.

6 References

1. Bellaire G, Graschew G, Engel-Murke F, Krauss M, Neumann P, Schlag PM: Interactive telemedicine in surgery: Fast 3-D visualization of medical volume data, Minimal Invasive Medizin:. Vol.8, no.1-2, 1997
2. CTN, DICOM Software Documentation, ftp://ftp.erl.wustl.edu/pub/dicom/software/ctn/doc
3. Informix Video Foundation DataBlade Module User's Guide, Version 1.1
4. Koschan A: A Framework for Area-Based and Feature-Based Stereo Vision. Machine GRAPHICS & VISION, Vol. 2, No. 4, 1993, pp. 285-308.
5. MPEG Draft International Standard. ISO/IEC 13818-2: Generic Coding of Moving Pictures and Associated Audio: Video, 1995
6. MPEG Software Simulation Group: mpeg2encodeVersion 1.2, ftp://mm-ftp.cs.berkeley.edu/pub/multimedia/mpeg2/software
7. Schlag PM., Rau B, Quack A, Below C, Graschew G, Meyer zur Heyde M, Rakowsky S, Engel-Murke F, Papst M, Balanos E, Breide S, Gaus H: New Technologies in Surgical Oncology. 3-D Video conference via Satellite from Berlin to Paris, CAR 96. Minimal Invasive Medizin 7: 184-186, 1996.
8. Siegel MW, Gunatilake P, Sethuraman S, Jordan AG: Compression of Stereo Image Pairs and Streams. Proc. SPIE Vol 2177, p. 258-268, Stereoscopic Displays and Virtual Reality Systems, 1994.
9. Tseng BL, Anastassiou D: Multi-Viewpoint Video Coding with MPEG-2 Compatibility. IEEE Transactions on Circuits and Systems for Video Technology, Vol.6, No.4, 1996
10. Tzovaras D, Grammalidis N, Strintzis MG: Object-Based Coding of Stereo Image Sequences using Joint 3-D Motion/Disparity Compensation, IEEE Trans. Video Technology 7(2), 1997
11. Woo O, Ortega A: Dependent Quantization for Stereo Image Coding. Proc. of PW-EI-VCIP, San Jose, USA, Jan., 1998

Interaktive Segmentierung von medizinischen Schichtbilddatensätzen verifiziert durch 3D-Visualisierung mittels "Volume Rendering" Methoden

R.Kottenhoff[1], J.Krone[1], R.Grebe[2], I.Wurdack[3], J.Jansen[3]

[1]Phys. Technik, MFH, Frauenstuhlweg 31, D-58644 Iserlohn, Germany
Email: kotti@physiology.rwth-aachen.de
[2]Département Génie Biologique, UTC, F-60205 Compiègne, France
[3]Inst. f. Physiologie, RWTH, Pauwelsstr. 30, D-52057 Aachen, Germany

Zusammenfassung. In diesem Beitrag wird eine Methode und deren interaktive Steuerung zur 3D-Segmentierung medizinischer Schichtbilddatensätze vorgestellt. Das Segmentierungsverfahren nutzt dabei einen Bereichswachstumsalgorithmus (*region growing*) [3] basierend auf der lokalen Grauwertstatistik mit zusätzlicher wachstumsabhängiger Terminierung. Eine direkte Verifizierung der Ergebnisse anhand der Visualisierung von so extrahierten Objekten bildet die Grundlage zur Verbesserung der Segmentierung. Die Ergebnisse werden nach einer Veränderung der Steuerungsparameter durch den Anwender, z.B. den entsprechenden Facharzt, unmittelbar überprüft und führen somit zu einer auf Expertenwissen basierenden Segmentierung.

Schlüsselwörter: Interaktive Segmentierung, Region Growing, Visualisierung, Volumerendering

1 Einleitung

In vielen Bereichen der medizinischen Diagnostik fallen durch bildgebende Verfahren Schichtbilddatensätze unterschiedlicher Modalitäten an. Neben bekanntem Bildmaterial aus (Spiral)CT- und MR-Scannern können auch Datensätze durch Zusammenfügen der Mikroskopaufnahmen von histologischen Gewebeschnitten erstellt und digitalisiert werden.

Zusätzlich zur Frage nach der korrekten Positionierung der Schichtbilder zueinander (*Registrierung*) ergibt sich die Problematik der Extraktion von räumlichen Strukturen und dreidimensionalen Objekten (*3D-Segmentierung*) zur weiteren digitalen Verarbeitung wie z.B. Operationsplanung, CAS, Volumetrie [1] und vieles mehr.

Erst eine 3D-Visualisierung von extrahierten Strukturen bietet die Möglichkeit der Überprüfung von Registrierung und Segmentierung [2]. Im folgenden wird eine Methode zur Segmentierung von Schichtbilddatensätzen genauer beschrieben.

2 Segmentierung mittels Bereichswachstum

Ausgehend von festgelegten Keimpunkten werden Segmente (Bereiche, Regionen) durch iteratives 3D-Wachstum der Segmentkontur (Regionoberfläche) gebildet [3]. Dabei wird in Abhängigkeit von Wachstumsparametern (siehe Abschnitt 2.3) anhand der lokalen Grauwertdynamik die Region bis zu den Objektgrenzen hin ausgedehnt.

2.1 Problematik von Regionenwachstumsalgorithmen

Neben der Wahl der Keimpunkte (siehe Abschnitt 2.2) und der Bestimmung der Wachstumsparameter ist die Wachstumsbegrenzung (siehe Abschnitt 2.4) der Region ein wesentlicher Gesichtspunkt für die Güte der Segmentierung. Zu grobe Wachstumsparameter führen zu einem „Auslaufen" der Region bzw. zu einem Verschmelzen mit Bereichen, die zu anderen Objekten gehören (*chaining effect*), während bei zu feinen Einstellungen der Parameter die Objektgrenzen durch das Bereichswachstum nicht mehr erreicht werden [3].

2.2 Auswahl der Keimpunkte

Die Auswahl der Keimpunkte für das Regionenwachstum ist ein wesentlicher und sensibler Aspekt der Segmentierung. Eine automatische Wahl durch Anwendung von lokalen Operatoren mit Schwellwertsetzung oder ähnlichen Verfahren führt oft zu unbefriedigenden Ergebnissen. Dagegen kann Expertenwissen über die zu segmentierenden Objekte mittels interaktiver Keimpunktwahl (Abb.1) einfließen, was zu besseren Resultaten führt.

2.3 Wachstumsparameter

Wachstumsparameter sind Bedingungen (z.B. Distanzmaße), die die Zugehörigkeit eines Voxels zum Segment festlegen. In diesem Verfahren wurde eine lokaladaptive Methode gewählt. Für die Aufnahme des Voxels $v := (x, y, z)$ mit dem Grauwert $f(v)$ am Rande der Region R müssen dabei zwei Bedingungen erfüllt sein:

$$|f(v) - \mu_R| \leq s_1, \quad \text{mit} \quad \mu_R := \frac{1}{\|R\|} \sum_{w \in R} f(w) \tag{1}$$

und

$$\frac{|f(v) - \mu_N|}{\kappa \cdot \sigma_N{}^2} \leq s_2, \quad \text{mit} \quad \sigma_N{}^2 := \frac{1}{\|N\|} \sum_{w \in N} (f(w) - \mu_N)^2. \tag{2}$$

Die globalen Eigenschaften des Segmentes werden durch μ_R, dem mittleren Grauwert des bisher gewachsenen Gebietes erfaßt. Die lokale Grauwertdynamik wird durch $\sigma_N{}^2$, der mittleren quadratischen Grauwert-Abweichung (*Varianz, Kontrast*) in der $n{\times}n{\times}n$-*Nachbarschaft* N (mit mittlerem Grauwert μ_N) des Aufnahmekandidaten berücksichtigt.

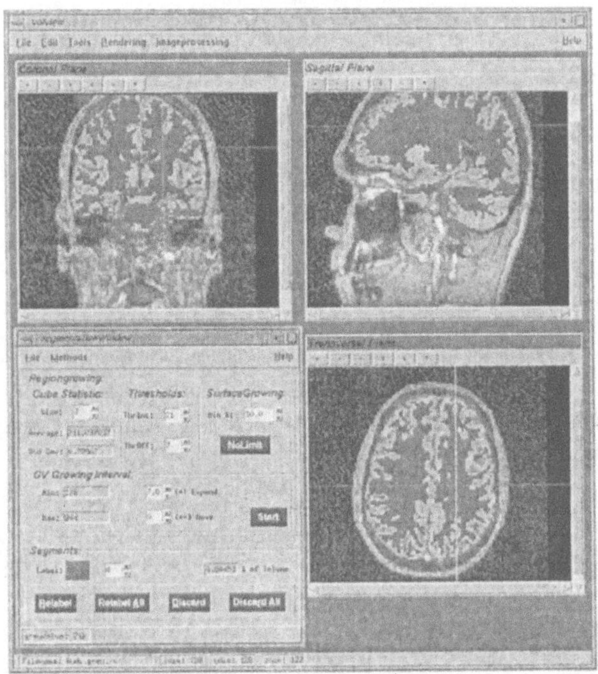

Der Faktor κ des Vertrauenintervalls der lokalen Grauwertdynamik kann aus der Tabelle einer entsprechenden Gaußverteilung gewählt werden. Die Größen s_1 und s_2 sind die interaktiv veränderbaren Schwellwerte des Verfahrens, die bei der Auswahl der Keimpunkte schon vorbesetzt werden.

Durch diese Wahl der Aufnahmebedingungen können auch Objekte segmentiert werden, die zu ihren Konturen hin eine nichtsprunghafte Grauwertdynamik aufweisen. Dieser Vorteil wird dagegen durch die Gefahr des „Auslaufens" in benachbarte Regionen hinein erkauft. Sie muß durch weitere Abbruchkriterien gemindert werden.

2.4 Wachstumsbegrenzung

Ein sprunghaftes Verhalten der Oberflächenzunahme bei der Wachstumsiteration ist ein Indiz für das Erreichen der Objektgrenzen. Dies gilt sowohl für glatte Oberflächen, wie der einer Kugel, als auch für stark verworfene Strukturen, wie dem Kortex des Gehirns. Für eine Kugel wächst das Volumen-zu-Oberfläche-Verhältnis linear mit dem Radius ($\frac{V}{A} = \frac{1}{3}r$). Entsprechend läßt sich für das Bereichswachstum ein dynamisch mitgeführter Sprungschwellwert definieren:

Seien $C(R_n)$ und $C(R_{n-1})$ die 3D-Konturen der gewachsenen Bereiche R_n bzw. R_{n-1} der n-ten bzw. $(n-1)$-ten Iteration, so ergibt sich die Abbruchbedingung zu:

$$\frac{1}{n}\left|\frac{\|R_n\|}{\|C(R_n)\|} - \frac{\|R_{n-1}\|}{\|C(R_{n-1})\|}\right| \leq s_3 \tag{3}$$

Die Segmentierung bricht also ab, falls ein „Auslaufen" über eine Grauwert-brücke hinweg in andere Regionen hinein droht.

3 Verifizierung durch 3D-Visualisierung

3.1 Volume rendering

Es gibt zwei prinzipielle Ansätze zur Visualisierung von Volumendaten:

- die Darstellung einer Oberflächenrepräsentation von Objekten im Volumen. Die Voraussetzung dafür ist immer eine Segmentierung.
- die Strahlverfolgung durch das Volumen mit der grauwertabhängigen Intensitätsaddition entlang der Strahlen.

Eine Überprüfung der segmentierten Strukturen erfolgt durch das erste Verfahren, nämlich die Darstellung der Oberflächenrepräsentation der segmentierten Objekte [4].

3.2 Überprüfung der Segmentierung

Nach dem Segmentierungsprozeß wird das *volume rendering* angestoßen und neben der Darstellung von orthogonalen 2D-Schnittbildern durch den Volumendatensatz werden die extrahierten Strukturen visualisiert (Abb. 2). Der Anwender hat so die Möglichkeit, die Qualität seiner Segmentierung zu prüfen und eine Fehlsegmentierung rückgängig zu machen. Durch die Wahl geeigneter neuer Wachstumsparameter für das Bereichswachstum kann die Segmentierung sukzessive verbessert werden.

4 Ergebnisse und Ausblick

Das beschriebene Verfahren zeigt gute Ergebnisse für MR-Datensätze des Kopfes (Abb.2), die allerdings noch durch einen Facharzt (Neuroanatomen) zu verifizieren sind. Ebenfalls steht noch ein Vergleich mit anderen Segmentierungsverfahren aus.

Eine Verbesserung der Segmentierung ist durch die Erweiterung der Wachstumsbegrenzung um Parameter entsprechend dem elastisch verformbaren Konturmodell (*deformable contour model*) zu erwarten. Hierbei wird durch die Minimierung einer Energiefunktion ein Gleichgewicht zwischen Adhäsion zu Bilddatenmerkmalen und interner Biegeenergie (*internal deformation energy*) bzw. Oberflächenspannung der Segmente hergestellt.

Hat man eine gute Segmentierung durch interaktive Veränderung der Wachstumsparameter erreicht, kann man einen automatischen *region growing* Prozeß

Abb. 2. Visualisierung des segmentierten Kortex

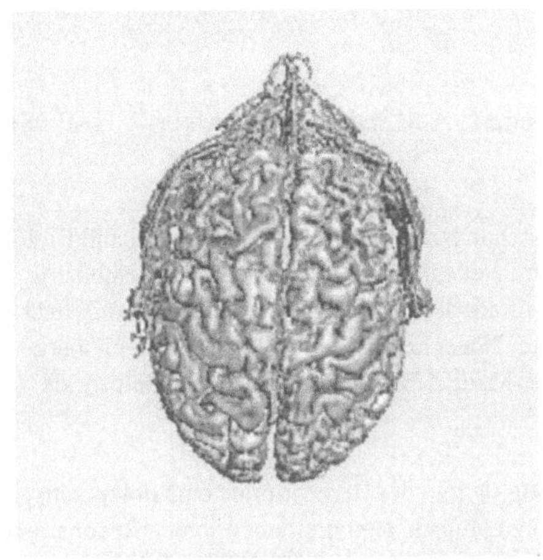

auf Basis der so evaluierten Parameter ansetzen. Dieser wird aber nur optimal für Regionen funktionieren, die die gleiche Dynamik in der Grauwertstatistik aufweisen, wie die Regionen, für die die Parameter ermittelt wurden. Wesentliche, aber noch nicht betrachtete Aspekte sind dabei die automatische Wahl des Keimpunktes sowie eine *region linkage strategy* für die Verschmelzung verschiedener Regionen mit gemeinsamen Kanten.

Literatur

1. Zellerhoff M, Reul J, Klusmann A, Schwarz M: Segmentierung und Volumenbestimmung gesunder und pathologischer Hirnstrukturen aus dreidimensionalen MRT Datensätzen. Proceedings des 1. Aachener Workshop. Bildverarbeitung für die Medizin. Algorithmen · Systeme · Anwendungen. Lehmann T, Scholl I, Spitzer K (Hrsg.), Verlag der Augustinus Buchhandlung, Aachen, 1996

2. Wolsiffer K, Mayer A, Niebsch R, Evers H, Meinzer HP: Die Integration des Heidelberger Raytracers in OpenGL zur integrierten Segmentierung und Visualisierung dreidimensionaler medizinischer Volumendaten. Proceedings des 1. Aachener Workshop. Bildverarbeitung für die Medizin. Algorithmen · Systeme · Anwendungen. Lehmann T, Scholl I, Spitzer K (Hrsg.), Verlag der Augustinus Buchhandlung, Aachen, 1996

3. Lehmann T, Oberschelp W, Pelikan E, Repges R: Bildverarbeitung für die Medizin. Grundlagen, Modelle, Methoden, Anwendungen. Springer-Verlag, Berlin, 1. Auflage 1997

4. Vandenhouten R, Kottenhoff R, Grebe R: 3D color visualization of label images using volume rendering techniques. Medical Informatics, Vol.20, No.2, 1995, pp.149-159.

Hierarchische Identifikation von Merkmalen zur automatischen Orientierung im Bildmaterial des Herzens

A. Schroeder[a], A.M. Demiris[a], J. Albers[b], H.-P. Meinzer[a]

[a] Deutsches Krebsforschungszentrum, Abt. Medizinische und Biologische Informatik,
Im Neuenheimer Feld 280, 69120 Heidelberg
[b] Chirurgische Klinik der Universität Heidelberg, Klinik für Herzchirurgie,
Im Neuenheimer Feld 110, 69120 Heidelberg
e-Mail: A.Schroeder@DKFZ-Heidelberg.de

Zusammenfassung: Um in der Herzchirurgie eine präoperative Operationsplanung durchführen zu können, sind dreidimensionale Rekonstruktionen des vermuteten Defekts basierend auf unterschiedlichem Bildmaterial wünschenswert. Dazu ist eine Identifikation der defekten Region und beteiligter Strukturen in Bildern unterschiedlicher Modalitäten und Schichtrichtungen nötig. In diesem Beitrag wird ein Ansatz vorgestellt, der sich mit der Identifikation statistischer und bildinhärenter Merkmale für eine automatische Orientierung beschäftigt.
Schlüsselwörter: Cardiochirurgische OP-Planung, automatische Orientierung, Merkmalsidentifikation

1 Einleitung und Motivation

In der Herzchirurgie ist eine präoperative Planung eines Eingriffs besonders wichtig, da die Operationen unter einem enormen Zeitdruck stattfinden. Grundlage für eine derartige Operationsplanung bilden beispielsweise MR- und EBT- Schichtaufnahmen. Da die Orientierung in diesem Bildmaterial aufgrund der vielfältigen Aufnahmemöglichkeiten schwierig ist, vereinfachen standardisierte dreidimensionale Rekonstruktionen die Interpretation der Bilder. Anhand dieser Rekonstruktionen soll dem Herzchirurgen ein Eindruck vom Defekt vermittelt werden, um ihn bei der Entscheidung für eine Operationsstrategie zu unterstützen.

Um derartige standardisierte Ansichten automatisch erzeugen zu können, ist eine Orientierung in dem Ausgangsbildmaterial notwendig. Es muß also das Wissen über die Anatomie des Herzens und die Bildakquisition algorithmisch abgebildet werden. Im folgenden wird die Fragestellung näher erläutert und auf Aspekte eingegangen, die für eine automatische Orientierung berücksichtigt werden müssen.

1.1 Fragestellung

Für eine automatische Orientierung in beliebigen Schichtaufnahmen des Herzens ist eine Auswertung des Bildmaterials unter zwei Gesichtspunkten notwendig. Zum einen muß die Orientierung und die Lage (basal, apical, ...) der Schichten sowie des Herzens darin ermittelt werden. Zum anderen ist eine Identifikation intracardialer Strukturen (Klappen, Vorhöfe, Kammern, Septum, ...) notwendig. Grundlage dafür ist eine Identifikation statistischer und bildinhärenter Merkmale.

Da es für cardiochirurgische Fragestellungen keine standardisierten Aufnahmeprotokolle gibt, muß man mit einer großen Vielfalt unterschiedlicher Bilder rechnen. Neben den unterschiedlichen Modalitäten MR und EBT mit ihren bildinhärenten Eigenschaften ist auch die Schichtführung zu betrachten. Es muß also geklärt werden, ob es sich um sagittale, transversale, coronale oder oblique Schichten handelt. Gerade das MR stellt in dieser Hinsicht große Anforderungen, da es das komplette Spektrum möglicher Schichtführungen zuläßt. Bei der Merkmalsidentifikation sind also die unterschiedlichen Ausprägungen der Merkmale in Abhängigkeit von der Schichtführung zu ermitteln. So entspricht in einem Kurzachsenschnitt der linke Ventrikel ungefähr einem Kreis, wohingegen er sich in einem Langachsenschnitt als längliche Struktur darstellt (siehe Abb. 1)

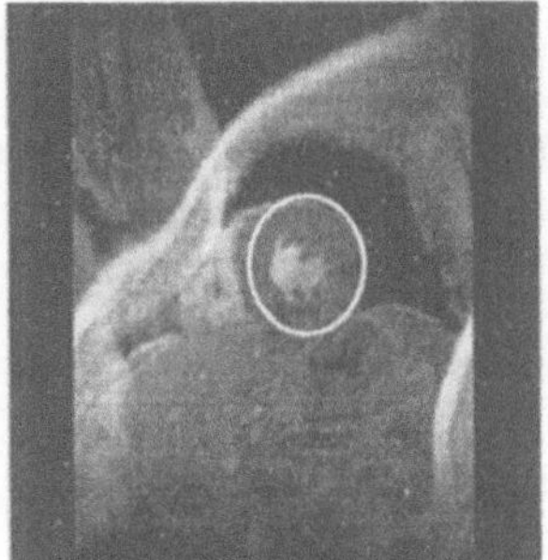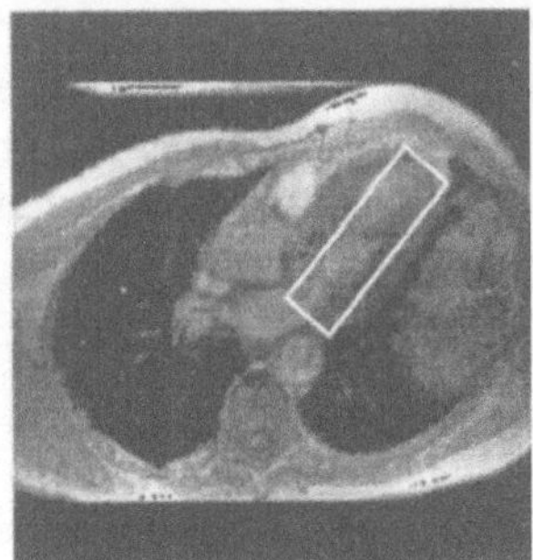

Abb. 1:   Linker Ventrikel in einem Kurz- und einem Längsachsenschnitt

Ein weiterer Punkt, der eine Identifikation von Merkmalen für eine automatische Orientierung erschwert, hängt mit den unterschiedlichen Aufnahmesequenzen zusammen. Je nach Sequenz (T1-, T2-, protonendichtegewichtet) erhält man gänzlich unterschiedliche Signale. So erscheint das Blut in T1-gewichteten Sequenzen dunkel und in T2-gewichteten hell (siehe Abb. 2).

2 State of the Art

In der Herzchirurgie findet derzeit eine präoperative Operationsplanung hauptsächlich mit Hilfe zweidimensionalen Bildmaterials wie beispielsweise Herzkatheterfilmen statt [1]. Durch den Einsatz dreidimensionaler Visualisierungen ist eine Verbesserung der chirurgischen Therapie zu erwarten. Allerdings stellt die Herzchirurgie in dieser Hinsicht besonders hohe Anforderungen. So muß einerseits eine Unterscheidung unterschiedlicher Weichteilgewebe (Myocard, Tumor) und andererseits eine Identifikation feiner Strukturen (Papillarmuskel, Trabekel, Klappen) möglich sein [2].

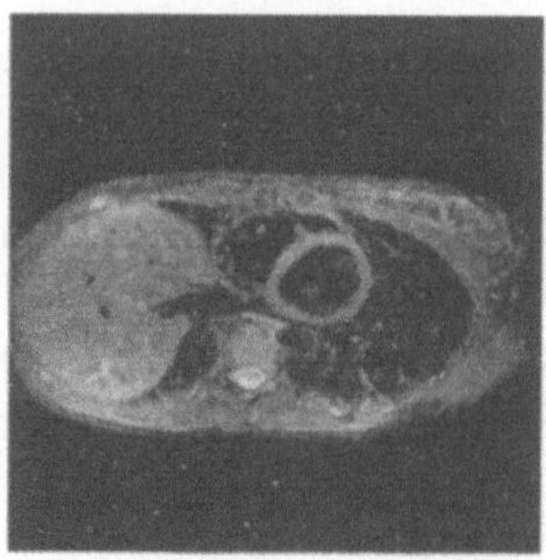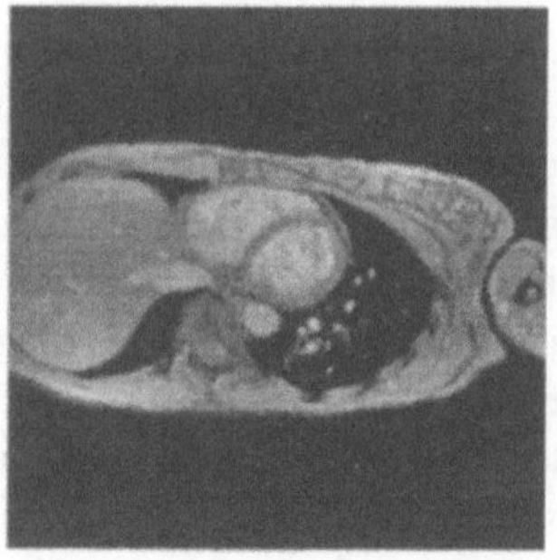

Abb. 2:   Kurzachsenschnitt einer T1- und einer T2-gewichteten Sequenz

Desweiteren ist eine Beurteilung dynamischer Vorgänge von großer Wichtigkeit.

Diese Forderungen führten zur Entwicklung des Konzepts der problemorientierten Segmentierung. Danach wird ausgehend von einer Verdachtsdiagnose eine dem Defekt angepaßte Bildakquisition durchgeführt. Anschließend soll eine Visualisierung des Defektes erstellt werden, die eine vorangehende Orientierung in dem Bildmaterial voraussetzt. Ein möglicher Ansatz beruht auf der Ermittlung der langen Herzachse [3]. Voraussetzung für diese Vorgehensweise ist allerdings, daß das gesamte Herz im Bildmaterial dargestellt ist, was in der Praxis allerdings selten realisiert ist. Aus diesem Grund wird ein Ansatz benötigt der eine Orientierung in beliebigen Ausschnitten des Herzens ermöglicht.

3 Merkmalsidentifikation

Um der in Abschnitt 1.1 beschriebenen Vielfalt möglicher Bilder gerecht zu werden, wurde ein mehrstufiges Konzept entwickelt. Danach werden zum einen im Bildmaterial vorhandene Informationen ausgewertet und zum anderen anatomische Merkmale identifiziert.

3.1 Auswertung des DICOM-Headers

Zunächst werden die Bilder in Abhängigkeit von Bildgebungsmodalität Kontrastverhalten und Schichtorientierung vorher definierten Klassen zugeordnet. Diese Zuordnung erfolgt anhand der Informationen aus dem DICOM-Header. So kann beispielsweise aus den DICOM-Feldern Scanning Sequence, Sequence Name, Contrast/Bolus Agent auf das Kontrastverhalten zurückgeschlossen werden. Um die Schichtorientierung zu ermitteln, müssen die Felder Patient Orientation und Image Orientation ausgewertet werden. Diese beinhalten zum einen die Lage des Patienten im Gerät (kopf-/fußwärts, Bauch-/Rücken-/Seitenlage) und zum anderen die Vektoren, die das Bild aufspannen.

3.2 Ableitung anatomischer Merkmale

Nach Auswertung der explizit vorhandenen Informationen werden anatomische Merkmale aus den Bildern abgeleitet. Entsprechend der Unterteilung der Bilder in verschiedene Klassen können auch die Merkmale unterschieden werden. So werden zunächst modalitätsunabhängige Merkmale identifiziert und anschließend auf eine Abhängigkeit von der Schichtrichtung untersucht und mögliche Ausprägungen ermittelt. Nach einer Identifikation modaltitätsunabhängiger Merkmale müssen Problemfälle, die durch dieses Vorgehen nicht abgedeckt werden, anhand modalitätsspezifischer Merkmale einbezogen werden.

Nach Identifikation der Merkmale müssen diese nun auf das Bildmaterial angewendet werden. Um zunächst einen Anhaltspunkt über die Lage und die Größe des Herzens zu erhalten, kann die Größe des Field of View betrachtet werden. Genauere Informationen erhält man, indem man für die jeweilige Schichtrichtung spezifische Merkmale anwendet. In Transversal- oder Kurzachsenschnitten einer EBT-Aufnahme kann auf die Lage des Herzens anhand einer Geraden durch Wirbelkörper und Brustbein rückgeschlossen werden. Die Größe des in Frage kommenden Suchraums läßt sich statistisch aus vorhandenem Bildmaterial ermitteln. Brustbein und Wirbelkörper können mit Grauwertprofilen im unteren und oberen Bildbereich identifiziert werden, da diese aufgrund ihrer hohen Dichtewerte sehr hell erscheinen. Neben der Lokalisation des Herzens innerhalb der Schicht ist auch die Lage der Schicht innerhalb des Herzens (basal, apical, ...) von Interesse. Hierzu kann das Verhältnis der rechten zur linken Lungenfläche herangezogen werden.

4 Ergebnisse und Diskussion

Der vorgestellte Ansatz ermöglicht unter Ausnutzung der Informationen über die Bildakquisition aus dem DICOM-Header und des explizit vorhandenen Wissens über die Anatomie des Herzens eine Orientierung in tomographischem Bildmaterial. Es können auf diese Art sowohl MR- als auch EBT-Aufnahmen verarbeitet werden. Es genügt auch, wenn lediglich Schichten aus dem interessierenden Bereich und nicht das gesamte Herz in den Aufnahmen dargestellt ist, da eine Lokalisation der Schichten innerhalb des Herzens durchgeführt wird. Da bei der Merkmalsidentifikation die unterschiedlichen Schichtorientierungen berücksichtigt worden sind, bestehen hinsichtlich des Bildmaterials keine Einschränkungen.

Nachteilig bei dieser Vorgehensweise ist, daß man auf die Informationen aus dem DICOM-Header angewiesen ist. Diese werden aber nicht immer vollständig ausgefüllt, bzw. einzelne Parameter werden in Abhängigkeit vom Gerät oder vom Personal in unterschiedlichen Feldern abgelegt. Außerdem ist dieser Ansatz recht aufwendig, da für alle unterschiedlichen Bildkategorien eine Vielzahl möglicher Merkmale und Ausprägungen identifiziert und angewendet werden müssen.

5 Ausblick

Das bisher beschriebene Vorgehen basiert auf einer rein statistischen Ermittelung der Merkmale. Es wurde vorhandenes Bildmaterial untersucht und die Signifikanz potentieller Merkmale überprüft. Damit wird aber anatomischen Abweichungen nicht ausreichend Rechnung getragen. Deshalb soll in einem weiteren Schritt eine Fuzzy-Komponente eingeführt werden, die aufgrund treffenderer heuristischer Regeln, die auftretenden Fehler gegenüber der Verwendung rein statistischer Merkmale minimiert.

6 Zusammenfassung

Es wurde ein Konzept zur automatischen Orientierung in tomographischen Aufnahmen des Herzens vorgestellt. Dieses beruht auf der Identifikation statistischer und bildinhärenter Merkmale in Abhängigkeit von Schichtorientierung und Kontrastverhalten. Dem Verfahren liegt ein mehrstufiges Konzept zugrunde, das sowohl die Informationen aus dem DICOM-Header ausnutzt als auch aus dem Bildmaterial abgeleitete anatomische Merkmale. Dadurch ist eine Orientierung in Bildmaterial beliebiger Schichtführung möglich, in dem zusätzlich nicht das gesamte Herz abgebildet sein muß, sondern nur die jeweils defekte Region.

Danksagung

Diese Arbeit wird von der Deutschen Forschungsgemeinschaft im Rahmen des SFB 414, Informationstechnik in der Medizin „Rechner- und Sensorgestützte Chirurgie " unterstützt.

Das verwendete Bildmaterial wurde im Institut für klinische Radiologie im Klinikum der Stadt Mannheim während der Kooperation im SFB 414 aufgenommen.

Literatur

1. Hagl S, Vahl C.: Intraoperative Diagnostik: Messung des Herz-Zeit-Volumens, Darstellung von Shunts. Z f Kardiologie 79: Suppl. 4, 1990, S. 107-111.
2. Vahl CF, Meinzer HP, Hagl S: Three-dimensional Presentation of Cardiac Morphology. Thorac Cardiovasc Surgeon 39 (Suppl), S. 198-204.
3. Schroeder A, Makabe MH, Glombitza G, Heiland M, Albers J, Vahl CF, Gaa J, Hagl S, Georgi M, Meinzer HP: Die automatische Orientierung in Bilddaten des Herzens - Voraussetzung für die problemorientierte Segmentierung in der computerunterstützten Planung cardiochirurgischer Eingriffe. In Arnolds B., Müller H., Saupe D., Tolxdorff T. (Eds): Tagungsband zum 5. Freiburger Workshop digitale Bildverarbeitung in der Medizin, März 1997, Freiburg: Technologie Transferstelle (1997), S. 202-207.

MeVisTo-Jaw
Ein Visualisierungstool für die kieferchirurgische OP-Planung

Patrick Neumann, Gabriele Faulkner, Klaus Haarbeck und Thomas Tolxdorff

Institut für Medizinische Statistik, Epidemiologie und Informatik
Universitätsklinikum Benjamin Franklin (UKBF)
Freie Universität Berlin, Hindenburgdamm 30, D-12200 Berlin
Email: neumann@medizin.fu-berlin.de

Zusammenfassung. Im folgenden soll ein, auf einer 3-D-Visualisierung basierendes, kieferchirurgisches Planungstool vorgestellt werden. Ausgehend von rekonstruierten Bildern aus CT-Volumendaten ist der Arzt in der Lage, eine computergestützte dreidimensionale Profilanalyse und Operationsplanung durchzuführen. Das von uns entwickelte Konzept für „Medical Visualization Tools" (MeVisTo) bietet hierfür die Voraussetzungen. Neben einer einfachen Benutzerschnittstelle wurde dabei im besonderen eine hohe Geschwindigkeit und Qualität des Volumenrenderings für die Visualisierung angestrebt. Mit dem „Virtual Sphere Rendering" (VSR) ist ein Verfahren integriert, das es durch Vorberechnung von Ansichten ermöglicht, eine Visualisierung der Daten in Echtzeit, also mit mehr als 25 Bildern pro Sekunden, zu erreichen.

Schlüsselwörter: Echtzeitvisualisierung, Volumenrendering, Operationsplanung, Client-Server System

1 Einleitung

Ziel unserer Forschung ist eine Unterstützung bei der Planung und Durchführung von kieferchirurgischen operativen Eingriffen. Derzeit werden für die Planung in diesem Bereich maßgeblich Gips- und Kunststoffmodelle eingesetzt, um ein Verständnis der räumlichen Anordnung von Knochen, Zähnen und Gelenken zu erhalten. Für die notwendige kephalometrische Analyse wird eine 2-D Planungssoftware eingesetzt.

Ein Projektziel ist die gewinnbringende Ergänzung der herkömmlichen Verfahren um eine schnelle und hochwertige 3-D Visualisierung [1] und Analyse.

2 Das MeVisTo-Konzept

Für die Visualisierung und Bearbeitung wird bei MeVisTo ein Client-Server-Ansatz verfolgt. Die mit hoher Rechenleistung und großem Hauptspeicher ausgestatteten Server übernehmen das Abarbeiten der Berechnungswünsche eines MeVisTo-Clients.

Mehrere Server sind in einem Cluster zusammengefaßt, wodurch eine hohe Gesamtrechenleistung zur Verfügung steht. Ein Dämon übernimmt die Verteilung der Bearbeitungswünsche im Cluster und sorgt für ein ausgewogenes Belastungsprofil.

Mit dem MeVisTo-Client erstellt und verändert der Benutzer die Bearbeitungsabläufe. Dem Client fällt zudem die Aufgabe zu, berechneten Ergebnisbilder vom Server anzuzeigen und Interaktionen des Benutzers zum Server weiterzuleiten.

Die Kommunikation zwischen Client, Dämon und Server erfolgt über TCP-IP. Nach dem Verbindungsaufbau von Client und Server (Abb. 1) werden die Daten in Skriptform ausgetauscht.

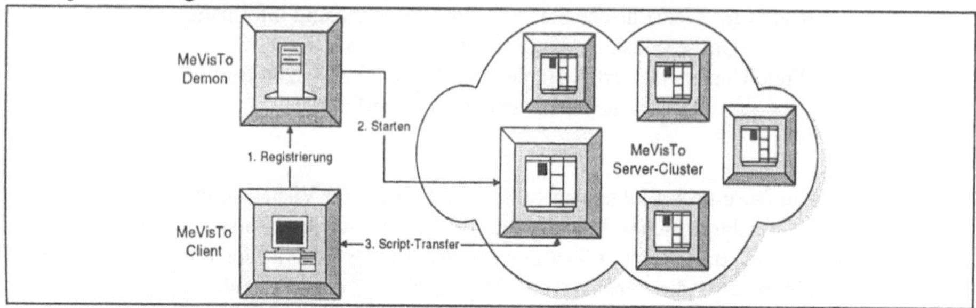

Abb. 1, Schritte für den Verbindungsaufbau zwischen MeVisTo-Client und - Server.

Neben immer zu verwendenden Grundfunktionalitäten bei der Bearbeitung gibt es für die verschiedenen denkbaren Einsatzgebiete von MeVisTo sehr spezielle Anforderungen. MeVisTo trägt dem durch sein offenes Konzept Rechnung, indem beliebige Bearbeitungsabfolgen in Skripten zusammengestellt und übertragen werden.

Ein Bearbeitungsskript besteht aus einem oder mehreren Bearbeitungsobjekten. Jedes dieser Objekte ist in einer Objekthierarchie eingebunden, aus der hervorgeht, von welchem anderen Ergebnis eines Bearbeitungsobjektes das Objekt abstammt beziehungsweise welche anderen Objekte fertig berechnet sein müssen, um mit der eigenen Berechnung beginnen zu können.

In jedem Objekt gibt es einen Bearbeitungsteil, der eine Aneinanderreihung von Funktionen enthält. Diese sind entsprechend einem Pipelinekonzept abzuarbeiten, was bedeutet, daß jeweils das Ergebnis einer Funktion die Eingabe für die nächste Funktion bildet. Die Funktionen werden in einem Funktionswörterbuch definiert, welches als Wörterbuchskript ebenfalls wieder zwischen Client und Server ausgetauscht wird. Funktionen können sich selbständig verteilen, indem sie entsprechende Skripte erzeugen und dem Dämon schicken.

Sowohl der Objektstatus als auch die Bearbeitungszustände der einzelnen Funktionen in der Pipeline werden bei jeder Veränderung dem Client gesandt, wodurch der Benutzer zu jedem Zeitpunkt über die Fortschritte bei der Bearbeitung des Skriptes informiert ist. Wird in der Pipeline vom Benutzer eine interaktive Eingabe erwartet, sei es numerisch oder über ein graphisches Eingabedevice im Bild, so stoppt die Abarbeitung des entsprechenden Objektes. Wenn möglich wird mit der Pipeline eines anderen Objektes im Skript fortgesetzt.

Nach dem Starten eines MeVisTo-Servers durch den Dämon beginnt die Bearbeitung des übermittelten Skriptes in zwei Schritten (Abb. 2). Die Bilddaten werden mittels DICOM von einem, im Haus entwickelten, DICOM-Server [2] zum MeVisTo-Server übermittelt. Im DICOM-Format werden anschließend auch wieder die Berechnungs- und Planungsergebnisse für eine spätere Verwendung abgelegt.

Abb. 2: Auswertung eines MeVisTo-Skripts durch den Server in zwei Schritten.

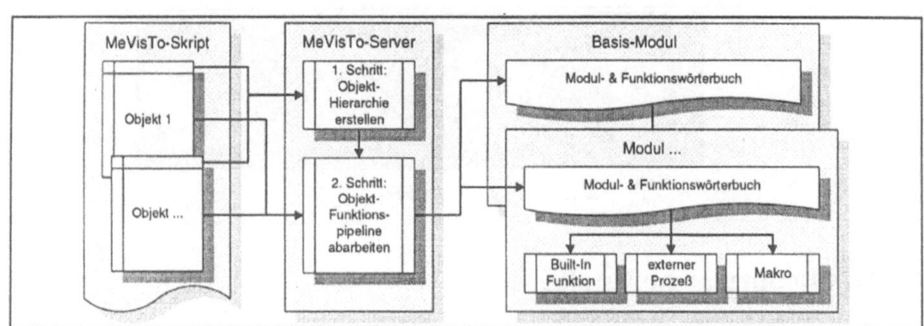

3 Die Visualisierung

Jedes Objekt in einem MeVisTo-Skript erzeugt bei seiner Bearbeitung durch den Server ein Ergebnisbild, das dem Client zum Darstellen zugesandt wird.

Der Kern für die Beschleunigung der 3-D-Visualisierung ist das „Virtual Sphere Rendering" (VSR) [3]. VSR visualisiert medizinische Volumendaten in Echtzeit durch Vorberechnung von Ansichten.

Auf einer imaginären Sichtkugel, die den Datenwürfel aus Volumendaten umschließt, werden 5000 Blickrichtungen auf das Objekt entlang der Längen- und Breitengrade ausgewählt (Abb. 3). Alle korrespondierenden Ansichten werden offline durch den Einsatz eines prinzipiell beliebigen Volumenrendering Verfahrens berechnet und zum Client übertragen. Die Reihenfolge, in der die Ansichten berechnet werden, ergibt sich nach einer Heuristik, die versucht das Benutzerverhalten abzubilden.

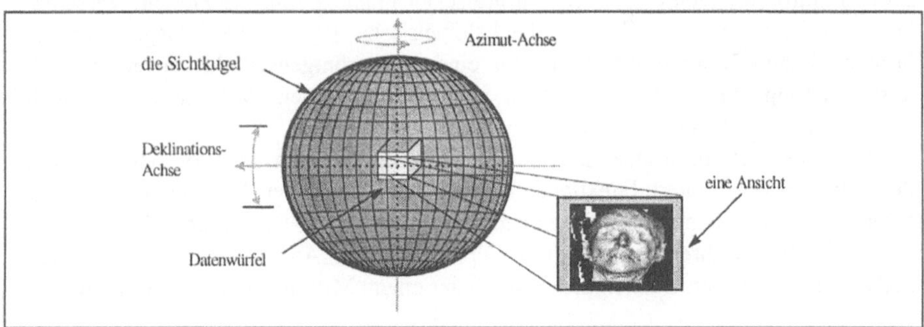

Abb. 3: Die virtuelle Sichtkugel mit den vorzuberechnenden Ansichten.

Je nach Objektgröße liegt das berechnete Datenvolumen dabei zwischen 20 und 400 Megabyte. Bei einer Berechnungszeit von einigen Sekunden für eine hochwertige Ansicht ergibt sich eine Gesamtzeit von mehreren Stunden für die Sichtkugel. Die Berechnung der Ansichten kann auf den Servern im Cluster verteilt werden.

Wünscht der Benutzer die Betrachtung einer noch nicht berechnete Ansicht, kann diese vom Server durch eine schrittweisen Verbesserung der Bildqualität sehr schnell in einer zunächst schlechten Qualität berechnet und übertragen werden (Abb. 4).

Abb. 4: Schnelle online Visualisierung durch schrittweise Verbesserung der Bildqualität.

Auflösung:	1/64	1/16	1/4	1
Berechnungszeit:	0.06s	0.20s	0.73s	6.63s

4 Das Benutzerschnittstelle

Voraussetzung für die Akzeptanz der Planungssoftware beim Arzt ist neben einer hohen Geschwindigkeit insbesondere eine einfache und intuitive Benutzerschnittstelle. Diese soll plattformunabhängig als Java-Client implementiert werden, um auch auf low-cost-Rechnern zur Verfügung zu stehen. Da die Ausführungsgeschwindigkeit von Java zur Zeit noch nicht ausreicht, um Bilder in Echtzeit auszugeben, erfolgt deren Ausgabe momentan in einem eigenen X-Windows-Fenster.

Java ist für die Darstellung und Manipulation der hierarchischen Baumstruktur mit den jeweils aktuellen Verarbeitungszuständen der Objekte verantwortlich. In ihr hat der Arzt die Möglichkeit Objekte zu erzeugen, anzuordnen und zu manipulieren.

Interaktionen des Benutzers in der Objektstruktur werden mit der Skriptsprache aufgezeichnet und sofort zum Berechnungskern von MeVisTo weitergereicht.

5 Das MeVisTo-Jaw Modul

Zu den Anforderungen einer kieferchirurgischen Planung zählt neben dem Verschieben von Knochensegmenten eine kephalometrische Profilanalyse. Gegenüber der herkömmlichen Analyse, basierend auf einem Fernröntgenseitbild, bietet die 3-D Visualisierung aus CT-Daten deutlich mehr Informationen. Mit ihr können auch Asymmetrien der beiden Gesichtshälften gut erfaßt werden.

Nach der Definition einer lateralen Bezugsebene werden die Profilpunkte durch den Benutzer positioniert. Funktionen für eine Auswertung der Winkel und Distanzen zwischen den Punkten bilden zusammen eine vollständige 3-D Profilanalyse.

Das VSR Verfahren wird für die kieferchirurgischen Anforderungen so angepaßt, daß die erforderlichen Genauigkeiten von unter einem Millimeter erreicht werden.

6 Ergebnisse und Ausblick

Neben der Realisierung des Client-Server Mechanismus mit Dämon, Kommunikation über TCP-IP und des Server-Clusters wurde die VSR-Visualisierung vollständig und der Skriptmechanismus in wesentlichen Teilen verwirklicht. Für die graphische Benutzerschnittstelle existiert ein Prototyp.

Es wurde ein einfaches, schwellwertbasiertes Verfahren für die Berechnung der Objektoberflächen implementiert (Abb. 5a). Das Verfahren ist geeignet um Knochen vollständig opaque darzustellen. Weiterhin wurde das Transparenzrendering nach Levoy implementiert [4]. Bei diesem Ansatz werden die Gewebegrenzschichten über den Gradienten ermittelt und Anhand einer am Grauwert orientierten Funktion gewichtet. Diese Verfahren ist sehr gut geeignet um sowohl Knochen, als auch Weichteilgewebe darzustellen (Abb. 5b). Zusätzlich wurden auch die Maximum- (Abb. 5c), die Summen- (Abb. 5d), und eine Art Textur-Projektion (Abb. 5e) implementiert und vom Arzt als gewinnbringend eingestuft. Bei der Textur-Projektion wird die Textur einer Objektoberfläche direkt ohne Beleuchtung dargestellt.

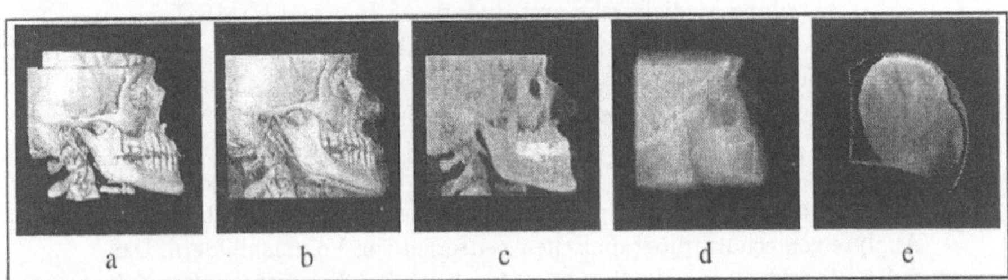

Abb. 5: (a) Schwellwertrendering, (b) Transparenzrendering, (c) Maximumprojektion, (d) Summenprojektion eines Kopfes, (e) Texturprojektion einer sphärischen Fundusaufnahme.

Zukünftig soll die Visualisierung von MeVisTo mit verschiedenen Eingabe- (3-D Trackingsystem) und Ausgabedevices („see through" Displays) gekoppelt werden.

Die Darstellung der Planung intraoperativ soll neben der Operationskontrolle auch zu Lehrzwecken eingesetzt werden. Durch die Benutzung eines 3-D-Ausgabegerätes soll es dem Studenten möglich sein, eine Darstellung von Planung und Operation nachvollziehen zu können, ohne dieser persönlich beiwohnen zu müssen.

7 Danksagung

Das Forschungsprojekt „Intraoperative Navigationsunterstützung" wird von der DFG und dem UKBF gefördert. Dank für die Unterstützung gilt auch der Klinik für Kieferchirurgie und Plastischen Gesichtschirurgie des UKBF.

8 Literatur

1. Faulkner G, Tolxdorff T: Einsatz von „Virtual Reality" Techniken in der Medizin. Arnolds B, Müller H, Saupe D, Tolxdorff T (Eds.): 5. Workshop Digitale Bildverarbeitung in der Medizin, 37-42, 1997.
2. Thiel A, Bernarding J, Hohmann J, Cosics D, Tolxdorff T: Security concepts in clinical applications using DICOM, SPIE's International Symposium Medical Imaging 1998, Vol. 3339, im Druck, 1998.
3. Neumann P: Interaktive dreidimensionale Visualisierung von medizinischen Volumendaten durch Vorberechnung von Ansichten. Diplomarbeit, Technische Universität Berlin, Fachgebiet Computer Graphics, 1996.
4. Levoy M: Display of Surfaces from Volume Data, IEEE Computer Graphics & Applications, Vol. 8, Nr. 3, 29-37, 1988.

Echokardiographische Flußberechnung durch Integration von Doppleraufnahmen und vierdimensionale Winkelkorrektur

M.Merdes[1], G.Glombitza[1], R.De Simone[2], H.P.Meinzer[1], C.F.Vahl[2], S.Hagl[2]

[1]Deutsches Krebsforschungszentrum
Abteilung Medizinische und Biologische Informatik (MBI)
INF 280, 69120 Heidelberg
[2]Chir. Universitätsklinik Heidelberg, Abteilung Herzchirurgie
Email: Matthias.Merdes@DKFZ-Heidelberg.de

Zusammenfassung. Wir präsentieren in diesem Artikel Methoden zur Analyse von echokardiographischen Zeitserien von Volumenbildern. Darauf basierend wurde ein System entwickelt, das die zeitliche Entwicklung intrakardialer Flüsse visualisiert und durchgesetzte Volumina berechnet. Wir beschreiben die Datenakquisition durch multiplane Transducer und die anschließende Extraktion der für die Flußmessung relevanten anatomischen Strukturen durch interaktive Segmentierung. Die fehlerhafte Abtastung der so erhaltenen Kurve wird korrigiert und eine Filterung im Fourierraum durchgeführt. Ein Modell für die notwendige Oberflächenintegration wird vorgestellt. Nach einer zeitabhängigen Winkelkorrektur führt die zeitliche Integration zum gesuchten Volumen.

Schlüsselwörter: Echokardiographie, Flußmessung, Doppler, Integration, Winkelkorrektur

1   Einleitung

1.1   Bedeutung intrakardialer Flüsse und Möglichkeiten ihrer Bestimmung

Die Bestimmung von Flüssen im Herzen ist aus mehreren Gründen wichtig. Kann man nämlich den Fluß durch ein Gefäß an einer Stelle des Herzens messen, so erhält man damit auch Aufschluß über das vom Herzen in einer gewissen Zeit durchgesetzte Volumen, das Herzzeitvolumen. Dies ermöglicht eine Beurteilung der (Pump-)Leistung des Herzens, die sowohl beim gesunden Menschen als auch im Zusammenhang mit Erkrankungen von größter Bedeutung ist.

Neben den hier diskutierten echokardiographischen Methoden können Flüsse durch Thermodilution, Anwendung des Fickschen Prinzips, elektromagnetische Flußmessung und Magnetresonanzflußkodierung gemessen werden, die aber teilweise ungenau, invasiv oder sehr aufwendig und teuer sind. Die Echokardiographie bietet daher eine kostengünstige und schonende Möglichkeit zur vierdimensionalen synchronen Akquisition von Gewebe- und Doppleraufnahmen.

1.2 Klinische Routineanwendung und andere Ansätze

Für die klinische Routine gibt es heute kommerzielle Geräte, mit deren Hilfe sich
zweidimensionale Standardmethoden anwenden lassen [1]. Man verwendet dabei
Gewebeaufnahmen für Längenmessungen und gepulste Doppleraufnahmen für
die Geschwindigkeitsmessungen. Die potentielle Ungenauigkeit dieser Messungen
liegt vor allem in zwei stark vereinfachenden Annahmen begründet. Um aus Ge-
schwindigkeitswerten das durch eine Oberfläche geflossene Volumen berechnen
zu können, müssen eine räumliche und eine zeitliche Integration durchgeführt
werden. Konventionell wird für das zeitliche Integral, "Velocity Time Integral"
(VTI) nur in einem begrenzten Gebiet ("Sampling Region") gemittelt und dann
zeitlich aufintegriert. Multiplikation mit einer als kreisförmig angenommenen,
zweidimensional bestimmten Fläche, führt zum gesuchten Volumen.

Jüngere Veröffentlichungen [2, 3] betonen vor allem die Form der Integrationsfläche. Verwendet man nämlich Kugelsegmente als Integrationsfläche, so kann
auf eine Winkelkorrektur verzichtet werden. Oft ist die verwendete Auflösung in
Rotationsrichtung aber so gering, daß man kaum von einem vierdimensionalen
Verfahren sprechen kann. Der Schwerpunkt dieser Arbeit liegt nun darauf, bei
hoher räumlicher Auflösung die Integrationsfläche für jeden Patienten individuell
aus der Analyse seiner anatomischen Gegebenheiten zu bestimmen. Da die vorgestellte Methode dazu plane Integratiosflächen benutzt, wurde außerdem eine
zeitabhängige Winkelkorrektur entwickelt.

2 Akquisition, Segmentierung und Filterung

Die von uns verwendeten vierdimensionalen Aufnahmen werden mit einem HP
Sonos 2500 und einer multiplanen TEE-Sonde mit Atem- und EKG-Triggerung
rotationsaquiriert. Dabei entstehen Aufnahmen von bis zu 90 Schichten in Rotationsrichtung. Eine derart hohe Auflösung von Zwei-Grad-Schritten geht jedoch
zu Lasten der zeitlichen Auflösung und ist in der Praxis meist ohnehin nicht notwendig. Die eigentlichen Doppleraufnahmen sind aus Gründen der Zeitersparnis
auf einen kleineren Sektor innerhalb der Gewebeaufnahme beschränkt.

2.1 Individuelle Anatomie und Interaktive Segmentierung

Da unser Ansatz von der individuellen Anatomie eines Patienten ausgeht, gilt
es nun, aus der so erhaltenen Folge von N zweidimensionalen Schichten die
relevante Information durch Segmentation des den Fluß umschließenden Herzklappenrings zu extrahieren. Neben der Erprobung vollautomatischer Verfahren findet zur Zeit eine interaktive Segmentierung Verwendung. Dazu klickt ein
erfahrener Herzchirurg in jeder der zu Verfügung stehenden Schichten die beiden Schnittpunkte der Bildebene mit dem Herzklappenring an, wobei Schichten
schlechter Qualität ausgelassen werden können.

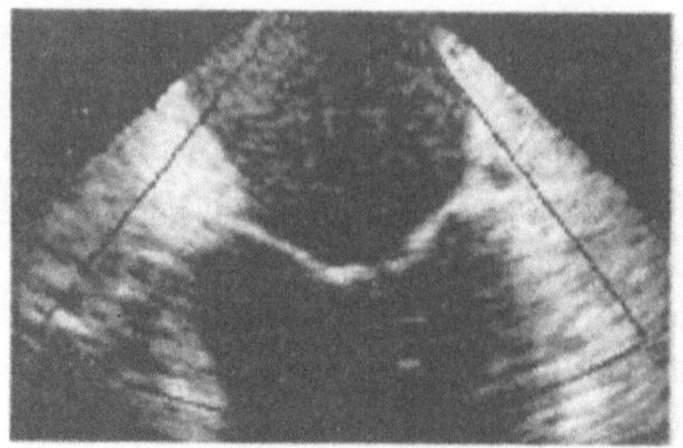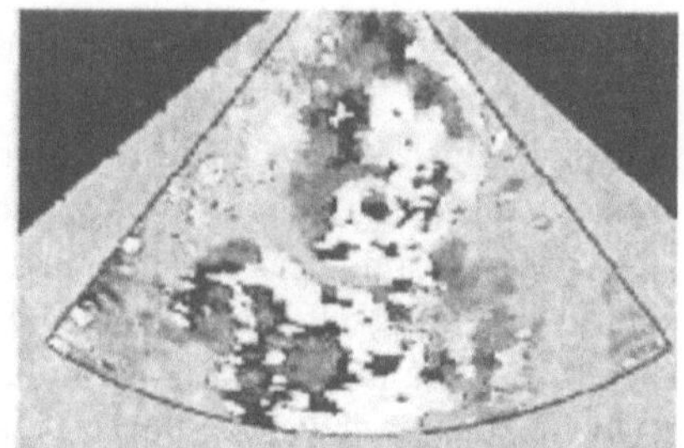

Abb. 1. Originalschichtbilder von Gewebe- und Doppleraufnahmen

2.2 Filterung

Die so erhaltene Liste von maximal $2N$ Punkten im Raum muß nun sortiert und weiterverarbeitet werden. Da die Genauigkeit des Triggermechanismus begrenzt ist, kommt es zu Artefakten im Bild. Durch Segmentierungsfehler und Rauschen entstehen zusätzliche Fehler.

Zur Korrektur dieser fehlerbehafteten Punktliste erschien eine direkte Filterung im Fourierraum besonders geeignet, d. h. Fouriertransformation, idealer Tiefpaß und Rücktransformation. Dazu ist es notwendig, daß die vorliegenden Daten Werte einer (hier unbekannten) auf einem äquidistanten Gitter abgetasteten Funktion sind. Dies ist aber durch die beschriebenen Einflüsse und zusätzlich durch schlechte Zentrierung der Rotationsachse bei der Aufnahme i. A. nicht der Fall. Eine direkte Filterung führt also zu Verzerrungen der gesuchten Struktur. Zur Lösung dieses Problems wurde ein Algorithmus entwickelt, der längs der Kurve im Raum neue Abtastpunkte so verteilt, daß sie kartesisch äquidistant sind. Dies entspricht zwar nicht der eigentlich geforderten Abtastung im Raum des Parameters, der die Kurve beschreibt, stellt für hinreichend glatte Kurven jedoch eine akzeptable Näherung dar. Dieser Algorithmus hat auch gewisse ungewollte Glättungseigenschaften; jedoch nur auf Skalen kleiner als realistische anatomische Details.

Danach kann die erwähnte Filterung im Fourierraum stattfinden, wobei so stark geglättet wird, daß Strukturen anatomisch sinnvoller Größe gerade noch dargestellt werden können. Dies entspricht gleichzeitig einem optimalen Fit an eine trigonometrische Entwicklung beliebigen Grades, da die verwendeten Basisfunktionen ein orthogonales Funktionensystem darstellen. Die nach der Filterung erhaltene geschlossene Raumkurve hat eigenständige anatomische Bedeutung und ist auch für andere echokardiographische Verfahren relevant. Ein Teil dieser Ergebnisse ist in [4] beschrieben.

3 Oberflächenintegration und Flußmessung

3.1 Diskretisierung der Oberflächenintegration

Für eine Oberflächenintegration benötigt man eine beliebige einfach zusammenhängende Fläche und eine sie begrenzende Randkurve. Wenn man die im

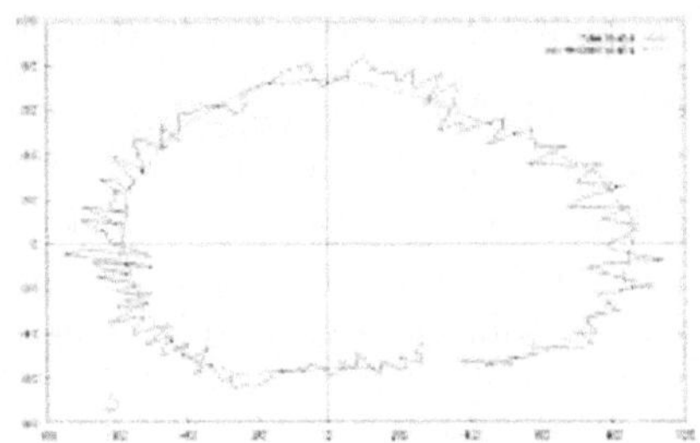

Abb. 2. Winkelkorrektur (links) und Filterung des Herzklappenrings (rechts)

nächsten Abschnitt beschriebene Winkelkorrektur verwendet, kann man für nur mäßig gekrümmte Randkurven eine plane, aus dem Berandungspolynom konstruierte Fläche verwenden. Nach Triangulierung der eingeschlossenen Oberfläche definiert die Mittelung der N Teilflächenvektoren einen neuen Flächenvektor und damit eine Schar von Ebenen. Seien also $\mathbf{x}_i, i = 1, \ldots, 2N$ die Stützvektoren entlang der Randkurve, und $\mathbf{s} = \frac{1}{2N} \sum_{i=1}^{2N} \mathbf{x}_i$ ihr Schwerpunkt. Für den globalen Flächenvektor $\mathbf{F}$ kann man dann schreiben:

$$\mathbf{F} = \frac{1}{2} \left\{ \sum_{i=1}^{2N-1} (\mathbf{x}_i - \mathbf{s}) \times (\mathbf{x}_{i+1} - \mathbf{s}) + (\mathbf{x}_{2N} - \mathbf{s}) \times (\mathbf{x}_1 - \mathbf{s}) \right\} \tag{1}$$

Fordert man noch, daß der Schwerpunkt $\mathbf{s}$ in der gesuchten Ebene enthalten sein soll, so ist diese eindeutig definert. Durch Projektion der Berandungskurve auf diese Ebene erhält man eine plane Fläche, deren Orientierung durch $\mathbf{F}$ bestimmt ist. Für ein Verfahren erster Ordnung ist die räumliche Integration damit auf die Summation aller in dieser Fläche enthaltenen Voxel reduziert.

3.2 Winkelkorrektur

Da die Dopplermessung nur die Projektion des Geschwindigkeitsvektors auf die Schallrichtung enthält, ist bei ebenen Integrationsfläche folgende zusätzliche Korrektur nötig: Unter der Annahme, daß die Hauptrichtung des Flusses in guter Näherung senkrecht auf der Klappenebene steht, kann der Kosinus des Winkels zwischen der Flächennormalen und der Richtung des Ultraschallstrahls zur Korrektur der Momentanflüsse Φ_t verwendet werden:

$$\Phi_{korrigiert} = \frac{\Phi_{gemessen}}{|\cos(\alpha_{korr})|} \quad \text{mit} \quad \cos(\alpha_{korr}) = \frac{\mathbf{sF}}{|\mathbf{s}||\mathbf{F}|} \tag{2}$$

Der Vorteil gegenüber der zweidimensionalen Methode besteht nun darin, daß zur Berechnung der Flächennormalen die Kenntnis der gesamten räumlichen Struktur des Herzklappenrings ausgenutzt wird und nicht nur ein willkürlich gewählter zweidimensionaler Schnitt. Hinzu kommt, daß sich diese Korrektur in jedem Zeitschritt seperat anwenden läßt, womit der räumlichen Bewegung des Herzklappenrings während des Herzzyklus Rechnung getragen wird.

3.3 Zeitliche Integration und durchgesetzte Volumina

Um die für den Arzt interessanten durchgesetzten Volumina durch eine zeitliche Integration zu gewinnen, muß das beschriebene Verfahren zuerst auf jeden Zeitpunkt angewandt werden. Interpolation dieser diskreten Momentanflüsse Φ_t liefert die zeitliche Entwicklung des Flusses, die zwischen interaktiv wählbaren Grenzen, z.B. während der Systole, integrierbar ist.

4 Zusammenfassung und Ausblick

Entwurf und Implementierung dieser neuen Methode stellen ein leistungsfähiges Tool zur Analyse der Dynamik des fließenden Bluts durch Herzklappen basierend auf Routineaufnahmen bereit. Die Zuverlässigkeit von Flußmessungen im Herzen wird durch Verzicht auf i.A. falsche Annahmen konventioneller Methoden gesteigert. Unser Ansatz betont die individuelle Anatomie eines Patienten und trägt ihrer zeitlichen Veränderung Rechnung.

Prinzipiell scheint eine Weiterentwicklung für die Quantifizierung von Herzklappeninsuffizienzen möglich, wobei ein Verfahren zur Aliasing-Korrektur zu hoher Geschwindigkeiten verwendet werden müßte. Neben der Entwicklung der automatischen Segmentierung würde ein Test anderer Integrationsflächengeometrien sinnvoll erscheinen. Für den Routineeinsatz könnte die automatische Berechnung von zeitlichen Integrationsgrenzen aus dem EKG oder aus einer Bewegungsanalyse des Herzklappenrings von Bedeutung sein. Vor einem möglichen klinischen Einsatz wird eine klinische Studie zur Validierung der Methode durchgeführt werden.

Danksagung

Diese Arbeit wurde von der Deutschen Forschungsgemeinschaft im Rahmen des SFB 414, "Informationstechnik in der Medizin: Rechner- und Sensorgestützte Chirurgie" unterstützt.

Literatur

1. Feigenbaum H: Echocardiography. Lea & Febiger, Philadelphia, 181 ff. 5. Auflage 1993
2. Sun Y, Ask P, Janerot-Sjöberg B, Eidenvall L, Loyd D, Wranne B: Estimation of volume flow rate by surface integration of velocity vectors from color doppler images. Journal of the American Society of Echocardiography, 8:904–914, 1995
3. Kim WY, Poulsen JK, Terp K, Staalsen N: A new doppler method for quantification of volumetric flow: In vivo validation using color Doppler. Journal of the American College of Cardiology, 27: 182–192, 1996
4. De Simone R, Glombitza G, Albers J, Nakamura G, Merdes M, Meinzer HP, Vahl CF, Hagl S: Three-dimensional analysis of mitral and tricuspid annuli for improving Doppler assessment of cardiac output. Echocardiography 14(6), Part 2, Nov 1997 Abstracts of the First Annual and Plenary Meeting of the Working Group on Echocardiography of the ESC, Prague 1997

Multimodale Bildauswertung zur rechnergestützten Bestrahlungsplanung von Augentumoren

Sebastian Nöh[1], Klaus Haarbeck[1], Norbert Bornfeld[2] und Thomas Tolxdorff [1]

[1] Institut für Medizinische Statistik, Epidemiologie und Informatik
[2] Augenklinik und Poliklinik
Universitätsklinikum Benjamin Franklin (UKBF)
Freie Universität Berlin, Hindenburgdamm 30, D-12200 Berlin
Email: noeh@medizin.fu-berlin.de

Zusammenfassung. Bei dem zugrundeliegenden Projekt wird eine Verbesserung der aktuellen Bestrahlungstherapie von intraokularen Tumoren durch den Einsatz von Protonenstrahlen angestrebt. Ausgehend von CT-Schnittbildern, MRT-Schnittbildern, Fundusphotographien und Ultraschallaufnahmen wird ein Bestrahlungmodell für die Durchführung der Bestrahlungstherapie ermittelt. Durch wissensbasierte Bildauswertung und Kombination aller zur Verfügung stehenden Informationen erreicht dieses Modell eine Präzision, die eine Ausnutzung der Dosierungsgenauigkeit von Protonenstrahlen erst möglich macht.

Schlüsselwörter: Segmentierung, Registrierung, Bestrahlungsplanung

1 Einleitung

Aktuelle Verfahren der Strahlentherapie, die vorwiegend auf Röntgenstrahlen oder radioaktiven Elementen basieren, können durch die Anwendung von Protonenstrahlen deutlich verbessert werden. Die Absorptionseigenschaften der Protonenstrahlen ermöglichen Dosierungsgenauigkeiten von deutlich unter einem Millimeter sowohl in axialer als auch in lateraler Ausbreitungsrichtung [1,2]. Dadurch können Dosisverteilungen im Zielvolumen maximiert und Schädigungen von umgebendem physiologischem Gewebe effektiv vermieden werden [3]. Grundlage für eine solche Verbesserung der Bestrahlungstherapie ist ein präzises Bestrahlungsmodell, das die physiologischen und pathologischen Strukturen im Bereich der Orbita des Patienten präzise nachbildet. Aktuelle Ansätze zur Bestrahlungsplanung basieren in ihrer Bestrahlungssimulation auf schematischen Augenmodellen, wie dem Gullstrandschen Normalauge [4,5]. Das Modell wird dabei zur Anpassung an das Auge des Patienten anhand des Bulbusdurchmessers aus CT-, Ultraschall- oder anderen Bilddaten in den drei Raumachsen verzerrt. Bei diesen Ansätzen kommt es zu grundlegenden Fehlern bei der Bestimmung der Bestrahlungsparameter, da sich in den meisten Fällen die Form des menschlichen Auges deutlich von den schematischen Modellen unterscheidet. Bereits Abweichungen von wenigen Millimetern können den Verlust des Augenlichts oder das unvollständige Abtöten des Tumors bedeuten, da die zu bestrahlenden Tumoren und essentiellen Strukturen wie Makula und Papille eng beieinander liegen. In dem hier beschriebenen Projekt wird eine Verbesserung der Bestrahlungstherapie von intraoku-

Abbildung 1: Bildverarbeitungspipeline zur Bestimmung des Bestrahlungsmodells

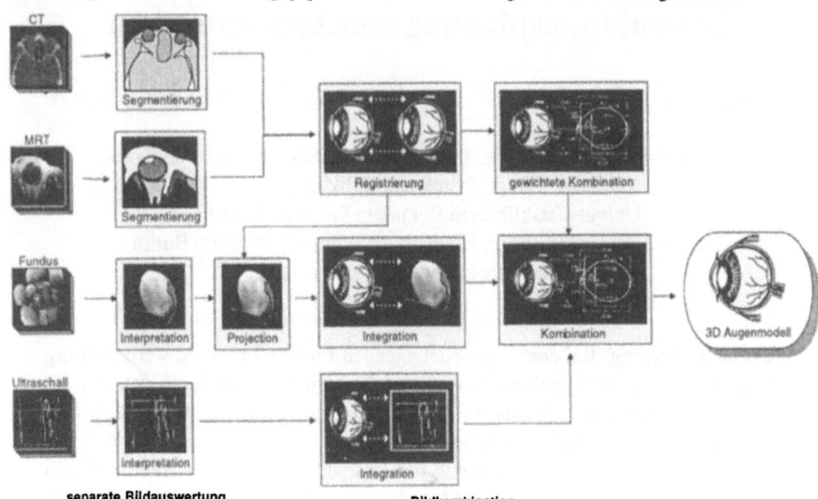

laren Tumoren mittels Protonenstrahlen angestrebt. Ausgehend von CT-Schnittbildern, MRT-Schnittbildern, Fundusphotographien und Ultraschallaufnahmen wird ein Bestrahlungsmodell ermittelt, das durch die angepaßte Kombination aller zur Verfügung stehenden Informationen die Präzisionsanforderungen erfüllt. Die CT-Daten dienen wegen der großen Darstellungskorrektheit und der Abbildung der Absorptionskoeffizienten der einzelnen anatomischen Strukturen als Grundlage für die Bestrahlungssimulation. Die schlechte Grauwertauflösung im Bereich der Weichgewebsstrukturen erfordert zusätzlich die Verwendung von hochauflösenden MRT-Daten, die eine zuverlässige Segmentierung der einzelnen Strukturen, wie Bulbus, Linse, Papilla und Tumor ermöglichen. Fundusphotographien erweisen sich bei der Bestimmung der Abstände zwischen Papilla, Makula und Tumor als besonders wertvoll, da ihre Darstellungskorrektheit im lateralen Bereich des Auges außerordentlich groß ist. Die Kenntnis dieser Abstände spielt eine besondere Bedeutung für die Bestrahlungplanung, wenn Tumor und essentielle Strukturen sehr eng beieinander liegen und somit die Präzision des Modells über Erfolg und Nebeneffekte der Therapie entscheidet. Die Ultraschalltiefenmessung erlaubt eine präzise Rekonstruktion der Distanzen zwischen den einzelnen anatomischen Strukturen entlang der Transducer-Achse. Sie kann für eine zuverlässige Verifikation des zuvor bestimmten Augenmodells herangezogen werden.

2 Bildverarbeitungskonzept

Die Bildverarbeitung ist in zwei Verarbeitungseinheiten untergliedert. In der ersten wird durch Segmentierung eine inhaltliche Interpretation der unterschiedlichen Bilddaten gewonnen. In der zweiten werden die Ergebnisse durch eine angepaßte Registrierung oder Integration in einem Augenmodell vereint. Ein wissensbasierter Ansatz zur semiautomatischen Bildauswertung reduziert den Arbeitsaufwand für den Benutzer, um die Kosten für die Bestrahlungsplanung trotz des großen Datenvolumens in einem für die klinische Praxis akzeptablen Rahmen zu halten.

Die semiautomatische Bildauswertung orientiert sich in ihrer Konzeption an der Wahrnehmung von visuellen Informationen durch den Menschen. Bildmaterial wird in Form von Hypothese-Verifikation Ansätzen auf unterschiedlichen Komplexitäts- und Abstraktionsebenen analysiert. Die Interpretationsschritte sind in die Einheiten „preattentive stage", „preattentive analysis", „attentive analysis" und „overall interpretation" untergliedert. Die einzelnen Bearbeitungsmodule werden mittels Skripten, Statistiken, Heuristiken und objektspezifischen Beschreibungen realisiert. Auswahl und Parametrisierung der angewandten Bildverarbeitungsalgorithmen werden auf der Basis von bereits bearbeiteten und in einer Falldatenbank abgelegten Fällen abgeleitet. Um Bildverarbeitungsergebnisse und die Fälle in der Datenbank miteinander zu korrelieren, werden Ähnlichkeiten mittels direkter Bildvergleiche oder Klassifikation von Parametern durchgeführt. Direkte Bildvergleiche werden mittels cepstraler Analysen realisiert. Analyseparameter werden mittels des Bayes-Klassifikators mit den Werten der Datenbank verglichen. Eine Beschreibung dieses Ansatzes zur wissensbasierten Bildverarbeitung findet sich in [6].

2.1 Segmentierung und Interpretation

CT- und MRT-Daten werden mit verschiedenen Segmentierungsverfahren bearbeitet, die in der gängigen Literatur beschrieben wurden. Verfahren wie Snakes, Region-Growing oder Thresholding werden an das zu segmentierende Objekt angepaßt und auf das Bildmaterial angewandt. Auswahl und Parametrisierung der Verfahren stützt sich auf dem Wissen der zuvor behandelten Fälle und dem abgeleiteten Wissen über das aktuell bearbeitete Bildmaterial. Anschließend werden die Ergebnisse aus den einzelnen Schichten zu dreidimensionalen Objektmodellen zusammengesetzt. In den Fundusphotographien werden Farbwert-basierte Region-Growing-Verfahren angewandt, um Papilla und Makula automatisch zu segmentieren. Liegen keine Anomalien wie Netzhautablösungen vor, lassen sich beide Objekte leicht durch ihre jeweils gelbe und dunkle Einfärbungen ermitteln. Tumoren sind aufgrund ihrer komplexen und lokal schwach ausgeprägten Texturierung nur sehr schwer zu bestimmen. Daher wird in diesem Fall auf eine manuelle Segmentierung zurückgegriffen. Bei den Ultraschallaufnahmen markiert der behandelnde Arzt schon während der Untersuchung die Positionen von Tumor und Sklera. Die Interpretation des Bildmaterials liegt in dem manuellen Markieren dieser Punkte und dem Hinzufügen des Eintrittspunktes an der Kornea.

2.2 Registrierung und Kombination

Aufgrund der stark variierenden Bildeigenschaften müssen unterschiedliche Strategien zur Kombination der Interpretationsergebnisse angewandt werden. CT- und MRT-Daten werden in zwei Schritten miteinander korreliert. Im ersten werden beide Datensätze auf der Basis der ermittelten Augenmodelle grob aneinander ausgerichtet. Dabei wird zunächst der translatorische Unterschied durch das Zusammenfassen der Massenzentren der beiden Bulbi eliminiert. Anschließend werden die Vektoren zur Linse, den Markern und der Papille benutzt, um den Rotationsunterschied festzustellen. Auf der Basis des mittleren Bulbusdurchmessers wird eine Skalierung der beiden Datensätze durchgeführt. Im zweiten Schritt werden beide Datensätze durch die gewichtete Kombination von oberflächenbasierter und landmarkenbasierter Registrierung miteinander korreliert. Hierzu sind zunächst beide, durch Partialvolumeneffekte zum Teil unvollständigen Datensätze sinnvoll zu interpolieren. Die Interpolation wird durch einen modifizierten Ansatz der Surface-based-deformation-Methode (Warping) erreicht. Die Unterschiede unseres Ansatzes zu gängigen Warping-Verfahren [10,11] bestehen vor allem in dem automatischen Finden der Korrespondenzvektoren und der Interpolation der Deformationen mittels eines Catmull-Rom-Splines. Die oberflächenbasierte Registrierung wird durch die Erweiterung des Warping-Ansatzes auf die dritte Dimension erreicht [6]. Die landmarkenbasierte Registrierung wird auf die Marker und die Papille angewandt. Korrespondierende Landmarken werden mittels dreidimensionaler Visualisierung [7] interaktiv eingegeben. Anschließend werden die Korrespondenzvektoren mittels Radial-Basis-Funktionen interpoliert [8] und lokal gewichtet mit den Korrespondenzvektoren der oberflächenbasierten Registrierung kombiniert. Wichtungskriterium bei der Kombination ist der Abstand der betrachteten Korrespondenzvektoren zu ihren jeweiligen Registrierungsreferenzen.

Die Korrelation der Fundusaufnahmen mit dem Augenmodell aus CT- und MRT-Daten wird durch die folgenden Schritte ermöglicht: Auf der Basis des Augenmodells werden die Voxel der Bulbusoberfläche aus CT- und MRT-Daten auf eine Ebene projiziert [9]. Ein gleichzeitig projizierter Kreis mit zwei Millimeter Durchmesser kann mit der Papille, die einen nahezu konstanten Durchmesser von 1,2 Millimetern aufweist, zur Skalierungsanpassung angewandt werden. Die Papillen der Fundusaufnahme und des projizierten Bildes werden zentriert und anschließend der Rotationsunterschied anhand der Marker eliminiert. Im letzten Schritt werden die Fundusaufnahmen mit den gleichen Parametern wie im ersten Schritt zurück projiziert, um die Fundusaufnahmen mit den drei dimensionalen CT- und MRT-Daten zu korrelieren.

Um die Ultraschalltiefenmessung auf das Augenmodell anzuwenden, sind zunächst Position und Einfallswinkel des Transducers während der Aufnahme zu rekonstruieren. Derzeit werden die Ärzte angehalten den Transducerkopf im Zentrum der Pupille möglichst senkrecht zu halten. Anschließend können die Distanzen mit jenen des Augenmodells verglichen werden. Kommt es zu deutlichen Abweichungen, sind die Bildverarbeitungsschritte zu revidieren, um mögliche Fehlerquellen zu eliminieren.

3 Ergebnisse und Diskussion

Die wissensbasierte Bildverarbeitung zeigte gute Segmentierungsergebnisse für Objekte wie Hintergrund, Bulbus, und Linse (Abb. 2a). Da jedoch Objektkanten durch Partialvolumeneffekte oft unregelmäßig wurden, werden im weiteren Verlauf des Projektes bei Objekten mit spezifischen Oberflächeneigenschaften die Segmentierungsergebnisse verbessert, indem Umrißlinien kontextabhängig modifiziert werden. Die Anpassung der regionenbasierten Segmentierungsverfahren konnten einfach und stabil realisiert werden. Das Snakes-Verfahren endet hingegen oft in lokalen Minima, da interne und externe Energiefunktion global und mit eingeschränkten Anpassungsmöglichkeiten definiert sind. Daher wird die Energiefunktion zukunftig modellbasiert mit lokal begrenzbaren Grauwert- und Kontureigenschaften konstituiert.

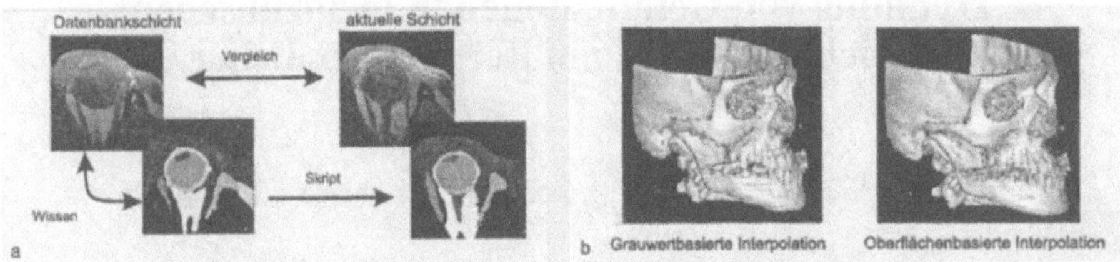

Abbildung 2: Ergebnisse der wissensbasierten Segmentierung und der Interpolation

Die oberflächenbasierte Interpolation produzierte gute Ergebnisse mit weichen Objektoberflächen (Abb. 2b). Unser Algorithmus für die automatische Bestimmung der Korrespondenzvektoren für die oberflächenbasierte Interpolation und Registrierung arbeitet stabil und stimmt mit den von einer Versuchsperson intuitiv eingegebenen weitgehend überein. Durch die immer besser werdenden Auflösungen von CT- und MRT-Daten wird die Interpolation von Datensätzen jedoch an Bedeutung verlieren. Notwendig sind statt dessen Objektparametrisierungen, die Fehler oder Löcher in den Modellen detektieren und durch angepaßte Interpolation kompensieren.

Wir bedanken uns bei der Deutschen Forschungsgemeinschaft für die Förderung dieses Projektes unter der Fördernummer (To 108/7-1).

4 Literatur

1. U Linz: Tumortherapie mit Ionenstrahlen. Spektrum der Wissenschaft 6/1996, 70-79, 1996.

2. W Schlegel. Impact of 3D Treatment Planning on Treatment Techniques. In Pierre Minet, editor, Three-Dimensional Treatment Planning, pages 131-142. Service d'oncologie radiothèrapie, Lieége, Belgique, 1993.

3. A Höss, J Debus, R Bendl, R Engenhart-Cabillic, und W Schlegel: Computerverfahren in der dreidimensionalen Strahlentherapieplanung. Radiologe 35, 583-586, 1995.

4. DD Michaels. Visual Optics and Refraction: A Clinical Approach. The CV Mosby Company, St. Louis, Missouri, USA, 1985.

5. M Goitein and T Miller: Planing proton therapy of the eye. Med Phys 10, 275-283, 1983.

6. S Nöh, K Haarbeck, N Bornfeld, and T Tolxdorff. Knowledge-based Image Processing for Proton Therapy Planning of Ocular Tumors. In Kenneth M Hanson, editor, SPIE-Mathematical Methods in Medical Imaging, volume 25, San Diego, USA, 1998.

7. P Neumann, G Faulkner, M Krauss, T Tolxdorff und B Hoffmeister: 3-D-Visualisierung in Echtzeit zur intraoperativen Navigationsunterstützung. 42. Jahrestagung der GMDS, Ulm, 15-18. September 1997.

8. D Ruprecht, R Nagel, and H Mueller. Spatial Free Form Deformation with Scattered Data Interpolation Methods. Computer and Graphics, 19:63-72, 1995.

9. MDC Evans, MA Astrahan, and R Bate: Tumor Localization Using Fundus View Photography for Episcleral Plaque Therapy. Med Phys 20, 769-775, 1993.

10. D Ruprecht and H Mueller. Deformed Cross-Dissolves for Image Interpolation in Scientific Visulization. In Workshop Freiburg, volume 1, pages 1-15, Freiburg, 1994.

11. S Sandor and R Leahy. Surface-Based Labeling of Cortical Anatomy Using a Deformable Atlas. IEEE Trans. On Medical Imaging, 16:41-53, 1997.

Trennung von Gefäßbäumen in medizinischen Schichtbildserien am Beispiel der Leber

M.R. Göpfert[a], G. Glombitza[a], A.M. Demiris[a], W. Lamadé[b], H.-P. Meinzer[a]

[a] Deutsches Krebsforschungszentrum, Abt. Medizinische und Biologische Informatik,
Im Neuenheimer Feld 280, 69120 Heidelberg
[b] Chirurgische Klinik der Universität Heidelberg, Abt. Allgemeine Chirurgie,
Im Neuenheimer Feld 110, 69120 Heidelberg
e-Mail: M.Goepfert@DKFZ-Heidelberg.de

Zusammenfassung: Für eine präoperative Bestimmung der individuellen Leberanatomie ist eine sichere Segmentierung und Rekonstruktion der Pfortader sowie ihrer intrahepatischen Verästelungen notwendig. In kontrastmittelverstärkten CT-Aufnahmen ist dies nicht immer eindeutig möglich, da das venöse Gefäßsystem der Leber ebenfalls kontrastiert ist. Dadurch kommt es zu Pseudoverbindungen zwischen den beiden Gefäßbäumen, die mit Hilfe eines hier vorgestellten Verfahrens getrennt werden. Dabei werden in der symbolischen Beschreibung der Gefäßbäume, in der die Verzweigungs- und Endpunkte als Knoten repräsentiert sind, alle falschen Verbindungen lokalisiert und nacheinander eliminiert.
Schlüsselwörter: Blutgefäße, Leberanatomie, Operationsplanung, Graph.

1 Einleitung und Motivation

In der Medizin ist die Kenntnis des individuellen anatomischen Aufbaus eines zu operierenden Organs von zentraler Bedeutung. Im Falle der Leber stehen dem Chirurgen zur Beurteilung der Operabilität eines Patienten kontrastmittelverstärkte CT- bzw. MR-Aufnahmen zur Verfügung, die es ihm erlauben beispielsweise die Lage und Ausmaße eines eventuell in ihr befindlichen Tumors grob zu lokalisieren. Für eine genaue und anatomisch korrekte Einteilung der Leber in ihre acht Funktionseinheiten (Lebersegmente) ist eine sichere Segmentierung und Rekonstruktion der Pfortader sowie ihrer intrahepatischen Verästelungen notwendig, da ein Lebersegment als Versorgungsgebiet eines bestimmten Pfortaderteilbaumes definiert ist [1].

Diese Verästelungen gehen über das Kapillarsystem der Leber in die Lebervenen über, so daß sich das Kontrastmittel bei der Datenaufnahme in den meisten Fällen nicht nur im Portalbaum befindet, sondern bereits in das venöse Gefäßsystem geflossen ist. Die anschließende Segmentierung dieser Daten liefert zwei Gefäßbäume, deren Äste an mehreren Stellen eng benachbart verlaufen. Einige dieser Blutgefäße liegen so nah beieinander, daß die Computertomographie diese miteinander verbunden darstellt; d.h. die Bildpunkte des einen Gefäßes gehen fließend in die des anderen über, ohne daß ein die beiden trennendes Voxel dazwischen liegt (s. Abb. 3a).

Ein zur Analyse von Gefäßbäumen entwickelter Algorithmus kann daher nicht feststellen, welche Äste dem venösen und welche dem portalvenösen Gefäßsystem der Leber zuzuordnen sind. Dadurch ergeben sich Probleme bei der Ermittlung der Verzweigungsstruktur der Pfortader und einer darauf basierenden Segmenteinteilung der Leber. Deshalb wurde von uns im Rahmen eines Operationsplanungssystems für die onkologische Leberchirurgie [2] ein Verfahren entwickelt, mit dem eine automatische Trennung fälschlicherweise verbundener Gefäßbäume möglich ist.

2 Vorverarbeitung

Die *Segmentierung* der Blutgefäße kann wegen des Kontrastmittels mit einem einfachen Schwellwert-Verfahren, das nur innerhalb der Leber angewendet wird, automatisch erfolgen. Ein solches Verfahren liefert in der Regel mehrere mögliche Schwellwerte, die mehr oder weniger Voxel segmentieren. Zur Identifizierung des optimalen Schwellwertes wird ein wissensbasierter Algorithmus eingesetzt, der speziell für diese Fragestellung.

Für die Analyse von Blutgefäßen in medizinischen Schichtbildern ist es wichtig, diese als möglichst homogene, zusammenhängende Bereiche aus dem umliegenden Lebergewebe herauszulösen. Deshalb werden die Bilddaten vorher mit einem dreidimensionalen Tiefpaßfilter geglättet. Die besten Ergebnisse haben wir mit einem Median-Filter (3×3×3-Maske) und einer adaptiven Filterung (Tiefpaß nach lokalem Region-Growing) erzielt, da beide konturerhaltend vorgehen.

3 Gefäßbaumtrennung

Der eigentliche Trennalgorithmus basiert nun nicht auf den segmentierten, voxelbasierten Gefäßbäumen, sondern auf ihrer symbolischen Beschreibung. Deshalb wird nach der Erzeugung eines *nicht-kreisfreien Graphen* dieser in zwei voneinander unabhängige Bäume zerlegt. Anschließend werden diese zur Weiterverarbeitung der Gefäßbäume und zur Beurteilung der Trennung auf die Volumendaten übertragen.

3.1 Grapherzeugung

Zur Erzeugung der symbolischen Beschreibung aus den Volumendaten werden die segmentierten Blutgefäße ausgehend von der Leberpforte durchlaufen. Dabei werden alle gefundenen Verzweigungs- und Endpunkte als Knoten in einem Graphen gespeichert, die mit ihren jeweiligen Vorgängern verbunden werden. Hierzu wird ein Algorithmus von Zahlten et. al. [3] verwendet, der dem hier beschriebenen Problem angepaßt wurde.

Mit der Speicherung von *Bifurkations-* und *Endknoten* kann die Verzweigungsstruktur eines Gefäßbaumes symbolisch als (kreisfreier) Graph beschrieben werden. Handelt es sich jedoch um mehrere miteinander verbundene Gefäßbäume, genügt diese Form der Beschreibung nicht. Durch die Pseudoverbindungen entstehen Kreise

(Zyklen), die nicht auf einen Baum abgebildet werden können. Aus diesem Grund wurde eine dritte Knotenart eingeführt, der *Hilfsknoten*. Dieser kann zwei direkte Vorgänger haben und wird als eine Art Verbindungsstück eingesetzt, um einen Zyklus zu beschreiben.

3.2 Lokalisierung der Trennpunkte

Um einen so erzeugten, allgemeinen Graphen in zwei Bäume zerlegen zu können, müssen zuerst die Wurzeln dieser Bäume ermittelt werden. Dies geschieht zur Zeit interaktiv durch den Benutzer. Die untere Wurzel befindet sich an der Leberpforte und entspricht dem Startpunkt der Grapherzeugung. Die zweite Wurzel liegt in der unteren Hohlvene kurz nach dem Eintritt der Lebervenen (s. Abb. 3a).

Danach wird der Graph nach allen *Pfaden*, die von der einen Wurzel zur anderen führen, durchsucht. Diese falschen Verbindungen der beiden Gefäßbäume werden

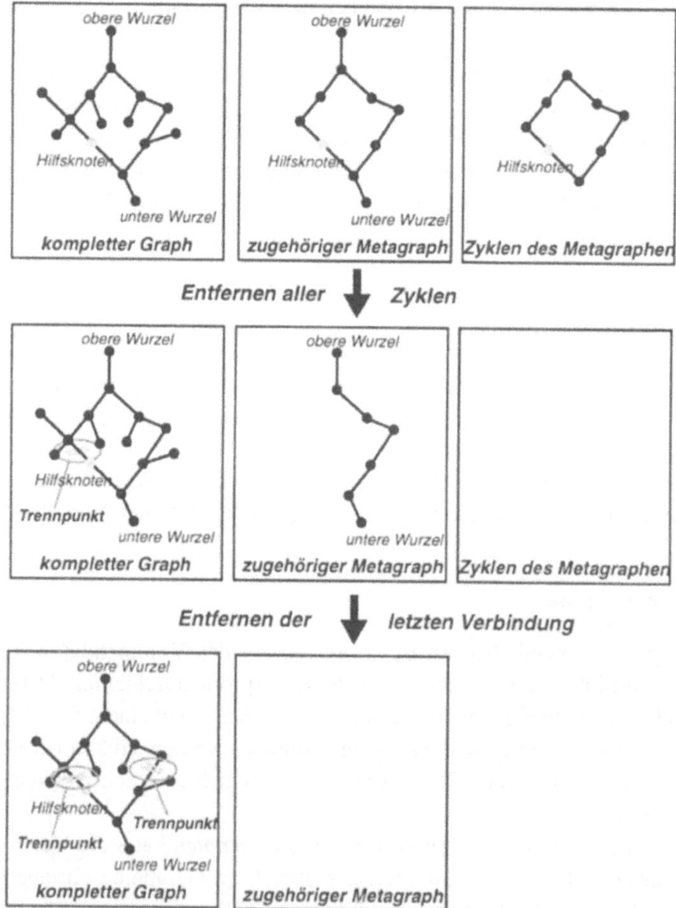

Abb. 1:   Demonstration des Trennverfahrens anhand eines einfachen Beispiels.

zunächst in einem *Metagraphen* gespeichert, wodurch der komplette Graph auf seine, für die Trennung nötigen Informationen reduziert wird. Es muß also das Ziel des Verfahrens sein, jede falsche Verbindung zwischen den Wurzeln der Reihe nach zu eliminieren und aus dem Metagraphen zu streichen bis dieser verschwunden ist und damit der eigentliche Graph in zwei voneinander unabhängige Bäume zerlegt ist.

Um zu verhindern, daß der Graph durch eine ungeschickte Trennung, beispielsweise in der Nähe einer der Wurzeln, in mehr als zwei Teile gespalten wird, werden alle im Metagraphen enthaltenen *Kreise* ermittelt. Da diese Zyklen der Grund für die Einführung des Hilfsknotens in das Datenmodell waren, ist gewährleistet, daß der Graph exakt so viele einfache Kreise enthält wie Hilfsknoten für seine Speicherung nötig waren. Es müssen also genau $n+1$ Trennpunkte (mit n = Anzahl Hilfknoten) gefunden werden, um zwei unverbundene Bäume zu erhalten[1]. Abbildung 1 zeigt anhand eines einfachen Beispiels den schematischen Ablauf des Verfahrens.

Das Finden der optimalen Trennpunkte sowohl in den Zyklen, als auch in der letzten Verbindung basiert auf der Dicke der Blutgefäße an dieser Stelle. Das bedeutet, für jede Kante zweier Knoten wird der mittlere Durchmesser des entsprechenden Gefäßabschnitts herangezogen und mit denen der anderen Kanten verglichen. Dadurch daß die beiden Gefäßsysteme nicht wirklich miteinander verbunden sind, sondern nur an manchen Stellen so nah aneinander vorbeilaufen, daß sie aufgrund der Auflösung der Computertomographie verbunden erscheinen, sind die Berührungspunkte meist sehr schmal. Dies bedeutet, daß die optimalen Trennpunkte sich zwischen den Knoten eines Zyklus (oder der letzten Verbindung) befinden, deren Kante den kleinsten mittleren Durchmesser besitzt.

3.3 Bestimmung der Trennungsart und Übertragung auf die Volumendaten

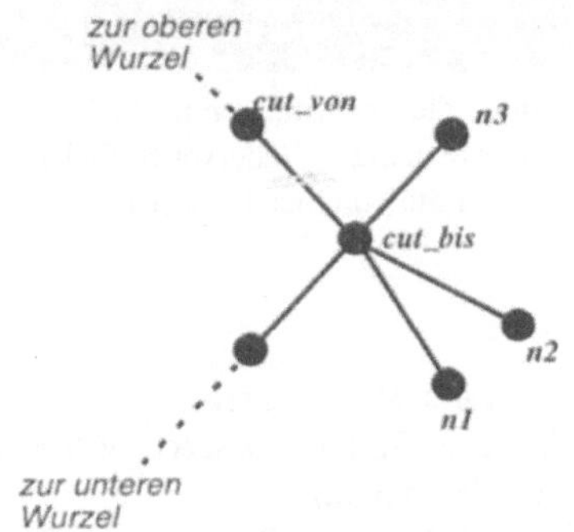

Abb. 2: Bestimmung der Trenungsart.

Wurden auf diese Weise n+1 Kanten zwischen zwei Knoten des Metagraphen gefunden, muß noch entschieden werden, wie die Trennung an diesen Stellen durchgeführt werden soll. Dieser Schritt ist nötig, da jeder dieser Knoten mindestens zwei weitere Nachbarn besitzt, die einem der entstandenen Teilbäume zugeordnet werden müssen. Abbildung 2 zeigt beispielhaft für dieses Problem den Ausschnitt eines Graphen, der zwischen den Knoten *cut_von* und *cut_bis* getrennt werden soll. Aufgrund der Richtung ihrer

---

[1] Die Anzahl $n+1$ kommt daher, daß durch die Entfernung aller n Zyklen in einem Graphen zwar ein kreisfreier Graph entsteht, dessen Knoten aber alle noch miteinander verbunden sind. Da es aber das Ziel des Trennungsverfahrens ist, zwei nicht mehr verbundene Bäume zu erzeugen, muß noch genau eine Kante des Graphen eliminiert werden.

Kanten werden die Nachbarknoten *n1* und *n2* (sowie alle ihre eventuellen Nachfolger) dem oberen und *n3* dem unteren Gefäßbaum zugeordnet.

Anschließend werden die Graphinformationen mit einer modifizierten Distanztransformation [4] auf die Volumendaten übertragen. Hierfür muß jedem Voxel der segmentierten Blutgefäße in der Leber ein Label zugewiesen werden, das die Zugehörigkeit zu einem der beiden Gefäßbäume beschreibt. Bei der anschließenden Visualisierung wird dieses Label dann durch eine bestimmte Farbe (blau für die Lebervenen und rot für die Gefäße der Pfortader) ersetzt (s. Abb. 3b)[2].

4 Ergebnisse und Diskussion

Mit dem hier vorgestellten Verfahren kann die Verzweigungsstruktur der Pfortader ermittelt und von den ebenfalls kontrastierten Lebervenen getrennt werden, wodurch eine anatomisch korrekte, präoperative Segmenteinteilung der Leber erst ermöglicht wird. Außerdem ist es unabhängig von der verwendeten Modalität und kann in allen medizinischen Datensätzen Anwendung finden, bei denen sich die Blutgefäße gut vom umliegenden Gewebe abgrenzen.

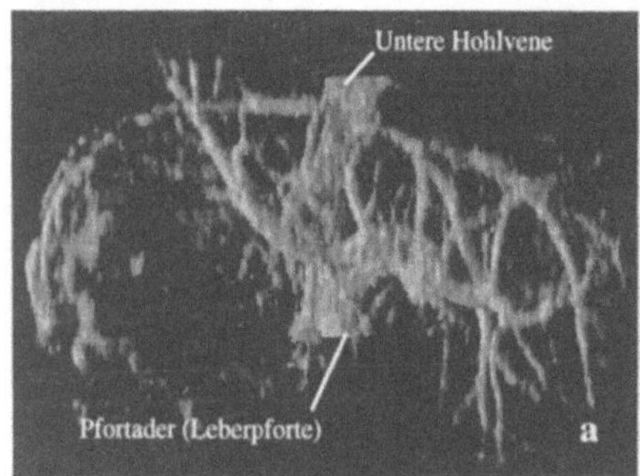

Abb. 3: Visualisierte intrahepatische Gefäßsysteme, die an mehreren Stellen miteinander verbunden sind (**a**). Ergebnis der Trennung in Lebervenen (hell) und Pfortader (dunkel) nach der Übertragung auf die Volumendaten (**b**).

Literatur

1. Couinaud C: Le Foie - Etudes anatomiques et chirurgicales. Masson, Paris, 1957
2. Glombitza G, Lamadé W, Demiris AM, Göpfert MR et al: Technical Aspects of Virtual Liver Resection Planning. Proc. MedInfo'98, Seoul 1998 (in print)
3. Zahlten C, Jürgens H, Peitgen H-O: Reconstruction of Branching Blood Vessels from CT-Data. In: Göbel M, Müller H, Urban B (Hrsg.): Visualization in Scientific Computing, Springer-Verlag Wien, 41-52, 1995
4. Borgefors G: On Digital Distance Transforms in Three Dimensions. Computer Vision and Image Understanding, 64(3): 368-376, 1996

---

[2] Die getrennten Blutgefäße sind als Farbvisualisierungen im Internet unter *http://mbi.dkfz-heidelberg.de/mbi/projects/liver/liver.html* zu finden.

Die Problemorientierte Segmentierung des Herzens am Beispiel des Myocardödems

A. Schroeder[a], M.H. Makabe[a], J. Albers[b], R. Möckel[c], H.-P. Meinzer[a]

[a] Deutsches Krebsforschungszentrum, Abt. Medizinische und Biologische Informatik,
Im Neuenheimer Feld 280, 69120 Heidelberg
[b] Chirurgische Klinik der Universität Heidelberg, Klinik für Herzchirurgie,
Im Neuenheimer Feld 110, 69120 Heidelberg
[c] Universität Heidelberg, Klinikum der Stadt Mannheim, Institut für Klinische Radiologie,
Theodor-Kutzer-Ufer 1-3, 68167 Mannheim
e-Mail: A.Schroeder@DKFZ-Heidelberg.de

Zusammenfassung: Eine nichtinvasive Erkennung myocardialer Ödeme stellt
für den Herzchirurgen gerade im Bereich der Frühdiagnostik und der Verlaufskontrolle ein wichtiges Hilfsmittel dar. In einer Studie, die sich mit der Identifikation von Ödemen in Bildern beschäftigt, wurden von sechs explantierten
Schweineherzen (drei mit und drei ohne Ödem) MR-Aufnahmen erstellt und
mit Methoden der Bildverarbeitung ausgewertet. Darin ergab sich, daß es generell möglich ist, qualitative Aussagen über das Vorhandensein myocardialer
Ödeme zu machen.
Schlüsselwörter: Myocardiales Ödem, Schwellwertverfahren, 3D-Rekonstruk-
tion

1 Einleitung und Motivation

Für die Herzchirurgie spielt die frühzeitige Erkennung myocardialer Ödeme unter den
Gesichtspunkten:
- Frühdiagnostik und
- Verlaufskontrolle

eine wichtige Rolle.

Ödeme treten u.a. aufgrund einer Mangeldurchblutung (Ischämie) auf. Die betrof-
fenen Zellen werden nicht mehr ausreichend mit Sauerstoff versorgt, wodurch es im
weiteren Verlauf zu einer Wassereinlagerung kommt, die eine Schädigung der entsprechenden Zellen zur Folge hat. Gründe dafür sind beispielsweise Herzinfarkte, Abstoßungsreaktionen nach Herztransplantationen, Vergiftungen oder Reaktionen auf eine
Strahlentherapie.

Aufgrund der großen klinischen Relevanz dieser Fragestellung wurde untersucht,
ob sich Ödeme mit Hilfe geeigneter bildgebender Verfahren darstellen und anschlies-
send mit Methoden der Bildverarbeitung auswerten lassen. Auf diese Art ist eine nicht-
invasive Diagnostik möglich ist. In diesem Zusammenhang interessieren den

Herzchirurgen die Lage des Ödems innerhalb der Herzwand (subendo-, subepicardial, intra-, transmural) sowie dessen Größe, um den Schweregrad beurteilen zu können. Neben diesen beiden Informationen ist auch die Topographie, also die Lokalisation innerhalb des Herzens, hinsichtlich der Beurteilung möglicher Funktionsstörungen bzw. der Bypassfähigkeit ein wichtiger Parameter [1].

2 State of the Art

Die Identifikation myocardialer Ödeme wurde bisher hauptsächlich in vitro experimentell am Tiermodell durchgeführt. Die dabei angewandten Verfahren beruhen auf der Berechnung des myocardialen Wassergehaltes und der linksventrikulären Masse. Der myocardiale Wassergehalt berechnet sich aus der Differenz zwischen Feucht- und Trockengewicht. Zur Berechnung der linksventrikulären Masse werden u.a. 2D-Echoaufnahmen verwendet. Anhand eines Ellipsenmodells berechnet man aus zwei aufeinander senkrechtstehenden Längsachsenschnitten mit Hilfe der Simpson-Regel das Volumen. Da es sich hierbei nicht um ein dreidimensionales Verfahren handelt, sondern Modellannahmen über die Geometrie zugrundegelegt werden, ist dieses Vorgehen fehleranfällig. Bei vorhandenen Ödemen nehmen der myocardiale Wassergehalt und die linksventrikuläre Masse erhöhte Werte an, wodurch es ebenfalls zu einer erhöhten Wandsteifheit kommt [2]. Diese tritt als diastolische Funktionsstörung in Erscheinung und ist somit eine der am frühesten erkennbaren Veränderungen.

Durch die Weiterentwicklungen im Bereich der Magnetresonanztomographie können Ödeme nunmehr mit Hilfe der STIR (Short Time Inversion Recovery)-Sequenz dargestellt und für eine Herzinfarktlokalisation herangezogen werden [3].

3 Segmentierung der Ödeme

Als Grundlage für die Erkennung myocardialer Ödeme mit Mitteln der digitalen Bildverarbeitung dienten sechs explantierte Schweineherzen. Drei der Herzen wurden direkt nach der Entnahme mit BDM, einer Cardioplegie-Lösung die bekanntermaßen Ödeme verursacht, perfundiert, um zu gewährleisten, daß Ödeme im Bildmaterial vorhanden sind. Die übrigen drei Herzen wurden zur Kontrolle mit einer Standardlösung perfundiert, die keine Ödeme verursacht.

Die derart vorbehandelten Herzen wurden in der jeweiligen Cardioplegielösung im MR aufgenommen. Dazu wurde die in Abschnitt 2 erwähnte STIR-Sequenz verwendet. Bei dieser Sequenz handelt es sich um eine T1-gewichtete Sequenz, die allerdings nicht das T1-Signal darstellt, sondern vielmehr den Unterschied zwischen Geweben mit verschiedenen T1-Zeiten hervorhebt. Daher ist sie gut geeignet, Ödeme darzustellen, die im resultierenden Bildmaterial heller erscheinen als das umliegende Myocard.

Das Datenmaterial mußte zunächst einer geeigneten Vorverarbeitung unterzogen werden. Deren Ziel bestand in der Trennung des Myocards von der umgebenden Cardioplegie und der Segmentierung des Ödems innerhalb des Myocards.

Die Segmentierung des Herzens erfolgte durch eine Kombination aus einem

Schwellwertverfahren zur Ausblendung der das Herz umgebenden Cardioplegielösung und einer anschließenden Connected-Component-Analyse zur Elimination des Rauschens außerhalb der ROI. Das Ödem innerhalb des Myocards wurde durch ein Schwellwertverfahren segmentiert. Da dabei aber das Problem der Partialvolumeneffekte beim Übergang von Myocard zur Cardioplegie eine Falschklassifikation der Pixel in den Randbereichen zur Folge hatte, wurden diese mit Hilfe eines datenangepaßten Schwellwertes, der auf das zugehörige Absolutgradientenbild angewendet wurde, eliminiert. Im Anschluß an die Segmentierung, bei der allen Ödempixeln ein verglichen mit dem Myocard extrem hoher Grauwert zugewiesen worden ist, wurde eine Visualisierung mit dem Heidelberger Raytracing-Verfahren [4] durchgeführt. Anhand dieser 3D-Rekonstruktionen aus verschiedenen Blickrichtungen soll die räumliche Lage und Ausdehnung beurteilt werden.

Neben der Auswertung des Bildmaterials wurde nach Durchführung der Bildakquisition eine myocardiale Trockengewichtsbestimmung durchgeführt, um zu überprüfen, ob in den drei Herzen aus der BDM-Gruppe Ödeme vorhanden waren. Dazu wurde das Gewicht der Myocard-Proben aus definierten Regionen (Vorderwand, Hinterwand, Septum, rechter Ventrikel, Apex) vor und nach dem Austrocknen (3 Stunden bei 80°C) verglichen.

4 Ergebnisse

Im vorangegangenen Abschnitt wurde ein Vorgehen beschrieben, um myocardiale Ödeme in MR-Aufnahmen darzustellen und sie mit Methoden der digitalen Bildverarbeitung zu segmentieren und 3D zu rekonstruieren. Wendet man das beschriebene Verfahren auf das Bildmaterial der explantierten Herzen an (Abb. 1b) so erkennt man nach der Segmentierung (Abb. 1c) subepicardiale Ödeme, deren räumliche Verteilung sich hauptsächlich über die Wand des linken Ventrikel bis hinein in das Septum erstreckt (Abb. 2). In den Aufnahmen der Kontrollherzen zeigen sich erwartungsgemäß keine Ödeme.

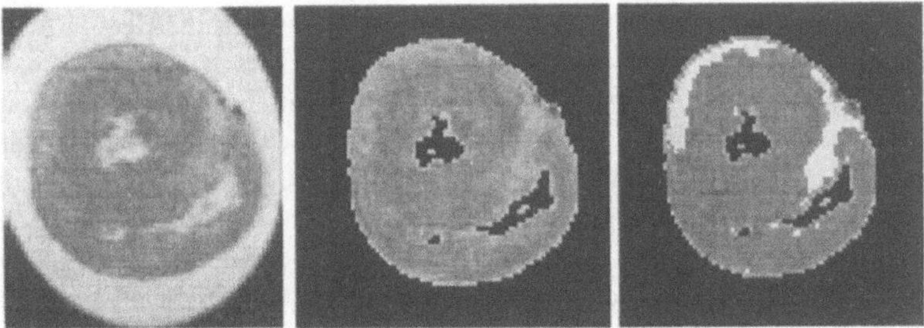

Abb. 1: Segmentierung der Daten: (a) Originalschicht, (b) nach Segmentierung des Herzens, (c) nach Segmentierung des Ödems (hell dargestellt)

Diese Ergebnisse decken sich qualitativ mit denen der Trockengewichtsbestimmung. Bei den ödematösen Herzen ergab sich die erwartete Reduktion des Gewichtes nach Austrocknen der Myocardproben, die sich bei den Herzen ohne Ödem nicht zeigte.

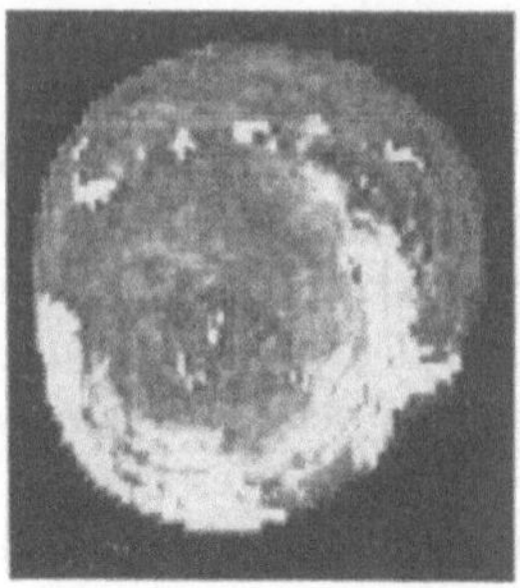 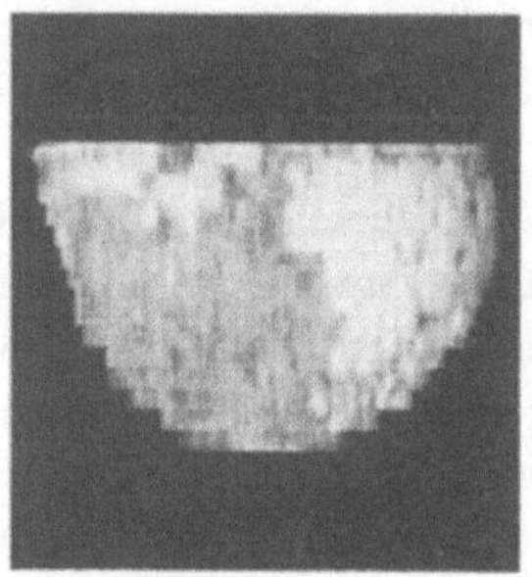

Abb. 2: 3D-Rekonstruktion des Myocardödems in einem Kurzachsenschnitt unterhalb der Klappenebene und in einer Frontalansicht

5 Diskussion und Ausblick

Im Rahmen dieser Untersuchungen wurde gezeigt, daß es generell möglich ist, mit Hilfe geeigneter bildgebender Verfahren und digitaler Nachbearbeitung der Bilder Hinweise auf das Vorhandensein myocadialer Ödeme zu erhalten.

Dabei handelt es sich um eine Methode, die dem Herzchirurgen die Möglichkeit bietet, nichtinvasiv das Herz auf Ödeme hin zu untersuchen. Somit kann das Verfahren in einem zweiten Schritt auch in vivo für die Patientenbehandlung getestet werden. Um diese Vorgehensweise in die klinische Routine integrieren zu können, sind sowohl von Bildgebungs- als auch der Bildverarbeitungsseite noch einige Probleme zu lösen.
Seitens der Bildgebung sind dabei vor allem die Reduktion der Aufnahmezeiten und der Partialvolumeneffekte zu nennen. Die verwendete STIR-Sequenz kann nur im Singleslice-Modus bei Atemanhalt gefahren werden. Bei einer Akquisitionsdauer von 15-20 Sekunden pro Schicht stellt dies besonders für herzkranke Patienten eine Belastung dar, da für eine anschließende quantitative Auswertung das gesamte Herz abgebildet sein muß. Aufgrund der genannten Partialvolumeneffekte ist es in den Randbereichen nicht eindeutig möglich, die Pixel dem Ödem zuzuordnen. Somit sind quantitative Aussagen über dessen Größe derzeit nicht möglich. Da diese Effekte aufnahmebedingt sind und selbst bei geringeren Schichtdicken als den derzeitigen 5mm nicht umgangen werden können, muß eine Strategie entwickelt werden, anhand der man die einzelnen Ödempixel gewichtet. Da auch noch nicht bekannt ist, welche Ausdehnung Ödeme beim Patienten verglichen mit den hier dargestellten haben, muß geklärt werden, wie sich Partialvolumeneffekte auf Ödeme geringer Ausdehnung auswirken. Wenn diese Probleme gelöst sind, kann zu einer quantitativen Auswertung der Ödeme übergegangen werden, so daß eine objektive Beurteilung möglich ist.

Die in dieser Studie verwendeten Schwellwertverfahren, um das Herz von der Cardioplegie zu trennen, sind auf in-vivo-Aufnahmen, auf denen das Herz aus dem umgebenden Brustkorb segmentiert werden muß, nicht übertragbar. Außerdem werden bei den derzeit möglichen Schichtdicken für die 3D-Rekonstruktion geeignete Interpolationsverfahren benötigt, um die Auflösung in der dritten Raumrichtung an die Auflösung in der Schichtebene anzupassen. Nur so können realitätsnahe Abbildungen erzeugt werden, anhand derer der Schweregrad der Ödeme beurteilt werden kann.

6 Zusammenfassung

Da für die Herzchirurgie der Nachweis von Myocardödemen ein wichtiges Hilfsmittel darstellt, um beispielsweise Abstoßungsreaktionen nach Herztransplantationen rechtzeitig zu erkennen, wurde hier ein nichtinvasives Verfahren beschrieben. Dieses wurde an sechs explantierten Schweineherzen, von denen drei künstlich mit Ödemen versehen worden sind, getestet. Die Herzen wurden mit der STIR-Sequenz im MR aufgenommen, anschließend mit einem Schwellwertverfahren segmentiert und 3D rekonstruiert. Diese Bilder ermöglichen dem Herzchirurgen qualitative Aussagen über das Ödem zu machen.

Danksagung

Diese Arbeit wird von der Deutschen Forschungsgemeinschaft im Rahmen des SFB 414, Informationstechnik in der Medizin „Rechner- und Sensorgestützte Chirurgie " gefördert.

Literatur

1. Albers J, Makabe MH, Schroeder A, Heiland M, Meinzer HP, Vahl CF, Hagl S: Cardiale MR in der Herzchirurgie - Forderungen des Herzchirurgen an die cMR-Bildgebung am Beispiel der 3D-Rekonstruktion des Myocardödems. Aktuelle Radiologie 7(6): S. 361-262 (1997).
2. Spotnitz HM, Hsu DT: Myocardial Edema: Importance in the Study of Left Ventricular Function. Advances in Cardiac Surgery, Mosby Year Book, Vol. 5, S. 1-25, (1994).
3. Voigtländer T, Kreitner KF, Wittlinger T, Kalden P, Möbius S, Thelen M, Meyer J: Neue Aspekte in der MR-Diagnostik von Herzinfarkten. Aktuelle Radiologie 7(6) (1997).
4. Meinzer HP, Metz K, Scheppelmann D, Engelmann U, Baur HJ: The Heidelberg Raytracing Model. IEEE Computer Graphics & Applications, Nov. 1991, S. 34-43 (1991).

Modellbasierte Segmentation klinischer MR-Aufnahmen

Christian D. Werner, Frank B. Sachse, Karsten Mühlmann und Olaf Dössel

Institut für Biomedizinische Technik,
Universität Karlsruhe, 76128 Karlsruhe
Email: cw@ibt.etec.uni-karlsruhe.de

Zusammenfassung Die in dieser Arbeit vorgestellte Strategie zur Segmentation und Klassifikation drei- und vierdimensionaler MR-Datensätze ermöglicht die Erstellung anatomischer Modelle des menschlichen Körpers. Zur Segmentation dieser Datensätze kommen unterschiedliche Verfahren zum Einsatz. Schwerpunkte bilden dabei das Region Growing und die Aktiven Konturen. Bei beiden Segmentationsverfahren werden zur Filterung der Datensätze unterschiedliche Filter (u. a. Gauß-, Sobelfilter, nichtlineare adaptive Diffusionsfilter, morphologische Filter) angewendet. Das Aktive Konturen-Verfahren wird weiterhin durch die Wahl geeigneter Potentialfunktionen unterstützt.

Schlüsselwörter: Segmentation, Aktive Konturmodelle, Region Growing, Diffusionsfilter, Klassifikation

1   Einleitung

Rechnerbasierte drei- und vierdimensionale anatomische Modelle des menschlichen Körpers gewinnen in vielen Bereichen der Medizin zunehmend an Bedeutung. Anwendungsgebiete dieser Modelle finden sich bei der Optimierung diagnostischer und therapeutischer Verfahren.

Um aus medizinischen tomographischen Aufnahmen dreidimensionale anatomische Modelle zu erstellen, bedarf es der Segmentation und Klassifikation dieser Aufnahmen. Im Allgemeinen geht der Segmentation und Klassifikation eine Vorverarbeitung der Aufnahmen voraus, die zum Ziel hat, die Bildqualität zu erhöhen und die Fehler in den Aufnahmen zu reduzieren. Bei der Segmentation der Bilddaten wird eine Unterteilung des Bildes in homogene Regionen durchgeführt [1]. Durch die Klassifikation wird jeder dieser homogenen Regionen eine Gewebeart zugeordnet.

Die in dieser Arbeit vorgestellte Strategie zur Segmentation klinischer MR-Aufnahmen basiert auf zwei unterschiedlichen Segmentationsverfahren, Region Growing und Aktive Konturen. Beiden Segmentationsverfahren gehen Filterungen der Ausgangsdatensätze voraus. Neben Mittelwert-, Gauss- und Sobelfiltern werden auch nichtlineare adaptive Diffusionsfilter eingesetzt. Die Segmentation mittels Aktiver Konturen wird durch die Wahl einer geeigneten, durch einen statistischen Klassifikator gewonnene Potentialfunktion unterstützt.

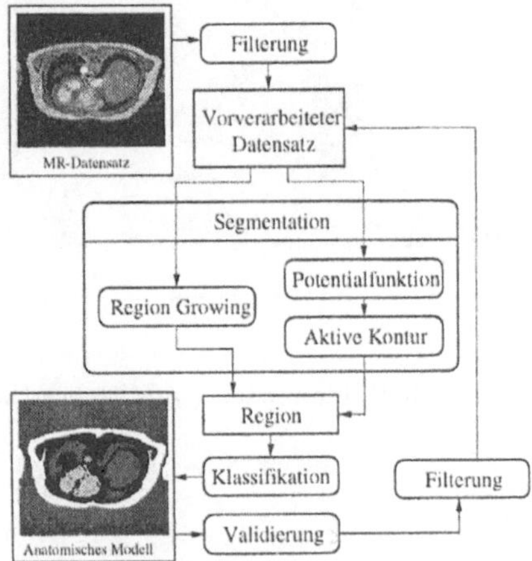

Abb. 1. Segmentationsstrategie für klinische MR-Aufnahmen

2 Methodik

2.1 Segmentationsstrategie

Die dieser Arbeit zugrundeliegende Segmentationsstrategie (Abb. 1) basiert im Wesentlichen auf dem iterativen Anwenden der Segmentationsverfahren Region Growing und Aktive Konturen. Bei jedem Iterationsschritt kommen unterschiedliche Filteroperationen zum Einsatz.

Nach einer initialen Filterung der MR-Ausgangsdaten erhält man einen vorverarbeiteten Datensatz. Dieser Datensatz wird zur Segmentation herangezogen, einerseits durch Region Growing oder andererseits mit Aktiven Konturen, wobei er hier zur Bestimmung der Potentialfunktion dient. Als Segmentationsergebnis erhält man eine Region, der bei der Klassifikation eine Gewebeart zugeordnet wird. Das Ergebnis der Klassifikation ist ein anatomisches Modell. Nach der Validierung dieses Modells kann gegebenenfalls erneut gefiltert, segmentiert und klassifiziert werden.

2.2 Datenmaterial

Als Ausgangsdaten dienen klinische 4D-MR-Aufnahmen unterschiedlicher Patienten in Voxelrepräsentation. Diese 4D-Aufnahmen liegen als Sequenzen dreidimensionaler Datensätze vor. Jeder dieser T1-gewichteten Datensätze [2] besteht aus $256 \times 256 \times 16$ Voxeln der Kantenlängen $2\,mm \times 2\,mm \times 8\,mm$.

2.3 Filterung

Neben der Mittelwert-, Median- und Gauss-Filterung [1] kommt zur Reduktion von Rauschen ein nichtlinearer adaptiver Diffussionsfilter (Adaptive Smoothing) [3] zum Einsatz.

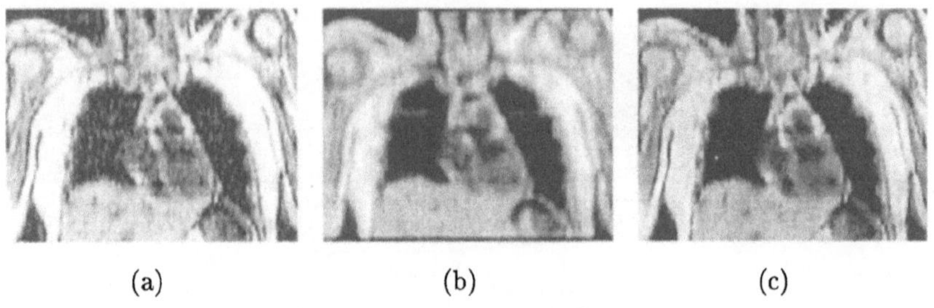

Abb. 2. Filterung von (a) 3D-MR-Daten mittels (b) Mittelwertfilter und (c) Adaptive Smoothing

Beim Adaptive Smoothing werden in Abhängigkeit der Bildgradienten Gewichtungsfaktoren bestimmt, mittels derer für jedes Voxel die Parameter zur Filterung neu definiert werden. Aus den Bilddaten I ergeben sich die gefilterten Daten F folgendermaßen:

$$F(x,y,z) = \frac{\sum\limits_{i,j,k=-1}^{+1} I(x+i,y+j,z+k)w(x+i,y+j,z+k)}{\sum\limits_{i,j,k=-1}^{+1} w(x+i,y+j,z+k)} \tag{1}$$

Hierbei ist w die Gewichtungsfunktion, die sich aus G, dem Betrag des Bildgradienten, wie folgt bestimmen läßt:

$$w(x,y,z) = e^{-\frac{G^2(x,y,z)}{2\sigma^2}} \tag{2}$$

Mit dem Parameter σ läßt sich die Filtercharakteristik beinflussen. Wird σ groß gewählt, nähert sich das Verhalten einem Mittelwertfilter an, d. h. man erhält eine starke Glättung der Ausgangsdaten. Bei kleinem σ bleiben Kanten weitgehend unverändert erhalten.

Der Betrag des Gradienten wird wie folgt bestimmt [3]:

$$G(x,y,z) = \max(|I(x,y,z) - I(x-i,y-i,z-i)|) \tag{3}$$

Ein Vergleich der Filterung von 3D-MR-Daten mit Gaussfilter bzw. Adaptive Smoothing ist in Abb. 2 dargestellt.

2.4 Region Growing

Das Region Growing Verfahren ermöglicht die Segmentierung eines zusammenhängenden Gebietes. Das Verfahren wird durch die Vorgabe von Saatpunkten, Segmentationskriterien und Nachbarschaftsbeziehungen parametrisiert [1].

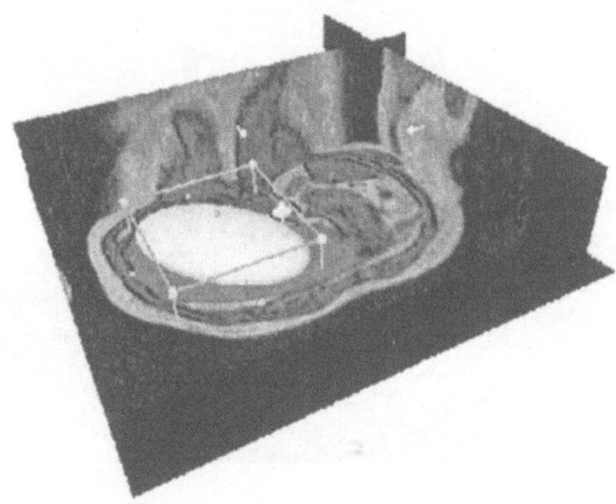

Abb. 3. Initale Kontur zur Segmentierung der Leber mittels eines Aktiven Konturmodells. Die Kontur wird interaktiv skaliert, rotiert und plaziert.

2.5 Aktive Konturen

Mit Aktiven Konturen werden die elasto-mechanische Eigenschaften einer dünnen Oberfläche nachgebildet. Dieses Oberflächenmodell steht dabei unter dem Einfluß unterschiedlicher Kräfte, die sich zum einen aus den inneren, durch Materialeigenschaften definierten Kräften und den äußeren, durch die Bildinformation eingebrachten Kräften zusammensetzen.

Die Energie einer Aktiven Kontur $\mathbf{x}(u,v)$ wird durch folgendes Energiefunktional beschrieben [4]:

$$\mathcal{E}(\mathbf{x}) = \mathcal{S}(\mathbf{x}) + \mathcal{P}(\mathbf{x}) \tag{4}$$

wobei $\mathcal{S}(\mathbf{x})$ die innere Deformationsenergie und $\mathcal{P}(\mathbf{x})$ die äußere durch die Bildinformation eingebrachte Energie ist. Es ergeben sich nach [4]:

$$\mathcal{S}(\mathbf{x}) = \iint \alpha_{10} \left|\frac{\partial \mathbf{x}}{\partial u}\right|^2 + \alpha_{01} \left|\frac{\partial \mathbf{x}}{\partial v}\right|^2 + \beta_{20} \left|\frac{\partial^2 \mathbf{x}}{\partial u^2}\right|^2 + \beta_{11} \left|\frac{\partial^2 \mathbf{x}}{\partial u\,\partial v}\right|^2 + \beta_{02} \left|\frac{\partial^2 \mathbf{x}}{\partial v^2}\right|^2 \, du\,dv, \tag{5}$$

$$\mathcal{P}(\mathbf{x}) = -\iint P(\mathbf{x}(u,v))\,du\,dv, \tag{6}$$

wobei die Parameter α_{01}, α_{10}, β_{20}, β_{02} und β_{11} die elasto-mechanischen Eigenschaften der Kontur bestimmen und $P(\mathbf{x}(u,v))$ eine aus den Bilddaten gewonnene skalare Potentialfunktion darstellt. Diese Potentialfunktion kann durch Gradientenbildung und durch Einsatz eines statistischen Klassifikators gebildet werden. Die Aktive Kontur $\mathbf{x}$ minimiert das Energiefunktional $\mathcal{E}$.

In dieser Arbeit wurde eine Diskretisierung der Kontur mittels eines Dreiecksnetzes durchgeführt. Durch geschickte Wahl der initialen Kontur (Abb. 3), der Potentialfunktion und der elasto-mechanischen Eigenschaften wird angestrebt, daß die Kontur das Energieminimum an Organ- oder Gewebegrenzen erreicht und somit eine Segmentierung der MR-Daten erfolgt.

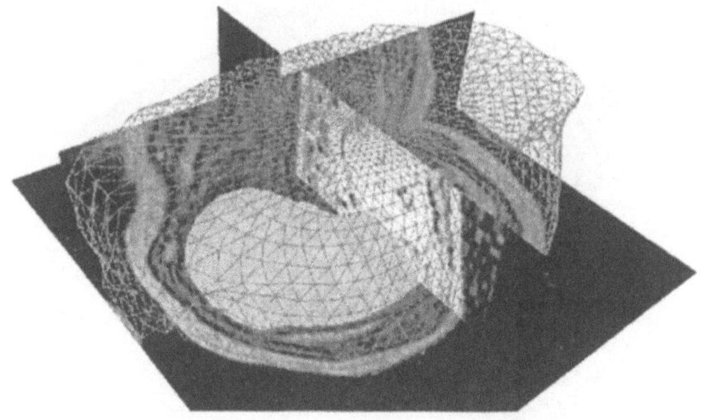

Abb. 4. Ergnisse der Segmentation: Segmentation der Leber und des Aussenbereichs.

3 Ergebnisse

Mit der vorgestellten Segmentationsstrategie wurde ein anatomisches Modell des Thorax erstellt. Dabei konnten in den Datensätzen folgende Gewebeklassen unterschieden werden: Aussenbereich, Haut, Lunge, Aorta, Subkutanes Fett, Muskel, Leber und Herz. Der Aussenbereich, die Lunge und die Aorta wurden hierbei durch Region Growing segmentieren. Durch Anwendung aktiver Konturen wurden Leber, Subkutanes Fett, und Muskulatur abgegrenzt. Die Kenntnis von Lage und Form der an das Herz grenzenden Gewebearten ermöglichte dessen Segmentierung. Hierbei wurden u. a. morphologischer Filter eingesetzt.

Danksagung

Wir danken Herrn Bornstedt vom Deutschen Herzzentrum Berlin für die freundliche Unterstützung unserer Arbeit, insbesondere für die Erstellung der 4D-MR-Aufnahmen.

Literatur

1. R. C. Gonzalez and R. E. Woods, *Digital Image Processing*. Reading, Massachusetts; Menlo Park, California; New York; Bonn: Addison-Wesley, 1992.
2. H. Morneburg, Siemens Aktiengesellschaft, ed., *Bildgebende Systeme für die medizinische Diagnostik*. Erlangen: Publicis MCD, 3 ed., 1995.
3. I. Matalas, R. Benjamin, and R. Kitney, "An edge detection technique using the facet model and parametrized relaxation labeling," *IEEE Transactions on Pattern Analysis and Machine Intelligence*, vol. 19, pp. 328–341, April 1997.
4. T. McInerney and D. Terzopoulos, "Deformable models in medical image analysis: A survey," *Medical Image Analysis*, vol. 1, no. 2, 1996.

Filterbankstrukturen zur verlustfreien Kompression medizinischer Bilddaten

Andreas Klappenecker, Frank U. May und Thomas Beth

Universität Karlsruhe, IAKS, D-76128 Karlsruhe
`wavelet@ira.uka.de`

Zusammenfassung In der modernen medizinischen Diagnostik werden eine Vielzahl von bildgebenden Verfahren verwendet. Hierdurch fallen jährlich radiologische Bilddaten in der Größenordnung von mehreren Petabytes an. In Deutschland wird vom Gesetzgeber zur Archivierung nur eine *verlustlose* Kompression dieser Bilddaten erlaubt. Wir stellen zwei neue verlustlose Kompressionsverfahren vor. Beide Verfahren benutzen eine Filterbank zur Reduktion der Signalentropie und verwenden eine Erweiterung der arithmetischen Codierung zur Entfernung der Redundanz.

Schlüsselwörter: Verlustfreie Kompression, Filterbänke, modulare Arithmetik, nichtlineare Rundungsoperationen, Leiterstrukturen.

1   Einleitung

Die bekannten *verlustbehafteten* Kompressionsverfahren (wie z.B. JPEG) lassen sich häufig in die drei Schritte Signaltransformation, Quantisierung und Entropiecodierung unterteilen. Die ersten beiden Schritte reduzieren die Entropie der Eingabedaten und erhöhen damit die Effizienz der Entropiecodierung.

Bei *verlustfreien* Kompressionsverfahren kann ebenfalls eine Signaltransformation (ohne Quantisierung) zur Reduktion der Entropie benutzt werden. Wir stellen zwei verschiedene Verfahren vor, welche auf diesem Prinzip beruhen. Beide benutzen im ersten Schritt eine Filterbankstruktur [1] und im zweiten Schritt eine Erweiterung der arithmetischen Codierung. Die Verfahren unterscheiden sich in den Operationen, die zur Realisierung der Filterbank verwendet werden.

Wir demonstrieren den Nutzen dieser Kompressionsverfahren für CT- und MRT-Schichtbilder. Es handelt sich hierbei um monochromatische Bilder, die typischerweise eine Größe von 256×256 oder 512×512 Pixeln mit einer Tiefe von 12-16 Bit aufweisen.

2   Filterbänke mit modularer Arithmetik

Die Implementierung der Filterbank muß eine perfekte Rekonstruktion des Signals erlauben und soll – trotz exakter Rechnung – eine Explosion der transformierten Koeffizienten vermeiden. Dies legt eine Verwendung von modularer

Arithmetik nahe. Die Pixel der Bilddaten werden hierbei als Elemente aus einem Restklassenring $\mathbf{Z}/2^n\mathbf{Z}$ (etwa mit $n \in [12..16]$) interpretiert. Entsprechend werden in der Filterbank alle Additionen und Multiplikationen modulo 2^n gerechnet. Im folgenden untersuchen wir die Bedingungen, denen eine modulare Filterbank genügen muß, um eine perfekte Rekonstruktion zu garantieren.

Die Eingabedaten interpretieren wir als Elemente des Laurentpolynomrings in zwei Unbestimmten mit Koeffizienten aus dem Restklassenring $A := \mathbf{Z}/2^n\mathbf{Z}$. Aufgrund der Tensorproduktstruktur

$$A[x, x^{-1}] \otimes_A A[y, y^{-1}] \cong A[x, x^{-1}, y, y^{-1}]$$

bietet sich eine zeilen- und spaltenweise Verarbeitung der Daten an.

Die Zeilen des Eingabebildes werden mit einer sogenannten Zweikanal-Filterbank horizontal in zwei Teilsignale zerlegt. Danach führen wir dasselbe Verfahren auf den Spalten der erhaltenen Teilbilder durch und erhalten so insgesamt vier Teilbilder. Dieser Zerlegungsschritt wird auf einem Teilbild rekursiv wiederholt. Der Datenfluß ist wie bei der schnellen Wavelettransformation [1, 2], lediglich die verwendeten Operationen unterscheiden sich. Die Funktionsweise der verwendeten Zweikanal-Filterbank erläutern wir in den nächsten beiden Abschnitten.

Analyse. Ein Eingabesignal $s(z) \in A[z, z^{-1}]$ wird mit den Filtern $\tilde{\alpha}(z)$ und $\tilde{\beta}(z)$ multipliziert (gefaltet). Danach wird die Abtastrate auf die Hälfte reduziert. Wir erhalten in diesem Schritt zwei Signale $d_\alpha(z) := [\downarrow 2]\,\tilde{\alpha}(z)s(z)$ und $d_\beta(z) := [\downarrow 2]\,\tilde{\beta}(z)s(z)$, wobei

$$[\downarrow 2] : \begin{cases} A[z, 1/z] \longrightarrow A[z, 1/z], \\ a(z) \longmapsto a_g(z), \end{cases} \quad \text{mit} \quad a(z) = a_g(z^2) + z a_u(z^2).$$

Diese Analysefilterbank ist in der linken Hälfte der folgenden Abbildung skizziert:

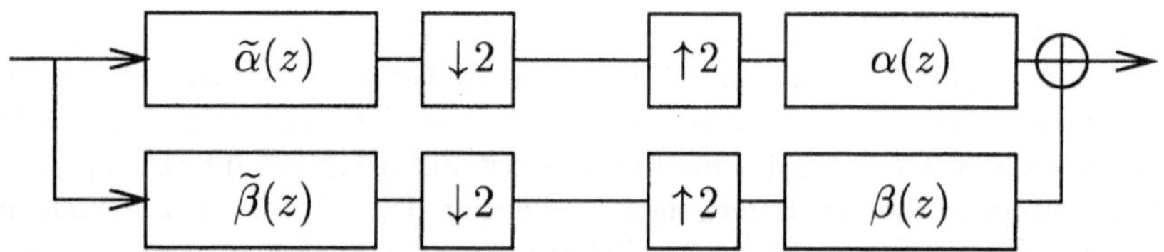

Synthese. Im Syntheseschritt wird die Abtastrate der Signale $d_\alpha(z)$ und $d_\beta(z)$ wieder erhöht, mit $\alpha(z)$ bzw. $\beta(z)$ multipliziert und addiert. Wir erhalten hierbei das Ausgabesignal

$$\hat{s}(z) := \alpha(z)d_\alpha(z^2) + \beta(z)d_\beta(z^2). \tag{1}$$

Auf der rechten Seite der vorigen Abbildung ist diese Synthesefilterbank skizziert.

Perfekte Rekonstruktion. Eine Filterbank wird **perfekt rekonstruierend** genannt, wenn das Ausgabesignal $\hat{s}(z)$ mit dem Eingabesignal $s(z)$ für alle Signale $s(z) \in A[z, z^{-1}]$ übereinstimmt.

Wenn wir sogenannte Polyphasenmatrizen [1]

$$H_p := \begin{pmatrix} \widetilde{\alpha}_g(z) & \widetilde{\alpha}_u(z) \\ \widetilde{\beta}_g(z) & \widetilde{\beta}_u(z) \end{pmatrix}, \qquad \text{mit} \qquad \begin{aligned} \widetilde{\alpha}(z) &= \widetilde{\alpha}_g(z^2) + z^{-1}\widetilde{\alpha}_u(z^2), \\ \widetilde{\beta}(z) &= \widetilde{\beta}_g(z^2) + z^{-1}\widetilde{\beta}_u(z^2), \end{aligned}$$

und

$$G_p := \begin{pmatrix} \alpha_g(z) & \alpha_u(z) \\ \beta_g(z) & \beta_u(z) \end{pmatrix}, \qquad \text{mit} \qquad \begin{aligned} \alpha(z) &= \alpha_g(z^2) + z\alpha_u(z^2), \\ \beta(z) &= \beta_g(z^2) + z\beta_u(z^2), \end{aligned}$$

definieren, dann erhalten wir mit einer kleinen Rechnung [3] die folgende Charakterisierung der perfekt rekonstruierenden Filterbänke:

Theorem 1. *Eine Zweikanal-Filterbank für Signale aus $A[z, z^{-1}]$ ist genau dann perfekt rekonstruierend, wenn die Polyphasenmatrizen H_p und G_p die Bedingung $G_p^t H_p = I$ erfüllen.*

Diese Polyphasenmatrizen lassen sich vollständig parametrisieren [4, Kap. 4]:

Theorem 2. *Jede Polyphasenmatrix einer perfekt rekonstruierenden Zweikanal-Filterbank läßt sich als Produkt von elementaren Transvektionen und einer Diagonalmatrix aus $\mathrm{GL}_2(A[z, z^{-1}])$ schreiben.*
[Eine elementare Transvektion unterscheidet sich von der Identitätsmatrix durch einen Eintrag aus $A[z, z^{-1}]$ auf der Nebendiagonalen.]

3 Filterbänke mit Rundungsoperationen

In der klassischen Filterbanktheorie werden die Koeffizienten A der Signale und Filter als reelle Zahlen interpretiert. Es läßt sich zeigen, daß Theorem 1 und 2 auch für Signale und Filter aus $A[z, z^{-1}] = \mathbf{R}[z, z^{-1}]$ gelten [3]. Nachteilig ist jedoch, daß die Transformationskoeffizienten im allgemeinen mit einer erheblich größeren Genauigkeit als die reellen Signalwerte dargestellt werden müssen, sofern die Filterbank-Implementierung eine perfekte Rekonstruktion des Signals erlauben soll.

Eine andere Vorgehensweise wird durch Theorem 2 (mit $A := \mathbf{R}$) nahegelegt. Die elementaren Transvektionen entsprechen bei einer Polyphasen-Filterbank [1, S. 259] direkt einem Leiterschritt (oder *lifting step* in der Terminologie von Sweldens). Ein kleines Beispiel soll dieses Prinzip verdeutlichen:

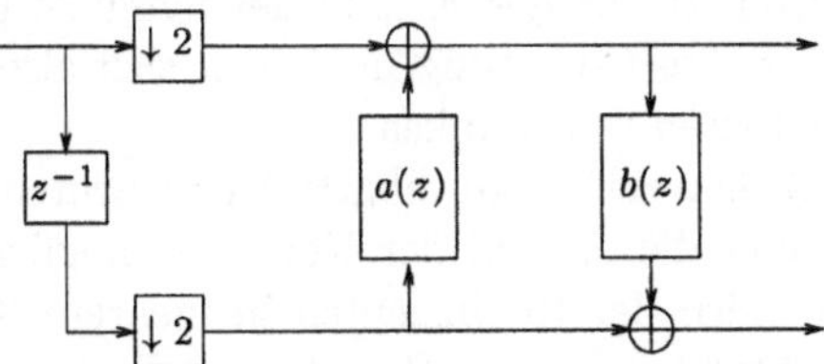

Die Struktur der Filterbank zeigt, daß man perfekte Rekonstruktion erreichen kann, indem die Operatoren $a(z)$ und $b(z)$ mit negativem Vorzeichen in umgekehrter Reihenfolge angewendet werden. Eine naheliegende Verallgemeinerung dieser Filterbankstruktur ist, statt der Faltungsoperatoren beliebige Operationen (wie Rundungsoperationen) zuzulassen. Die perfekte Rekonstruktion wird bereits durch die Struktur der Filterbank garantiert [5].

4 Arithmetische Codierung

Die Redundanz in den Bilddaten wird erst durch die Entropiecodierung entfernt. Es erweist sich als vorteilhaft, die Koeffizienten nach einer der vorgestellten Transformationen zu codieren, anstatt die Codierung direkt auf die Bilddaten anzuwenden.

Die arithmetische Codierung ist eine optimale verlustfreie Entropiecodierung. Sie basiert auf einer Idee von Elias, Symbole auf Teilintervalle von $[0, 1)$ abzubilden, wobei die Intervallbreite proportional zur Auftrittswahrscheinlichkeit des Symbols gewählt wird. Eine Symbolfolge wird gliedweise codiert, wobei jedes codierte Symbol das Ausgangsintervall $[0, 1)$ weiter verkleinert. Die Intervallbreite entspricht nach jedem Schritt der Wahrscheinlichkeit des bis dahin codierten Folgenpräfixes. Der Codierer überträgt dann eine beliebige Zahl aus dem letzten Intervall. Der Decodierer kann anhand dieser Zahl die Operationen des Codierers nachvollziehen, und dabei die Symbolfolge gliedweise rekonstruieren.

Abgesehen von der Einschränkung, daß Codierer und Decodierer dasselbe Modell benutzen müssen (d. h. zur Codierung und Decodierung eines Symbols muß jeweils dieselbe Wahrscheinlichkeitsverteilung benutzt werden), sind die Verteilungen in jedem Schritt frei wählbar. Ein adaptiver arithmetischer Codierer wird realisiert, indem man nach der (De-)Codierung eines Symbols das Modell mit einem vorgegebenen Algorithmus anpaßt.

Die Flexibilität des Modells erlaubt es, die Abhängigkeiten zwischen benachbarten Transformationskoeffizienten zu berücksichtigen. Dazu berechnet man aus den bereits codierten Koeffizienten einen *Codierungskontext*, der die tatsächlich benutzte Wahrscheinlichkeitsverteilung aus einer vorgegebenen Menge auswählt. Das zugehörige Modell enthält für jeden möglichen Kontext eine eigene Wahrscheinlichkeitsverteilung. Die einzelnen Verteilungen werden unabhängig voneinander adaptiert.

Eine adaptive Codierung arbeitet erst dann wirklich effizient, wenn das Modell die tatsächliche Statistik der Koeffizienten ungefähr widerspiegelt. Das ist zu Beginn der Codierung jedoch meist nicht der Fall. Die Adaption dauert umso länger, je mehr unterschiedliche Symbole und Codierungskontexte das Modell enthält, denn die Anzahl der adaptierten Wahrscheinlichkeiten im Modell entspricht gerade dem Produkt aus der Anzahl der Symbole und der Anzahl der Kontexte. Für eine effiziente Codierung muß man sich also auf eine möglichst kleine Anzahl von Kontexten beschränken.

Um einerseits möglichst viele benachbarte Koeffizienten berücksichtigen zu können, andererseits aber die Anzahl der Kontexte möglichst klein zu halten, teilt man den Wertebereich der Koeffizienten in mehrere Klassen (sogenannte *buckets*) ein und berücksichtigt bei der Berechnung des Codierungskontexts nur die Klassenzugehörigkeit der benachbarten Koeffizenten.

5 Erste Ergebnisse

In der folgenden Tabelle werden unsere beiden Verfahren (Modular und Rundung) mit bekannten Standardkompressionsverfahren für ein MRT- und ein CT-

Bild mit jeweils 512 × 512 Pixeln und 12 Bit Tiefe verglichen. Die Tabelle zeigt das Verhältnis von der Größe der Rohdaten (384 KByte) zur komprimierten Dateigröße und die Bits pro Pixel. Mit den weitverbreiteten universellen Kompressionsverfahren GZIP und BZIP2 wurden die Bilddaten (ohne *header*-Information) komprimiert. Hierfür wurden zwei Dateiformate verwendet: eine Datei enthielt die Bilddaten in gepackter 12-Bit-Form, bei der anderen wurde jeder 12-Bit-Wert in zwei Bytes eingebettet (16 Bit). Das GIF-Bildformat ist lediglich für Bilder mit bis zu 8 Bit Tiefe definiert. Wir haben zum Vergleich das Nachfolgeformat PNG herangezogen, das deutlich besser komprimiert als GIF und auch für Bilder mit 12 Bit Tiefe definiert ist. Leider stand uns keine Implementierung des „lossless JPEG"-Standards oder des kommenden JPEG-LS-Standards zur Verfügung, die unsere 12 Bit Bilder korrekt komprimieren konnte.

	CT			MRT		
Verfahren	Rate	BpP	Größe (KB)	Rate	BpP	Größe (KB)
GZIP 16 Bit	1.042	11.519	368.62	1.041	11.526	368.83
GZIP 12 Bit	1.096	10.945	350.25	1.089	11.021	352.66
BZIP2 12 Bit	1.202	9.981	319.39	1.247	9.619	307.82
BZIP2 16 Bit	1.365	8.794	281.40	1.453	8.262	264.37
PNG	1.368	8.772	280.69	1.489	8.061	257.97
Modular	1.398	8.583	274.64	1.546	7.764	248.43
Rundung	1.519	7.902	252.87	1.753	6.845	219.04

Aus der Tabelle wird ersichtlich, daß die vorgeschlagenen Kompressionsverfahren im Vergleich zu den Standardverfahren deutlich besser abschneiden. Die Parametrisierung der Codierung und der Filter bietet noch viele Möglichkeiten zur weiteren Optimierung der Verfahren.

Danksagung. Wir danken der Deutschen Forschungsgemeinschaft für die Unterstützung durch den Sonderforschungsbereich SFB 414 „Informationstechnik in der Medizin – Rechner und sensorgestützte Chirurgie" (Projekte Q1 und Q6).

Literatur

1. N. Fliege: *Multiraten-Signalverarbeitung*. B. G. Teubner, Stuttgart, 1993.
2. A. K. Louis, P. Maaß und A. Rieder: *Wavelets – Theorie und Anwendungen*. B.G. Teubner, Stuttgart, 1994.
3. A. Klappenecker, A. Nückel und F. U. May: *Lossless image compression using wavelets over finite rings and related architectures*. In: A. Aldroubi, A. F. Laine und M. A. Unser (Herausgeber): *Wavelet Applications in Signal and Image Processing V*, Band 3169, Seiten 139–147. SPIE, 1997.
4. A. Klappenecker: *Algebraische Wavelets*. (In Vorbereitung), Universität Karlsruhe, 1998.
5. A. R. Calderbank, I. Daubechies, W. Sweldens und B. L. Yeo: *Wavelet transforms that map integer to integers*. Erscheint in ACHA, 1996.

Kompensation von Metallartefakten in der Computertomographie

D. Zerfowski

Institut für Algorithmen und Kognitive Systeme
Universität Karlsruhe
76128 Karlsruhe
Email: zerfowsk@ira.uka.de

Zusammenfassung. Metallische Fremdkörper wie z. B. Zahnfüllungen oder implantierte Schrauben wirken sich in computertomographischen Aufnahmen negativ auf die Bildqualität aus, indem sich streifenförmige Artefakte über große Bereiche des Bildes ausbreiten und für die Diagnostik relevante Informationen überdecken. Für eine zuverlässigere Befundung ist die Kompensation solcher Artefakte von besonderer Bedeutung. Das vorgestellte Verfahren lokalisiert in den gemessenen Rohdaten die durch das Metallobjekt verursachten Störungen, um diese mittels eines an die Geometrie des Tomographen angepaßten Verfahrens zu kompensieren.
Da das vorgestellte Verfahren unabhängig von nachfolgend angewandten Rekonstruktionsalgorithmen ist, handelt es sich um einen reinen Vorverarbeitungsalgorithmus, der sich einfach auf bereits existierenden Tomographieanordnungen implementieren läßt.

Schlüsselwörter: Computertomographie, Metallartefakte, Bildverbesserung, Radon-Transformation.

1 Einleitung

Die mathematisch-physikalische Grundlage der Computertomographie stellt die Radon-Transformation (Gleichung 1) dar [1, 2, 3]. Diese überführt die im durchstrahlten Objekt vorliegende Verteilung des Absorptionskoeffizienten $f(x, y)$ mittels Linienintegrale über alle möglichen, das Objekt durchquerenden Projektionsgeraden in eine Darstellung $g(l, \theta)$, wie sie in Abbildung 1 wiedergegeben wird. Dabei entspricht jeder Wert

$$g(l, \theta) = \begin{cases} \int\limits_{-\infty}^{\infty} f\left(\sqrt{l^2 + z^2}, \theta + \arctan(\tfrac{z}{l})\right) dz, & \text{falls } l \neq 0, \\ \int\limits_{-\infty}^{\infty} f(z, \theta + \tfrac{\pi}{2}) \, dz, & \text{falls } l = 0 \end{cases} \tag{1}$$

dem Wert des Linienintegrals entlang einer Projektionsgeraden mit dem Abstand l vom Rekonstruktionszentrum und einem Normalenwinkel θ zur x-Achse.

Aufgrund des im Vergleich zum körpereigenen Gewebe hohen Absorptionskoeffizenten von Metallen werden eine erhebliche Anzahl von Messungen verfälscht.

Abb. 1. Geometrische Interpretation der Radon-Transformierten.

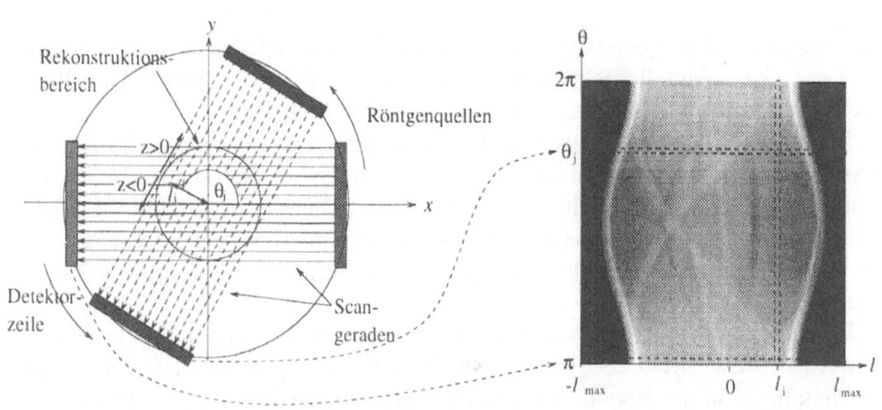

Ein in einer tomographischen Aufnahmeschicht liegendes, metallisches Objekt mit elliptischem Querschnitt (z. B. schräg durch die Aufnahmeschicht hindurchtretende Schraube) verursacht somit (Abb. 2 b) einen deutlich aus der restlichen Radon-Transformierten hervortretenden, sinusförmigen Streifen variabler Breite. Ohne vorherige Kompensation werden diese Fehler während des Rekonstruktionsprozesses über das gesamte Bild verteilt.

Kalender et al. [4] stellten ein halbautomatisches Verfahren vor, bei dem der Mediziner in den rekonstruierten Bilddaten das metallische Objekt manuell identifizieren muß. Mit diesen Angaben werden in der Radon-Transformierten die gestörten Daten gesucht, um nach einer nicht näher beschriebenen Korrektur und einer nochmaligen Rekonstruktion ein verbessertes Bild zu erhalten.

Wang et al. [5] wählen hingegen einen automatischen, dafür jedoch wesentlich rechenintensiveren Ansatz, indem sie ein an die Problemstellung angepaßtes, iteratives algebraisches Rekonstruktionsverfahren verwenden.

Das hier vorgestellte Verfahren sucht in der gemessenen Radon-Transformierten den Bereich der gestörten Daten unter Verwendung eines durch eine Histogrammanalyse vorgegebenen Schwellwertes. Aufgrund des endlichen Absorptionskoeffizienten von Metall, lassen sich die Ränder der gestörten Daten nicht exakt lokalisieren. Somit wird für alle Randpunkte über einen hinreichend großen Bereich in der Radon-Transformierten ein Schätzwert, basierend auf parallelen Projektionen, bestimmt. Hieraus ergibt sich für jeden Rotationswinkel θ (also einer Zeile in Abb. 1 rechts) ein guter Schätzwert für eine knapp am Metall vorbeiführende Messung.

Die anschließende Interpolation der in der Radon-Transformation verfälschten Daten nutzt die zuvor gemittelten Messungen, wobei neben parallelen auch nicht parallele Messungen entsprechend ihrer örtlichen Nähe im Objektbereich in die Schätzung eingehen.

Das Verfahren wurde in der Simulationsumgebung TomAS [6] implementiert und erprobt.

2 Kompensation in der Radon-Transformation

Ausgehend von einer gemessenen Radon-Transformierten (Abb. 2 b) eines Phantoms mit einem Metallobjekt (helles kreisförmiges Objekt in Abb. 2 a), soll im folgenden das Kompensationsverfahren beschrieben werden.

In einem ersten Schritt wird eine Histogrammanalyse über die in der Radon-Transformierten auftretenden Werte $g(l, \theta)$ durchgeführt. Hieraus ergibt sich eine untere Schranke für die durch die Metallkomponenten beeinflußten Projektionen. Unter Verwendung des so bestimmten Schwellwertes wird zeilenweise in der Radon-Transformierten der linke $(d_l(\theta))$ und rechte $(d_r(\theta))$ Rand des Metall ¡einflusses lokalisiert.

Für eine zeilenweise lineare Interpolation der Werte $g(d, \theta)$ für $d_l < d < d_r$ werden nicht direkt die Werte $g(d_l, \theta)$ und $g(d_r, \theta)$ verwendet. Um lokale Schwankungen in der Radon-Transformierten auszugleichen, wird als Schätzung für eine knapp außerhalb des Metalls verlaufende Projektion eine Mittelung über Projektionen durchgeführt, die in einem 3 mm breiten Streifen parallel verlaufen. Formal ergibt sich für die Interpolation der gestörten Daten $g(d, \theta)$ mit $d_l(\theta) < d < d_r(\theta)$ und P der Anzahl der zu mittelnden Geraden

$$\bar{g}(d, \theta) = \frac{d - d_l(\theta)}{d_r(\theta) - d_l(\theta)} m_l(\theta) \; + \; \frac{d_r(\theta) - d}{d_r(\theta) - d_l(\theta)} m_r(\theta) \quad \text{mit} \tag{2}$$

$$m_l(\theta) = \frac{1}{P} \sum_{i=0}^{P-1} g(d_l - i \cdot \Delta d, \theta) \; \text{und} \; m_r(\theta) = \frac{1}{P} \sum_{i=0}^{P-1} g(d_r + i \cdot \Delta d, \theta). \tag{3}$$

Bereits diese einfache Interpolationsmethode liefert nach der Rekonstruktion eine deutlich verbesserte Bildqualität. Jedoch weißt die Radon-Transformierte im Bereich der interpolierten Daten deutliche horizontale Strukturen auf. Sie verläuft somit in θ-Richtung nicht glatt. In Abbildung 2 d) ist ein entsprechender Ausschnitt aus der Radon-Transformierten wiedergegeben. Aus dem genannten Grund wird hier eine weitere Interpolationsmethode vorgestellt.

Die Erweiterung der zuvor beschriebenen eindimensionalen Interpolation in die zweite Dimension, also in θ-Richtung, durch Verwendung einer einfachen zweidimensionalen Filterung auf der Radon-Transformierten ist nicht von Vorteil. Der Grund hierfür liegt darin, daß für festes d bei kleinen Veränderungen in der θ-Koordinate, bereits über Daten gemittelt würde, die sich entlang von Projektionsgeraden ergeben, die das Metallobjekt in einem relativ großen Abstand passieren. Es würde somit über Daten gemittelt, die wenig Informationen aus der örtlichen Nähe des metallischen Fremdkörpers enthalten. Dieses gilt in besonders starkem Maße für Metallobjekte, die vom Rekonstruktionszentrum weit entfernt liegen.

Wünschenswert ist es also für jede durch (d, θ) festgelegte Gerade, die den im Metall liegenden Punkt (x, y) durchläuft, alle die Projektionsgeraden in der Schätzung zu berücksichtigen, die mit einem geringen Abstand zu (x, y) außerhalb des Metalls verlaufen und außerdem nahezu parallel zu (d, θ) liegen.

Die Einschränkung auf nahezu parallele Geraden und damit auf kleine Variationen von θ bewirkt, daß lediglich Projektionsgeraden berücksichtigt werden,

Abb. 2. Metallartefakte in der Radon-Transformierten und Rekonstruktion.

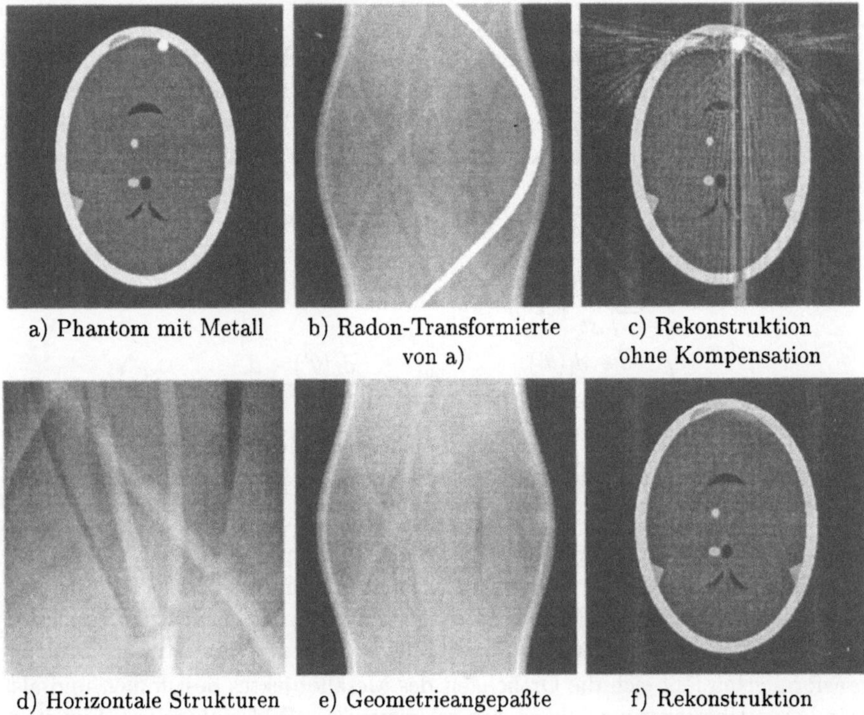

a) Phantom mit Metall   b) Radon-Transformierte   c) Rekonstruktion
von a)   ohne Kompensation

d) Horizontale Strukturen   e) Geometrieangepaßte   f) Rekonstruktion
bei zeilenweiser Interpolation   Interpolation   nach Kompensation

die auf ihrem Weg durch das Objekt eng benachbarte Gebiete durchlaufen und damit eine hohe Korrelation zueinander besitzen. Geht man von einem inkrementellen Rotationswinkel $\Delta\theta$ zwischen zwei, sich im Rekonstruktionszentrum schneidenden Geraden aus, so besitzen die zwei Punkte, die mit einem radialen Abstand r vom Ursprung auf den Geraden liegen, einen Abstand

$$a = 2r \left| \sin\left(\frac{\Delta\theta}{2}\right) \right|.$$

Für den in den Simulationen verwendeten Paralleltomographen mit 256 Sichten und Detektoren bedeutet dies, daß die Positionen des auf der durch den Ursprung verlaufenden Projektionsgeraden und dem Rand des Rekonstruktionsbereiches (mit dem Durchmesser $2r = 300\,\mathrm{mm}$) liegenden Punktes zwischen zwei Sichten einen Abstand von $\approx 1{,}84\,\mathrm{mm}$ besitzen. Nach vier Sichten beträgt der entsprechende Abstand bereits $\approx 7{,}4\,\mathrm{mm}$. Mit einem größer werdenden Rotationswinkel durchlaufen diese Gebiete fast vollständig verschiedene Regionen innerhalb des Objektes (mit Ausnahme ihres Schnittpunktes), und eine entsprechende Mittelung ergibt keine Vorteile.

Die geometrieangepaßte Bestimmung der für die Korrektur der gestörten Daten $g(d, \theta)$ benötigten Werte in der Radon-Transformierten ergibt sich unter

Berücksichtigung des Gesagten wie folgt (Abb. 2 e).

- Analog zur zeilenweisen Interpolation, bestimme über einen mittels einer Histogrammanalyse bestimmten Schwellwert den linken und rechten Rand $(d_l(\theta)$ und $d_r(\theta))$ der gestörten Daten in der Radon-Transformierten.
- Analog zur zeilenweisen Interpolation (Gleichung 3), berechne die Mittelwerte $m_l(\theta)$ und $m_r(\theta)$ außerhalb der beiden Ränder, linear gewichtet mit dem Kehrwert ihres Abstands vom Rand.
- Schätze den Wert $\bar{g}(d,\theta)$ mit $d_l(\theta) < d < d_r(\theta)$ gemäß

$$\bar{g}(d,\theta) = \sum_{\theta'=\theta-j\cdot\Delta\theta}^{\theta+j\cdot\Delta\theta} \frac{1}{1+|\theta'-\theta|} \cdot \tag{4}$$
$$\left(\frac{d-d_l(\theta')}{d_r(\theta')-d_l(\theta')} \cdot m_l(\theta') + \frac{d_r(\theta')-d}{d_r(\theta')-d_l(\theta')} \cdot m_r(\theta') \right),$$

wobei die Anzahl j der bei der Interpolation berückichtigten unterschiedlichen Winkel einmalig der verwendeten Scannergeometrie angepaßt werden muß.

Im Idealfall ist nach der zuvor beschriebenen Kompensation im rekonstruierten Bild das metallische Objekt nicht mehr erkennbar (Abb. 2 f). Um den Bereich des kompensierten Metalls im Bild zu markieren, können die Randkurven $d_l(\theta)$ und $d_r(\theta)$ ausgenutzt werden. Aufgrund ihres Verlaufes in der Radon-Transformierten läßt sich die Örtlichkeit des Metallobjektes bestimmen und als zusätzliches Überlagerungsbild in das rekonstruierte Bild einblenden. Für eine detaillierte Beschreibung der Korrespondenzen zwischen den Randkurven und Strukturen im rekonstruierten Bild sei auf [7] verwiesen.

Danksagung. Wir danken der Deutschen Forschungsgemeinschaft für die Unterstützung durch den Sonderforschungsbereich SFB 414 „Informationstechnik in der Medizin – Rechner und sensorgestützte Chirurgie" (Teilprojekt Q1).

Literatur

1. G. T. Herman: *Image reconstruction from projections.* Academic Press, 1980.
2. F. Natterer: *The Mathematics of Computerized Tomography.* Wiley, 1986.
3. A. C. Kak und M. Slaney: *Principles of Computerized Tomography.* New York: IEEE Press, 1987.
4. W. A. Kalender, R. Hebele und J. Ebersberger: *Reduction of CT artifacts caused by metallic implants.* Radiology, 164(2):576–577, 1987.
5. G. Wang, D. L. Snyder, J. A. O'Sullivan und M. W. Vannier: *Iterative Deblurring for CT Metal Artifact Reduction.* IEEE Transactions on Medical Imaging, 15(5):657, Oktober 1996.
6. D. Zerfowski, T. Rohlfing, U. Mende und Th. Beth: *TomAS – Tomographic Algorithms and Ultrasound Simulation.* In: Lemke (Herausgeber): *CAR'97,* Seite 1017. Elsevier Science, 1997.
7. D. Zerfowski: *A new Method for Motion Artifact Compensation in CT.* In: *Proceedings Medical Imaging,* San Diego, California, USA, 1998. SPIE.

A new stereotaxic multiarchitectonic atlas of the human thalamus in a 3D MRI navigation system

Klaus Niemann [1], Dagmar Noelchen [1], Daniel Jeanmonod [2], Anne Morel [2]

[1] Department of Neuroanatomy, University of Technology (RWTH),
D-52057 Aachen, Germany and
[2] Laboratory for Functional Neurosurgery, Neurosurgical Clinic, University Hospital,
CH-8091 Zürich, Switzerland
Email: niemann@cajal.medizin.rwth-aachen.de, amorel@nch.unizh.ch

Summary. In the context of MRI-guided stereotaxy a new stereotaxic atlas of the human thalamus was developed in order to improve anatomical definition and precision in the prediction of the exact location of thalamic targets. It is based on multiarchitectonic parcellation (Nissl, myelin, calcium-binding proteins). Sagittal atlas data were digitized and registered together with 3D MRI data sets. In a coarse to fine strategy the atlas-to-patient transformation matrix is refined. Thus the atlas is tailored to the individual anatomy of the patient. The effects of the rigid transformation are directly monitored on the computer screen using visible anatomical landmarks as control.

Keywords: Brain atlas, calcium-binding proteins,   magnetic resonance imaging, 3D navigation, stereotaxy, thalamus

1 Introduction

1.1 Stereotaxic atlases of the thalamus

Stereotaxic histological atlases provide information concerning the location of brain structures in a Cartesian coordinate system based on anatomical landmarks related to the ventricular system. The atlases date back to an era when CT and MR imaging of the brain were not yet available and the exact 3D location of intracerebral targets could only be inferred from their position relative to the intracerebral fluid spaces. In stereotaxic interventions for the treatment of chronical functional disorders such as neurogenic pain and Parkinson's disesase [1], the tip of a probe is advanced through a burrhole in the skull along a precalculated trajectory towards a target situated in deep diencephalic areas of the brain. Microelectrode recordings on the fly as well as electrical stimulation serve as control for the trajectory and the correct target site. At the target site, coagulation of the target or implantation of depth electrodes is performed. Although thalamic contours are partly discernible in MR imaging, intrathalamic targets cannot be visually identified in pre-operative low-field MR images. This is due to the fact that signal intensities within the thalamus are homogeneous and that the definition of a target relies on microstructural and microfunctional criteria which have no direct correlate in routine MRI data sets.

1.2 Advantages of multiarchitectonic parcellation

The definition of thalamic nuclei and territories on the basis of cyto- and myeloarchitectonic criteria has in the past been a matter of constant debate. In the lateral nuclear group, Hassler [3] differentiated 30 nuclei, Andrew and Watkins [4] only eleven. Whereas Hassler described 8 nuclei in the medial group, Andrew and Watkins saw no justification for a subdivision of the medial thalamic mass. The classical, partly contradictory anatomical descriptions rely on cyto- and myeloarchitectonic definitions which imply fuzzy morphological classification schemes prone to subjective interpretation. Hassler [3] 'finds it impossible to recognize in many illustrations in van Buren and Borke's atlas [5], the indicated architectonic subdivisions' and relates the fact to the different morphological criteria delineating a region. Because of different categorization criteria as well as species differences in thalamic organization consequently different thalamic terminologies came into being [2]. In recent years Hirai and Jones [6] presented a unified terminological concept of thalamic subdivision. It provides easy comparison of human thalamic organization with the wealth of information on thalamic organization available, for the most part, only in non-human primates. Classical descriptions are supplemented by more objective histochemical criteria (e.g. histochemical staining for acetylcholinesterase). Calcium-binding proteins like parvalbumin, calbindin D-28K, calretinin are especially suited for histochemical parcellation because there is evidence that their thalamic distribution pattern is related to distinct cell populations [7]. Craig et al. [8] demonstrated an association of calbindin with a posterolateral thalamic area relaying pain and temperature information.

2 Co-registration of Atlas and Patient Data in 3D MRI scans

2.1 Stereotaxic atlas data

The atlas presented by Morel et al. [9] is based on multiarchitectonic parcellation (Nissl, myelin, calcium-binding proteins) on sections parallel or perpendicular (frontal and sagittal) to the horizontal intercommissural (anterior commissure-posterior commissure, AC-PC) reference plane.

2.2 Digitization and co-registration of atlas data

Besides anatomical labels the atlas supplies closed contours of the histological entities. Thus it is well suited for digital 3D representation. From the sagittal atlas data (3.6 - 19.4 mm lateral to the interhemispheric plane) 55 anatomical structures were digitized. Apart from thalamic structures, the subthalamic nucleus, substantia nigra as well as the (incomplete) section profile of the caudate nucleus were included. Data were interpolated in the direction of the cuts using an algorithm suggested by Akima [10, 11]. The data were manually re-edited after the interpolation so as to eliminate unwanted side effects of the interpolation and resolve ambiguities in the definition of bordering structures. The outcome is an isotropic 3D contour and volume representation with a resolution of .225 mm.

The atlas data are co-registered with the MRI scans and shown in superimposition. Atlas data may be subjected to rigid transformations (translation, rotation, and scaling) in a correlated triplanar display (axial, frontal, and sagittal sections, correlated cursor movements). Thus the morphological quality of the atlas-to-patient registration is interactively assessed and improved. Reference structures which are discernible both in the atlas and in the MR images (e.g. thalamic surface, section profiles of mamillothalamic tract, caudate nucleus, red nucleus) serve as control for the quality of the fit. Following a coarse-to-fine strategy, the initial transformation matrix for the co-registration of atlas and patient data is thus gradually refined under direct visual control [cf. 12]. After correct adjustment of the atlas [Fig. 1] the course of the planned trajectory is thoroughly checked and alternatives can be evaluated. Target and trajectory coordinates may then be transferred to the Radionics planning system.

2.3 Target determination

Target planning during the stereotactic intervention is performed with the MRI-related fiducial-based Radionics system coupled to the Cosman-Roberts-Wells (CRW) stereotactic frame. During MRI examination (T1-weighted images, Philips Gyroscan S 15 with MRI-compatible head ring fixed to the patient earlier under local anesthesia), a rapid series of 5 mm thick horizontal slices through the diencephalic area is acquired so as to determine the midsagittal plane. Then a series of 2 mm thick sagittal slices is performed which is centered on the midsagittal plane. The midsagittal scan allows for determination of AC and PC and thus for the definition of the intercommissural plane DV0 which is orthogonal to the midsagittal plane. From a series of 2 mm thick horizontal slices (with 0.2 mm interslice gap) planned parallel to DV0, one is centered on the dorso-ventral coordinate of the intended target. In the latter slice the other anterior-posterior (measured from the PC or mid-commissural point) and medial-lateral (measured from the ventricular border) target coordinates are determined. The final XYZ coordinates of the intended target are set on the CRW frame using the fiducial-related Radionics stereotactic program. The penetration angles are determined according to the pre-planned electrode trajectory on the atlas and the intended frontal precoronal approach.

3 Discussion

The advent of MRI-guided stereotaxy in conjunction with digital atlas representation enables the direct visual control of the atlas-to-patient transformation above.

Arguments for fitting the thalamic contours from the atlas to the MRI data of the patient is superior to solely ACPC-based target determination can be extrapolated from the work of Brierley and Beck [13]. In 53 hemispheres they found a proportional arrangement of the thalamic nuclei in the antero-posterior axis but failed to demonstrate a constant relationship of the thalamic nuclei to PC in frontal sections. As there are hints that interindividual differences in the spatial arrangement of thalamic nuclei exist [9, 12, 13], digital representation of histological data from different brains is to our opinion a prerequisite for the consistent evaluation of the degree and nature of this variation.

Subsequently fuzzyfication [14] applied to the different histological data sets helps to overcome problems of interindividual variation. Recent advance in high-field MR imaging - yet at an experimental stage - [15,16] is expected to have a positive impact

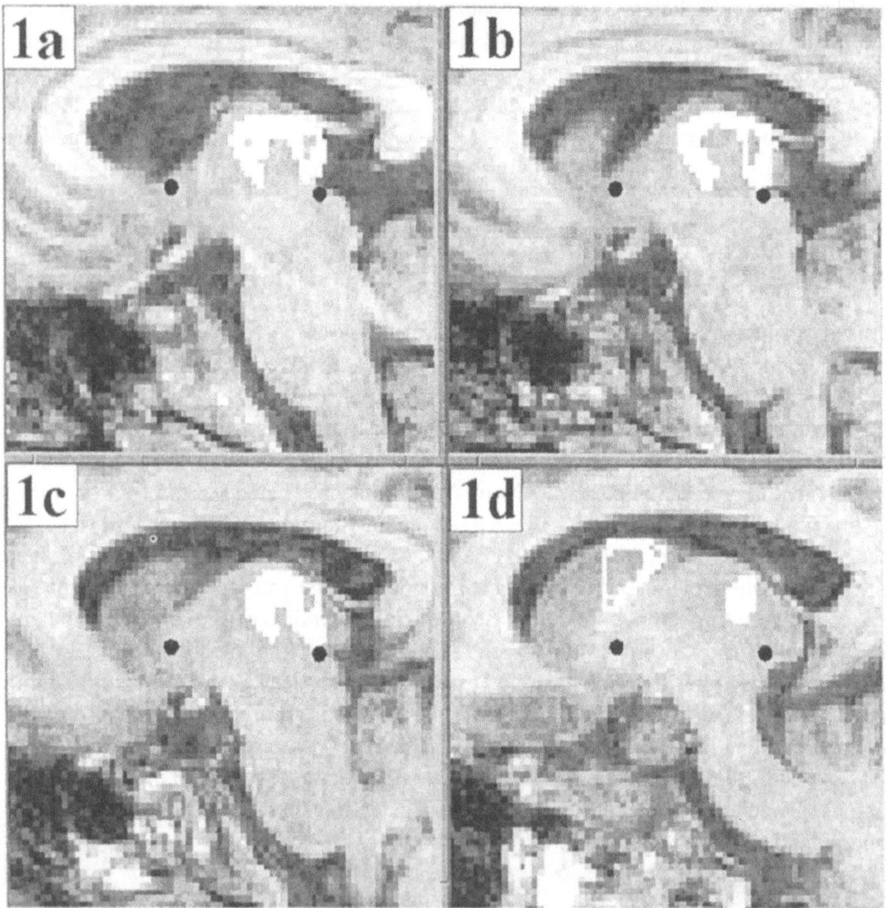

Figure 1. Central lateral nucleus of thalamus in superimposition with sagittal MRI scans after adjustment of atlas to patient. Slices are 5 mm (1a), 7 mm (1b), 9 mm (1c), 11 mm (1d) apart from the midsagittal plane. Central lateral nucleus shown in white. Section profile of caudate nucleus indicated in 1d serves as reference structure. AC and PC represented by black dots.

in this area because it enables a more specific discrimination of intrathalamic landmarks.

4 References

1. Jeanmonod D, Magnin M, Morel A: Low-threshold calcium spike bursts in the human thalamus. Brain 119:363-375, 1996.
2. Axer H, Niemann K: Terminology of the thalamus and ist representation in a part-whole relation. Meth. Inform. Med. 33:488-495, 1994.
3. Hassler R: Architectonic organization of the thalamic nuclei. In: Stereotaxy of the Human Brain, Schaltenbrand G, Walker AE (eds). Thieme, Stuttgart, New York, 2nd ed. 1982, 140-180.
4. Andrew J, Watkins ES: A stereotaxic atlas of the human thalamus and adjacent structures. A variability study. Williams and Wilkins, Baltimore, 1969.
5. Van Buren JM, Borke RC: Variations and connections of the human thalamus. Vol. 1. The nuclei and cerebral connections of the human thalamus. Vol. 2. Variations of the human diencephalon. Springer, Heidelberg, 1972.
6. Hirai T, Jones EG: A new parcellation of the human thalamus on the basis of histochemical staining. Brain Res. Rev. 14:1-34, 1989.
7. Jones EG, Hendry SHC: Differential calcium binding protein immunoreactivity distinguishes classes of relay neurons in monkey thalamic nuclei. Eur. J. Neurosci. 1: 222-246, 1989.
8. Craig AD, Bushnell MC, Zhang ET, Blomquist A: A thalamic nucleus specific for pain and temperature sensation. Nature 372: 770-773, 1994.
9. Morel A, Magnin M, Jeanmonod D: Multiarchitectonic and stereotactic atlas of the human thalamus. J. Comp. Neurol. 387: 588-630, 1997.
10. Akima H: A new method of interpolation and smooth curve fitting based on local procedures. JACM 17: 589-602, 1970.
11. Akima H: A method of bivariate interpolation and smooth surface fitting based on local procedures. Comm. ACM 17: 18-20, 1974.
12. Niemann K, Naujokat C, Pohl G, von Keyserlingk D: Verification of the Schaltenbrand and Wahren stereotactic atlas. Acta Neurochir. (Wien) 129: 72-81, 1994.
13. Brierley JB, Beck E: The significance in human stereotactic brain surgery of individual variation in the diencephalon and globus pallidus. J. Neurol. Neurosurg. Psychiat. 22: 287, 1959.
14. Niemann K, van Nieuwenhofen I, Berks G, von Keyserlingk DG: The Schaltenbrand and Wahren stereotaxic atlas: Conflicts in a histological database resolved by fuzzy set representation. In: Eufit '96. Proc. Fourth European Congress on Intelligent Techniques an Soft Computing, ELITE-European Laboratory for Intelligent Techniques Engineering, Zimmermann HJ (ed). Mainz, Aachen, 1996, 2117-2122.
15. Vandersteen M, Beuls E, Gelan J, Adriaensens P, van Ormelingen L, Palmers Y, Freling G: High field magnetic resonance imaging of normal and pathologic human medulla oblongata Anat. Rec. 283: 277-286, 1994.
16. Pan JW, Vaughan JT, Kuzniecky RI, Pohost GM, Hetherington HP: High Resolution Imaging at 4.1 T. Magn. Res. Imag. 13: 915-921, 1995.

Anatomically Guided Neuronavigation:
Sample Applications of the SulcusEditor in a Clinical Setting

Volker A. Coenen[1], Klaus Niemann[1], Uwe Spetzger[2], Armin Thron[3]

Departments of [1]Neuroanatomy, [2]Neurosurgery, and [3]Neuroradiology
University of Technology (RWTH), 52057 Aachen, Germany
Email: niemann@cajal.medizin.rwth-aachen.de

Summary. The clinical use of the SulcusEditor (SE) on an everyday basis for preoperative analysis of 3D MRI data sets of neurosurgical patients is reported. The SE is applied to MRI data sets of patients with tumors in the central and the temporal region of the brain in order to trace the individual sulcal pattern. This leads to a better understanding of the topographical relationships between the tumor and the surrounding tissue. Hence the operating neurosurgeon is provided preoperatively with detailed knowledge concerning the area of interest, eventually leading to a reduction of the operating trauma. Three cases of patients with tumors in the central region are shown examplarily.

Keywords: Neuronavigation, brain tumors, magnetic resonance imaging

1 Introduction

To provide the operating neurosurgeon with knowledge concerning the topography of a brain tumor is an important goal of preoperative magnetic resonance imaging. Yet the neurosurgeon has to create a three-dimensional 'mental image' of the anatomical relationships by looking at plane MR slides. Although workstations for neuronavigation using correlated triplanar displays support the surgeon, an automatical detection of eloquent cortical regions is not yet feasible. Since functional aspects are closely related to morphology a sensitive detection of anatomical structures is needed. There is, however, a substantial lack of exact lesion site definition with regard to the 'functional environment' of the tumor. Although the SulcusEditor (SE) essentially uses a morphological approach, it provides detailed information concerning the exact localization of a mass and its relationship to the surrounding functionally intact nervous tissue. So far 41 patients underwent the SE procedure.

2 Methods

For SE analysis T1-weighted 3D FLASH data sets were acquired using a Magnetom 1.5T imaging system (Siemens Medical Systems, Erlangen, Germany, SL=1.6 mm) as well as a Gyroscan T5-NT (Philips Medical Systems, Best, The Netherlands, SL=

3.0 mm, Easy-Guide MR scan protocol). The results of the SE procedure had to be made available to the neurosurgeons within a period of 48 hours after acquisition of the MR sequence including bidirectional data transfer. The individual tumor site was scrutinized by identifying and interactively labelling 10 to 12 sulci neighbouring the lesion. The selection of the sulci took into account the intended trepanation site as well as the eloquent areas that had to be bypassed during operation.

3 Results

Case p0056: A 65-year-old female presenting with an isolated right-sided hemiparesis (power 4/5). Initial MRI scanning was interpreted as a left-sided centrally located contrast enhancing lesion with surrounding edema. Preoperative SE analysis showed that the tumor was situated posterior to the central sulcus within the postcentral gyrus and also embraced the dorsal tip of the superior postcentral sulcus. The vertical branch of the cingulate sulcus was displaced posteriorly. In its medial aspect the tumor was confined to the paracentral lobule. During operation the SE findings were confirmed. Histological analysis showed a metastasis of an adenocarcinoma.

Case 179: A 50-year-old male who presented with a loss of consciousness, a left-sided hemiparesis, and a hemihypesthesia. Initial CT and subsequent MR imaging both showed parietal postcentral atypical bleeding, suspectible for a tumor. Further investigation revealed a mass with a rim enhancement and a diameter of 3-4 cm that was located in the parietal region. SE analysis showed that the vertical branch of the cingulate sulcus was displaced anteriorly. The superior portion of the postcentral gyrus was also shifted rostrally. Concludingly the tumor was located in the precuneus. Since the interparietal sulcus passed the tumor laterally in its complete extent the tumor was solely situated in the superior parietal lobule [Fig.1]. During intraoperative preparation along the pseudo-membrane the rostral demarcation of the mass by the postcentral sulcus was corroborated. The tumor appeared to be reaching the midline. Postoperative histological workup revealed a glioblastoma.

Case 1131: A 33-year-old female who exhibited a seizure with loss of consciousness during work. Initial CT and MR imaging showed a huge mass with a right medial frontal location that compressed the anterior horn of the lateral ventricle. Preoperative analysis with the SE revealed that the huge tumor was situated in the superior and middle frontal gyri, displacing the superior and middle frontal sulcus laterally. Seen from the medial aspect the cingulate sulcus traversed the tumor area although the corpus callosum was displaced ventrally. Thus the tumor additionally involved the cingulate gyrus. During operation the neurosurgeon removed the tumor - histologically a grade II astrocytoma - essentially from the superior frontal and cingulate gyri. However in the area of the posterior margin the brain tumor interface was not clearly visible.

Figure 1. *Case 179.* Example of the tracing results in correlated triplanar display. Frontal (1a), axial (1b), and sagittal (1c) view. Sulci labelled: cingulate sulcus (CIS), central sulcus (CS), inferior postcentral sulcus (IPOS), interparietal sulcus (IPS), superior postcentral sulcus (SPOS), subparietal sulcus (SPS), vertical branch of cingulate sulcus (VCMG)

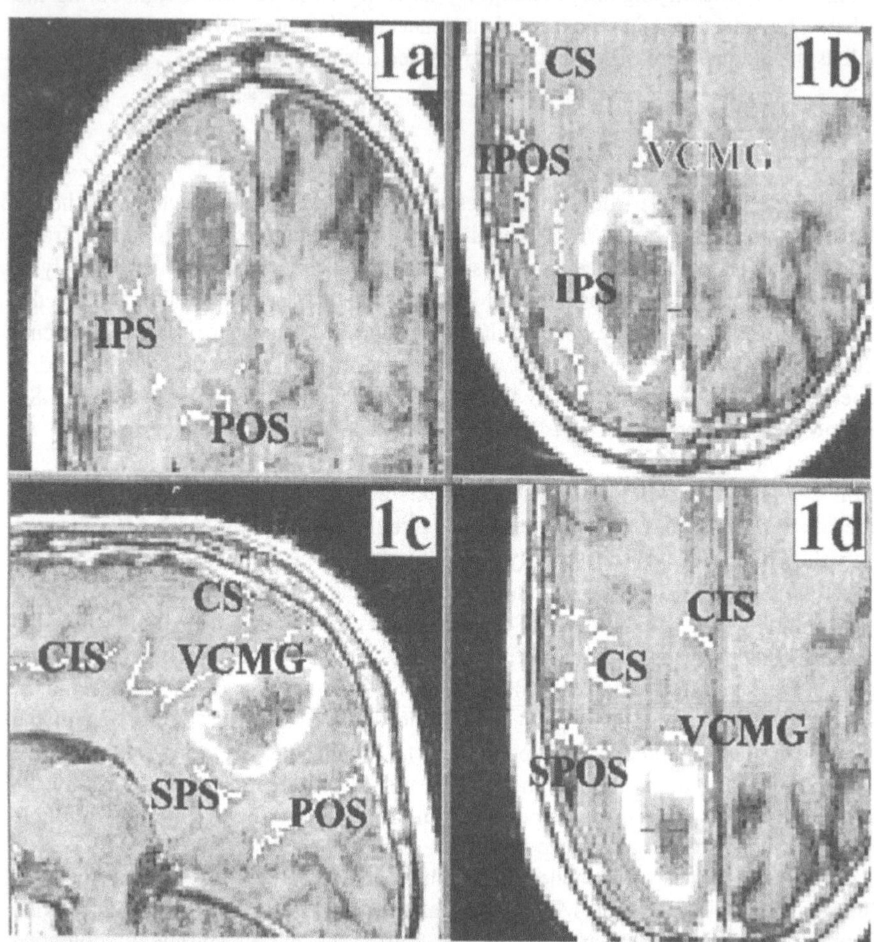

4 Discussion

Interactive definition of the sulcal topography of a tumor in a triplanar correlated display has several advantages. The labelling procedure enables initial definition of segments of a sulcus which can unequivocally be defined in a slice. Using these definitions as starting points 3D continuity detection of the sulcus even in unfavourable section planes is possible. Thus reviewing the data set a definite recognition of the structure in every section plane is possible. Unravelling the cortical landscape the tumor is embedded in enables a specific detailed verbal representation of its topography. This verbal representation complements the surgeon's 'mental image' with detailed information for the minimally invasive neurosurgical approach.

5 References

1. Niemann K, van Nieuwenhofen I, Huetter BO, Thron A, Gilsbach JM, v. Keyserlingk DG: The Sulcus Editor: An interactive tool for atlas generation and surgical planning. Human Brain Mapping Suppl. 1:66, 1995.
2. Niemann K, Spetzger U, Coenen VA, Huetter BO, Kueker W, v. Keyserlingk DG: Anatomically Guided Neuronavigation: First Experience with the SulcusEditor. In: Minimally Invasive Techniques for Neurosurgery, Hellwig D, Bauer BL (eds). Springer, Stuttgart, 1997, 215-221.

CT-basierte 3D-Planung für die dentale Implantologie

W. Stein, S. Haßfeld, J. Brief, I. Bertovic, R. Krempien*, J. Mühling

Mund-, Kiefer- und Gesichtschirurgie
*Radiologiesche Klinik, Abteilung klinische Radiologie
Universität Heidelberg, Im Neuenheimer Feld 400, 69120 Heidelberg
http://www.rzuser.uni-heidelberg.de/~v97
v97@ix.urz.uni-heidelberg.de

Zusammenfassung. Beschrieben wird ein 3D-Planungssytem für die dentale Implantologie. Wir haben einen Algorithmus für die automatisierte Detektion Alveolarnervs entwickelt, der nur eine minimale Benutzerinitialisierung erfordert. Um eine interaktive Implantatpositionierung auf vergleichsweise preiswerter PC-Hardware zu ermöglichen, wurden Methoden zur Hybridvisualisierung entwickelt, die auch ohne große Texturspeicher und spezielle Graphikprozessoren auskommen.

Schlüsselwörter: Dentale Implantologie, Nervdetektion, Hybridvisualisierung

1 Einleitung

Computergestützte Chirurgie (CAS) war bisher ein Anwendungsgebiet für Hochleistungsgraphikrechner und wurde fast ausschließlich an Universitätskliniken für Forschungszwecke eingesetzt. Die schnelle Weiterentwicklung von PC-Hardware, sinkende Preise und neue und sorgfältig überarbeitete Softwarealgorithmen ermöglichen es, CAS einem wesentlich erweiterten Benutzerkreis zugänglich zu machen.

Wir stellen ein interaktives 3D-Planungssystem für die dentale Implantologie vor, welches auf einer Workstation implementiert wurde. Zudem zeigen wir einige der notwendigen Schritte auf, die es ermöglichen, die Abhängigkeit von spezialisierter (teurer) Hardware, große Texturspeicher und Graphikprozessoren, zu überwinden und CAS auf einem PC auch dem niedergelassenen Zahnarzt zugänglich zu machen.

2 Klinischer Hintergrund und Ziel der Arbeit

Das bisherige klinische Protokoll verwendet für die Implantatplanung das Orthopantomogramm (OPG), eine 2D Panorama-Röntgenprojektion. Dies stellt jedoch nicht die notwendigen Tiefeninformationen für komplexe klinische Fälle zur Verfügung, z.B. bei atrophierter Maxilla oder in der Nähe von nervösen oder vaskulären Strukturen.

Bei Implantationen im Seitenzahnbereich des Unterkiefers ist die Kenntnis über die exakte Lage des nervus alveolaris inferior, der innerhalb des Unterkieferknochens vom foramen mandibulae zum foramen mentale verläuft, für den Operationserfolg entscheidend. Um genaue 3D Daten des Patientenkiefers zu erhalten wird deshalb eine Computertomogramm-Untersuchung durchgeführt.

Die Nervdetektion stellt sich als eine anspruchsvolle Aufgabe dar, da Nerven nur einen sehr kleinen Durchmesser besitzen und sich gekrümmt durch den dreidimensionalen Raum winden. Erschwerend kommt hinzu, daß sie von Gewebe mit ähnlichen Abbildungscharakteristika im CT umgeben sind und sich nur ein schwacher Kontrastunterschied zum umgebenden Gewebe ergibt. Der nervus alv. inf. verläuft zusammen mit einer Arterie und Vene innerhalb eines schmalen Kanals mit sehr dünnen und perforierten Seitenwänden. Mit der z.Z. verfügbaren Technologie scheint es nicht möglich zu sein, den Nerv allein zu detektieren, aber das Innere dieses Kanals kann detektiert und so die kritische Struktur angezeigt werden.

Basierend auf Knochenverfügbarkeit, Abstand zu kritischen Strukturen und der geplanten Funktionalität entscheidet der Zahnarzt über die Plazierung des Implantates. Um ein effizientes Werkzeug in der Hand des Zahnarztes darzustellen, muß das System für eine genaue, hochaufgelöste 3D Detektion und Visualisierung von Nerven und Knochen sorgen. Für eine interaktive, intuitive Positionierung des Implantes werden Bildwiederholraten von mehreren Bildern pro Sekunde benötigt.

3 Nervdetektion

Der Benutzer identifiziert durch Mausklick im Schichtbild oder in der 3D-Visualisierung jeweils den gut sichtbaren Eintritts- und Austrittspunkt des Nervs am Knochen und wählt den für den Nerv spezifischen Grauwert aus. Der gesamte Voxeldatensatz wird jetzt wie Graph behandelt, bei dem jedes Voxel als ein Knoten betrachtet wird. Das Fortschreiten von einem Voxel zu einem seiner 26 Nachbarn wird dabei als gewichtete Kante aufgefaßt *(Abb. 1)*. Die Gewichtung der Kanten basiert auf den Grauwerten der Bilddaten:

$$g_i = \text{Grauwert am } Knoten_i$$

$$g_{best} = \text{Grauwert mit der höchsten Wahrscheinlichkeit für Nerv}$$

$$dist_{ij} = \text{Euklidische Distanz zwischen } Knoten_i \text{ und } Knoten_j$$

$$\textbf{Gewicht}_{ij} = (const \cdot |g_i - g_{best}|^n + 1) \cdot dist_{ij}$$

$$= \text{Kosten beim Schritt von } Knoten_i \text{ zu } Knoten_j \text{ entlang } Kante_{ij}$$

Die Leitdrahtsuche im Voxelraum läßt sich jetzt als Suche nach dem günstigsten Pfad zwischen zwei Knoten betrachten. Eine drastische Einschränkung der

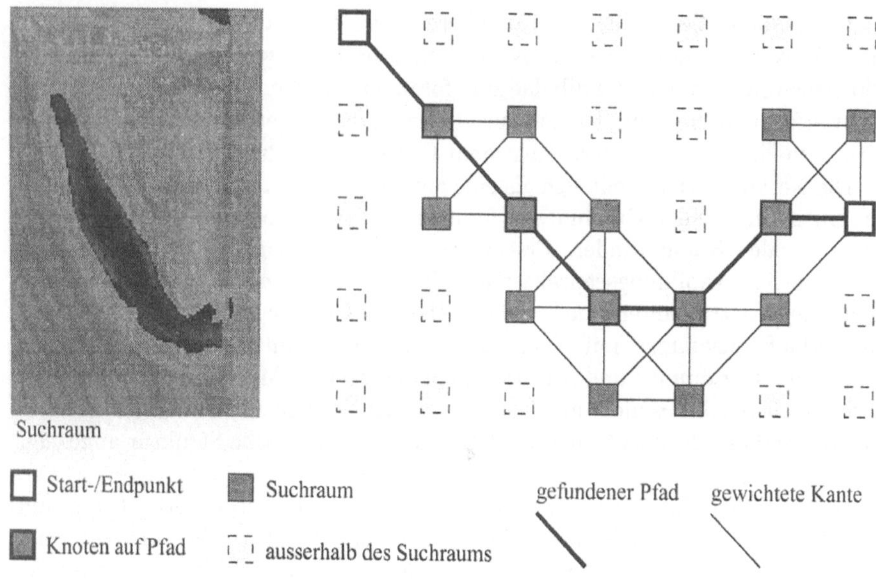

Abb. 1. Graphensuche für Detektion des Leitdrahtes

Suchzeiten um ungefähr 95% wird durch eine vorangehende Folge von Erosionen und Dilatationen erreicht, wodurch der Suchraum auf die Voxel eingeschränkt wird, die von Knochen umschlossen sind oder sich zumindest in der Nähe von Knochen befinden.

Bei der Breitensuche werden vom Startknoten ausgehend die Kosten der gewichteten Kanten beim Fortschreiten zum Nachbarvoxel aufsummiert. Wenn die aktuelle Summe kleiner ist, als der in diesem Knoten gespeicherte Wert, so wird dieser Wert ersetzt und der Knoten wird in der Liste der auf ihre Nachbarn noch zu untersuchenden Knoten vermerkt. Sobald keine Knoten mehr untersucht werden müßen, haben alle Knotenwerte ihr Minimum erreicht und die Breitensuche wird beendet. Ausgehend vom Endknoten kann nun der günstigste Pfad zurück zum Startknoten, an dem sich das globale Minimum befindet, ausgelesen werden.

Hierdurch wird eine fuzzy-Klassifizierung erreicht, die im Vergleich zu einer harten Klassifizierung Artefakten gegenüber robuster ist. Bei einer harten Klassifizierung könnte es passieren, daß ein Artefakt den einzigen Pfad blockiert. Bei der unscharfen Klassifizierung kann der Pfad durch kleine Regionen passieren, die aufgrund ihres Grauwertes eine niedrige Wahrscheinlichkeit zeigen, den Nerv zu enthalten, jedoch durch ihre Nachbarn bedingt, mit hoher Wahrscheinlichkeit den Nerv enthalten.

Der Leitdraht wird im nächsten Schritt zur Initialisierung eines länglichen 3D-Ballons verwendet, um dadurch das gesamte Volumen des Mandibularkanals, in dem der Nerv enthalten ist, auszufüllen [1]. Da der Leitdraht eine sehr gute Initialisierung bietet, kann das Ballonmodell einfach und robust realisiert werden.

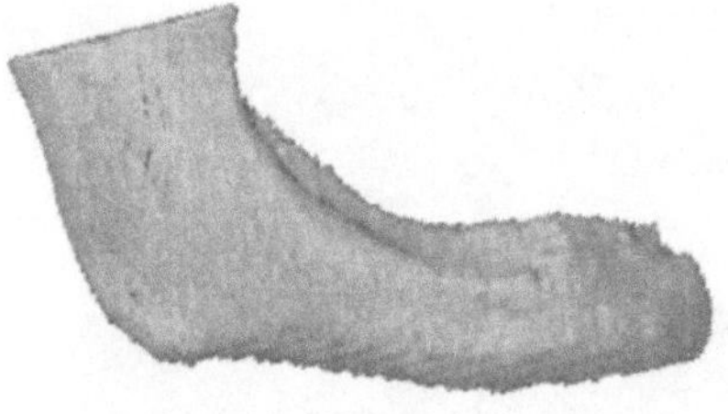

(a) Volumenvisualisierung der CT-Aufnahme

(b) Aufsicht von oben

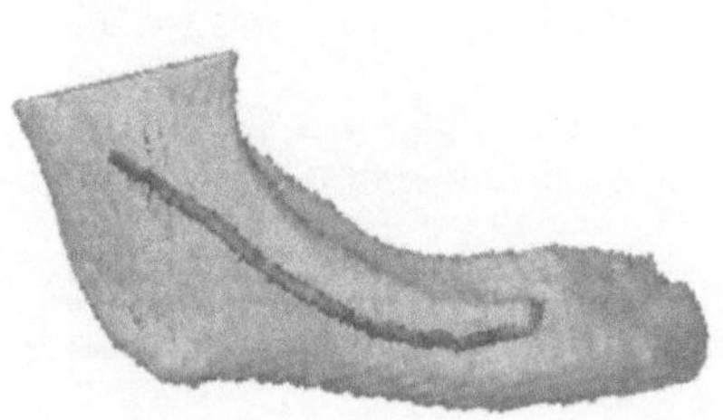

(c) Darstellung des Nervs aus CT-Daten

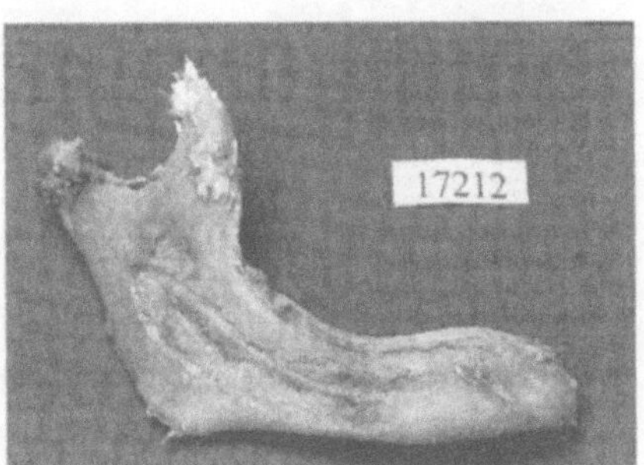

(d) Anatomisches Präparat, Knochen teilweise entfernt

Abb. 2. Validierung durch Vergleich der CT-Volumenvisualisierung mit Photo des anatomischen Präparates

4 Validierung der Segmentierung

Zur Validierung der Nervdetektion wurden fünf anatomische Präparate einer CT-Aufnahme unterzogen und der Datensatz wie oben beschrieben analysiert. Nach der Entfernung von Gewebe und der den Nerv verdeckenden Knochenschichten wurden die Präparate photographiert *(Abb. 2, d)*. In den CT-Aufnahmen wurde der Alveolarnerv detektiert und das Ergebnis mittels Volumenvisualisierung der Voxeldaten sichtbar gemacht *(Abb. 2, a-c)* und mit den Photographien verglichen. Zudem erfolgte auch eine Überprüfung der Segmentierungsergebnisse manuell in den einzelnen CT-Schichten.

Sowohl bei den Präparaten, wie auch bei Patientendaten zeigten 3D-Visualisierung und schichtweise Überprüfung der Segmentierung äußerst realistische und vielversprechende Ergebnisse *(Abb. 2, c und d)*.

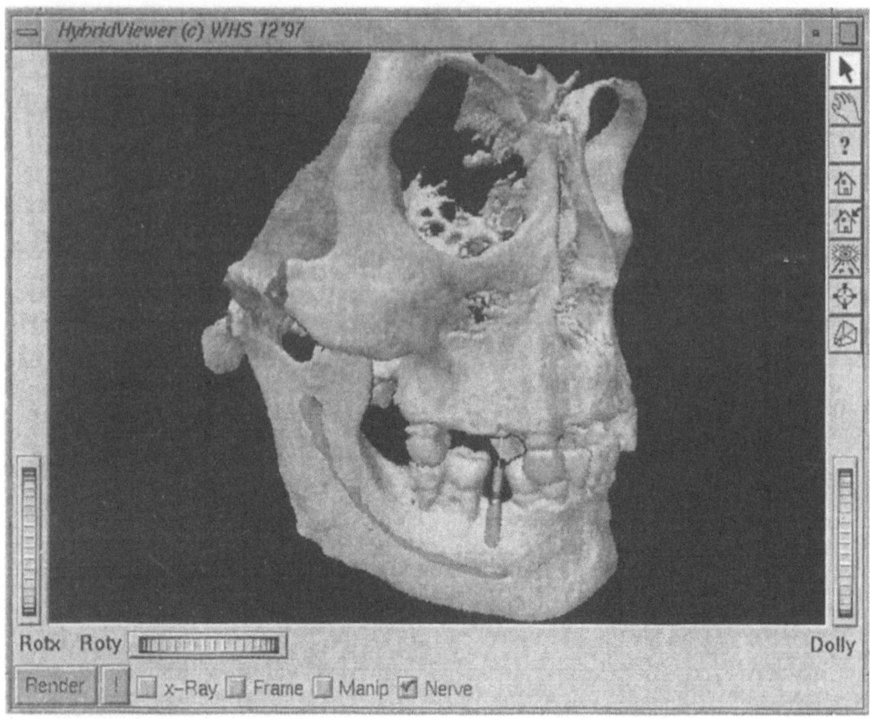

Abb. 3. Hybridvisualisierung: Volumenvisualisierung in Bildreihenfolge und Oberflächenvisualisierung in Objektreihenfolge mittels Tiefenpufferverschmelzung

5 Hybridvisualisierung

Da spezielle Texturspeicher, Geometrie- und Rasterprozessoren für eine schnelle, interaktive Volumenvisualisierung nicht zur Verfügung stehen, haben wir einen neuen Ansatz mit hybriden Techniken gewählt. Das fertige Bild setzt sich aus Projektionen in Bildreihenfolge (raycasting) und Objektreihenfolge aus Volumenobjekten und Oberflächenobjekten zusammen, die in ein quasi-stationäres Hintergrundbild und ein dynamisches Vordergrundbild aufgespaltet werden. Anschließend erfolgt mittels des Tiefenpuffers eine Verschmelzung beider Visualisierungsprozesse [2]. Dies erlaubt auch auf PCs ohne spezielle Graphikhardware eine sehr hohe Bildauflösung und gleichzeitig ein interaktives Positionieren von Zahnarztbohrer oder Implantat *(Abb. 3)*.

Literatur

1. D. Terzopoulos, T. McInerney: Deformable models in medical image analysis: a survey. Medical Image Analysis 1(2), 1996
2. W. Stein, S. Haßfeld: Integrierte Steuerung eines Hybrid-Visualisierers durch Open Inventor. Digitale Bildverarbeitung in der Medizin, Tagungsband zum 5. Freiburger Workshop, 1997.

Region-Oriented Segmentation of Vascular Structures from DSA Images Using Mathematical Morphology and Binary Region Growing

Marco Donizelli

CRS4 (Center for Advanced Studies, Research and Development in Sardinia)
via Nazario Sauro 10, 09123 Cagliari (Italy)
Email: donza@crs4.it

Abstract. In this paper we describe a region-oriented segmentation algorithm suited for the detection and extraction of large blood vessels in angiographic images. The algorithm is based on the mathematical morphology top-hat operator followed by a binary region growing process. The combination of these two steps generates an image containing only the largest vessels regions, allowing a fully automatic segmentation without any manual interaction. We demonstrate the advantages of our approach comparing its results with those of other classical and morphological algorithms.

Keywords: DSA image processing, Blood vessel segmentation, Mathematical morphology

1 Introduction

Blood vessel delineation in angiograms forms an essential step in solving several practical applications, such as diagnosis of vascular diseases (e.g. stenosis or malformations), blood flow studies and three-dimensional reconstruction of vascular structures. Many authors have previously developed segmentation procedures to extract the regions corresponding to the blood vessels in DSA images [1-3]. Unfortunately, the results of these classical segmentation techniques are not optimal: noise, overlapping structures, variations in background, and variations in the structures themselves, all combine to make the use of such well-established techniques inadequate. This paper describes a region-oriented segmentation technique that overcomes all these problems, by employing the mathematical morphology top-hat operator followed by a binary region growing process. The combination of these two steps generates an image containing only the large vessels regions, devoid of shorter capillaries or background noise artefacts, allowing a fully automatic segmentation without any manual interaction. The results of our approach are compared with those of other classical and morphological region segmentation algorithms [1, 3, 4], using the two test images representing two different kinds of vascular structures shown in fig. 1.

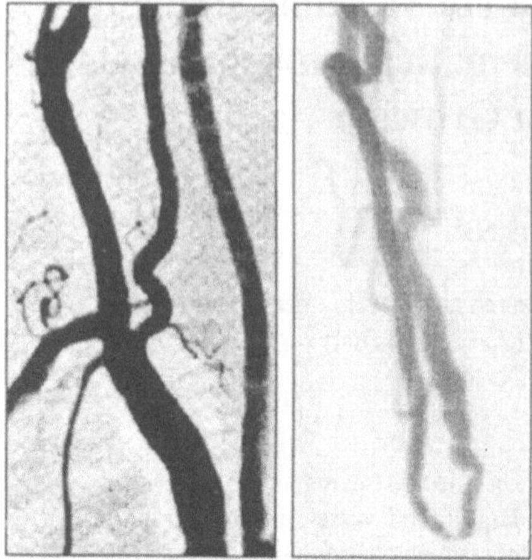

Figure 1. The two angiographic images used to test the algorithms.

2 The Previous Approaches

Three previously developed region oriented segmentation techniques have been implemented in order to compare the results of our algorithm.

The first one is the *multiphase region analysis process* (MRAP) described in [1]. It starts with the creation of a binary image via a regional thresholding algorithm, followed by a second phase that picks out the connected components in the binary output of the first phase and eliminates the spurious noise points. The third region analysis phase then attempts to grow the regions detected by the previous two processes, in order to compensate for the gaps in the larger objects left as a result of the thresholding algorithm. The two leftmost images of fig. 2 and fig. 3 show the results of the application of the MRAP algorithm on the images of fig. 1.

The second technique is the *region splitting* approach based upon *bimodality analysis* (RSBA) developed in [3]. Here, the input image is subdivided successively into smaller and smaller regions according to a bimodality measure and a bimodality threshold. That is, if a region is labelled bimodal, it is subdivided into four subregions, otherwise the grey scale values of the pixels within the region are assigned to the mean of the region, and no further subdivision is made. In our implementation, at the end of the splitting process we interactive threshold the output in order to obtain a binary image. The two central images of fig. 2 and fig. 3 show the results of the application of the RSBA technique on the images of fig. 1.

The third technique is the *morphological-thresholding* (ROSE) algorithm described in [4]. In this approach, a first morphological step produces eight different images by applying eight separate *opening* operations to the input image using eight differently oriented linear structuring elements, and combines these eight images into one containing the maximum pixel values. A second step thresholds the output of the morphological step using a dual feature thresholding. In our implementation, instead of this methodology that doesn't perform well on our images, we simply use an interactive threshold. The two rightmost images of fig. 2 and fig. 3 show the results of the application of the ROSE algorithm on the images of fig. 1

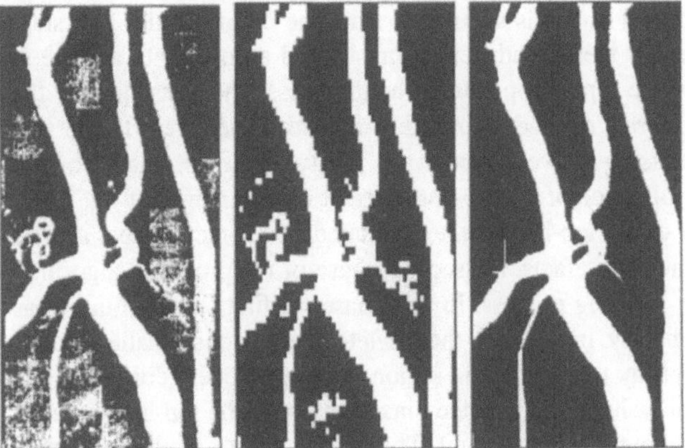

Figure 2. From left to right, respectively the result of the application of the MRAP, RSBA and ROSE techniques on the leftmost image of fig. 1.

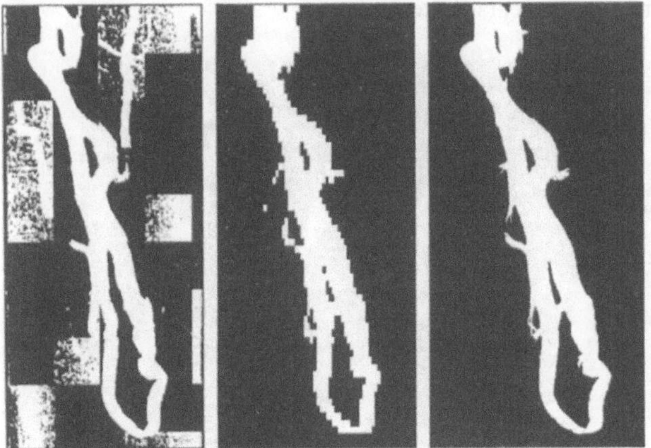

Figure 3. From left to right, respectively the result of the application of the MRAP, RSBA and ROSE techniques on the rightmost image of fig. 1.

3 The Proposed Algorithm

Within an angiographic image, large vessels have well-defined structural properties: continuous, connected line-like structures with slowly changing thickness, orientation and intensity, except for stenosis or other malformations [5]. The idea underlying our approach is to exploit these properties using operators defined in the field of mathematical morphology [6]. In particular, we use the *top-hat* operator described in [7], a morphological filter well-suited to identify and extract line-like patterns of a certain size and contrast, and then optimised to produce a binary image predominantly containing the regions corresponding to the large vessels. The implementation of the top-hat operator involves three steps. First, the morphological *closing* of the original image is obtained using a flat circular structuring element of size r (the width of the top-hat operator. Then, the original image is subtracted from the output of the first step. Finally, the image produced by the second step is thresholded according to a value h, which defines the height of the top-hat operator. The thickness, and consequently the typology, of the outlined vessels depend on r and h, related respectively to the size and to the contrast characterising the vessels regions. The two leftmost images of fig. 4 show the results of the application of the top-hat operator on the images of fig. 1.

Since the binary output of the top-hat operator contains also some residual shorter capillaries or background noise artefacts, the second phase of the proposed algorithm consists in a *binary region growing* process. In this phase we first compute the areas of all the regions of the binary image and then delete the regions smaller than a threshold area value (chosen by the user). The region growing process considers any object point (e.g., those with value of 255) in the binary output of the top-hat operator, and extracts the 8-connected region containing it. Then, if the area (e.g., the number of pixels) of the region is greater then the threshold, the region is outlined in the final image, otherwise it is not. The two rightmost images of fig. 4 show the results of the binary region growing run on the two leftmost images of the same figure, and represent the final result of our region segmentation technique.

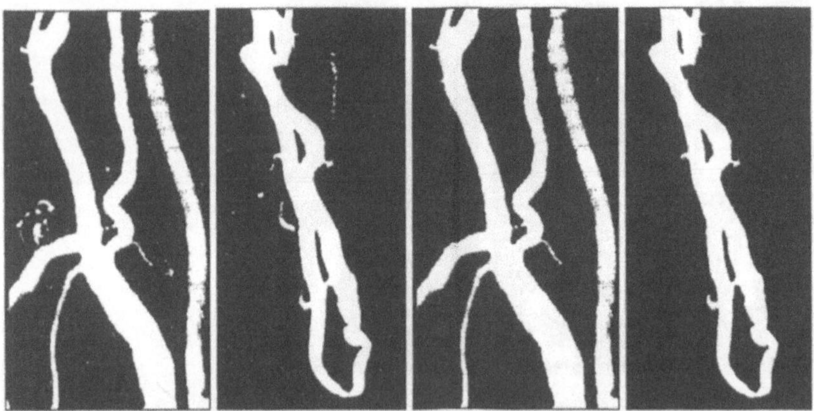

Figure 4. The two leftmost images show the result of the top-hat operator applied on the images of fig. 1, while the two rightmost images represent the final results of the proposed segmentation procedure, after the binary region growing process run on the leftmost ones.

4 Comparison of Segmentation Results

We have compared the results of the four region segmentation techniques considering the number of shorter capillaries or background noise artefacts present in the output images and the shape of the extracted large vessel.

Regarding the first aspect, the worse result is produced by the MRAP technique while both the morphological based operators give optimal outputs because of their capability to exploit not only the pictorial properties of the object to segment, but also their structural characteristics. The structuring element that is used in the morphological operation is constructed so that its shape matches the shape of the objects to be retained. For the ROSE operator, the use of linear structuring elements long enough to fit into the large vessels but not the more tortuous capillaries yields to an image which predominantly includes the large vessels, as happens for the top-hat operator. This operator, however, filters the undesired objects using mostly its height h rather than its width s. Being in fact correlated to the contrast of the region to be segmented, an appropriate high value of h assures that the top-hat operator selectively extracts only the regions characterised by an higher contrast, as the large vessels. This selective distinction carried out by the top-hat operator makes very simple for the binary region growing process to delete the few residual artefacts due to smaller vessels or background variations, and thus to produce the final image containing only the large vessels. We cannot obtain the same optimal result applying the region growing process on the outputs of the MRAP algorithm.

Concerning the shape of the segmented vessels, the RSBA technique gives unsatisfying results due the methodology itself. The output can be improved increasing the value of the bimodality threshold, but this leads to a very time-consuming segmentation process. The MRAP performs better on the first image than on the smoother second one, where the effects of the initial regional thresholding are more evident. The ROSE operator, employing linear non-isotropic structuring elements, leaves some artefacts in the outlined vessels, unlike the top-hat operator, which uses an isotropic structuring element. In addition, the top-hat operator is also superior to the ROSE operator from a computationally point of view, requiring only one closing operations instead of eight openings.

References

1. Stansfield S.: ANGY: a rule-based expert system for automatic segmentation of coronary vessels from digital subtracted angiograms. IEEE Trans. on Pattern Analysis and Machine Intelligence, 8(2):188-199, 1986.
2. Kottke D. P., Sun Y.: Segmentation of coronary arteriograms by iterative ternary classification. IEEE Transactions on Biomedical Engineering, 37(8):778-785, 1990.
3. Kottke D. P., Sun Y.: Region splitting of medical images based upon bimodality analysis. IEEE Engineering Conference In Medicine and Biology, 12(1):154-155, 1990.
4. Thackray B. D., Nelson A. C.: Semi-automatic segmentation of vascular network images using a rotating structuring element (ROSE) with mathematical morphology and dual feature thresholding. IEEE Transactions on Medical Imaging, 12(3):385-392, 1993.
5. Smeets C., Verbeeck G., Suetens P., Oosterlinck A.: A knowledge-based expert system for the delineation of blood vessels on subtraction angiograms. Pattern Recognition Letters, 8(2):113-121, 1988.
6. Maragos P., Schafer R. W.: Morphological systems for multidimensional signal processing. Proceedings of the IEEE, 78(4):690-710, 1990.
7. Zamperoni P.: Metodi dell'elaborazione digitale delle immagini. Masson, Italy, 1990.

An Object-Oriented Client-Server System for Interactive Segmentation of Medical Images Using the Method of Active Contours

Alan L. Scheinine, Marco Donizelli and Marco Pescosolido

CRS4 (Center for Advanced Studies, Research and Development in Sardinia)
via Nazario Sauro 10, 09123 Cagliari (Italy)
Email: donza@crs4.it

Abstract. In this paper we describe the first prototype of a distributed medical imaging system suitable for the visualisation and processing of medical images. The prototype is an object-oriented client-server system that provides a complete framework for the interactive segmentation of blood vessel contours from X-Ray Computed Tomography (CT) or Magnetic Resonance Imaging (MRI) scans, through the method of snakes or active contours. The system has been implemented exploiting the benefits of recent software developments, such as the Java language programming and the CORBA distributed object technology, which simplify the building, the maintenance and the portability of this kind of distributed applications.

Keywords: Distributed medical imaging systems, Distributed computing, Java, CORBA, Active contours

1 Introduction

Beyond the immediate diagnostic value of medical images from X-Ray Computed Tomography (CT), Magnetic Resonance Imaging (MRI) and ultrasound scans, image data can be used for physical analysis and simulation. For example, the reconstruction as a geometric data set of a section of an artery could be used for medical procedural planning and for conducting research in vascular physiophathology through fluid dynamic simulations [1]. This key role played by medical imaging has led to an increasing demand for electronic medical imaging systems (EMISs, [2]) that allow visualisation and processing of medical images. Recently, the growing demand for EMISs has been coupled with a need to access medical images and other diagnostic information remotely across networks, and to integrate and analyse data from various sources. These requirements, together with the development of data interchange standard formats such as DICOM [3], has also led to an increasing demand for *distributed* EMISs [1]. These systems go far beyond the original previsions of the instruments as stand-alone diagnostic workstations, and must have the capabilities to access images across networks, provide powerful image processing tools, as well image retrieval and storage mechanisms, manage various data from various sources, and integrate different software packages. Recent software developments, such as the Java programming language [4] and the CORBA distributed object technology [5], meet the needs underlying these *distributed* EMISs, simplifying their development, maintenance and portability. This paper describes the design and implementation of the first prototype of a *distributed* EMIS suitable for the visualisation and processing of medical images from different modalities. The prototype is an *object-oriented* client-server system that provides a complete framework for the interactive segmentation of CT or MRI scans of carotid artery sections including the first bifurcation, through the method of *snakes or active contours* [6].

2 The System Requirements

In the design of the system prototype, the following requirements have been considered:

- The prototype must provide a complete, usable and efficient graphical user-interface (GUI), with all the controls needed to manage, visualise and process a sequence of images. In particular, the GUI must provide all the tools useful to interact with a snake-based edge detection algorithm and to evaluate the algorithm results (due to the poor definition of medical images and the complexity of anatomical structures a user interaction is essential to guide the segmentation process [7]).
- The prototype GUI must be portable, in order to lead the visualisation and the processing of the images on any platform.
- The prototype GUI must be flexible, in order to permit the implementation of time-consuming segmentation algorithms using the most appropriate fast computer language and, possibly, the execution on special-purpose machines.
- The framework for the communication and the data exchange among the prototype components must be able to work with different languages and platforms.
- The prototype architecture must be scalable, in order to lead the simple addition of new segmentation algorithms or other useful system components without requiring the rewriting of the system.

3 Solution: Java and Distributed Object Technology

The Java programming language [4] and the CORBA distributed object technology [5] have met the requirements underlying the design of the system listed above.

Java is an object-oriented programming language that has sparked over the past two years considerable interest among software developers. Besides the properties that it has in common with other OO languages (modularity, reusability, security), three features supported by Java has been particularly relevant to its choice as the language used to implement the prototype GUI:

- Java is a complete programming environment that provides a complete set of services and packages that support GUI development, graphics and image visualisation and treatment.

- Java is a platform-independent language, so an application written in Java is completely portable and executable on any platform.
- Java has built-in support for multi-threading programming, relevant for an application like a medical imaging system characterised by time-consuming processing algorithms.

In addition to these three properties, Java has also built-in support for TCP/IP based networking and for distributed computing middleware (Java RMI). Even if this feature guarantees the possibility of developing distributed applications within the Java environment, a different technology has been chosen to implement the framework that manages the communication among the system prototype components: the CORBA distributed object technology. CORBA, the Common Object Request Broker Architecture defined by the Object Management Group (OMG), specifies how software objects distributed over a network can work together without regard to client and server operating systems and programming languages. The kernel of the CORBA architecture is the CORBA Object Request Broker (ORB), the middleware that establishes the client-server relationships between objects. Using an ORB, a client object can invoke a method on a server object that can be on the same machine or across the network. The ORB intercepts the call and finds an object that implements the request, passes it the parameters, invokes its method, and returns the result. The client does not have to know the object's location, neither its programming language nor its operating system: the ORB takes care of all these details. An ORB can manage various servers on different hosts, and this guarantees the complete scalability of a CORBA-based distributed system. Since the Java and C++ binding of CORBA are based on the object method invocation, CORBA is completely compatible with object-oriented languages as Java or C++, leading in this way the simple development of distributed application as the proposed medical system.

4 The System Architecture

Figure 1 shows the object-oriented distributed architecture of the system prototype.

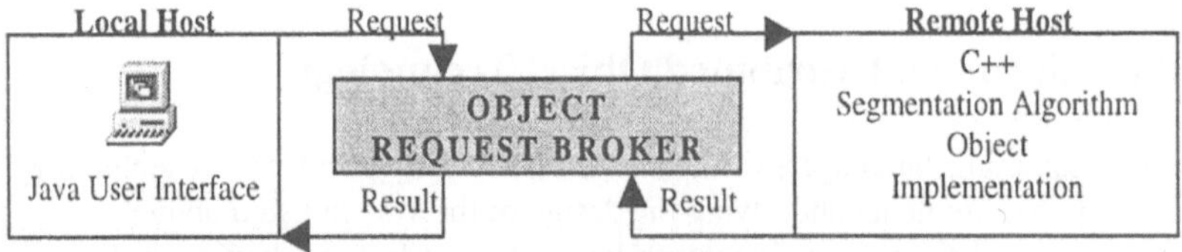

Figure 1. The OO distributed architecture of the system prototype.

The client side of the system is represented by a GUI written in Java. It has been implemented developing a set of packages and classes that represent both the visual components of the interface and the underlying modules needed to perform the retrieving, the treatment and the visualisation of a sequences of images, some simple image processing routines, and the complex remote snake-based segmentation procedures:

- *Package slice*: contains the classes useful to the creation and storage in memory of the images that form the CT or MRI scan sequence to analyse. The image data can be retrieved from graphic files of various formats (GIF, JPEG, BMP, and raw data), or from URL locations, or from a DICOM archive through a TCP/IP socket-based DICOM server.
- *Package sequence*: contains the classes that build the GUI components useful to visualise in various ways the entire sequence of images.
- *Package slicedisplayer*: contains the classes that build the GUI component useful to visualise an image of the sequence, in which it is possible to perform simple image processing operations and to draw interactively overlays on the image.
- *Package image*: contains classes that build the GUI components useful both to display some characteristics of the visualised image (histogram, cross-section, bit-planes) and to modify interactively the appearance of the image (contrast stretching, grey-scale slicing, intensity mappings).
- *Package overlay*: contains all the classes needed to draw, modify and store in memory the overlays on the visualised image.
- *Package segmentation*: contains the classes that build the GUI components by which the user can employ the remote snake-based segmentation algorithms.

A generic snake-based edge detection algorithm written in C++ represents the server side of the system. For now, in the prototype only one algorithm is available, based on the Generalized Active Contour Model theory [8]. It has been implemented using the public-domain C++ library GSNAKE API [9], jointly developed by the Information Technology Institute (ITI), Singapore, and the School of Applied Science, Nanyang Technological University (NTU), Singapore.

The client side and the server side of the system are connected through the functionalities of a CORBA Object Request Broker. The data types and methods useful to perform a complete remote segmentation procedure have been defined following the CORBA specifications and using an Interface Definition Language (IDL), which has been subsequently mapped both to the Java language and to the C++ language. The classes so obtained have been integrated into the Java GUI and the C++ algorithm, and their methods invocation represent the modality by which the client side and the server side of the system interoperate through the ORB during a segmentation session. These methods concern the connection and the disconnection between client and server, the posting of the image data and of the initial contour points from the client to the server for being processed, the posting of the extracted contour from the server to the client for being visualised and postprocessed.

5 Discussion

Fig. 2 shows the contours extracted from three different CT scans of a carotid artery using the functionalities provided by the described system. The good result obtained, together with the good performances of the system and its relative simplicity of implementation, indicate that the technologies such as Java and CORBA are suitable for the design and development of medical imaging systems. The object-oriented feature of the system guarantees its simple maintenance and scalability, while its client-server architecture allows the different components of the system to be implemented using the most appropriate computer language and platform.

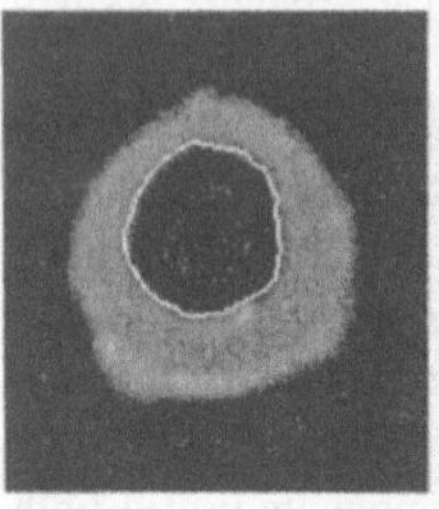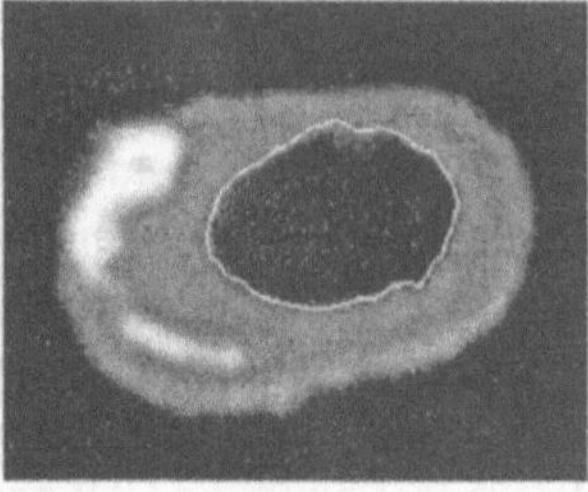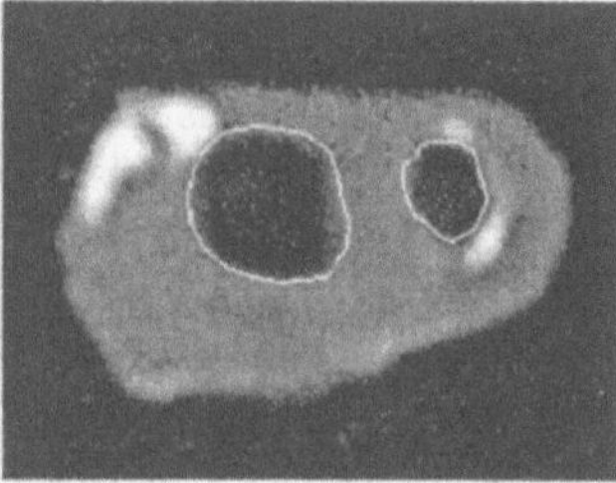

Figure 2. The contours extracted from three different CT scans of a carotid artery using the functionalities provided by the described system.

Acknowledgements

The authors gratefully acknowledge Dr. Massimiliano Tuveri for his important help in providing vascular image sequences.

References

1. D. P. Giddens, C. K. Zarins and S. Glagov: The Role of Fluid Mechanics in Localization and Detection of Atherosclerosis. Journal of Biomechanical Engineering 115:588-594, 1993.
2. P. Jain, S. Widoff, D. C. Schmidt: The Design and Performance of MedJava. USENIX Conf. On Object-Oriented Technologies and Systems, Sante Fe, New Mexico, April 1998.
3. NEMA Standard Publication PS3.X: Digital Imaging and Communications in Medicine Parts 1-10, 1994.
4. M. Campione and K. Walrath: The Java Tutorial - Object-Oriented Programming for the Internet. Addison-Wesley, 1996.
5. R. Ben-Natan: CORBA - A Guide to Common Object Request Broker Architecture. McGraw-Hill, 1995.
6. M. Kass, A. Witkin and D. Terzopoulos: Snakes: Active Contour Models. IEEE Conf. On Computer Vision and Pattern Recognition:259-268, 1987.
7. G. J. Sicewright, J. M. Knapman, W. Dickson and P. J. Elliot: Interactive Image Segmentation Applied to CT and MR Images, Proc. of CAR:328-333, 1993.
8. K. F. Lai and R. T. Chin: Deformable Contours: Modeling and Extraction. IEEE Transactions on Pattern Analysis and Machine Intelligence 17(11):1084-1090, 1995.
9. K. F. Lai, S. Chan, C. W. Ngo, E. L. Ang and K. W. Ong: GSnake API version 1.0: reference manual. 1995.

Automatische 3D-Volumetrie und Visualisierung von Insuffizienzjets in der Echokardiographie

G. Glombitza[1], R. De Simone[2], M. Merdes[1], A. Mayer[1],
H.P. Meinzer[1], C.F. Vahl[2], S. Hagl[2]

[1]Deutsches Krebsforschungszentrum Heidelberg,
Abt. Medizinische und Biologische Informatik
[2]Chir. Universitätsklinik Heidelberg, Abt. Herzchirurgie
Email: G.Glombitza@dkfz-heidelberg.de

Zusammenfassung. Die Bestimmung des Volumens von Insuffizienzjets stellt in der Echokardiographie einen wichtigen Parameter bei der Beurteilung von defekten Herzklappenstrukturen dar. Für diese Volumenbestimmung gibt es in der klinischen Routine keine Standardmethode. Wir stellen zum einen ein Verfahren für die dreidimensionale Volumetrie der Insuffizienzjets vor, das auf der Verteilung der Geschwindigkeiten im Blutfluß beruht, zum anderen wird ein neues Verfahren für die dreidimensionale Rekonstruktion in diesem Gebiet vorgestellt, bei dem die Flußinformation auf die gleiche Weise farblich kodiert werden kann, die auch bei der zweidimensionalen Darstellung während der Aufnahme verwendet wurde.

Schlüsselwörter: Echokardiographie, Insuffizienzjets, Visualisierung, Volumetrie

1 Einleitung

Für die Beurteilung der Schwere von Herzklappenfehlern sind transösophageale (von der Speiseröhre aus aufgenommene), getriggerte dreidimensionale Ultraschallaufnahmen das optimale bildgebende Verfahren[1]. Neben der guten Auflösung der im Backscattermodus abgebildeten kardialen Strukturen bietet diese Methode mit dem ebenfalls möglichen Dopplermeßverfahren eine gute Darstellung der Flußstrukturen [2]. Dadurch ist es möglich, Blutströme, die durch die defekte, geschlossene Klappe fließen, sogenannte Insuffizienzjets, abzubilden.

Ein wichtiger Parameter bei der Beurteilung des Klappendefekts ist das Volumen dieses Insuffizienzjets. Bisher übliche Methoden bestimmen dieses Volumen entweder durch indirekte Messungen oder näherungsweise durch zweidimensionale Messungen. Keine der bisher zur Verfügung stehenden Methoden kann als Referenzmethode bezeichnet werden.

Bei den indirekten Messungen werden durch punktuelle Doppler-Flußmessungen an der Eintritts- und der Austrittsöffnung einer Kavität Volumendifferenzen festgestellt, die dann der Insuffizienz zugeordnet werden.

Die zweidimensionalen Verfahren nähern die Form des Insuffizienzjets durch Messungen in einer 2D-Aufnahme. Sie haben gemeinsam, daß ihnen Symmetrieannahmen bezüglich der Form des Insuffizienzjets zu Grunde liegen, die im Allgemeinen nicht gegeben sind. Hier durch treten insbesondere dann Schwierigkeiten auf, wenn die Jets durch Kontakt mit der Vorhofwand eine eventuell vorhandene Symmetrie verloren haben. Die zwei-dimensionalen Messungen lassen sich daher nur bei freien Jets, die zentral in den Vorhof strömen, einsetzen.

Der drei-dimensionale Ansatz, der in dieser Arbeit verfolgt wird, verspricht, diese Schwierigkeiten zu überwinden und biete außerdem, die Möglichkeit, die Flußstrukturen zu visualisieren [3, 4].

Die bisher kommerziell erhältlichen Auswertungsmöglichkeiten für dreidimensionale Ultraschallaufnahmen boten bei der Visualisierung der Flüße allerdings nur die Möglichkeit der Erzeugung von Grauwertbildern, in denen der Jet nicht von den umgebenden Strukturen isoliert werden konnte. Mit dem hier vorgestellten Visualisierungsverfahren ist es erstmals möglich die bei der Untersuchung verwendete Farbkodierung der Dopplerdaten auf die Visualisierung zu übertragen und damit auch komplexe Flußstrukturen deutlich zu machen.

2 Material

Es wurden 45 Patienten mit einer Insuffizienz der Mitralklappe untersucht. Alle Daten wurden mit dem Echogerät HP Sonos 2500 aufgenommen, das die digitale Speicherung der Bilddaten ermöglicht.

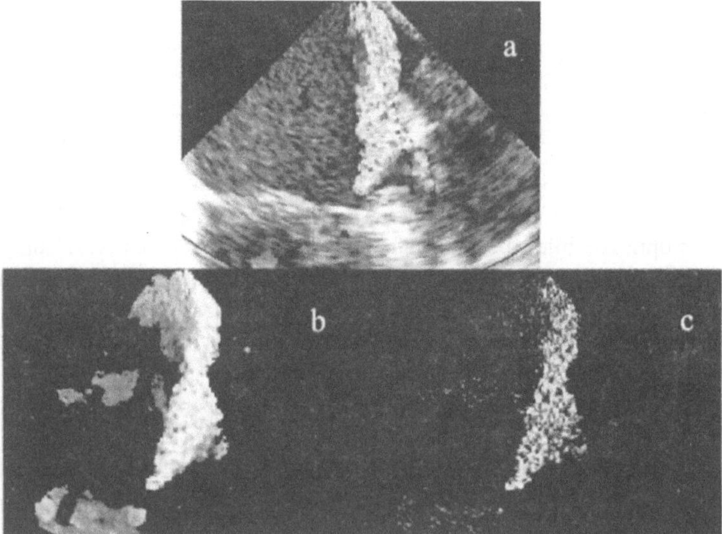

Abb. 1: Gemeinsame Darstellung der Backscatter- und der Doppler-Messung durch Farbkodierung (a). Transformation der Dopplerwerte zu Absolutgeschwindigkeiten (b) und Turbulenzinformation (c).

Hierbei werden die Backscatterdaten von den Dopplerdaten als getrennte Bilder abgelegt und können dementsprechend auch getrennt weiterverarbeitet werden. Beide

Bilder sind mit 8 bit aufgelöst, wobei die Dopplerdaten selbst wiederum Informationen sowohl über die Geschwindigkeit (5 bit) als auch über die Turbulenz (3 bit) enthalten.

Bei den Dopplerdaten wird für Jets mit hohen Geschwindigkeiten ein sogenanntes Aliasing beobachtet: Die Abtastrate des Ultraschallsignals beschränkt die aufnehmbaren Geschwindigkeiten nach oben. Ein Übeschreiten dieses Nyquist-Limits führt zu den Farbumschlägen in der Abb. 1a.

Die Daten werden im Rotationsmodus aufgenommen, liegen also primär in Zylinderkoordinaten vor. Die Daten werden EKG- und Atem-getriggert aufgenommen. Die zeitliche Auflösung des Triggermechanismus hängt bei dem verwendeten Gerät von der Größe des für die Dopplermessung ausgewählten Bereichs ab. Dies kann bei großen Jets zu einer entsprechenden Absenkung der Genauigkeit des Triggermechanismus führen. Auf dieses Problem wird in der Diskussion näher eingegegangen.

3 Segmentierung und Visualisierung des Insuffizienzjets

Trotz des bereits angesprochenen Aliasing-Problems wurde eine Segmentierung des Jets durch Analyse der Verteilung der Dopplerwerte angestrebt. Die Transformation der Dopplerdaten zu Absolutgeschwindigkeiten $|v|$ (siehe Abb. 1b) zeigt trotz der auftretenden Farbumschläge im Originalbild flächendeckend hohe Geschwindigkeiten an und kann damit gut für eine Segmentierung verwendet werden.

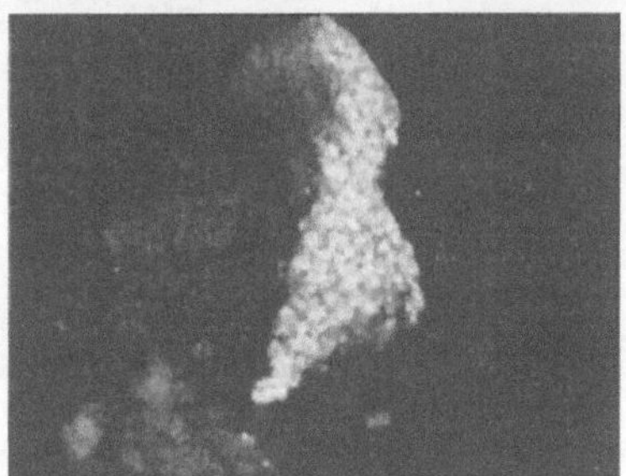

Abb. 2: Die aus Absolutgeschwindigkeit und Turbulenz kombinierte Größe J hebt den Jet deutlich hervor.

Die besten Ergebnisse wurden mit einer gemeinsamen Auswertung der Geschwindigkeits- und der Dopplerwerte erzielt. Wegen der unterschiedlichen Auflösung der beiden Größen wurden dabei verschiedene Gewichtungen für Geschwindigkeit und Turbulenz eingeführt.

$$ J \;=\; \frac{1}{2}\left(|v|^2 \;+\; 8t^2\right) \tag{1} $$

Eine entsprechende Transformation der Daten mit anschließender Glättung ist in Abb. 2 gezeigt. Man kann sehen, daß der Insuffizienzjet deutlich hervorgehoben ist und mit Hilfe eines Schwellwertes segmentiert werden kann. Dieser Schwellwert wird automatisch mit Hilfe einer Histogramm-Methode bestimmt.

3.1 Volumetrie

Die Volumen der segmentierten Jets lassen sich direkt in den durch die Aufnahme gegebenen Zylinderkoordinaten berechnen [5]. In wenigen Fällen treten zeitgleich an verschiedenen Orten des Herzens schnelle Blutströme auf. Da für die Beurteilung einer Klappeninsuffizienz nur die Flüße im Vorhof interessieren, müssen diese isoliert werden. Hier kommen momentan noch interaktive Methoden zum Einsatz.

Die 3D-Volumetrie wurde mit den üblichen Verfahren zur Volumenbestimmung von Insuffizienzjets verglichen. Dabei zeigte sich, daß das neue Verfahren im Vergleich mit zwei-dimensionalen Methoden deutliche Vorteile bei Jets mit Wandkontakt hat, da es ohne Symmetrieannahmen auskommt. Mit der indirekten Flußdifferenzmethode konnten sehr hohe Korrelationen erzielt werden, allerdings mit leichten systematischen Abweichungen.

3.2 Visualisierung des Jets

Neben der volumetrischen Auswertung der Daten bietet die drei-dimensionale Rekonstruktion wichtige Information über die Lage und die Schwere des Klappendefekts.

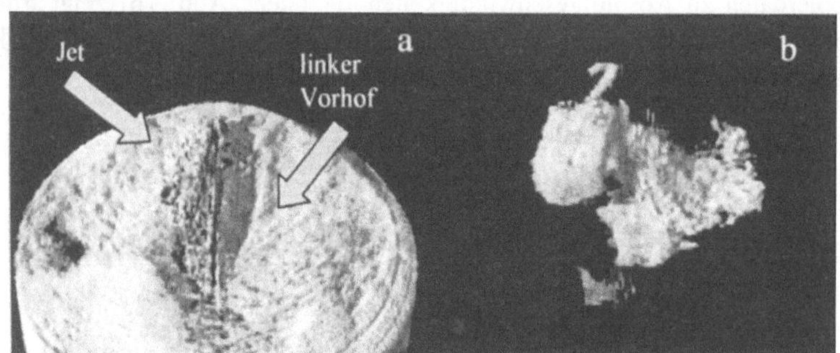

Abb. 3: Beispiele für die Jetvisualisierung. Ein Blick in den linken Vorhof zeigt einen großen Insuffizienzjet mit Wandkontakt (a). Ein anderer Jet ist isoliert von den Myokardstrukturen visualisiert (b). Vorne links ist das Einflußgebiet zu erkennen. (Die Original-Farbbilder und die entsprechenden Animationen können im Internet unter der Adresse http://www.mbi.dkfz-heidelberg.de/mbi/sfb414/us.html eingesehen werden.)

Die Visualisierung der Jets war auf kommerziell verfügbaren Auswertungsgeräten bis jetzt nur in Grauwertbildern möglich. Zusätzlich zur Trennung der Flußstrukturen von den Gewebestrukturen durch Farbvisualisierungen war es unser Ziel, die gleiche Farbkodierung zu verwenden, die auch in der zweidimensionalen Kombination der beiden Messungen verwendet wurde (siehe Abb. 1).

An dem verwendeten Ultraschallgerät wird diese Farbkombination über eine frei auswählbare Farbtabelle erzeugt. Mit dieser sind bis zu 65536 verschiedene Farben möglich. Diese Farbtabelle wurde in den Visualisierungsprozeß integriert. In einer ersten Version wurde ein farbfähiges Volumenvisualisierungsverfahren, das Heidelberg Raytracing Modell (HRM), an die Visualisierung dieser Jets angepaßt. Dieses

Modell war ursprünglich für die Visualisierung von bis zu 16 verschiedenen Objekten implementiert worden und stellte dementsprechend 16 verschiedene Farben zur Verfügung. Diese können mit Hilfe einer statistischen Auswertung der Farbvektoren optimiert werden, die bei dem jeweiligen Bilddatensatz nach Kombination mit der zugeordneten Farbtabelle entstehen.

4 Zusammenfassung und Diskussion

Das vorgestellte Verfahren für die Volumetrie von Insuffizienzjets wurde an dem vorhandenen Datenmaterial getestet. Dabei ergab sich, daß die drei-dimensionale Volumetrie große Vorteile gegenüber den zweidimensionalen Methoden hat und sich auch für Jets mit Wandkontakt hohe Korrelation mit der Messung der Flußdifferenz ergibt.

Die vorgestellte, neue Methode zur Visualisierung dieser Flußstrukturen ist in der Lage, die Jets isoliert von den Wänden der Herzkammern darzustellen und verwendet zudem die dem Echokardiographen vertraute Farbkodierung der Geschwindigkeiten, die auch während der Aufnahme der Daten eingesetzt wird, was die Interpretation der Daten erleichtert.

Momentane Probleme liegen noch in dem Triggermechanismus, mit dem die Bilder aufgenommen werden. Die zeitliche Ungenauigkeit hängt von der Größe des ausgewerteten Dopplerfensters ab und kann auf fast 100ms ansteigen. Diese Bildeigenschaft läßt sich auch gut in den Visualisierungen wiedererkennen. Eine volumetrische Aussage auf der Basis dieser Daten läßt sich aber durch die Mittelung über alle aufgenommenen Schichten begründen. Die hohe Korrelation mit den Ergebnissen der bisher üblichen Verfahren bekräftigen diese Annahme.

Der nächste Schritt in der Insuffizienzvolumetrie ist die Automatisierung der Separation schneller Flüße in unterschiedlichen Kavitäten.

Die Arbeiten wurden im Rahmen des SFB 414 „Rechner- und sensorgestützte Chirurgie" durchgeführt.

5 Literatur

1. Ofili EO, Nanda NC: Three-dimensional and four-dimensional echocardiography. Ultrasound in Medicine and Biology, 20 (8): 669-675, 1994
2. Feigenbaum H: Echocardiography, Lea & Febiger, Philadelphia , 5th Edition 1994
3. Behlolavek M, Foley DA, Gerber ThC, Greenleaf JF, Seward JB: Three-Dimensional Reconstruction of Color Doppler Jets in the Human Heart. Journal of the American Society of Echocardiography, 7(6): 553-560, 1994
4. Delabays A, Sugeng L, Pandian NG, Hsu T-L, Chen C-H, Marx G,Schwartz SL, Cao Q-L: Dynamic Three-Dimensional Echocardiographic Assessment of Intracardiac Blood Flow Jets. The American Journal of Cardiology, 76: 1053-1058, 1995
5. Glombitza G, Makabe MH, Hardt S, Kücherer H, Meinzer H-P: Vergleich verschiedener volumetrischer Methoden für rotationsakquirierte echokardiographische Bilddaten. In Mustererkennung 1996, 18. DAGM-Symposium (Hrsg. Jähne B, Geißler P, Haußecker H, Hering F), Heidelberg, Springer-Verlag 1996, 661-668

Neuronale Netze zur automatischen Auswertung der Zirkulationsstörungen der Netzhaut auf den SLDF-Perfusionsbildern

István Pál[1], Heinrich Niemann[2] und Georg Michelson[1]

[1] Augenklinik mit Poliklinik Universität Erlangen–Nürnberg
Schwabachanlage 6. (Kopfklinikum), D–91054 Erlangen
Email: inpal@cip.informatik.uni-erlangen.de
[2] Lehrstuhl für Mustererkennung (Informatik5)
Universität Erlangen–Nürnberg, Martenstraße 3. D–91058 Erlangen

Zusammenfassung. Scanning Laser Doppler Flowmetrie (SLDF) bietet ein nicht-invasives Verfahren zur Untersuchung der Zirkulationsstörungen des Augenhintergrundes. Die mit SLDF hergestellten Perfusionsbilder können mit neuronalem Netz automatisch ausgewertet werden.

Schlüsselwörter: neuronales Netz, Laser Doppler Flowmetrie

1   Einleitung

Eine Reihe von Augenerkrankungen beruhen auf Zirkulationstörungen in der retinalen und papillären Strombahn. Neuere Untersuchungen ergaben, daß auch bei Glaukom Zirkulationstörungen betrachtet werden können, wobei die rechtzeitige Erkennung wegen der irreversibilen Veränderung und Absterben des Gefäßsystems sehr wichtig ist. Bei diesen Erkrankungen ist es notwendig, die retinalen Kapillaren und Gefäßsysteme zu untersuchen. Dazu eignet sich die "Scanning Laser Doppler Flowmetrie" (SLDF), ein nicht-invasives Verfahren, das die zweidimensionale Darstellung der retinalen Blutzirkulation und die Visualisierung des retinalen Gefäß- und Kapillarsystems ermöglicht [1]. Durch dieses Verfahren wird der Augenhintergrund sequentiell, mehrmalig mit einem Laserstrahl abgetastet. Die Wellenlänge des Laserlichtes verändert sich gemäß optischem Doppler-Effekt und wird von einer empfindlichen Photodiode empfangen. Diese Meßwerte von Photodiode werden mit Fast-Fourier Transformation (FFT) verarbeitet und schließlich normiert. Nach der Normierung können die Perfusionsbilder, d.h. das anatomische (DC), volume, (Vol), flow (Flw) und velocity (Vel) Bilder errechnet werden. Diese Bilder (64 Pixel x 256 Pixel) visualisieren das retinale Gefäß- und Kapillarsystem (siehe Abb. 1). Auf den von SLDF hergestellten Bildern können zwischen dem gesunden und kranken Auge Unterschiede beobachtet werden (verändertes und abgestorbenes Gefäßsystem). Diese Eigenschaften sind auch auf den Bildern eines glaukomatösen Auges zu sehen (siehe Abb. 1). In dieser Arbeit möchten wir die computerunterstüzte Verarbeitung und die automatische Auswertung der SLDF-Bilder mit neuronalen Netzen vorstellen.

Abb. 1. *linke Spalte*: gesundes Auge; *rechte Spalte*: glaukomatöses Auge

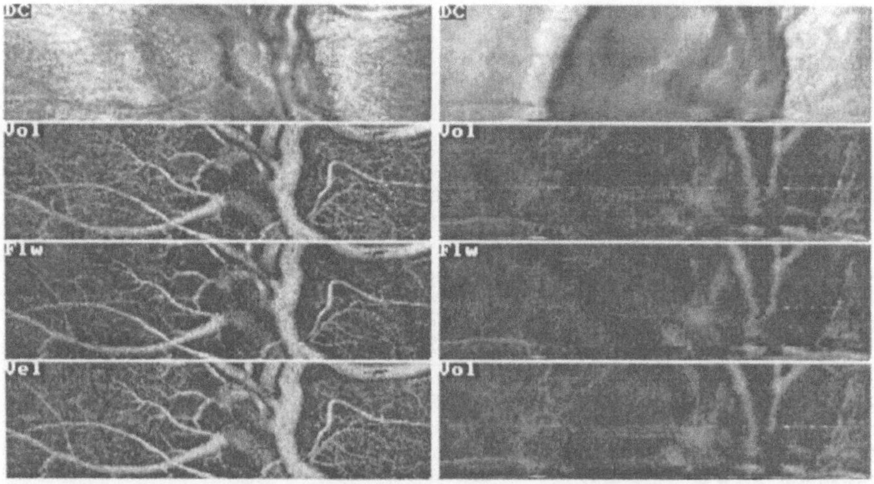

2 Vorverarbeitung und Merkmalgewinnung

2.1 Vorverarbeitung

Zu der Auswertung der Perfusionsbilder werden die volume Bilder verwendet. Es ist notwendig, die unerwünschten Linienstörungen (Sakkaden) auf den Retinabildern zu eliminieren, die bei einer Augenbewegung des Patienten auftreten. Die Sakkaden werden mit einem zeilenlangen Kantenfilter (Abb. 2) mit Hilfe eines Schwellwertverfahrens erkannt und eliminiert (Abb. 3). Das Bild wird danach mit einem Gaussian Filter gefiltert, um die Rauschen zu unterdrücken. Schließlich wird ein nichtlineares Kapillarhervorhebungsverfahren mit einer Binarisierung durchgeführt, wodurch das Kapillarsystem und die dickeren Gefäße besser visualisiert werden [2]. Dieses Bild wird zu der Merkmalextraktion verwendet.

2.2 Die Komponenten des Merkmalvektors

Infolge Makro- oder/und Mikrozirkulationserkrankungen wird das Gefäßsystem des Auges verändert bzw. es stirbt ab. Dadurch wird die Kapillardichte kleiner, nur die größeren Gefäße sind sichtbar, das interkapillare Gebiet vergrößert sich. Diese Eigenschaften der Zirkulationserkrankungen können auch bei dem sehr häufigen Glaukom auf den SLDF-Bildern beobachtet werden (siehe Abb. 1).

$$
\begin{array}{cccc}
-1 & -1 & -1 & -1 \\
2 & 2 & 2 & 2 \\
-1 & -1 & -1 & -1
\end{array}
$$

Abb. 2. Kantenmaske

Abb. 3. Ergebnisse des Kantenfilters

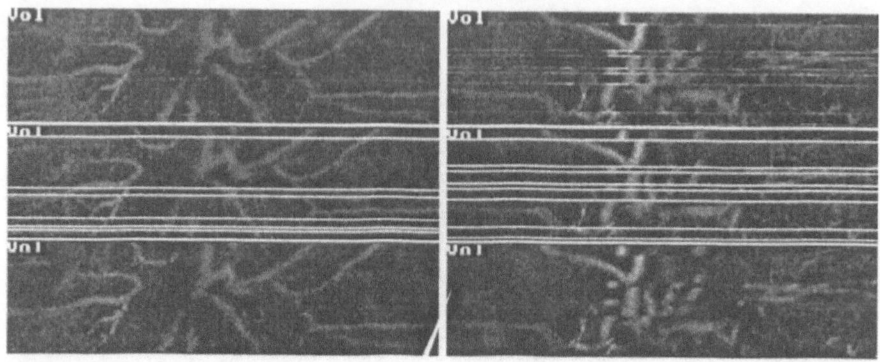

Abb. 4. *obere Reihe*: Skelettbilder de' Binärbilder; *untere Reihe*: Ausfüllung der interkapillaren Bereiche mit Quadraten

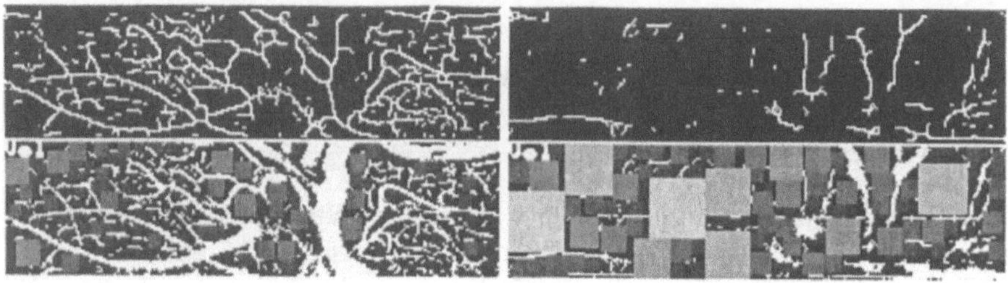

Diesen Eigenschaften entsprechend werden die Komponenten des Merkmalvektors [3] nach folgenden gewählt und errechnet:

1. Die Länge der Gefäße: aus dem Binärbild der Gefäßstruktur kann mit einem Skelettierungsverfahren [4] eine Gefäßmittellinie in der Breite von 1 Pixel hergestellt werden (Abb. 4 oben), diese Gefäßmittellinie gibt die Länge der Gefäße an

2. Die Größe des interkapillaren Gebietes: der Mittelwert der fünf größten Quadrate; das kapillarfreie Gebiet wird hierzu mit möglichst großen disjunkten Quadraten iterativ ausgefüllt [2] (Abb. 4 unten)

3. Die Kapillardichte bzw. die Proportion der Länge der dickeren Gefäße und der Kapillaren: aus dem Skelettbild und aus dem Gefäßbild kann ein Wert bestimmt werden, der mit der Kapillardichte proportional ist

4. Die Anzahl der "Y-Verzweigungen": kann aus dem Skelettbild mit der Hilfe der "connectivity number" der Gefäßmittelpunkte bestimmt werden

Diese vier Merkmale bilden die Komponenten des Merkmalvektors und die Inputs der Klassifikatoren bzw. des neuronalen Netzes.

Abb. 5. 4-Input Netz

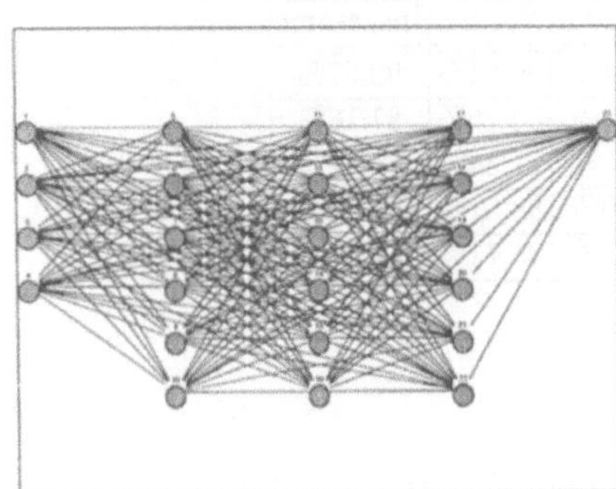

Abb. 6. Polynomklassifikator Netz

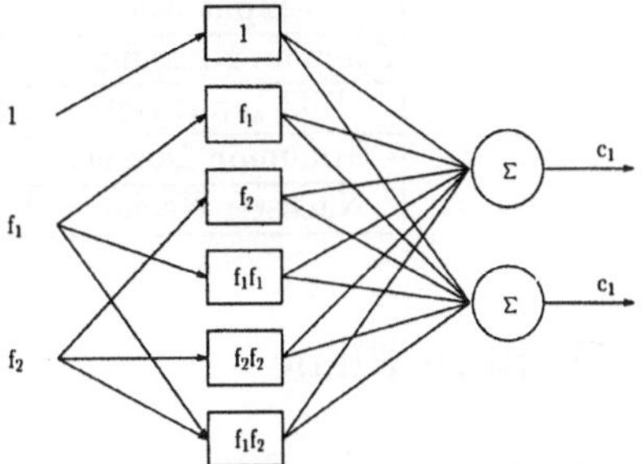

3 Neuronale Netze zur Auswertung der Retinabilder

3.1 "4-Input" Netz

Hier wurde ein feedforward, vollverbundenes (shortcut) Netz mit drei verborgenen Schichten verwendet (Abb. 5). Die Aktivationsfunktion der Neuronen ist die Sigmoide Funktion. Als Lernverfahren wird der Rprop Algorithmus [5, 6] verwendet, der schnellere Konvergenz als Backpropogation oder Quickpropogation Algorithmus zeigte. Das Netz hat vier Inputs den Komponenten des Merkmalvektors (Abschnitt 2.2) entschprechend und ein Output für das Ergebnis "krank" oder "gesund".

3.2 Polynomkassifikator Netz

Der Polynomkassifikator wird mit einem neuronalen Netz realisiert [7]. Die Abbildung 6. stellt ein Netz dar, das einen vollständig quadratischen Polynomklassifikator für zwei Merkmale und für zwei Klassen realisiert. Für vier Merkmale wird der Input des Netzes entsprechend erweitert.

3.3 "Bild-Input" Netz

Bei diesem Netz wird das Bild ohne Vorverarbeitung ausgewertet. Das Bild wird mit einem bilinearen Verkleinerungsverfahren mit einem Verkleinerungsfaktor von $0,25$ (Breite und Höche) verkleinert und zeilenweise als ein 1024-komponentiger Input Vektor verarbeitet [8]. Das Netz besteht wieder aus drei verborgenen Schichten und aus einem Ausgang, wie in dem Abschnitt 3.1.

3.4 Ergebnisse der Auswertungen

Zur Training wurden 38 "gesunde" und 82 "glaukomatöse" und zum Testen 77 "gesunde" 164 "glaukomatöse" Aufnahmen verwendet. Die Ergebnisse der verschiednen Netztypen sind in Tabelle 1 zu sehen. Hier sind zusätzlich die Ergebnisse des minimum Distanz- und des nächsten Nachbar Klassifikators [9] dargestellt.

Tabelle 1. Die Erkennungsergebnisse

Klassifikator	Glaukom	Normal	Insgesamt
4-Input Netz	90.24%	90.91%	90.57%
Polynom Klassifikator	89.61%	84.76%	87.18%
Bild-Input Netz	88.31%	71.34%	79.82%
Minimum Distanz	87.80%	88.31%	88.05%
Nächster Nachbar	82.31%	85.71%	84.01%

4 Weitere Pläne

Zur Verbesserung der Erkennungsrate des "4-Input" Netzes: weitere Merkmale als Input verwenden, die Merkmale der Temporal-, Nasalseite des Auges und des Papillenbereiches getrennt errechnen und verarbeiten, da wegen der Konfokalität des Lasergeretes der Papillenbereich "unscharf" sein kann. Die Anzahl der Training und Tesmuster muß erhöht werden.

Literatur

1. Michelson G, Groh M, Langhans MJ, Schmauß B: Zwiedimensionale Kartierung der retinalen und papillären Mikrozirkulation mittels Scanning Laser Doppler Flowmetrie. Klinische Monatsblätter für Augenheilkunde, Bd. 207, Nr. 3, 1995, S. 180–190.

2. Pál I, Michelson G, Niemann H, Welzenbach J: Erkennung von Mikrozirkulationsstörungen der Netzhaut mittels "Scanning Laser Doppler Flowmetrie". in Bildverarbeitung für Medizin Proceedings des Aachener Workshop, Bd. 1., Verlag der Augustinus Buchh., Aachen, Nov. 1996, S. 89–94.

3. Pál I, Niemann H, Michelson G: Evaluation of retina pictures using "Scanning Laser Doppler Flowmetrie" with neuronal networks. in Magyar Képfeldolgozók és Alakfelismerők Országos Konferenciája, Konferenciakiadvány, Keszthely, Okt. 1997, S. 18–24.

4. Zhou RW, Quek C, Ng GS: A novel single-pass thinning algorithm and an effective set of performance citeria. IEEE Trans. on Pattern Recognition Letters, Bd. 16, 1995, S. 1267–1275.

5. Zell A, et. all: SNNS. User Manual Version 4.1, 1995.

6. Zell A: Simulation Neuronaler Netze. Addison–Wesley (Deutschland) GmbH, Bonn, 1. unv. nachdruck. Ausg., 1996.

7. Sagerer G: Neuronal, Statistisch, Wissenbasiert: Ein Beitrag zur Paradigmendiskussion für die Mustererkennung. Mustererkennung 93, 15. DAGM-Symposium Bielefeld, Informatik aktuell, Springer-Verlag, 1993, S. 158–177.

8. Kulkarni AD: Artificial Neural Networks for Image Understanding. International Tomhomson Publishing, New York, 1994.

9. Niemann H: Klassifikation von Mustern. Springer–Verlag, Berlin, Heidelberg, New York, Tokyo, 1983.

Multimodale Registrierung mit effizienten Lernverfahren für neuronale Netze

Torsten Rohlfing, Jürgen Beier, Oliver Schulte, Norbert Hosten
und Roland Felix

Virchow-Klinikum, Medizinische Fakultät der Humboldt-Universität zu Berlin,
Strahlen- und Poliklinik, Augustenburger Platz 1, 13353 Berlin
Email: torsten@ukrv.de

Zusammenfassung. Ausgangspunkt ist die mathematische Äquivalenz von voxelbasierter Registrierung und dem Training neuronaler Netze als multidimensionales Optimierungsproblem. Die Lernverfahren Quickprop und Rprop wurden implementiert, modifiziert und als Optimierungsverfahren für ein voxelbasiertes Ähnlichkeitsmaß verwendet. Tests mit realen Daten zeigten eine deutliche Überlegenheit beider Verfahren gegenüber einfachem Gradientenabstieg, wobei sich ein Vorteil zugunsten von Rprop andeutete. Der Vergleich mit einem konjugierte-Gradienten-Verfahren ergab keine signifikanten Unterschiede bezüglich Effizienz und Stabilität.

Schlüsselwörter: Voxelbasierte Registrierung, Optimierung, adaptive neuronale Lernverfahren

1 Einleitung

Die Registrierung zweier medizinischer Bilddatensätze (Referenz- und Modelldatensatz) erfordert das Finden einer geometrischen Transformation, welche die Koordinaten des Modells in die der Referenz überführt.

Durch Definition eines Maßes S für die erreichte Qualität der Registrierung und Festlegung der zulässigen Transformationen Ω ergibt sich in natürlicher Weise folgendes Optimierungsproblem: Unter allen Transformationen $\omega \in \Omega$ ist diejenige zu finden, welche angewendet auf den Modelldatensatz bezüglich des (ortsfesten) Referenzdatensatzes die Funktion $S(\omega)$ maximiert.

Dabei ist prinzipiell unerheblich, welche Transformationen (affin, elastisch) zugelassen sind und wie S definiert ist (Kreuzkorrelation, mittleres Abstandsquadrat, gewichtete Varianzen, mutual information).

Analog läßt sich das Lernproblem bei neuronalen Assoziativspeichern (feed forward Netze) als Optimierungsproblem formulieren. Die Optimierungsfunktion ist in diesem Fall der (zu minimierende) Lernfehler des Netzes. Ebenso wie daher gängige Optimierungsverfahren (downhill-Suche, konjugierte Gradienten, simulated annealing etc.) zum Trainieren neuronaler Netze verwendet werden, können umgekehrt effiziente Lernverfahren auch allgemeinere Optimierungsprobleme lösen.

Gefördert von der Deutschen Forschungsgemeinschaft, GRK 331–1/97.

2 Material und Methoden

2.1 Bildakquisition

Für den Vergleich der Optimierungsverfahren wurden dreidimensionale Computer- (CT) und Magnetresonanztomographien (MRT) aus dem Schädelbereich von 7 Tumorpatienten verwendet.

Für die CT-Akquisition wurden folgende Geräte und Einstellungen verwendet: Somatom Plus S (Siemens AG, Erlangen), Spiraltechnik, axiale Schichtung, Schichtabstand 5mm, Schichtauflösung $0,57$–$0,70$mm, Rekonstruktionsmatrix 512×512 Pixel.

Die MRT-Aufnahmen wurden auf einem Magnetom (Siemens AG, Erlangen) mit folgenden Parametern durchgeführt: T1-gewichtete axiale Schichten, Schichtabstand 5–6mm, Pixelgröße $0,90$–$1,17$mm, Matrixgröße 256×256 Pixel.

2.2 Iterative Optimierungsverfahren

Die Registrierung der Datensätze mittels starrer-Körper-Transformation erfolgte durch Maximierung des entropiebasierten Ähnlichkeitsmaßes "mutual information" nach Wells et al. [1]. Aufbauend auf dem kommerziellen Bildverarbeitungssystem AVS/Express (AVS/UNIRAS, Erkrath) wurden eigene Softwarekomponenten implementiert, welche die Optimierungsverfahren Gradientenabstieg, Quickprop, Rprop und konjugierte Gradienten realisieren.

Beginnend mit einer Ausgangsnäherung $\omega^{(0)}$ (initiale Registrierung) wird in einem iterativen Prozeß jeweils aus einer Näherungslösung $\omega^{(i)}$ die nächste Approximation $\omega^{(i+1)}$ durch einen Schritt $\Delta\omega^{(i)}$ berechnet:

$$\omega^{(i+1)} = \omega^{(i)} + \Delta\omega^{(i)}. \tag{1}$$

Gradientenabstieg (GD). Wird $\Delta\omega^{(i)}$ in (1) immer in Richtung des lokalen Gradienten von S gewählt als

$$\Delta\omega^{(i)} = \delta\frac{d}{d\omega}S(\omega^{(i)}), \tag{2}$$

erhält man einen reinen Gradientenabstieg. Ein freier Parameter δ regelt hierbei die Schrittweite. Angewendet auf das Training neuronaler Netze ist dies äquivalent zum Backpropagation-Algorithmus. Rumelhart et al. [2] führen ein *Trägheitsmoment m* ein und modifizieren (2) zu

$$\Delta\omega^{(i)} = \delta\frac{d}{d\omega}S(\omega^{(i)}) + m\Delta\omega^{(i-1)}. \tag{3}$$

Quickprop. Das von Fahlman entwickelte *Quickprop*-Verfahren [3] basiert auf der Annahme, die zu optimierende Funktion verhalte sich in jeder Dimension unabhängig von den anderen Parametern lokal quadratisch. Die mehrdimensionale Verallgemeinerung des Newton-Verfahrens führt für diese Approximation zu

$$\Delta\omega_j^{(i)} = \frac{\frac{\partial}{\partial\omega_j}S(\boldsymbol{\omega}^{(i)})}{\frac{\partial}{\partial\omega_j}S(\boldsymbol{\omega}^{(i)}) - \frac{\partial}{\partial\omega_j}S(\boldsymbol{\omega}^{(i-1)})}\Delta\omega_j^{(i-1)}. \tag{4}$$

In der Praxis wird die Schrittweite auf ein ν-faches des jeweils letzten Schrittes beschränkt, um die numerische Stabilität der Iteration zu gewährleisten. Zusätzlich wird jedem Schritt ein mit ε gewichteter Gradiententerm überlagert.

Resilient Backpropagation (Rprop). Bei dem von Riedmiller und Braun [4] unter dem Namen "resilient backpropagation" vorgestellten Verfahren entfällt die Abhängigkeit der Schrittweite vom Betrag des Gradienten. Lediglich seine Richtung wird für den nächsten Schritt in Betracht gezogen, während die Schrittweite unabhängig vom lokalen Gradienten bestimmt wird:

$$\Delta\omega_j^{(i)} = \begin{cases} -\Delta_j^{(i)} & \text{falls } \frac{\partial}{\partial\omega_j}S(\boldsymbol{\omega}^{(i)}) < 0 \\ +\Delta_j^{(i)} & \text{falls } \frac{\partial}{\partial\omega_j}S(\boldsymbol{\omega}^{(i)}) > 0 \\ 0 & \text{falls } \frac{\partial}{\partial\omega_j}S(\boldsymbol{\omega}^{(i)}) = 0 \end{cases} \tag{5}$$

Nach Komponenten getrennt wird die Schrittweite adaptiv um einen Faktor η^- verringert oder um η^+ vergrößert, wobei gilt $0 < \eta^- < 1 < \eta^+$:

$$\Delta_j^{(i)} = \begin{cases} \eta^+ \cdot \Delta_j^{(i-1)} & \text{falls } \frac{\partial}{\partial\omega_j}S(\boldsymbol{\omega}^{(i-1)})\frac{\partial}{\partial\omega_j}S(\boldsymbol{\omega}^{(i)}) > 0, \\ \eta^- \cdot \Delta_j^{(i-1)} & \text{falls } \frac{\partial}{\partial\omega_j}S(\boldsymbol{\omega}^{(i-1)})\frac{\partial}{\partial\omega_j}S(\boldsymbol{\omega}^{(i)}) < 0, \\ \Delta_j^{(i-1)} & \text{falls } \frac{\partial}{\partial\omega_j}S(\boldsymbol{\omega}^{(i-1)})\frac{\partial}{\partial\omega_j}S(\boldsymbol{\omega}^{(i)}) = 0. \end{cases} \tag{6}$$

Conjugate Gradients (CG). Als Referenz wurde ein klassischer Optimierer nach der Methode der konjugierten Gradienten in der Variante von Polak und Ribiere eingesetzt (vgl. Press et al. [5]).

2.3 Eigene Anpassungen der Algorithmen

Für die spezielle Situation wurden die oben beschriebenen Standardverfahren modifiziert und an die Besonderheiten der Registrierung angepaßt.

Gradientenabstieg. Um die Konvergenz zu verbessern, erfolgte nach einer geeignet gewählten maximalen Anzahl von Verschlechterungen ein erzwungenes Rücksetzen (backtracking) auf die beste bisher gefundene Transformation.

Resilient Backpropagation. Abweichend von (6) erfolgte auch bei $\frac{\partial}{\partial\omega_j}S(\boldsymbol{\omega}^{(i)}) = 0$ ein Verringern der Schrittweite um η^- mit dem Ziel, die Zerstörung von Stabilität einer Variablen durch plötzliche große Schritte zu verhindern.

Conjugate Gradients. Die Optimierung von Translation und Rotation geschah zwar parallel, doch mathematisch unabhängig voneinander, da durch unterschiedliche Basiseinheiten (Millimeter vs. Grad) die partiellen Gradienten nicht kompatibel sind.

Initiale Translation. Alle Optimierungsverfahren wurden sowohl mit als auch ohne eine initiale Translation getestet, durch die vor der eigentlichen Registrierung die Mittelpunkte beider Datensätze zur Deckung gebracht wurden.

3   Ergebnisse

Im Durchschnitt konvergierten sowohl Rprop als auch Quickprop zuverlässiger und schneller als einfacher Gradientenabstieg (vgl. Tab. 1). Das Konvergenzverhalten der konjugierte-Gradienten-Methode war den lokalen Optimierern dabei nur knapp überlegen.

In insgesamt 20/56 Fällen schlug die Registrierung fehl (GD 8/14, Rprop 5/14, Quickprop 6/14, CG 1/14). Initiale Translation des Modelldatensatzes ermöglichte in 7/13 zuvor erfolglosen Fällen das Finden einer akzeptablen Registrierung. In einem Fall (Quickprop bei Patient #2) wurde eine vorher erreichte Lösung mit initialer Translation nicht mehr gefunden.

Initiale Translation beschleunigte die Konvergenz in 16/28 Fällen, in 4/28 Fällen konvergierten die Iterationen ohne sie besser. War die Registrierung sowohl mit als auch ohne initiale Translation erfolgreich (14/28 Fälle), wurde die Qualität der Registrierung in 7/14 Fällen durch die initiale Translation verbessert (Tab. 2).

4   Diskussion

Die insgesamt große Zahl nicht gefundener Registrierungen erklärt sich durch die teilweise stark unterschiedlichen Bildausschnitte der einzelnen Modalitäten. Daran vermag die verwendete initiale Registrierung kaum etwas zu ändern.

Optimierer	Patient						
	1	2	3	4	5	6	7
GD	–/–	–/–	30/20	–/–	23/19	20/21	–/–
Rprop	–/–	16/14	9/11	–/8	–/11	10/8	–/6
Quickprop	–/–	18/–	14/11	–/10	–/12	11/9	–/8
CG[†]	–/11	5/5	3/3	7/2	14/6	5/1	6/7

Tabelle 1. Iterationen bis zur Konvergenz ohne (erster Wert) und mit initialer Translation (zweiter Wert). Ist kein Eintrag vorhanden, lieferte die jeweilige Iteration kein brauchbares Ergebnis. [†]Die Anzahl der Iterationen beim konjugierte-Gradienten-Verfahren ist nicht mit den übrigen Angaben vergleichbar, da pro Iteration eine projizierte Optimierung erforderlich ist.

Optimierer	Patient						
	1	2	3	4	5	6	7
GD	-/-	-/-	0.93/0.94	-/-	0.88/0.89	0.88/0.89	-/-
Rprop	-/-	0.98/0.96	0.85/0.86	-/1.03	-/0.88	0.83/0.87	-/0.95
Quickprop	-/-	0.98/-	0.87/0.87	-/1.06	-/0.88	0.86/0.88	-/0.93
CG	-/0.76	0.99/0.99	0.85/0.85	1.05/1.05	0.86/0.88	0.85/0.85	0.93/0.93

Tabelle 2. Erreichte Registrierungsqualität entsprechend Ähnlichkeitsmaß "mutual information" (Wertebereich $\mathbb{R}^+$, höhere Werte zeigen bessere Qualität an) nach Wells et al. [1]. Der jeweils zweite Wert wurde mit initialer Translation berechnet.

Hiervon abgesehen zeigten die durchgeführten Tests, daß sowohl Rprop als auch Quickprop dem Gradientenabstieg überlegen sind und dem konjugierte-Gradienten-Verfahren hinsichtlich Effizienz und Stabilität kaum nachstehen. Dabei deutete sich eine leichte Überlegenheit von Rprop gegenüber Quickprop an, was auch Trainings-Benchmarks für neuronale Netze belegen [4].

Daß allerdings die Optimierung eines Ähnlichkeitsmaßes nicht notwendigerweise identisch mit dem Auffinden einer geeigneten Registrierungstransformation ist, zeigen insbesondere die Resultate für Patient #6 mit initialer Translation. Das vom Gradientenabstieg erreichte Ergebnis lag über dem der anderen Verfahren, obwohl nach visueller Beurteilung den von letzteren gelieferten Transformationen eindeutig der Vorzug zu geben wäre.

Insofern ist der Einwand berechtigt, ein abstraktes Ähnlichkeitsmaß (Tab. 2) sei kein geeignetes Kriterium für den Vergleich von Registrierungsverfahren. Dem ist zu entgegnen, daß das Fehlen eines globalen Maximums bei der korrekten Transformation ein Mangel des Ähnlichkeitsmaßes und nicht etwa des Optimierungsverfahrens ist. Dessen Leistungsfähigkeit kann daher durchaus anhand der angegebenen Daten bewertet werden, weswegen auf einen Vergleich mit manuell oder mittels Landmarken gefundenen Registrierungen verzichtet wurde.

Literatur

1. Wells WM, Viola P, Atsumi H, Nakajima S, Kikinis R: Multi-Modal Volume Registration by Maximization of Mutual Information. In: *Medical Image Analysis*, 1(1), 1996
2. Rumelhart DE, Hinton GE, Williams RJ: Learning internal representations by error propagation. In: *Parallel Distributed Processing: Explorations in the Microstructure of Cognition*, 1:318–362. MIT Press, Cambridge, MA, 1986
3. Fahlman SE: An Empirical Study of Learning Speed in Back-Propagation Networks. Technical Report CMU-CS-88-162, School of Computer Science, Carnegie Mellon University, Pittsburgh, PA, 1988
4. Riedmiller M, Braun H: A direct adaptive method for faster backpropagation algorithm learning: The RPROP algorithm. In: *Proc. of IEEE Int. Conf. on Neural Networks (ICNN)*, 586–591, San Francisco, 1993
5. Press WH, Teukolsky SA, Vetterling WT, Flannery BP: *Numerical Recipes in C: The Art of Scientific Computing.* Cambridge University Press, 1988

Automatische Objekterkennung in 3D-Echokardiographiesequenzen auf Basis aktiver Oberflächenmodelle und modellgekoppelter Merkmalsextraktion

M. Schreckenberg, G. von Dziembowski, O. Ziermann, D. Meyer-Ebrecht

Lehrstuhl für Meßtechnik
Rheinisch-Westfälische Technische Hochschule (RWTH), 52057 Aachen
Email: Schreckenberg@lfm.rwth-aachen.de

Zusammenfassung. Die in der kardiologischen Routine anfallende Menge echokardiographischer Aufnahmen kann mit manuellen Methoden nicht mehr quantitativ ausgewertet werden. Wir stellen daher einen auf aktiven Oberflächen basierenden Ansatz vor, der ein automatisches Konturieren von TEE Echokardiographiesequenzen erlaubt. Im Gegensatz zu bestehenden Ansätzen erfolgt dabei die Extraktion von lokalen Bildmerkmalen nicht in einem Vorverarbeitungsschritt, sondern iterativ mit einem an das globale Modell angekoppelten anisotropen Extraktor.

Schlüsselwörter: 3D Echokardiographie, aktive Oberflächen, Automatische Konturfindung

1 Einleitung

Für zahlreiche Fragestellungen in der Kardiologie ist die Kenntnis von Lage bzw. zeitlichem Verhalten anatomischer Oberflächen eine wesentliche Grundlage der Diagnose (Herzklappendefekte, Septumdefekte, Beurteilung des Ausflußtraktes, Analyse der regionalen Herzwandbewegung). Als Rohinformation stehen dafür überwiegend 2D- und 3D-Echokardiographiesequenzen zur Verfügung, da Ultraschallverfahren eine hervorragende zeitliche Auflösung bei moderatem apparativen Aufwand liefern.

Eine rein visuelle Begutachtung dieser Daten ermöglicht dabei vor allem qualitative Aussagen, während die Ableitung quantitativer Parameter im allgemeinen noch manuelle Konturierung/Segmentierung voraussetzt. Bei 3D-Daten wird dabei schichtweise vorgegangen, wodurch der räumliche Zusammenhang verloren geht. Zudem beeinträchtigt die hohe Variabilität bei der Handsegmentierung sowohl Objektivierbarkeit als auch Reproduzierbarkeit der gewonnenen Parameter. Die vollständige manuelle Auswertung der bei modernen Systemen verfügbaren Datenmenge (1600 - 6000 Einzelbilder pro 3D-Sequenz) ist darüber hinaus routinemäßig nicht mehr durchführbar.

In diesem Beitrag stellen wir daher einen Ansatz zur automatischen Oberflächendetektion vor. Aufgrund der spezifischen Probleme bei echographischen Aufnahmeverfahren (Speckles, Abschattung, tangentiale Anschallung, Mehrfachechos) kann man sich dabei nicht allein auf lokale Bildmerkmale stützen. Ein automatisches Verfahren muß vielmehr den komplexen Erkennungsprozeß des menschlichen Betrachters zumindest ansatzweise nachvollziehen und auf eine hinreichende Modellierung von Abbildungssystem und abgebildetem Objekt aufbauen. Das hier eingesetzte Verfahren der aktiven Oberflächen auf Basis einer FEM Approximation schafft hierzu die notwendigen Voraussetzungen. Insbesondere ist bei dem von uns vorgestellten Ansatz bereits die Extraktion lokaler Bildmerkmale an das globale Objektmodell gekoppelt. Dies ermöglicht den Einsatz spezialisierter anisotroper Merkmalsextraktoren, was Qualität und Ortsauflösung der Grenzflächenerkennung erheblich verbessert.

2 Das aktive Oberflächenmodell

Bei der Erkennung anatomischer Objektoberflächen kann a-priori-Wissen sowohl über deren Verlauf und Beschaffenheit als auch über die Eigenschaften des bildgebenden Systems eingesetzt werden. Wir machen folgende Annahmen:
Die Objektoberfläche ist glatt und zusammenhängend (mind. C_1-stetig). Die Bildsignale sind durch Specklerauschen und Aufnahmefehler (lokale Signalausfälle, Abschattungen, Mehrfachechos) beeinträchtigt. Die Grauwerte können näherungsweise als Rayleigh-verteilt angenommen werden.

Daraus ergeben sich notwendige Eigenschaften des Oberflächenmodells, das Bereiche mit lokalen Störungen überbrücken und statistische Fluktuationen der Objektkante approximierend unterdrücken muß.

Das hier realisierte aktive Oberflächenmodell bildet das physikalische Verhalten einer sowohl elastischen als auch biegesteifen Schale nach, die unter Einwirkung der Bildinformation so verformt wird, daß sie die gesuchte Objektoberfläche approximiert. Derartige Ansätze sind bereits mit Erfolg auf MR und CT Daten angewendet worden [1, 2].
Die Lage des Oberflächenmodells ist über die Abbildung X vollständig definiert.

$$X:\Omega=[0,1]\times[0,1]\to\Re \quad X(u,v)=(x(u,v),y(u,v),z(u,v)) \tag{1}$$

Physikalisch betrachtet nimmt das Oberflächenmodell den Verformungszustand an, bei dem äußere und innere Energie im Gleichgewicht stehen. Die innere Energie ergibt sich dabei aus den Materialeigenschaften und den vorherrschenden Dehnungen, Biegungen und Scherungen, die äußere Energie resultiert aus den angreifenden Kräften, die diese Verformungen verursachen.

$$E_{ext}(X)=\iint \vec{f}(u,v)dudv \tag{2}$$

$$E_{int}(X)=\iint \alpha_{01}\left|\frac{\partial X}{\partial u}\right|^2+\alpha_{10}\left|\frac{\partial X}{\partial v}\right|^2+\beta_{02}\left|\frac{\partial^2 X}{\partial u}\right|+\beta_{11}\left|\frac{\partial^2 X}{\partial u\partial v}\right|+\beta_{20}\left|\frac{\partial^2 X}{\partial v}\right|$$

Das Schalenmodell wurde mit der Methode der Finiten Elemente approximiert. Dabei wurden Hermite C_1 Dreieckselemente mit 3 Knoten und 6 Freiheitsgraden pro Knoten und Raumrichtung verwendet [1, 4].

3 Merkmalsextraktion

Für die Berechnung der Modellverformung ist es notwendig, die Bildinformationen in geeignete äußere Energieterme zu überführen. Bisherige Ansätze bereiten die Bilddaten dazu in einem Vorverarbeitungsschritt auf [1, 2, 3]. Die lokalen Merkmalsextraktoren müssen dabei ohne globale Kontextinformation auskommen. Gerade bei Echographieaufnahmen bereitet dies Schwierigkeiten, da die lokale Information alleine nicht hinreichend zuverlässig ist. Bei unserem Ansatz wird der Merkmalsextraktor an die Modelloberfläche angekoppelt, die eine stetig genauer werdende Approximation der gesuchten Objektoberfläche darstellt. Damit ist eine Schätzung von lokaler Position und Orientierung der gesuchten Oberfläche möglich, was wir durch Verwendung von entsprechenden anisotropen Merkmalsextraktoren ausnutzen.

3.1 Ankopplung und Realisierung

Der hier realisierte Merkmalsextraktor vergleicht die statistischen Eigenschaften in zwei benachbarten quaderförmigen Voxelgruppen A und B. Die Trennfläche zwischen den Quadern wird jeweils parallel zur Modelloberfläche ausgerichtet. Die gesamte Anordnung wird dann innerhalb eines Suchradius in Normalenrichtung bewegt (Abb.1). Die statistischen Merkmale werden für die Gruppen getrennt in Vektoren eingetragen. Wenn deren Differenz ein lokales Maximum erreicht, wird die gegenwärtige Position S_l der Trennfläche als wahrscheinlichste Position für die gesuchte Objektfläche angenommen. Der Betrag der Vektordifferenz dient dabei als Maß für die Wahrscheinlichkeit, beziehungsweise Güte.

Durch die Ausrichtung der Trennfläche ist es möglich, auch schwach ausgeprägte Objektgrenzen in unmittelbarer Nachbarschaft starker lokaler Störungen zu detektieren.

Ausgehend von einer Rayleighverteilung werden derzeit Mittelwert und Varianz der Amplitudenverteilung als statistische Maße verwendet. Vielversprechend sind jedoch auch Ansätze mit Rangordnungsoperatoren.

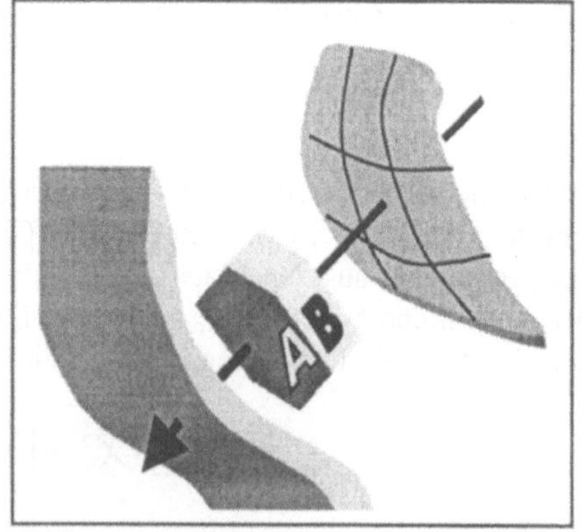

Abb.1 Ankopplung des anisotropen Merkmalsextraktors

3.2 Berechnung der äußeren Kräfte

Die Richtung der zu ermittelnden Kraftvektoren wird auf die Normalenrichtung der Modelloberfläche gesetzt (Blendenproblem). Ihre Orientierung ergibt sich jeweils aus dem Vorzeichen der Differenz S_1-S_0, d.h. die Kräfte sind stets von Modell- zu Objektoberfläche orientiert. Die Beträge werden über ein Abstandsgesetz festgelegt, das dem Gravitationsfeld einer Masseverteilung mit Schwerpunkt S_1 nachempfunden ist.

4 Resultate

Für die Detektion der Innenfläche des linken menschlichen Ventrikels wurden zeitlich aufeinanderfolgende 2D-Einzelbilder einer 3D-TEE Sequenz hintereinander zu einem Datenvolumen angeordnet. Da die Sequenz aus technischen Gründen keinen kompletten Herzzyklus umfaßt, wurde das Ende der Sequenz mit Leerbildern aufgefüllt (Abb.2). Zur Vermeidung von Randeffekten ist es notwendig, die Sequenz in beide Richtungen der Zeitachse periodisch fortzusetzen. Das Oberflächenmodell wurde mit einem in Richtung der Zeitachse projizierten Ellipsenabschnitt initialisiert (Abb.3, Abb.5), der automatisch auf den dunklen Bereich des Cavums zentriert wird.

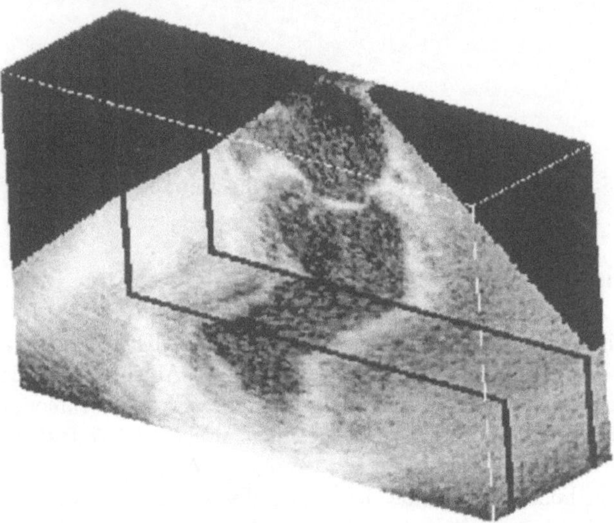

Abb.2 2D-Einzelbilder hintereinander zu einem Datenvolumen angeordnet

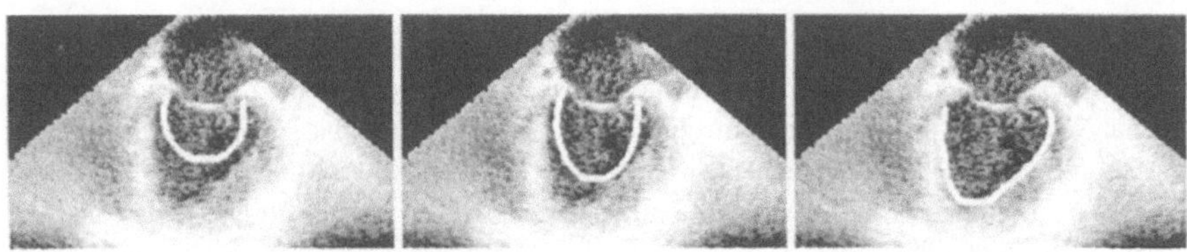

Abb.3 Iterative Oberflächenverformung in einer Herzphase

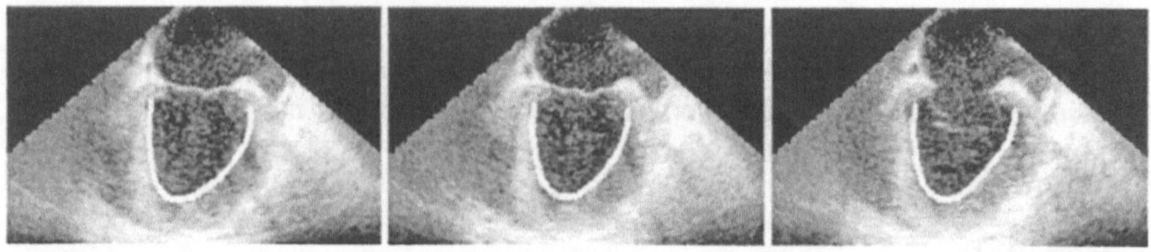

Abb.4 Lage der Oberfläche zu unterschiedlichen Zeitpunkten innerhalb eines Herzzyklus

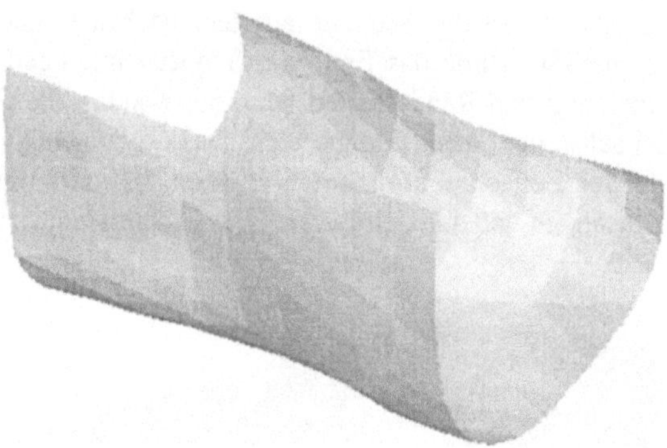

Abb.5 Angepasste FEM-Modelloberfläche für einen kompletten Herzzyklus

5 Diskussion

Das vorgestellte Verfahren erlaubt eine stabile Detektion der inneren Wandfläche des linken Ventrikels in 2D-Echokardiographiesequenzen (Abb.4). Das Verfahren eignet sich - bei entsprechend geänderter Initialisierung des Oberflächenmodells - auch für die Oberflächendetektion in statischen und dynamischen 3D-Aufnahmen. Der nicht unerhebliche Rechenaufwand bei der FEM Approximation legt es allerdings nahe, bei Aufnahmen mit hoher Bildqualität die Verwendbarkeit alternativer Oberflächenmodelle, z.B. auf Basis approximierender B-Splineflächen, zu untersuchen.

6 Literatur

1. McInerney T,. Terzopoulos D: A dynamic finite element surface model for segmentation and tracking in multidimensional medical images with application to cardiac 4D image analysis, Computerized Medical Imaging and Graphics, Vol. 19, No. 1, pp.69-83,1995
2. Cohen L, Cohen I: Finite-Elemente Methodes for Active Contour Models andBalloons for 2-D and 3-D Images, CERAMADE Centre de Recherche de Mathématiques de la Décision, No. 9124, Nov. 1991
3. Ronfard R: Region-Based Strategies for Active Contour Models, International Journal of Computer Vision,13:2, 229-251 (1994)
4. Dhatt G:Finite Elemente Methode Displayed, Wiley & Sons 1985, ISBN 047190110 5

Benutzergeführte Auswertung von Bildsequenzen mikroskopierter Mikrozirkulationsgebiete
Anwendungen der Digital Video Workbench

Jens Hektor[1], Florian Zschocke[1], Thomas Förster[1],
Reinhard Grebe[2], Holger Schmid-Schönbein[1]

[1]Inst. f. Physiologie, RWTH, Pauwelsstr. 30, D-52057 Aachen, Germany
[2]Département Génie Biologique, UTC, F-60205 Compiègne, France

Zusammenfassung. Rheoskopie ist eine Methode, Blutzellen unter wohldefinierten fluiddynamischen Bedingungen studieren zu können. Bei der seit kurzem verfügbaren Invivo-Rheoskopie werden Blutzellen auf ihren Bahnen durch bestimmte Mikrozirkulationspräparate (Mesenterien) mit Hilfe eines computergesteuerten Mikroskops verfolgt. Diese Verfolgungsfahrten werden mittels einer CCD auf Videoband aufgezeichnet und können später offline mit Hilfe einer geeigneten Software ausgewertet werden.

In diesem Beitrag wird eine Methode zur benutzergeführten Auswertung solcher Bildsequenzen vorgestellt. Nach Bewegungskorrektur der Einzelbilder der Aufzeichnung werden anschließend mit einer Kombination aus einem einfachen Subtraktionsverfahren und einem modifizierten Isoseg-Algorithmus die Lage der Blutzellen in den Einzelbildern bestimmt und daraus relevante Parameter wie Geschwindigkeit, Lage und Orientierung im Gefäß sowie Verformung der Zellen bestimmt. Mit dieser Methode läßt sich das unterschiedliche Verhalten normaler und gehärteter Zellen miteinander vergleichen und quantifizieren.

Schlüsselwörter: Mikrozirkulation, Rheoskopie, Segmentierung, Digitalisierung

1 Einleitung

Aufgabe der Mikrozirkulation ist es, die Vitalität und Funktionalität eines Gewebes sicherzustellen. Dazu muß sie den An- bzw. Abtransport von O_2 und CO_2 gewährleisten, das Gewebe ausreichend mit Nährstoffen versorgen und den Transport von Stoffwechselprodukten übernehmen. Weiterhin dient sie als "Autobahn" für den Informationsaustausch z.B. bei der Immunabwehr. Wegen dieser zentralen Bedeutung der Mikrozirkulation ist es wichtig, quantitative Aussagen über deren Zustand machen zu können. Hierbei sind auch rheologische Parameter von Belang, da sowohl Adsorption wie auch Resorption von der Fließfähigkeit des Blutes abhängen. Für diese ist neben der Plasmaviskosität das Verhalten des hauptsächlichen zellulären Anteils im Blut, der roten Blutzellen (Erythrozyten), entscheidend.

Trotz zahlreicher Invitro- und wegen seltenerer Invivo-Experimente besteht weiterhin ein Bedarf, Daten über die fluiddynamischen Eigenschaften roter Blutzellen invivo zu sammeln. Dazu wurde kürzlich die Methode der "Invivo Rheoskopie" vorgestellt [1]. Bei dieser Methode wird der Objekttisch eines Mikroskops so bewegt, daß die beobachteten Blutzellen bei Ihrer Passage durch die Mikrozirkulation im Sichtfeld des Objektivs bleiben. Hierzu ist es notwendig, zunächst einen Weg entlang interessierender Gefäße festzulegen und dann die Bahngeschwindigkeit der der Erythrozyten anzupassen. Solche Fahrten mit im Bild "stehenden" Zellen können auf Video aufgezeichnet werden, um später einer digitalen Bildverarbeitung zu Auswertungszwecken zugeführt zu werden.

Aufgabe der Bildverarbeitung ist hier zunächst einmal die Akquirierung solcher Sequenzen, sowie eine Identifikation der Zellen in den Bildern, weiterhin die Bestimmung ihrer Geschwindigkeit und Form, der Position innerhalb des Gefäßes und ihrer Orientierung relativ zur Flußrichtung. Des weiteren ist die zeitliche Entwicklung dieser Größen unter wechselnden fluiddynamischen Bedingungen von Interesse. Da Erythrozyten als sehr gut verformbare Zellen sich den ständig wechselnden Anforderungen durch äußere Kräfte anpassen können, erwartet man auch hier die Beobachtung von Veränderungen während Ihrer Passage.

Aufgrund des nicht zu standardisierenden Bildmaterials (wechselnder Untergrund, variable Beleuchtungsbedingungen) kann hierbei kein unüberwachtes Verfahren zum Einsatz kommen, so daß bei der Auswertung solcher Bildsequenzen eine Interaktion mit dem Benutzer notwendig bleibt.

2 Material

Die vorliegenden aufgezeichneten Sequenzen stammen von Versuchen mit isoliert perfundierten Rattenmesenterien am Institut für Physiologie der RWTH Aachen. Hierbei werden "normale" bzw. mit Dimaid gehärtete Erythrozyten bei einem niedrigen Hämatokrit von $10 - 20$ aus einem Vorratsgefäß mit definiertem hydrostatischen Druck in das unter dem Mikroskop gut sichtbare Mikrozirkulationsnetzwerk geleitet.

Die Steuerung des Mikroskops (Leitz, invertierter Aufbau) wurde einer Workstation (SGI Indy) mit der "travelling microscope" Software [2] übertragen. Die Sequenzen wurden mit Hilfe einer CCD auf Videoband aufgezeichnet. Wegen der teilweise hohen Geschwindigkeiten ($\sim 1 - 3\ mm\ s^{-1}$) der Zellen, wird als Lichtquelle ein Stroboskop (Chadwick & Hellmuth, 50 Hz) eingesetzt, so daß scharfe Aufnahmen erzielt werden. Um einen gut konstrastierten Erythrozyten darzustellen, wird ein die Soretbande des Hämoglobins absorbierender Filter eingesetzt.

Die Digitalisierung und Auswertung der Sequenzen wird derzeit mit Hilfe der "Digital Video Workbench" (DVW) [3] durchgeführt. Hierbei handelt es sich um eine frei verfügbare Software für SGI Indy/O2 und Linux Workstations [4]. In diese Digitalisiersoftware lassen sich zur Laufzeit selbsterstellte Auswerteroutinen hinzuladen, die den Bedürfnissen des jeweiligen Bildmaterials angepasst sind. Hiermit können Digitalisierung der Sequenz und Auswertung in einem Schritt vorgenommen werden.

3 Methode

Da Videosignale im Zeilensprungverfahren mit Halbbildern ("interlacing") aufgezeichnet werden, hat man in Videobildern schnell bewegter Objekte in jedem Halbbild eine andere Information, so daß als erster Verarbeitungsschritt ein Trennen des Vollbildes I in die Halbbilder I_1, I_2 durchgeführt wird. Da sich hierbei die vertikale Auflösung reduziert, aber aus Gewöhnungsgründen ein Vollbildformat gewünscht ist, ergibt sich folgende Abbildungsvorschrift, bei der fehlende Zeilen $y, y = 0 \dots Y - 1$ interpoliert werden:

$$I_1(x,y) = \begin{cases} I(x,y) & : \quad y = 0, 2, \dots Y - 3 \\ \frac{1}{2}\left(I(x, y-1) + I(x, y+1)\right) & : \quad y = 1, 3, \dots Y - 2 \\ 0 & : \quad y = Y - 1 \end{cases}$$

$$I_2(x,y) = \begin{cases} 0 & : \quad y = 0 \\ I(x,y) & : \quad y = 1, 3, \dots Y - 1 \\ \frac{1}{2}\left(I(x, y-1) + I(x, y+1)\right) & : \quad y = 2, 4, \dots Y - 3 \end{cases}$$

Anschließend muß die durch die Bewegung des Objektträgers bedingte Verschiebung der (Halb-) Bilder gegeneinander bestimmt werden. Als bestes Maß zur Bestimmung der Verschiebung des schwach texturierten Gewebes hat sich hier die Kreuzkorrelationsfunktion K erwiesen:

$$K_{I_k I_{k+1}}(x, y, \Delta x, \Delta y) = \sum_{-w}^{w} \sum_{-w}^{w} I_k(x + \Delta x, y + \Delta y) - I_{k+1}(x, y)$$

Hierbei wird vom Benutzer als Referenzpunkt eine gut zu erkennende Struktur im Bild mit der Maus vorgegeben. Als typischer Fensterbereich w sind acht bis 16 Pixel zu wählen.

Um eine einfache Detektion der Erythrozyten in den überlappenden Bereichen aufeinanderfolgender Bilder zu erreichen, wird ein Subtraktionsverfahren angewendet, so daß der Hintergrund zu großen Teilen den Wert 0 annimmt. Aufgrund des Rechnens mit vorzeichenlosen acht-Bit Werten und des Clippens negativer Werte, werden hier im wesentlichen neben nicht vollständig eliminierten Gewebestrukturen die Zellen eines Bildes dargestellt.

Dieses Subtraktionsbild kann nun mit Hilfe eines K-Means Clustering Algorithmus [5] binarisiert werden, so daß die im Überlappungsbereich befindlichen Zellen gegen das Gewebe getrennt werden.

Dieses Binärbild wird jetzt in einzelne Objekte aufgeteilt ("gelabelt"), indem zusammenhängende Pixelmengen ein Label erhalten. Label, die eine für

Erythrozyten zu geringe Fläche einnehmen, stellen in diesen Bildern Gewebestrukturen dar, die vom Subtraktionsverfahren nicht vollständig eliminiert wurden, aber vom Segmentierungsalgorithmus nicht dem Hintergrund zugeordnet wurden. Diese werden an dieser Stelle mit Hilfe eines Schwellwertkriteriums für die Fläche entfernt.

Aus diesen Labeldaten können bereits die Position der Zelle innerhalb des Gefäßes und die Orientierung der Zellen relativ zur Gefäßrichtung quantifiziert werden. Diese ergeben sich aus den Momenten erster und zweiter Ordnung der jeweiligen Label [6]. Hierbei ist eine weitere Interaktion notwendig, da die Orientierung des Blutgefäßes ebenfalls vom Benutzer mit der Maus vorzugeben ist.

Durch wiederholte Anwendung dieses Verfahrens auf die gesamte Bildsequenz kann jetzt noch zusätzlich die Geschwindigkeit der Zellen in den Gefäßen bestimmt werden. Insgesamt ergeben sich die für die Beurteilung des Strömungsverhaltens des Blutes notwendigen Daten.

4 Implementierung

Die im Abschnitt 3 beschriebenen Routinen wurden in "C++" unter Verwendung einer am Institut für Physiologie entwickelten Klassenbibliothek zur Bildverarbeitung als "shared object" für Unix-Workstations implementiert. Zusammen mit den Routinen zur Benutzerinteraktion, welche in "TCL/TK" implementiert wurden, bilden sie ein ladbares Modul für DVW. DVW stellt für den Zugriff auf die Daten und die Darstellung errechneter Bilder ein Programmierinterface (API) bereit, so daß Ein/Ausgabeoperationen größerer Datenmengen vermieden werden können.

5 Zusammenfassung

Die hier vorgestellte Methode zur Auswertung mikroskopierter Verfolgungsfahrten befindet sich derzeit im Einsatz im Rahmen einer medizinischen Doktorarbeit. Hierbei soll das Verhalten größerer Zahlen einzelner roter Blutzellen in der Mikrozirkulation in statistisch auswertbaren Größenordnungen erfaßt und beschrieben werden. DVW bietet hier eine Unterstützung, dies effizient durchzuführen.

Insgesamt sind am Institut bereits mehrere solcher Plugins für DVW realisiert worden. Diesen bieten den Vorteil einer einheitlichen Oberfläche für verschiedenste Anwendungen (Fluoreszenzangiografie, Analyse von Ultraschalldopplerbildern, Auswertung mikroskopischer Erythrozytenaufnahmen verschiedenster Art). Dies verkürzt die Einarbeitungszeit des Personals bei Bearbeitung neuer Fragestellungen erheblich.

Literatur

1. Schmid-Schönbein H, Jansen J, Heidtmann H, Horstkott H, Grebe R: High resolution flow visualization in microvascular networks; the travelling microscope applied to microrhelogical studies in vivo. Int. J. Microcirc., 16(suppl. 1), 1996.

2. Hektor J, Jansen J, Heidtmann H, Schmid-Schönbein H, Grebe R: A Setup for Computer Assisted Tracking of Erythrocytes in Microvascular Networks. Journal of Computer Assisted Microscopy, to be published in 1998.
3. Hektor J, Jansen J, Broicher F, Grebe R: Digital Video Workbench (DVW) - Ein Hilfsmittel zur Online Bildverarbeitung. Proceedings des 1. Aachener Workshop Bildverarbeitung für die Medizin. Algorithmen · Systeme · Anwendungen. Lehmann T, Scholl I, Spitzer K (Hrsg.), Verlag der Augustinus Buchhandlung, Aachen, 1996
4. ftp://ftp.Physiology.RWTH-Aachen.DE/pub/DVW/, http://WWW.Physiology.RWTH-Aachen.DE/bs/image/DVW.html .
5. Wittkop S: Parallele statistikbasierte und geometrieorientierte Segmentierung von multivarianten dreidiemsionalen Bilddaten. Diplomarbeit Informatik, Institut für Physiologie, RWTH Aachen, 1994.
6. Pratt W K: Digital Image Processing. John Wiley & Sons Inc., New York, 1991.

Visualisierung und Kommentierung von DICOM-Daten
Ein Java-Applet

Thomas Balbach, Thomas Liß, Alexander Horsch

Institut für Medizinische Statistik und Epidemiologie
Klinikum rechts der Isar der TU München, 81675 München
Email: alexander.horsch@imse.med.tu-muenchen.de

Zusammenfassung. Zum Zweck einer orts- und plattformunabhängigen Möglichkeit der Visualisierung von DICOM 3.0-Daten wurde ein Java-Applet erstellt, das in jede Intra- und Internetanwendung eingebunden werden kann. Dieses Java-Applet interpretiert Bilddaten nach dem DICOM 3.0-Standard wie zum Beispiel CT- und MRT-Daten.

Die Bilddaten selbst liegen auf einem HTTP-Server in Dateiverzeichnissen relativ zur jeweils aufrufenden HTTP-Seite. Die Visualisierung erfolgt auf beliebigen Java-fähigen WWW-Clients in Originalqualität, also in 12-Bit-Graustufen, und ermöglicht eine Grauwertfensterung nach Hounsfield mit frei wählbaren Einstellungen von Fensterzentrum und Fensterweite.

Innerhalb des Applets können ganze Schichtbildserien mit ca. 40 bis 120 Bildern durchgesehen werden. Ferner ist es möglich, die Schichtbilder einzeln zu kommentieren und mit Overlays zu versehen, die mit Hilfe des Applets generiert werden. Als geometrische Primitive für die Overlays werden hier Pfeile, Polygone, Kreise, Ellipsen und Textfelder angeboten.

Das Speichern der Overlay- und Kommentardaten übernimmt ein CGI-Skript nach Senden der Daten an den HTTP-Server. Dabei bleiben die DICOM-Dateien unverändert, indem unabhängig davon auf dem HTTP-Server Annotationsdateien in einem speziell dafür entworfenen ASCII-Format angelegt werden.

Eingesetzt wird das Applet im verteilten radiologischen Lehrbuch ODITEB (gefördert vom DFN-Verein, Berlin, mit Mitteln des BMBF, Förderkennzeichen TK598-VA/M04.3), das fallorientiert aufgebaut ist und die Bilddaten verschiedener Provider visualisiert. Entscheidend ist dabei die Benutzerfreundlichkeit der Overlay- und Kommentarerstellung für die medizinisch-radiologischen Experten bei der Fallaufbereitung.

Schlüsselwörter: DICOM, Radiologie, computergestützte Lehre, Java, WWW

1 Einleitung

Im Zuge der fortschreitenden weltweiten Kommunikation und des Datenaustausches etabliert sich im Bereich bildgebender Verfahren in der Medizin die Standardisierung der Daten nach dem DICOM-Format. Dieser vom American College of Radiology (ACR) und der amerikanischen National Electrical Manufacturers Association (NEMA) erstellte Standard liegt inzwischen in der dritten überarbeiteten Version vor. DICOM-fähige Anwendungsprogramme zur Visualisierung der Bilddaten [1] sind schon seit längerer Zeit verfügbar. Allerdings sind sie plattformabhängig und setzen die lokale physikalische Verfügbarkeit der Daten voraus. Sie erfüllen daher nicht die Anforderung des Web-basierten radiologischen Lehrbuchs ODITEB [2,3] mit seinen bei verschiedenen Providern im Internet verteilten Falldatenbeständen. Aus diesem Grund wurde ein DICOM-Viewer mit Kommentiermöglichkeit in Java implementiert.

2 Material und Methoden

Entwickelt wurde unter IRIX 5.3 auf einer SGI-Indy mit Perl Version 5.004 und Java Development Environment 3.0.1 (Sun JDK 1.1.3). Das Lehrbuch wird bereitgestellt über einen Apache-HTTP-Server.

Lauffähig ist der Viewer mit den Java-fähigen HTML-Browsern Netscape Navigator 3.x, 4.x, Microsoft Internet Explorer 4.x.

3 Das Java-Applet

3.1 Interpretation der DICOM-Daten und Zugriff im WWW

Das DICOM-Format [4,5] ist *TAG*-basiert, das heißt, daß Datenfelder durch Kennungen in Form von standardisierten Einzelfeld- und Gruppennummern gekennzeichnet sind. Dadurch ist ein Datenzugriff unabhängig von der Reihenfolge der Datenfelder möglich. Außerdem ergeben sich nach diesem Prinzip optionale, nicht obligatorisch vorhandene Datenfelder abhängig vom gewünschten Dateiinhalt. Gleichzeitig wird zu einzelnen Datenfeldern die Länge des Datenfeldes gespeichert.

Für die Interpretation der Bilddaten bedeutet dies, daß aus einer entsprechenden Bilddatei die Informationen zu Bildgröße, Länge des Bildrohdatenblocks und bitweisem Aufbau der Pixeldaten ausgelesen werden.

Die durch DICOM definierten Übertragungsprotokolle werden für die Darstellung im WWW nicht genutzt. Statt dessen stellen lokal installierte *WAIS-Server* (Wide Area Information Service) den Zugriff auf die in strukturierten Verzeichnissen abgelegten DICOM-Dateien her.

Abb. 1: Screenshot des Viewers mit einem CT-Bild und 3 Kommentaren

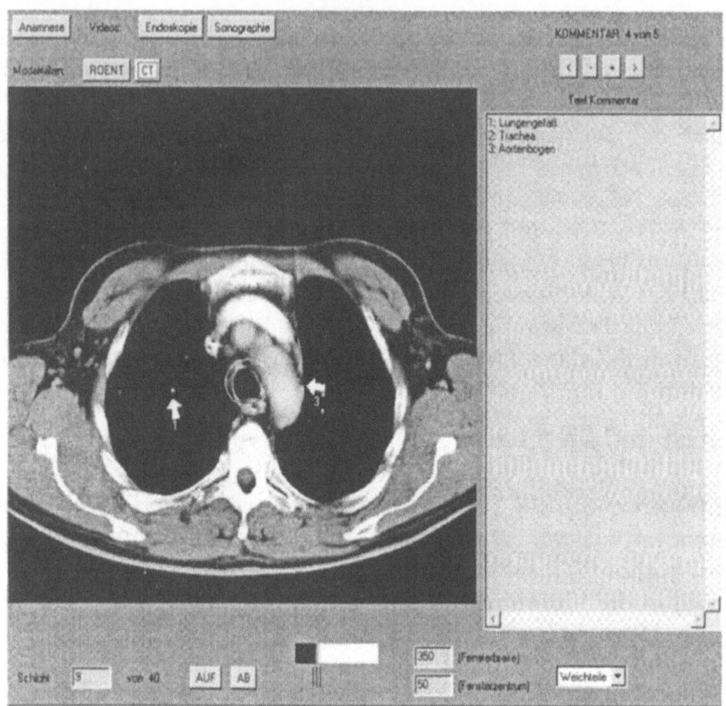

3.2 Features

Für die Anzeige der Bilder steht innerhalb des Applets ein Bereich von 512 x 512 Pixeln zur Verfügung (Abb. 1). Eine Statusanzeige im unteren Bereich informiert über die aktuell angezeigte Schicht und die Gesamtzahl der für den Fall zur Verfügung stehenden Schichten. Zum Durchmustern der Schichten stehen die Buttons AUF und AB zur Verfügung. Die Grauwertfensterung nach Hounsfield ist zunächst standardmäßig auf ein Weichteilfenster (Hounsfieldfenster 350/50) eingestellt, jedoch hat hier der Benutzer mehrere Möglichkeiten zur eigenen Anpassung. Einerseits lassen sich über eine Auswahl andere in der Radiologie verwendete Standardfenster abrufen (z. B. Knochen- und Lungenfenster), andererseits sind zwei Eingabefelder vorhanden, die gleichzeitig fortwährend die aktuellen Werte anzeigen, aber auch eine Direkteingabe von neuen Werten über die Tastatur zulassen. Ergänzt wird dieses System durch zum Experimentieren animierende, mit der Maus verschiebbare Balken, die, unterhalb eines Graukeils angeordnet, Fenstermitte und Fensterränder darstellen. Durch Verschieben der Balken mit der Maus lassen sich beliebige Fensterwerte einstellen.

Ein Mausklick innerhalb eines Bildes schaltet den Zoommodus ein oder aus. Der Zoomfaktor liegt fest bei 2. Bei eingeschaltetem Zoommodus werden auch andere Schichten gezoomt dargestellt.

Rechts des Bildanzeigebereichs ist das Kommentarfeld angeordnet. Zur Bedienung der Kommentarauswahl hat der Benutzer oberhalb des Textfelds die Buttons <, –, +

und > mit den Funktionen *Alle Kommentare aus*, *Alle Kommentare ein*, *Einen Kommentar mehr anzeigen*, *Einen Kommentar weniger anzeigen* (aus einer Anzahl von Kommentaren). Standardmäßig startet das Applet ohne Anzeige von Kommentaren, um dem Benutzer die Möglichkeit zu geben, sich zunächst unabhängig einen Überblick über das Bildmaterial zu verschaffen, bevor er sich über die Kommentarauswahl zu wichtigen Bereichen und Schichtbildern in Stufen hinführen lassen kann. Da Kommentare immer mit Schichtbildern verknüpft sind, wird zum Kommentar gleichzeitig das zugehörige Schichtbild geladen.

Die Auswahl unterschiedlicher Modalitäten wie CT, MRT, Durchleuchtung, Endoskopie und Endosonographie geschieht mittels über dem Bild angeordneten Buttons. Es können auch JPEG-Bilder angezeigt werden. Für diese Bilder mit ihren je 8 Bit pro Farbkanal (RGB) ist aber, im Gegensatz zu den 12-Bit-DICOM-Daten, keine Fensterung vorgesehen. Im Falle der Modalitäten Endoskopie- und Endosonographie lässt sich vom Applet aus die Anzeige von Videos im AVI- und MPEG-1-Format über den Browser starten.

3.3 Kommentierung und Overlayerstellung über das Applet

Die Fallaufbereitung und Kommentierung übernehmen die Provider selbst; dazu müssen sie sich über eine Zugangsberechtigung autorisieren. Nach Eingabe von Benutzername und Passwort erscheint ein zusätzliches Appletfenster, das das gleichzeitig im normalen Applet zu sehende Bild anzeigt. Dem Fallautor steht jetzt eine Palette von Werkzeugen ähnlich denen einer Bildbearbeitungssoftware zur Verfügung.

Zur Overlayerstellung im Bild kann er zwischen Pfeil, Polygon, Kreis und Ellipse wählen, aber auch Klartext oder Zahlen sind als Overlay in mehreren Farben möglich.

Jedes Overlay-Element erhält eine fortlaufende Nummer, unter der im nebenstehenden Textfeld Kommentartext eingegeben werden kann. Die Anzahl von Overlayobjekten und die jeweilige Kommentartextlänge sind unbeschränkt, genauso können die erstellten Kommentare und Overlays sofort oder auch in späteren Sitzungen modifiziert oder gelöscht werden.

Einzelne Kommentare sind fest mit einem gewählten Bild verknüpft. Diese Verknüpfung ist für die stufenweise Kommentarauswahl (siehe oben) erforderlich.

Die Speicherung der Overlay-und Kommentartextdaten geschieht unabhängig von den DICOM-Bilddaten in einer eigenen Datei, die einmal pro Fall angelegt wird und im jeweiligen Fallverzeichnis liegt, so daß die im Original vorliegenden DICOM-Dateien unangetastet bleiben.

3.4 Overlay-und Kommentarspeicherung

Aufgrund des Java-Sicherheitskonzepts für Applets wurde für das serverseitige Speichern der Overlay- und Kommentierungsdaten der Weg über CGI-Skripts gewählt, die ihrerseits neue Dateien anlegen und in diese Dateien Daten hineinschreiben. Damit verbunden ist die fortlaufende Überprüfung der Zugangsberechtigung des anfordernden Applets.

4 Einsatz des Java-Applets

Das Applet ist zentraler Bestandteil des ODITEB-Lehrbuchs für die Diagnostik von Tumoren des Gastrointestinaltrakts einschließlich Leber und Pankreas sowie des Thoraxbereichs mit CT, MRT, Durchleuchtung, Videoendoskopie und Endosonographie. Innerhalb dieses fallorientiert aufgebauten Lehrbuchs werden die Bilddaten bei den Providern (Institut für radiologische Diagnostik, Chirurgische Klinik und II. Med. Klinik der TU München, Institut für Diagnostische Radiologie der FAU Erlangen-Nürnberg und Institut für Röntgendiagnostik der JMU Würzburg) gespeichert und über das Viewer-Applet auf dem Client visualisiert.

Zielgruppen sind Studenten der Medizin und Ärzte in Weiterbildung einerseits, Medizininformatiker mit Schwerpunkt Bildverarbeitung andererseits. In einer späteren Ausbaustufe sollen Möglichkeiten der direkten Bildverarbeitung implementiert werden.

Seit Januar 1998 werden mit dem Viewer ODITEB-Fälle kommentiert. Bis zum Ende der vorlesungsfreien Zeit, das heißt bis Ende April, ist die Bearbeitung von 70 Fällen geplant. Bei der anschließenden Evaluierung des Lehrbuchs im Sommersemester 98 wird der Viewer als Frontend für die Studenten eingesetzt.

5 Literatur

1. OSIRIS DICOM-Viewer der Division of Medical Informatics of the University Hospital of Geneva: http://www.expasy.ch/www/UIN/html1/projects/osiris/osiris.html
2. Horsch A, Hellerhoff P, Hogg M, Ahlbrink A, Balbach T, Liß T, Minov K, Gerhardt P: Concepts of a Web-based Open Distributed Textbook for the Multimodal Diagnostics of Gastrointestinal Tumours with MRI, CT and Video-endoscopy Adressing Students of Medicine and Students of Medical Informatics as two different Target Groups. Accepted paper, Medinfo '98, August 18-22, Seoul, Korea
3. Findling A, Horsch A, Zink A: An Open Distributed Medical Image and Signal Data Server Network with World Wide Web Front-End. In: Pappas C, Maglavera N, Scherrer J-R (eds.) Medical Informatics Europe '97. Amsterdam: IOS Press, 1997, 591-595.
4. the ACR/NEMA Standard Homepage: http://www.xray.hmc.psu.edu/dicom/dicom_home.html
5. NEMA Official Homepage of DICOM: ftp://ftp.nema.org/medical/dicom.htm

Erstellung detaillierter Finite Elemente Modelle des menschlichen Körpers

Marcus Müller, Thilo Franz und Karsten Meyer-Waarden

Institut für Biomedizinische Technik,
Universität Karlsruhe, 76128 Karlsruhe
Email: mm@ibt.etec.uni-karlsruhe.de

Zusammenfassung Wir präsentieren einen Algorithmus zur Erstellung von Finite Elemente Modellen des menschlichen Körpers. Ein von uns entwickelter Netzgenerator zerlegt ein durch Voxeldaten vorgegebenes Volumen in ein unstrukturiertes Tetraedergitter, welches das *Delaunay Kriterium* erfüllt. Sind die Ausgangsdaten gewebeklassifiziert, so erfolgt die Modellerzeugung basierend auf einem Teile und Herrsche Algorithmus automatisch, bei unklassifizierten Voxeldaten können unterstützend Grenzflächen mit *Aktiven Konturen* oder *Marching Cubes* erzeugt werden.

Schlüsselwörter: Finite Elemente, automatische Netzgenerierung

1   Einleitung

Körpereigene Stromquellen, wie aktive Nervenzellen der Hirnrinde oder Muskelzellen des Herzens, verursachen ebenso wie externe Quellen bei der Defibrillation oder der Elektrostimulation die Ausbildung elektrischer und magnetischer Felder. Die numerische Feldberechnung in detaillierten Modellen des menschlichen Körpers ermöglicht Aussagen über die resultierende Verteilung von Potentialen und von Strom-, Energie- oder Leistungsdichten. Damit eröffnet sie Möglichkeiten der Erforschung oder der Optimierung verschiedener Anwendungsbereiche.

Stationäre Strömungsfelder werden durch das folgende Randwertproblem beschrieben:

$$\nabla\left(\hat{\kappa}(\mathbf{x})\nabla\varphi(\mathbf{x})\right)=0$$

$$\varphi(\mathbf{x})=f_D(\mathbf{x}),\quad \mathbf{x}\in\Gamma_D \tag{1}$$

$$\nabla_{\mathbf{n}}\,\varphi(\mathbf{x})=\mathbf{f}_N(\mathbf{x}),\quad \mathbf{x}\in\Gamma_N$$

$\varphi(\mathbf{x})$ ist die gesuchte Potentialverteilung wie sie sich bei gegebenen Randbedinungen $f_D, \mathbf{f}_N$ in einem inhomogenen und u.U. anisotropen Volumenleiter mit der Leitfähigkeitsverteilung $\hat{\kappa}(\mathbf{x})$ einstellt. Die Finite Elemente Methode (FEM) eignet sich aufgrund ihrer Fexibilität bei der mathematischen Formulierung und der geometrischen Diskretisierung für dieses Problem besonders [1]. Die Lösung $\varphi(\mathbf{x})$ wird innerhalb jedes einzelnen Elements durch ein Polynom niederen Grades approximiert, welches in der Darstellung der *Formfunktionen*

Abbildung1. Darstellung eines aus gewebeklassifizierten Voxeldaten automatisch erzeugten Ganzkörpermodells. Es besteht aus etwa $1,3\cdot10^6$ Tetraederelementen variabler Form und Größe und unterscheidet mehr als 30 Gewebearten.

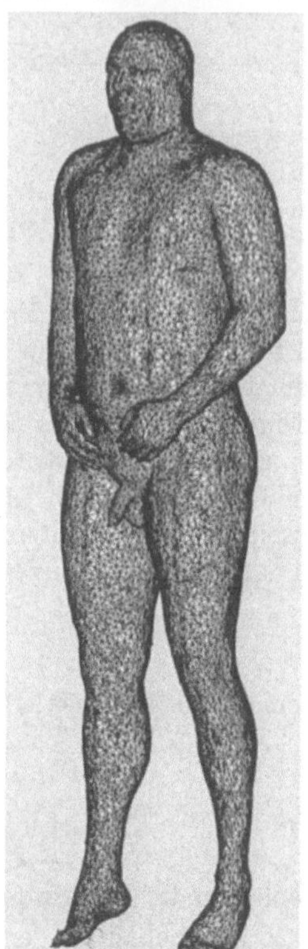

$f_i(\mathbf{x})$ von n *Elementfreiheitsgraden* $\varphi_i^{\triangle}$, z.B. den Potentialwerten an den Elementecken, abhängt:

$$\varphi^{\triangle}(\mathbf{x}) = \sum_{i=1}^{n} \varphi_i^{\triangle} f_i(\mathbf{x}) \tag{2}$$

Durch Anknüpfbedingungen zwischen benachbarten Elementen wird ein stetiger Potentialverlauf im gesamten Modell sichergestellt, der dann von den N Freiheitsgraden φ_i des gesamten Systems abhängt. Die Forulierung der Bedingungsgleichungen führt auf ein lineares Gleichungssystem:

$$\mathbf{Ax} = \mathbf{b} \tag{3}$$

Bei entsprechender Sortierung der Freiheitsgrade ist $\mathbf{A}$ eine schwach besetzte, symmetrische Bandmatrix der Dimension N. Zur Lösung wird das iterative *Konjugierte Gradienten Verfahren* eingesetzt, dessen Konvergenz durch eine Vorkonditionierung der Matrix $\mathbf{A}$ mit Hilfe einer *unvollständigen Cholesky Zerlegung* wesentlich beschleunigt wird (ICCG).

2 Geometrische Modellerstellung

Eine detaillierte geometrische Modellierung des menschlichen Körpers beinhaltet die Abbildung komplexer Gewebestrukturen und -grenzflächen. Um hierbei die Anzahl benötigter Elemente zu minimieren, werden Tetraeder variabler Form und Größe verwendet. Der von uns entwickelte Netzgenerator zerlegt ein vorgegebenes Objektvolumen in ein Startgitter aus Tetraedern und ermittelt deren Güte. Dieses Tetraedernetz erfüllt das *Delaunay Kriterium* und stellt somit die gleichwinkligste Vernetzung der Stützstellen sicher [2]. Die am schlechtesten bewerteten Elemente werden durch das Einbringen weiterer Knotenpunkte an geeigneten Positionen sukzessive entfernt. Die im verfeinerten Gitter erzeugten Elemente werden neu bewertet.

Grundlage für die Bewertung bilden entweder gewebeklassifizierte Volumendaten, zum Beispiel der *MEET Man* [3] Datensatz oder unklassifizierte Aufnahmen, wie sie verschiedene bildgebende Verfahren der Medizintechnik, z.B. Kernspin- oder Computertomographie, liefern. Die Bewertungs- oder Gütefunktion und die Wahl der Position neuer Knotenpunkte sind folglich die beiden wesentlichen Parameter, welche die Qualität des Modells beeinflussen. Grundsätzlich stehen als lokale Gütekriterien die Form und Größe und das Histogramm der Elemente zur Verfügung.

Gewebeklassifizierte Volumendaten Liegt ein gewebeklassifizierter Datensatz zugrunde, so definiert das größte der im Element vorgefundenen Gewebevolumina die dem Tetraeder zugeordnete Gewebeklasse. Das restliche Volumen oder auch Fehlvolumen bestimmt als absolute oder relative Größe die Güte des aktuellen Elements [4].

Unklassifizierte Volumendaten Das für klassifizierte Volumendaten beschriebene Verfahren läßt sich in abgewandelter Form zur Segmentation von unklassifizierten Ausgangsdaten, also zur Zerlegung des Objektvolumens in homogene Teilbereiche, einsetzen. Liegen einmodale Aufnahmen zugrunde, der Intensitätswert wird im folgenden als Grauwert bezeichnet, so wird für jedes zu bewertende Element der Mittelwert und die Varianz der Grauwerte ermittelt. Der Mittelwert definiert die Grauwertklasse des Elements, die Varianz ist ein Maß für dessen Homogenität.

Zusätzlich können Grenzflächen, wie sie beispielsweise mit Hilfe *Aktiver Konturen* [5] oder des *Marching Cubes Algorithmus* [6] erzeugt werden, in das Volumenmodell eingebracht werden. Hierbei wird im Verlauf der Netzgenerierung sichergestellt, daß die einzelnen Oberflächendreiecke ihre Entsprechung in Form von Grenzflächen benachbarter Tetraederelemente im Volumenmodell besitzen. Allerdings werden dabei automatische Modifikationen der Ausgangsoberfläche, wie das *Swappen* (das Vertauschen der Diagonalkante benachbarter Dreiecke), oder das Hinzufügen feinerer Dreiecke zugelassen.

Im Anschluß an die Zerlegung des Objektraums in Tetraeder erfolgt eine Klassifikation der Elemente. Hierzu werden eine einfache Grauwertklassifikation oder ein Regionenwachtumsverfahren auf Tetraederebene eingesetzt.

Abbildung2. Aus Kernspintomographie gewonnenes Torsomodell. Die Torsooberfläche wurde mit Hilfe einer Aktiven Kontur erzeugt. Im Anschluß an eine Zerlegung in Elemente homogener Grauwerte erfolgte eine Gewebeklassifikation mit Hilfe von Schwellwert- und Regionenwachstumsverfahren auf Tetraederebene.

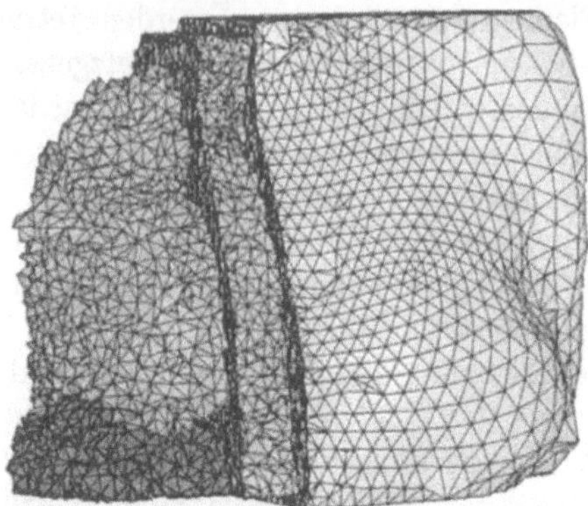

Position neuer Knotenpunkte Neue Knotenpunkte werden innerhalb zu entfernender Tetraeder positioniert. Zur Bestimmung der genauen Lage wird das Gewebehistogramm des zu zerteilenden Elements analysiert. Hierbei werden Grauwerte ermittelt, welche die Modi des mehrmodalen Elementhistogramms voneinander trennen. Entlang vorgegebener Linien (z.B. Verbindung Mittelpunkt des Tetraeders mit Mittelpunkt einer Seitenfläche) wird nach diesen Grauwerten gesucht. Aus der Menge der gefundenen Trennpunkte wird beispielsweise derjenige mit dem größten Abstand zu allen Eckpunkten gewählt.

Aspect Ratio Tetraeder mit extrem großem Kantenlängenverhältnis (*Aspect Ratio*) verschlechtern die Konvergenz und die numerische Stabilität des Verfahrens. Aus dem Verhältnis von Inkugelradius r_i zu Umkugelradius r_u wird der *Sliverwert* $s = 3\ r_i/r_u$ berechnet. Er ist ein Maß für die Gleichwinkligkeit des Tetraeders. Unterschreitet s eines Elements einen kritischen Grenzwert von $s_{min} = 0.001$, so wird dieses im Laufe der Modellerstellung durch Hinzufügen geeigneter Knotenpunkte entfernt.

3 Ergebnisse

Der vorgestellte Netzgenerator ist in der Lage, ausgehend von Voxeldaten, unstrukturierte Tetraedergitter zu erzeugen. Im Fall gewebeklassifizierter Daten geschieht dies automatisch (Abbildung 1 und 3. Im Fall unklassifizierter Daten kann das Verfahren durch die Definition von Grenzflächen unterstützt werden (Abbildung 2). Die Datenstrukturen sind auf Modelle mit mehreren 10^5 Elementen ausgelegt, womit auch komplexe Gewebestrukturen realistisch abgebildet werden können.

Abbildung3. Aus gewebeklassifizierten Voxeldaten automatisch erzeugtes Kopfmodell bestehend aus ca. 350000 Tetraederelementen. Differenziert wurden u.a. Knochen, Muskulatur, Fett, Blut, Liquor, graue- und weiße Hirnsubstanz.

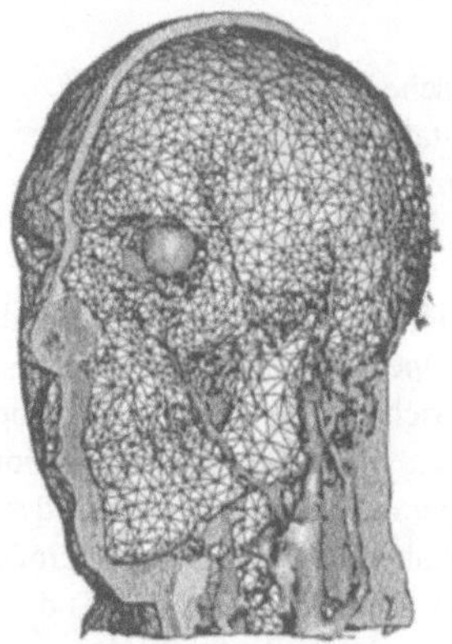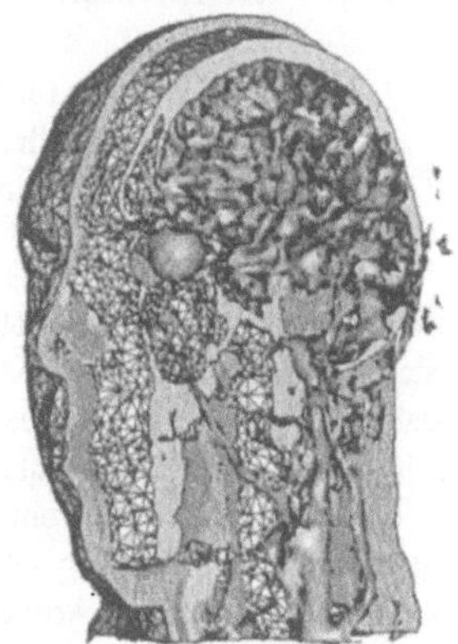

Literatur

1. Brenner S. C., Scott L. R.: The mathematical therory of finite element methods. Texts in Applied Mathematics, Springer-Verlag, New York, 1994.
2. Shenton D. N., Cendes Z. J.: Three-dimensional finite element mesh generation using Delaunay tesselation. IEEE Transactions on Magnetics, Vol. MAG-21, No. 6, pp. 2535-2538, 1985.
3. Sachse F., Müller M., Glas M., Meyer-Waarden K.: Segmentation and tissue-classification of the visible man dataset using the computertomographic scans and the thin-section photos. Proc. First Users Conference of the National Library of Medicine's Visible Human Project, 1996.
4. Müller M., Sachse F., Meyer-Waarden K.: Creation of finite element models of human body based upon tissue-classified voxel representations. Proc. First Users Conference of the National Library of Medicine's Visible Human Project, 1996.
5. Cohen L. D., Cohen I.: Finite-elements methods for active contour models and balloons for 2-D and 3-D images. IEEE Transactions on Pattern Analysis and Marching Intelligence, Vol. 15, pp. 1131-1147, 1993.
6. Lorensen, W. E. and Cline, H. E.: Marching Cubes: A high resolution 3d surface construction algorithm. Computer Graphics, Vol. 21, No. 3, pp. 163-169, July 1987.

Computerbasierte Planung für die roboterunterstützte zementlose Implantation von Hüftendoprothesen

K.Wolsiffer, R. Petzold, W.A. Kalender

Institut für Medizinische Physik
Friedrich Alexander Universität, 91054 Erlangen
Email: kerstin@imp.uni-erlangen.de

Zusammenfassung. Die Implantation von Hüftendoprothesen ist eine der am häufigsten durchgeführten orthopädischen Operationen. Der Operationserfolg hängt dabei vor allem von der Auswahl der richtigen Prothese und der optimalen Positionierung des Implantats im Knochen ab. Bei der konventionellen Operationsmethode stellen sowohl die präoperative Planung als auch deren genaue intraoperative Umsetzung selbst für erfahrene Chirurgen eine große Herausforderung dar. In diesem Artikel wird ein System vorgestellt, das den Chirurgen bei der Planung und Durchführung eines Hüftgelenkersatzes unterstützt. Die Planung erfolgt auf der von uns entwickelten Planungsstation anhand von Spiral-CT-Daten von Hüfte und Femur sowie CAD-Daten der Prothesen. Die exakte Umsetzung des präoperativen Plans wird durch den intraoperativen Einsatz eines Roboters gewährleistet, der die Markhöhle zur Aufnahme der Femurschaftkomponente einer Hüftendoprothese mit hoher Genauigkeit entsprechend der präoperativen Planung präpariert.

Schlüsselwörter: Computerunterstützte Chirurgie (CAS), Hüftgelenk, Registrierung, Computer Tomographie, Roboter

1 Problemstellung

Beim totalen Hüftgelenksersatz (THE) wird ein (beispielsweise infolge einer Arthrose) degeneriertes Hüftgelenk (Abb. 1) durch ein künstliches ersetzt .

Dazu wird während der Operation zunächst der Femurkopf entfernt und die Hüftpfanne (Acetabulum) zur Aufnahme der künstlichen Gelenkpfanne vorbereitet. Anschließend erfolgt die Präparation der Markhöhle im proximalen Femur, in welches der Schaft der Femurkomponente des Implantats eingeführt wird (Abb. 2).

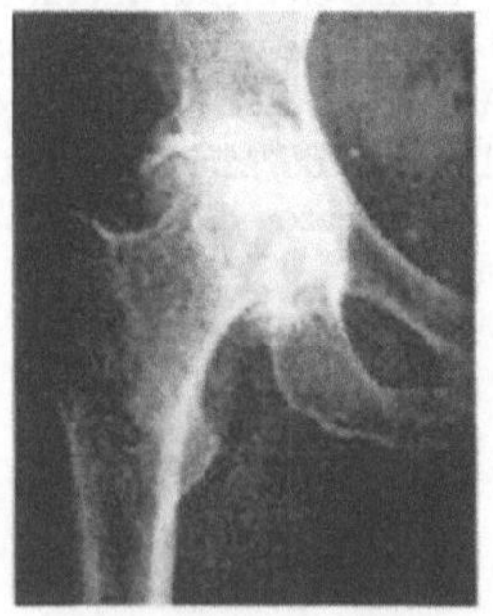

Abb 1: Ein arthrotisches Hüftgelenk

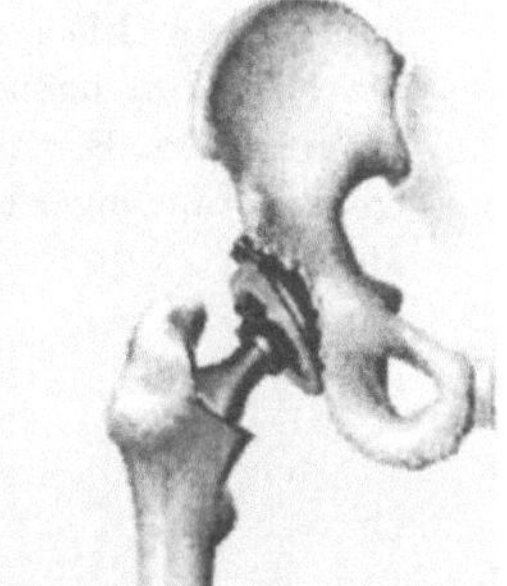

Abb. 2: Ein künstliches Hüftgelenk

Die Befestigung der Prothesenkomponenten kann dabei entweder durch Verwendung von Knochenzement oder zementlos durchgeführt werden. Bei der zementlosen Implantation wird die Prothese durch Press-Fit-Mechanismen oder durch Einwachsen des Knochens in die poröse Prothesenoberfläche fixiert. Daher hängen *Sitz* und *Haltbarkeit* zementloser Prothesen im Wesentlichen von der *Paßgenauigkeit* („*fit*") der Markhöhle für das verwendete Implantat ab. Der Oberflächenkontakt zwischen Prothese und Knochen sollte also so groß wie möglich sein.

Bei der konventionellen Methode wird die Markhöhle mit Hammer und Formraspeln präpariert. Da der Knochen bei der Bearbeitung splittern und reißen kann, wird dabei selten eine Kontaktfläche von mehr als 30 Prozent erreicht [1]. Daher kommt es häufig zu schmerzhaften Lockerungen und Verschiebungen, was im schlimmsten Fall eine erneute Operation erforderlich macht.

Für die *postoperative Funktionalität* ist eine gründliche präoperative Planung von Lage und Größe der Prothesenkomponenten entscheidend. Die *Lage* der Prothese muß dabei so geplant werden, daß eine optimale Kraftübertragung und ein möglichst natürlicher Bewegungsumfang erreicht werden kann.

Die *Größe* der Prothese muß so dimensioniert sein, daß die Prothese einerseits groß genug ist, um eine ausreichende Stabilität zu gewährleisten, und andererseits es nicht zu Frakturen und Schmerzen infolge einer zu großen Prothese kommt [2].

Bei der konventionellen, manuellen Operationsmethode werden zur Planung konfektionierte Prothesenschablonen auf Röntgenbildern verschoben. Da es sich dabei lediglich um zweidimensionale Projektionen handelt, ist diese Methode relativ fehleranfällig und ungenau. Insbesondere die exakte operative Umsetzung des präoperativen Plans verlangt vom Operateur ein hohes Maß an Erfahrung und Intuition.

2 Ansatz

Zur Verbesserung der präoperativen Planung und zur Überwindung der Probleme bei der Umsetzung des präoperativen Plans wurden Methoden der computerunterstützten Chirurgie (Computer Assisted Surgery, CAS) angewendet.

Das erste CAS-basierte System im Bereich der Hüftgelenksendoprothetik wurde vonTaylor et al. [3] vorgestellt. Dieses System wurde schon bei einem großen Patientenkollektiv erfolgreich eingesetzt und die dadurch gewonnen Erkenntnisse stellen eine wichtige Grundlage für das von uns entwickelte System dar [3].

Abb. 3 zeigt die drei Hauptschritte eines CAS-basierten Systems zum THE [4].

Der Bezug zwischen dem prä- und intraoperativen System wird dabei durch die Registrierung hergestellt.

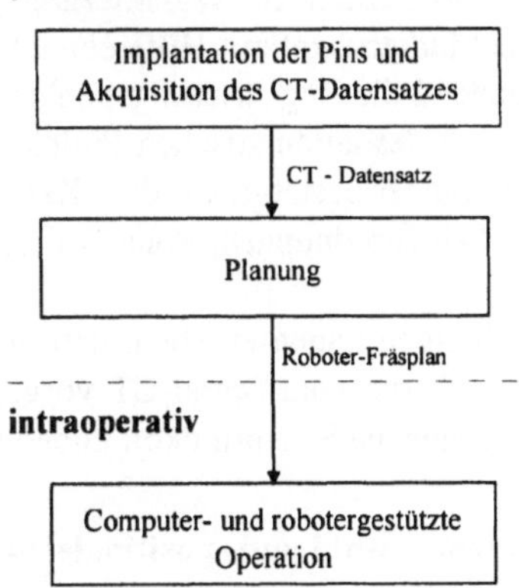

Abb. 3: Ablaufplan zu einem CAS-basierten THE

3 Implantation der Marker und CT-Datenakquisition

In der präoperativen Phase werden dem Patienten zunächst in einer separaten Operation jeweils eine Titanschraube (Marker) in den lateralen und medialen Femurkondylus sowie in den Trochanter major implantiert. Diese dienen zur späteren Registrierung des Planungs- mit dem Roboterkoordinatensystem.

Um eine dreidimensionale Planung zu ermöglichen, wird anschließend ein Spiral-CT-Scan im Bereich des proximalen Femur und der Femurkondylen akquiriert. Es wurde eine spezielles Scan-Protokoll entwickelt, das den Patienten einer möglichst geringen Strahlenbelastung aussetzt und gleichzeitig den Genauigkeitsanforderungen der vorliegenden Anwendung gerecht wird. Der gesamte Datensatz umfaßt dann etwa 200 Schichten mit 512*512 Pixeln .

4 Planung

Die Planungssoftware wurde für Standard-PCs und das Windows95® Betriebssystem entwickelt. Die Planung basiert auf den Spiral-CT-Daten des Femur und Prothesendaten, die in einer Prothesendatenbank gespeichert sind.

Die Prothesendatenbank enthält Daten zu Typ, Größe und Form verschiedener Prothesen sowie CAD-Daten zur Beschreibung der Prothesengeometrien. Außerdem sind darin Bahnplanungsdaten der Prothesen gespeichert, die zur Generierung des Roboterprogramms benötigt werden.

Der Benutzer wird bei der Planung automatisch durch drei Hauptschritte geführt: Die Lokalisation der Pins, die Prothesenauswahl und –positionierung und schließlich der Export des Roboterprogramms und der Planungsdaten.

4.1 Pinlokalisation

Die Komponente zur Pinlokalisation berechnet vollautomatisch die vom Roboter intraoperativ abzutastenden Registrierungspunkte im CT-Datensatz. Hierzu werden zunächst die Markervoxel mit Hilfe eines Volume-Growing-Algorithmus segmentiert und anschließend die Registrierungspunkte durch ein Geradeneinpassungs-Verfahren bestimmt. Nach der automatischen Pinlokalisation muß jeder gefundene Marker explizit vom Benutzer bestätigt werden. Kam es, z.B. infolge weiterer metallischer Implantate, zu Fehlzuordnungen, können diese in einem interaktiven Modus korrigiert werden.

Untersuchungen haben ergeben, daß die Genauigkeit der Pinlokalisation im wesentlichen durch die vom Spiral-CT vorgegebene Auflösung bestimmt wird. Daher muß das vorgegebene Scanprotokoll unbedingt eingehalten werden.

4.2 Prothesenauswahl und -positionierung

Zur Planung von Prothesenmodell, -größe und -lage im Femur werden die CT-Daten im 4-Quadrantenmodus angezeigt (Abb. 4). In den ersten drei Quadranten können transversale, sagittale und koronale Schnitte durch das CT-Volumen frei gewählt werden. Gleichzeitig stehen die in der Radiologie üblichen Bildverarbeitungsoperationen, wie z.B. Fensterung, Zooming oder Paning, zur Verfügung. Dies ermöglicht dem Operateur eine genaue Analyse der Knochenverhältnisse am Femur sowie den Zugriff auf die gesamte Volumeninformation. Im vierten Quadranten wird zusätzlich eine 3D-Ansicht der Prothese zur visuellen Kontrolle der Prothesenlage und Erleichterung der Orientierung bereitgestellt.

Zu Beginn der eigentlichen Planung wählt der Operateur zunächst eine Prothese nach Typ, Form und Größe aus der Prothesendatenbank aus. Daraufhin wird die Prothese in einer Default-Position im Volumen positioniert und in den vier Quadranten zusammen mit den CT-Daten angezeigt.

Die endgültige Positionierung der Prothese erfolgt interaktiv durch Bewegung der Prothesenschnitte mit der Maus. Dem planenden Operateur stehen also alle sechs Freiheitsgrade zur Verfügung, so daß eine echte dreidimensionale Planung stattfinden kann. Dadurch läßt sich ein optimaler Oberflächenkontakt zwischen dem kortikalen Femurknochen und dem Prothesenschaft sowie eine optimale Größe und Lage der Femurkomponente erreichen.

4.3 Export des Roboterprogramms und der Planungsdaten

Nach Beendigung der interaktiven Positionierung wird, basierend auf den Bahnplanungsdaten aus der Prothesendatenbank sowie den Ergebnissen der Pinlokalisation und der Prothesenplanung, der Roboter-Fräsplan berechnet. Dieser wird zusammen mit den Pinkoordinaten, den Patienten- und Prothesendaten sowie weiteren Planungsdaten auf einem externen Datenträger gespeichert und an die Robotersteuerung übergeben.

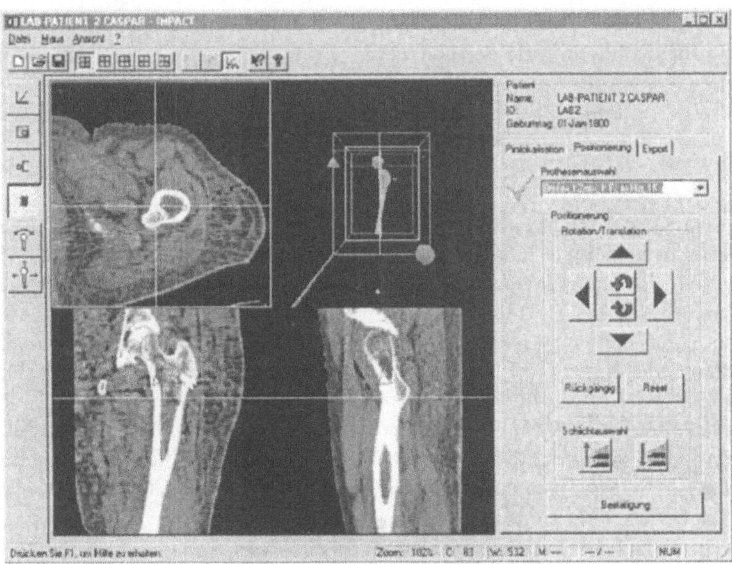

Abb. 4: Benutzerschnittstelle bei der Prothesenpositionierung

5 Computer- und roboterunterstützte Operation

Bei der eigentlichen Operation wird der Patient wie gewöhnlich gelagert und vorbereitet. Der Femurkopf wird entfernt, die Hüftpfanne auf konventionelle Art und Weise von Hand präpariert und die Acetabulumkomponente eingesetzt. Anschließend werden die Planungsdaten in den Roboter geladen und der Roboter kalibriert. Der Femur wird fixiert und die Registrierung durch Abtastung der Regstrierpunkte der Marker mit dem Roboter durchgeführt. Nach erfolgreicher Registrierung wird die Markhöhle durch den Roboter entsprechend den Planungsdaten ausgefräst, die Femurkomponente eingesetzt und die Operation auf konventionellem Wege zu Ende geführt.

6 Schlußfolgerung und Ausblick

Mit diesem CAS-basierten Planungssystem hat der Operateur Zugriff auf die gesamte Volumeninformation und kann somit eine dreidimensionale präoperative Analyse, Planung und Simulation durchführen. Durch den Robotereinsatz wird eine sehr genaue Umsetzug des präoperativen Plans gewährleistet und der Knochen-Implantatkontakt deutlich erhöht. Daher wird eine Verbesserung der postoperativen Funktionalität erwartet, bei gleichzeitiger Verkürzung des Aufenthalts des Patienten im Krankenhaus. Desweiteren ist mit einer höheren und längerfristigeren Stabilität des Implantats zu rechnen.

7 Kooperation

Diese Arbeit entstand in Zusammenarbeit mit Firma orto Maquet in Rastatt und der Abteilung für Unfallchirurgie der Universität Erlangen unter Leitung von Herrn Prof. Dr. Hennig.

8 Literatur

1. Paul HA, Bargar, WL, Mittelstadt, B: Development of a Surgical Robot for Cementless Total Hip Arthroplasty. Clinical Orthopaedics and Related Research, 285:57-66, 1992.
2. Balgar WL, Carbone, EJ: Robotic Femoral Canal Preparation. Total Hip Revision Surgery, Raven Press, 1994.
3. Taylor, RH, Mittelstadt, BD, Paul HA et al.: An Image-Directed Robotic System for Precise Orthopaedic Surgery. IEEE Transactions on Robotics and Automation, 10(3):261-275, 1994.
4. Kalender WA, Blank M, Engelke K, Freund J, Fuchs T, Kachelrieß M, Krause J, Petzold R, Prevrhal S, Schneider J, Schnütgen G, Wahl S, Wolf H, Wolsiffer K: Computer Assisted Hip Implant Surgery: Prerequisites on CT Imaging and Quality. Computer Aided Surgery, in press, 1998.

Automatische Segmentierung und morphometrische Analyse von Nervenbiopsien

A. Knepper[1], A. Dölemeyer[1], M. Mugler[2], J. M. Schröder[2], D. Meyer-Ebrecht[1]

[1] Lehrstuhl für Meßtechnik
Rheinisch-Westfälische Technische Hochschule (RWTH), 52056 Aachen
Email: achim@lfm.rwth-aachen.de

[2] Institut für Neuropathologie
Klinikum der RWTH Aachen, 52057 Aachen
Email: neupath@alpha.imib.rwth-aachen.de

Zusammenfassung. Lichtmikroskopische Aufnahmen gefärbter Semidünn-schnitt-Präparate von Nervenbiopsien müssen bei einer Vielzahl von neuromuskulären Erkrankungen morphometrisch analysiert werden. Es wird hier eine weitgehend automatische Ermittlung klinisch relevanter Parameter vorgestellt. Die nach Vorverarbeitung, Kantendetektion und region growing noch verbundenen Objekte werden mit einem statistischen und einem geometrischen Ansatz aufgetrennt. Für die klassifizierten Nervenfasern wird die Axon-Markscheiden-Relation bestimmt. Außerdem werden neue Beschreibungen der Rundheit der Nervenfasern eingeführt.

Schlüsselwörter: Nervenbiopsie, Segmentierung, Canny-Operator, Distanztransformation, Morphometrie

1 Einleitung

Am Institut für Neuropathologie des Klinikums der RWTH Aachen befindet sich das Referenzzentrum für neuromuskuläre Krankheiten bei der Deutschen Gesellschaft für Neuropathologie. Die Mehrzahl der hier im Jahr untersuchten ca. 400 Nervenbiopsien bedürfen einer diagnostischen Präzisierung mit Hilfe morphometrischer Methoden. Die Bildanalyse ist wegen der Komplexität und Größenverteilung der beteiligten Strukturen und wegen des oft nur quantitativ, weniger qualitativ erfaßbaren Ausfalls bestimmter Größenklassen und Fasertypen von entscheidender diagnostischer Bedeutung. Das gilt insbesondere für die Quantifizierung von De- und Regenerationsvorgängen sowie von Therapieerfolgen (Kompensation und Rehabilitation) oder Mißerfolgen und Prognosefaktoren [1].

Derzeit erfolgen die Auswertungen der zu messenden Strukturen "von Hand" am Mikroskop mit dem Meßokular oder auf Fotografien. Es wurden daher in Zusammenarbeit mit dem Institut für Neuropathologie, gefördert von dem START-Programm der RWTH, analyseunterstützende Verfahren zur weitgehend automatischen Ermittlung signifikanter morphometrischer Parameter (Faserdichte, Größenverteilungen, Axon-Markscheide-Relation, Markscheidendicke, Formmerkmale) entwickelt.

2 Segmentierung

Die als Eingangsbilddaten verwendeten lichtmikroskopischen Aufnahmen von einge-
färbten Semidünnschnitt-Präparaten werden in ein für die nachfolgende Segmentierung optimales Merkmalsbild transformiert.

Hierbei wird als Gütekriterium der Kontrast des bei der Transformation entstehenden Graustufenbildes gewählt. Es wird eine Regressionsgerade durch die im dreidimensionalen RGB-Farbraum eingetragenen Bildpunkte berechnet. Die Projektion
jedes Bildpunktes auf die linear skalierte Regressionsgerade definiert dann seinen
monochromatischen Grauwert [2].

Für die Einteilung des Bildinhaltes nach Objekt (Markscheideflächen) und Hintergrund (Axone, Bindegewebe) kann neben Formwissen (z.B. jede Markscheide umgibt
nur ein Axon) auch die homogene Verteilung des Hintergrunds ausgenutzt werden.
Die Segmentierung erfolgt mit einem durch ein Kantenmerkmalsbild gesteuertem
region growing und einer anschließenden Objekttrennung von fehlerhaft zusammengefaßten Strukturen. Das verwendete Verfahren des region growing entspricht dem zugrunde liegenden biologischen Modell der Nervenfaser und der hier angewandten
Färbetechnik, da ausgehend von Keimpunkten im Objektinnern räumlich zusammenhängende, kompakte Regionen gebildet werden.

2.1 Kantendetektion

Ausgangsbasis des region growing ist ein Kantenmerkmalsbild sowie eine adaptive
Schwellwertbildung für Bereiche mit nicht geschlossenen Konturen. Der Kantendetektor sollte so gewählt werden, daß drei Kostenfunktionen [3] gleichzeitig optimiert
werden.

- Fehlerrate - nur Kanten werden detektiert.
- Lokalisation - der Abstand zwischen den vom Kantendetektor gefundenen Kanten-
  pixeln und der korrekten Kante soll so klein wie möglich sein.
- Filterantwort - auf eine einzige Kante nur eine Filterantwort.

Der Operator nach Shen-Castan (infinite symmetric exponential filter) [4] berücksichtigt nur die ersten beiden Bedingungen, zeigt aber bei Eingangsdaten mit schlechtem
Signal-Rausch-Verhältnis eine gute Performance. Bei dem hier vorliegenden Bildmaterial ist der Canny-Operator [5], trotz seiner Approximation des optimalen Detektors
durch den Gradienten des Gauß-Filters, besser geeignet, da alle drei Kostenfunktionen berücksichtigt werden.

Die Bildfunktion wird mit den Richtungsableitungen der Gauß-Funktion in beiden
Richtungen gefaltet. Der Gradientenbetrag liefert ein gutes Maß für die Stärke der
Kante. In einem abschließenden Schritt werden alle Punkte entfernt, die kein lokales
Maximum bilden (nonmaximum-suppression).

2.2 Objekttrennung

Kontrastarme Übergänge zwischen eng anliegenden Nervenfasern müssen nachbearbeitet werden, wenn die Gradienteninformation nicht ausreicht um Kantenpunkte zu detektieren. Zur Separierung der beim region growing verschmolzenen Objekte werden zwei Ansätze verfolgt, die beide die morphometrische Analyse nur vernachlässigbar beeinflussen.

Die statistische Objekttrennung orientiert sich an der Grauwertintensität des Objektes. Für alle Objekte des Gesamtbildes werden sequentiell die Bildpunkte in sichere und unsichere Pixel eingeteilt. Bei sicheren Pixeln ist die Differenz zum mittleren Grauwert der Region größer als die Standardabweichung der Grauwerte der Region. Die Auftrennung erfolgt, indem nur solche unsicheren Bereiche gelöscht werden, die an mindestens zwei unverbundene sichere Bereiche grenzen [6].

Bei der nachfolgende geometrischen Objekttrennung dient die Form des Objektes als einziges Kriterium der Separation. Hierzu wird mit einem effizienten sequentiellen Algorithmus [7] innerhalb von zwei Iterationen die Distanztransformation des binarisierten Markscheidenmerkmalbildes mit vorher aufgefüllten Axonen berechnet. Die resultierenden Distanzwerte der Objekte (in Abb. 1 grauwertkodiert dargestellt) können auch eine dreidimensionale Struktur bilden, wenn die Distanzwerte als Höhenkoordinate aufgefaßt werden. Ein kreisförmiges Objekt z.B. wird dann einen Kegel bilden. An der Verbindungsstelle zweier Objekte entsteht ein Sattelpunkt, d.h. benachbarte Distanzwerte weisen in einer Richtung aufsteigende und orthogonal dazu abfallende Werte auf. Beginnend von diesen Sattelpunkten werden Trennungslinien für verschmolzene Objekte gebildet, indem in Richtung fallender Distanzwerte der kürzeste Pfad zum nächst gelegenen Objektrand berechnet wird.

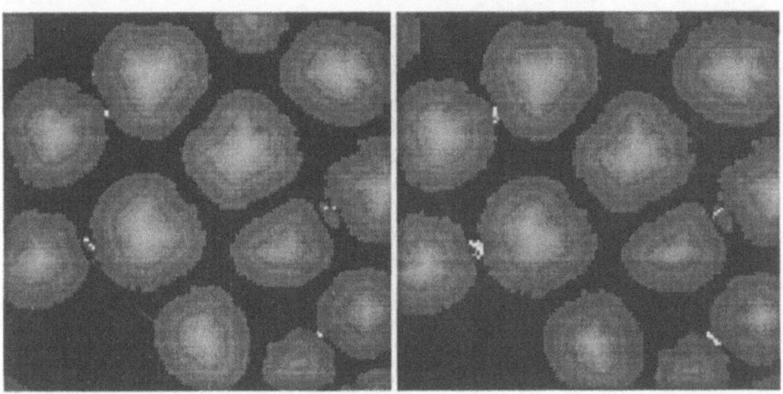

Abb. 1: Sattelpunkte (links) und Trennungslinien (rechts) im distanztransformierten Bild.

3 Morphometrische Messungen

Bei der anschließenden morphometrischen Analyse werden klinisch relevante Parameter aus den gewonnenen Objektklassen extrahiert. Neben den in der klinischen

Routine schon verwendeten Maßen wurden neue, differenziertere Beschreibungen der Form und der Größenverteilung von Nervenfasern entwickelt.

Während bei der Bestimmung der Faserdichte (prozentualer Anteil der Objektfläche an der Gesamtbildfläche) auch vom Rand beschnittene Objekte mit erfaßt werden, sind Randobjekte bei der Berechnung aller anderen Parameter nicht berücksichtigt worden. Neben der Berechnung der Axon- und Markscheideflächen und ihrer Größenverteilung ist vor allem ihr Verhältnis, die Axon-Markscheide-Relation, von entscheidender diagnostischer Bedeutung.

Der unscharf gefaßte Begriff der Rundheit wurde durch drei unter klinischen Aspekten entworfenen Beschreibungen präzisiert. Diese Definitionen einer allgemeinen, globalen und lokalen Rundheit genügen den notwendigen Bedingungen der Rotations-, Skalierungs- und Verschiebungsinvarianz. Eine allgemeine Formbeschreibung wird durch das Verhältnis von Fläche zu quadriertem Umfang gewonnen, die globale Rundheit läßt sich mittels Bestimmung normierter Zentralmomente zweiter Ordnung, bezogen auf die Kreisform, analytisch beschreiben [8]. Ein lokales Rundheitsmaß beschreibt die hochfrequenten Anteile der Außenkontur. Welligkeiten der Markscheideumhüllungen, ungeachtet einer globalen Deformation des Objektes, weisen auf spezielle pathologische Veränderungen hin (z.B. an den Schmidt-Lantermanschen Inzisuren [9]). Dieses lokale Maß ergibt sich aus der energetischen Betrachtung höherer Koeffizienten der in ihr Spektrum zerlegten Kontur [10].

Die abschließende Bestimmung der mittleren Markscheidedicke erfolgt aus einer Distanztransformation der Objekte mit anschließender Skelettierung. Im Vergleich zu Erosionsverfahren wird so sensibler auf Irregularitäten des Konturbereiches reagiert und werden Abhängigkeiten von einer Vorzugsrichtung vermieden.

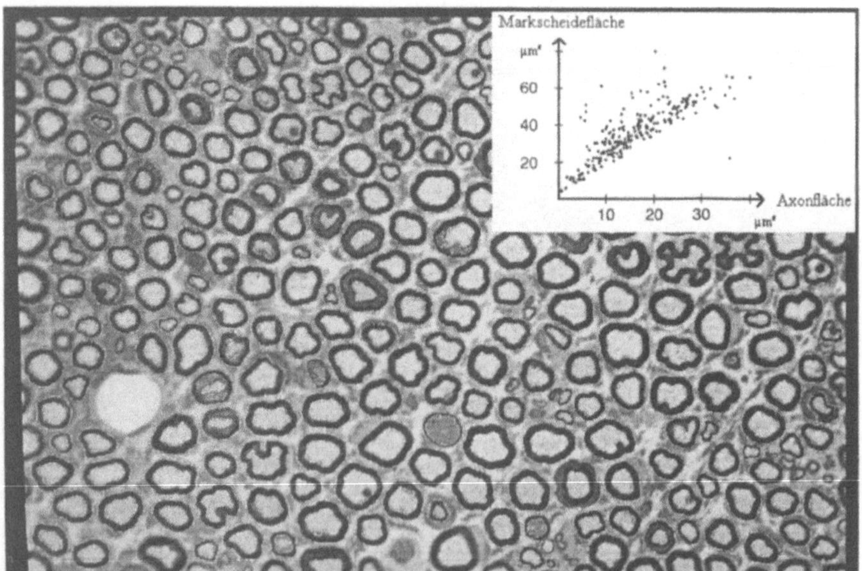

Abb. 2: Segmentiertes Ergebnisbild mit Scatterdiagramm der Axon-Markscheide-Relation.

4 Zusammenfassung

In dieser Arbeit wurde ein Mustererkennungssystem zur Klassifikation, Vermessung und Formbeschreibung von Nervenfasern vorgestellt. Damit ist eine objektive und reproduzierbare morphometrische Auswertung der Präparate möglich geworden.

Es wurden gefärbte Semi-Dünnschnitt-Präparate benutzt, in denen Markscheiden besonders kontrastreich sind. Bei den lichtmikroskopischen Aufnahmen der Nervenbiopsien reicht eine 160-fache Vergrößerung der Präparate für eine hinreichend genaue automatische morphometrische Auswertung aus. Die Auswertung erfolgte an digitalisierten Diapositiven und an mit einer hochauflösenden CCD-Farbkamera (1950x1300 Pixel) aufgenommenen Bildern. Neben den bisher in der klinischen Routine benutzten Parametern Faserdichte, Faseranzahl, Axon- und Markscheidefläche und deren Relation sowie Durchmesser des flächengleichen Kreises können jetzt zusätzlich drei Formbeschreibungen und die mittlere Markscheidedicke automatisch bestimmt werden. Die klinische Relevanz der jetzt neu zur Verfügung gestellten morphometrischen Maße ist gegenwärtig noch Gegenstand von weiterführenden Untersuchungen.

5 Literatur

1. Bertram M, Schröder JM: Developmental changes at the node and paranode in human sural nerves: Morphometric and fine-structural evaluation. Cell Tissues Res 273:499-509, 1993.
2. Russ JC: Optimal Grey Scale Images from Multiplane Color Images. J. Comp. Ass. Microsc., 7(4):221-233, 1995.
3. Parker JR: Algorithms for image processing and computer vision. John Wiley & Sons, New York, 1997.
4. Canny J: A Computational Approach to Edge Detection. IEEE Trans. Pattern Anal. Machine Intell., 8(6):679-698, 1986.
5. Shen J. Castan S: An Optimal Linear Operator for Step Edge Detection. Comp. Vision, Graphics, and Image Proc., 54(2):112-133, 1992.
6. Renn T: Entwicklung von Algorithmen zur Analyse von Nerven- und Muskelbiopsien bei neuromuskulären Krankheiten. Diplomarbeit, RWTH Aachen, 1997.
7. Russ JC: Computer-Assisted Microscopy. Plenum Press, New York, 1990.
8. Schalkoff RJ: Digital Image Processing and Computer Vision. John Wiley & Sons, New York, 1989.
9. Schröder JM, Seiffert KE: Untersuchungen zur homologen Nerventransplantation. Morphologische Ergebnisse. Zentrbl Neurochir, 2:103-118, 1972.
10. Zabele GS, Koplowitz J: Fourier Encoding of Closed Planar Boundaries. IEEE Trans. Pattern Anal. Machine Intell., 7:98-102, 1989.

Ein schneller Algorithmus zur Erkennung und Kompensation von Augenbewegungen zur automatischen Durchführung der funduskontrollierten Mikroperimetrie

A. Dölemeyer[1], H. Liebau[1], F. Toonen[2], S. Wolf[2], D. Meyer-Ebrecht[1].

[1]Lehrstuhl für Meßtechnik
[2]Augenklinik der Medizinischen Fakultät
Rheinisch-Westfälische Technische Hochschule (RWTH), 52056 Aachen
Email: doelemeyer@rwth-aachen.de

Zusammenfassung. Bei der mikroperimetrischen Untersuchung der Funktion des visuellen Systems des Menschen führen unvermeidbare Augenbewegungen zu großen Meßungenauigkeiten. Eine bislang eingesetzte manuelle Nachführung bedeutet eine erhebliche Belastung für den Patienten und den Untersucher. Es wird ein Algorithmus vorgestellt, mit dem Augenbewegungen in Echtzeit erkannt und ausgeglichen werden können. Dabei wird a-priori-Wissen über das Bildmaterial genutzt, um die Bewegungserkennung stark zu vereinfachen. In einer Kontrollstufe wird die Validität des Ergebnisses überprüft. Die Performance wurde an Hand von Videomitschnitten verschiedener Untersuchungen ermittelt. Bei der Implementierung unter WindowsNT konnte die videofrequente Bestimmung der Augenposition erreicht werden. Es gelang weiterhin, falsch positive Ergebnisse völlig auszuschließen.

Schlüsselwörter: Bewegungserkennung, Mikroperimetrie, Echtzeit

1 Einleitung

Wie bei vielen Untersuchungen am Auge stören dessen unwillkürliche und kaum zu beeinflussenden Bewegungen auch die Perimetrie, die „Gesichtsfeldmessung". Diese Untersuchung ist ein psychophysisches Meßverfahren zur Bestimmung der Lichtunterschiedsempfindlichkeit der menschlichen Retina. Sie dient der funktionalen Analyse der Wahrnehmung durch das visuelle System von den Rezeptoren bis zum Visuellen Kortex. Das Verfahren liefert wichtige Erkenntnisse über die Netzhautphysiologie und unterstützt die Diagnostik unterschiedlicher Augenerkrankungen [1]. Darüber hinaus können die Auswirkungen pathologischer Veränderungen der Durchblutung oder der Morphologie der Netzhaut auf die Funktion der Wahrnehmung untersucht werden.

Im Unterschied zur normalen (Kugel-)Perimetrie [2] bedient sich die Mikroperimetrie des Scanning-Laser-Ophthalmoskops (SLO, Rodenstock Inst.), mit dem ein Videobild des Augenhintergrunds erzeugt wird [3]. Dies erlaubt die permanente Kontrolle auf Fundusbewegungen. Gleichzeitig können über einen akusto-optischen Modulator synchron zum Bildsignal beliebige Videobilder auf die Retina projiziert werden. Das wird ausgenutzt, um dem Patienten Lichtpunkte in einem vom Untersucher festgelegten Raster zu präsentieren (s. Abb 1), deren Wahrnehmung mit Hilfe eines Drucktasters bestätigt werden muß. An den Rasterpunkten werden die Intensitäten solange variiert, bis die Wahrnehmungsschwelle festgestellt ist.

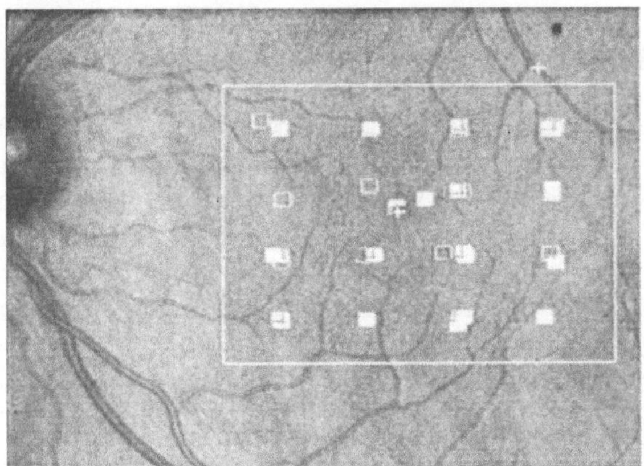

Abb.1 Fundusbild mit Fixationskreuz, Stimulusraster und Referenzpunkt.

Augenbewegungen bilden hierbei ein grundlegendes Problem. Sie führen einerseits zu einer Verwischung des individuellen Stimulus, der eine Präsentationszeit von etwa 200 ms (5 Videobilder) hat. Andererseits kann das Stimulusraster nicht mehr eingehalten werden, wenn zwischen Stimuli mit unterschiedlichen Intensitäten an derselben Position eine Bewegung auftritt. Diese Fehler können es im schlimmsten Fall notwendig machen, eine Untersuchung vollständig zu wiederholen.

Bisher eingesetzte experimentelle Perimetrie-Software [4] erlaubt die Berücksichtigung von Augenbewegungen nur über eine manuelle Markierung eines Referenzpunktes nach oder direkt vor der Präsentation des Stimulus. Dieses Vorgehen verlangt vom Untersucher während der gesamten Untersuchungszeit ein hohes Maß an Aufmerksamkeit und gestaltet die Untersuchung schwierig und aufwendig. Eine automatische Durchführung ist somit bisher nicht möglich.

Ansätze für die automatische Erkennung von Augenbewegungen sind in der Ophthalmologie bereits bei der Unterstützung der Laserkoagulation verfolgt worden [7,8]. Die dabei erzielten Positionsbestimmungsraten von etwa 5 Positionen/sec reichen jedoch bei der hier betrachteten Problematik nicht aus.

Der hier vorgestellt Lösungsansatz macht sich den typischen Inhalt von Fundusbildern zunutze, um die Bestimmung der Verschiebung stark zu vereinfachen. Aufgrund der besonderen Lage und des Verlaufs der Blutgefäße in den Fundusbildern kann der Verschiebungsvektor aufeinanderfolgender Bilder in zwei orthogonale Komponenten separiert werden, deren sukzessive Bestimmung schnell und einfach durchführbar ist. Die Korrektheit der so bestimmten Position wird erst in einem nachfolgenden Kontrollschritt sichergestellt. Dabei werden auch Bildstörungen durch Lidschlag oder starke Verzerrungen automatisch erkannt.

Der Algorithmus wurde in ein neu entwickeltes Mikroperimetrie-Untersuchungsprogramm [5] integriert [6]. Eine sehr wichtige Anforderung war dabei eine schritthaltende Verarbeitung, also die Positionsbestimmung mit Videofrequenz.

Die Funktion des Gesamtsystems wurde an Hand von Videoaufzeichnungen von Untersuchungen überprüft und bewertet.

2 Bewegungserkennung, Suchalgorithmus

Der Lösungsansatz basiert auf dem Template-Matching-Verfahren, mit dem die Verschiebung in aufeinanderfolgenden Bildern aus dem Bewegungsvektor von Bilddetails bestimmt wird, die so lange verschoben werden, bis eine Übereinstimmung gefunden wird. Um den Zeitanforderungen bei der Perimetrie (25 Positionsbestimmungen/sec) genügen zu können, muß der Suchbereich stark verkleinert werden, ohne dabei jedoch den Bereich detektierbarer Verschiebungen einzuschränken. Dazu ist eine Reihe von Vereinfachungen notwendig.

Aufgrund der typischen Augenbewegungen, die durch Einblenden einer Fixationshilfe (Fixationskreuz) beeinflußt sind, können die zu erkennenden Verschiebungen eingeschränkt werden:

- Rotationen des Auges um die optische oder Visuelle Achse sind selten und klein gegen Verschiebungen. Sie werden vernachlässigt.

- Verzerrungen des Bildes durch große Sakkaden brauchen nur erkannt zu werden. Es muß keine Korrektur vorgenommen werden.

- Kopfbewegungen werden durch eine Kinn- und Stirnstütze am Aufnahmegerät SLO weitgehend unterdrückt und resultierende Maßstabsänderungen o.ä. daher ebenfalls vernachlässigt.

Die typische Fundusmorphologie kann dazu ausgenutzt werden, den Suchbereich einzuschränken. Bei der Mikroperimetrie wird in der Regel in der Nähe der Makula untersucht. Die Papille ist meist (zumindest teilweise) sichtbar. Vom Sehnerv aus verlaufen die großen Gefäße in die vier retinalen Quadranten. In der Regel lassen sich so Gefäßabschnitte finden, die annähernd senkrecht zueinander verlaufen und stückweise gerade sind. Unter diesen Bedingungen kann die Bestimmung der Verschiebung in einer stufenweise Bestimmung von zueinander senkrechten Verschiebungskomponenten entlang von Linien aufgeteilt werden (Abb 2.). Die Gefäßkanten lassen sich dabei wegen ihres guten Kontrastes mit dem Template-Matching unter Benutzung des Kreuzkorrelationskoeffizienten als Übereinstimmungsmaß sehr sicher und weitgehend unabhängig von Beleuchtungsschwankungen entlang der Suchlinien wiederfinden. Gegenüber einem Template-Matching mit einem 2D-Bildbereich ist so der Suchbereich stark verkleinert.

Die Suche läuft in 3 Stufen ab (s. Abb 2). Zu Beginn der Untersuchung werden zwei Punkte auf Gefäßkanten manuell ausgewählt. Die Richtungen der Kanten werden automatisch bestimmt und die initialen Suchrichtungen der ersten Stufe senkrecht dazu festgelegt. Entlang dieser beiden Suchrichtungen wird nun die neue Position der Kanten gesucht. Die Verschiebung der Kante, die das bessere Qualitätsmaß liefert wird als die erste Komponente der Verschiebung übernommen. Sämtliche Anfangspositionen werden nun entsprechend nachgeführt. In der zweiten Stufe wird die zweite Komponente der Verschiebung analog zur ersten senkrecht zu dieser bestimmt. In der dritten Stufe werden die Kandidatenpositionen mit einer relativ kleinen 2D-Referenzmaske in einem sehr kleinen Suchbereich überprüft und die „richtige"

Position ausgewählt. In diesem Schritt werden Ungenauigkeiten bei der resultierenden Verschiebung durch kleine Fehler bei der Bestimmung der einzelnen Komponenten ausgeglichen.

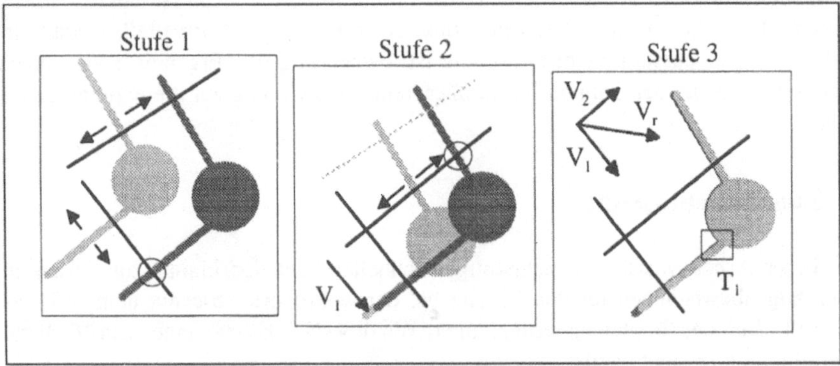

Abb. 2: Die 3-stufige Suche zur Bestimmung der resultierenden Verschiebung V_r aus
den orthogonalen Komponenten V_1 und V_2. Das Template T_1 dient zur Validierung
der ermittelten Verschiebung. Zu beachten ist, daß in Stufe 1 die Richtungen nur näherungsweise orthogonal sein müssen.

Das Qualitätsmaß bei der Bestimmung der Gefäßkanten-Position wird auch für
die Erkennung von Bildstörungen durch Lidschlag herangezogen. Bildverzerrungen
durch schnelle Sakkaden können an Hand der Lage der Matchpunkte auf den Gefäßkanten zueinander identifiziert werden.

3 Ergebnisse

Verschiebungen bis zu 20% der horizontalen Bilddimension (CCIR-Auflösung 768
Bildpunkte) - entsprechend etwa 6 Grad Raumwinkel - können sicher erkannt werden.
Die Rechenzeit beträgt dafür auf einem 200MHz Pentium im Mittel 18,5 ms, maximal 20 ms. Damit steht bei der Bildrate von 25 Bildern/sec noch genug Zeit für Be-
triebssystem-Aufgaben und Steuerprogrammfunktionen zur Verfügung.

Die Performance des Algorithmus und seiner Implementierung wurden an realen
und an künstlich erzeugten Bildsequenzen überprüft. Dabei wurde der Einfluß der
Parameter des Algorithmus und die Rauschempfindlichkeit untersucht. Folgende vier
Ergebnisfälle wurden unterschieden:

- falsch negativ: richtige Position fälschlicherweise abgelehnt. Fehler!
- richtig negativ: falsche Position zu recht als solche erkannt und abgelehnt.
- falsch positiv: falsche Position als richtige erkannt. Gravierender Fehler!
- richtig positiv: richtige Position erfolgreich bestimmt.

Bildausfälle durch Lidschlag und schnelle Augenbewegungen, die zu Bildverzerrungen führen, werden mit hoher Zuverlässigkeit automatisch erkannt und die Ergebnisse
entsprechend verworfen. Die Prüfung eines solchen Rasterpunktes wird dann mit der
entsprechenden Intensität wiederholt. Die Ergebnisse bei realen Bildsequenzen zeigen ein gutmütiges Verhalten der Parameter „Maskengröße" (Linienlänge) und der

„Vertrauensschwelle" (Bewertung des Matching-Qualitätsmaßes und der Validie-rungsstufe). Bei den durchgeführten Experimenten konnten auch unter schlechten Bedingungen – Lidschlag und sich aus dem Bildbereich bewegende Kanten – die Parameter immer so gewählt werden, daß falsch positive Ergebnisse auszuschließen waren. Die so gefundenen Parameter funktionieren auch im Normalfall, so daß eine individuelle Anpassung nicht notwendig ist. Falsch negative Ergebnisse verschlech-tern die Ausbeute der Stimuli, haben aber keine Auswirkung auf die erzielte Genau-igkeit.

4 Zusammenfassung

In dieser Arbeit wurde ein mehrstufiger schneller Suchalgorithmus zur Erkennung von Augenbewegungen für den Einsatz bei der Mikroperimetrie mit dem SLO ent-wickelt. Bei der Implementierung unter WindowsNT konnte eine schritthaltende Verarbeitung erreicht werden.

Mit dem vorgestellten System kann durch die Einhaltung des Stimulusrasters nunmehr die hohe Ortsauflösung des SLO bei der Untersuchung auch kleiner mor-phologischer Veränderungen genutzt werden. Die Untersuchung vereinfacht sich für den Mediziner deutlich, da eine manuelle Nachführung entfällt. Die notwendige Zeit für eine Untersuchung wird deutlich reduziert. Die Anforderungen an die Konzentra-tionsfähigkeit der Patienten sind damit herabgesetzt, so daß mit glaubwürdigeren Ergebnissen zu rechnen ist.

Mit dem System ist die Grundlage dafür gelegt, die Mikroperimetrie vollständig zu automatisieren und die Durchführung durch geschultes Hilfspersonal zu ermögli-chen.

5 Referenzen

1. Reim M: Augenheilkunde, Enke, Stuttgart, 1993
2. Dannheim F: Computer-Perimeter. Ophthalmologisch-optische Instrumente, Rassow B (Hg.). Enke, Stuttgart, 1987
3. van de Felde FJ, Jalkh AE, Elsner AE: Microperimetry with the scanning laser oph-thalmoskop. Perimetry Update, Proc Ixth Intenational Perimetric Society Meeting. Kugler Pub, pp. 93-101, 1990
4. Rohrschneider K, Becker M, Fendrich T, Völcker HE: Kinetische funduskontrollierte Perimetrie mit dem Scanning-Laser-Ophthalmoskop. Klinische Monatsblätter für Augen-heilkunde, 2 (207):102-110. Okt 1995
5. Buchholtz E: Konzeption und Aufbau einer Steuereinheit zur durchführung der Mikrope-rimetrie mit dem Scanning-Laser-Ophthalmoskop. Diplomarbeit am Lehrstuhl für Meß-technik, RWTH Aachen, 1996
6. Liebau H: Integration eines Verfahrens zur automatischen Verfolgung von Augenbewe-gungen in eine Steuereinheit für die Mikroperimetrie, Diplomarbeit am Lehrstuhl für Meßtechnik, RWTH Aachen, 1997
7. Markow MS, Rylander HG, Welch AJ: Real-Time Algorithm for Retinal Tracking. IEEE Trans. Biomed. Eng. 40(12), 1993
8. Barrett SF, Jerath MR, Rylander HG, Welch AJ: Digital tracking and control of retinal images. Optical Engineering 33(1), 150-159, 1994

Robuste Anpassung digitaler Bilddaten auf mehreren Auflösungsstufen

Stefan Henn[1,2], Thorsten Schormann[2],
Knut Engler[1], Karl Zilles[2] und Kristian Witsch[1]

[1] Institut für Angewandte Mathematik,
Heinrich-Heine Universität Düsseldorf, Deutschland
[2] C. und O. Vogt Institut für Hirnforschung,
Heinrich-Heine Universität Düsseldorf, Deutschland

e-mail: henn@sunserver1.rz.uni-duesseldorf.de

Zusammenfassung. In dieser Arbeit wird ein Verfahren zur elastischen Modellierung zweier Bilddatensätze auf mehreren Auflösungsstufen beschrieben. Durch die automatische Modellierung ist es möglich die verschieden frequenten Bildstrukturen auf den verschiedenen Auflösungsstufen ohne jede Vorabinformation elastisch so zu deformieren, daß eine deckungsgleiche Anpassung möglich ist. Hierfür wird auf jeder Auflösungsstufe ein von der gewählten Modellierung abhängiges Funktional sukzessiv minimiert. Dadurch entsteht eine Folge von Verschiebungsvektoren, die die Bilddatensätze elastisch ineinander überführt.

1 Einführung

Verfahren zur räumlichen Überlagerung digitaler Bilddaten sind in der medizinischen Forschung ein notwendiges Werkzeug zur Klärung von Fragestellungen zur Organisation und Variation des menschlichen Gehirns.

Das Problem eine bestmögliche Überlagerung der Bilddaten zu erreichen, führt durch das Prinzip vom Minimum der potentiellen Energie auf die Aufgabe das Funktional

$$J(U) = a(U,U) - 2 \cdot l(U) \quad \text{mit} \quad U \in (H_0^1(\Omega))^n \tag{1}$$

zu minimieren [3], wobei

$$J : I\!\!R^n \to I\!\!R \quad \text{mit} \quad J : U(x_1,..,x_n) \to J(U(x_1,..,x_n))$$

die potentielle Energie einer elastischen Verschiebung beschreibt. Hierbei ist $a(U,U)$ eine Bilinearform und $l(U) = \int_\Omega (F,U)_0 \, dX$ eine Linearform (vgl. [3]) mit dem Vektor $F = \nabla T(T - R)$ der Volumenkräfte, die auf das Template T wirken. R bezeichnet hierbei das Referenzvolumen. Äquivalent zur Minimierung von (1) ist die Lösung der Variationsgleichung

$$a(U,\phi) = l(\phi) \quad \forall \phi \in (H_0^1(\Omega))^n.$$

Das ist die schwache Form des Systems partieller Differentialgleichungen nach Navier-Lamé:

$$\mathbf{NLE}(\mu, \lambda)U := \mu \Delta U + (\lambda + \mu)\nabla(\nabla)U = F(U) \quad \text{auf} \quad \Omega \qquad (2)$$
$$U = 0 \quad \text{auf} \quad \partial\Omega$$

mit den elastischen Konstanten λ und μ.

Die Minimalstelle U^* des Funktionals $J(U)$ entspricht dem Verschiebungsfeld, welches die Bilddatensätze aufeinander transformiert. Um eine maximale Volumenänderung zu erzielen, wird $\lambda = 0$ gesetzt [1], so daß nur μ zum Ausbalancieren der äußeren und inneren Kräfte verwendet wird. Hierbei verhält sich für große μ das Ausgangsvolumen wie ein starrer Körper, der kaum Deformationen zuläst. Ist anderseits μ sehr klein, so wird der Einfluß der Kräfte so groß, daß kleinste Störungen (wie z.B. Rauschen) zu unerwünschten Fehlanpassungen führen. Deshalb wird im folgenden Text die Verschiebung U neben der Abhängigkeit vom Ort $X \in I\!R^n$ auch in Abhängigkeit der Modellierungskonstante μ geschrieben $U(X) = U(X, \mu)$. Zur Bestimmung des Minimums $U^*(X, \mu)$ von J bzgl. μ wird

$$\Omega^n = \{(x_1, ..., x_n) \in I\!R^n \mid x_1, ..., x_n \in (0, 1)^n\}$$

so diskretisiert, daß das Gitter Ω_h^n mit der Schrittweite $h = 1/N$ (N =Anzahl der Bildpunkte in einer Koordinatenrichtung) mit den Bildelementen korrespondiert. Als Restriktion des Minimierungsproblems ergibt sich $X - U(X) \in \Omega$, was bedeutet, daß die Bildelemente durch die Verschiebung $U(X)$ nicht den Bildbereich verlassen dürfen. Die Suche nach einer Minimalstelle von J beginnt nun mit der Berechnung der Suchrichtung $V_h(X, \mu)$ durch Lösen von (2). Anschließend wird an der berechneten Stelle $(V_0, J(V_0))$ wieder (2) gelöst und $U_1 = V_0 + V_1$ berechnet. Dieser Iterationsprozeß (elastische Iteration vgl. [3]) wird solange durchgeführt, bis ein geeignetes Abbruchkriterium erfüllt ist.

Die Berechnung der Näherungslösungen $\{V_{i,h}(X, \mu)\}_{i=0,...,k}$ auf Ω_h^n von (2) ist trotz effizienter numerischer Methoden (vgl. [2], [3]) sehr zeitaufwendig und sollte deshalb so selten wie möglich bestimmt werden. Eine geeignete Modellierung der Bilddaten ist hierfür notwendig.

In dieser Arbeit wird eine Vorschrift zur Modellierung der Bilddaten vorgeschlagen, die es ermöglicht auf verschiedenen Diskretisierungsstufen des Funktionals $J_h(U(X, \mu)), J_{2h}(U(X, \mu)), ..., J_{Lh}(U(X, \mu))$ (bzw. der Auflösungsstufen der Bilddaten $\Omega_h, \Omega_{2h}, ..., \Omega_{Lh}$), die jeweiligen existierenden Bildstrukturen einander robust (d.h. unabhängig gegenüber kleineren Störungen) anzupassen. Die Anzahl der Auflösungsstufen wird hierbei mit L bezeichnet.

2 Mathematische Beschreibung des Verfahrens

Um auf einer Diskretisierungsstufe $\{\Omega_{lh}\}_{l \in \{1,...,L\}}$ die existierenden Bildstrukturen anzupassen wird eine Folge von Verschiebungsvektoren $\{U_i(X, \mu)\}_{i=0,..,k}$ gesucht, die sukzessiv das Funktional J bzw. den quadratischen Abstand der

Bilddaten $D_2(U(X,\mu)) = h^2 \cdot \int_{X \in \Omega_h^n} (T(X-U) - R(X))^2 dX$ minimiert.
D.h. für $\{U_i(X,\mu)\}_{i=0,..,k}$ gilt

$$J(U_0(X,\mu)) > J(U_1(X,\mu)) > \cdots > J(U_k(X,\mu)) \quad \text{bzw.} \tag{3}$$
$$D_2(U_0(X,\mu)) > D_2(U_1(X,\mu)) > \cdots > D_2(U_k(X,\mu)),$$

wobei $U_0(X,\mu) = V_0(X,\mu)$ die erste berechnete Verschiebung ist. Ist ein $k \in I\!N$ gefunden, für das

$$J(U_k(X,\mu)) < J(U_{k+1}(X,\mu)) \quad \text{oder} \quad D_2(U_k(X,\mu)) < D_2(U_{k+1}(X,\mu))$$

gilt, so ist keine weiter Minimierung des Funktionals J bzw. des quadratischen Abstands der Bilddaten D_2 mehr möglich. Anschließend wird der Verschiebungsvektor U_k^l auf die nächst feinere Auflösung $\Omega_{(l-1)h}$ interpoliert. Dort wird der Minimierungsprozeß erneut gestartet, bis die feinste Auflösung erreicht ist. Die Modellierung der Bilddaten auf den verschiedenen Auflösungsstufen erfolgt hierbei so, daß die Verschiebung U_0^l bzgl. der Norm

$$\|U\|_{\infty,2} := \max_{X \in \Omega_h^n} \sqrt{\sum_{i=1}^n u_i(X)^2}$$

etwa ein bis zwei Bildelemente beträgt, daß dies stets möglich ist zeigt der folgende Satz:

Satz. *Ein Bilddatensatz T mit dem Referenzsystem R kann für ein $\mu > 0$ und $\lambda = 0$ stets so modelliert werden, daß der Verschiebungsvektor $U(X,\mu)$ die Eigenschaft $\|U\|_{\infty,2} = c \in I\!R^{>0}$ besitzt.*

Beweis. Mit $\lambda = 0$ folgt für den Differentialoperator aus (2)

$$\mathbf{NLE}(\mu,\lambda) \stackrel{\lambda=0}{=} \mathbf{NLE}(\mu,0) \stackrel{(2)}{=} \mu\Delta + \mu\nabla(\nabla) =: \mathbf{L}(\mu).$$

Da $\mathbf{L}$ linear in μ ist (d.h. $\mathbf{L}(a \cdot \mu) = \mu \cdot \mathbf{L}(a)$ für ein $a \in IR^{>0}$), folgt aus (2)

$$(\mathbf{L}(\mu))(U) = \mu \cdot (\mathbf{L}(1))(U) = F.$$

Da die Lösung U^* von Gleichung (2) eindeutig existiert, existiert auch der inverse Operator $\mathbf{L}^{-1}$ [2]. Sei nun $\mu > 0$ beliebig aber fest.
Dann gilt:

$$\mu \cdot (\mathbf{L}(1))(U) = F \Longleftrightarrow \mu \cdot U = \mathbf{L}(1)^{-1} F \Longleftrightarrow U = \frac{\mathbf{L}(1)^{-1} F}{\mu} =: U(\mu) \tag{4}$$

Setze mit $c \in I\!R^{>0}$:

$$\tilde{\mu} = \frac{\mu \cdot \|U(\mu)\|_{\infty,2}}{c}, \tag{5}$$

damit gilt:

$$\|U(\tilde{\mu})\|_{\infty,2} \stackrel{(4)}{=} \frac{\|\mathbf{L}(1)^{-1} F\|_{\infty,2}}{\|\tilde{\mu}\|_{\infty,2}} \stackrel{(5)}{=} \frac{\|\mathbf{L}(1)^{-1} F\|_{\infty,2} \cdot c}{\mu \cdot \|U(\mu)\|_{\infty,2}} \stackrel{(4)}{=} \frac{\|\mathbf{L}(1)^{-1} F\|_{\infty,2} \cdot c}{\mu \cdot \frac{\|\mathbf{L}(1)^{-1} F\|_{\infty,2}}{\mu}} = c.$$

$\square$

Gemäß (5) können also auf jeder Auflösungsstufe die Bilddaten so modelliert werden, daß die Verschiebung $\|U_0\|_{\infty,2} = \nu \cdot h$ ist, und somit das Template T um maximal ν Bildelemente verschoben wird.

3 Ergebnisse

Anhand zweier Bilddatensätze soll die Zweckmäßigkeit der oben vorgeschlagenen Modellierung der Bilddaten verdeutlicht werden. Dazu werden die Bildaten auf drei verschiedene Arten ($c_1 = h$, $c_2 = 2h$ und $c_3 = 4h$ gemäß (5)) modelliert. In Abbildung 3 erkennt man gut, daß für c_1 und c_2 der quadratische Abstand der Bilder D_2 sowie die potentielle Energie der elastischen Verschiebung J kontinuierlich minimiert werden. Wählt man μ zu klein (bzw. c zu groß), so wird der quadratische Abstand und das Funktional zunächst käfig minimiert. Jedoch nach einigen elastischen Iterationen beginnen die Werte zu alternieren, was zur Folge hat, daß das Templatebild um das Referenzsystem alterniert. Die Anpassung ist nicht mehr robust.

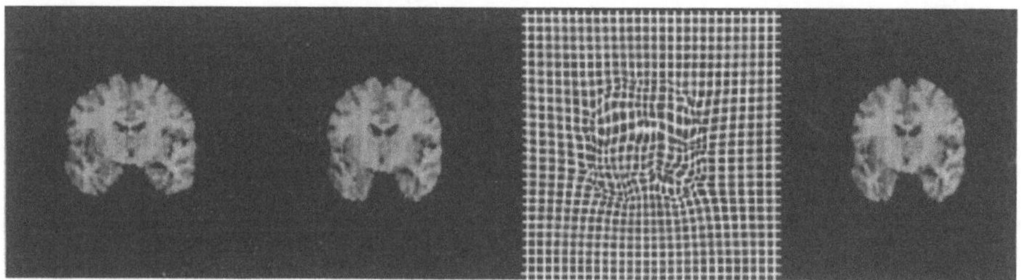

Abb. 1. Von links nach rechts: Referenz-Bild, Template-Bild, Verschiebungsfeld angewendet auf ein äquidistantes Gitter, Ergebnisbild nach 10 elastischen Iterationen wobei die Ausbangsbilder gemäß $\|U_0\|_{\infty,2} = h$ modelliert worden sind.

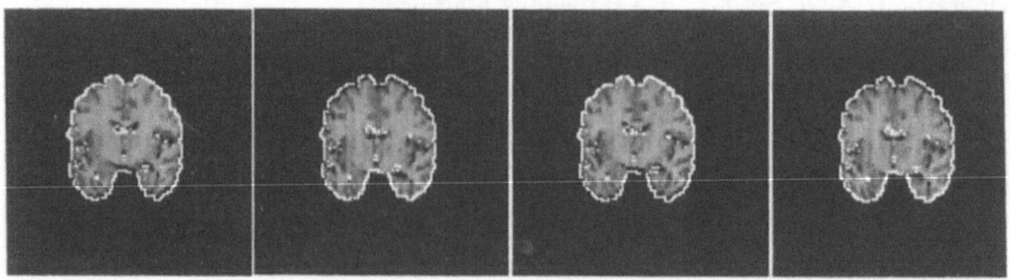

Abb. 2. Das transformierte Template nach der 7, 8, 9 und 10 -ten elastischen Iteration, wobei die Ausgangsbilder gemäß $\|U_0\|_{\infty,2} = 4h$ modelliert worden sind.

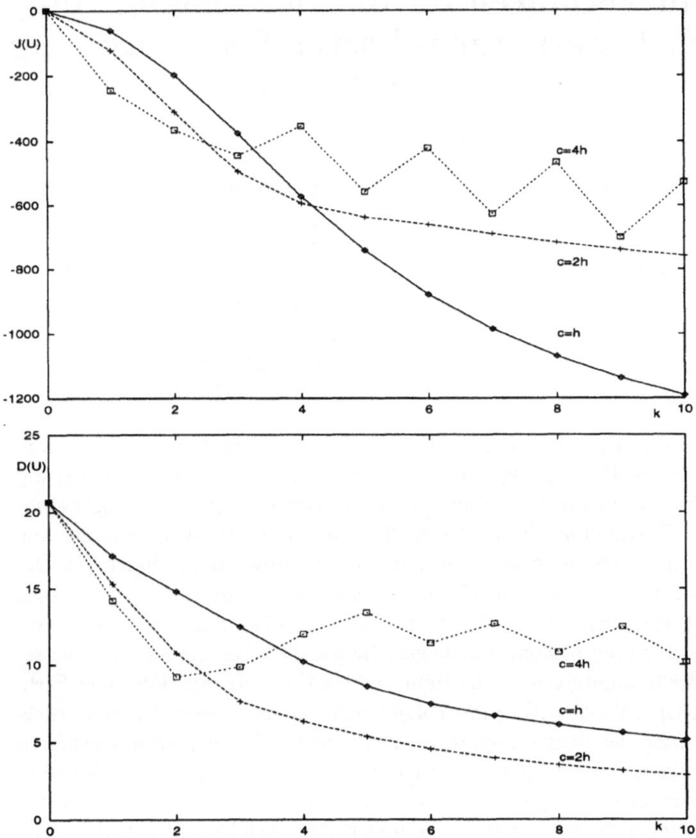

Abb. 3. Entwicklung der potentiellen Energie der elastischen Verschiebung J (oben) und des quadratischen Abstandes der Bilddaten D_2 (unten) bzgl. der elastischen Iteration für die Modellierungen c_1, c_2 und c_3.

Literatur

1. Bajcsy R. and Kovacic S. (1989): Multiresolution Elastic Matching, *Computer Vision, Graphics and Image Processing 46, 1-21.*
2. Henn S. (1997): Schnelle elastische Anpassung in der digitalen Bildverarbeitung mit Hilfe von Mehrgitterverfahren, *Diplomarbeit Heinrich-Heine Universität Düsseldorf,* http://www.hirn.uni-duesseldorf.de/˜stef/
3. Henn, S., Schormann, T., Engler, K., Zilles, K., Witsch, K. (1997): Elastische Anpassung in der digitalen Bildverarbeitung auf mehreren Auflösungsstufen mit Hilfe von Mehrgitterverfahren. *Springer Series: "Informatik-Aktuell", Springer-Verlag (1997), 392-399.*
4. Schormann T., Henn S. and Zilles K. (1996): A New Approach to Fast Elastic Alignment with Applications to Human Brains. *Lecture Notes in Computer Science 1131, Springer-Verlag (1996), 437-442.*

Ein Verfahren für die Berechnung von Farbclustern zur robusten Segmentierung von Farbflächen

Hermann Hienz, Kirsti Grobel und Markus Tan

Lehrstuhl für Technische Informatik
Rheinisch-Westfälische Technische Hochschule Aachen (RWTH)
Ahornstrasse 55, D-52074 Aachen
Phone: +49-241-8026105   Fax: +49-241-8888308
Email: hienz@techinfo.rwth-aachen.de

Zusammenfassung Dieser Beitrag beschreibt ein interaktives Verfahren für die Berechnung von Farbclustern zur robusten Segmentierung von Farbflächen in Videobildern. Die entwickelte Segmentierungsmethode ist Bestandteil eines Bildverarbeitungssystems zur Erkennung von Gebärden, wie sie in der Gebärdensprache Anwendung finden [1]. Der Benutzer trägt einen mehrfarbig markierten Handschuh an der rechten Hand, einen einfarbigen Handschuh an der linken Hand und eine Farbmarkierung am rechten Ellenbogen. Insgesamt sollen die zehn Farben sowie der Bildhintergrund, die Haut und die Kleidung mit Hilfe einer Farb-Look-Up-Tabelle (LUT) in Echtzeit segmentiert werden. Unter Berücksichtigung der Echtzeitanforderungen wird ein Segmentierungsverfahren entwickelt, das robust bezüglich der Kleidung des Benutzers, des Bildhintergrunds und gegenüber Änderungen der Beleuchtungsintensität ist. Das implementierte Segmentierungsverfahren ermöglicht dem Benutzer, eine Segmentierung von sehr hoher Qualität zu erzielen, welche eine gute Grundlage für die anschließende Merkmalsextraktion und Klassifikation der Gebärde darstellt.

Schlüsselwörter: Punktorientierte Segmentierung, Farb-Look-Up-Tabelle, RGB-Farbraum, HSV-Farbraum, Gebärdenerkennung

1   Einleitung

Eine wichtige Verarbeitungsstufe der Bildanalyse stellt die Segmentierung dar. Mit Segmentierung bezeichnet man das Zusammenfassen inhaltlich zusammenhängender Regionen, die einem bestimmten Homogenitätskriterium genügen [2].

In diesem Beitrag wird ein interaktives Verfahren vorgestellt, mit dessen Hilfe die Berechnung von Farbclustern zur robusten Segmentierung von Farbflächen in Videobildern möglich ist. Das entwickelte Verfahren findet Anwendung in einem automatischen Gebärdenerkennungssystem, das den gesamten Gebärdenraum (Bereich in dem alle Bewegungen der Gebärdensprache gebildet werden) mit einer einzigen Videokamera erfaßt und auf einem handelsüblichen PC mit zusätzlicher Bildverarbeitungshardware implementiert ist [1].

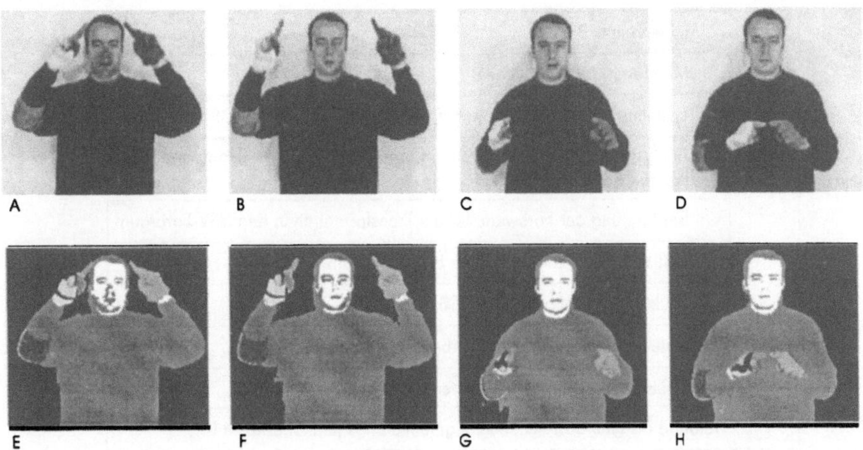

Abbildung 1. Die Gebärde *Fenster* dargestellt durch vier Einzelbilder (A bis D). Die Bilder E bis H zeigen die korrespondierende segmentierte Bildfolge. Der Benutzer trägt einen mehrfarbig markierten Handschuh an der rechten Hand, einen einfarbigen Handschuh an der linken Hand und eine Farbmarkierung am rechten Ellenbogen

Damit genügend Information über die Gebärde für die anschließende Klassifikation zur Verfügung steht, muß die Segmentierung der Bildfolgen in Echtzeit erfolgen. Des weiteren muß die Qualität der Segmentierung gute Ergebnisse liefern, damit eine schnelle weitere Verarbeitung des segmentierten Bildes erfolgen kann, ohne daß aufwendige Korrekturverfahren durchgeführt werden.

Um sowohl Echtzeitfähigkeit als auch eine ausreichende Robustheit zu ermöglichen, trägt der Benutzer farbig markierte Handschuhe und eine Markierung am rechten Ellenbogen. Die Aufgabe der Segmentierung besteht darin, diese farbigen Flächen (Zeigefinger, Ringfinger, Kleiner Finger, Handücken, Handgelenk, Handballen, Haut, Mittelfinger, Daumen, Ellenbogen, Linke Hand) sowie den Bildhintergrund (Wand) und die Haut des Benutzers zu segmentieren. Kleidung und Haare des Benutzers repräsentieren den Hintergrund im Sinne der Bildverarbeitung, während die Farbmarkierungen, die Haut und der Bildhintergrund (Wand) die Objekte der Bildszene darstellen [3]. Abbildung 1 zeigt vier Einzelbilder einer Bildfolge.

Ein weiteres Problem ergibt sich aus der Tatsache, daß die Bildszene sowohl mit Halogenscheinwerfern als auch mit Tageslicht beleuchtet wird. Aufgrund der Farbtemperaturschwankungen des Tageslichts (und auch der Scheinwerfer) verändern die Farbcluster der Markierungsfarben ihre Lage im Farbraum. Daraus ergibt sich die Anforderung, daß die Segmentierung auf eine einfache Art und Weise an Farbtemperaturänderungen anpassbar sein muß. Eine adaptive Segmentierung, die sich automatisch an eine veränderte Farbtemperatur anpaßt, ist in Echtzeit nicht zu realisieren und wird daher nicht näher betrachtet. Im Gegen-

Laden eines Bildes
Markieren der Farbflächen
Erstellen von Farbhistogrammen für jede Farbfläche im RGB-Farbraum
Analyse der berechneten Histogramme und eindeutige Zuordnung eines Farbwerts zu einem Objekt
Bestimmung der Farbwerte für die Transformation in den HSV-Farbraum
Festlegen der Schwellwerte im HSV-Farbraum
Rücktransformation in den RGB-Farbraum
Erstellen einer vorläufigen Farb-Look-Up-Tabelle
Visuelle Beurteilung der Segmentierung
Solange bis eine ausreichende Segmentierungsqualität erreicht ist
Erstellen der Farb-Look-Up-Tabelle im RGB-Farbraum

Abbildung2. Struktogramm des interaktiven Verfahrens für die Berechnung der Farbcluster zur Aufteilung einer Farb-Look-Up-Tabelle

satz zur Veränderung der Farbtemperatur können Helligkeitsschwankungen bei der Entwicklung des Segmentierungsverfahrens berücksichtigt werden, sodaß sie keinen bzw. nur einen geringen Einfluß auf das Segmentierungsergebnis haben.

Bei der Auswahl der verwendeten Markierungsfarben werden eine hohe Intensität sowie ein möglichst großer Farbtonunterschied zwischen den Farben gefordert.

2 Interaktives Verfahren für die Berechnung der Farbcluster

Um die Segmentierung in Echtzeit durchführen zu können, wird eine punktorientierte Segmentierung mit Hilfe einer Farb-LUT realisiert [4].

Die wesentlichen Schritte zur Berechnung einer neuen Farb-LUT zeigt Abbildung 2.

Das Einlesen eines Bildes repräsentiert den ersten Schritt des Verfahrens. Eine interaktive Vorgehensweise erlaubt dem Benutzer die einzelnen Farben sukzessive im Videobild zu markieren. Die Markierung kann entweder manuell (Markierung unter Verwendung von Rechtecken) oder mit Hilfe des Bereichswachstumsverfahren durchgeführt werden, wobei die Keimpunkte manuell gesetzt werden [5].

Nachdem alle Objekte markiert sind, wird für jedes Objekt ein Histogramm im RGB-Farbraum ermittelt. Mit Hilfe des Histogramms wird für jeden Farbwert des Objekts die Häufigkeit seines Vorkommens im markierten Bildausschnitt bestimmt (Abbildung 3).

Im Anschluß daran erfolgt die Analyse der berechneten Histogramme mit dem Ziel eine eindeutige Zuordnung eines Farbwerts zu einem Objekt zu erreichen. Für jeden Farbwert der Farb-LUT wird geprüft, ob ein Farbwert eindeutig einem Objekt zugeordnet werden kann. Dazu werden die Histogramme betrachtet und daraufhin geprüft, ob nur für ein Objekt Einträge vorliegen und ob die Anzahl der Einträge einen Mindestwert übersteigt. Ist beides der Fall, wird dieser Farbwert innerhalb der Farb-LUT dem jeweiligen Objekt zugeordnet. Tritt ein Farbwert in zwei Objekten auf, wird der Farbwert grundsätzlich dem Hintergrund (Kleidung und Haare) zugeordnet. Dabei muß zwischen einer Über- und einer Untersegmentierung unterschieden werden [2]. Eine Übersegmentierung tritt dann auf, wenn außerhalb des zu segmentierenden Objekts eine Farbfläche fälschlicherweise diesem Objekt zugeordnet wird. Dagegen bedeutet eine Untersegmentierung, daß nur Teile des Objekts richtig segmentiert werden. Für die Erkennung von Gebärden ist eine Untersegmentierung weit weniger störend, als eine Übersegmentierung, sodaß bei einer Überlappung zweier Farbcluster die Schnittmenge dem Hintergrund zugeordnet wird. Mit dieser Zuordnung wird bei annähernd konstanten Beleuchtungsverhältnissen eine gute Segmentierung erreicht.

Um die Segmentierung gegenüber Änderungen der Beleuchtungsintensität invariant zu halten, werden die Kerngebiete der Farbbereiche in den HSV-Farbraum transformiert. Für jeden dieser Farbbereiche werden Schwellwerte festgelegt. Die Schwellen für den Farbton H und die Sättigung S sind dabei die Minimal- bzw. Maximalwerte der transformierten Kernbereiche. Für die Intensität werden die Schwellen erweitert, um Helligkeitsschwankungen ausgleichen zu können.

Anschließend wird jeder Farbwert in der Farb-LUT, der noch nicht eindeutig zugeordnet werden konnte, darauf geprüft, ob eine eindeutige Zuordnung im HSV-Farbraum vorliegt. Alle Farbwerte, die sich nicht eindeutig zuordnen lassen, fallen dem Hintergrund zu. Die so erstellte Aufteilung der Farb-LUT kann direkt getestet und visuell beurteilt werden. Ist die Qualität der Segmentierung ausreichend, ist die Erstellung der Farb-LUT beendet. Ist dagegen die Qualität der Segmentierung nicht ausreichend, kann ein neues Bild geladen und die Farb-LUT verbessert werden. Abbildung 1 (E-G) zeigt die segmentierten Bildsequenzen der Gebärde *Fenster*.

3 Ergebnisse

Das vorgestellte Verfahren ermöglicht mit wenigen Messungen eine weitgehend fehlerfreie Segmentierung. Fehlsegmentierungen aufgrund von Schattenbildung am Hintergrund oder durch das Tragen farbiger Kleidung werden fast vollständig eliminiert. Besonders die für die anschließende Handformerkennung kritische Übersegmentierung wird erfolgreich beseitigt. Leichte Fehlsegmentierungen können durch Interreflexionen an Farbübergängen auftreten, sie lassen sich jedoch durch zusätzliche Messungen ebenfalls beseitigen.

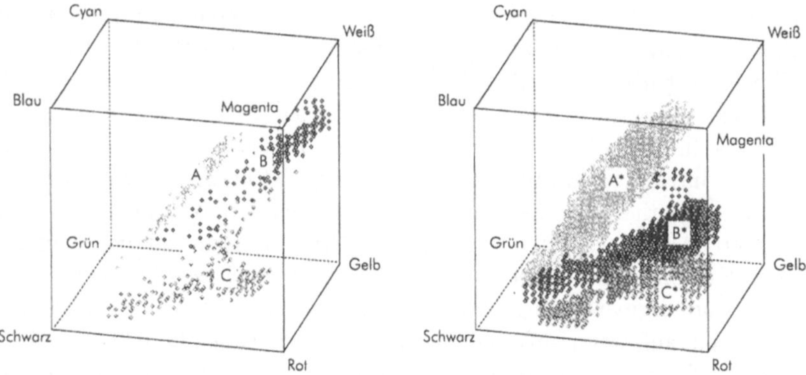

Abbildung3. Im linken Bild sind beispielhaft die markierten Farbwerte für drei Objekte im RGB-Farbraum dargestellt. Die Farbwerte bilden streuende Farbcluster (A - kleiner Finger, B - Handgelenk, C - Daumen) im Farbraum. Der rechte Teil der Abbildung zeigt die berechneten kompakten Cluster (A*, B*, C*), wie sie zur Erstellung der Farb-Look-Up-Tabelle verwendet werden

4 Zusammenfassung

Diese Arbeit präsentiert ein interaktives Verfahren für die Berechnung von Farbclustern zur robusten Segmentierung von Farbflächen in Videobildern. Die punktorientierte Segmentierung ist durch eine Farb-LUT realisiert und arbeitet in Echtzeit. Die Nutzung der Eigenschaften des HSV-Farbraums ermöglicht, die Segmentierung gegenüber Änderungen der Beleuchtungsstärke invariant zu halten.

Das entwickelte Verfahren wird erfolgreich in einem Bildverarbeitungssystem zur automatischen Erkennung von Gebärden eingesetzt.

Literatur

1. Grobel, K., Hienz, H.: Videobasierte Gebärdenerkennung. In: Kraiss, K.-F., Hrsg.: Jahresbericht - Lehrstuhl für Technische Informatik 1995/96, S. 21-28. Shaker-Verlag Aachen, 1997.
2. Lehmann, T., Oberschelp, W., Pelikan, E., Repges, R.: *Bildverarbeitung für die Medizin. Grundlagen, Modelle, Methoden, Anwendungen.* Springer-Verlag, Berlin, 1. Auflage 1997.
3. Tan, M.: *Ansichtenbasierte Handformerkennung in Bildfolgen.* Diplomarbeit, Lehrstuhl für Technische Informatik der RWTH Aachen, 1997.
4. Jähne, B.: *Digitale Bildverarbeitung.* Springer-Verlag, Berlin, 1993.
5. Wahl, F.M.: *Digitale Bildsignalverarbeitung - Grundlagen, Verfahren, Beispiele.* Springer-Verlag, Berlin, 1984.

Multimediale Darstellung und Verarbeitung medizinischer Bilddaten in Rechnernetzen

Prof. Dr. W.Hillen, Dipl.Ing. N.Jansen, F.Unglauben, R.Indefrey

Medizinische Informatik
FH - Aachen Abt. Jülich, Biomedizinische Technik
Email: hillen@fh-aachen.de

Zusammenfassung. Auf der Basis der Java-Programmiertechnik wird eine Anwendung erstellt, mit der medizinische Bilddaten, Befunde und Patienteninformationen in digitaler Form innerhalb und außerhalb des Krankenhauses dargestellt und verarbeitet werden können. Die Java-Anwendung ermöglicht eine Informationsübertragung im Intra- und Internet, die unabhängig ist von der Hardware und vom Betriebssystem des Clients. Der Funktionsumfang der auf den Client übertragenen Software zur Visualisierung und Verarbeitung der Bilddaten wird vom Server genau auf die jeweils ausgewählte medizinische Anwendung abgestimmt.

Schlüsselwörter: medizinische Bilddarstellung, Bildverarbeitung, verteilte Informationssysteme, Java - Applikation.

1 Einleitung

Medizinische Bildinformation wird in der klinischen Diagnostik weitgehend digital aufgenommen und verarbeitet. Die Bilddaten von CT-, MR-, Angiographie- und nuklearmedizinischen Geräten werden hierbei in der Regel zentral verwaltet (Bild- / Patientendatenbank) und auf speziellen Befundungskonsolen ausgewertet. Die Weiterleitung der Bilddaten und Befunde z.B. zur chirurgischen Abteilung, zu den Klinikstationen oder auch zum niedergelassenen Arzt (außerhalb des Krankenhauses) erfolgt allerdings oft noch in Form von Filmkopien und Textdokumenten. Die Übertragung der Bilddaten, Befunde und Patienteninformationen in digitaler Form innerhalb und außerhalb des Krankenhauses im Intra- und Internet sowie die multimediale Darstellung und Verarbeitung der Informationen ist das generelle Ziel der vorliegenden Aktivität.

2 Systemkonzept

Das Konzept des Informationssystems zur Darstellung und Verarbeitung medizinischer Bilddaten im Intra- und Internet ist in Abb. 1 dargestellt. Typischerweise werden die Bilddaten der unterschiedlichen diagnostischen Systeme (CT, MR u.s.w) auf speziellen Befundungskonsolen ausgewertet und in einem zentralen Bildarchiv gespeichert. Ebenfalls werden im Zentralarchiv die Patientendaten und Befundungsergebnisse verwaltet. Im dargestellten Systemkonzept verbindet ein spezieller Web-Server das zentrale Datenarchiv der radiologischen Abteilung mit den dezentralen Arbeitsplätzen (Clients). Die Kopplung zwischen Web-Server und Clients erfolgt über Intra- oder Internet. Die Clients können sowohl in den verschiedenen Klinikbereichen (Intranet-Kopplung) als auch in den Praxen niedergelassener Ärzte (Internet-Kopplung) plaziert sein. Auf dem Web-Server ist ein verteiltes Informationssystem installiert, das auf den Datenbestand des Zentralarchivs zugreift. Zu diesen Daten zählen die Patientendaten, die patientenbezogenen Applikationen sowie die Daten , die einer einzelnen Applikation zugeordnet sind. Die applikationsbezogenen Daten bestehen im allgemeinen Fall aus den Bilddaten, den Ergebnissen der Befunde (in Form von Textdokumenten und/oder grafischen Overlays) sowie spezifischen Parametern der Aufnahmesysteme und Parametern zur Steuerung der Java-Anwendung auf dem Client. Dieser „Datensatz" einer medizinischen Applikation wird zusammen mit dem Java-Code bei einer User-Anfrage vom Web-Server auf den Client übertragen.

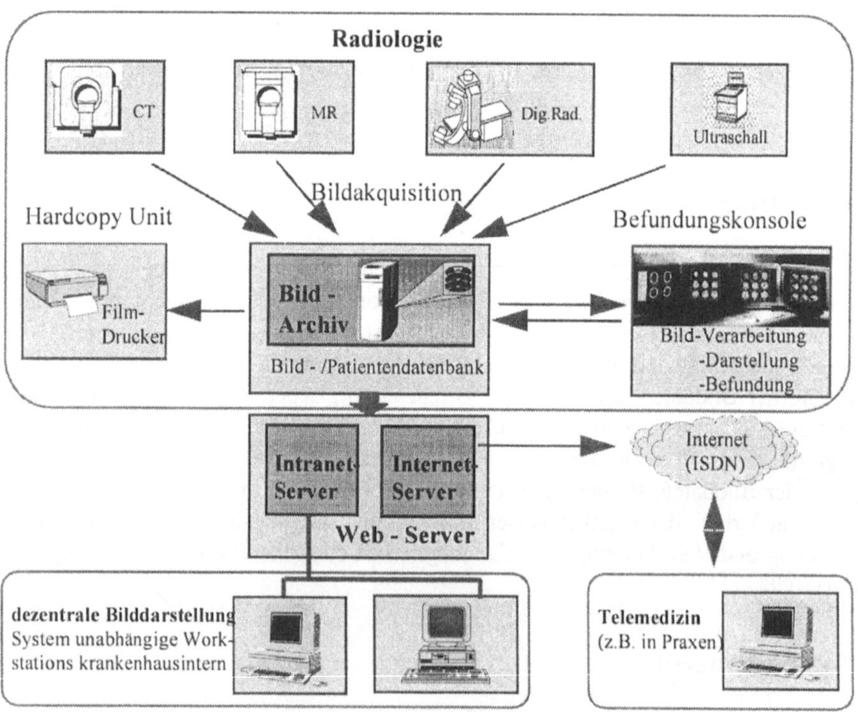

Abb.1: Systemkonzept eines verteilten, multimedialen Informationssystems im Bereich der bildgebenden Diagnostik.

Der Systembenutzer benötigt auf dem Client (PC, Mac, Sun, ...) mit Ausnahme eines Netz-Browsers keine spezielle Softwareinstallation. Damit entfallen sowohl die Erstinstallation der Software als auch spätere Software-Updates auf den dezentralen Arbeitsplätzen. Die Pflege der Bild- und Patientendatenbank, die Einstellung der applikationsbezogenen Parameter sowie der vollständige Sevice der Software erfolgen auf dem Web-Server.

Das Java-Framework garantiert eine von der Hardware und von dem Betriebssystem der Client - Rechner unabhängige Anwendung. Diese Plattformunabhängigkeit stellt eine der generellen Vorteile der Java-Applikation dar. Hierdurch wird gewährleistet, daß die Vielfalt der heute eingesetzten Systeme in gleicher Weise unterstützt wird.

3 Programm - Funktionen

Innerhalb der Java-Anwendung wählt der Benutzer die gewünschte medizinische Applikation eines Patienten aus und aktiviert damit die Übertragung der Bilddaten sowie der zugehörigen Befunde und Patienteninformationen (applikationsbezogene Daten) vom Server auf den Client. Ebenfalls werden sämtliche Java-Komponenten zum Einlesen, Darstellen und Verarbeiten der Daten auf den Client übertragen und zur Ausführung gebracht.

In der Anwendung werden verschiedene Methoden der Bilddarstellung und der interaktiven Bildverarbeitung sowie Verfahren zur Visualisierung von Patienteninformationen und Befunden bereitgestellt. Zu den bislang realisierten Möglichkeiten der Darstellung und Verarbeitung der Bilder und Informationen gehören:

- Darstellung von Einzelbildern und Bildgruppen sowie Darstellung von Bildsequenzen (z.B. CT- / MR- Applikationen) mit interaktiv einstellbaren Ablauffolgen.

- Interaktive Bildoperationen zur optimalen Wiedergabe der Bilder (z.B. Kontrast- / Helligkeitsanpassungen, Bildfilter, Zoomfunktionen).

- Überlagerte Darstellung von Befundungsergebnissen in Form von Text- und/oder Grafik-Overlays.

Die Anwendung unterstützt sowohl Bilder mit einer Digitalisierungstiefe von 8-Bit als auch Bilder mit maximal 16 Bits pro Pixel. Alle Bildverarbeitungsschritte werden in voller Digitalisierungstiefe durchgeführt. Zur Darstellung von Bildern mit mehr als 8-Bit ist ein eigenes Color-Model entwickelt worden. Das Color-Model führt eine Projektion der Daten in den 8-Bit Darstellungsbereich durch über eine beliebig einstellbare 16- auf 8-Bit LUT-Operation.

Eine wichtige Anforderung für medizinische Anwendung ist das Einlesen von Bildformaten, die Java nicht direkt unterstützt (z.B. TIFF oder DICOM). Zur Zeit werden in der Anwendung 8- bzw. 16-Bit Bilder im TIF-Format eingelesen und weiterverarbeitet.

Die Methoden und der Funktionsumfang der zur Anwendung gebrachten Software-Module sind genau auf die jeweils ausgewählte Applikation abgestimmt. So sind z.B. Bildverarbeitungsschritte wie Restaurationsfilter auf den einzelnen Anwendungsfall und das verwendete Aufnahmesystem optimiert. Ebenso werden im Gegensatz zu einer fest installierten Software dem Benutzer nur Operationen und Visualisierungsverfahren bereitgestellt, die für die gewählte Applikation sinnvoll sind. Damit wird eine einfache, applikationsbezogene und zielgerichtete Programmanwendung realisiert mit einer intuitiv bedienbaren und auf den Anwendungsfall zugeschnittenen Benutzeroberfläche.

Die Benutzeroberfläche des Programms wird automatisch angepaßt und optimiert in Bezug auf unterschiedliche Bildschirmauflösungen und benutzerabhängige Browser-Einstellungen. Ein Beispiel für die Organisation der Benutzeroberfläche mit dem Zusammenwirken von Netz-Browser, HTML-Elementen und der Java-Applikation zeigt Abb.2. Im dargestellten Beispiel wird eine CT-Bildsequenz wiedergegeben, wobei Darstellungsart und Benutzerführung der Anwendung entsprechend gestaltet sind. Analog zur Darstellung von Bildsequenzen bietet das Programm spezielle Darstellungsmoden zur Wiedergabe von Einzelbildern und Bildgruppen.

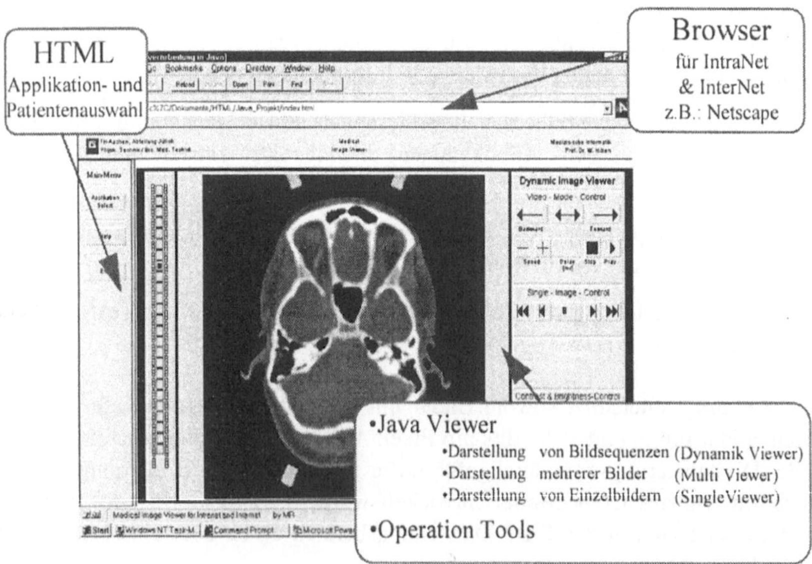

Abb. 2: Organisation der Benutzeroberfläche
(Beispiel: Visualisierung dynamischer Bildsequenzen (CT))

4 Programm - Evaluation

Die Java-Anwendung wurde in einer Laborumgebung mit den Browsern Netscape Communicator 4.01 und MS Explorer 3.02 getestet und insbesondere hinsichtlich der Funktionalität und der Ausführungsgeschwindigkeit ausgewertet. Die Anwendung erwies sich unter beiden Browsern im Betrieb als absolut stabil. Ein besonderer Schwerpunkt der Evaluation lag in der Untersuchung der Ausführungszeiten beim Einlesen der TIFF-Bilddaten und bei komplexen Bildoperationen. Das vorcompilierte Java-Programm benötigt im Netscape-Browser zum Einlesen eines 1k*1k großen 16-Bit Bildes ca. 1 s (Pentium-PC 133 MHz mit 100 MB/s Netzanbindung unter Win-NT 4.0). Eine beliebige 16- auf 8-Bit Transformation des Bildes erfolgt in 0.6 s. Damit ist die Java Anwendung nur wenig langsamer als eine entsprechende compilierte Programmversion einer herkömmlichen Hochsprache.

Die bisherigen Studien zeigen, daß unter Java ein relativ schnelles, verteiltes Informationssystem für den Bereich der bildgebenden Diagnostik realisiert werden kann mit vielfältigen Möglichkeiten der Bilddarstellung und der interaktiven Bildverarbeitung, das den besonderen Vorteil der Plattformunabhänigkeit besitzt.

Danksagung: Die Autoren möchten an dieser Stelle Herrn Dipl. Ing. M. Rawanschad für seine wichtigen Vorarbeiten im Rahmen des Projektes danken.

Automatische Extraktion von Referenzpunkten zur Inhomogenitätskorrektur in kernspintomographischem Bildmaterial des menschlichen Gehirns

S. Romainczyk[1,2], G. Wagenknecht[1,2] und U.Büll[2]

1 Lehrstuhl für Allgemeine Elektrotechnik und Datenverarbeitungssysteme
2 Klinik für Nuklearmedizin des Universitätsklinikums der RWTH Aachen
Rheinisch-Westfälische Technische Hochschule (RWTH), 52057 Aachen
Email: g.wagenknecht@nuk-gate.nukmed.rwth-aachen.de

Zusammenfassung. Grauwertinhomogenitäten in kernspintomographischem Bildmaterial erschweren die automatische Klassifikation des Gehirngewebes. Das eingesetzte Korrekturverfahren basiert auf der Hypothese, daß von der Grauwertinhomogenität eines Gewebetyps (Referenzgewebe) auf die Gesamtinhomogenität geschlossen werden kann. Die zur Schätzung des Inhomogenitätsverlaufs benötigten Referenzpunkte werden mit Hilfe eines zweistufigen Extraktionsverfahrens bestimmt, welches Merkmale des Referenzgewebes und der Referenzpunkte mit Verfahren der digitalen Bildverarbeitung aus den Bilddaten ermittelt und analysiert.

Schlüsselwörter: Inhomogenitätskorrektur, Gaußhomogenitäts-Operator, MRT, Klassifikation, Segmentierung

1 Einleitung

Im Rahmen eines Forschungsprojektes zur multimodalen Bildanalyse (PET, SPECT, MRT) des menschlichen Gehirns ist die Klassifikation kernspintomographischer Bilddaten von besonderem Interesse. Auftretende Grauwertinhomogenitäten erschweren die Differenzierung der Gewebeklassen in weiße Substanz (WM), graue Substanz (GM), cerebrospinale Flüssigkeit (CSF) und Hirnhäute, Knochen, Fettgewebe (SB). Gelingt es, diese Inhomogenitäten mit vertretbarem Aufwand zu reduzieren, so kann die Genauigkeit einer anschließenden Klassifikation gesteigert werden. Im Rahmen dieses Beitrags wird ein Verfahren vorgestellt, das unabhängig von der Ursache der Grauwertinhomogenität [1] und der Art des kernspintomographischen Aufnahmeverfahrens arbeitet.

2 Voraussetzungen

Die Grundlage der Inhomogenitätskorrektur bildet die idealisierte Hypothese, daß Gewebe gleichen Typs denselben Grauwert besitzt und von der Grauwertinhomogenität innerhalb eines Gewebetyps auf die Gesamtinhomogenität geschlossen werden kann [2]. Hierzu muß sich dieser Gewebetyp großflächig und weiträumig über das gesamte Bild erstrecken, weshalb die weiße Substanz als *Referenzgewebe* gewählt wird. Innerhalb des Referenzgewebes werden dann weiträumig verteilte Stützstellen, die *Referenzpunkte*, für eine Spline-Interpolation bestimmt. Diese Spline-Interpolation wird als eine Schätzung der Gesamtinhomogenität betrachtet und zur Korrektur des akquirierten Bildes herangezogen.

Zur Extraktion der weißen Substanz und mit ihr der Referenzpunkte ist es erforderlich, diese durch Merkmale zu beschreiben. Untersucht man kernspintomographische Aufnahmen des menschlichen Gehirns, so kann die weiße Substanz als weitgehend homogenes Gewebe beschrieben werden, das sich durch seinen Grauwert (Intensität) von anderen Gewebetypen abhebt und sich über große zusammenhängende Gebiete erstreckt. Daraus lassen sich die *Homogenität*, der *Grauwert* und die *Größe* als Merkmale der weißen Substanz ableiten. Für die Referenzpunkte wird gefordert, daß sich diese innerhalb der homogensten Teilbereiche der weißen Substanz und fernab von Übergängen (*Kanten*) zu anderen Gewebetypen befinden. Diese Merkmale lassen sich mit Verfahren der digitalen Bildverarbeitung aus dem Bild ermitteln.

3 Merkmalsextraktion

Zur Extraktion des Referenzgewebes und der anschließenden Bestimmung der Referenzpunkte ist ein zweistufiges Extraktionsverfahren (Abb.1) entwickelt worden, das die Merkmale der weißen Substanz und der Referenzpunkte in geeigneter Weise miteinander kombiniert.

In der ersten Extraktionsstufe werden zunächst die Regionen innerhalb des Grauwertebereichs der weißen Substanz durch die Auswertung des Histogramms und einer anschließenden Schwellwertsegmentierung bestimmt. Diese Regionen werden durch eine Homogenitätsanalyse auf ihre homogensten Bereiche beschränkt und die größten Regionen ausgewählt. Zur Verringerung von Fehlextraktionen werden die Grauwertebereiche der so gewonnenen Regionen einzeln untersucht und Pixel am Rand des Grauwertebereichs verworfen.

Innerhalb dieser Regionen werden, in der zweiten Extraktionsstufe, die Referenzpunkte bestimmt. Als Referenzpunkte werden diejenigen Pixel ausgewählt, die in den homogensten Teilbereichen der weißen Substanz liegen und nur von Kanten mit geringer Kantenstärke umgeben sind. Gehäufte Referenzpunkte werden im Sinne einer 4er-Nachbarschaft zu einem Referenzpunkt zusammengefaßt. Diesem werden als Koordinaten der Schwerpunkt

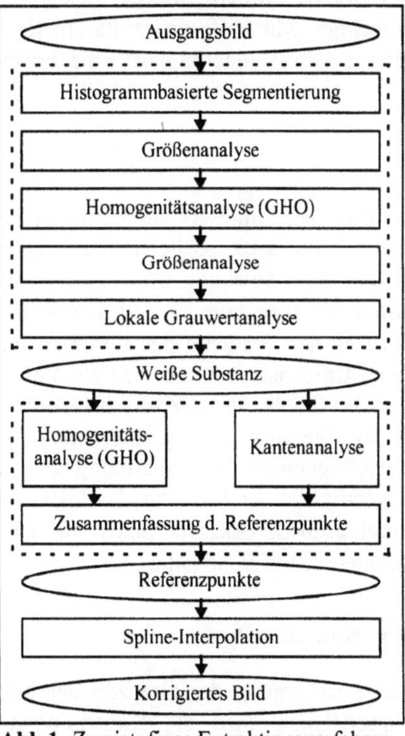

Abb.1: Zweistufiges Extraktionsverfahren.

und als Grauwert der mittlere Grauwert der zusammengefaßten Punkte zugewiesen.

Zur Schätzung der Gesamtinhomogenität wird mit Hilfe der multiquadratic method [3] eine Spline-Interpolation durch die zuvor bestimmten Referenzpunkte berechnet. Die Division des akquirierten Bildes durch den geschätzten Inhomogenitätsverlauf liefert das korrigierte Ergebnisbild.

3.1 Histogrammbasierte Schwellwertsegmentierung

Zur Bestimmung des Grauwertebereichs der weißen Substanz wird das Grauwerthistogramm des Bildes berechnet. Bedingt durch ihre Größe bildet die weiße Substanz ein deutliches Maximum aus. Nach der Glättung der Kurve wird der Histogrammverlauf in der Umgebung des Maximums durch eine Parabel approximiert. Die Schnittpunkte der Parabel mit der x-Achse werden als Grenzen des Grauwertebereichs der weißen Substanz angenommen. Eine Schwellwertsegmentierung mit den so ermittelten Grenzen liefert eine erste Abschätzung der Regionen der weißen Substanz.

3.2 Homogenitätsanalyse

Zur Bestimmung des Merkmals Homogenität ist ein neuartiger Operator entwickelt worden. Dazu wird zunächst aus den Grauwerten aller Pixel innerhalb des Operatorfensters der mittlere Grauwert a und eine Schätzung der Streuung σ der Grauwerte berechnet. Mit Hilfe dieser Parameter kann dann die Verteilfunktion (Gaußverteilung) der Pixel innerhalb des Operatorfensters beschrieben werden.

$$f(x_i) = \frac{1}{\sqrt{2\pi}\,\sigma}\,e^{-\frac{(x_i-a)^2}{2\sigma^2}}$$

(1)

Wird der Grauwert des zentralen Pixels x_i des Operatorfensters in die Gaußverteilung eingesetzt, so liefert das Ergebnis einerseits eine Aussage darüber, wie homogen die Umgebung des Pixels ist (bedingt durch die Streuung σ) und gleichzeitig wie gut sich der Grauwert des zentralen Pixels in seine Umgebung einpaßt. Da als Verteilfunktion die Gaußverteilung gewählt wurde, wurde dieser Operator *Gaußhomogenitäts-Operator* (GHO) genannt [4]. Abbildung 2 zeigt das Ergebnis der Anwendung des GHO mit 9x9 Pixel großem Operatorfenster auf ein ρ-gewichtetes Spin-Echo Bild.

3.3 Kantenanalyse

Zur Bestimmung der Grenzen der einzelnen Gewebetypen wird als Kantenoperator der

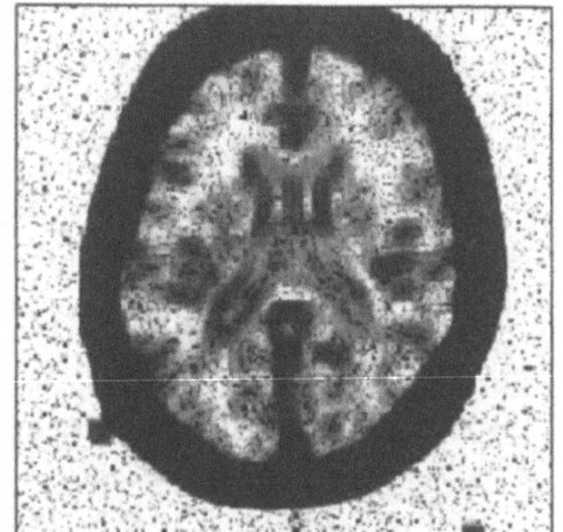

Abb.2: Anwendung des GHO auf ein ρ-gewichtetes Spin-Echo Bild.

Kirsch-Operator eingesetzt [5]. Dieser zeichnet sich durch eine Kantendetektion in acht Raumrichtungen und seine einfache Implementierung aus.

4 Diskussion und Ergebnisse

Zum Test des Verfahrens wird ein dreischichtiges Simulationsmodell herangezogen, welches auf einem, in die fünf Klassen: Weiße Substanz (WM), graue Substanz (GM), cerebrospinale Flüssigkeit (CSF), Hirnhäute, Knochen, Fettgewebe (SB) und Hintergrund (BG) unterteilten Datensatz basiert. Die Grauwerte der einzelnen Klassen werden entsprechend den mittleren Grauwerten ρ-, T1- bzw. T2-gewichteter Spin-Echo Datensätze gewählt. Diesen Grauwerten wird ein Partialvolumeneffekt, ein quadratischer Inhomogenitätsverlauf $I(x,y)=c(x^2+y^2)$ und gleichverteiltes Rauschen überlagert. In den oberen beiden Schichten (Schicht1 und 2) beträgt das Verhältnis von weißer Substanz zu den restlichen Gewebetypen etwa 1:2, in der unteren Schicht (Schicht3) nur noch 1:5,6, so daß an dieser Schicht die Grenzen des Verfahrens aufgezeigt werden können.

Nach Durchlaufen der ersten Extraktionsstufe sind in den oberen beiden Schichten, unabhängig von der simulierten Wichtung, etwa 30% der insgesamt enthaltenen weißen Substanz extrahiert worden (Extr. WM). Der Anteil der fehlerfrei zugeordneten Pixel (Trefferquote1) liegt dabei zwischen 85% und 100%. An den Ergebnissen der unteren Schicht sind bereits die Grenzen des Verfahrens zu erkennen. Durch die Verletzung der Grundvoraussetzung, wonach sich das Referenzgewebe großflächig und weiträumig über das Bild erstrecken soll, sinkt der Anteil der fehlerfrei zugeordneten Pixel (Trefferquote1) auf teilweise unter 30% ab (Tab.1).

Sim. Modell		1.Extraktionsstufe		2.Extraktionsstufe	
		Extr. WM (%)	Trefferquote1 (%)	Anz. RP	Trefferquote2 (%)
ρ	Schicht1	34,5	100	180	100
	Schicht2	37,9	92,2	173	98,8
	Schicht3	41,1	62,1	119	71,7
T1	Schicht1	30,2	100	97	100
	Schicht2	29,2	86,8	170	98,8
	Schicht3	27,2	50	81	80,2
T2	Schicht1	32,4	100	90	100
	Schicht2	31,5	85,7	172	98,8
	Schicht3	21,2	29,6	48	48

Tab.1: Simulationsergebnisse des zweistufigen Extraktionsverfahrens.

Für die in der zweiten Extraktionsstufe bestimmten Referenzpunkte zeigt sich, daß diese in den oberen beiden Schichten, bis auf einen zu vernachlässigen Teil, innerhalb der weißen Substanz liegen. Deutlich zu erkennen ist die weiträumige Verteilung der Referenzpunkte (Abb.3). In der unteren Schicht sind zwar noch genügend viele Referenzpunkte mit einer Trefferquote von bis zu 80% extrahiert worden, jedoch werden weite Teile des Gehirns und somit auch der Inhomogenität nicht mehr durch Referenzpunkte erfaßt (Tab. 1).

382

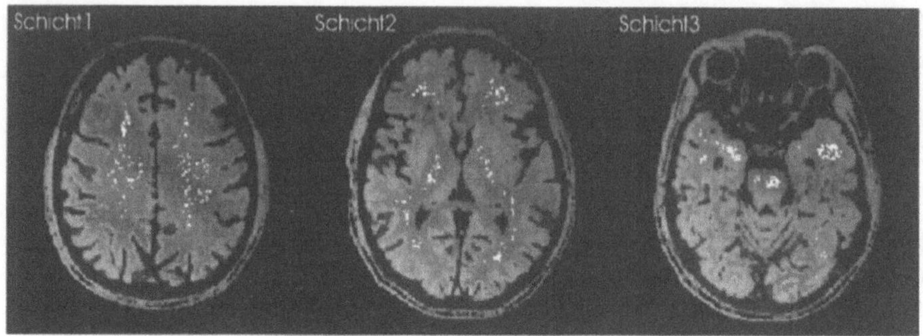

Abb.3: Referenzpunkte (weiß überlagert) eines ρ-gewichteten Simulationsmodells.

Auch an realen Bilddaten zeigt sich eine gute Verteilung der extrahierten Referenzpunkte. Das auf der Basis dieser Referenzpunkte erzielte Korrekturergebnis läßt sich anschaulich durch eine Schwellwertsegmentierung der weißen Substanz vor und nach der Korrektur darstellen (Abb.4).

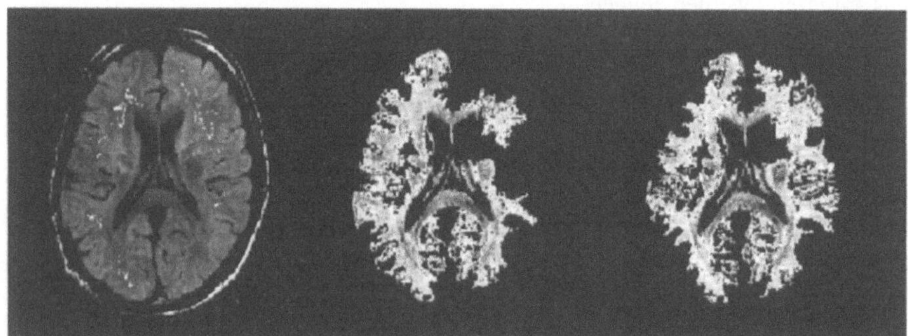

Abb.4: Links: Referenzpunkte für ein ρ-gewichtetes Spin-Echo Bild; Mitte: Segmentierungsergebnis der weißen Substanz vor und Rechts: nach der Inhomogenitätskorrektur.

Danksagung: Wir danken dem IZKF/ZNS der medizinischen Fakultät der RWTH Aachen für die Förderung des Forschungsprojektes NUKMED1, in dessen Rahmen diese Arbeit angefertigt wurde.

5 Literatur

1. Rothschild P, Solomon M, Carlson J: Magnetic Resonance Imaging of Children. B.C. Decker, Inc., 1990.
2. Dawant BM, Zijdenbos AP, Margolin RA: Correction of Intensity Variations in MR Images for Computer-Aided Tissue Classification. IEEE Transactions on Medical Imaging, Vol. 12: 770-781, 1993.
3. Hardy RL: Multiquadratic Equations of Topography and Other Irregular Surfaces. Journal of Geophysics, Vol. 76: 1905-1915, 1971.
4. Romainczyk S: Inhomogenitätskorrektur in kernspintomographischem Bildmaterial des menschlichen Gehirns. Diplomarbeit am Lehrstuhl für Allgemeine Elektrotechnik und Datenverarbeitungssysteme der RWTH Aachen, 1997.
5. Klette R, Zamperoni P: Handbuch der Operatoren für die Bildverarbeitung. Vieweg Verlag, 1995.

Verlustbehaftete Bilddatenreduktion von digitalen Koronarangiogrammen

Vergleich der subjektiven Bildqualität mit verschiedenen objektiven Parametern

U. Bürgel, R. Brennecke, H.P. Fritsch, J. Meyer

II. Medizinische Klinik und Poliklinik,
Universitätsklinikum Mainz, 55101 Mainz
Email: buergel@2-med.klinik.uni-mainz.de

Zusammenfassung Zum Testen und Entwickeln von neuen verlustbehafteten Algorithmen für die Bilddatenkompression benötigt man leicht zu ermittelnde, berechnete Bildqualitätsparameter. Die Korrelation solcher berechneter, „objektiver" Parameter mit der visuellen, subjektiven Beurteilung der Bildqualität wurde für JPEG-komprimierte Koronarangiogramme untersucht. Zusätzlich zu drei auf der mittleren quadratischen Abweichung basierenden Bildqualitätsparametern wurde dabei ein neu entwickeltes, die Bildstrukturen berücksichtigendes Bildqualitätsmaß getestet. Die visuelle Bildqualitätsbeurteilung wurde von sechs Beobachtern anhand einer fünfstufigen Skala durchgeführt. Als Bildmaterial dienten 40 verschiedene Bilder (acht Koronarangiogramme in fünf verschiedenen Kompressionsstufen). Mit Hilfe des neuen Qualitätsparameters konnte die Korrelation zur visuellen Qualitätsbeurteilung von ca. 92% ($PSNR$) auf ca. 96% gesteigert werden.

Schlüsselwörter: subjektive Bildqualität, objektive Bildqualität, JPEG, Koronarangiogramme

1   Einleitung

In digitalen Systemen für die Koronarangiographie entstehen sehr große Bilddatenmengen (ca. 400 MByte pro Untersuchung), daher wird zur Zeit im Rahmen der DICOM-Standardisierung die Zulässigkeit der Datenreduktion nach dem JPEG-Standard bewertet. Dies geschieht mittels zeitaufwendiger und kostenintensiver psychovisueller Verfahren. Zum Testen und Entwickeln von neuen Algorithmen für die verlustbehaftete Bilddatenkompression benötigt man leichter zu ermittelnde Bildqualitätsparameter. Diese berechneten Bildqualitätsparameter müssen möglichst gut mit den Ergebnissen aus visuellen Tests korrelieren. In dieser Arbeit sollen daher die üblicherweise verwendeten Qualitätsparameter MSE (*mean square error*), $NMSE$ (*normalised mean square error = MSE/Varianz*), $PSNR$ (*peak to peak signal to noise ratio = $10 * log_{10}(255^2/MSE)$*) sowie ein neu entwickelter Parameter Q bezüglich ihrer Korrelation mit visuellen Bildqualitätsbewertungen getestet und verglichen werden.

2   Verfahren

2.1   Bildmaterial und visuelle Bildqualitätsvergleiche

Als Bildmaterial wurden acht verschiedene Koronarangiogramme (Einzelbilder, 512x512 Pixel, digitale Kardioangiographieanlage Siemens HICOR) verwendet, welche in jeweils fünf Kompressionsstufen (Qualitätsfaktor = 79, 84, 89, 94, 98) mittels des JPEG-Verfahrens komprimiert wurden. Die Bildqualitätsbewertung erfolgte nach Kantenanhebung (unsharp masking). Die visuellen Beurteilungen wurden nach Interpolation auf 1024x1024 Pixel von sechs Beobachtern vorgenommen [1]. Dabei bewertete jeder Beobachter jedes Bild in allen fünf Kompressionsstufen mittels einer fünfstufigen Skala:

1. slight difference - just detectable
2. small difference; image usable and very adequate
3. image quality passable; image usable but below standard
4. low image quality; image usable but difficult to use
5. image not generally usable; changes in structures

Durch Mittelung über die Scores der verschiedenen Beobachter erhält man hieraus einen mittleren subjektiven Bildqualitätsparameter *MOS* (*mean opinion score*).

2.2   Entwicklung und Test eines neuen Fehlermaßes

Zur Berechnung des neu entwickelten, berechneten Bildqualitätsparameters segmentiert man, analog zu dem bei Hosaka-Plots [2] verwendeten Verfahren, die Koronarangiogramme in Gebiete unterschiedlicher Blockgröße und „Aktivität" (Bildkanten-Regionen). Man erhält dabei fünf Klassen bestehend aus quadratischen Blöcken mit Kantenlängen von 1,2,4,8 und 16 Pixeln. Kleinere Blöcke befinden sich in Bildkantenregionen und größere Blöcke repräsentieren homogenere Gebiete. Diese in dem Originalbild berechnete Segmentierungsmaske wird gleichermaßen auf Original- und entkomprimiertes Bild angewendet. Für jede der Klassen werden vier verschiedenen Parameter berechnet, welche die Bildveränderungen beschreiben. Hierzu werden zunächst die Bildinhalte korrespondierender Blöcke im Original- und entkomprimierten Bild verglichen, indem Standardabweichung σ und Mittelwert μ für jeden Bildblock berechnet werden. Auf diese Art und Weise erhält man im Original- und entkomprimierten Bild für jede Klasse k die Verteilungen:

$$\mathbf{S}_k^{orig} = \{\sigma_{1_k}^{orig}, \sigma_{2_k}^{orig}, \ldots, \sigma_{N_k}^{orig}\} \qquad \mathbf{S}_k^{komp} = \{\sigma_{1_k}^{komp}, \sigma_{2_k}^{komp}, \ldots, \sigma_{N_k}^{komp}\}$$

$$\mathbf{M}_k^{orig} = \{\mu_{1_k}^{orig}, \mu_{2_k}^{orig}, \cdots, \mu_{N_k}^{orig}\} \qquad \mathbf{M}_k^{komp} = \{\mu_{1_k}^{komp}, \mu_{2_k}^{komp}, \cdots, \mu_{N_k}^{komp}\}$$

Dabei bezeichnet N_k die Anzahl der Blöcke in der jeweiligen Klasse. Basierend auf diesen Verteilungen wird der von Hosaka eingeführte Parameter

$$dS_k = |Mittelwert(\mathbf{M}_k^{orig}) - Mittelwert(\mathbf{M}_k^{komp})| = |\overline{\mathbf{M}}_k^{orig} - \overline{\mathbf{M}}_k^{komp}|$$

berechnet. Als neue Parameter werden außerdem die Korrelationen der korrespondierenden Verteilungen berechnet:

$$KS_k = Korrelation(\mathbf{S}_k^{orig}, \mathbf{S}_k^{komp})$$

$$KM_k = Korrelation(\mathbf{M}_k^{orig}, \mathbf{M}_k^{komp})$$

Einen weiteren Parameter erhält man, indem basierend auf der Segmentierung die Entropie erster Ordnung des Differenzbildes aus Original- und entkomprimierten Bild berechnet wird:

$$Ent_k = E\big(h(orig_k - komp_k)\big)$$

wobei: E: Entropiefunktion
          h: Histogramm
          $orig_k$: Pixel im Originalbild welche zur Klasse k gehören
          $orig_k$: Pixel im entkomprimierten Bild welche zur Klasse k gehören

Aus diesen Parametern wird nun durch Bildung einer geeigneten Linearkombination ein neues Bildqualitätsmaß Q abgeleitet. Die Koeffizienten dieser Linearkombination wurden durch Anpassung an die *MOS*-Werte gewonnen. Die Anpassung wurde anhand von fünf Angiogrammen in fünf Kompressionsstufen (25 Bilder) durchgeführt und an den restlichen drei Angiogrammen getestet. Zur Bestimmung der Koeffizienten der einzelnen Parameter wurden zunächst, mittels einer Hauptachsentransformation, die Hauptkomponenten des Parameterraumes bestimmt. Es zeigt sich, daß der Parameterraum für die untersuchten Angiogramme im wesentlichen 4-dimensional ist. In diesen vier Dimensionen sind 95% der Eigenwertenergie enthalten. Basierend auf dieser Hauptachsendarstellung wurden nun die Koeffizienten mittels der Methode der kleinsten Fehlerquadrate angepasst. Anschließend wurde die Korrelation des so gewonnenen, neuen Bildqualitätsmaßes Q mit den *MOS*-Werte der restlichen 15 Bilder (drei Angiogramme in fünf Kompressionsstufen) getestet.

3 Ergebnisse

3.1 Vergleich der MSE-basierten Fehlermaße

Die Korrelationen von *MSE, NMSE* und *PSNR* mit den Ergebnissen aus den visuellen Beurteilungen (*MOS*) über alle Bilder betragen:

MSE	NMSE	PSNR
0.898	0.742	-0.902

3.2 Vergleich mit dem neuen Fehlermaß

Da ein Teil der Bilder für die Anpassung des neuen Qualitätsmaßes benötigt wird, ist die Angabe der Korrelation von Q mit dem MOS über alle Bilder nicht sinnvoll. Statt dessen wurden die Korrelationen aufgrund der Testbilder für alle 70 möglichen Kombinationen von Test- und Anpassungsbildern berechnet. Die Mittelwerte und Standardabweichungen der Korrelationen sind in Tabelle1 dargestellt.

Tabelle1. Mittelwerte und Standardabweichungen der Korrelationen mit MOS

	Q	MSE	PSNR
Mittel	0.959	0.915	-0.922
Stdabw.	0.013	0.042	0.033

3.3 Diskussion

Der neue Bildqualitätsparameter Q zeigt im Vergleich mit den bisher üblicherweise verwendeten Parametern eine deutlich höher Korrelation zu den Ergebnissen aus visuellen Tests. Wünschenswert ist die Erprobung an einem größeren Bilddatensatz und die Anwendung auf andere Bildkompressionsverfahren wie zum Beispiel waveletbasierte Methoden.

Literatur

1. J.P. Fritsch, F. Negwer, U. Renneisen, R. Brennecke, J. Meyer: „Visual and quantitative analysis of coronary angiograms after irreversible data compression", European Heart Journal 15(1994), 46 Abstract supplement
2. K. Hosaka: „A new picture quality evaluation method", Proceedings International Picture Coding Symposium, 86(1986), 17-18, Tokyo
3. Ho, Bruce K., Tseng V., Marco M., Doris C.: „A mathematical model to quantify JPEG block artifacts", SPIE Vol. 1897, 269-275 Image Capture, Formating and Display

Colored 3D-CT Reconstruction
A Planning Tool in Skull Base Surgery

Erck Elolf, Marcos Tatagiba, Madjid Samii

Krankenhaus Nordstadt, Neurochirugische Klinik,
Haltenhoffstr. 41, D-30167 Hannover, Germany
phone: ++ 49 511 970 1245
fax: ++ 49 511 970 1606
e-mail: Elolf@t-online.de

Abstract. Introduction: Planning of skull base surgery involves a large number of conventional pictures. Three-dimensional CT-reconstruction added a different perspective in demonstrating spatial relationships of bone, tumor and vessel in a single illustration. Methods: 70 patients with skull base lesions (63 neoplastic and 7 vascular) were examined with spiral CT and 3D-reconstruction preoperatively. The reconstruction both visualized the pathology in its relationship to the adjacent bone and vessels -labelled in different colors - and simulated the possible surgical approaches. A General Electric High Speed Advantage CT and a maximum of 95 ml intravenous contrast media were used. A Spiral CT covering the area of interest was performed and transformed to 1 mm slices. Reconstruction was done after transfering the data set to an Advantage Windows Workstation; this required about 3 to 5 minutes. Editing the 3D-reconstruction took between 20 minutes and 1.5 hours (average one (1) hour) depending on the pathology´s complexity. Results: Preoperative 3D-reconstruction of CT-data renders spatial representation of the lesion in relationship to neighboring structures using data usually acquired in preoperative routine. Complex anatomy is visualized with a handful of pictures including cinematografic presentations. Using the reconstructed 3D-computer model it was easily possible to compare different surgical approaches and its specific exposure. The short time necessary for reconstruction allows the application of this method as a routine preoperative procedure for selected skull base pathologies. Computing time of 1.5 hours in complex cases is acceptable due to the information gained with 3D-imaging. Since a preoperative CT in thin slices is mandatory in skull base surgery, no additional costs are caused. Conclusion: 3D-imaging in skull base surgery is a useful tool for visualizing complex anatomy and for finding the most feasible approach. It represents an application of "virtual surgery" in a standard hospital environment. Since CT data is acquired during preoperative routine, no additional examinations become necessary. We recommend this procedure as a routine preoperative procedure for selected skull base lesions.

Keywords: 3D-reconstruction, computer assisted surgery, skull base surgery

3 Results

Preoperative 3D-reconstruction of CT-data renders very useful and informative visualizations. The complex anatomy of selected skull base pathologies can be visualized with only a handful of pictures 5. It is easily possible to simulate the surgical approaches in question thus delivering specific arguments for certain surgical options. Problematic anatomical entities are identified and the "surgeon's view" can be presented preoperatively. Even cinematographic representations are possible to enhance the spatial impression.

The method simplifies the presentation of the tumor's anatomy and orientation and is a useful tool for the discussion of surgical options. In certain cases the surgical approach was altered secondary to information gained from 3D-reconstruction. Before using this technique the planning of skull base surgery was done using a large number of conventional, two-dimensional MR- and CT-films. Approach options were discussed on the basis of individual "mental" reconstructions of these pictures.

With this technique different approaches can be rehearsed and the location of vessels, tumor and bony skull base structures and their spatial relationship is clearly depicted. This makes discussions and decision-making much easier since everyone literally sees the same picture. The explanation of different approaches and their specific advantages is simplified compared to the conventional means. The three-dimensional understanding of the pathology is markedly enhanced since the pictures are based on nondistorted data.

Certain decisions concerning approaches are eventually altered based on the 3D pictures. It is possible to clarify with the 3D pictures whether a combined subtemporal and presigmoid approach is really necessary or whether a lateral suboccipital craniotomy is sufficient. Thus the pictures are requested more often to enhance the understanding of the relationship between vessel and tumor and to evaluate the necessary surgical exposure. Whether an experienced neurosurgeon will ultimately change his "approach" to the surgery is uncertain.

4 Discussion

3D-imaging in skull base tumors is a useful tool, since the time-consuming process of reviewing multiple pages of two-dimensional axial pictures to understand the spatial orientation can be shortened. Evaluating the images still requires imaginative three-dimensional reconstruction, but for discussion or teaching of surgical options all participants talk about the same picture, if this method is applied. Since the CT data set is acquired during the preoperative imaging routine, no additional examinations become necessary. Using the mentioned method with a helical CT does not increase the cost of preoperative examinations, the amount of radiation or contrast media used. The method can be used on an outpatient basis, so the length of stay is unchanged. The mentioned protocol is an efficient use of the available resources; if a surgeon wants to use the method to plan skull base surgery, the necessary infrastructure usually is in place [12,13].

1 Introduction

Three-dimensional (3D) computed tomography (CT) reconstructions have developed into a routine method of imaging [1-3]. They add a different perspective to the data usually acquired during the standard preoperative routine. 3D-CT imaging from helical CT data [4,5] demonstrates the spatial relationship of bones, tumors, vessels and ventricles simultaneously in a single illustration thus providing a very helpful tool to understand the anatomical situation 6-8. Additionally, 3D-CT provides a simple way to demonstrate surgical approaches to the skull base and to show the individual exposure of the pathology [9,10]. Since pathology, bone and vessel are shown in color, their spatial orientation is easily appreciated and with a simulation of the "surgeon's view" critical anatomical relations can be demonstrated preoperatively. Therefore the rehearsal and comparison of different surgical approaches is easily performed [11].

2 Material and Methods

In this series we examined 70 patients with skull base related pathologies. 63 had neoplastic pathologies, while 7 presented with vascular pathologies. All patients were examined with helical CT and subsequent 3D-reconstruction as part of their preoperative imaging.

The examination is carried out using a General Electric High Speed Advantage CT Scanner (General Electric Medical Systems, Milwaukee, WI, USA). A maximum of 95 ml iodized contrast media (Optiray 300, Mallinckrodt; Injektron, Medtron) is used to enhance either tumor or vessels or both, according to the specific pathology. A spiral CT with 3 mm table feed and a pitch of one covering the area of interest is performed. The data set is transformed to 1 mm slices.

The data set is processed using the Advantage Windows 3D Analysis Package Version 1.2 which comes bundled with the 3D-workstation of GE Scanner. The module uses a semiautomatic or manual, Hounsfield-unit oriented, separation tool, so different partial models can be produced and later merged together. The model allows "freehand" cutting either to remove certain parts or to uncover hidden anatomy. The model can be magnified to a certain extent, but quality is lost since the voxels become visible. As output we produce 35mm screen shots, x-ray laser prints or color prints.

Reconstruction is performed on an Advantage Windows Workstation (Sun Sparcstation 10) requiring about 3 to 5 minutes. The reconstruction demonstrates the pathology and its relationship to bones of the skull base and neighboring intracranial vessels. Editing the 3D-reconstruction took between 20 minutes and 2.5 hours depending on the complexity of the pathology (average 1 hour). Using the computer model the simulation of the surgical approach is done to simulate the pathology´s accessibility and the actual "view of the surgeon".

Since computation time for the images has dropped dramatically with the advent of high speed workstations and recent software, it is easily possible to apply the 3D-reconstruction as a routine preoperative procedure. No specific timing is necessary, there is no "down time" of the CT scanner. Image processing can be done independently from a hospital or a radiological office, thus theoretically allowing the surgeon to manipulate the image data the day before surgery in the privacy of his or her own office. With even faster computers and more sophisticated software at a reasonable price, this form of virtual skull base surgery may become available at any place with a spiral CT. Since a preoperative CT in thin slices is mandatory in skull base surgery, no additional costs are caused [14]. We recommend the method as a routine preoperative procedure for selected skull base lesions [9].

5 References

1. Becker H (1988) 3-dimensional cranial and spinal computed tomography. Radiologe 28(5): 239-42.
2. Gillespie JE, Isherwood I (1986) Three-dimensional anatomical images from computed tomographic scans. Br J Radiol 59(699): 289-92.
3. Yune H Y (1993) Two-dimensional-three-dimensional reconstruction computed tomography techniques. Dent Clin North Am 37(4): 613-26.
4. Heiken JP, Brink JA, Vannier MW (1993) Spiral (helical) CT. Radiology 189(3): 647-56.
5. Kalender WA, Vock P, Polacin A, Soucek M (1990) Spiral-CT: a new technique for volumetric scans. I. Basic principles and methodology. Rontgenpraxis 43(9): 323-30.
6. Elolf E, Steinau U, Samii M (1997) Skull Base Tumors and Related Pathologies. PC CD-ROM, Fa. U. Steinau, Hannover, Germany
7. Rubin GD (1994) Three-dimensional helical CT angiography. Radiographics 14(4): 905-12.
8. Schwartz RB (1994) Neuroradiological applications of spiral CT. Semin Ultrasound CT MR 15(2): 139-47.
9. Leboucq N, Montoya P (1992) 3D imaging and pathology of the base of the skull in children. Ann Radiol Paris 35(6): 424-9.
10. Elolf E, Tatagiba M, Samii M (1997) Colorcoded 3D-CT for pathologies in and around the petrous bone. Klinische Neuroradiologie 7(2): 72-6
11. Becker D, Bertalanffy H, Tacke J, Prescher A, Gilsbach JM (1997) Morphometric analysis of the transcondylar approach and its correlation with spiral CT findings. Zentralbl Neurochir (1997) Suppl:70
12. Elolf E, Tatagiba M, Samii M (1997) Colorcoded 3D-CT - computer assisted planning of skull base surgery. Clinical Neurology and Neurosurgery 99(Suppl.1):99
13. Elolf E, Tatagiba M, Samii M (1997) Colorcoded 3D-CT reconstructions in skull base surgery. Computer Aided Surgery 2(Suppl.):2
14. Dietrich J, Fried H (1994) Intracranial 3-dimensional computerized tomography in preoperative diagnosis of brain tumor. Zentralbl Neurochir 55(1): 42-7.

In vitro Kalzifizierung biologischer Herzklappen- prothesen: Computergestützte Bestimmung des Kalzifizierungsgrads aus Mikroradiographien

Birgit Glasmacher, Helmut Reul und Günter Rau

Helmholtz-Institut für Biomedizinische Technik an der RWTH Aachen
Pauwelsstr. 20, D-52074 Aachen
Email: glasmacher@hia.rwth-aachen.de

Zusammenfassung. Die Lebensdauer biologischer Herzklappenprothesen (Bioprothesen) wird durch strukturelles Klappenversagen beeinträchtigt. Das Hauptproblem liegt in der dystrophischen Kalzifizierung des implantierten Gewebes. Die meisten implantierten Bioprothesen stammen entweder vom Schwein (porcine Klappen) oder werden aus Rinderperikard (bovine Klappen) gefertigt. Ziel der vorliegenden Studie ist, in vitro den Einfluß dieser beiden Gewebearten auf die Kalzifizierung zu untersuchen. Dabei wird das Ausmaß der Kalzifizierung zerstörungsfrei mittels Mikroradiographie detektiert. Mit Hilfe einer Bildverarbeitungssoftware war es möglich, die kalzifizierten Areale der untersuchten Herzklappenprothesen aus den Röntgenbildern zu berechnen. Die bovinen Bioprothesen weisen in dieser Studie eine geringere Kalzifizierungsneigung gegenüber den porcinen auf.

Schlüsselwörter: In vitro Kalzifizierung, Bioprothesen, Kalzifizierungsgrad, Mikroradiographie

1 Einleitung

Die Lebensdauer biologischer Herzklappenprothesen (Bioprothesen) wird nach über 30jähriger klinischer Anwendung auch bei neueren Klappen-Generationen durch strukturelles Klappenversagen beeinträchtigt [1]. Das Hauptproblem liegt in der dystrophischen Kalzifizierung des implantierten Gewebes, die nach unvorhersehbarem Zeitintervall zum Versagen der Bioprothese führt. Obwohl gerade bei jüngeren Patienten und insbesondere bei Kindern ein erheblicher Bedarf für biologische Herzklappen besteht, gibt es für diese Patientengruppe bislang keine Prothese mit ausreichend guten Ergebnissen im Langzeitverlauf [2]. Die Analyse von Ursachen und Einflußparametern der Prothesenkalzifizierung ist daher von großer Bedeutung. Die meisten implantierten Bioprothesen stammen entweder vom Schwein (porcine Klappen) oder werden aus Rinderperikard (bovine Klappen) gefertigt. Ziel der vorliegenden Studie ist, in vitro den Einfluß dieser beiden Gewebearten auf die Kalzifizierung zu untersuchen. Dabei wird das Ausmaß der Kalzifizierung zerstörungsfrei mittels Mikroradiographie detektiert und mit der Bildverarbeitungssoftware „AdOculos" (Version 3.0 von BDS) berechnet.

2 Material und Methode

2.1 Klappen

Zehn gerüstmontierte (stented) bovine und porcine Mitral-Bioprothesen (Fa. Baxter USA, Tissue Annulus Diameter (TAD) 27 und 29mm) wurden parallel in einem am Institut entwickelten pulsatilen Klappentestgerät [3] einem 6wöchigen Test unterzogen. Vor Testbeginn wurden die Klappen geröntgt (Nativwerte).

2.2 Klappendauertestgerät

Das Funktionsprinzip des Testgeräts basiert auf dem einer Kolbenpumpe. Die Kolbenbewegung wird durch eine Taumelscheibe, die durch einen Elektromotor mit einstellbarer Geschwindigkeit bis zu 800/min angetrieben wird, erzeugt. Die Klappen schließen während der Aufwärtsbewegung der Kolben unter einer einstellbaren sinusförmigen Druckdifferenz (Δp) an den Klappen. Δp wird durch Druckaufnehmer (Cobe, München, 2 kHz), Meßverstärker (HIA) und Oszilloskop (HM 1007 Hameg) gemessen. Die Druckeinstellung erfolgt über die Einstellung der Schräglage der Taumelscheibe und durch eine Drossel im Bypass. Das Testgerät wird mittels Wasserbad mit Heizstab und Minipumpe zum konvektiven Wärmeaustausch auf 37 °C temperiert.[3,4]

2.3 In vitro Kalzifizierungsmethode

Die Untersuchung erfolgte nach einem standardisierten Versuchsprotokoll [3], das bisher bereits zur Untersuchung von über 40 porcinen Bioprothesen verwendet wurde [4,5], unter Berücksichtigung der Vorgaben der amerikanischen Food and Drug Administration bei 37 °C, $\Delta p = 110$ mmHg und mit einer Testrate von 300 Zyklen/min in einem synthetischen Kalzifizierungsfluid [3]. Die Klappen wurden nach 4 und 6 Wochen Versuchsdauer ($\cong$ 12 und $19 \cdot 10^6$ Zyklen) mittels Mikroradiographie (Standardmammographiegerät, 700 mAs, 22 kV, MoAl-Filter ohne Folie) auf Kalzifizierungsablagerungen untersucht. Die mit Hilfe dieser zerstörungsfrei arbeitenden Methode ermittelte Verkalkung der Klappen korreliert mit dem chemisch nachweisbaren Calciumphosphatgehalt [6].

2.4 Computergestützte Bestimmung des Kalzifizierungsgrads

Zur Berechnung der kalzifizierten Klappenareale wurden die Röntgenbilder eingescannt (HP ScanJet 4c, Pixelauflösung 600 dpi). Vor der eigentlichen Bildverarbeitung mit „AdOculos" (Version 3.0 von BDS) wurde der Klappenring unter Corel PhotoPaint herausgeschnitten. Mit Hilfe der Funktion *Spreizen* wurde der Grauwertbereich, innerhalb der der Kalk liegt, verstärkt dargestellt. Die Flächenberechnung der verkalkten Klappenareale sowie der Gesamtklappenfläche erfolgte über die Funktion *Zählen*. [7,8] Zur Charakterisierung der Kalzifizierung der individuellen Klappen wird der Kalzifizierungsgrad als prozentualer Anteil der radiologisch erfaßten verkalkten Segelareale bezogen auf die Gesamtfläche der Klappensegel definiert.

3 Ergebnisse

Je nach Klappengröße betrugen die mittels AdOculos ermittelten Gesamtklappenflächen 570 mm^2 (TAD 27mm) und 660 mm^2 (TAD 29mm). Alle getesteten Klappen wiesen radiologisch Kalzifizierungen auf. Der Anteil der kalzifizierten Areale lag nach 4 Wochen Versuchsdauer zwischen 8% und 31% und stieg nach 6 Wochen auf 15% bis 44%. Abbildung 1 vergleicht exemplarisch die Ergebnisse der bovinen Klappen #5 und #7 mit denen der porcinen Klappen #9 und #10. Die obere Bildreihe zeigt die makroskopische Ansicht der Klappen nach 6 Wochen Versuchsdauer, in der zwei-

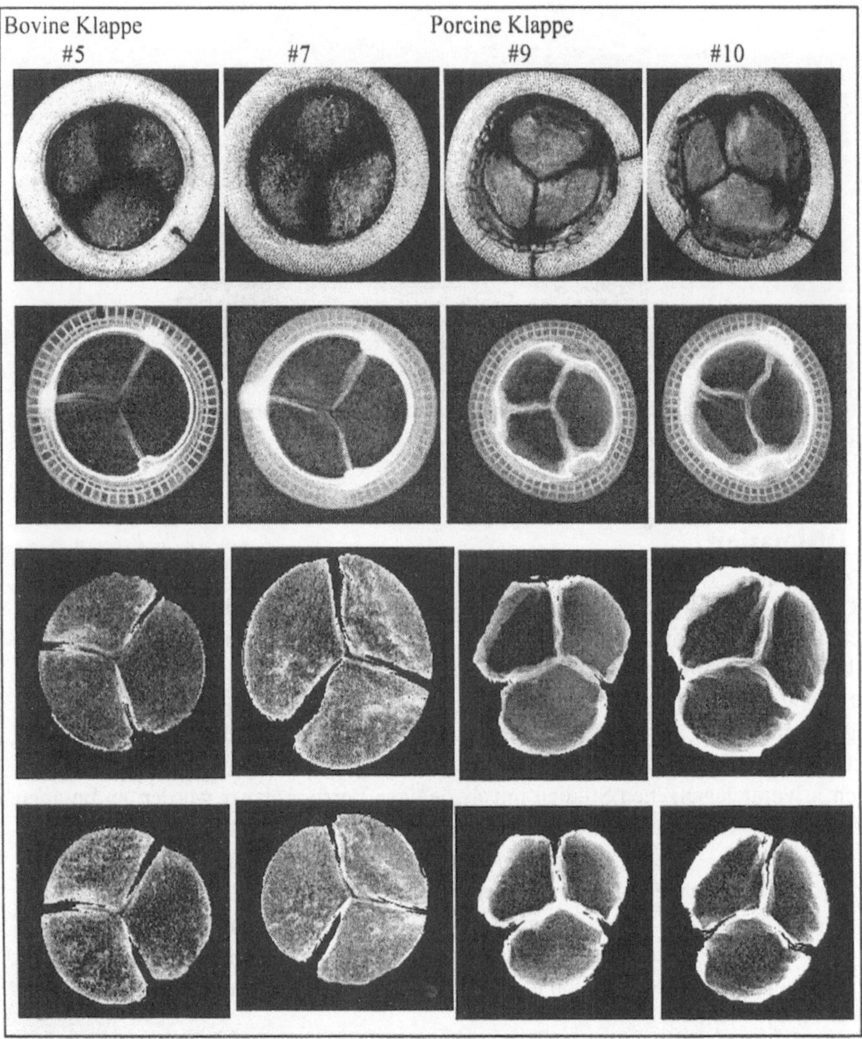

Abb. 1. Ergebnisse der Klappen #5, #7, #9 und #10. Makroskopische Ansicht nach 6 Wo in vitro Kalzifizierung (oben); Mikroradiographien nach 6 Wo (2. Reihe); mittels AdOculos hinsichtlich Kalzifizierungsablagerungen ausgewertete Radiographien nach 4 und 6 Wo (untere Reihen).

ten Reihe sind die entsprechenden Mikroradiographien dargestellt. Die mittels AdOculos hinsichtlich Kalzifizierungsablagerungen ausgewerteten Radiographien nach 4 und 6 Wochen Versuchsdauer sind in den unteren Bildreihen dargestellt. Erwartungsgemäß steigt die Kalzifizierung mit der Versuchsdauer an (Abb. 1 und 2). Der mittlere Kalzifizierungsgrad der Rinderperikardklappen beträgt nach 4 Wochen 14% und nach 6 Wochen 20%. Die Schweineaortenklappen weisen mit 28% (4 Wo) und 37% (6 Wo) eine höhere Verkalkung auf (vgl. Abb. 2).

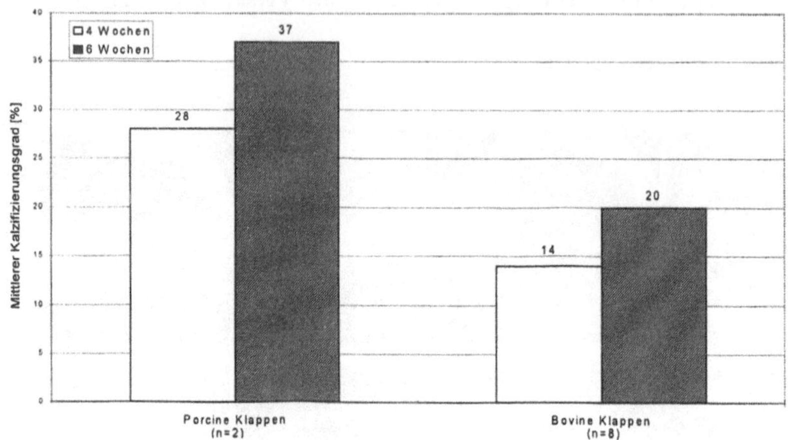

Abb. 2. Mittlerer Kalzifizierungsgrad der untersuchten bovinen und porcinen Bioprothesen nach 4 und 6 Wochen in vitro Kalzifizierung.

4 Diskussion

Mit Hilfe der gewählten Bildverarbeitungssoftware war es möglich, die kalzifizierten Areale der untersuchten biologischen Herzklappenprothesen aus den Röntgenbildern zu berechnen. Erwartungsgemäß steigt die Kalzifizierung mit der Versuchsdauer an. Die bovinen Bioprothesen weisen in dieser Studie eine geringere Kalzifizierungsneigung gegenüber den porcinen auf. Dieses Ergebnis wird durch eigene statische Inkubationsversuche mit Schweineaortenklappensegeln und Rinderperikard bestätigt. Auch in vorangegangenen Studien mit 4wöchiger Versuchsdauer wurden an bovinen Klappen mit vergleichbarem TAD geringere Kalzifizierungsgrade von 25.4% (n=5) im Vergleich zu 39.3% (n=4) an porcinen Bioprothesen ermittelt. Eine positive Bewertung der bovinen Klappen findet sich auch bei anderen Autoren [9-12]. Zur weiteren Überprüfung muß eine größere Zahl an Herzklappenprothesen untersucht werden, da neben der Gewebeherkunft noch weitere Faktoren wie mechanische Belastung und Gewebeanomalien [4,13] und/oder Lipidansammlungen [13] eine Rolle in der Klappenkalzifizierung spielen.

5 Danksagung

Wir bedanken uns für die wertvolle Unterstützung bei Dr. A. Stargardt (Klinik für Radiologische Diagnostik, RWTH Aachen), D. Keus und S. Schneppershoff (HIA) und bei der Fa. Baxter für die Bereitstellung der Herzklappenprothesen.

6 Literatur

1. Schoen FJ, Golomb G Levy RJ: Editorial Calcification of Bioprosthetic Heart Valves: A Perspective on Models. J Heart Valve Dis. 1:110-142, 1992.
2. Deiwick M: persönliche Mitteilung 1997
3. Glasmacher B, Deiwick M: Kalzifizierung porciner Bioprothesen: Korrelation von holographischer Interferometrie und dynamischer in vitro Kalzifizierung. Forschungsbericht des Helmholtz-Instituts Aachen Nr. 10:41-47, 1997.
4. Deiwick M, Glasmacher B, Zarubin AM, Reul H et al.: Quality control of bioprosthetic heart valves by means of holographic interferometry. J Heart Valve Dis, 5:441-47, 1996.
5. Glasmacher B, Deiwick M, Reul H, Knesch H, Keus D, Rau G: A new in vitro test method for calcification of bioprosthetic heart valves. Int J Artif Organs, 20:267-71, 1997.
6. Schoen FJ, Kujovich JL, Webb CL, Levy RJ: Chemically determined mineral content of explanted porcine aortic valve bioprostheses: correlation with radiographic assessment of calcification and clinical data. Circulation, 76(5):1061-6, 1987.
7. N.N.: AdOculos Benutzerhandbuch DBS GmbH Bremen 1996.
8. Bässmann H, Besslich Ph.W: Bildverarbeitung Ad Oculos. Springer-Verlag Berlin 2. Auflage 1993.
9. Grunkemeier GL, Dodnar E: Comparative assessment of bioprosthesis durability in the aortic position. J Heart Valve Dis, 4:49-55, 1995.
10. Cosgrove DM, Bruce WL, Taylor PC et al.: The Carpentier-Edwards pericardial aortic valve. Ten-year results. J Thorac Cardiovasc Surg, 110:651-62, 1995.
11. Aupart MR, Sirinelli AL, Diemont FF, Meurisse YA, Dreyfus XB, Marchand MA: The last generation of pericardial valves in the aortic position: Ten-year follow-up in 589 patients. Ann Thorac Surg, 61:615-20, 1996.
12. Aupart MR, Neville PH, Hammami S, Sirinelli AL, Meirisse YA, Marchand MA: Carpentier-Edwards pericardial valves in the mitral position: Ten-year follow-up. J Thorac Cardiovasc Surg, 113:492-8, 1997.
13. Deiwick M, Glasmacher B, Geiger A, Zarubin AM, Baba HA, Reul H et al.: In vitro testing of bioprostheses: Influence of mechanical stresses, and lipids. Ann Thorac Surg 1997 (in press).

Medizinische Bildverarbeitung
-Aktueller Stand und Zukunftsperspektiven-

Erdmuthe Meyer zu Bexten[1] und Jens Hiltner[2]

[1]Fachhochschule Gießen-Friedberg
Fachbereich Mathmatik, Naturwissenschaften und Informatik
Wiesenstr. 14, 35390 Gießen
Email: erdmuthe.meyer-zu-bexten@mni.ls1.informatik.fh-giessen.de

[2]Universität Dortmund
Fachbereich Informatik, Lehrstuhl I
Otto-Hahn-Str. 16, 44227 Dortmund
Email: hiltner@ls1.informatik.uni-dortmund.de

Zusammenfassung: Der Bereich der Medizinischen Bildverarbeitung ist ein
sehr umfangreiches Anwendungsgebiet in der großen Disziplin der Bildverarbeitung. Er hat in den letzten Jahren zunehmend an Bedeutung gewonnen
(siehe beispielsweise die verschiedenen Konferenzen und Workshops, neu er-
schienene Bücher und die unterschiedlichen Lehrveranstaltungen an den
Hochschulen). Neben der Entwicklung immer besser werdender bildgebender
Verfahren hat auch gerade die Anwendung „Intelligenter Systeme" (Unscharfe
Logik, Neuronale Netze und Evolutionäre Algorithmen) in den siebziger Jahren bis heute dieses Forschungsgebiet zusätzlich neu „belebt", was sich auch
in den vielen neuen positiven Forschungsergebnissen widerspiegelt.

Schlüsselwörter: Medizinische Bildverarbeitung, Industrie, Wissenschaft,
Aktueller Stand, Zukunftsperspektive

1 Einleitung

Um einmal mit verschiedenen Wissenschaftlern zu analysieren, wie sich der aktuelle
Stand und die Zukunftsperspektiven der Bildverarbeitung in der Medizin wirklich in
der Praxis darstellen, wurde auf dem 3. Anwendersymposiums für Bildverarbeitung
in Aachen eine Podiumsdiskussionssitzung mit dem Thema „Bedeutung und Perspektiven der Medizinischen Bildverarbeitung" veranstaltet. Der Kreis der Diskussionspartner [1] war bewußt sehr breit gewählt worden, damit während der Sitzung
verschiedene Meinungen und Standpunkte zur Sprache kommen und diskutiert werden konnten: Vertreter aus der Industrie waren ebenso eingeladen, wie auch Vertreter der Hochschulen mit unterschiedlichsten Fachrichtungen, wie Medizin, Informatik und Ingenieurwesen. Zu Beginn dieses Beitrages richtet sich nochmals ein recht
herzlicher Dank an die Diskussionspartner, denn ohne ihre rege Teilnahme hätte
keine so lange und erfolgreich Diskussion stattfinden können. Im Rahmen dieses
Beitrages werden nun die verschiedenen Standpunkte der Experten zur Bedeutung

der medizinischen Bildverarbeitung und ihrer Zukunftsperspektiven vorgestellt und diskutiert.

2 Bildverarbeitung

Die Bildverarbeitung ist eine traditionelle Disziplin. Der Begriff als solches wird in verschiedenen Kontexten unterschiedlich ausgelegt. Im engeren Sinne sollte zwischen *Bildbearbeitung* und *-verarbeitung* unterschieden werden. Bildbearbeitung umfaßt dabei die manuelle oder automatische Modifikationen von Bildern, die ohne a priori Wissen über den konkreten Inhalt des einzelnen Bildes realisiert wird. Hierunter fallen also z.B. histogrammbasierte Algorithmen zur Kontrastverbesserung oder einfache Faltungsoperationen zur Kantenverstärkung. Die Bildverarbeitung hingegen umfaßt solche Verfahren, die auf einer höheren Abstraktionsebene a priori Information zur Segmentierung, Klassifikation oder Interpretation integrieren [4].

Die medizinische Bildverarbeitung stellt immer einen Teil eines komplexen medizinischen Entscheidungsprozesses dar. Das Ziel der medizinischen Bildverarbeitung besteht darin, diagnostische Fehler zu reduzieren und den therapeutischen Eingriff zu unterstützen, wobei der Arzt im Mittelpunkt steht und die medizinischen Bildverarbeitungssysteme ihm hilfreich zur Seite.

Mit der Entwicklung großer und leistungsfähiger Rechnersysteme, d.h. mit dem großen Fortschritten im Bereich der Halbleitertechnologie und dem Voranschreiten der Weltraumforschung in den sechziger Jahren gewann die Bildverarbeitung zunehmend an Bedeutung [6]. Auf Seiten der Medizin war dies die rasanteste Weiterentwicklung im Bereich der bildgebenden Verfahren. Neben den in der Bildverarbeitung am häufigsten zur Bildgewinnung eingesetzten CCD-Kameras kommen hier eine große Zahl anderer bildgebender Verfahren zum Einsatz, wie z. B. Ultraschall, Thermo-, Kernspintomo- und Röntgen-Computer-Tomographie (PET), Single-Photon-Emissions-CT (SPECT), digitale Angiographie (DA). Dieser Trend hat sich bis heute stetig anwachsend gehalten. Gerade durch den „Einsatz" Intelligenter Systeme in den siebziger Jahren wurde dieses Forschungsgebiet zusätzlich neu „belebt", was sich auch in den vielen positiven Forschungsergebnissen widerspiegelt. Die Ergebnisse der im Rahmen der Diskussionsrunde diskutierten Fragen werden im folgenden vorgestellt.

2.1 Wie wird es speziell in dem Anwendungsbereich Medizin weitergehen?

Einheitlicher Konsens bei der Diskussion herrschte darüber, daß der Einsatz von Methoden der Bildverarbeitung in der Medizin eine immens gestiegene Bedeutung in den letzten Jahren erfahren hat. Sie hat neben der Medizin auch in vielen anderen Anwendungsbereichen erfolgreich Einzug gehalten, wie z.B. in der Technik, der Produktionsautomatisierung, der Qualitätskontrolle, der Umwelttechnik oder Robotik. Dieser Trend in der Medizin, der sich in den kommenden Jahren eher noch verstärken wird, ist hauptsächlich auf die Einführung moderner bildgebender Verfahren wie Computer- und Magnetresonanztomographie zurückzuführen. Darüber hinaus wird die Bildverarbeitungstechnologie [7] noch mehr Anwendungsbereiche in der Medizin erschließen.

Dieser Aufschwung wird auch zusätzlich bekräftigt durch die steigende Zahl an Konferenzen u.ä. (z.B. [1, 2, 3]) in den letzten zehn Jahren zu diesem Thema. Darüber hinaus werden seit vielen Jahren verstärkt die theoretischen Grundlagen immer mehr an Hochschulen in Form von Vorlesungen, Seminaren und andern Lehrveranstaltungen vermittelt, unterstützt durch die zunehmende Zahl an neu erscheinenden Büchern zu dieser Thematik. Was für Probleme gibt es?

Wie bei der Diskussion deutlich wurde, sind die Probleme in der medizinischen Bildverarbeitung vielseitig und von verschiedener Größe, trotzdem aber wohl nicht unlösbar. Die Probleme reichen von Akzeptanzproblemen für Bildverarbeitungssysteme bei den Ärzten bis hin zur Datensicherheit von erzeugten Bilddaten, deren Übermittlung zu verschiedenen Einrichtungen (wie z.B. Praxen und Krankenhäuser) sowie Zugriffssicherheit und der Vertraulichkeit der übermittelten Informationen.

Viele Mediziner nehmen gegenüber Bildverarbeitungssystemen eine passive, kritische Haltung ein. Zum einen sind sie nicht vertraut mit der Bedienung von Computersystemen, zum anderen haben sie Bedenken bezüglich der neuen Methoden. Sie fragen nach der Qualitätskontrolle für die neuen Systeme: Wie sicher sind die präsentierten Ergebnisse der Computersysteme? Deshalb setzen sich neue und gute Systeme, die an den Universitäten entwickelt wurden, bei den Ärzten nicht durch. Weniger als 5% der Forschungsergebnisse werden nur in die Industrieentwicklung umgesetzt. Wie kann diese Problematik entschärft werden? Der Ruf nach einheitlichen Standards wird immer lauter. Zur Zeit gibt es aber nur Insellösungen. Verschiedene Fachverbände bemühen sich um Standards, aber es ist noch kein harmonischer Prozeß. Es wird demzufolge noch einige Zeit dauern, bis es fest definierte Standards gibt. In den USA ist die Situation besser: Mediziner sehen sich dort intensiver nach Neuerungen um und stehen diesen auch viel aufgeschlossener gegenüber.

Darüber hinaus fürchten viele Ärzte um ihre Akzeptanz. Lösen wirklich die neuen Systeme mit neuen Methoden die Ärzte ab? Dies ist auf keinen Fall so! Die neuen Systeme sollen die Ärzte bei der Diagnose lediglich unterstützen und somit die getroffene Diagnose sicherer machen.

Zwar interessieren sich viele Mediziner für die Bildverarbeitung und entwickeln in Zusammenarbeit mit Informatikern Bildverarbeitungssysteme. Aber leider reicht der Enthusiasmus der jungen Mediziner nur bis zur Vollendung ihrer Dissertation oder Habilitation. Nur wenige interessieren sich noch später weiter für die neuen Technologien, zudem fehlt ihnen die Zeit dafür.

Ein weiteres Problem bei der Bildverarbeitung in der Medizin liegt in der Verfügbarkeit der gewonnenen Bilddaten. Die Radiologen haben allgemein den Wunsch nach Zusammenfügung der verschiedenen bildgebenden Verfahren an eine Arbeitsstation. Von einem Patienten möchten sie alle bereits erstellten Aufnahmen zur gleichen Zeit zur Verfügung haben, um eine bessere Diagnose durchführen zu können.

Viele Mediziner meinen auch, daß sich etwas politisch ändern muß. Es muß nach ihrer Meinung eine zweite Diagnose gesetzlich festgeschrieben werden, was eine schnelle Kommunikation über Datenhighways erfordert, denn viele Radiologen fragen auch jetzt schon Kollegen zwecks Festlegung einer genauen Diagnose. Aber die

Radiologen fragen nicht gerne den Kollegen in der Nachbarschaft, sondern lieber weiter entfernt wohnende. Das ist ein weiteres Problem, wie selbst die Radiologen von sich sagen. Die deutschen Radiologen untereinander befinden sich im großen Konkurrenzkampf, was auch bei der Bewertung von Projekten deutlich wird: Deutsche untereinander lehnen ihre Projekte ab, während ausländische Kollegen die eingereichten Projekte der Deutschen sehr gut finden.

2.2 Welche Probleme müssen vorrangig gelöst werden?

Das Wissen des Arztes muß angemessen in den Bildverarbeitungsprozeß einbezogen werden, dazu sind geeignete Systeme zu entwickeln. Zudem wird eine hohe Anforderung an diese System bzgl. ihrer Bedienbarkeit und Verständlichkeit gefordert, da die Mediziner bzw. die Anwender in der Regel keine Informatiker sind. Auch die im System selbst ablaufenden Prozesse müssen klar nachvollziehbar sein, um sowohl die Anwendung als auch die Akzeptanz zu sichern.

Ein weiteres wichtiges Problem ist, daß das Wissen aus der Industrie auch den Forschern an den Hochschulen und den Medizinern in der Praxis Preis gegeben werden muß. Technisches Wissen, d.h. wie die einzelnen Aufnahmegeräte wirklich arbeiten, ist in den Hochschulen kaum bekannt. Der Arzt muß die Entscheidung fällen, welche bildgebenden Verfahren eingesetzt werden, um zu einer guten Diagnose zu kommen. Denn erst dann kann er zu einer Therapie übergehen.

2.3 Was brachte bzw. bringt der Einsatz intelligenter Systeme?

Durch den Einsatz intelligenter Systeme (Unscharfe Logik, Neuronale Netze und Evolutionäre Algorithmen) und wissensbasierter Systeme wird die Leistungsfähigkeit der Bildverarbeitungssysteme verbessert (z. B. in [5, 8]). Durch bessere und leistungsfähigere Systeme wiederum wird die Menge der praktisch lösbaren Probleme beträchtlich erhöht. Es können somit immer mehr umfangreiche und komplexe Verfahren eingesetzt werden. Ein wenig pauschal gesagt, handelt es sich bei den intelligenten Systemen um Methoden, die zum einen eine abweichungstolerante Bildverarbeitung garantieren und zum anderen das spezifische Wissen aus der Medizin berücksichtigen. Ein klassisches Anwendungsbeispiel aus der Medizin die Behandlung interindividueller Variabilitäten, also die sehr patientenspezifischen verschiedenartigen Ausprägungen eines an sich gleichen Objektes, beispielsweise das menschliche Gehirns. Toleranz gegenüber Abweichungen wird insbesondere durch Methoden wie Neuronale Netzwerke und Fuzzy-Systeme, aber auch bezüglich gewisser Eigenschaften invarianter Transformationen gewährleistet. Die weitere Erforschung dieser Methoden kann die Akzeptanz von Informatikmethoden in der Medizin deutlich unterstützen.

Um die Leistungsfähigkeit dieser Methoden zu optimieren, sind intelligent wirkende Werkzeuge vonnöten. So wie ein Mediziner, der bei der visuellen Auswertung eines Bilddatensatzes über eine Vielzahl von Standardwissen in Kombination mit Wissen über den zugrundeliegenden Fall verfügt, reicht auch in leistungsfähigen Bildverarbeitungssystemen nicht allein ein gut elaborierter Satz an Bildverarbeitungsoperatoren aus. Eine Wissenskomponente, die nahtlos an die Bildverarbeitung anschließt und mit dieser im Dialog steht, spiegelt einen zentralen Aspekt zukünftiger Systeme wider.

Die Kombination von Bildverarbeitungsmethoden mit effizienten wissensbasierten Systemen bietet sich an, um zu einer genauen Analyse des Bildmaterials und einer besseren Unterstützung des praktizierenden Arztes zu gelangen.

Es gibt aber auch viele Ärzte, die von den intelligenten Systemen enttäuscht sind, da sie ja nicht das "Allheilmittel" darstellen, als das sie viele Jahre hingestellt wurden. Auch viele Entwickler stehen diesen Methoden der intelligenten Systeme kritisch gegenüber und die Firmen, die sie eingesetzt haben, haben damit noch nicht so viel Geld machen können, wie sie sich erhofft hatten: Nur die Ministerien fördern an den Hochschulen diese Methoden sehr stark.

2.4 Was bringt die Zukunft hervor?

Das Interesse an medizinischen Bildverarbeitungssystemen ist auf jeden Fall gerade in den letzten Jahren sehr stark gestiegen und immer mehr Wissenschaftler beschäftigen sich mit diesem Themengebiet. Und das wird sich auch in der nächsten Zukunft nicht so plötzlich ändern. Wenn man die verschiedenen Probleme, wie sie zuvor geschildert wurden, versucht weitestgehend zu beheben, hat die medizinische Bildverarbeitung eine große Zukunft. Es wird dann viele Systeme geben, die die Ärzte bei ihrer Diagnose unterstützen und auch Veränderungen frühzeitig zu erkennen hilft. Somit ist dann nicht nur den Medizinern mit derartigen modernen Systemen geholfen, sondern auch den Patienten in Bezug auf die Vorsorge.

3 Zusammenfassung

In der Diskussion kamen Leistungen der unterschiedlichen medizinischen Bildverarbeitungssyteme, konzeptionelle Fragen, bestehende Probleme und kritische Positionen zur Sprache. Aus Unternehmersicht wurden Bildverarbeitungs- und Archivierungssysteme als Marktsegment mit großem Wachstumspotential dargestellt, andererseits wurde auf die gleichzeitige Stagnation in Deutschland bei Forschung und Innovation hingewiesen: Nahezu alle neuen Entwicklungen und Methoden der Bildverarbeitung haben ihren Ursprung in den USA. Den künftigen Beitrag der Informatik zu technischen Fortschritten auf diesem Gebiet und zur Ausweitung der Einsatzfelder betrachteten alle Experten als positiv. Dazu muß aber das Wissen der Mediziner noch stärker in den Bildverarbeitungsprozeß mit einbezogen werden und die Systeme sehr benutzerfreundlich gestaltet werden, da die Anwender dieser Systeme in der Regel keine Informatiker sind.

4 Literatur

1. Meyer zu Bexten E u.a.: Bedeutung und Perspektiven in der medizinischen Bildverarbeitung, 3. Anwendersymposium ‚Aktuelle Entwicklungen und Realisierungen der Bildverarbeitung‘, 11. und 12. September, Aachen, S. 89-96, 1997
2. 1. Aachener Workshop „Bildverarbeitung für die Medizin“, Aachen, November 1996
3. Freiburger Workshop „Digitale Bildverarbeitung in der Medizin“, Freiburg, März 1997
4. Lehmann T, Oberschelp W, Pelikan E, Repges R: Bildverarbeitung für die Medizin – Grundlagen, Modelle, Methoden, Anwendungen. Springer Verlag, 1997
5. Tizhoosh H.R: Fuzzy-Bildverarbeitung in Theorie und Praxis. Springer Verlag, 1997
6. Medizinische Bildverarbeitung. Spektrum der Wissenschaft, Juni 1997
7. Bildverarbeitungs-Systeme - Applikationsberichte, VITRONIC Dr.-Ing. Stein Bildverarbeitungssysteme GmbH, Wiesbaden, 1997
8. J. Hiltner, M. Jäger, E. Meyer zu Bexten, C. Tresp, M. Fathi: Analyse Medizinischer Bilddaten mit Hilfe unscharfen Wissens, Tagungsband zum 5. Workshop Digitale Bildverarbeitung in der Medizin, Freiburg, März 1997

Neural network analysis of functional MRI time-series - hierarchical clustering by deterministic annealing

A. Wismüller[1], D. R. Dersch[2], B. Lipinski[3], K. Hahn[1], and D. Auer[3]

[1]Dept. of Radiology, Klinikum Innenstadt, University of Munich, Germany
Email: Axel.Wismueller@physik.uni-muenchen.de
[2]Dept. of Electrical Engineering, University of Sydney, Australia
[3]Max Planck Institute of Psychiatry, Munich, Germany

Abstract. In this paper, we present a neural network approach to hierarchical unsupervised clustering of functional magnetic resonance imaging (fMRI) time-sequences of the human brain by self-organized fuzzy minimal free energy vector quantization (VQ). In contrast to conventional model-based fMRI data analysis techniques, this deterministic annealing procedure does not imply presumptive knowledge of expected stimulus-response patterns, and, thus, may be applied to fMRI experiments in which the time course of the stimulus is unknown like in spontaneously occurring events, e.g. hallucinations, epileptic fits, or sleep. Moreover, as minimal free energy VQ represents a hierarchical data analysis strategy implying repetitive cluster splitting, it can provide a natural approach to the subclassification task of activated brain regions on different scales of resolution with respect to fine-grained differences in pixel dynamics.

Keywords: functional magnetic resonance imaging, neural networks, deterministic annealing, vector quantization, time-series

1 Introduction

fMRI experiments induce spatio-temporal patterns of changing imaging properties in the human brain. Interpretation of these patterns as a response to a given experimental stimulus is the key problem of fMRI data analysis. Model-based approaches like cross-correlation techniques are commonly used to perform this task. However, as they imply presumptive knowledge of expected stimulus-response patterns, they may sometimes fail in unveiling complex signal changes, thus discarding valuable information about the fMRI signal. Moreover, in fMRI studies of spontaneously occurring events like hallucinations, epileptic fits, or sleep, even the exact time course of the stimulus is unknown.

Unsupervised clustering techniques offer a powerful strategy to overcome these problems. In this context, different vector quantization (VQ) algorithms have been proposed for a wide scope of biomedical signal processing problems including fMRI data analysis [6]. Here, the time-sequences of pixel grey values obtained from fMRI experiments can be interpreted as feature vectors representing a multidimensional probability distribution. VQ procedures map a data space onto a finite set of prototypical feature vectors, a so-called codebook. Examples of this class of algorithms are Kohonen's self-organizing maps (SOMs) [3], minimal free energy VQ [5], and the

$Z = \sum_k \exp(-E_k(\vec{x}_i)/2\rho^2)$ and ρ is the cooperativity parameter of this model. That so-called 'fuzzy range' ρ defines a length scale in data space and is annealed to repeatedly smaller values in the VQ procedure. The learning rule (1) with a_k given by (2) describes a stochastic gradient descent on the error function

$$F_\rho(W) = -\frac{1}{2\rho^2} \int P(\vec{x}_i) \ln Z \, dx^n, \tag{3}$$

which is a free energy in a mean-field approximation. Here, $P(\vec{x}_i)$ denotes the probability density of feature vectors $\vec{x}_i$. For the minimal free energy VQ procedure, the codebook vectors mark local centers of this multidimensional probability distribution. Thus, for the application to fMRI signal analysis, the codebook vector $\vec{w}_k$ is the weighted average fMRI signal of all the time-sequences $\vec{x}_i$ belonging to group k with respect to a fuzzy tesselation of the feature space.

In contrast to SOMs, minimal free energy VQ
(i) can be described as a stochastic gradient descent on an explicitly given energy function [5],
(ii) preserves the probability density without distortion, and
(iii)allows hierarchical data analysis on different scales of resolution.

In the beginning of the VQ process, there is only one cluster representing the center of the whole data set. As the deterministic annealing procedure continues, phase transitions occur and large clusters split up into smaller ones marking increasingly smaller regions of the feature space. Tracing this repetitive cluster splitting through the whole VQ procedure leads to a 'genealogy' of cluster centers, i.e. a resemblance tree of codebook vectors. Thus, the manual merging of cluster centers into larger meta-clusters like in the SOM approach to fMRI analysis can be avoided. At the same time, the scope of resolution can be adapted according to the observer's needs. The similarity of different codebook vectors can easily be derived by back-tracking the clustering tree. The procedure can be monitored by various control parameters like the free energy, entropy, reconstruction error etc. which allow an easy detection of cluster splitting.

3 Methods

Functional imaging was performed on a 1.5 T system (Signa, General Electrics, Milwaukee) using a GI-EPI sequence (TR/TE = 4,000/66 msec) with 8 slices and 64 images per experiment. Resolution was 3x3x4 mm, and three periods of photic stimulation (8 Hz alternating checkerboard, central fixation point) were interleaved by four control periods (dark background, central fixation point). The first scan was discarded from analysis for remaining saturation effects. Movement artifacts were compensated by automatic image alignment (AIR software, [7]). Average-corrected time-sequences of each pixel were clustered by minimal free energy VQ employing 30 codebook vectors. The results were compared with classical cross-correlation images (e.g. [1]).

'neural gas' algorithm [4]. The mathematical properties of these algorithms, their motivation from statistical mechanics, as well as their strengthes and weaknesses in the field of biosignal analysis have been thoroughly investigated in the literature (see e.g. [6]). SOMs have already been applied to fMRI data analysis [2]. Minimal free energy VQ is a deterministic annealing procedure minimizing the free energy of a multiparticle system in analogy to a canonical ensemble tending towards thermal equilibrium. In contrast to SOMs, this algorithm offers a specific advantage for practical data analysis problems [6]: it provides a *hierarchical* clustering scheme *on different scales of resolution.*

In the field of fMRI time-sequence analysis, this offers a convenient method for subclassification of activated areas according to similarities in signal time-sequences. At the same time, heuristic manual merging of pixel clusters belonging to different codebook vectors like in the SOM approach can be avoided. Merging into larger meta-clusters can be replaced by back-tracking the codebook hierarchy tree to an earlier stage of the annealing procedure. Thus, the coarse-grained structure of the data set can be explored in a natural manner.

2 Theory

Let n denote the number of subsequent scans in a fMRI experiment. The dynamics of each voxel i , i.e. the sequence of grey values $x_i(t)$ over all scan acquisition time spots t can be interpreted as a vector $\vec{x}_i \in R^n$ in the n -dimensional feature space of possible fMRI signal time-sequences. Clustering identifies groups k of pixels with similar dynamics. These groups are represented by prototypical time-sequences called codebook vectors $\vec{w}_k$. Soft-competing VQ procedures determine these cluster centers by an iterative adaptive update according to

$$\vec{w}_k(t+1) = \varepsilon \, a_k(\vec{x}_i(t); W(t); \kappa) \, (\vec{x}_i(t) - \vec{w}_k(t)), \tag{1}$$

where ε denotes a learning parameter, a_k a so-called cooperativity function which, in general, depends on the codebook $W(t)$, a cooperativity parameter κ , and the presented feature vector $\vec{x}_i(t)$ itself. In the fuzzy clustering scheme proposed by Rose, Gurewitz, and Fox [5], the cooperativity function a_k reads

$$a_k(\vec{x}_i; W; \kappa \equiv \rho) = \frac{\exp(-E_k(\vec{x}_i)/2\rho^2)}{Z}. \tag{2}$$

Here, the 'energy' $E_k(\vec{x}_i) = \left\| \vec{w}_k - \vec{x}_i \right\|^2$ measures the distance between the codebook vector $\vec{w}_k$ and the data vector $\vec{x}_i$. Z denotes a partition function given by

Fig. 1:   (a) Stimulus. (b) Cross-correlation image. (c) anatomical image.

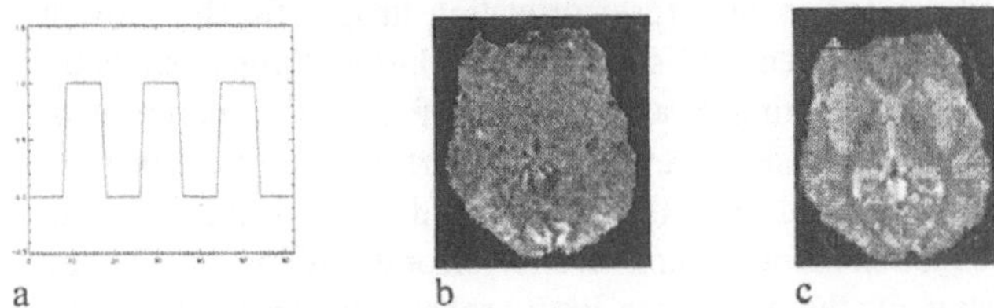

a   b   c

Fig. 2: Part of the hierarchical clustering tree demonstrating cluster separation during deterministic annealing. (a) Cluster center before phase transition, i.e. cluster separation. (b) Corresponding pixel cluster before phase transition according to a minimal distance criterion. (c), (d) Cluster centers after phase transition. (e),(f) Corresponding pixel clusters after phase transition.

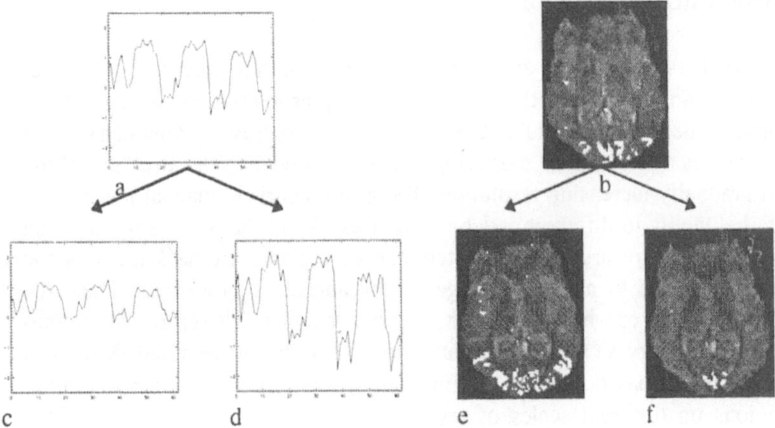

c   d   e   f

4 Methods

Functional imaging was performed on a 1.5 T system (Signa, General Electrics, Milwaukee) using a GI-EPI sequence (TR/TE = 4,000/66 msec) with 8 slices and 64 images per experiment. Resolution was 3x3x4 mm, and three periods of photic stimulation (8 Hz alternating checkerboard, central fixation point) were interleaved by four control periods (dark background, central fixation point). The first scan was discarded from analysis for remaining saturation effects. Movement artifacts were compensated by automatic image alignment (AIR software, [7]). Average-corrected time-sequences of each pixel were clustered by minimal free energy VQ employing 30 codebook vectors. The results were compared with classical cross-correlation images (e.g. [1]).

5 Results

Fig.2 shows a part of the hierarchical clustering tree covering two subsequent VQ steps of the deterministic annealing procedure. Fig.2a presents one of 17 cluster centers present at the observed stage of VQ. Note the apparent similarity compared with the stimulus (fig.1a). Fig.2d shows all the pixels belonging to this cluster center according to a minimal distance criterion in the metric of the time-sequence feature space. The highlighted regions can be attributed to the visual cortex. They clearly correspond to the activated regions in the cross-correlation image (fig.1b). Now a phase transition occurs in the subsequent VQ step, and the cluster of fig.2a splits up into two descendant clusters representing smaller regions of the visual cortex with different pixel dynamics. They are presented in the lower part of fig.2. Note that the sum of the activated areas in fig.2e and fig.2f is greater than the area of the cluster in fig.2b. This is based on a reduction in local reconstruction error due to the fact that the new codebook structure better fits the underlying local probability density. Thus, the descendant clusters can take over pixels which formerly were attributed to adjacent codebook vectors.

6 Discussion and Conclusion

The study shows that deterministic annealing by the minimal free energy VQ is a useful strategy for the analysis of fMRI data sets without presumptive knowledge of stimulus-response models or the stimulus function itself. In contrast to Kohonen's SOM algorithm, it realizes a hierarchical clustering procedure unveiling the structure of the data set with gradually increasing resolution. Therefore, heuristic manual merging of pixel clusters belonging to different codebook vectors like in the SOM approach can be avoided. Merging into larger meta-clusters can be replaced by back-tracking the codebook hierarchy tree to an earlier stage of the annealing procedure. Thus, the structure of the data set can be explored in a natural manner. Therefore, we recommend minimal free energy VQ as an alternative to SOMs for unsupervised fMRI data analysis. Especially, it may be helpful in situations where subclassification of activated brain regions on different scales of resolution is focused with respect to fine-grained differences in pixel dynamics.

7 References

1. P.A. Bandettini, et al. Processing strategies for time-course data sets in functional MRI of the human brain. *Magn. Reson. Med.*, 30:161-173, 1993
2. H. Fischer, M. Buechert, and J. Hennig. Assessing the dynamics of fMRI data using self-organizing map clustering, *Proceedings of the 5th SMR meeting*, 1997
3. T. Kohonen. The self-organizing map. *Proceedings of the IEEE*, 78(9):1464-1480, 1990
4. T.M. Martinetz and K.J. Schulten. A 'neural gas' network learns topologies. In *Proceedings of the International Conference of Artificial Neural Networks ICANN*, pages 397-402, Amsterdam, 1991. Elsevier Science Publishers.
5. K. Rose, E. Gurewitz, and G.C. Fox. Vector quantization by deterministic annealing. *IEEE Transactions on Information Theory*, 38(4):1249-1257, 1992
6. A. Wismüller and D.R. Dersch. Neural network computation in biomedical research: chances for conceptual cross-fertilization. *Theory in Biosciences*, 116:290-301, 1997
7. R.P. Woods, S.R. Cherry, and J.C. Mazziotta. Rapid automated algorithm for aligning and reslicing PET images. *Journal of Computer Assisted Tomography*, 16:620-633, 1992

Detektion und Quantifizierung der Membranstrukturen von Nervenzellen

J. Bredno, V. Metzler, W. Nacimiento[*], T. Lehmann, K. Spitzer

Institut für Medizinische Informatik und [*]Neurologische Klinik
Rheinisch-Westfälische Technische Hochschule (RWTH), 52057 Aachen
Email: jbredno@bootes.imib.rwth-aachen.de

Zusammenfassung. Quantitative diagnostische Aussagen aufgrund histologischer Untersuchungen erfordern eine reproduzierbare Auswertung von Zellbildern. Der Einsatz eines rechnergestützten Auswertungssystems kann die Qualität der Aussagen steigern, indem der subjektive Einfluß des Untersuchers minimiert wird. Mit einem für die Aufgabe der Zelldetektion spezialisierten deformierbaren Membranmodell können geometrische Informationen über die Form einer Zelle im Bild gewonnen werden. Die Geometrie und ein zusätzlich ermitteltes lokales Qualitäts- und Wichtungsmaß für die aufgefundene Kontur werden verwendet, um diagnostisch relevante Membranstrukturen zu extrahieren und quantitative Kennwerte zu ermitteln. Das Verfahren wird zur quantitativen Auswertung bei einer neurobiologischen Fragestellung eingesetzt. Hier werden histologisch präparierte Zellen automatisch ausgewertet und in 94% der Fälle korrekt erkannt.

Schlüsselwörter: Deformierbares Membranmodell, Computer-Assisted Microscopy, Konturdetektion, Quantitative Mikroskopie

1 Einleitung

Um in einer histologischen Versuchsreihe relevante Ergebnisse zu messen, muß eine sichere Methode vorliegen, um Aussagen über den Zustand von präpariertem Gewebe zu erhalten. Die Begutachtung und Einordnung durch eine geschulte Person ist zeitintensiv und vom subjektiven Eindruck des Betrachters abhängig. Eine Rechnerunterstützung *(Computer-Assisted Microscopy)* bietet hier mit der Automatisierung des Vorgangs und dem Ausschalten subjektiver Eindrücke Vorteile gegenüber der herkömmlichen visuellen Beurteilung der Präparate [1]. Ergebnisse werden vergleichbar und können statistisch verifiziert werden. Zu diesem Zweck benötigt man robuste Algorithmen, die insbesondere den Anforderungen mikroskopischen Bildmaterials und biologischer Präparate gerecht werden. Dort sind komplexe Strukturen oft undeutlich und mit großen Variationen im Erscheinungsbild gegeben.

In der Neurologischen Klinik der RWTH Aachen werden motorische Nervenzellen aus dem Rückenmark von Ratten untersucht, um Aussagen über pathologische Veränderungen von synaptischen Boutons an der Oberfläche dieser Zellen nach einer Rückenmarksläsion zu erhalten. Die Präparation der Schnitte erfolgt mit unterschiedlichen immunhistochemischen Färbetechniken, die bestimmte Neurotransmitterstoffe einfärben. Die nachgewiesene Reduktion von inhibitorischen axosomatischen Boutons nach einer Läsion [2] ist zu quantifizieren. Dazu wird die unterschiedliche Farbintensität markierter Boutons gemessen und auf objektive Parameter abgebildet. Ein Präparat ist in Abbildung 1 gezeigt.

Eine rechnerunterstützte Auswertung muß als schwierige Teilaufgabe geometrische Informationen über die Lage der Zellmembran in einem Bild gewinnen [3]. Diese Bildsegmentierung ist bei biologischem Material oft schwierig [4]. Algorithmen auf Basis deformierbarer Konturmodelle ermöglichen es, in einem Bild Formen aufzufinden und geometrisch zu repräsentieren. Speziell die formgebenden Eigenschaften biologischer Objekte können dabei modelliert werden [5, 6].

Mit den Algorithmen werden diagnostisch relevante Bereiche eines Bildes extrahiert, aus denen Kennwerte erarbeitet werden. Diese Kennwerte werden dem Nutzer als Protokolle zur Verfügung gestellt, anhand derer eine Qualitätskontrolle durchgeführt wird.

2 Konturdetektion mit dem deformierbaren Membranmodell

Die auszuwertenden Zellen wurden unter dem Mikroskop so plaziert, daß sich in der Mitte des Bildes der Zellkern befindet. Mit dieser a-priori-Information wird mit dem deformierbaren Membranmodell, ausgehend von einem Punkt im Zellinnern, die Zellkontur bestimmt. Das verwendete Modell wurde als aktives Konturverfahren realisiert. Solche Modelle und Algorithmen werden zur Bestimmung einer Kontur in undeutlichem Bildmaterial eingesetzt [6]. Sie können nicht klar erkennbare Abschnitte interpolieren, die Detektion verläuft objekt-, statt punkt- oder frequenzorientiert. Für die deformierbare Membran werden Verhaltensweisen festgelegt, die dazu führen, daß sie iterativ die Lage der im Bildmaterial enthaltenen Formen annimmt. Die Dynamik der definierten Kontur wird durch mechanische Membraneigenschaften festgelegt, die möglichst genau das Verhalten einer biologischen Membran unter Innendruck simulieren sollen. Aus diesem Grunde werden Eigenschaften wie Elastizität oder Splineinterpolation hier nicht verwendet.

2.1 Modellierung der Kontur

Die Membran wird beim verwendeten Modell durch eine Abfolge von geraden Kanten repräsentiert, die von Knoten unterstützt werden. Die Anzahl der Kanten und Knoten ist variabel, eine maximale und minimale Kantenlänge kann eingestellt werden. Auf die Membran wirken mehrere Einflüsse, die mechanisch modelliert wurden.

- Der wichtigste innere Einfluß, der das Suchverhalten der Kontur bestimmt, ist ein Innendruck. Dieser führt zu einer Ausdehnung der modellierten Membran aus der Startlage im Zellinneren heraus.
- Als äußerer Einfluß resultierend aus dem Bild, werden dessen Grauwerte als energetische Höhen und Potentiale interpretiert. Eine Kante erfährt durch anliegende Potentialdifferenzen Normalkräfte. Die Kräfte entlang einer Kante summieren sich zu Momenten um die stützenden Knoten. Die Stützkräfte zur Aufnahme dieser Momente und die Resultierende des Innendrucks wirken auf angrenzende Knoten einer Kante.

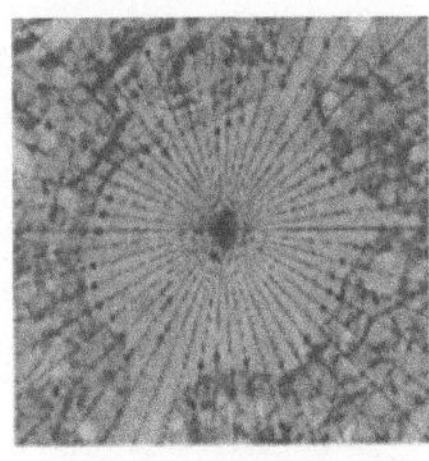

Abb. 1. Im Bild einer Nervenzelle sind Schnittverläufe eingezeichnet, die zur adaptiven Zuordnung energetischer Profilhöhen zu den Grauwerten des Bildes ausgewertet werden. Auf den Strahlen eingezeichnete Marker kennzeichnen Stellen, an denen eine konservative Kantenerkennung die Zellmembran gefunden hat.

- Mit inneren Einflüssen des deformierbaren Membranmodells kann der Detektionsalgorithmus den Verlauf von undeutlichen Zellabschnitten rekonstruieren. Diese können mit der pathologischen Reduktion von Neurotransmitterstoffen oder einem tangentialen Anschnitt der Zellmembran erklärt werden. Eine Zellmembran ist vander-Waals-gebunden, sie nimmt immer eine Form an, die durch eine minimale Verformungsenergie (zweite Ableitung der Kontur) gekennzeichnet ist. Undeutliche Bereiche der Membran können durch das Modell rekonstruiert werden, indem auf Knoten Deformierungskräfte wirken, die die lokale zweite Ableitung minimieren und die Kontur dadurch glätten.

Die Zuordnung der Grauwerte eines Bildes zu energetischen Höhen erfolgt nach einer Voranalyse (Abbildung 1). Mit dieser wird erreicht, daß die zu erkennende Kontur im Bild sich dem deformierbaren Modell als eine Energiebarriere darstellt, die vom Innendruck nicht überwunden werden kann. Die in der Abbildung eingezeichneten Schnittverläufe werden analysiert, um Informationen über die Grauwerte im Innern und am Rand einer Zelle zu erhalten.

Die Knoten bewegen sich proportional zu den einwirkenden Kräften. Im Laufe der Iteration wird das Membranmodell so deformiert, daß Knoten eine Lage an der Zellmembran einnehmen und sich hier stabilisieren. Diese Punkte werden eingefroren. In der Nähe solcher stabilisierter Bereiche können undeutliche Konturabschnitte durch Verfolgung des Verlaufs der Kontur rekonstruiert werden. Implizit sinkt damit die Aktivität der modellierten Membran in der Nähe der zu erkennenden Zellmembran, ähnlich wie dies in einem *Annealing-Prozess* vom Algorithmus vorgegeben wird. Abbildung 2 zeigt die Einflüsse auf eine deformierbare Membran.

2.2 Bewertung der Kontur mit Konfidenzwerten

Eine fehlerfreie automatische Detektion kann bei der Formerkennung von bio-

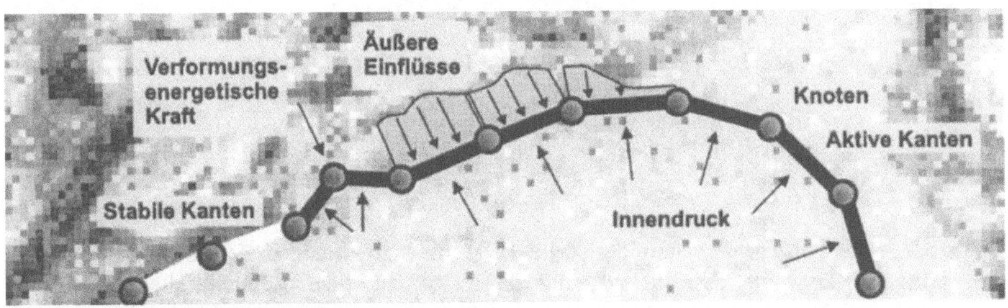

Abb. 2. Die Einflüsse auf die deformierbare Membran während der Konturdetektion

logischen Strukturen nicht erreicht werden. Dennoch ist es auch bei Bildmaterial mit leichten Erkennungsfehlern noch möglich, diagnostisch relevante Kennwerte aus den gut erkannten Bereichen zu extrahieren. Zur Unterstützung der nachfolgenden Quantifizierung wird jeder Kante eine Konfidenz zugeordnet, die die lokale Detektionsqualität angibt, also die Wahrscheinlichkeit, mit der eine Kante korrekt erkannt wurde und entlang einer Zellmembran im Bild verläuft. So erhalten Kanten, die eine glatte Kontur entlang einer Energiebarriere bilden, hohe Konfidenzwerte. Unstetigkeiten in der Kontur oder ein nicht erwünschtes Energieprofil über eine Kante führen zur Abwertung der Konfidenz. Die Aufgabe der Konfidenz ist es, zu verhindern, daß sich Detektionsfehler auf ermittelte Kennwerte einer Zelle auswirken. Im folgenden Abschnitt wird beschrieben, wie die lokale Konfidenz der Kontur zur Verbesserung der Robustheit quantitativer Parameter eingesetzt wird.

2.3 Kennwerte

Nachdem die Kontur detektiert und den einzelnen Membranabschnitten ein Konfidenz- und damit ein Qualitätsmaß zugewiesen ist, werden die Bildinformationen entlang der Membran unter Annahme einer vorgegebenen Membrandicke als *Region of Interest* aus dem Bild extrahiert. Nun werden verschiedene diagnostisch relevante Kennwerte bestimmt. Dies sind die durchschnittliche Schwärzung der Membran und die Besetzung mit synaptischen Boutons, in denen Neurotransmitterstoff enthalten ist. Eine morphologische Analyse ermittelt deren Größenverteilung. Dabei werden in einer Abfolge von morphologischen Öffnungen Kreisscheiben verschiedenen Durchmessers in der binarisierten Darstellung der Zellmembran aufgefunden [7]. Jede Kreisscheibe ist die Abbildung eines synaptischen Boutons. Deren Anzahl wird über die Membranlänge normiert angegeben. Bei der Kennwertbestimmung werden Beleuchtungseinflüsse durch Regressionsrechnungen unterdrückt.

Die Bestimmung der Kennwerte wichtet die gelesenen Bildinformationen jeweils mit der Konfidenz der entsprechenden Kante. Unsicher erkannte Bereiche mit niedriger Konfidenz tragen damit wenig zu den ermittelten Kennwerten einer Zelle bei, leichte Fehler bei der Konturdetektion wirken sich nicht auf diese aus.

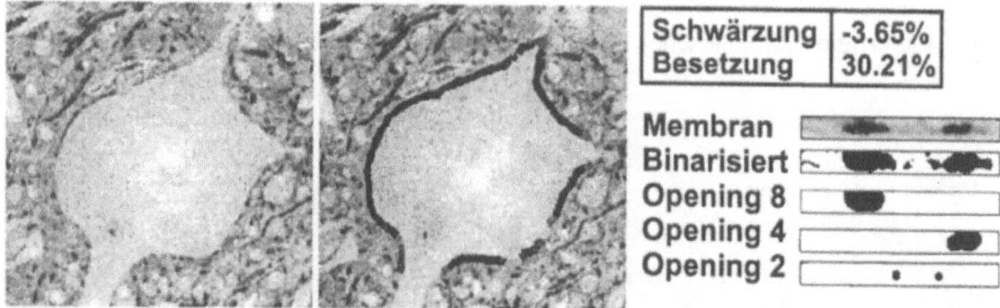

Abb. 3.   Die Auswertung zu einer Zelle zeigt die aufgefundene Zellmembran und die zugehörigen Kennwerte. Die Schwärzung ist relativ zu einer Referenzzelle angegeben. Zusätzlich ist für einen kurzen Abschnitt der Zellmembran die morphologische Auswertung dargestellt.

3 Ergebnisse und Ausblick

In Abbildung 3 ist die ausgewertete Zelle mit der vom System ermittelten Kontur dargestellt. Je heller die Membran eingezeichnet wurde, desto geringer ist die Konfidenz an den entsprechenden Stellen. Der Nutzer erhält eine einfache Qualitätskontrolle des Detektionsalgorithmus. Bei günstigen Bedingungen, also einer möglichst konstanten Färbeantwort und identischer Ausleuchtung der Präparate, konnten in einer Versuchsreihe Erfolgsraten von 94% erreicht werden. Bei den übrigen Bildern sind deutliche Fehler in der detektierten Kontur zu erkennen, so daß die Kennwerte zu diesen Zellen bei der visuellen Kontrolle zurückgewiesen werden können.

Allgemein steht mit dem deformierbaren Membranmodell jetzt ein System zur Verfügung, das biologische Formen auf Bildmaterial gut erkennen kann und eine detektierte Kontur für beliebige Auswertungen zur Verfügung stellt. Dieses wird im beschriebenen Auswertungssystem für die histologische Untersuchungsreihe der Neurologischen Klinik der RWTH Aachen eingesetzt, um Kennwerte zu Nervenzellen zu bestimmen. Das System wird zur Zeit verifiziert und in naher Zukunft in der neurobiologischen Routine Einsatz finden. Durch die Methode der Konfidierung von Abschnitten einer erkannten Kontur kann der Einfluß eventueller Detektionsfehler auf ermittelte Kennwerte verringert werden. Das Verfahren wird auch auf verschiedene andere Fragestellungen aus dem Bereich der quantitativen Mikroskopie angepaßt. Als sehr günstig erwies sich dabei die Konfigurierbarkeit des Systems auf unterschiedlichstes Bildmaterial. Von etwa 40 externen Parametern, die die Verhaltensweisen des Membranmodells bestimmen, müssen dabei lediglich fünf nachgestellt werden. Allgemein können histologische Problemstellungen untersucht werden, bei denen sich Kennwerte, die einem Gewebe zugeordnet werden sollen, an Grauwerten des Bildes oder Geometrien im Bild ablesen lassen.

4 Literatur

1. J.C. Russ: *Computer-Assisted Microscopy*. Plenum Press, New York, 1990
2. W. Nacimiento, J. Noth: Zelluläre Pathomechanismen und experimentelle Therapien nach Rückenmarkstrauma. *Nervenheilkunde*, 16: 1-11, 1997
3. C.A. Glasby, G.W. Hogan: *Image Analysis for the Biological Sciences*. John Wiley & Sons, New York, 1994
4. T. Lehmann, W. Oberschelp, E. Pelikan, R. Repges: *Bildverarbeitung für die Medizin, Grundlagen, Modelle, Methoden, Anwendungen*. Springer-Verlag, Berlin, 1. Auflage, 1997.
5. S. Lobregt, A. Viergerer: A discrete dynamic contour model. *IEEE Trans. Med. Imaging*, 14(1): 12-24, 1995
6. D. Rückert, P. Burger, S. Forbat, R. Mohiaddin, G. Yang: Automatic tracking of the aorta in cardiovascular MR images using deformable models. *IEEE Trans. Med. Imaging*, 16(5): 581-590, 1997
7. R. Haralick, S. Sternberg, X. Zhuang: Image Analysis using mathematical morphology. *IEEE Trans. Pattern Analysis and Machine Intelligence*, 9(4): 532-550, 1987

Quantitative Farbmessung
in laryngoskopischen Bildern

Christoph Palm, Ingrid Scholl, Thomas Lehmann und Klaus Spitzer

Institut für Medizinische Informatik,
Rheinisch-Westfälische Technische Hochschule (RWTH), 52057 Aachen
Email: cpalm@imib.rwth-aachen.de

Zusammenfassung. Quantitative Farbmessungen sollen die Diagnostik laryngealer Erkrankungen unterstützen. Dabei wird der Farbeindruck nicht nur durch die Reflexionseigenschaften des Gewebes sondern auch durch die Farbe der verwendeten Lichtquelle beeinflußt. Der hier vorgestellte Farbkonstanz-Algorithmus basiert auf dem dichromatischen Reflexionsmodell und liefert eine pixelweise Trennung des Farbbildes in seine beiden Farbanteile. Die Körperfarbe entspricht dabei der gewebespezifischen Reflexion, die Oberfächenfarbe der Strahlung der Lichtquelle.

Schlüsselwörter: Farbkonstanz, quantitative Farbmessung, dichromatisches Reflexionsmodell, Laryngoskopie

1 Einleitung

In der medizinischen Diagnostik spielt die Farbe bei der Beurteilung des zu untersuchenden Gewebes seit jeher eine zentrale Rolle. Sie ist auch ein wichtiger Parameter zur Befundung von organischen Kehlkopferkrankungen. Dazu wird der Larynx mit Hilfe eines starren Endoskops mit einer Lupenoptik eingesehen. Bislang erfolgt die Begutachtung der Farbe der Stimmlippen und des umliegenden Gewebes ausschließlich durch den Arzt, so daß das Ergebnis von seiner Beobachtungsgabe und Erfahrung abhängt und so zu einer recht groben Klassifizierung des Krankheitsbildes führt. Zusätzlich wirkt sich die Beleuchtungsfarbe auf den Farbeindruck aus, die sich durch Alterung oder Lichtquellenwechsel verändert.

Eine quantitative Farbmessung, die gleichzeitig den Einfluß der Lichtquellenfarbe eliminiert, würde die Objektivierung der Diagnostik fördern, eine genauere Zuordnung von Farbmessung und Erkrankung ermöglichen und so auch die Verlaufskontrolle über einen längeren Zeitraum hinweg unterstützen. In dem Projekt *Quantitative Digitale Laryngoskopie*[1] erfolgt die Farbmessung durch Einsatz einer Farb-CCD-Kamera und Videoaufzeichnung des Endoskopbildes mit nachfolgender Digitalisierung. Zur Elimination der Lichtquellenfarbe wird in dieser Arbeit ein Farbkonstanz-Algorithmus vorgestellt, der die beleuchtungsunabhängige Gewebefarbe bestimmt und Farbfehler durch Überbelichtung und Interreflexion detektiert.

---

[1] Das Projekt wird von der Deutschen Forschungsgemeinschaft gefördert (Sp 538/2-1 und We 2147/1-1).

2 Methodik

Das Verfahren basiert auf dem dichromatischen Reflexionsmodell [1], das den Farbeindruck aus der Linearkombination zweier Farben erklärt: der Farbe der Oberflächen- und der der Körperreflexion. Mit der Annahme einer achromatischen Reflexion an der Objektoberfläche kann die Lichtquellenfarbe als Farbe der Oberflächenreflexion und die Gewebefarbe als Körperreflexionskomponente identifiziert werden. Ziel der quantitativen Farbmessung ist die Bestimmung der reinen Gewebefarbe, die der Unterscheidung von verschiedenartigem Gewebe, insbesondere zur Differenzierung zwischen gesundem und pathologischem Gewebe, dient. Der hier vorgestellte Farbkonstanz-Algorithmus ist dreistufig. Dabei wird zunächst die Lichtquellenfarbe ohne Einsatz von a-priori verfügbarem Wissen aus den Bilddaten ermittelt. Aufgrund dieser Zusatzinformation läßt sich die gesuchte Gewebefarbe schätzen. Bei Verfügbarkeit beider Farbanteile werden die Faktoren der dichromatischen Linearkombination berechnet, so daß das Bild pixelweise in die jeweiligen gewichteten Farbkomponenten aufgeteilt wird.

2.1 Bestimmung der Lichtquellenfarbe

Die zu messenden Farbwerte $[R, G, B]^{tr}$ eines einfarbigen Objekts mit spektralem Remissionsgrad $[\beta_k^R, \beta_k^G, \beta_k^B]^{tr}$ des Körpers und einer wellenlängenneutralen Reflexion der Objektoberfläche $[\beta_o^R, \beta_o^G, \beta_o^B]^{tr} = [\beta_o, \beta_o, \beta_o]^{tr}$, das mit einer Lichtquelle der Farbe $[s^R, s^G, s^B]^{tr}$ beleuchtet wird, stellen sich nach dem dichromatischen Reflexionsmodell wie folgt dar:

$$
\begin{bmatrix} R \\ G \\ B \end{bmatrix} = g_o \beta_o \begin{bmatrix} s^R \\ s^G \\ s^B \end{bmatrix} + g_k \begin{bmatrix} \beta_k^R \cdot s^R \\ \beta_k^G \cdot s^G \\ \beta_k^B \cdot s^B \end{bmatrix}, \tag{1}
$$

mit den positiven Gewichtsfaktoren g_o und g_k.

Im auf die Summe der drei Farbkanäle normierten CIE–Farbdiagramm liegen diese Farbwerte auf einer Geraden, deren Geradengleichung explizit angegeben werden kann:

$$
\frac{G}{R+G+B} = a \cdot \frac{R}{R+G+B} + b \tag{2}
$$

mit

$$
a = -\frac{1 - \frac{s^B}{s^R} \cdot \frac{\beta_k^B - \beta_k^G}{\beta_k^G - \beta_k^R}}{1 + \frac{s^B}{s^G} \cdot \frac{\beta_k^B - \beta_k^R}{\beta_k^G - \beta_k^R}} \quad \text{und} \quad b = \frac{1}{1 + \frac{s^B}{s^G} \cdot \frac{\beta_k^B - \beta_k^R}{\beta_k^G - \beta_k^R}}. \tag{3}
$$

Für zwei verschiedenfarbige Objekte, die mit einer Lichtquelle der gleichen Farbe S bestrahlt werden, gilt:

$$
\begin{bmatrix} \beta_{k,1}^R \\ \beta_{k,1}^G \\ \beta_{k,1}^B \end{bmatrix} \neq \begin{bmatrix} \beta_{k,2}^R \\ \beta_{k,2}^G \\ \beta_{k,2}^B \end{bmatrix} \quad \text{und} \quad S = \begin{bmatrix} s_1^R \\ s_1^G \\ s_1^B \end{bmatrix} = \begin{bmatrix} s_2^R \\ s_2^G \\ s_2^B \end{bmatrix}. \tag{4}
$$

414

Das Gleichsetzen beider Geradengleichungen ergibt mit $r_s = s^R/(s^R + s^G + s^B)$ und $g_s = s^G/(s^R + s^G + s^B)$ die normierte Farbe der Lichtquelle als Schnittpunkt.

Um diese Eigenschaft ausnutzen zu können, müssen die Farbgeraden ohne Einsatz von a-priori-Wissen aus den Bilddaten extrahiert werden. Das Bild wird zunächst *farbsegmentiert*, um Objekte einer einheitlichen Körperfarbe in einem Cluster zu vereinen. Dazu wird ein spezieller Merkmalsraum verwendet, bei dem die Farbvektoren auf das orthogonale Komplement zur Unbuntachse projiziert und anschließend normiert werden [2, 3]. Da die Körperfarben nicht bekannt sind, kommt es dabei zu Ungenauigkeiten, die sich darin äußern, daß i. allg. mehrere Objekte mit ähnlichen Körperfarben in einem Cluster zu finden sind.

Im CIE-Farbdiagramm eines solchen Clusters sind dann auch mehrere mögliche Geraden zu finden. Die N Längsten dieser Geraden werden mit Hilfe einer *Hough-Transformation* detektiert. N sollte nicht zu klein gewählt werden, um die Zahl der Geradenhypothesen nicht bereits in diesem Schritt zu beschränken. In Abb. 1(a) wurden beispielhaft vier Geraden aus Farbdiagramm eines Clusters extrahiert.

Eine Selektion innerhalb dieser Hypothesen findet im Rahmen der *inversen Pfadsuche* statt. Dabei wird deren Konsistenz zum dichromatischen Reflexionsmodell überprüft und bewertet. Physikalische Grundlage der inversen Pfadsuche ist die sukzessive Änderung der Farbwerte entlang eines gekrümmten Objekts von einem Farbextrem (Körperfarbe) zum anderen Farbextrem (Beleuchtungsfarbe) des dichromatischen Modells [4]. Deshalb wird für jede Geradenhypothese eines Clusters ein lokaler Pfad im Bild gesucht (Abb. 1(b)), der die Farbwerte auf der Geraden in einen topologischen Zusammenhang bringt. Lange Pfade im Originalbild, die im Farbdiagramm einer Geraden zuzurechnen sind, entsprechen mit hoher Wahrscheinlichkeit einem der gesuchten Farbübergänge. Zur Bestimmung des längsten Pfades einer Geraden werden deren normierte Farbwerte nacheinander in das Originalbild zurückprojiziert und auf direkte Nachbarschaft zu bereits bestehenden Pfaden überprüft. Dabei ist zu beachten, daß zwar entlang eines Pfades Farben im Diagramm übersprungen werden können, die Rei-

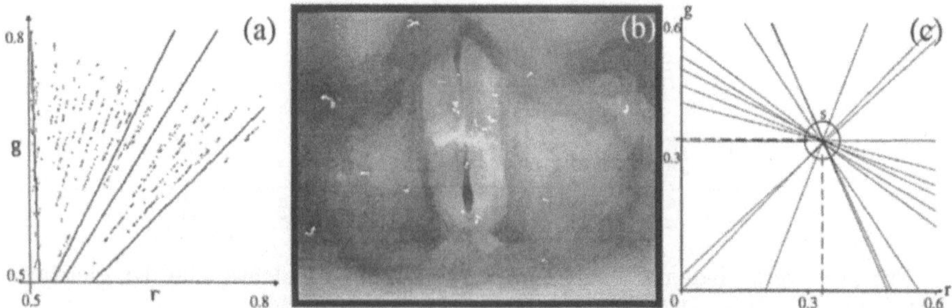

Abb. 1. (a) Ausschnitt des CIE-Farbdiagramms eines Clusters. (b) Die lokalen Pfade der repräsentativen Farbgerade eines Clusters sind als weiße *Schlangenlinien* im Farbbild eingetragen. (c) Die Farbgeraden der einzelnen Cluster schneiden sich in der Lichtquellenfarbe S.

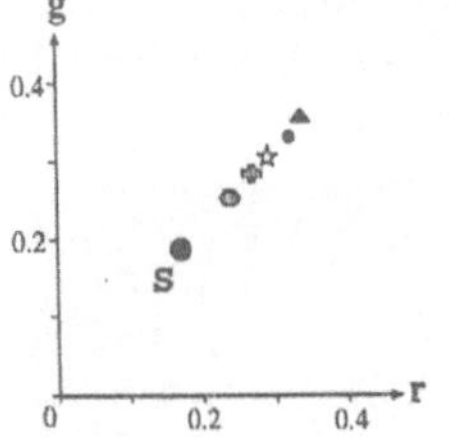

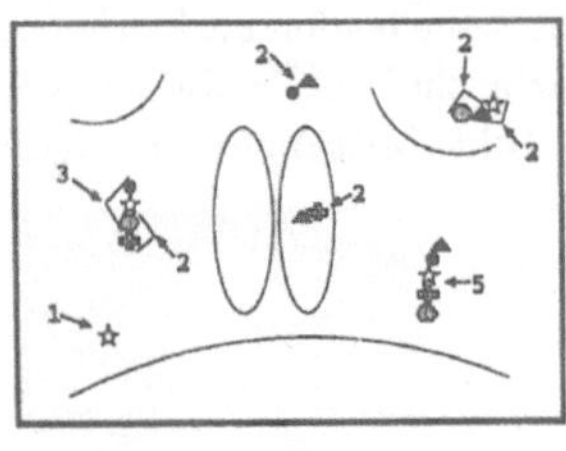

Abb. 2. Die Symbole im CIE-Farbdiagramm (links) entsprechen den normierten Farbwerten eines Clusters. Sie sind im normierten Originalbild wiederzufinden und bilden Pfade mit den angegebenen Längen.

henfolge aber erhalten bleiben muß. Abb. 2 verdeutlicht den Zusammenhang von Farbgerade im Diagramm und lokalem Pfad im Bild. Die Länge des längsten Pfades kann als Maß für die Gültigkeit des dichromatischen Reflexionsmodells interpretiert und so eine repräsentative Gerade für ein Cluster bestimmt werden.

Der Schnittpunkt der repräsentativen Geraden liefert die gesuchte Beleuchtungsfarbe (Abb. 1(c)). Allerdings ist in diesem Stadium nicht zwischen korrekten Farbgeraden und solchen, die z.B. das Ergebnis von *Color-Clipping* sind, zu unterscheiden. Da die Anzahl der fehlerhaften Geraden verhältnismäßig gering ist, kann dennoch der korrekte Schnittpunkt bestimmt werden.

2.2 Schätzung der Gewebefarbe

Eine Methode zur Bestimmung der Gewebefarbe ist die Viertelkreisanalyse [5], bei der die Farben eines Objekts mit Hilfe zweier orthonormaler Eigenvektoren beschrieben werden. Diese werden so rotiert, daß einer von beiden in Richtung der Lichtquellenfarbe S weist. Die transformierten Werte sind dann im ersten Quadranten des Einheitskreises zu finden. Eine robuste Schätzung der Körperfarbe liefert der Wert, der *am weitesten* von S entfernt ist.

2.3 Pixelweise Trennung

Sind beide Farbanteile des dichromatischen Modells bekannt, so können auch die Gewichtsfaktoren berechnet und so das Bild pixelweise in seine Farbbestandteile zerlegt werden. Dazu wird die Moore-Penrose-Pseudoinverse eingesetzt. Damit wird die Gewichtung so vorgenommen, daß der quadratische Abstand zwischen Schätzwert und Originalwert minimiert wird [3].

3 Ergebnisse und Diskussion

Das hier vorgestellte Verfahren zur Trennung von Oberflächenreflexion und Körperreflexion wurde sowohl an Bildern des Larynx als auch an Phantombildern getestet. Die Phantombilder zeigen Plastikkugeln, die in einem neutralreflektierenden Kasten unter Einsatz eines üblichen Lupenparyngoskops aufgenommen wurden. Für beide Bildmaterialien konnte die Lichtquellenfarbe bestimmt und eine pixelweise Separierung der Bilder in ihre gewichteten Farbanteile erzielt werden. In Abbildung 3 wird dieses Ergebnis als mathematische Gleichung wie (1) dargestellt.

416

Abb. 3. Das Originalbild (links) wird in seine beiden Farbanteile (rechts) gesplittet. Die Gewichtsfaktoren g_k und die Körperfarbe sind als Produkt (rechts) zu sehen, während g_o und die Lichtquellenfarbe in einem Bild (Mitte) zusammengefaßt sind.

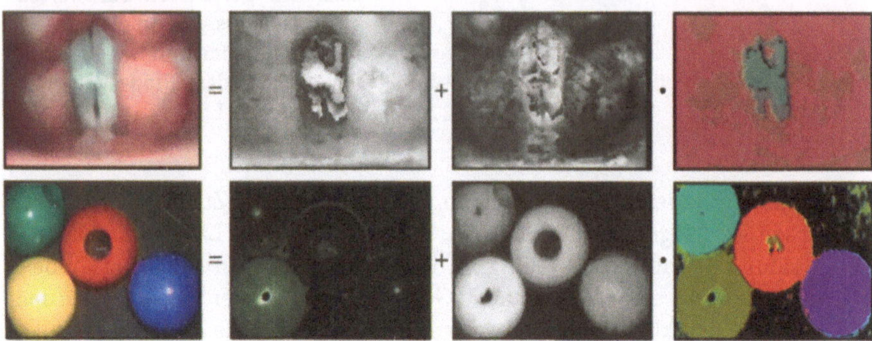

In beiden Bildern der Körperfarbe fallen die geschwärzten Teile ins Auge. Eine Schwärzung erfolgt bei negativen Farbanteilen bei der dichromatischen Trennung. Da diese innerhalb des zugrundeliegenden physikalischen Modells nicht auftreten, können so Farbfehler aufgespürt werden. Im Glanzlichtbereich der gelben Kugel (Abb. 3 (unten links)) sind *Color Clipping*-Effekte in Folge von Überbelichtung zu beobachten. Im Randbereich der Stimmlippen treten dagegen Interreflexionen auf, d.h. die benachbarten rötlichen Objekte beleuchten die Stimmlippen zusätzlich. Diese dritte Farbkomponente kann nicht mit dem dichromatischen Modell beschrieben werden. Die Markierung dieser Farbfehler ist nützlich, um eine Störung der anschließenden Farbanalyse zu verhindern und evtl. Korrekturmaßnahmen einzuleiten.

Insgesamt führt der beschriebene Algorithmus zur Elimination des Einflusses der Beleuchtung auf die quantitative Farbmessung. Die farbkonstanten Farbwerte sollen in der weiteren Arbeit zur Diskriminierung verschiedener Gewebearten und Klassifikation verschiedener Krankheitsbilder eingesetzt werden.

Literatur

1. Shafer SA: Using Color to Separate Reflection Components. Color Research and Application, 10(4):210-218, 1985.
2. Tominaga S: Surface Identification Using the Dichromatic Reflection Model. IEEE PAMI, 13(7): 658-670, 1991
3. Palm C, Scholl I, Lehmann T, Spitzer K: Trennung von diffuser und spiegelnder Reflexion in Farbbildern des Larynx zur Untersuchung von Farb- und Formmerkmalen der Stimmlippen. In: Lehmann T, Scholl I, Spitzer K (Hrsg.), Bildverarbeitung für die Medizin. Augustinus Buchhandlung Aachen, 229-234, 1996
4. Lee H-C: Method for computing the scene-illuminant chromaticity from specular highlights. JOSA A, 3(10):1694-1699, 1986
5. Tominaga S, Wandell BA: Standard surface-reflectance model and illuminant estimation. JOSA A, 7(2):312-317, 1990

Schadensbeurteilung von Zellpopulationen durch morphologische Formanalyse

V. Metzler[1], H. Bienert[2], T. Lehmann[1], K. Spitzer[1]

[1]Institut für Medizinische Informatik
[2]Interdisziplinäres Zentrum für klinische Forschung "Biomat"
Rheinisch–Westfälische Technische Hochschule (RWTH), 52057 Aachen
Email: metzler@imib.rwth-aachen.de

Zusammenfassung. Im IZKF "Biomat" wird die Bioverträglichkeit von Biomaterialien über den Schädigungsgrad von Zellpopulationen beurteilt. Dazu werden spezielle Zellinien (hier L-929 Fibroblasten) dem Material im indirekten oder direkten Kontakt unter definierten Bedingungen ausgesetzt, wodurch die Zellen ihre Morphologie proportional zur Toxizität des zu untersuchenden Materials verändern. Die automatische Analyse des Schädigungsgrads der Zellen liefert dem Untersucher, im Gegensatz zur üblichen Beschreibung eines visuellen Eindrucks, quantitative Maße, die erst eine objektive Vergleichbarkeit von Ergebnissen ermöglichen. Darüber hinaus kann das Laborpersonal von einer zeitaufwendigen und fehlerintensiven Routinetätigkeit entlastet werden. Nach der digitalen Aufnahme der Präparate mit einer CCD Kamera werden die Zellbilder mit Methoden der mathematischen Morphologie analysiert. Der Algorithmus besteht aus drei Phasen: Der Binarisierung, der morphologischen Trennung zusammenhängender Zellen und der Vermessung der Objekte. Im Gegensatz zu herkömmlichen morphologischen Analysemethoden liefert das Verfahren im praktischen Einsatz zufriedenstellende diskriminative Papameter.

Schlüsselwörter: Quantitative Zytologie, mathematische Morphologie, adaptives Thresholding, Formanalyse, Zytotoxizität, Biomaterialien

1 Einleitung

Bisher werden Zytotoxizitätsstudien vorzugsweise qualitativ oder semiquantitativ durchgefüht. Durch Fortschritte in der digitalen Bildgebung und der Molekularbiologie (immunhistochemische Färbetechniken), wurde in den letzten Jahren die quantitative Auswertung zytologischer Präparate ermöglicht [1, 2].

Zur Beurteilung der Toxizität von Biomaterialien werden standardisierte Zellinien unter wohldefinierten Bedingungen einem Biomaterial ausgesetzt. Dabei signalisieren morphologische Veränderungen der Zellen einen toxischen Einfluß des Biomaterials. Zur quantitativen Beurteilung pathologischer Veränderungen wird, nachdem die Zellpopulationen entsprechend gefärbt, mikroskopiert und digital aufgenommen wurden, eine Formanalyse durchgeführt. Hierzu müssen zwei wesentliche Verarbeitungsschritte vorgenommen werden. Zunächst werden

* Das Projekt *Quantitative Mikroskopie* wird vom Bundesministerium für Bildung, Wissenschaft, Forschung und Technologie gefördert (BMBF 01ks9503/9).

die zytologischen Präparate segmentiert, was die Binarisierung mit adaptiven Schwellwerten erfordert, um robuste Ergebnisse auch für inhomogene Beleuchtungen und Zelldichten erreichen zu können (Abschn. 2). Anschließend werden die binären Objekte mit Hilfe verschiedener morphologischer Filtertechniken [3] in einzelne, getrennt zu analysierende Zellen zerlegt (Abschn. 3).

Die Evaluierung der Methode wurde mit Hemalaun–gefärbten (blau) L–929 Fibroblasten durchgeführt, welche sich unter Einfluß eines Toxins (hier Ethanol) abrunden und schrumpfen. Als Merkmale der Zellmorphologie werden verschiedene Parameter, wie z.B. Zellgröße und –umfang oder ihre Kompaktheit extrahiert. Die experimentellen Ergebnisse zeigen die Signifikanz der gewählten Parameter (Abschn. 4).

2 Lokal–adaptive Schwellwertbinarisierung

Unter den existierenden Segmentierungsverfahren gibt es nur wenige, die zur Segmentierung zytologischer Aufnahmen eingesetzt werden können [4, 5]. Bei der Segmentierung lichtmikroskopierter Zellpopulationen müssen verschiedene Problemfälle berücksichtigt werden. In der Regel ist die Lichtintensität nicht konstant, die Schichtdicke und die Konzentration des Farbstoffs kann variieren und die Zellen können sehr inhomogen auf dem Bild verteilt sein. Da es sich aber um Zellen gleichen Typs mit ähnlichen Grauwertcharakteristiken handelt, kann eine Schwellwertsegmentierung vorgenommen werden [6]. Globale Verfahren, die eine Schwelle für das gesamte Bild berechnen sind hier allerdings aus den oben genannten Gründen nicht einsetztbar (Abb. 1b). Auch der Einsatz

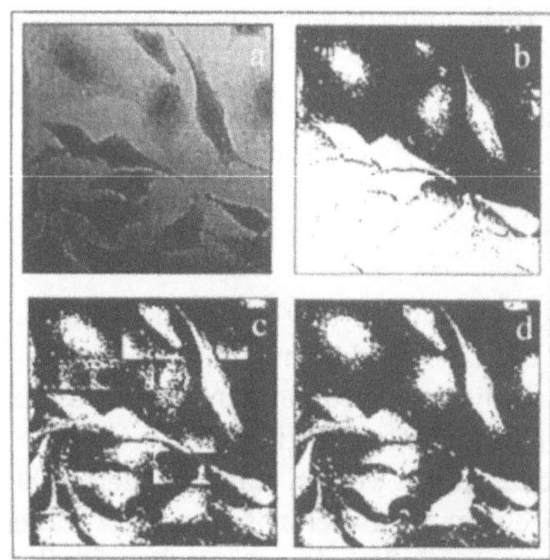

Abb. 1. Das cytologische Präparat in (a) ist inhomogen ausgeleuchtet und variiert in der Zelldichte. Eine globale Schwellwertbinarisierung (b) führt dabei ebenso zu schlechten Ergebnissen wie ein lokales Schwellwertverfahren mit konstanter Fenstergröße (c). Erst das lokal adaptive Schwellwertverfahren, das die Fenstergröße auf die lokale Grauwertverteilung abstimmt, liefert zufriedenstellende Ergebnisse (d).

lokaler Schwellen für Teilbilder konstanter Größe führt nicht zu befriedigenden Ergebnissen, denn es entstehen oft Artefakte in Fenstern, die keine Objektinformation enthalten (Abb. 1c). Die optimale Fenstergröße kann also nur abhängig von der lokalen Grauwertverteilung bestimmt werden. Grundidee der Strategie ist, daß hohe lokale Standardabweichungen der Grauwerte die Präsenz von Hintergrund– und Objektinformation im Fenster signalisieren. Umgekehrt sind niedrige Standardabweichungen darauf zurückzuführen, daß nur Hintergrund erfaßt wurde. Die lokale Fenstergröße zur Schwellwertberechnung wird, ausgehend von einem minimalen Fenster (i.d.R. 25 × 25 Pixel) sukzessive vergrößert, bis die Standardabweichung einen Schwellwert erreicht hat. Dieser kann abhängig von der Standardabeichung des ganzen Bildes angegeben werden. Das Verfahren liefert für jedes Pixel eine individuelle Fenstergröße, die zur Berechnung der Schwelle verwendet wird. Die Strategie der lokalen Adaption der Fenstergöße kann prinzipiell mit jedem beliebigen Schwellwertverfahren realisiert werden, in diesen Fall wurde das Verfahren von Otsu verwendet [7].

3 Morphologische Zelltrennung

Die morphologische Trennung binärer Objekt in einzelne Zellen kann in zwei Schritten vorgenommen werden. Zunächst müssen für alle abgebildeten Zellen *Marker* gefunden werden, danach kann die Form der Zellen ausgehend von den sie repräsentierenden Markern rekonstruiert werden. Dieses Vorgehen ist insbesondere dann möglich, wenn es sich um konfluente Zellen handelt, die in Monolayern vorliegen. In der Praxis kommen im wesentlichen zwei Verfahren zur Markerextraktion zum Einsatz: Entweder werden die *ultimate–eroded–points*[1] [8], oder die *Distanz–Transformierte* beginnend mit ihren Maxima, rekonstruiert [9]. Dabei wird jeweils das Verschmelzen von Markern verhindert. Beide Verfahren sind zur zuverlässigen Quantifizierung morphologischer Veränderungen ungeeignet, denn einerseits kommt es meist zu Übersegmentierungen und andererseits werden die Trennlinien zwischen den Objekten nur ungenau rekonstruiert. Diese Nachteile werden durch das hier vorgestellte mehrstufige Verfahren vermieden (Abb 2).

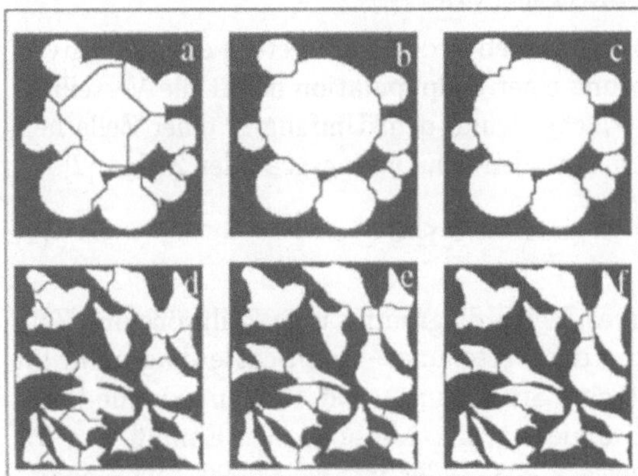

Abb. 2. Die Separierungen (a) und (d) wurden von den ultimate–eroded–points, bzw. (b) und (e) von den Maxima der Distanztransformation rekonstriert. Die Markerzahl wurde durch Filtern reduziert. Das einfachere Problem (oben) ist mit der Distanzrekonstruktion noch befriedigend zu lösen. Das mehrstufige Verfahren errechnet in beiden Fällen (c) und (f) jeweils gute Trennungen.

▷ Die Marker werden durch sukzessives Anwenden eines *erweiterten Erosionsoperators* ermittelt. Dieser besteht aus einer einfachen Erosion, gefolgt von einem maskierten Opening. Durch das nachgeschaltete Opening werden nach jedem Erosionsschritt 'falsche Marker', die immer bei mehrfacher Erosion strukturreicher binärer Objekte entstehen, entfernt. Eine Übersegmentierung wird dadurch vermieden.

---

[1] dabei wird ein Objekt solange erodiert, bis eine weiter Erosion das Objekt vollständig entfernen würde.

▷ Die Rekonstuktion wird entsprechend den ursprüngliche Objektgrößen durch sukzessive Anwendung eines *erweiterten Dilatationsoperators* durchgeführt. Dabei werden die Marker verschiedener Erosionsstufen sukzessive addiert, um sie anschließend durch eine SKIZ–Operation[2] bis zur Größe der Objekte der entsprechenden Stufe zu dilatieren, ohne deren Verschmelzung zuzulassen. Diese Art der Rekonstruktion liefert sinnvolle Separierungen, selbst wenn die zu trennenden Objekte unterschiedlich groß sind.

4 Ergebnisse und Ausblick

Abb. 3 zeigt die verschiedenen Schritte der Formanalyse. Nach der Binarisierung des Präparats (Abschn. 2) können mit einem nicht–linearen Rekonstruktionsfilter unerwünschte Objekte effizient entfernt werden [10], da die minimale Größe der zu detektierenden Zellen bekannt ist. Aus den separierten Zellen werden

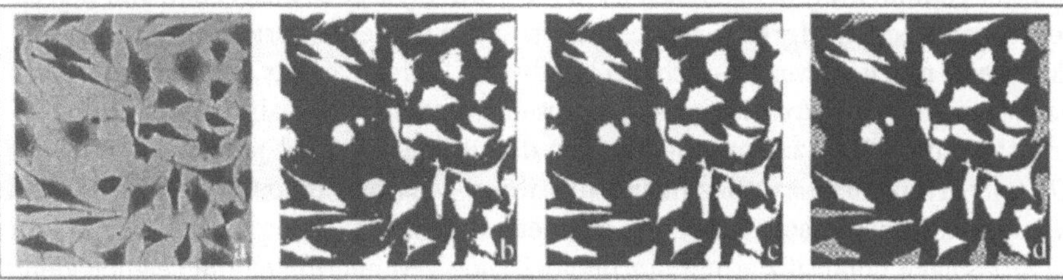

Abb. 3. Der Ausschnitt (a) wird zur Formanalyse zunächst binarisiert (b). Ein Rekonstruktionsfilter entfernt sowohl falsche Objekt– als auch falsche Hintergrundpixel (c). Nach der morphologischen Trennung werden diejenigen Objekte entfernt, deren Formparameter nicht zu ermitteln sind (d).

verschiedene Formparameter extrahiert. Neben den Parametern der Größenverteilung, der Dichte und der Besetzung einer Zellpopulation liefert die Verteilung der Kompaktheit C, die aus der Fläche A und dem Umfang U einer Zelle hergeleitet wird, wichtige Information über den Schädigungsgrad der Zellen [2].

$$C = \frac{4\pi A}{U^2} \quad \text{mit} \quad 0 \leq C \leq 1 \tag{1}$$

Ebenso ist der Schwerpunkt eines Scatterdiagramms über Zellgröße und Zellumfang von Interesse. Abb. 4 zeigt das Verteilungs– und Scatterdiagramm für die Ethanolkonzentrationen 0% (keine Schädigung) und 10% (maximale Schädigung). Zusätzlich wurde zur Evaluierung der Methode der Einfluß von 5% Ethanol untersucht. Es wurden jeweils 268 Bilder mit ca. 60000 Zellen analysiert. Die Tabelle in Abb. 4 stellt die extrahierten Parameter gegenüber. Die pathologischen Veränderungen, abhängig von der Konzentration des Toxins sind deutlich zu erkennen. Ziel ist es zunächst eine Dosis/Wirkung–Kurve für Ethanol zu erstellen und daraus eine Schwelle für die Toxizität zu definieren. Anschließend wird das Verfahren für verschiedene Biomaterialextrakte normiert um deren Toxizität quantifizieren zu können.

---

[2] Die *SK*eleton–of–*I*nfluence–*Z*one berechnet die Skelettierung des Hintergrundes. Sie ist das binäre Analogon der Watershed–Transformation.

Das Verfahren wird im Zellkulturlabors des IZKF "Biomat" eingesetzt. Auf diese Weise können Bioverträglichkeitstests standardisiert und das Laborpersonal von fehleranfälligen Routinetätigkeiten entlastet werden. Die Qualitätskontrolle solcher Laborversuche wird ebenfalls ermöglicht, denn der Vergleich mit den Extremdosen (Negativ– und Positvkontrolle) ermöglicht eine Beurteilung der Tauglichkeit erstellter Präparate. Eine Erweiterungen des Verfahrens zur Beurteilung der Thrombozyten–Adhäsion wird zur Zeit vorgenommen.

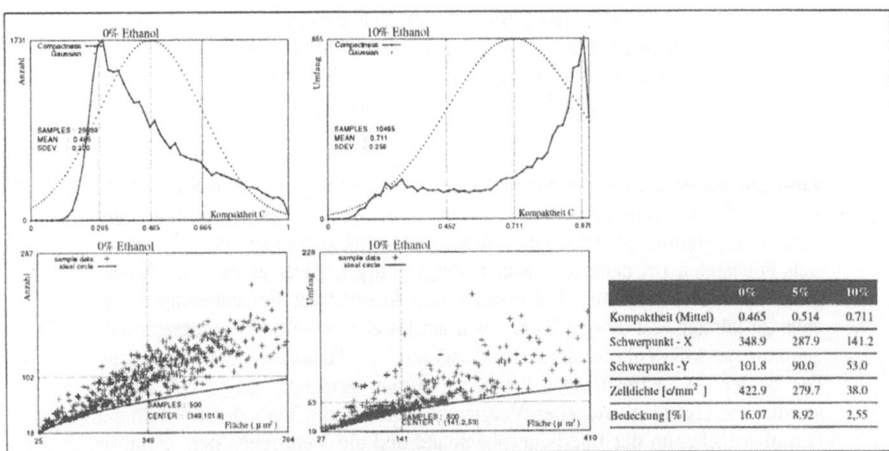

	0%	5%	10%
Kompaktheit (Mittel)	0.465	0.514	0.711
Schwerpunkt - X	348.9	287.9	141.2
Schwerpunkt - Y	101.8	90.0	53.0
Zelldichte [c/mm^2]	422.9	279.7	38.0
Bedeckung [%]	16.07	8.92	2,55

Abb. 4. Die Diagramme zeigen die Ergebnisse der L-929 Zellinie, bei jeweile 0% und 10% Ethanol. Die Parameter der Verteilung der Kompaktheit C (links) sind durch eine Gaußkurve veranschaulicht. Rechts sind Scatterdiagramme (Zellgröße aufgetragen gegen –umfang) mit je 500 Zellen dargestellt. Der Schwerpunkt der Plots ist jeweils angegeben. Die Tabelle zeigt zusätzlich die Parameter für 5% Ethanol–geschädigte Zellen und weitere einfache diskriminative Parameter.

Literatur

1. I.T. Young. Quantitative microscopy. *IEEE EMB*, 15(1):59–66, 1996.
2. J.C. Russ. *Computer–Assisted Microscopy*. Plenum Press, New York, 1990.
3. R.M. Haralick, S.R. Sternberg, X. Zhuang. Image analysis using mathematical morphology. *IEEE PAMI*, 9(4):532–550, 1987.
4. R.M. Haralick, L.G. Shapiro. Image segmentation techniques. *CVGIP*, 29:100–132, 1985.
5. C. Garbay. Image structure representation and processing: A discussion of some segmentation methods in cytology. *IEEE PAMI*, 8(2):140–146, 1986.
6. C. McAulay, B. Palcic. A comparison of some quick and simple threshold selection methods for stained cells. *Analyt. Quantit. Cytol. Histol.*, 10(2):134–138, 1988.
7. N. Otsu. A threshold selection method from grey level histograms. *IEEE SMC*, 9:62–66, 1979.
8. J. Serra. *Image Analysis and Mathematical Morphology*. Academic Press, London, 1982.
9. G. Borgefors. Distance transforms in digital images. *CVGIP*, 34:679–698, 1986.
10. P. Salembier, J. Serra. Morphological multiscale image segmentation. In *Procs. SPIE*, 1818:620–631, 1992.

Quantifizierung von Brain-Shift durch Vergleich von prä- und intraoperativ erzeugten MR-Volumendaten

K.A. Ganser*, H. Dickhaus*,

A. Staubert+, M.M. Bonsanto+, C.R. Wirtz+, V.M. Tronnier+, S. Kunze+

* Institut für Medizinische Informatik, Universität Heidelberg, Fachhochschule Heilbronn,
Max-Planck-Str. 39, 74081 Heilbronn
+ Neurochirurgische Klinik der Universität Heidelberg
Im Neuenheimer Feld 400, 69120 Heidelberg
Email: ganser@fh-heilbronn.de

Zusammenfassung. Bei der Neuronavigation tritt häufig ein Brain-Shift-Effekt auf: Das Gehirn verändert seine Form aufgrund mechanischer Einflüsse während der Operation. Da der Operationsplan, der anhand präoperativen Bildmaterials entstanden ist, dann nur mehr bedingt gültig ist, war es Ziel der Arbeit, quantitative Aussagen über Lokalisation und Ausmaß der Verschiebungen machen zu können. Zu diesem Zweck wurden jeweils prä- und intraoperativ aufgenommene MR-Volumendaten von insgesamt 10 Tumorpatienten untersucht. Die beiden Aufnahmen eines Patienten wurden gematcht, und anschließend wurden mit eigens entwickelten Vergleichsverfahren die Veränderungen an der Hirnoberfläche, an der Interhemisphärspalte und am Ventrikelsystem quantifiziert. Es wurden Unterschiede bis zu 2 cm beobachtet.

Schlüsselwörter: Brain-Shift, Matching, intraoperatives MR, Neuronavigation

1 Einleitung

In der Neurochirurgie werden Operationen häufig mit Computerunterstützung durchgeführt. Ein präoperativ aufgenommener dreidimensionaler CT- oder MR-Datensatz dient dabei als Grundlage für die OP-Planung. Der Arzt identifiziert z.B. Tumoren und legt im Sinne einer minimalen Schädigung des Patienten optimale Zugangswege fest. Während des Eingriffs werden die Planungsdaten mit Neuronavigationssystemen - z.B. dem MKM-Operationsmikroskop der Firma Carl Zeiss - in das Koordinatensystem des Patienten übertragen und dienen dem Operateur zur Orientierung.

Problematisch ist, daß sich das Gehirn nicht wie ein starrer Körper verhält: Durch die Trepanation und die Eröffnung der Dura können Veränderungen an der Geometrie des Gehirns auftreten, die man als Brain-Shift bezeichnet. Eine unmittelbare Ursache hierfür ist z.B. das Abfließen von CSF (Cerebro Spinal Fluid).

Da in der Regel bei neurochirurgischen Eingriffen dieser sogenannte Brain-Shift auftritt, stimmen die Daten aus dem Operationsplan häufig nicht mehr mit den tatsächlichen Gegebenheiten während des Eingriffs überein. Damit die Qualität solcher Operationen dennoch gesichert ist, müssen die präoperativen Planungskoordinaten intraoperativ korrigiert werden. Derzeit beruht die Korrektur auf der Erfahrung des Neurochirurgen; wünschenswert wäre es jedoch, Brain-Shift bereits bei der Planung berücksichtigen zu können. Hierfür ist es aber notwendig, umfangreiches Wissen über die Verschiebungsvorgänge zu besitzen. Da über Brain-Shift bislang wenig bekannt ist, war es Ziel der Arbeit, quantitative Aussagen über dessen Ausmaß und Lokalisation zu machen.

2 Material und Methode

Grundlage unserer Untersuchung sind Magnetresonanztomogramme, die vor und während neurochirurgischer Eingriffe am Universitätsklinikum Heidelberg mit dem dort neben einem Operationssaal installierten offenen MR-Scanner Siemens Magnetom Open erstellt wurden (128 Schichten, Abstand 1,3 mm, T1-Flash) [1].Untersucht wurden 10 Patienten mit unterschiedlichen Hirntumoren. Von jedem Patient stand ein prä- und ein intraoperativer Datensatz für die Auswertung zur Verfügung. Als Referenz und zur Validierung wurden von einem gesunden Probanden und ebenfalls von einem Kopfphantom zwei Scans in unterschiedlicher Lage aufgenommen.

Da die beiden Aufnahmen der Patienten zu unterschiedlichen Zeitpunkten entstanden sind, werden sie in verschiedenen Koordinatensystemen abgebildet. Es war also notwendig, über ein Matching die räumliche Ausrichtung der jeweils korrespondierenden Datensätze aneinander anzugleichen. Die gematchten Bilder wurden anschließend verglichen, um die Auswirkungen des Brain-Shifts zu quantifizieren. Drei Bereiche des Gehirns wurden untersucht: Die Hirnoberfläche, an der sich Einsinken und Anschwellen ablesen läßt, die Interhemisphärspalte, die durch Shift-Vorgänge zwischen den beiden Hirnhälften lateral verschoben wird, und das Ventrikelsystem, das Deformationen in tieferen, stammhirnnahen Bereichen zeigt.

2.1 Matching

Für die Ausrichtung der Datensätze wurde ein Chamfer-Matching-basierter Algorithmus implementiert [2], der als Vergleichsfeature die Kopfoberfläche betrachtet. In beiden Aufnahmen wird diese halbautomatisch segmentiert. Die intraoperative Oberfläche wird gleichmäßig abgetastet und so auf eine Menge von 5000 Punkten p_j ($j=1..5000$) reduziert. Eine Kostenfunktion $c(T)$, die von sechs Transformationsparametern $T=(dx, dy, dz, \phi, \theta, \psi)$ abhängt, berechnet den Mittelwert der minimalen Abstände der Punkte p_j zur präoperativen Kopfoberfläche:

$$c(T) = \sum_j \overline{P_j T(p_j)} \,, \tag{1}$$

wobei P_j der zu p_j am nächsten gelegene Punkt auf der präoperativen Oberfläche ist. $T(p_j)$ bedeutet die Transformation von p_j mit T. Um diese Abstandsberechnung zu beschleunigen, werden alle Abstände vorberechnet, d.h. die präoperative Oberfläche wird einer Distance-Transformation unterzogen (Abstandsmetrik Chamfer-3-4-5 [3]). Es entsteht eine Distance-Map D, in der jedes Voxel als Grauwert den minimalen Abstand zum Objekt im Ausgangsbild, also zur präoperativen Kopfoberfläche, an-

Abb. 1. Darstellung der Matchgenauigkeit. Erläuterung im Text.

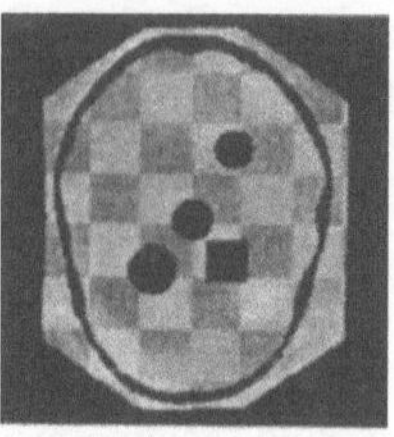

nimmt. Die Abstandsberechnung in der Kostenfunktion reduziert sich damit auf das Auslesen eines Wertes aus der dreidimensionalen Look-up-Tabelle **D**:

$$c(T) = \sum_j \mathbf{D}(T(p_j)).$$ (2)

$c(T)$ wird nach der Downhill-Simplex-Methode in sechs Dimensionen minimiert [4]. Als Ergebnis erhält man Schätzwerte für die Transformationsparameter T. Mit diesen Parametern wird der intraoperative Grauwertdatensatz unter Anwendung der trilinearen Interpolation in das Koordinatensystem des präoperativen transformiert. Untersuchungen mit teilweise synthetischen Daten ergaben eine Matchgenauigkeit im Submillimeterbereich, also unter der Voxelauflösung der Originaldaten. Abb. 1 demonstriert die Genauigkeit des Algorithmus durch schachbrettartige Überlagerung korrespondierender Schichten aus zwei gematchten Aufnahmen des Kopfphantoms. Die glatten Übergänge an den Kanten zwischen den Feldern belegen die Matchqualität.

2.2 Vergleich der Gehirnoberflächen

Im präoperativen und im gematchten intraoperativen Datensatz wird halbautomatisch das Gehirn segmentiert. Mit jedem der beiden Segmente wird anschließend folgendermaßen verfahren: Durch eine Triangulierung wird die Segmentoberfläche in ein Dreiecksnetz überführt. Die kartesischen Koordinaten der Gitterpunkte $g_i=(x_i,y_i,z_i)$ des Netzes werden über eine Kugelkoordinatentransformation bezüglich eines zentralen Fixpunkts f in neue Koordinaten $g_i'=(\alpha_i,\beta_i,r_i)$ umgerechnet. f ist der Ursprung des (x, y, z)-Koordinatensystems.

$$\alpha = \arctan(z/y) \quad \beta = \arctan(z/\sqrt{y^2+z^2})+90° \quad r = \sqrt{x^2+y^2+z^2}.$$ (3)

Dies entspricht anschaulich einer Projektion des Hirnreliefs auf die Ebene, wobei α und β vergleichbar sind mit den Längen- und Breitengraden auf dem Globus. r ist der Abstand des Netzpunkts zum Fixpunkt f. Zwischen den projizierten Punkten g_i' wird linear interpoliert, so daß sich eine vollständige "Relieffläche" ergibt.
Die Reliefbilder aus beiden Datensätzen werden schließlich subtrahiert. Im Ergebnisbild kann für jede Raumrichtung (α, β) die Veränderung - ein Anschwellen für negative und ein Absinken für positive Werte - quantitativ abgelesen werden (Abb. 2).

Abb. 2. Subtrahierte Reliefbilder eines Patienten (rechts) und des Probanden (links). Helle Bereiche kennzeichnen Anschwellungen, dunkle Absenkungen. Frontal in der rechten Hemisphäre des Patienten ist Brain-Shift als dunkler Bereich zu erkennen.

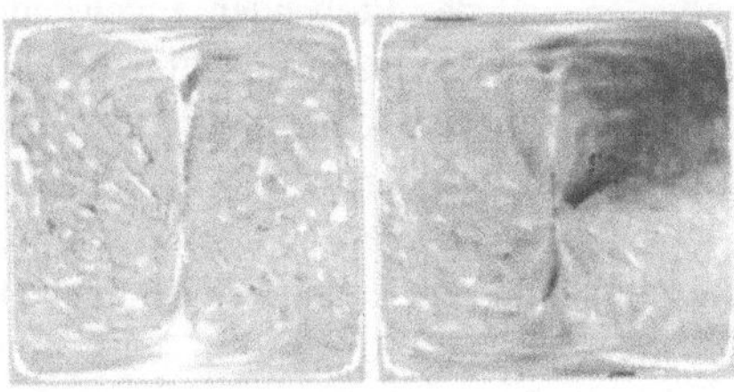

2.3 Vergleich der Interhemisphärspalten

In den gematchten Aufnahmen wird interaktiv der Verlauf der Interhemisphärspalte eingezeichnet. Zwischen den manuell festgelegten Punkten wird jeweils eine Fläche interpoliert. Der laterale Abstand dieser Flächen wird berechnet und als Grauwert über der *(y, z)*-Ebene aufgetragen. Positive Werte entsprechen einer Verschiebung nach links, negative einer Verschiebung nach rechts (Abb. 3).

2.4 Vergleich am Ventrikelsystem

In den gematchten Grauwertdatensätzen werden jeweils die beiden Seitenventrikel und der dritte Ventrikel halbautomatisch segmentiert. Für jedes Segment wird der Schwerpunkt s und die Trägheitsmatrix Θ berechnet:

$$s = (\overline{x}_s, \overline{y}_s, \overline{z}_s) \qquad \Theta = \begin{pmatrix} \theta_{xx} & \theta_{xy} & \theta_{xz} \\ \theta_{yx} & \theta_{yy} & \theta_{yz} \\ \theta_{zx} & \theta_{zy} & \theta_{zz} \end{pmatrix} \quad \text{mit} \quad \begin{aligned} \theta_{xx} &= \Sigma(y^2 + z^2) \\ \theta_{yy} &= \Sigma(x^2 + z^2) \\ \theta_{zz} &= \Sigma(x^2 + y^2) \\ \theta_{ab} &= -\Sigma(a \cdot b) \end{aligned} \tag{4}$$

Die Eigenvektoren der Trägheitsmatrix zeigen in Richtung der Hauptträgheitsachsen. Für die Bestimmung von Shiftvorgängen wird der Differenzvektor zwischen korrespondierenden Schwerpunkten und die Winkeldifferenz zwischen korrespondierenden Hauptträgheitsachsen ermittelt. Der Vektor macht hauptsächlich Aussagen über Verschiebungen, die Winkeldifferenzen über Rotationen und Verformungen.

 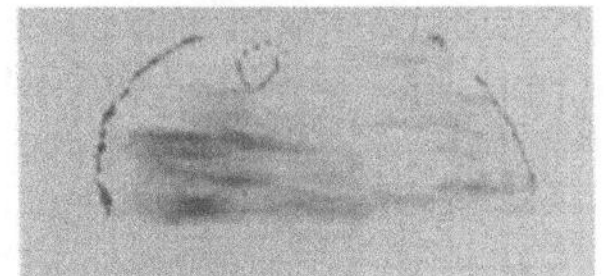

Abb. 3. Laterale Verschiebung an der Interhemisphärspalte (rechts Patient, links Proband). Helle Bereiche kennzeichnen Verschiebungen nach rechts, dunkle nach links Beim Patienten ist deutlich eine Verformung als dunkler Bereich zu erkennen.

3 Ergebnisse

Die im vorigen Abschnitt beschriebenen Vergleichsverfahren wurden auf die Datensätze der zehn Tumorpatienten und des Probanden angewendet, nachdem ein Matching der jeweils korrespondierenden Aufnahmen stattgefunden hat. An der Gehirnoberfläche wurden bei den Patienten Einsenkungen bis zu 20 mm und Anschwellungen bis zu 9 mm beobachtet. Die Interhemisphärspalte war um maximal 6 mm verschoben, wobei Verschiebungen in beide Richtungen auftraten. Am Ventrikelsystem zeigten sich Schwerpunktsverschiebungen bis zu 7 mm, die Differenzen zwischen den Hauptträgheitsachsen betrugen maximal 18 Winkelgrad. In den Aufnahmen des Probanden zeigten sich im Vergleich dazu an keiner Stelle nennenswerte Veränderungen.

4 Konsequenzen

Mit Hilfe des dargestellten Ansatzes konnte quantitativ gezeigt werden, daß die während einer neurochirurgischen Operation auftretenden Deformationen des Gehirns teilweise mit erheblichem Ausmaß in allen Bereichen des Gehirns auftreten. Die Oberfläche ist ebenso betroffen wie tiefe, stammhirnnahe Bereiche. Die Unterschiede bewegen sich z.T. in der Größenordnung von Zentimetern. Es muß demnach mit deutlichen Mißweisungen der Navigationssysteme gerechnet werden, wenn die Navigation einzig anhand präoperativen Bildmaterials durchgeführt wird. Da in den wenigsten Krankenhäusern die Möglichkeit besteht, durch intraoperative Bildgebung die Navigation neu zu kalibrieren, scheint es sinnvoll, nach Verfahren zu suchen, die die Brain-Shift-Effekte bereits bei der Planung berücksichtigen können. Es gibt für diese komplexe Aufgabe derzeit noch keine etablierte Lösung.

Wir haben vorgesehen, durch elastisches Matching den Gehirnatlas von Talairach und Tournoux [5] an die individuelle Patientenanatomie anzupassen. Durch eine geeignete Modellierung soll es möglich sein, Brain-Shift auch am Atlas vorzunehmen und so intraoperativ die Information über anatomisch und funktional wichtige Hirnstrukturen im verformten Gehirn bereitzustellen.

5 Literatur

1. Tronnier V.M., Wirtz C.R. et al.: Intraoperative diagnostic and interventional magnetic resonance imaging in neurosurgery. Neurosurgery 40 (5), 1997.
2. van Herk M., Kooy H.M.: Automatic three-dimensional correlation of CT-CT, CT-MR, and CT-SPECT using chamfer matching. Med. Phys. 21(7): 1163-1178, 1994.
3. Borgefors G.: Distance transformations in arbitrary dimensions. Computer Vision, Graphics and Image Processing (27): 321-345, 1984.
4. Press W.H., Teukolsky S.A., Vetterling W.T., Flannery B.P.: Numerical Recipes in C. Cambridge University Press, Cambridge, 1992.
5. Talairach J., Tournoux P.: Co-Planar Stereotaxic Atlas of the Human Brain. Georg Thieme Verlag, Stuttgart, New York, 1988.

Detektion von Leukozyten
mit Hilfe neuronaler Strukturen

U. Schreiner (1,2), M. Egmont-Petersen (1), T. Lehmann (2),
S. C. Tromp (3), D.W. Slaaf (1), T. Arts (1)

(1) Institut für Biophysik, Universität Maastricht
(2) Institut für Medizinische Informatik, RWTH Aachen
(3) Institut für Physiologie, Universität Maastricht

Email: uwe@vaire.imib.rwth-aachen.de

Zusammenfassung. Die Bestimmung der Anzahl und Geschwindigkeit von Leukozyten in Venolen ermöglicht Rückschlüsse auf den Aktivierungszustand des Immunsystems. In diesem Beitrag werden neuronale Netze zur Detektion von Leukozyten in Sequenzen von Mikrozirkulationsaufnahmen eingesetzt. Das Training der Netze erfolgt mit synthetischen Leukozytenbildern, die über ein stochastisches Modell gewonnen werden. Künstliche Zellenmuster bieten eine wesentlich bessere Anpassungsfähigkeit an neues Bildmaterial, als dies reales Bildmaterial ermöglicht. Um die Leistungsfähigkeit des Zellenmodells zu überprüfen, werden Netze mit echten und synthetischen Datensätzen trainiert. Dabei erzielen Netze auf Basis synthetischer Zellenmuster in fast allen Netzkonfigurationen bessere Ergebnisse als solche, die mit echten Zellenbildern trainiert wurden.

Schlüsselwörter: Neuronale Netze, Klassifikation, Leukozytenverfolgung, modellbasierte Bildverarbeitung

1 Einleitung

Zur Untersuchung des Einflusses verschiedener chemischer Substanzen auf das Immunsystem werden weiße Blutkörperchen in Videosequenzen erkannt und verfolgt. Hierzu wird eine automatische Auswertungsmethode vorgestellt. Dabei werden mehrschichtige Perzeptronen zur Zellenerkennung eingesetzt. Sie erhalten die Intensitäten eines diskreten Bildausschnittes als Eingabe und berechnen die Wahrscheinlichkeit, mit der das Fenster eine Leukozytenzelle enthält.

Neben der Topologie haben die Trainingsdaten entscheidenden Einfluß auf die Klassifikationseingenschaften des Netzes. In dieser Arbeit wird ein stochastisches Modell präsentiert, mit dem synthetische Trainingsdaten generiert werden können. Als Grundlage dienen Bilder, die mit einem Intravitalmikroskop aufgenommen wurden (Abb. 1). Sie enthalten eine Venole, in der sich Leukozyten (weiße Blutkörperchen) und die sehr viel kleineren Erythrozyten (rote Blutköperchen). Die Venole kann aus den Bildsequenzen leicht extrahiert werden [1].

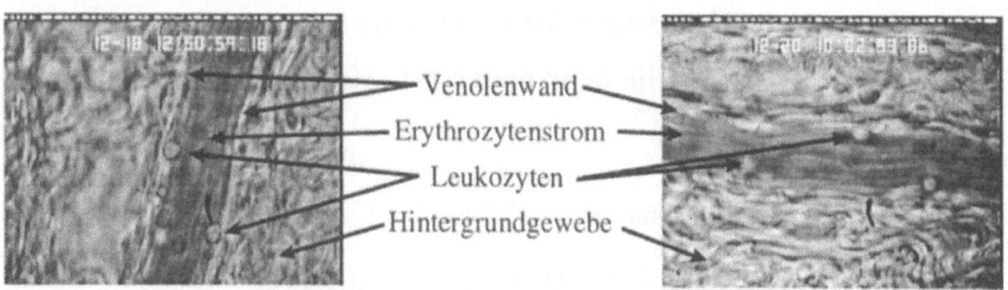

Abb. 1. In den Mikrozirkulationsaufnahmen sind die Leukozyten, die an der Venolenwand entlangrollen, deutlich erkennbar. Die roten Blutkörperchen sind erheblich kleiner und bewegen sich viel schneller, so daß sie als Strömungsmuster dargestellt werden.

2 Zellenmodell

Ein Leukozytenbild (Abb. 2a) kann durch wenige charakteristische Parameter beschrieben werden. Die oftmals ellipsenförmigen Zellen besitzen Dimensionsparameter, die ihre räumliche Ausdehnung und Lage in einem Bild charakterisieren: die Breite λ_1 (Länge der 1. Hauptachse), die Höhe λ_2 (Länge der 2. Hauptachse) sowie der Rotationsparameter α, der die Lage einer Ellipse im Raum beschreibt (Abb. 2b). Die Grauwerte eines Leukozyts weisen eine räumliche Intensitätsverteilung auf. Weiterhin hat ein Zellenbild eine Innen- und Außentextur. Die Zellenmembran wird von einem Schatten umgeben, der im folgenden als *Furche* bezeichnet wird. Innerhalb dieser Furche weisen die Intensitäten sowohl eine Längsverteilung (entlang der Ellipse) als auch eine Querverteilung (von innen nach außen) auf.

Die synthetische Erzeugung von Zellenmuster basiert auf folgendem mathematischen Modell. Das Zellenprofil wird zunächst über die Ellipsenfunktion

$$c^T M c = 1, \qquad \text{mit} \quad M = \begin{bmatrix} a & {}^o\!/_2 \\ {}^o\!/_2 & k \end{bmatrix} \tag{1}$$

mit dem Koordinatenvektor $c^T=(x,y)$ erzeugt. Die Eigenwerte der Matrix M bestimmen die Längen λ_1 und λ_2 einer Ellipse. Der Rotationswinkel α wird über die Eigenvektoren der Matrix beschrieben. Deren Parameter haben die Form

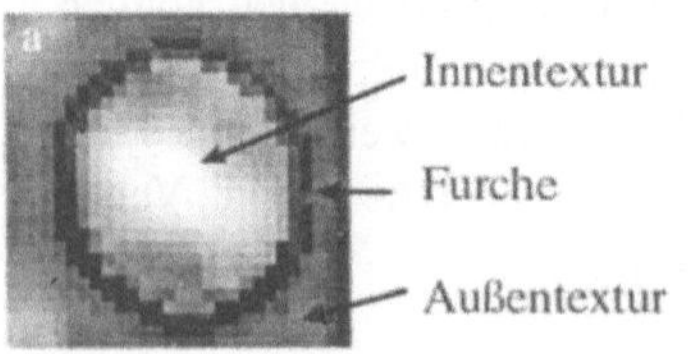

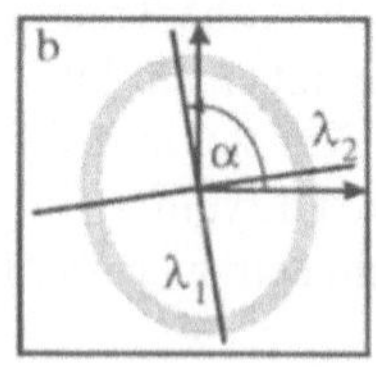

Abb. 2. Das Bild einer Zelle hat eine Innen- und Außentextur, die durch die Furche getrennt werden. Die Form kann als Ellipse modelliert werden

$$a = \lambda_1 \cos(\alpha)^2 + \lambda_2 \sin(\alpha)^2 \qquad (2)$$

$$k = \lambda_1 \sin(\alpha)^2 + \lambda_2 \cos(\alpha)^2 \qquad (3)$$

$$o = 2\cos(\alpha)\sin(\alpha)(\lambda_1 - \lambda_2) \qquad (4)$$

Der Intensitätsverlauf der Furche wird durch die Funktion

$$s \cdot \tanh(d - t(\phi)) - u \cdot \tanh(d - 1) \qquad (5)$$

bestimmt. Dabei stellen die Parameter s und u Kontrastmaße zur Beschreibung der mittleren Intensität innerhalb und außerhalb der Zelle dar, während d den radialen Abstand zum Zellenmittelpunkt beschreibt. Kombiniert man die Furchenfunktion (5) mit einem Ellipsenmodell, so kann ein zweidimensionaler Verlauf definiert werden:

$$e(x, y, x_0, y_0) =$$

$$s \tanh\{a(x - x_0)^2 + k(y - y_0)^2 + o(x - x_0)(y - y_0) - t(\phi)\} - \qquad (6)$$

$$u \tanh\{a(x - x_0)^2 + k(y - y_0)^2 + o(x - x_0)(y - y_0) - 1\}$$

Der Parameter $t(\phi)$ ermöglicht die Variation der Furchentiefe und -breite entlang der Winkel ϕ, $0 \leq \phi < 2\pi$. Damit liefert die Furchenfunktion (6) ein zweidimensionales Zellenbild (Abb. 3).

Zur Erzeugung synthetischer Texturen wird die Autokorrelationsfunktion 120 extrahierter Texturen im Fourierraum berechnet. Hierzu werden die extrahierten Muster in den Fourierraum transformiert und deren Powerspektren gemittelt. Zur Textursynthese wird die gemittelte Autokorrelation mit zufällig erzeugtem weißen Rauschen gestört und in den Ortsraum zurücktransformiert.

Die Erzeugung synthetischer Furchenverläufe erfolgt analog, mit dem Unterschied, daß hier eine eindimensionale Autokorrelationsfunktion berechnet wird. Für die Hintergrundtextur zeigt sich die Methode der Autokorrelation jedoch als unzureichend, da die Frequenzinformationen in Fließrichtung zu gering sind. Daher werden

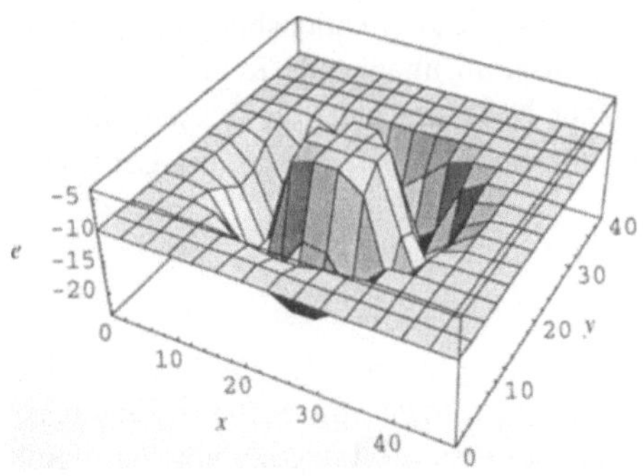

Abb. 3. Das synthetische Zellenbild enthält eine Zelle, die durch eine Furche begrenzt wird. Die Zelle als auch der Hintergrund enthalten noch keine Texturen.

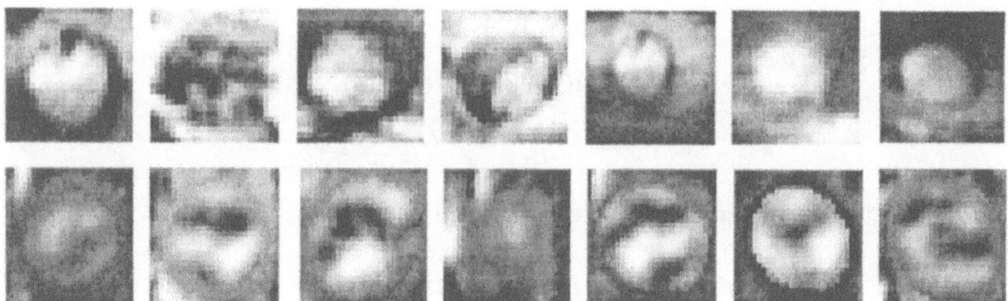

Abb. 4. Die obere Reihe zeigt reale Zellenmuster, mit denen der Trainingssatz für echte Zellen erstellt wurde. Dagegen sind in der unteren Zeile synthetisches Zellenmuster dargestellt. Diese dienten als Grundlage für die Erstellung des synthetischen Trainingsdatensatzes.

echte Hintergrundmuster aus verschiedenen Sequenzenbilder ausgeschnitten, um einen zufällig gewählten Winkel rotiert und dem Zellenbild hinzugefügt.

Alle Modellparameter sowie die zwei Autokorrelationsfunktionen (Furche und Zellentexturen) werden auf Basis 120 manuell extrahierter Zellenbildern bestimmt. Die Parameter eines künstlich generierten Zellenbildes werden zufällig gewählt und dienen zur Definition der Klasse der Leukozyten eines Trainingsdatensatzes (Abb. 4).

3 Training der Netze

Das Verhältnis der Klassen Zellenmuster und Hintergrund innerhalb des Trainingsdatensatzes muß sich an den *a priori* Wahrscheinlichkeiten dieser Klassen innerhalb realer Bilder (Abb. 1) orientieren, da nur so eine optimale Trennung erreicht werden kann [2]. Hier ist P(Hintergrund) wesentlich größer als P(Zelle).

Es werden Netze mit einer versteckten Schicht und sechs bis zwölf versteckten Knoten verwendet. Das Training der Netze erfolgt mit Backpropagation bei eine Trainingsrate von 0,0001, einem Momentum von 0,5 und einer maximal 3000 Iterationsschritten.

Als Ausgabe erzeugt das Netz ein sogenanntes Klassifikationsbild, das über einen Schwellwert binarisiert wird. Es enstehen zusammenhängende Regionen zu denen mit Hilfe eines Nachbarschaftskriterium (8er Nachbarschaft) die Schwerpunkte berechnet werden. Diese Punkte markieren nun die vom Netz ermittelten Leukozytenpositionen.

4 Ergebnisse und Ausblick

Die Bewertung der Netze, auf Basis synthetischer sowie mit echter Zellenmustern erfolgt mit ROC-Kurven. Als Vergleichsmaß wurden die Integrale unter den ROC-Kurven berechnet (Abb. 5). Das Netz mit dem größten Integral eignet sich dabei am

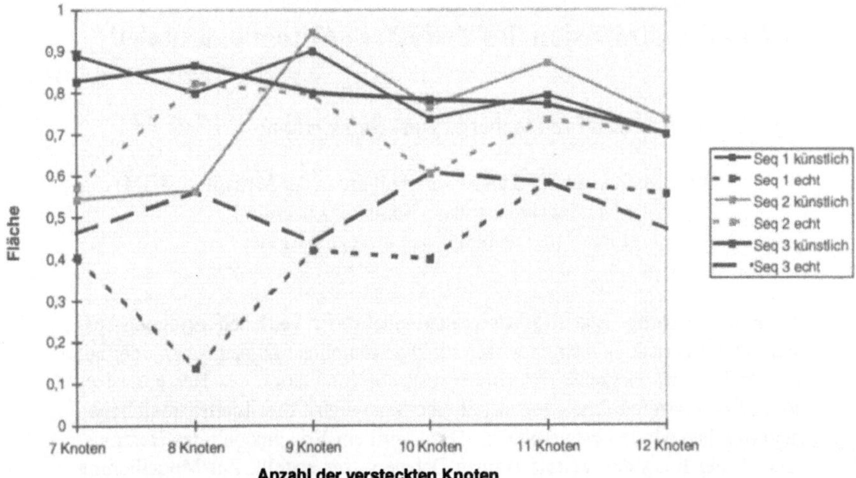

Abb. 5. Die Klassifikationseigenschaften der trainierten Netze werden mit drei neuen Sequenzen getestet. Die Netze auf Basis synthetischer Zellenmuster weisen fast durchgehend bessere Ergebnisse auf.

besten für die Detektion von Leukozyten. Hierbei zeigt das Netz mit neun versteckten Knoten die besten Klassifikationseigenschaften.

Durch die Klassifikation mit neuronalen Netzen, die auf Basis synthetisch generierter Daten trainiert wurden, ist es möglich, die Zellen auch visuell zur verfolgen. Das Verfahren kann um die automatische Verfolgung erweitert werden [3]. Hierzu können zeitvariante Informationen aller Sequenzenbilder ausgenutzt werden. Nicht nur für die Erkennung von Leukozyten, sondern auch für die Detektion von Rötgenmarkern [4], ist das Training mit teilweise modellgenerierten Objekten erfolgreich.

5 Literatur

1. Sato Y, Zoroofi RA, Harada N, Tamura S, Shiga T: Automatic extraction and measurement of leukocyte motion in microvessels using spatiotemporal image analysis. IEEE Trans. Biomedical Engineering 44(4):225-236, 1997.
2. Wolpert DH, Macready WG: No free lunch theorems for search. Technical Report SFI-95-02-010, The Santa Fe Institute, 1995
3. Anderson JA: Introduction to neural networks. MIT Press, Cambridge, 1995
4. Egmont-Petersen M, Arts T: Detection of implanted markers in radiographic image sequences. S.209-214. In: Lehmann T, Scholl I, Spitzer K (Hrsg.): Bildverarbeitung für die Medizin. Verlag der Augustinus Buchhandlung, Aachen, 1996

Modellierung und Visualisierung kardialer Erregungsausbreitungsmuster in einem Voxelmodell des Herzens
Ein dreidimensionales Zelluläres Automatenmodell

Jan Freudenberg , Karl Heinz Höhne

Institut für Mathematik und Datenverarbeitung in der Medizin (IMDM)
Universitätskrankenhaus Hamburg Eppendorf
Email: freudenberg@uke.uni-hamburg.de

Zusammenfassung. Bisherige Computermodelle der kardialen Erregungsausbreitung beschränkten sich entweder auf zwei räumliche Dimensionen oder auf Teilbereiche des Herzens. Für eine realistische Simulation des Herzens ist es nötig, das physiologische Modell mit einem möglichst detaillierten räumlichen anatomischen Modell zu verbinden. Dazu wird ein Voxelmodell des Herzmuskels auf der Basis des Visible Human Datenersatzes erstellt. Zur Modellierung der Erregungsausbreitung wird das von Gerhardt et al. (1) entwickelte Zelluläre Automatenmodell den verschiedenen Zelltypen des Herzmuskels angepasst. So lassen sich erstmals sowohl normale als auch pathologisch veränderte Erregungsmuster auf einer makroskopischen Ebene in einem verschiedene Zelltypen umfassenden dreidimensionalen Modell des gesamten Herzens modellieren. Derartige Modelle könnten es in Zukunft ermöglichen, Auswirkungen lokalisierter Defekte oder anatomischer Fehlbildungen auf die Erregungsausbreitung zu untersuchen.

Schlüsselwörter: Visible-Human, Herz, Anatomie, Physiologie, 3D Visualisierung, Simulation, Zelluläre Automaten

1 Einleitung

Als Grundlage für die Verwirklichung einer möglichst vollständigen Simulation des menschlichen Organismus initierte die National Library of Medicine der USA 1994 das sogenannte Visible Human Project (VHP), das hochaufgelöste Volumendaten der menschlichen Anatomie zur Verfügung stellt. Die Simulation der Dynamik von Lebensvorgängen auf der Basis dieser anatomischen Daten ist eine große Herausforderung dieses Projektes.
In unserem VOXEL-MAN-Projekt (2) wurden Methoden entwickelt, die es erlauben visuelle anatomische Computermodelle mit symbolischem anatomischen Wissen zu verbinden. Die vorliegende Arbeit versucht diesen Ansatz zu erweitern, indem physiologische Eigenschaften dieser Objekte modelliert und ihr Verhalten als Teil des Organismus simuliert werden. Dieses simulierte Verhalten anatomischer Objekte kann dann wieder mit dem anatomischen Modell visualisiert werden.

Als Ausgangspunkt der Simulation der Physiologie sollte die Erregungserregungsausbreitung im Herzmuskel modelliert werden. Für eine realistische Simulation der Erregungsausbreitung ist es nötig, physiologische Modelle mit möglichst detaillierten räumlichen anatomischen Modellen zu verbinden. Zur Modellierung der Membranerregungsphysiologie des Herzmuskels sind Differentialgleichungssyteme, wie das FitzHugh-Nagumo (3) oder Beeler-Reuter Modell (4), bekannt. Da die numerische Lösung dieser Gleichungen extem rechenintensiv ist, kann eine Modellierung des gesamten Herzens mittels dieser Gleichungen auf gewöhnlichen Rechenanlagen noch nicht realisiert werden. Auf der anderen Seite hat es einige Versuche gegeben erregbare Medien mittels Zellulärer Automaten zu simulieren (5, 6). Diese sind intuitiv verständlich und leicht zu berechnen. Als Nachteil galt, daß essentielle Eigenschaften erregbarer Medien wie das Kurvatur- und Dispersionsverhalten sich ausbreitender Wellen in ihnen nicht dargestellt wurden. Diese Nachteile wurden überwunden durch den von Gerhardt et al. entwickelten GST-Algorithmus zur Modellierung erregbarer Medien (1). Unser Ziel ist es diesen Algorithmus zur Simulation der Erregungsausbreitung in einem anatomischen Herzmodell zu verwenden.

2 Methoden

Auf der Basis des Visible Human Female Datensatzes wurde mit den früher beschriebenen Methoden (7, 8) ein Voxelmodell des Herzens, bestehend aus Vorhöfen, Kammern, Herzklappen, Aorten- und Pulmonalisabgang, Hohl- und Lungenvenenmündung, Koronararterien, Herzvenen sowie umgebendem Fett- und Bindegewebe, erstellt. Das aus den VHP-Daten erstellte anatomische Modell wurde mittels eines Volumeneditors um die für Reizbildung und Reizausbreitung wichtigen Strukturen des Sinusknoten, des Atrioventrikularknoten (AV-Knoten) sowie des Hiss-Purkinje-System (HPS) ergänzt. In einem getrennten Datenvolumen wird dabei jedes Voxel mit einem anatomischen Label versehen. Da im Herzmuskel der VHF-Daten die Leichenstarre bereits eingetreten war, wurde die sich daraus ergebende Hyperkontraktion des Muskels mittels einer digitalen „Ausschabung" im Computermodell korrigiert. Dies führte zum Verlust der Papillarmuskeln im linken Ventrikel.

Zur Modellierung der Erregungsausbreitung im Myocard wurde der oben genannte GST Algorithmus zur Modellierung erregbarer Medien dem Herzmuskel angepasst. Durch Variation der Parameter können die unterschiedlichen Eigenschaften verschiedener Zelltypen, die vegetative Steuerung des Herzens oder ein ischämisches Myocardareal modelliert werden. Die für Ausbreitung von Wellen wichtige Geschwindigkeit-Kurvatur-Relation kann bei einer räumlichen Auflösung von 1/3 mm^3 mit den bekannten physiologischen Meßdaten des Myocards in Übereinstimmung gebracht werden. Für die Abhängigkeit der Dauer eines „Aktionspotentials" von der Dauer des vorangegangenen Zellzyklus wurde die von Winfree in (9) referierte Formel verwendet.

Zur Visualisierung mit dem Programm VOXEL-MAN wird davon ausgegangen, daß ein einzelner Zellzyklus eine Mindestdauer besitzt. Dem Zeitpunkt der Veränderung des Aktivierungszustandes eines Voxel kann so ein eindeutiges zeitliches Label innerhalb dieser Mindestdauer zusätzlich zu dem anatomischen Label zugewiesen werden. Auf Basis dieser zeitlichen Labels werden aktive Voxel farbig markiert. Die Diffusion der Erregungsvariablen im Volumen wird dabei im zeitlichen Ablauf dargestellt. Hierfür ist eine Zwischenspeicherung der Simulationsergebnisse auf einem Massenspeichermedium notwendig.

3 Ergebnisse

Wie in der Bilderserie dargestellt, wird die Entstehung der Erregung im Sinusknoten mit folgender Ausbreitung über die Vorhöfe zum Atrioventrikuluarknoten, die verzögerte Überleitung auf die Kammern sowie die schnelle Erregung des Kammerseptums aufgrund erhöhter Leitungsgeschwindigkeit im Hiss-Purkinje-System durch das Modell wiedergeben und visualisiert. Dies zeigt, daß das Modell als Ganzes, das aus der Physiologie bekannte Verhalten des Herzmuskels als Ganzem, wie erwartet abbildet.

Verschiedene Störungen der Reizbildung und Reizausbreitung lassen sich durch Variation von Parametern einzelner Zelltypen oder manuelle Veränderung des anatomischen Modells darstellen.

4 Schlußfolgerungen

Durch unsere Anpassung des von Gerhardt et al. entwickelten Zellulären Automaten an die verschiedenen Zelltypen des Herzmuskels ist es uns möglich ein dreidimensionales Modell der Erregungsausbreitung im gesamten Herzen zu konstruieren. Eine Zelle des Automaten muß als Volumenelement des Herzmuskels aufgefasst werden und darf nicht mit einem Kardiomyozyten verwechselt werden. Als Näherung wird davon ausgegangen, daß die Kardiomyzyten innerhalb dieses Volumenelementes sich aufgrund ihrer räumlichen Nähe gleich verhalten.

Hauptmangel des hier vorgestellten Modells der Reizausbreitung ist das Fehlen der Faseranisotropieeigenschaften des Herzmuskels. Dieser Mangel ist behebbar durch Betrachtung anderer Nachbarschaften, was jedoch eine noch höhere räumliche Auflösung erfordert. Desgleichen ist eine detaillierteres Modellieren des Reizleitungssystems nötig, was ebenfalls eine höhere räumliche Auflösung vorausetzt. Interessant wäre es, neben der Diffusion der Aktivierungsvariablen auch die Diffusion der Erholungsvariablen im dreidimensionalen Modell zu beobachten. Dies macht genauso wie eine interaktive Variation der Parameter eine Weiterentwicklung der Volumenvisualisierungsmethoden notwendig.

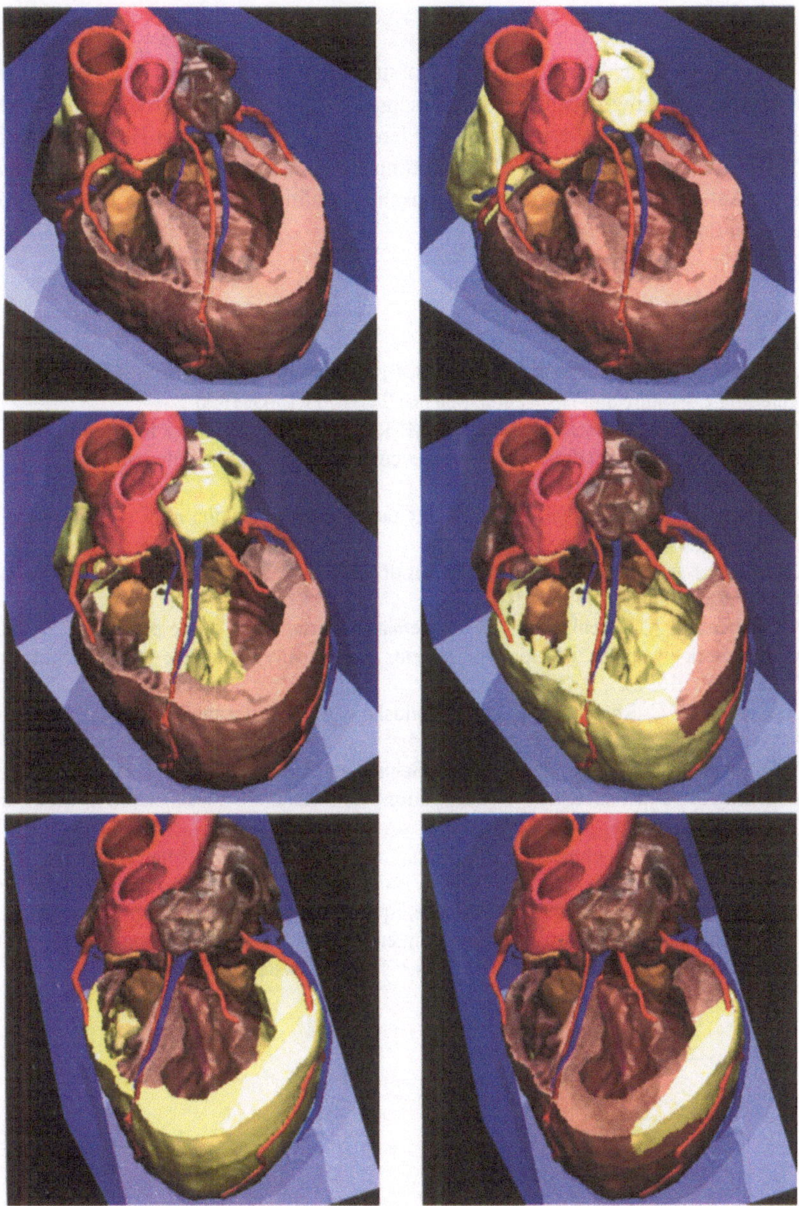

Abb. 1: Visualisierung der Erregungsausbreitung (gelb markiert) im Volumenmodell des Herzens. Die Erregung geht aus vom Bereich um den Sinusknoten (oben links), zur vollständigen Erregung der Vorhöfe (oben rechts); es folgt die Überleitung der Erregung auf die Ventrikel am AV-Knoten und frühzeitige Erregung des Kammerseptums mit anschließender Ausbreitung über die Ventrikel bei gleichzeitiger Erholung der Vorhöfe (Mitte), zuletzt die Rückbildung der Ventrikelerregung (unten links und rechts).

Mit der vorgestellten Arbeit lassen sich erstmals sowohl normale als auch pathologisch veränderte Erregungsmuster dreidimensional auf einer makroskopischen Ebene in einem verschiedene Zelltypen umfassenden Modell des gesamten Herzen modellieren und visualisieren. Derartige Modelle könnten es in Zukunft ermöglichen, Auswirkungen lokalisierter Defekte oder anatomischer Fehlbildungen auf die Erregungsausbreitung zu untersuchen

5 Literatur

1. M. Gerhardt, H. Schuster and J.J. Tyson: A Cellular Automaton Model of Excitable Media Including Curvature and Dispersion. Science 247:1563-1565, 1990
2. K.H. Höhne , B. Pflesser, A. Pommert, M. Riemer, Th. Schiemann, R. Schubert and U. Tiede: A new representation of knowledge concerning human anatomy and function. Nature Medicine 1(6):506-511, 1995
3. R.A Fitzhugh: Mathematical Models of Excitation and Propagation in Nerve. In Biological Engineering:1-85, Mc Graw Hill 1969
4. G.W. Beeler and H. Reuter: Reconstruction of the Action Potential of Ventricular Myocardial Fibres. J Physiol 268:177-210, 1977
5. N. Wiener and A. Rosenblueth: The mathematical formulation of the problem of impulses in a network of connected exitable elements, specifically in cardiac muscle. Arch. Inst. Cardiol Mex. 16: 295, 1946
6. G.K. Moe , W.C. Rheinboldt and J.A. Abildskov: A computer model of atrial fibrillation. Am Heart J 67(2):200-220, 1964
7. A. Pommert, R. Schubert, M. Riemer, T. Schiemann, U. Tiede and K.H. Höhne: Symbolic modelling of human anatomy for vizualisation and simulation. Visualization in Biomedical Computing, Rochester 1994
8. Th. Schiemann, J. Nuthmann, U. Tiede and K. H. Höhne: Segmentation of the Visible Human for High Quality Volume based Visualization. Visualization in Biomedical Computing, Lecture Notes in Computer Science, Springer Verlag, 1996
9. A. T. Winfree: Rotors, Fibrillation and Dimensionality. In: Computational Biology of the Heart, A v. Holden and A.V. Panfilov (Eds.): 101-135, Wiley 1997

Interaktive Deformation volumenbasierter Körpermodelle

Thomas Schiemann und Karl Heinz Höhne

Institut für Mathematik und Datenverarbeitung in der Medizin
Universitätskrankenhaus Hamburg-Eppendorf
http://www.uke.uni-hamburg.de/idv

Zusammenfassung Üblicherweise sind digitale Körpermodelle starr. Für einen realistischen Umgang mit den Modellen ist es jedoch nötig, diese auch verformen zu können. Da der volumenbasierte Charakter für einen umfassenden Einsatz der Modelle entscheidend ist, kommt es darauf an, daß echte Volumendeformationen anstelle von Oberflächenverformungen berechnet werden. Die Deformationen werden zur Simulation interaktiver Eingriffe benutzt, so daß die entwickelten Methoden sich vor allem durch schnelle Berechenbarkeit auszeichnen.

Schlüsselwörter: Deformation, Thin-Plate-Splines, Finite Elemente, Virtuelle Körpermodelle

1   Einleitung

Mit Hilfe tomographischer Bildgebung werden überlagerungsfreie Schnittbildserien des menschlichen Körpers erzeugt. Mit Segmentierungsverfahren werden den Voxeln dieser Datenvolumen Attribute für Zugehörigkeiten zu morphologischen Bereichen gegeben, so daß man volumenbasierte Körpermodelle erhält [1].

Diese Modelle sind a priori starr, was für viele Anwendungen keine Einschränkung darstellt (Abb. 1). Eine wichtige Gruppe von Applikationen ist jedoch mit bildverändernden Manipulationen (Schneiden, Drücken, Biegen) verbunden, die mit einem starren Modell nicht simuliert werden können. Es gibt zwar verschiedene Ansätze zur interaktiven Deformation von Objekten [2, 3], diese beziehen sich jedoch auf Oberflächenmodelle, die nur beschränkt realistisch sind, weil sie aus hohlen Hüllen ohne innere Struktur bestehen. Ein anderer Bereich, in dem Volumendeformationen benötigt werden, ist die Fusion mehrerer Bildvolumen aus verschiedenen Akquisitionen desselben Patienten oder auch verschiedener Individuen. Bei diesen Problemen ist das Ziel der Deformation in Form eines Bildvolumens vorgegeben. Bei den Manipulationen hingegen muß der Benutzer die Deformation nach seinen Vorstellungen spezifizieren können.

Unser Projekt verfolgt deshalb zwei Ziele: Zum einen sollen Verfahren für echte Volumendeformationen untersucht werden, die sich für einen interaktiven Einsatz eignen. Andererseits sollen Verfahren entwickelt werden, mit denen die Deformationsfunktion intuitiv spezifiziert werden kann.

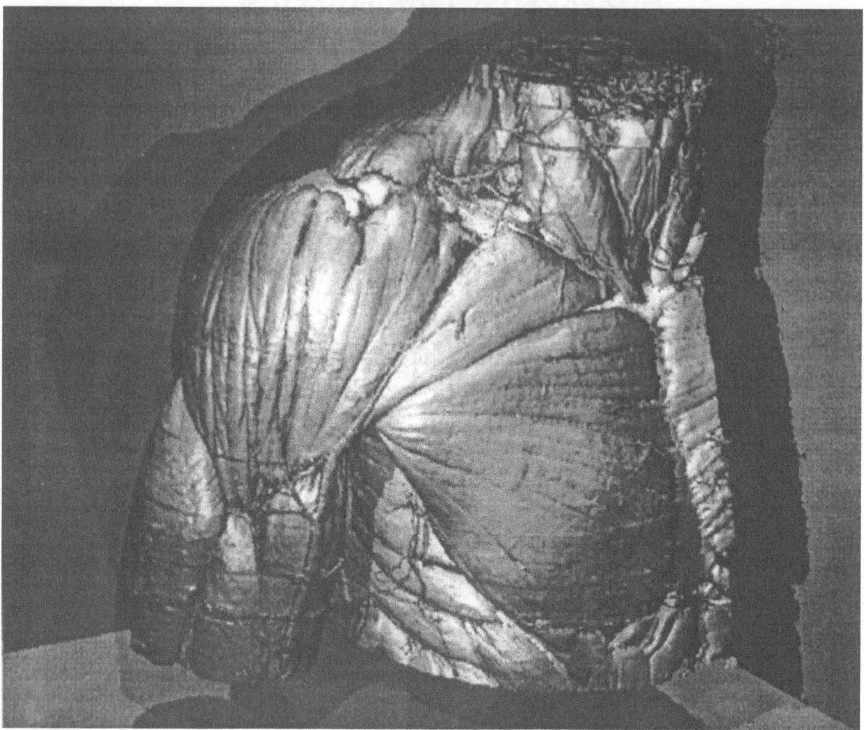

Abb. 1. Volumenbasiertes Modell der rechten Schulter des Visible Human. Aufgrund der hohen Auflösung der Daten kann dieses starre Modell z.B. zu Lehrzwecken sehr realistisch visualisiert werden. Realistische Manipulationen (Schneiden, Drücken, Biegen) setzen jedoch ein deformierbares Modell voraus.

2 Deformation

Im Idealfall müßte die Deformation über ein vollständiges biomechanisches Modell berechnet werden. Dies ist jedoch beim gegenwärtigen Stand der Forschung aus verschiedenen Gründen nicht realisierbar: Es fehlen die organspezifischen mechanischen Parameter, die Auflösung der geometrischen Modelle ist zu grob, und schließlich reichen die allgemein verfügbaren Computerressourcen nicht aus. Deshalb muß man sich für operable Methoden auf vereinfachte Deformationsverfahren beschränken.

Die Methode der *Finiten Elemente* ist prinzipiell die Methode der Wahl für komplexe mechanische Berechnungen. Bei Beschränkung auf ein lineares physikalisches Modell kann in einem Vorverarbeitungsschritt eine direkte Inversion der Steifigkeitsmatrix ausgeführt werden. Für ein belastetes Objekt kann die Verformung dann schnell berechnet werden, indem der Lastvektor mit der invertierten Matrix multipliziert wird [4, 5]. Dieses Verfahren benötigt allerdings große Speicherkapazität und hat den weiteren Nachteil, daß bei Modifikation der

Randbedingungen der aufwendige Inversionsschritt wiederholt werden muß. Für einen flexiblen Einsatz ist diese Methode also nur eingeschränkt nützlich.

Deshalb werden im folgenden vorrangig *Thin-Plate-Splines* benutzt. Diese lassen sich sehr schnell berechnen und erzeugen unter Minimierung des Energiepotentials einer dünnen Platte eine Volumeninterpolation zwischen Verschiebungsvektoren, die an gewissen Landmarken gegeben sind. Diese Landmarken sind im Prinzip frei wählbar, so daß nicht automatisch sichergestellt ist, daß die mit Thin-Plate-Splines berechneten Deformationen auch realistisch sind. Mit Hilfe von Vergleichsrechnungen mit Finiten Elementen konnten jedoch für typische Belastungen solche Parametereinstellungen gefunden werden, mit denen die Thin-Plate-Splines zu sehr ähnlichen Ergebnissen führen wie die Finiten Elemente.

3 Spezifikation

Nach Berechnung der Koeffizienten der Deformationsfunktion muß für jedes Voxel ein Verschiebungsvektor berechnet werden, und in einem Resampling-Schritt werden die deformierten Bildvolumen erzeugt. Selbst bei einfachster Deformationsfunktion sind diese beiden Schritte so aufwendig, daß sie nicht in einem interaktiven Rahmen durchgeführt werden können. Deshalb wurde ein hybrides Oberflächenmodell entwickelt. Mit diesem wird einerseits die Deformation der Volumenobjekte durch zugehörige deformierte Oberflächenrepräsentanten schnell dargestellt, und andererseits werden Werkzeuge zur Interaktion im Kontext des Volumens modelliert (Abb. 2).

Das Oberflächenmodell besteht aus einer Menge von Hüllen, die entweder über eine analytische Parametrisierung gegeben sind oder durch Triangulierungsverfahren aus den Volumenrepräsentationen extrahiert werden. Auf den Hüllen sind gewisse Punkte als Sensorpunkte ausgezeichnet, mit denen Wechselwirkungen zwischen den Hüllen und dem Volumenmodell registriert werden. Daraus lassen sich die Eingabegrößen zur Berechnung der Koeffizienten der Deformationsfunktion ableiten.

Das Modell ist in dem Sinne hybrid, daß es zwar mit Oberflächen umgeht, wie es in weiten Bereichen der Computergraphik üblich ist. Diese Oberflächen sind jedoch in den Kontext der volumenbasierten Darstellungen eingebunden. Damit verbindet sich der Vorteil der hohen Bearbeitungsgeschwindigkeiten der oberflächenbasierten Methoden mit den Vorteilen des volumenbasierten Modells.

4 Anwendung

Die Methoden wurden innerhalb des Systems VOXEL-MAN implementiert, das eine Vielzahl von Möglichkeiten zur Erstellung, Visualisierung und anderer Exploration virtueller Körpermodelle auf Basis von Volumenbildern bereitstellt [1].

Aufgrund ihrer allgemeinen Konstruktion lassen sich die Verfahren für verschiedenartige Aufgaben verwenden [6]. Dazu gehören Simulationen laparosko-

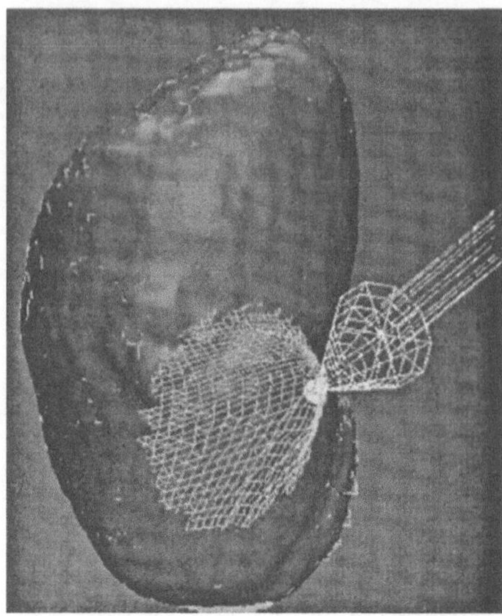

Abb. 2. Oberflächenbasierte Vorschau auf die Volumendeformation einer Niere. Eine stilisierte Nadel dient als Repräsentant für eine Zange während einer laparoskopischen Operation. Die Kugel an der Spitze der Nadel ist ein Sensorpunkt, der das Berühren der Niere registriert. Wenn interaktiv an der Niere gezogen wird, so wird die resultierende Deformation mit Hilfe eines Oberflächenrepräsentanten der Niere visualisiert. (Zur Verdeutlichung des Effekts ist die Deformation hier künstlich überhöht.) Die Berechnung der vollständigen Volumendeformation erfolgt außerhalb der Interaktion und muß gesondert ausgelöst werden.

pischer und endoskopischer Eingriffe, Planungen von Operationen oder geometrisch motivierte Verformungen etwa zur Illustration. Abbildung 3 zeigt exemplarisch die Anwendung im Rahmen einer laparoskopischen Operation der Gallenblase.

5   Schlussfolgerungen

Es wurde ein methodischer Rahmen beschrieben, mit dem sich interaktive Deformationen volumenbasierter Körpermodelle durchführen lassen. Dazu wurden schnelle Deformationsfunktionen und ein hybrides Oberflächenmodell aufeinander abgestimmt, um zu einem operablen Gesamtverfahren zu kommen. So wurden drei wesentliche Ziele erreicht: Es werden vollständige Volumendeformationen berechnet, die zugehörige Spezifikation erfolgt interaktiv und eine allgemeine Anwendbarkeit unter verschiedenartigen Bedingungen ist gewährleistet. So lassen sich die Methoden z.B. zur virtuellen Gastroskopie, zur Simulation von Weichteilverformungen in der Kiefer- und Gesichtschirurgie oder auch zur nichtlinearen Registrierung von Atlas- und Patientendaten einsetzen.

Literatur

1. K. H. Höhne, B. Pflesser, A. Pommert, M. Riemer, T. Schiemann, R. Schubert, and U. Tiede, "A new representation of knowledge concerning human anatomy and function," *Nature Med.*, vol. 1, no. 6, pp. 506–511, 1995.
2. C. Kuhn, U. Kühnapfel, and H.-G. Krumm, "A virtual reality based training system for minimally invasive surgery," in *Computer Assisted Radiology (Proc. CAR '96)* (H. U. Lemke, K. Inamura, A. Farman, and M. W. Vannier, eds.), Amsterdam: Elsevier, 1996.

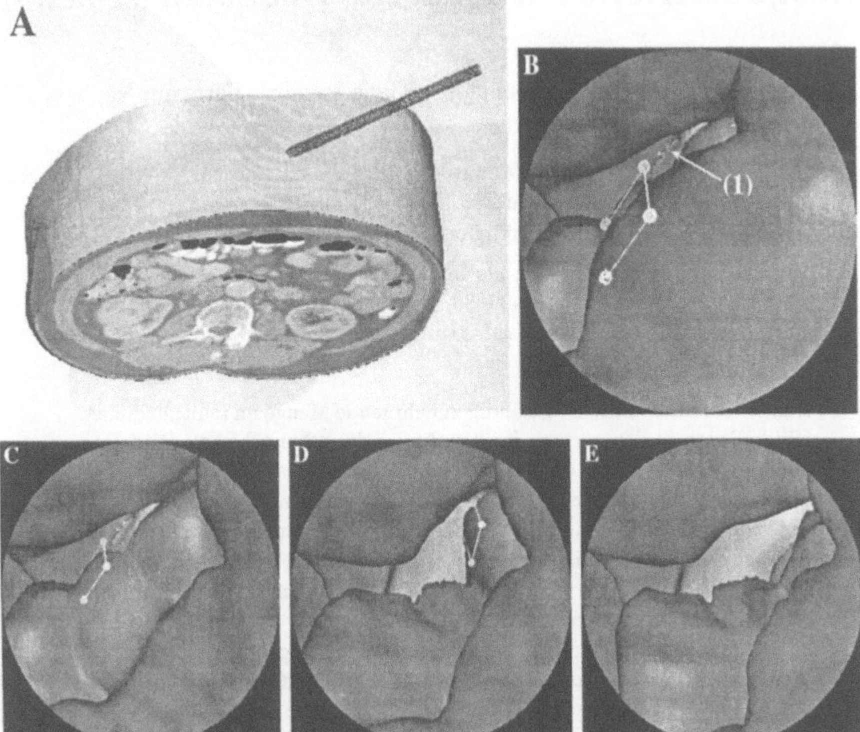

Abb. 3. Simulation des Zugangs zur Gallenblase an einem CT-basierten Modell des Oberbauchs. Das Modell eines Laparoskops wird in die Bauchhöhle vorgeschoben (A). Das laparoskopische Bild (B) zeigt einen kleinen Ausschnitt der Gallenblase (1), die überwiegend von Darmschlingen verdeckt wird. Mit einem Oberflächenelement werden diese sukzessiv zur Seite gedrängt (B–D), so daß schließlich der größte Teil der Gallenblase sichtbar wird (E).

3. R. M. Koch, M. H. Gross, F. R. Carls, D. F. von Büren, G. Frankhauser, and Y. I. Parish, "Simulating facial surgery using finite element models," in *SIGGRAPH '96 Conference Proceedings*, Computer Graphics Proceedings, pp. 421–428, New Orleans, LA: ACM SIGGRAPH, 1996.

4. S. Cotin, H. Delingette, and N. Ayache, "Real time volumetric deformable models for surgery simulation," in *Visualization in Biomedical Computing 1996, (Proc. VBC '96)* (K. H. Höhne and R. Kikinis, eds.), vol. 1131 of *Lecture Notes in Computer Science*, pp. 535–540, Berlin: Springer, 1996.

5. M. Bro-Nielsen, "Fast finite elements for surgery simulation," in *Medicine Meets Virtual Reality (Proc. MMVR 5)* (K. S. Morgan, H. Hoffman, D. Stredney, and S. Weghorst, eds.), vol. 39 of *Studies in Health Technology and Informatics*, pp. 395–400, Amsterdam: IOS Press, 1997. (ISBN 90-5199-299-8).

6. T. Schiemann, *Interaktive Verfahren für deformierende Eingriffe an volumenbasierten digitalen Körpermodellen.* Dissertation, Technische Universität Hamburg-Harburg, 1998. (in Vorbereitung).

Image Retrieval für klinische Bilddatenbanken

Jörg Dahmen[1], Thomas Lehmann[2], Klaus Spitzer[2], Hermann Ney[1]

[1] Lehrstuhl für Informatik VI der RWTH Aachen,
Ahornstraße 55, D-52056 Aachen
e-mail: dahmen@informatik.rwth-aachen.de

[2] Institut für Medizinische Informatik der RWTH Aachen,
Pauwelsstraße 30, D-52057 Aachen
e-mail: lehmann@imib.rwth-aachen.de

Zusammenfassung. Die ständig zunehmende Menge an multimedialen (Bild-)Daten in den verschiedensten Anwendungsbereichen stellt immer höhere Anforderungen an den Zugriff auf diese. Da eine manuelle Indizierung immer aufwendiger wird, sind in der Vergangenheit zahlreiche Systeme und Algorithmen entwickelt worden, mit denen Indizierung und Abfrage solcher Datenbanken erleichtert werden sollen. Ein möglicher Ansatz ist der Bildzugriff durch Bildanalyse, der eine automatische Indizierung von Bilddaten erlaubt. In dieser Arbeit wird ein Überblick über aktuelle Entwicklungen auf diesem Gebiet gegeben, insbesondere im Hinblick auf eine klinische Anwendbarkeit, und es wird ein neues Verfahren zur Leistungsbewertung solcher Systeme vorgeschlagen, das auf dem statistischen Ansatz von *Sensitivität* und *Spezifität* beruht.

Schlüsselwörter: Image Retrieval, Sensitivität, Spezifität

1 Einführung

Heute existierende Datenbanksysteme (DBS) bieten in der Regel nur die Möglichkeit, Anfragen textuell zu formulieren, üblicherweise über die Datenbankabfragesprache SQL. Um ein solches System zur Verwaltung von Bilddaten heranzuziehen, ist es daher nötig, jedes Bild manuell mit Schlüsselwörtern zu versehen. Eine solche Beschreibung ist jedoch aufwendig und zudem weder vollständig noch eindeutig, da abhängig von Erfahrungshorizont und Intention der Benutzer unterschiedliche Schlüsselwörter herangezogen werden. Auch eine nachträgliche Indizierung mit erweiterten Attributen ist oft nicht möglich, so daß in der Vergangenheit zahlreiche Versuche unternommen worden sind, neue Bildzugriffsverfahren zu entwickeln. Diese lassen sich unter dem Oberbegriff *Content-Based Image Retrieval* oder kurz *Image Retrieval* (ImR) zusammenfassen.

2 Aufbau eines Image Retrieval-Systems

ImR-Systeme beruhen in der Regel auf dem folgenden Ansatz. Bei der Eingabe in das DBS werden aus dem Bild Merkmale extrahiert, die den Merkmalsvektor bilden. Dieser wird nun zusätzlich zum eigentlichen Bild in der DB gespeichert. Anfragen geschehen fast immer über das 'Query by Example'-Paradigma (QBE). Aufgabe des Systems ist es dabei, alle Bilder zurückzuliefern, die einem vorgegebenen Anfragebild visuell ähnlich sind. Zu diesem Zweck wird der zu dem Anfragebild gehörige Merkmalsvektor bestimmt und mittels geeigneter Distanzmaße mit den in der DB gespeicherten verglichen. Unter *Query-Refinement* (QR) versteht man dabei die sukzessive Verfeinerung einer QBE-Anfrage. Eine spezielle Variante des QR ist das *Relevance Feedback*. In diesem Fall wird die Anfrage über die manuelle Einteilung des Suchergebnisses in erwünschte und unerwünschte Bilder verfeinert.

Die Definition der Ähnlichkeit zweier Bilder geschieht in der Regel über die Merkmale Farbe, Textur, Form sowie deren räumliche Anordnung [1]. Um das Merkmal Farbe sinnvoll einsetzen zu können, ist die Wahl eines geeigneten Farbraumes sehr wichtig. Nur perzeptive Farbräume wie das HVC-Farbsystem [2] haben die Eigenschaft, daß die visuell wahrnehmbaren Farbunterschiede den geometrischen Farbdistanzen entsprechen. Dies ist aber eine elementare Voraussetzung für ein farbbasiertes ImR [3][4]. Ausgangspunkt des texturbasierten Ansatzes ist HARALICK's Grundlagenwerk aus dem Jahr 1973 [5], in dem zahlreiche Texturdeskriptoren vorgestellt werden. Formbasierte Verfahren erlauben es dem Benutzer, das gesuchte Objekt zu skizzieren. Mittels eines Gradientenbildes kann dann untersucht werden, ob ein Bild dieses Objekt enthält oder nicht. Solche Verfahren sind, beispielsweise durch Verwendung der FOURIER-MELLIN-Transformation, invariant gegenüber Rotation, Translation und Skalierung oder anderen affinen Transformationen. Einige Systeme erlauben auch eine manuelle Segmentierung der Bilder in Regions of Interest (ROI). Diese Verfahren sind aber für große Datenmengen zu aufwendig, zumal die Suche dann auf Bilder beschränkt ist, deren ROIs zuvor ebenfalls manuell extrahiert wurden.

Zur Leistungsfähigkeit dieser Ansätze stellen SCASSELLATI et al. die These auf, die bislang verwendeten Formmerkmale korrelierten in keinster Weise mit der Wahrnehmung des Menschen [6]. In der Tat erzielen diese die schlechtesten Resultate [7], wohingegen das Merkmal Farbe nach FALOUTSOS et al. die besten Ergebnisse liefert [8]. Zur Komplexitätsreduktion werden Datenstrukturen wie der G-Baum [9] oder die Voronoi-Tesselierung [10] eingesetzt, die die Anzahl der zum ImR benötigten Vergleichsoperationen von N auf $log(N)$ reduziert.

3 Vorstellung von Image Retrieval-Systemen

Im folgenden werden einige ImR-Systeme vorgestellt, die nach Kriterien wie Beispielhaftigkeit und Innovativität ausgewählt wurden.

IBM's *QBIC*-System (Query by Image Content) war die erste kommerziell verfügbare ImR-Applikation und unterstützt im wesentlichen die in Kapitel 2 vorgestellten Merkmale [11]. Diesem System sehr ähnlich ist das *MARS*-System (Multimedia Analysis and Retrieval System) der University of Illinois [12]. Schwerpunkt von MARS sind Anfragen, die auf gewichteten Kombinationen mehrerer

Merkmale basieren. Eine automatische ROI-Extraktion findet in keinem der beiden Systeme statt.

VisualSEEK (Columbia University) beschränkt sich bislang auf die Analyse von Farben und ihrer räumlichen Anordnung zueinander [13], allerdings findet eine automatische ROI-Extraktion statt. *WebSEEK* ist eine Abwandlung des Systems für den WWW-Bereich. Das *Blobworld*-Projekt [14] der University of California at Berkeley, spezialisiert auf natürliche Bilder wie Landschafts- und Tieraufnahmen, arbeitet lediglich mit den Merkmalen Farbe und Textur, wobei auch und gerade räumliche Zusammenhänge berücksichtigt werden. Die Extraktion der durch Ellipsen (genannt Blobs) beschriebenen ROIs erfolgt automatisch unter Verwendung des Expectation-Maximization Algorithmus. *Photobook* (Massachusetts Institute of Technology) erlaubt unter anderem Anfragen über die sogenannte 'Appearance' eines Bildes [15]. Appearance-Merkmale sind solche, die eine möglichst exakte Rekonstruktion des Bildes erlauben (Semantics Preserving Compression); sie werden durch Anwendung einer KARHUNEN-LOÈVE-Transformation (KLT) gewonnen und beispielsweise zur Gesichtserkennung genutzt. Photobooks Formerkennungsmodul basiert auf einem Finite Elemente-Ansatz und erlaubt die Detektion von verformten 2D-Objekten. Neu ist auch der Anfrageunterstützungsagent 'Four Eyes', der den Benutzer bei der Auswahl von für ein Problem besonders geeigneten Merkmalen unterstützen soll.

Erwähnenswert ist auch das *IRIS*-Projekt (Image Retrieval for Information Systems), das 1994 als Kooperation von IBM und der Universität Bremen gestartet wurde [16] und heute unter dem Name *ImageMiner* weiterentwickelt wird. Durch den Einsatz einer regelbasierten Wissensbank können Bilder gewisser Domänen automatisch textuell beschrieben werden. Damit ist IRIS das bislang einzige ImR-System, welches auf semantischer Ebene arbeitet [7]. Systeme wie *Virage* (Virage, Inc, San Mateo, USA) oder *CORE* (National University of Singapore) sind keine eigenständigen ImR-Applikationen, stellen aber Datenstrukturen und Funktionalitäten zur Verfügung, mit denen solche implementiert werden können.

4 Systemevaluierung über Sensitivität und Spezifität

Die Effizienz von ImR-Systemen wird üblicherweise über die Größen *Precision* (P) und *Recall* (R) definiert [14]. P gibt an, wieviel Prozent der auf eine Anfrage zurückgelieferten Bilder tatsächlich korrekt sind, R hingegen, wieviel Prozent der Bilder in der DB, die die Anfrage erfüllen, zurückgeliefert wurden. Man beachte, daß bei diesen Effizienzmaßen die Größe der DB unberücksichtigt bleibt, obwohl es offensichtlich ein erheblicher Unterschied ist, ob ein ImR-System aus einer Gesamtmenge von 32 oder 1000 Bildern eine Menge von M Bildern extrahiert.

Ein Leistungsvergleich der vorgestellten Systeme ist nicht möglich, da das Konzept von P und R einerseits Schwächen aufzeigt und andererseits nicht von allen Autoren genutzt wird. Darüberhinaus existieren noch keine standardisierten Trainings-/ und Testcorpora. Aussagen über die Leistungsfähigkeit heutiger Systeme auf medizinischen Bilddaten gibt es somit praktisch nicht.

Als Bewertungskriterium für die Effizienz eines ImR-Systems bietet sich das statistische Bewertungskonzept von *Sensitivität* (SE) und *Spezifität* (SP) an, welches in der Medizin zum Vergleich von Diagnoseverfahren herangezogen wird [2]. Die Größen P und R sind in diesem Zusammenhang völlig analog definiert, P wird nun aber als *positiver Vorhersagewert* (PV), R als *Sensitivität* bezeichnet. Zusätzlich wird jedoch noch der Begriff der *Spezifität* eingeführt. Diese ist, übertragen auf eine Anwendung im Bereich ImR, definiert als $SP = rn/(rn+fp)$. Dabei ist rn die Anzahl der korrekterweise nicht zurückgelieferten Bilder (also Bilder, die dem Anfragebild unähnlich sind und auch nicht zurückgeliefert wurden) und fp die Anzahl der Bilder, die zwar zurückgeliefert wurden, aber falsch sind.

In Verbindung mit standardisierten, gelabelten Testcorpora ermöglichen die Kriterien SE, SP und PV nun einen aussagekräftigen Vergleich verschiedener ImR-Applikationen, was am folgenden Beispiel gezeigt werden soll. Liefert ein ImR-System 16 Bilder zurück, von denen 4 korrekt sind und waren insgesamt 5 korrekte in der DB, so bedeutet dies stets $R = 80\%$, $P = 25\%$. Enthielte die DB 32 Bilder, so entspräche dies $SE = 80\%$ und $SP = 55.6\%$. Wird das gleiche Ergebnis auf 1000 Bildern erzielt, so gilt $SP = 98.8\%$, bei gleichbleibendem $SE = 80\%$. Der Tatsache, daß die Komplexität eines ImR-Problems proportional zur Anzahl der Bilder in der DB wächst, wird also durch SP Rechnung getragen.

5 Zusammenfassung und Ausblick

Wie bereits die große Anzahl an Publikationen in diesem Bereich zeigt, ist ImR nach wie vor ein aktuelles Forschungsgebiet. Obwohl eine experimentelle Untersuchung noch aussteht kann prognostiziert werden, daß heutige Systeme in einer Domäne wie der Medizin versagen werden; sie scheinen eher für heterogene Bildsammlungen, wie etwa ein privates Photoalbum, geeignet, da dem bislang effektivstem Merkmal 'Farbe' [8] nur hier diskriminative Eigenschaften zukommen. Es besteht also ein Bedarf an neuen ImR-Algorithmen bzw. an der Weiterentwicklung der bestehenden. Darüberhinaus ist die Entwicklung von standardisierten Testcopora zum Leistungsvergleich verschiedener Systeme unumgänglich. Interessant erscheint auch eine Anwendung der KLT auf medizinische Daten, allerdings sollte, da eine Klassentrennung angestrebt wird, das Verfahren um eine sich anschließende Lineare Diskriminanzanalyse (LDA) erweitert werden [10]. Abschließend sei bemerkt, daß ein ImR-System nur dann in der klinischen Routine eingesetzt werden kann, wenn es Standards wie DICOM oder HL-7 unterstützt. Bislang erfüllt kein ImR-System diese Anforderung.

Literatur

1. M.D. Marsicoi, L. Cinque, S. Levialdi, "Indexing Pictorial Documents by their Content: A Survey of Current Techniques", Image and Vision Computing 15, pp. 119-141, 1997

2. T. Lehmann, W. Oberschelp, E. Pelikan, R. Repges, "Bildverarbeitung für die Medizin", Springer Verlag Berlin, 1997

3. J.R. Smith, S.F. Chang, "Tools and Techniques for Color Image Retrieval", Procs. SPIE, Vol. 2670, pp. 426-437, 1996

4. H.J. Zhang, Y. Gong, C.Y. Low, S.W. Smoliar, "Image Retrieval based on Color Features: An Evaluation Study", Procs. SPIE, Vol.2606, pp. 212-220, 1995

5. R.M. Haralick, K. Shanmugam, I. Dinstein, "Textural Features for Image Classification", IEEE Trans. on Systems, Man and Cybernetics, Vol.3, No.6, pp. 610-621, 1973

6. B. Scassellati, S. Alexopoulos, M. Flickner, "Retrieving Images by 2-D Shape: A Comparison of Computation Methods with Human Perceptual Judgements", Procs. SPIE, Vol.2185, pp. 2-14, 1994

7. J.P. Eakins, "Automatic Image Content Retrieval - Are we Getting Anywhere?", 3rd Int. Conf. Electronic Library and Visual Information Research, De Montford University, Milton Keynes, UK, pp.123-135, 1996

8. C. Faloutsos, R. Barber, M. Flickner, J. Hafner et al., "Efficient and Effective Querying by Image Content", Journal of Intelligent Information Systems, Vol.3, pp. 231-262, 1994

9. T.C. Wu, J. Cheng, "Retrieving similar Pictures from Iconic Databases using G-Tree", Pattern Recognition Letters 18, pp. 595-603, 1997

10. D.L. Swets, J.J. Weng, "Efficient Content-Based Image Retrieval using Automatic Feature Selection", Procs. International Symposium Computer Vision, Coral Gables, Florida, pp. 85-90, Nov. 1995.

11. W. Niblack, R. Barber, W. Equitz, M. Flickner et al., "The QBIC Project: Querying Images by Content using Color, Texture and Shape", Procs. SPIE, Vol.1908, pp. 173-187, 1993

12. S. Mehrotra, Y. Rui, M. Ortega-Binderberger, T.S. Huang, "Supporting Content-Based Queries over Images in MARS", IEEE Int. Conf. Multimedia Computing and Systems, Chateau Laurier, Canada, pp. 623-633, June 1997

13. J.R. Smith, S.F. Chang, "VisualSEEK: A Fully Automated Content-Based Image Query System", ACM Multimedia 96, Boston, USA, pp. 87-98, Nov. 1996

14. C. Carson, S. Belongie, H. Greenspan, J. Malik, "Color- and Texure-Based Image Segmentation using EM and its Application to Image Querying and Classification", to appear in: IEEE Pattern Analysis and Machine Intelligence

15. A. Pentland, R.W. Picard, S. Scarloff, "Photobook: Content-Based Manipulation of Image Databases", Procs. SPIE, Vol.2185, pp. 34-47, 1994

16. P. Alshuth, T. Hermes, C. Klauck, J. Kreyß, M. Röper, "IRIS - A System for Image and Video Retrieval", Center for Advanced Studies Conference '96, Toronto, Canada, Abstract: pp. 208, Paper: CDROM, Nov. 1996

Moderne Computertechnologie für die medizinische Bildverarbeitung

Dipl.-Betriebswirt Jörg Schwarz

Sun Microsystems GmbH, Ratingen
Email: Joerg.Schwarz@Germany.Sun.COM
http://www.sun.de

1   Einleitung

Für die Befundung und Diagnostik spielt die traditionelle Bilderstellung in zahlreichen Teilgebieten der Medizin eine immer wichtigere Rolle. Durch den Einsatz digitaler, bildgebender Geräte konnte die diagnostische Relevanz in den letzten Jahren drastisch gesteigert werden. Teilweise wurden durch die neuen Technologien auch die Belastung der Patienten (z.B. durch Minimierung der Röntgenstrahlung) reduziert.

Viele Verfahren, die in der Wissenschaft entwickelt und erprobt werden, konnten bisher noch nicht breit im Feld eingesetzt werden, weil der Kostenaufwand nicht finanzierbar erschien. Die Fortschritte in der Computertechnik machen nun sinnvolle Verfahren für einen breiteren Einsatz in der Medizin bezahlbar.

Die Produkte von Sun Microsystems, Workstations und Server, sind von vielen Herstellern bildgebender Geräte und bildverarbeitender Verfahren ausgewählt worden. Höchstleistung und Zuverlässigkeit waren dabei die Kriterien, die mit den heute verfügbaren Produkten auch einen kostengünstigen Einsatz in vielen Gebieten erst möglich machen. Im folgenden werden exemplarisch zwei Innovationen der medizinischen Bildverabeitung dargestellt, die leistungsstarke Rechner fordern und erst durch die Entwicklungen der letzten Jahre ermöglicht werden können.

2   Archivierung digitaler Bilder

Schon seit einigen Jahren sind bildgebende Großgeräte (CT, MRT, etc.) im Einsatz, die über entsprechende Schnittstellen digitale Bilder an eine Workstation zur Nachbearbeitung liefern. Vielfach werden auch heute noch die Bilder zwar digital bearbeitet, dann aber auf herkömmliche Filme belichtet. Befundung und Archivierung finden in der Regel analog statt.

Seit längerem sind Methoden und Lösungen bekannt, die Originalbilder auch in ihrer digitalen Form zu archivieren. Diese digitale Archivierung hat diverse Vorteile:

- Innerhalb kürzester Zeit können die Bigitalen Daten übermittelt werden. Hier ist einmal das Konzil mit Kollegen, aber auch der Service für den zuweisenden Arzt innerhalb des Krankenhauses oder sogar im niedergelassenen Bereich zu nennen. Bei der *Teleradiologie* gibt es derzeit zahlreiche Projektvorhaben in Deutschland, die durch den Einsatz von Intranet–Technologie die Übermittlung und auch Archivierung von Bilddaten ermöglichen sollen. Hier ist Sun als führender Anbieter von Internet–Technologie, leistungsfähigen Servern und Kommunikationsinfrastruktur engagiert.

– Bei der digitalen Archivierung entsteht kein Qualitätsverslust. Der Originaldatensatz kann jederzeit wieder weiterverarbeitet werden, z.B. um präoperativ durch eine 3D–Rekonstruktion dem Chirurgen die Navigation zu erleichtern. Inzwischen gibt es auch chirurgische Navigationssysteme, die aktiv auch perioperativ die Arbeit des Chirurgen unterstützen. Sun–Systeme kommen in diesem Bereich als leistungsfähige Workstations zur Aufbereitung der Bilddaten zum Einsatz.

– Die Integration von Bilddaten und anderen diagnostischen Daten in eine einheitliche Patientenakte, die alle relevanten Daten referenziert kann auf Anforderung einen aussagefähigen Gesamtüberblick vermitteln. Sun–Partner bieten heute Lösungen an, die Daten unterschiedlicher Genese in einem relationalen Datenbank–Management–System ablegen, verwalten und unter eindeutigen Zugriffskriterien für verschiedene Aufgaben auswertbar machen. Sicherlich ist die Erschließung von Bilddaten für epidemiologische Zwecke (Mustererkennung) noch nicht vollständig ausgreift, aber an dieser Stelle sind interessante Perspektiven eröffnet.

– Durch die Verwaltung und Konservierung von belichteten Filmen entstehen nennenswerte Kosten. Inzwischen stehen sowohl schnelle Massenspeichersysteme (Festplattensubsysteme), als auch Langzeitspeicher (CD–ROM, DVD, MOD etc.) zu Preisen zur Verfügung, die schon nach einer überschaubaren Dauer ihre Investitionskosten durch Kosteneinsparungen amortisieren (ROI). Nach der Amortisation zahlt sich dann die digitale Speicherung mit ihren Vorteilen auch durch günstige laufende Kosten aus.

– Inzwischen können durch leistungsfähige Workstations von Sun sogar Bewegtbildsequenzen in Echtzeit digitalisiert werden, um diese dann ebenfalls einer elektronischen Archivierung, Distribution und Auswertung zugänglich zu machen.

3 Die Vision: Echtzeitnavigation im MR–Tomographen

Das große Ziel industriellen Engagements in der medizinischen Bildverarbeitung, nämlich den Patienten zu schonen bei gleichzeitiger Kostensenkung, ist man in den USA ein Stück näher gekommen.

Am Brigham and Women's Hospital der Harvard Medical School, USA wird eine Vision in die Realität umgesetzt, die einige Aspekte der digitalen Bildverabeitung integriert, siehe hierzu auch `http://splweb.bwh.harvard.edu:8000/`.

Zunächst wurden dort präoperativ Bilddaten in 2D–Darstellung aufbereitet. Sehr schnell enstand der Wunsch, diese Daten auch während der Operation als Navigationsunterstützung zur Verfügung zu haben. Man entwickelte zusammen mit einem Großgerätehersteller ein System, welches die Operation in einem MR–Tomographen erlaubte. Die Bilddaten werden nun in Echtzeit aufbereitet, zu einem 2D–Modell aufgebaut und mit präoperativ erstellten 3D–Studien überlagert, so daß das OP–Team jederzeit über eine exakte Navigationsunterstützung verfügt. Diese Technik führt zur Reduktion von zerstörtem Gewebe, da z.B. ein Tumor gezielter extrahiert werden kann (Stichwort: minimalinvasive Chirugie). Es konnte in klinischen Studien nachgewiesen werden, daß durch den Einsatz dieser Technik Rekonvalszenzzeiten deutlich reduziert und somit auch die Verweildauer der Patienten im Krankenhaus signifikant verkürzt werden konnte.

Inzwischen arbeitet man an einer weiteren Verbesserung der 3D–Modellierung, die weitesgehend automatisiert werden soll. Höchstleistungsrechner von Sun führen die komplexen Rechenoperationen aus, um die 3D–Studien möglichst optimal vorzubereiten, den Nachbearbeitungsaufwand durch qualifizierte Fachleute auf ein Minimum beschränkend. Es ist auch daran gedacht, die automatisierte 3D–Modellierung über die Hochleistungsrechner als Dienstleistung auch extern zugänglich zu machen, z.B. niedergelassenen Radiologen oder kleineren radiologischen Abteilungen, die die Ausstattung und das Fachpersonal für 3D–Rekonstruktionen nicht effektiv vorhalten können oder wollen.

Für diese Arbeiten wurde das Institut zu einem *Sun Technology and Research Excellence Center* ausgebaut, in dem sich jeder interessierte über verschiedene Aspekte fortschrittlicher Verfahren in der Bildbearbeitung informieren kann.

4 Ausblick

Dieser kurzer Überblick über einige Anwendungsbeispiele moderner Computertechnik in der medizinischen Bildverarbeitung zeigt, das Techniken, die vor Jahren aufgrund der Kosten nur wenigen Großeinrichtungen vorbehalten waren, nun auch gerade unter dem Aspekt der Kostensenkung bei gleichzeitiger Qualitätsverbesserung zugänglich werden.

Der Einsatz von Intranet–Technologie ermöglicht darüber hinaus die sinnvolle Nutzung von Resourcen, zum Nutzen der Leistungserbringer, Leistungsträger und nicht zuletzt der Patienten.

Sun Workstations und 3D–Arbeitsplätze liegen heute preislich auf PC-Niveau und bewähren sich wegen Ihrer Leistungsfähigkeit und Zuverlässigkeit täglich im klinischen Einsatz.

Waveletbasierte Bildkompressionsverfahren
Vorteile bei der Archivierung und Übertragung hochaufgelöster Bilddaten

Michael Thierschmann, Uwe-Erik Martin

LuRaTech, Gesellschaft für Luft- und Raumfahrttechnologie & Multimedia mbH
Rudower Chaussee 5, 12489 Berlin
Email: thierschmann@luratech.de, martin@luratech.de

Zusammenfassung. Die elektronische Verarbeitung von Daten eröffnet neue Möglichkeiten auch im Bereich der Bildverarbeitung. Ihr Einsatz vereinfacht die Archivierung, Verwaltung und Übertragung von Bildern. Aufgrund der hohen Datenmenge, die bei der Arbeit mit digitalisierten Bildern entstehen, stoßen jedoch die Archivierungs- und Datenübertragungssysteme dabei an ihre Leistungsgrenzen. Obwohl die Leistungsfähigkeit der digitalen Bildaufnahmesysteme und der Rechentechnik ständig zunimmt, steigt die Datenmenge der digital zu verarbeitenden Bilder in höherem Maße, so daß derzeit die Speicher- und Übertragungsmedien den Engpaß bei der digitalen Bildverarbeitung darstellen. Eine Lösungsmöglichkeit besteht in einer effizienten Datenkompression. Der folgende Beitrag zeigt die Vorteile des Einsatzes moderner Bilddatenkompressionsverfahren am Beispiel des waveletbasierten LuraWave-Verfahrens.

Schlüsselwörter: Bildverarbeitung, Datenkompression, Wavelet-Verfahren, Bildarchivierung, Bildübertragung

1 Einleitung

Die heute verwendeten Bildkompressionsverfahren lassen sich prinzipiell in zwei Gruppen einteilen: *verlustfreie* und *verlustbehaftete* Kompressionsverfahren.

Die mit *verlustfreien* Verfahren erreichbaren Kompressionsraten für natürliche Bilder sind gering. Es sind bestenfalls Kompressionsraten bis 1:3 erreichbar, ein typischer Wert ist 1:1,5 (Bsp. TIF-LZW-Kodierung). Diese Verfahren erlauben die identische Rekonstruktion des Originalbildes aus den komprimierten Daten.

Verlustbehaftete Verfahren lassen höhere Kompressionsraten zu. Die dabei immer größer werdende Abweichung zwischen Originalbild und dem rekonstruierten Bild führt bei hohen Anforderungen an die Originaltreue des Bildes zu einer Beschränkung der möglichen Kompressionsrate. So sind Raten von 1:5 bis 1:30 mit dem Standardverfahren JPEG, Kompressionsraten bis 1:300 mit neueren Verfahren (Wavelet, Fraktale) erreichbar.

Für künstliche Bilder existieren spezielle, angepaßte Verfahren, die hohe Kompressionsraten erreichen. Dazu zählen beispielsweise die Fax-Kodierung und die Bildformate PCX und RLE.

2 Beschreibung der Wavelet-Kompression

Wavelet-Kompressionsverfahren benutzen zweidimensionale Transformationen, um die Bildinformationen zu dekorrelieren. Die Kompression mit Wavelet-Kompressionsverfahren läuft in mehreren Schritten ab (siehe auch [1,2])

2.1 Transformation

Die Diskrete Wavelet-Transformation benutzt im Gegensatz zur Diskreten Fourier-Transformation (DFT) nicht die örtlich unbegrenzten Sinus- und Kosinusfunktionen zur Analyse des Bildmaterials. Die Basisfunktionen sind die Scaling-Funktionen und die sogenannten Wavelets. Diese Funktionen verbinden die grundlegende Eigenschaft der Orthogonalität, die eine Transformation und eine identische Rekonstruktion erst ermöglicht, mit der Eigenschaft des „compact support", d.h. sie besitzen eine endliche Ausdehnung. Dies erlaubt die Analyse von Bilddaten ohne Fenstereffekte.

Eine Wavelettransformation ist eine mehrfach durchgeführte zweidimensionale Filteroperation. Teilergebnisse der zuerst durchgeführten Schritte dienen wiederum als Eingangswert der nachfolgenden Stufen, so daß eine hierarchische Transformationsstruktur entsteht. Das transformierte Abbild besteht aus einem Tiefpaßbereich, der die niederfrequenten Anteile des Originalbildes widerspiegelt, und mehreren Hochpaßanteilen, die die feineren Strukturen des Originalbildes repräsentieren.

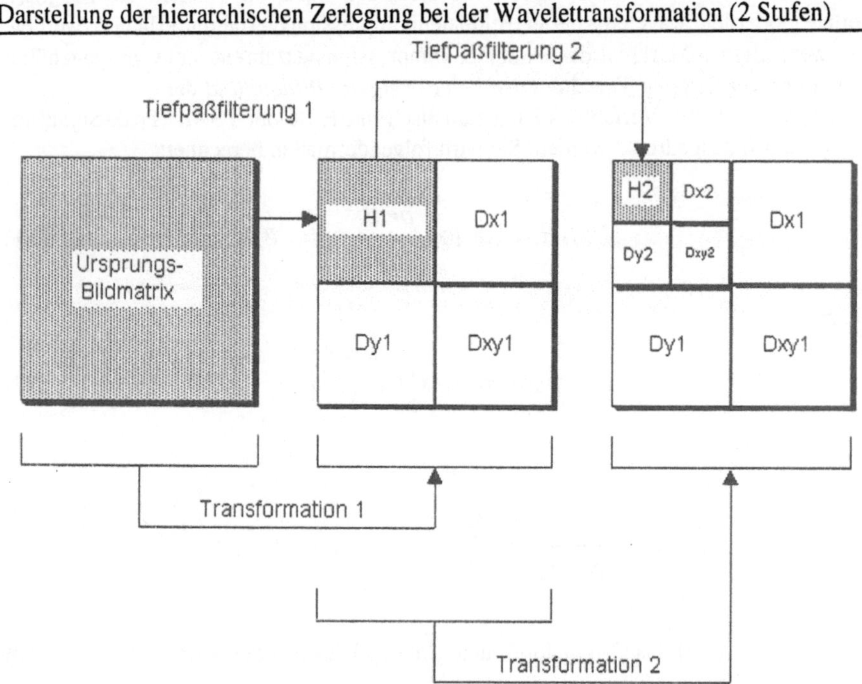

2.2 Quantisierung und Kodierung

Die Quantisierung und Kodierung sorgen für die Auswahl der Information im entstehenden Datenstrom. Dabei verwirft die Quantisierung die bei der geforderten Kompressionsqualität irrelevanten Informationen. Eine Kombination von Kodierung und Quantisierung ermöglicht eine genaue Steuerung der Kompressionsqualität (Bildqualität vs. Kompressionsrate). Die Länge des erzeugten Datenstromes kann exakt vorherbestimmt werden.

Zu Beginn des Quantisierungs- und Kodierungsvorganges werden die Koeffizienten der Wavelettransformation grob quantisiert. Nur die größten und daher für die Qualität des rekonstruierten Bildes wichtigsten Transformationskoeffizienten liefern einen Beitrag zum entstehenden Datenstrom. Anschließend werden die zu Beginn verwendeten Quantisierungsintervalle verfeinert, so daß weitere Koeffizienten übertragen werden. Es entsteht ein *eingebetteter* Datenstrom. Dies ermöglicht bei einer beliebigen Unterbrechung des Kodiervorganges eine vollständige Rekonstruktion des kodierten Bildes in einer entsprechend verminderten Qualität.

Wird der Quantisierungs- und Kodiervorgang nicht unterbrochen, dann werden die entstandenen Transformationskoeffizienten in voller Genauigkeit kodiert. Die Datenkompression ist dann verlustlos.

3 Vorteile der Wavelet-Kompression in der Anwendung

Am Beispiel des Bilddatenkompressionsverfahrens LuRaWave sollen die Möglichkeiten moderner, waveletbasierter Bilddatenkompressionsverfahren erläutert werden. Ein wesentliches Merkmal des Bilddatenkompressionsverfahrens stellt die gegenüber bisherigen verbreiteten Verfahren *deutlich gesteigerte Bildqualität* dar.

Die Qualität des Verfahrens kann statistisch mit Hilfe der PSNR (Peak-Signal-to-Noise-Ratio) ausgedrückt werden. Sie wird folgendermaßen berechnet:

$$PSNR = 10 \cdot \log \frac{peak^2}{noise} \; (\textit{in dB}) \tag{1}$$

mit

$$peak = \max\big[f(x,y)\big] \tag{2}$$

und

$$noise = \frac{1}{N \cdot M} \sum_{i=0}^{N-1} \sum_{j=0}^{M-1} \big[f(x_i,y_j) - \tilde{f}(x_i,y_j)\big]^2 \tag{3}$$

wobei $f(x,y)$ das Originalbild, und $\tilde{f}(x,y)$ das aus den komprimierten Daten rekonstruierte Bild repräsentiert.

Testbild der Kompression

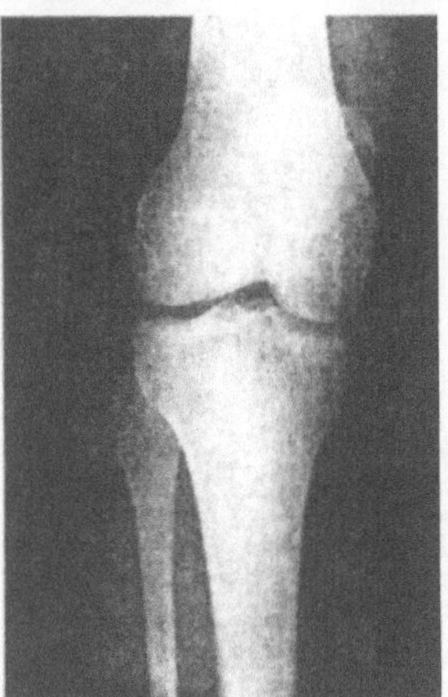

statistische Bildqualität LuRaWave vs. JPEG am Beispiel eines Röntgenbildes

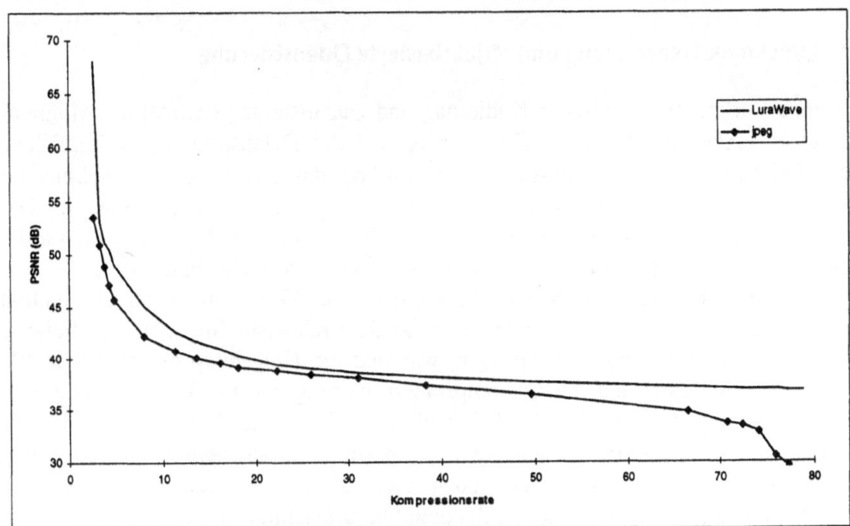

Im visuellen Vergleich ist ein Hauptunterschied der waveletbasierten Kompressionsverfahren im Vergleich zum Standardverfahren JPEG sichtbar. Während das Standardverfahren aufgrund seiner blockorientierten Arbeitsweise bei mittleren bis hohen Kompressionsraten deutliche Kachelartefacte zeigt, führt die hierarchische Zerlegung in Grob- und Feinstrukturen bei LuraWave zu einer angenehmeren Glättung des Bildes, ohne jedoch signifikant Kantenstrukturen des Originalbildes zu unterdrücken.

Desweiteren erlaubt die LuraWave-Datenkompression im Gegensatz zu anderen waveletbasierten Kompressionsverfahren die *verlustlose Datenkompression* als Grenzfall einer verlustbehafteten Kompression, falls kein Unterschied zum Originalbild akzeptiert wird.

Visueller Vergleich JPEG-LuraWave (Ausschnitte, Kompressionsrate 1:22)

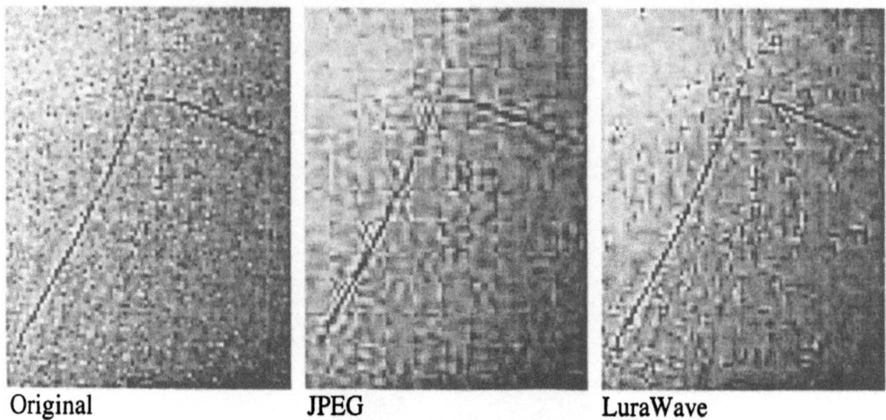

Original   JPEG   LuraWave

Das Beispielbild läßt sich mit LuraWave verlustfrei um den Faktor 2,6 komprimieren. (Zum Vergleich: TIFF LZW erzielt eine Kompressionsrate von 1:1,7).

3.1 Quicklook Generierung und objektbasierte Quantisierung

Die enge Verknüpfung zwischen Kodierung und Quantisierung eröffnet die Möglichkeit einer einfachen Quicklook-Generierung. Da der Datenstrom eines LuraWave komprimierten Bildes jederzeit die Information über das Gesamtbild in zunehmender Bildschärfe repräsentiert, kann durch die Übertragung nur eines Bruchteiles der Datenmenge ein Vorschaubild erzeugt werden. In digitalen Bildarchiven und in Bilddatenbanken entfällt dabei die separate Verwaltung kleiner Vorschaubilder.

Die Quantisierer/Kodierer Kombination erlaubt eine Verschiebung der Bildqualität innerhalb des Bildes. So ist es möglich, besonders relevante Bildanteile in höherer Qualität (auch verlustlos) zu übertragen, während die Umgebung dieser Bildanteile der Orientierung dient und stärker komprimiert übertragen wird. Bei einer progressiven Übertragung, bei der sich die Bildqualität mit zunehmend übertragener Datenmenge ständig verbessert, werden bei objektbasierter Quantisierung die relevanten Bildanteile zuerst übertragen, daher auch zuerst dargestellt, während die weniger relevanten Anteile zu einem späteren Zeitpunkt berücksichtigt werden.

4 Literatur

1. J.M. Shapiro, Embedded Coding Using Zerotrees of Wavelet Coefficients, IEEE Trans. Sign. Proc., Vol. 41, No. 12, Dec. 1993
2. A. Said, W.A. Pearlman, A New Fast and Efficient Image Codec Based on Set Partitioning in Hierarchical Trees, IEEE Trans. On Circuits and Systems for Video Tech., Vol. 6, June 1996

EEG/MEG Quellen Rekonstruktion
-Die Funktionen von *CURRY* und *CAUCHY^{par}*-

H. Buchner[1], S. Kaiser[2], P. M. A. Sloot[3], M. Fuchs[4], K. Waßmuth[5]

[1]Klinik für Neurologie RWTH Aachen, Pauwelsstraße 30, D-52057 Aachen,
Email: buchner@neurologie.rwth-aachen.de
[2]Parsytec Computer GmbH, Auf der Hüls 183, D-52068 Aachen
Email: stefan@parsytec.de
[3]Universiteit van Amsterdam, Kruislaan 403, NL-1098 SJ Amsterdam
Email: peterslo@wins.uva.nl
[4]Philips Forschungslabor, Roentgenstraße 24-26, D-22335 Hamburg
Email: m.fuchs@pfh.research.philips.de
[5]Biomagnetic Technologies, Grüner Weg 83, D-52070 Aachen
Email: kw@magnes.de

Zusammenfassung. In dem Programmpaket *CURRY-CAUCHY* wurden Werkzeuge erstellt, mit denen es möglich wurde, die Quellen der elektromagnetischen Aktivität des Zentralnervensystems in der individuellen Anatomie zu berechnen. Es wird der Weg von der Datenaufnahme bis zur Visualisierung der Ergebnisse vorgestellt. Ziel weiterer methodischer Entwicklung sind deutlich beschleunigte und „automatisierte" Programmabläufe. Als wesentlicher Schritt zum effizienten Einsatz der Methoden werden zeitintensive Teilfunktionen parallelisiert und das gesamte Programmpaket auf einen Parallelrechner portiert.

Schlüsselwörter: Elektroenzephalographie, Magnetoenzephalographie, EEG, MEG, Source Reconstruction, realistically shaped headmodeling, parallel computing, HPC

1 Einleitung

Die Zuordnung elektrischer Aktivität des Zentralnervensystems zu ihrer funktionell-anatomischen Entstehungsstruktur ist für die theoretische und klinische Medizin von hohem Interesse. Sie dient der Aufdeckung funktioneller Zusammenhänge im Zentralnervensystem und zur Lokalisation pathologischer elektrischer Aktivität mit daraus folgender Therapie.

Es wurde ein Programmpaket (*CURRY^{1}-CAUCHY^{2}*) mit einer Methodik zur elektrischen Quellenanalyse in einem der individuellen Anatomie angepaßten Kopfmodell entwickelt. In diesem wurde die Quellenanalyse der elektrischen Daten und die 3D-Darstellung bildgebender Verfahren (Magnetresonanztomographie, MR) gemeinsam realisiert.

---

^{1} *CURRY* ist Produkt der Philips Forschungslaboratorien Hamburg
^{2} *CAUCHY* wurde von einer interdisziplinären Arbeitsgruppe an der RWTH Aachen mit Förderung der Volkswagenstiftung entwickelt.

2 Aktueller Stand der Methodik

Im folgenden sollen zwischenzeitlich etablierte Methodik und aktuelle Trends für die einzelnen Komponenten eines Systems (Programmpaket) zur anatomischen Abbildung elektrischer Aktivität des ZNS vorgestellt werden:

2.1 Datenaufnahme

Die Notwendigkeit einer multikanalen Datenaufnahme für eine ausreichende räumliche Auflösung der elektrischen bzw. magnetischen Felder hat zur Entwicklung von kommerziellen Systemen mit bis zu 256 Kanal Aufnahme von EEG und MEG Helmsystemen mit 60 bis 306 Kanälen geführt. Zur Abbildung der individuellen Anatomie werden 3D-MR in einer stark T1-gewichteten Sequenz aufgenommen und in ein isotrophes Volumen umgerechnet.

2.2 Kopfmodell

Das einfachste Modell ist die Annahme einer Kugel mit multiplen Schalen, die die Schichten von Kopfhaut, Knochen, Liquor und Hirn abbilden. Die der individuellen Anatomie des Kopfes und seiner Kompartimente angepaßte Modelle wurden mit Boundary-Element-Modellen (BEM, Repräsentationen der Flächen durch Triangel) oder mit Finite-Element-Modellen (FEM, Repräsentationen des Volumens in den Flächen durch Tethraeder oder Kuben) möglich (Abb. 1) [1]. Der Lokalisationsfehler des Kugelmodelles relativ zu einem der individuellen Anatomie des Kopfes angepaßten Boundary-Element-Modells beträgt i.M. 2cm, wenn Quellen frontal bzw. temporal liegen. Desgleichen wurden Fehler etwa gleichen Ausmaßes bei der Auswertung von MEG-Daten mit dem Kugelmodell gefunden, wenn die Quellorte relativ tief (mehr als 3 cm von der Kopfoberfläche) lagen. Ein genereller Vorteil des MEGs besteht nicht, obwohl die Leiteigenschaften der Kompartimente für die Berechnungen nicht berücksichtigt werden müssen [2].

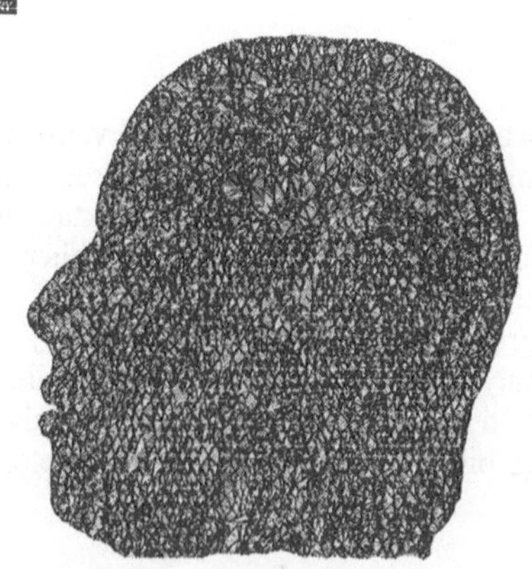

Abb. 1 Kopfmodell FEM

Zur Erstellung eines individuellen Kopfmodells ist eine spezielle Bildverarbeitung mit Segmentierung der Grenzflächen zwischen den Kompartimenten unterschiedlicher Leiteigenschaften erforderlich. Gezielt wurden bei den Philips-Forschungslaboratorien Werkzeuge zur Segmentierung, Oberflächen- und Volumendefinition sowie Visualisierung entwickelt.

In der aktuellen Diskussion wird davon ausgegangen, daß ein Kopfmodell die vorhandene Anisotropie der Leiteigenschaften von Haut, Knochen und Hirn berücksichtigen muß [3]. Dies wurde in einem FE-Modell realisiert.

2.3 Inverse Optimierung

In den letzten Jahren sind zwei methodische Wege zur inversen Optimierung erprobt worden: (1) Nichtlineare Optimierung und (2) spatiale Regularisierung.

Die nichtlineare Optimierung setzt zumeist nichtlineare Minimierungstechniken ein (z.B. Marquardt Algorithmus). Diese Gruppe von Optimierungsmethoden konvergiert häufig nicht auf das globale Minimum. Dagegen wurde gezeigt, daß simulated annealing bei ausreichend langsamer "Abkühlung" gegen das globale Minimum konvergiert [siehe in 1]. Dies ist bedeutsam, weil davon auszugehen ist, daß es komplizierteren Geometrien mehrere lokale Minima existieren.

Die spatiale Regularisierung erhöht die Anzahl der Gleichungen und führt eine Zusatzbedingung ein, durch die eine eindeutige Lösung erzeugt wird. Als Zusatzbedingung wurde entweder das Minimum-Norm-Kriterium (Minimierung der Summe der elektrischen Leistung) oder die Forderung nach einer glatten Verteilung der Quellstärke implementiert [siehe in 1,2]. Die regularisierte Lösung führt zu spatial "verschmierten" Quellverteilungen. Durch Nutzung zusätzlicher Randbedingungen, wie einem auf der Kortex-Oberfläche eingegrenzten Suchraum, kann die Lösung verbessert werden (BU). Eine Simulation zeigte, daß es mit Hilfe dieser Eingrenzung des Suchraums möglich ist, Quellen an gegenüberliegenden Hirnwindungen zu unterscheiden.

2.4 Visualisierung

Die Visualisierung von Ergebnissen inverser Optimierung erfolgte, nachdem das Kopfmodell an die Anatomie angepaßt wurde, in der Bildgebung des MR. Zumeist wurden Punktlokalisationen äquivalenter Dipole in Pseudo-3D-Schnitten gezeigt. Von den Philips-Forschungslaboratorien wurde zudem eine 3D-Darstellung von Oberflächen realisiert, in der die Quellokalisation als Punkt, Vektor oder farbcodiert wiedergegeben werden kann (Abb. 2).

2.5 Medizinische Anwendungen

Es liegen eine Vielzahl von Publikationen mit Untersuchungen experimenteller oder klinisch-medizinischer Anwendungen der Quellrekonstruktion vor.

Eine klinisch besonders interessierende Anwendung ist die Lokalisation der Entstehung epileptischer Aktivität bei Patienten mit Anfallserkrankungen die mit Medikamenten nicht ausreichend behandelt werden können. Unter Berücksichtigung verschiedener Voraussetzungen kann nach sicherer Bestimmung des Ursprungs der

Abb. 2 Epileptische Region rot markiert. Links Berechnung in einem FE-Modell; rechts Bestimmung mit Elektroden an der Hirnoberfläche und im Gehirn, Histogramm der Amplituden pathologischer Erregungen.

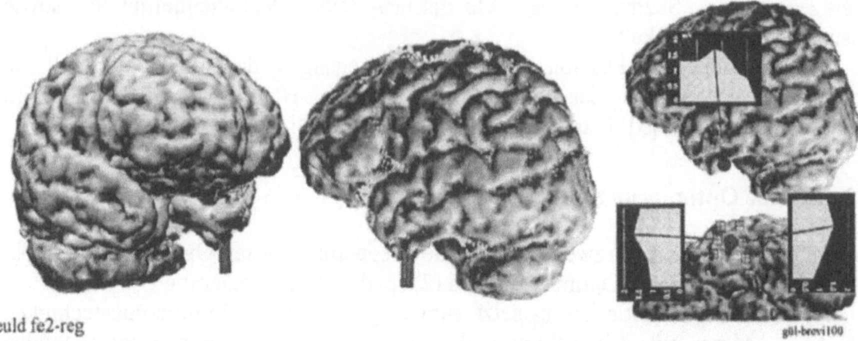

pathologischen Erregung dieser Ort am Gehirn operativ entfernt werden. Dazu ist es bisher in den meisten Fällen erforderlich, das EEG unmittelbar an der Hirnoberfläche oder im Gehirn aufzunehmen nachdem entsprechende Elektroden operativ plaziert wurden. Dies ist mit einem erheblichen technischen und logistischen Aufwand sowie einem operativen Risiko verbunden. Die nicht eingreifende Bestimmung des Ursprungs der epileptischen Aktivität mit Methoden der Quellrekonstruktion könnte die prächirurgische Bestimmung erheblich verbessern. Ein Beispiel zeigt die Abb. 2, in der vergleichend der invers berechnete Ursprung mit dem durch Elektroden an der Hirnoberfläche bzw. im Gehirn gegenübergestellt ist. Ausführlich wurde die Methodik dargestellt in [4].

3 Methodische Weiterentwicklungen

Trotz der nachgewiesenen Lokalisationsgenauigkeit der Programme *CURRY* und *CAUCHY* ist die Quellrekonstruktion noch weit von einer alltäglichen, in Forschung und Klinik praktizierbaren Anwendung entfernt. Dies hat zwei Ursachen: Erstens ist für die Auswahl der einzusetzenden Techniken zur inversen Berechnung und die Wahl der jeweiligen Parameter Wissen und Erfahrung erforderlich. Zweitens ist eine deutlich feinere Diskretisierung (2-4 mm) der Kopfmodelle für eine genauere Lösung erforderlich. Daraus ergeben sich sehr lange Rechenzeiten. Ein BE-Modell würde dann auf einer Workstation bei einem Hauptspeicherbedarf von ca. 2 GB etwa 2000 Stunden Rechenzeit benötigen, während ein FE-Modell ca. 100 MB RAM allokieren würde und über 600 Stunden zur Berechnung bräuchte. Eine Parallelisierung des FEM-Codes ermöglicht eine massive Beschleunigung der Berechnungen.

3.1 Parallelisierung

Im Januar 1998 startete das von der Europäischen Union im ESPRIT-Rahmen (HPCN Preparatory, Support and Transfer Activities) geförderte Projekt *CAUCHY^{par}* (Nummer 26433), dessen Ziel die Parallelisierung des sequentiellen Codes ist, um die Akzeptanz der Applikation im klinischen Umfeld zu erhöhen. Partner für die parallele Hardware ist die Aachener Parsytec Computer GmbH. Die Implementierung des Programms selber wird durch Experten der Universität Amsterdam vorgenommen.

Nach Projektende (voraussichtlich September 1998) soll eine Beschleunigung gegenüber der sequentiellen Applikation mit einem Faktor von ca. 10 bis 20 erreicht sein, die zum einen aus der erhöhten Anzahl der Prozessorknoten und zum anderen aus der Verbesserung der zugrundeliegenden Algorithmen resultiert. Weitere Geschwindigkeitserhöhung kann bei Bedarf durch Hinzufügen zusätzlicher Prozessorknoten erfolgen. Da die Parsytec-Systeme voll skalierbar sind, ist der Performance-Zuwachs nahezu proportional zur Anzahl der Knoten.

Die Zielplattform in diesem Projekt ist ein System der CCe- bzw. der CC/PP-Generation [siehe in 5] basierend auf PowerPC604e-Motherboards, die der CHRP Spezifikation entsprechen. In den CCe-Systemen werden Single Processor Boards mit einer Prozessortaktrate von 200 MHz integriert, während in den CC/PP-Systemen Double Processor Boards mit einer Taktrate von 300 MHz pro Prozessor eingesetzt werden. Die erforderliche hohe Bandbreite zur Interprozessorkommunikation wird in beiden Systemen durch ein dediziertes Hochgeschwindigkeitsnetzwerk erreicht, in dem die Rechenknoten durch HS-Link-PCI-Karten (high speed/IEEE 1355) über kaskadierbare 8x8-HS-Link-Routing-Module miteinander verbunden sind. Dabei werden Übertragungsraten von über 40 MB/sec. bidirektional bzw. 30 MB/sec. unidirektional erreicht. Das eingesetzte Betriebssystem AIX (IBM) wurde durch eine spezielle Laufzeit- und Kommunikationsschicht (EPX-Embedded Parallel Extensions to UNIX) erweitert, so daß sowohl AIX-basierte Standardsoftware (Compiler, Tools, etc.) als auch parallele Applikationen lauffähig sind. Jeder Rechenknoten kann dabei individuell konfiguriert werden. Der (lokale) Speicher ist dabei auf 512 MB limitiert. Die Erweiterung der Plattform kann u.a. durch diverse PCI-Karten erfolgen, die z.B. eine Einbindung des Parallelrechners in das LAN oder die Nutzung eines Framegrabbers ermöglichen.

3.2 Automatisierung

Für eine routinemäßige Anwendung der Quellrekonstruktion ist die Entwicklung allgemein einsetzbarer robuster inverser Verfahren erforderlich. Dies ist aktueller Inhalt eines interdisziplinären Forschungsprojekts (Förderung des BMBF).

Weiter sollen eine verbesserte Bedienerführung und Batchprozesse den Benutzer entlasten und zu einer Beschleunigung der Datenverarbeitung von deren Aufnahme bis zur Visualisierung führen.

4 Literatur

1. Fuchs M, Drenckhahn R, Wischmann H-A, Wagner M: An improved boundary element method for realistic volume conductor modeling. IEEE Trans. Biomed. Eng., 1998 in press.
2. Buchner H, Knoll G, Fuchs M, Rienäcker A, Beckmann R, Wagner M, Silny J, Pesch J: Inverse localization of electric current sources in finite element models of the human head. Electroenceph. clin. Neurophysiol., 102: 267-278, 1997.
3. Pohlmeier R, Buchner H, Knoll G, Rienäcker A, Beckmann R, Pesch J: The influence of skull-conductivity misspecification on inverse source localization in realistically shaped finfite element head models. Brain Topography, 9(3): 157-162, 1997.
4. Waberski TD, Buchner H, Lehnertz K, Hufnagel A, Fuchs M, Beckmann R, Rienäcker A: The properties of source localization of epileptiform activity using advanced headmodelling and source reconstruction. Brain Topography, 1998 in press.
5. Parsytec: Parsytec CCe - New Trends in HPC, Parsytec Aachen, 1996.

3D-Segmentierung in konfokalen Laserscans der Retina über das Dresdner 3D-Display
ESPRIT-Projekt 26 401 „VISPAR"

S. Böttcher, H.-J. Malig

Dresden Informatik GmbH
Tannenstr. 2A, D-01099 Dresden
Email: boettcher@dresden-informatik.de, malig@dresden-informatik.de

Zusammenfassung. Das ESPRIT-Projekt „VISPAR" stellt eine über den Technologie-Transfer-Knoten Thüringen (TTN-T) geförderte Demonstrationsaktivität dar. Deren Ziel ist die Erweiterung eines bestehenden Systems zur Unterstützung der medizinischen Diagnose, speziell von Glaukomerkrankungen. Durch autostereoskopische 3D-Visualisierung, online 3D-Segmentierung und wissensbasierte Diagnoseunterstützung soll die bisherige ophthalmologische Laserscanning-Untersuchung weiterentwickelt werden. Insbesondere soll die Reproduzierbarkeit der Segmentationsergebnisse, der darauf aufbauenden statistischen Daten und die Diagnosesicherheit entschieden verbessert werden.

Schlüsselwörter: Confocal Laser Scanning, Glaukom, 3D-Segmentierung, 3D-Display, Fuzzy-Entscheidungsunterstützung

1 Ziel des Projektes

Das über den Technologie-Transfer-Knoten Thüringen (TTN-T) geförderte ESPRIT-Projektes 26 401 „VISPAR" soll die Möglichkeiten zur Verbesserung eines bestehenden Systems zur Unterstützung der medizinischen Diagnose – speziell von Glaukomerkrankungen – demonstrieren, indem das Know-how der Projektpartner zusammengeführt und eine state-of-the-art Applikation beispielhaft implementiert wird. Durch autostereoskopische 3D-Visualisierung [1], online 3D-Segmentierung und Diagnoseunterstützung auf der Grundlage einer Wissenbasis soll die bisherige ophthalmologische Laserscanning-Untersuchung weiterentwickelt werden. Insbesondere soll die Reproduzierbarkeit der Segmentationsergebnisse, der darauf aufbauenden statistischen Daten und die Diagnosesicherheit entschieden verbessert werden.
Entsprechende Hardware und Programmierung sollen nutzerfreundliche Reaktionszeiten gewährleisten. Der modulare Systementwurf soll eine möglichst einfache Übertragung auf verwandte Aufgaben in anderen Bereichen der Medizin oder Technik ermöglichen.

2 Vorgehen

Bei der bisherigen ophthalmologischen Untersuchung mit dem Laser Scanning Tomograph von Heidelberg Engineering (HE) „Heidelberg Retina Tomograph" (HRT) ist ein manuelles Einzeichnen der Papillenbegrenzung notwendig. Diese Referenzlinie unterliegt relativ stark subjektiven Schwankungen seitens des Augenarztes, hat aber z.T. große Auswirkungen auf die dann vom HRT gelieferten automatisch bestimmten stereometrischen Daten. Durch die Verwendung des autostereoskopischen „Dresdner 3D-Displays" in Zusammenspiel mit der Visualisierung über OpenGL soll dieser subjektive Faktor deutlich eingeschränkt werden, indem die Papillenkontur im Raum eingezeichnet werden kann [2].

Eine Fuzzy-Entscheidungskomponente wird die vom HRT gelieferten Daten auf Plausibilität prüfen und den Arzt bei der Diagnose unterstützen.

Geplant ist außerdem die automatische Segmentierung der für die Verlaufsuntersuchung bedeutsamen Exkavation des Sehnervenkopfes, um erstens die bei der manuellen Lösung erhaltene Exkavation zu verifizieren und zweitens – mit dann eingeschränktem Datensatz – eine Offline-Auswertung der Bilder zu ermöglichen [3].

Tabelle 1. Die Projektpartner.

Organisation	Rolle im Projekt	projektbezogenes Arbeitsfeld
Dresden Informatik GmbH	Projektkoordinator, Technologieprovider	Bildverarbeitung, 3D-Visualisierung, Parallelverarbeitung
TU Dresden, Fakultät Informatik	Technologieprovider	Autostereoskopisches Display, 3D-Visualisierung
Fraunhofer Institut für zerstörungsfreie Prüfung, Außenstelle EADQ Dresden	Nutzeranforderungen, wissensbasierte Diagnoseunterstützung	Glaukomdiagnostik, Fuzzy-Expertensysteme
Augenklinik und Poliklinik der Universität des Saarlandes	medizinische Nutzeranforderungen	Laser-Scanning-Tomographie, Glaukomdiagnostik
Heidelberg Engineering GmbH	technische Nutzeranforderungen, Test	Laser-Scanning-Tomograph-Hersteller, Bildverarbeitung

3 Literatur

1. Schwerdtner A, Heidrich H: Dresden 3D display: a flat autostereoscopic display, Technische Univ. Dresden (FRG) [3295-28]. Stereoscopic Displays and Applications IX, 26-28 January 1998, part of Electronic Imaging/Photonics West 1998, San Jose, California
2. Fiedler U: Bildverarbeitung zur Diagnostik von Glaukomerkrankungen. Interner Bericht des Fraunhofer Instituts IzfP/EADQ Dresden, FIE-2/1992
3. Maier H, Siebert M, Gramer E: Unterschiede in der Form der Papillenexkavation bei Glaucoma chronicum simplex und Glaukom ohne Hochdruck. in: Gramer, Kampik (Hrsg.): Pharmakotherapie am Auge. Springer-Verlag, Berlin Heidelberg, 1992.

Bilddokumentation und –analyse am Beispiel der Augenmedizin

Werner Neubert

Soft Imaging System GmbH
Hammer Str. 89, D-48153 Münster
Email: info@soft-imaging.de, Website: http://www.soft-imaging.de

Zusammenfassung. Die digitale Erfassung und Dokumentation erlangt in der Augenmedizin eine immer größere Bedeutung. Der Einsatz herkömmlicher chemischer Photomaterialien (Sofortfilm) verbietet sich bei Dokumentationspflicht und bei Anfall von bis zu einem Dutzend Aufnahmen pro Untersuchung aus Preis- und Umweltschutzgründen. Die Erzeugung von Dias ist zeitaufwendig, das Material steht erst Stunden bis Tage später zur Begutachtung unsortiert zur Verfügung. Bei Fluoreszenzangiografie-, ICG und auch normalen Farbaufnahmen wird eine objektive, den Behandlungsverlauf dokumentierende Befundung mittels schneller Monitordarstellung und Ablage in die Bilddatenbank erst ermöglicht.

Schlüsselwörter: Fluoreszenzangiografie, Bilddatenbank, Funduskamera, affine Transformation, Differenzielle Kontrastverstärkung, Detektion, Exsudate.

1   Einleitung

Für das Sehen ist eine intakte Netzhaut (Fundus) im Auge erforderlich. Mannigfaltige Einflüsse können hier zu Beeinträchtigungen des Sehvermögens führen. Besonders die Gefäßschädigungen bei Diabetikern sind als Spätschäden gefürchtet. Eine Standardtherapie ist hier der Laser, durch dessen thermische Wirkung ausufernde Gefäße verödet werden. Bei anderen Krankheitsbildern kann es zu Gefäßläsionen kommen, Blut tritt aus und vernebelt den klaren Blick.

2   Historie

Bisher erfolgt die Dokumentation der Befundung in der Augenmedizin an der Funduskamera mittels herkömmlicher Fotografie (Dia) oder Sofortfilm. Im ersten Fall steht das Material erst Stunden bis Tage später zur Verfügung und muß in separaten Arbeitsschritten der Patientenakte wieder manuell beigefügt werden. Im Extremfall stellt man dann fest, daß eine wichtige Aufnahme unscharf oder mißlungen ist (Augenbewegung). Letzteres entfällt zwar bei der Sofortbildfotografie; neben den Kosten ist aber hier der Umweltschutzaspekt zu berücksichtigen. In vielen Fällen wird dem überweisenden Arzt zusätzlich auch Bildmaterial zur Verfügung gestellt.

Der erste Schritt in die richtige Richtung war der Einsatz einer Videokamera und der Ausdruck des Bildes mittels Videoprinters. Die erforderlichen Ausdrucke des digital eingefrorenen Bildes mußten aber sofort angefertigt werden. Die Ablage in einer Datenbank erfolgte nicht. Das Verfahren eignete sich in der Regel nicht für alle Untersuchungsmethoden.

3 Idealer Sollzustand

Die Bilder werden über die optische Schnittstelle der Funduskamera, der Spaltleuchte, des OP-Mikroskops oder des Perimeters mittels einer analogen oder voll digitalen Videokamera aufgenommen, in den Rechner übertragen, binnen Sekundenbruchteilen auf Wunsch formatfüllend auf dem Monitor in optimaler Qualität dargestellt und auf Tastendruck (auch per Voicecontrol!) mit den Aufnahme- und Patientendaten unverwechselbar in eine digitale Bilddatenbank abgelegt. Die Speicherung erfolgt für Pfennigbeträge in Sekundenbruchteilen. Die digitale Weitergabe des Bildmaterials über ISDN (Eurofiletransfer, Email Attachment, Internet) oder Datenträger ist sofort oder jederzeit später ohne Qualitätsverlust und manuellen Suchaufwand gegeben. Die Suche in der Datenbank ist sowohl nach Patient und oder Diagnose oder über einen Zeitraum möglich. Es können bei Bedarf (und nur dann!) auch jederzeit preiswerte digitale Farbausdrucke erstellt werden.

4 Spezielle Applikationen

Bei der Fluoreszenzangiografie wird nach Einspritzen des fluoreszierenden Farbstoffes Fluorescein in die Blutbahn abgewartet, bis der Farbstoff das Auge erreicht. Sind

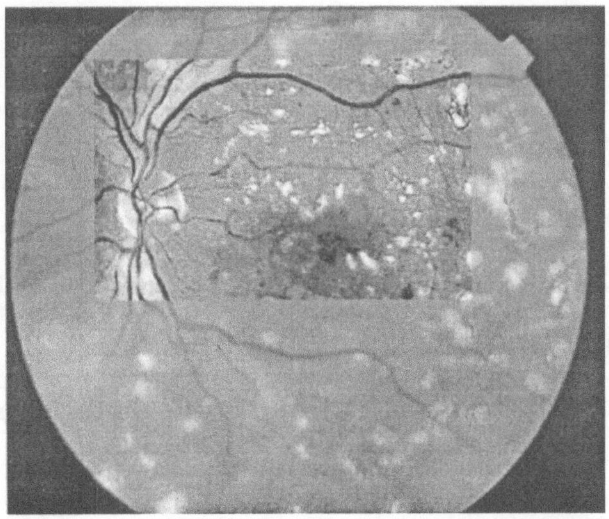

Abb. 1: Augenhintergrund, Rahmen mit DCE Filterung

Gefäßläsionen vorhanden, verteilt sich der Farbstoff auch außerhalb der Gefäße. Zu sicheren Diagnose muß dieser Austritt in Form einer Bildserie dokumentiert werden. Die hohe Anregungsenergiedichte und die erforderliche kurze Belichtung ist nur über Blitzlichtbeleuchtung möglich. Die gesamte Steuerung des Ablaufs vom Einschwenken der Anregungsfilter, dem Zünden des Blitzes, dem „Einfrieren" des Bildes und der Darstellung auf dem Monitor erfolgt über das Bildanalyse- und Dokumentationssystem analySIS vollautomatisch. Binnen einer Sekunde, sobald der Blitz wieder geladen ist, ist die nächste Aufnahme möglich. Eine automatische Bildoptimierung über Schärfe- und DCE (Differential Contrast Enhancement) – Filterung ist eingebunden. Es können sofort oder später alle oder nur ausgesuchte Bilder in die Patienten- Datenbank übernommen werden. Schnittstellen zu Praxissoftware(IFA, Medistar), Barcodeerfassung o.ä. sind möglich.

Die Datenbankstruktur ist auf medizinische Belange ausgerichtet: Name, Geburtsdatum, Aufnahmedatum, Aufnahmegerät, Diagnose1, Diagnose2, untersuchender Arzt. Das Wiederaufsuchen älterer Aufnahmen zur Verlaufskontrolle findet in sekundenschnelle in unveränderter Bildqualität statt.

Speziell beim Auge gibt es ein Problem beim visuellen Vergleich der Aufnahmen (z.B. Größe der Exsudate als Verlauf). Deckungsgleiche Aufnahmen lassen sich aufgrund der Augenbewegung und der wechselnden Augengröße! nur schwer oder gar nicht gewinnen.

Hier kommt die affine Transformation zum Einsatz. Durch wechselnde Markierung gleicher Strukturen (Aderverzweigungen) werden Bildpaare zur Deckung gebracht. Mittels Subtraktion werden die Veränderungen im Laufe der Behandlung objektiv sichtbar. Selbst eine quantitative Erfassung der Exsudatgröße ist auf Knopfdruck vorgesehen. Mangels eindeutiger Kalibriermöglichkeiten sind absolute Werte mit einem Fehler $\pm 10\%$ versehen. Zur Kalibrierung wird die Papille (Sehnervenkopf) verwendet.

Beim Einsatz von Laser Ophthalmoskopen entstehen auch durch die Kugelform des Auges bedingt Bilder mit geringer Tiefenschärfe. Es wird eine Bildserie von diversen Schichten aufgenommen. Durch automatisches Alignieren, Extraktion der „scharfen" Bildelemente und der Rekombination entstehen Bilder mit ausgedehnter Tiefeninformation und Auflösung.

5 Ausblick

Durch den Einsatz des Digitalen Bilddokumentation und –analyse analySIS von Soft Imaging System in Kombination mit dem Blitzsteuerungsinterface von PSI Pawlowski Medizintechnik Jena werden Dokumentationsabläufe in der Praxis und der Forschung kostengünstig beschleunigt und z.T. erst verfügbar gemacht. Die Hardwareplattform besteht neben Funduskameras verschiedener Hersteller aus Pentium und Pentium II PCs.

Autorenverzeichnis

Springer und Umwelt

Als internationaler wissenschaftlicher Verlag sind wir uns unserer besonderen Verpflichtung der Umwelt gegenüber bewußt und beziehen umweltorientierte Grundsätze in Unternehmensentscheidungen mit ein. Von unseren Geschäftspartnern (Druckereien, Papierfabriken, Verpackungsherstellern usw.) verlangen wir, daß sie sowohl beim Herstellungsprozess selbst als auch beim Einsatz der zur Verwendung kommenden Materialien ökologische Gesichtspunkte berücksichtigen.

Das für dieses Buch verwendete Papier ist aus chlorfrei bzw. chlorarm hergestelltem Zellstoff gefertigt und im pH-Wert neutral.